Dedication

This book is dedicated to our fallen and injured police officers who show us the true meaning of sacrifice. Rest in Peace to our brothers and our sister in the Baltimore City Police Department who have given their lives to the senseless violence of this city. They will not be forgotten, as we their brothers and sisters will keep them in our memories.

Acknowledgments

I would like to acknowledge my family, both at home and at work; as well as all those in whose footsteps I have walked, and those who someday will walk in mine. For without them we would have no history, and no future.

Written and composed by Retired Detective Kenny Driscoll

Edited and prepared for publication by Wesley R. Wise

© Copyright 2016 – Kenny Driscoll – Baltimore, MD
All Rights Reserved

ISBN-13: 978-1530877706
ISBN-10: 1530877709

This book is not a work of fiction. It is a comprehensive and exhaustive encyclopedia of the 250-year history of the Baltimore Police Department. This compendium is replete with stories of its officers' lives, deaths and heroism, successes and failures – a wide-ranging timeline history of the development and progress of policing in Baltimore.

Note that in this book the terms Officer, Police Officer, Patrolman and Watchman are used interchangeably, without regard to the specific term as it may have been used at the time, or as it may have changed over time.

The Baltimore City Police Department

~ Historical Timeline ~

The comprehensive information in this book is presented in a variety of ways, broken down into several sections:

- **Motto** – A History of our department's Motto, its meaning and derivation;

- **Year-by-Year Event Timeline** – a summary timeline of events going through the years, from the department's inception to the present;

- **Day-by-Day Incident Timeline** – a detailed timeline of our many fallen brothers and one fallen sister – beginning with January 1st and listing all significant incidents that took place on 1 January, regardless of the year, day-by-day from 1 January through 31 December, utilizing two distinct introductory phrases:

    - "*Today in Baltimore City Police History*" is an introduction used for certain historical events throughout our history

    - "*On This Day in Baltimore City Police History*" is an introduction used to list our fallen brothers and sister

- **Fallen Officers** – An alphabetical list of Baltimore's fallen officers whose names appear on the National Law Enforcement Memorial wall in Washington, DC. Each listing includes their wall location code and instructions on how to use these location codes. This aids visitors in finding loved one's names among the overwhelming number of fallen officers listed on the Memorial wall.

The Evolution of Baltimore Police Badges

Table of Contents

The Baltimore City Police Department 2
The Evolution of Baltimore Police Badges 3
Baltimore City Police Department Motto 17
Year-By-Year Event Timeline 18

1700's 18
1800's 21
1900's 35

1901 35
1902 35
1904 36
1905 36
1907 37
1908 37
1909 37
1910 37
1912 38
1913 38
1914 39
1915 39
1916 40
1917 40
1918 40
1919 40
1920 41
1921 41
1922 41
1923 41
1924 42

1925	42
1926	42
1927	42
1928	43
1929	43
1931	43
1932	43
1933	44
1934	44
1935	44
1936	44
1937	44
1938	45
1939	45
1940	46
1941	46
1943	46
1944	47
1945	47
1946	47
1947	47
1948	48
1949	48
1950	48
1951	48
1952	49
1953	49
1954	49
1955	49
1956	50
1957	51
1958	51
1959	51

1960	51
1961	51
1962	52
1964	52
1965	52
1966	53
1967	54
1968	54
1969	56
1970	56
1971	57
1972	58
1973	59
1974	60
1975	62
1976	63
1977	64
1978	64
1979	65
1981	65
1982	66
1983	66
1984	66
1985	66
1986	67
1987	67
1989	67
1990	68
1991	68
1992	68
1993	68
1994	69
1995	70

1996	70
1997	71
1998	71
2000's	**72**
2001	72
2002	72
2003	73
2004	73
2005	73
2006	73
2007	74
2010	74
2011	74
2012	74
2013	75
2014	76
2015	76
2016	77
Baltimore Police History	**78**
A Detailed Day-by-Day Look Through Our Past	78
1 January - 1857	78
1 January - 1960	79
1 January - 1976	80
2 January - 1925	81
2 January - 1932	81
6 January - 1884	85
6 January - 1951	86
6 January - 2014	86
7 January - 1931	88
9 January - 2007	89
9 January - 2011	91
9 January - 2015	93
10 January - 1964	95

11 January - 1959	96
11 January - 2015	100
12 January - 1871	100
12 January - 1873	104
12 January - 1873	104
13 January - 1947	104
14 January - 1941	107
15 January - 1983	108
16 January - 1905	108
16 January - 1970	109
20 January - 1965	112
20 January - 1982	114
22 January - 1917	114
25 January - 1947	115
25 January - 1967	115
26 January - 1905	116
29 January - 1944	118
29 January - 2014	118
1 February - 1900	118
2 February - 1860 - 2nd Issue Badge	122
4 February - 1929	123
6 February - 1964	124
7 February - 1904 - Great Baltimore Fire	126
8 February - 1904	144
9 February - 1904	164
10 February - 1967	166
12 February - 1928	167
12 February - 1934	168
13 February - 1948	168
14 February - 1935	172
14 February - 1966	173
14 February - 1954	175
15 February - 1915	176

18 February - 1845	176
21 February - 1938	176
22 February - 1928	176
26 February - 1799	177
1 March - 1857	178
1 March - 1972	178
1 March - 1946	178
1 March - 1957	179
2 March - 1924	180
4 March - 1909	182
4 March - 1909	187
4 March - 1933	188
5 March - 1989	189
8 March - 2000	190
9 March - 1807	194
9 March - 1826	194
9 March - 1826	194
9 March - 1826	195
9 March - 1826	195
9 March - 1835	195
9 March - 1977	195
9 March - 1963	196
12 March - 2001	196
15 March - 1808	197
15 March - 1875 – Marshal Gilmor	198
15 March - 2012	200
16 March - 1853	200
16 March - 1858	201
17 March - 2006	201
19 March - 1798	201
19 March - 1918	202
21 March - 2002	203
23 March - 1974	204

24 March - 1970 204
26 March - 1971 206
28 March - 1889 206
28 March - 1925 207
29 March - 1973 208
1 April - 1972 209
1 April - 1979 209
3 April - 1797 209
4 April - 1938 210
4 April - 1949 211
4 April - 1976 - 5th Issue Badge 212
5 April - 2013 213
6 April - 1968 213
6 April - 1973 214
7 April - 1962 218
7 April - 1994 - SCAN 219
16 April - 1976 221
17 April - 1957 222
18 April - 1915 223
18 April - 1968 230
19 April - 1861 231
April 19 - 1861 250
21 April - 1933 254
22 April - 1934 - Md. Tags 257
24 April - 1970 261
26 April - 2006 264
29 April - 1966 278
30 April - 1800 279
1 May - 1860 - 2nd Issue Badge 279
5 May - 1974 279
5 May - 1939 280
7 May - 1997 281
9 May - 2013 283

16 May - 1968	285
17 May - 1837	285
17 May - 1925	285
19 May - 2006	286
20 May - 1902	286
20 May - 2006	288
22 May - 1838	288
22 May - 1871	288
26 May - 1956	289
26 May - 1962	290
26 May - 1993	291
27 May - 1890 - 4th Issue Badge	295
28 May - 1937	295
28 May - 1994	296
29 May - 1914	296
2 June - 1945	297
4 June - 1975	298
8 June - 1994	298
11 June - 1973	298
12 June - 1943	299
12 June - 1971	304
13 June - 1940	306
17 June - 1965	309
19 June - 1912	311
20 June - 1894	312
20 June - 1896	313
20 June - 1924	314
22 June - 1860 - 2nd Issue Badge	316
22 June - 1967	316
23 June - 1978	316
26 June - 1946	316
27 June - 1861 - Fed Takeover	317
22 June - 1862 - 3rd Issue Badge	318

29 June - 1926	318
1 July - 1891	320
1 July - 1954	321
1 July - 1970	321
2 July - 1962	321
3 July - 1919	323
3 July - 1925	325
3 July - 2004	325
4 July - 1889	327
5 July - 1870	329
5 July - 1938 - Vice Squad Creation	331
5 July - 1938	339
11 July - 1958	339
11 July - 1974 - Police Strike	339
12 July - 1973	340
12 July - 1897 - Frey Retires	341
15 July - 1891	341
15 July - 1976	342
16 July - 1877	342
20 July - 1981	346
21 July - 1986	347
22 July - 1965	348
24 July - 1868 - Great Baltimore Flood	352
26 July - 1929	353
26 July - 1972	356
27 July - 1971	359
29 July - 1776	359
30 July - 1902	359
30 July - 1983	360
1 August - 1907	360
1 August - 1953	360
1 August - 1971	362
1 August - 1974	363

1 August - 1975	365
4 August - 1950	365
5 August - 1927	366
5 August - 1981	366
7 August - 1951	367
8 August - 1729	367
8 August - 1902 - Marshal Farnan	368
10 August - 1891	385
11 August - 1972	385
14 August - 1914 - Marshal Carter	385
15 August - 1857	386
15 August - 1974	386
19 August - 1979	387
20 August - 1902	389
21 August - 1967	393
22 August - 2002	393
23 August - 1872	394
25 August - 1974	395
27 August - 1926	396
29 August - 1899	396
29 August - 2012	399
30 August - 1972	400
31 August - 1959	400
31 August - 1959	401
9 September - 1977	401
10 September - 1945	401
11 September - 1964	402
12 September - 1926	404
13 September - 1975	404
14 September - 1871	406
14 September - 1940	407
17 September - 1857	407
17 September - 1922	407

18 September - 1914	408
19 September - 1958	410
19 September - 1975	410
20 September - 1986	411
21 September - 1915	412
21 September - 1992	413
22 September - 1858	414
22 September - 1973	416
23 September - 1968	418
27 September - 2010	418
29 September - 1956	418
31 September - 1971	421
2 October - 1920	421
2 October - 1978	423
October 3 - 1967	423
4 October - 1932	424
7 October - 1897 - Hamilton	425
7 October - 1944 - Helmet Type Hats	426
9 October - 1936	427
8 October - 1985	428
9 October - 1957	429
10 October - 1989	429
11 October - 1857	430
14 October - 1857	431
14 October - 1994	432
14 October - 2000	435
15 October - 1885	436
16 October - 1949	437
16 October - 2010	437
17 October - 1885	438
17 October - 1895	440
17 October - 1914	443
20 October - 1851 - 1st Issue Badge	445

20 October – 2010 445
22 October - 1971 446
22 October - 1987 446
23 October - 1955 448
23 October - 1973 449
24 October - 1978 449
24 October - 1987 449
27 October - 1975 449
27 October - 1978 451
29 October - 1936 453
30 October – 1998 454
31 October - 1935 455
1 November - 1935 456
1 November - 1925 456
1 November - 1938 457
2 November - 1934 458
4 November - 1968 459
4 November - 1998 459
5 November - 1858 463
7 November - 1908 – Round Hat 467
7 November - 1943 467
9 November - 1880 468
13 November - 1856 469
16 November - 1960 470
16 November - 1994 471
18 November - 1985 471
18 November - 1946 473
19 November - 1928 475
20 November - 1930 - Weitzel 477
22 November - 1872 480
23 November - 2002 480
25 November - 1912 482
26 November - 1904 - Fingerprints 483

28 November - 1955 484
28 November - 1995 486
1 December - 1973 487
3 December - 1937 489
3 December - 1984 495
3 December - 1970 498
7 December - 1904 498
10 December - 1974 508
11 December - 1856 511
13 December - 1988 512
18 December - 1948 - K9 513
18 December - 1956 513
20 December - 1934 516
20 December - 1977 519
25 December - 1964 519
28 December - 1936 526
30 December - 1948 528
31 December - 1937 531
Fallen Hero's Wall Locations 534
Line of Duty & On-Duty Deaths 542
Excerpts - 1856 Proceeding of City Council 549
Baltimore's Police Commissioners 551
Baltimore's Board of Police Commissioners 555
Baltimore Police Weapons 560
Highly Recommended 561

Baltimore City Police Department Motto

Ever Ready - Ever Faithful - Ever on the Watch

In the year of 1886, on the wall of the department's gym hung a large shield upon which was painted in gold letters the words, *"The Central Police Gymnasium, organized November 9, 1880 - Ever on the Watch."* In the center of the shield was a large round wooden plaque containing the image of two gladiators engaged in combat. Framing the plaque was a depiction, carved in wood, of a regulation patrolman's belt, upon which was inscribed in a flowing ribbon the Latin words **"Semper Paratus - Semper Fideles,"** which translated read **"Ever Ready - Ever Faithful."** The shield was presented to the "Central Police Athletic Association" by Mr. John Convery on 10 November, 1886, according to the book *"Our Police 1888."*

Our Motto, an important part of our departmental history, is part of everyone who has ever pinned on the badge of a Baltimore Police Officer. Our motto should make those who have enforced the laws on the streets of Baltimore proud, and it should give those ready to apply more reason to want to wear the uniform of a Baltimore Police Officer. For years Baltimore City Police Department families and in many cases their fathers, grandfathers, great grandfathers, and officers of Baltimore's Police have expressed pride, and seemed to walk with their heads a little higher. Because, Semper Paratus – Semper Fideles – Ever on the Watch is more than just words; Baltimore police live this motto, every time they walk their beat, handle their calls, and do their job.

As you will learn from the pages of this book, the Baltimore City Police Department has a rich history, every officer since the first officers have had big shoes to fill, and most of us have lived up to the oath we took, as if it were the words of this Motto... We have all, always been, "Ever Ready, Ever Faithful, and Ever on the Watch"

Semper Paratus - Semper Fideles - Semper Alapa Buris Pervigil

Ever Ready - Ever Faithful - Ever on the Watch

Year-By-Year Event Timeline

1700's

1729 – 8 August, 1729 - The preservation of the peace, protection of property and the arrest of offenders has been the goal of Baltimore residents since August 8, 1729, when the Legislature created Baltimore Town, 100 years before the "London Metropolitan Police Department" was founded by Sir Robert Peel (1829), and 47 years before the nation was established as a free and independent union of thirteen sovereign states, throwing off the rule of King George of England.

<u>Note</u>: Upon founding the London Metropolitan Police Department, their officers were quickly known as "Bobby Cops," or "Bobbies"; likewise their hats, "Bobby caps."

1775 – The year 1775 would be the start of what would come to be nine years of haphazard policing in "Baltimore Town." A series of mistakes were made in those nine years, but those mistakes were instructive, and in 1784, "Baltimore Town" decided to form a paid "Watch," in which the Watchmen could be fired, or otherwise penalized, for neglect of duty or certain other offenses. In the first abortive attempts to form the Nightwatch, every male inhabitant capable of duty signed an agreement, in which they swore to conform to police regulations adopted by the citizens, sanctioned by the Board of Commissioners, and to attend when summoned to serve as night watchmen. This citizen committee had some of the functions of the later 1888 Board of Police Commissioners. Baltimore Town was divided into Districts, and in each of these was stationed a company of Watchmen, commanded by a Captain of the Nightwatch.

1776 – The first **Captains of the Watch, or policemen**, in Baltimore under this primitive arrangement were Captain James Calhoun, of the First or Middle/Central District; Captain George Woolsey, had the Second District; Captain Benjamin Griffith, was in command of the Third District; Captain Barnard Eichelberger, the Fourth District; Captain George Lindenberger, the Fifth District; and Captain William Goodwin would manage the Sixth District. In Fell's Point, Captain Isaac Yanbidder served with two assistants, or Lieutenants. Each Captain had under his command a squad of sixteen men, every capable inhabitant being enrolled, and taking his turn. The streets were patrolled by these watchmen from 10 pm. until daybreak. None of these people were paid for their efforts to help their community.

1784 – The first attempt to organize a "**paid force**" to guard, or police Baltimore occurred in 1784. Constables were appointed, and given police powers to keep the peace. Baltimore's Police Department had been developing their police force since the formation of our "*Night Watch*" in 1784. In the beginning they were "Necessary to prevent fires, burglaries, and other outrages and disorders." This from Chapter 69 of the Acts of 1784, which was now 45 years before Sir Robert Peel's London Metropolitan Police Department was founded in *1829*. Baltimore would obtain Street Lights by order of the Police Department - These lights were oil lamps, and they were lit by order of the police, they were extinguished by the police, and they were maintained by order of the police. It was not so obvious to the public as it was to the panel of commissioners, and to the council of city hall, but the lighted streets in Baltimore served as a deterrent to decrease crime in and around a city known as "Mob Town". While at first many of the ideas, and or theories of the Panel of Commissioners, or "Our Marshals" were not approved, or put off until they either died in committee or were funded privately. Still, many of these ideas went on to become a norm in law enforcement throughout the country, and around the world. Furthermore, these concepts would eventually be paid for, and widely approved of and authorized by state legislatures throughout the country.

1797 – 3 April, 1797 – The City Council passed the first ordinance affecting the police. It directed that three persons were to be appointed Commissioners of the watch. They could employ for one year as many Captains and watchmen as had been employed in the night watch the year past for the same remuneration. The Commissioners prescribed regulations and hours of duty for the police.

1798 – 19 March, 1798 – An "officer" was known as a "High Constable." The position was created by an ordinance on 19 March, 1798. His duty was "to walk through the streets, lanes and alleys of the city daily, with "mace" in hand, taking such rounds, that within a reasonable time he shall visit all parts of the city, and give information to the Mayor or other Magistrate, of all nuisances within the city, and all obstructions and impediments in the streets, lanes, and alleys, and of all offences committed against the laws and ordinances." He was also required to report the names of the offenders against any ordinance and the names of the witnesses who could sustain the prosecutions against them, and regard the mayor as his chief. The yearly salary of the city constable was fixed at $350, and he was required to give a bond for the performance of his duty.

Note: Mace was not the "Chemical Mace" we think of today when we hear the word. A "Mace" is a weapon with a heavy head on one end of a solid shaft originally used to strike the opponent in self-defense, but in later years, it was learned that it served better for arm bars, and other holds, that prevent a suspect from injuring an officer or him/herself.

1798 – Baltimore made the first steps toward creating the **chief of police**, or marshal as he was later called. A high constable was appointed, and it was his duty to tour the city frequently, carrying a mace, the badge of authority, and to report on lawbreakers. By the turn of the century Baltimore had again became an unmanageable, riotous city. It was now a bustling community of 31,514 in population and one historian remarks naively, "The city was a rendezvous of a number of evil characters."

1799 – 26 February, 1799 - Authorized the appointment of a city constable in each ward. This ward constable was thus a policeman, and the term of city constable was not properly his although his duties were defined by the ordinance to be the same as those of the city or high constable.

1800's

1800 – 30 April, 1800 – At this meeting a committee of three persons from each ward was appointed to plan a reorganization of the "Night-watch." At a subsequent assembly on April 30, this committee recommended that the patrol be increased. The recommendation was approved and implemented, and by the vigilance of the watchmen disorder was suppressed for a time.

1807 – 9 March, 1807 - A general ordinance was passed defining the duties of the city **Board of Commissioners**. They were granted extensive powers. Among other things, with the Mayor they were authorized to employ as many captains, officers and watchmen as they might, from time to time, find necessary, but the expense should not exceed the annual appropriation for the service. The board was also required to make regulations and define the hours of duty of the watch, see that they attended to their duties with punctuality, receive their reports and cause those reports to be returned to the Mayor's office.

1808 – 15 March, 1808 – We lost our Brother **Night Watchman George Workner**.

1826 – 9 March, 1826 – The Mayor was given control of the city police by an ordinance which provided that there should be appointed, annually, two captains and two lieutenants of the watch for the **Eastern District**; two captains and four lieutenants of the watch for the **Middle District** and two captains and two lieutenants of the watch for the **Western District**. They were expected to perform such duties as the Mayor from time to time might direct. The latter was also given power to appoint as he chose any number of watchmen, and to dismiss them at his pleasure. He was also to prescribe their duties.

1826 – Central/Middle District History – 9 March, 1826 – a building built in 1802 at Holiday and Saratoga Streets housed the Central/Middle District, and was in use for that purpose until 1870. In that year, 202 N. Guilford Avenue (AKA North Street) was built for the district and used until 1908. At Saratoga and St. Paul Streets, a renovated school was used from March 4, 1908 until 1926, when the police headquarters building was built at Fallsway and Fayette Street, the first floor of which housed the Central District, as it was then known. The HQ/Central building was built in 1926 and used until 09-12-1977, when they moved to the current building at 500 E. Baltimore Street.

1826 – Eastern District History – 9 March, 1826 – The building at 1621 Bank Street, erected around 1822 and still standing today, was used for the Eastern District station house

from this date until 31 Aug 1959, at which time they opened their "new" station house at the old Northeastern station at Ashland and Rutland Avenue, pending the construction of a new building on Edison Highway at Federal Street. The Edison Highway building was completed in Dec of 1960 and remains the site of the Eastern District. When it opened, it was commanded by Capt. Millard B Horton.

1826 – **Western District History** – A building on Green Street, between Baltimore and Belvidere Streets, was used from 1826 until 1876 when they moved to their new location, Pine Street – which still stands today and is now used by the Maryland University Police Department. The Baltimore Police Department used the Pine Street station from 1876 until 31 Aug 1959 at 12:01 am, when they opened a new station house at Riggs Ave and Mount Street – 1034 N Mount Street continues to be the site of the Western District. When it opened, it was commanded by Capt. Wade H. Poole.

1835 – 9 March, 1835 – A "supplement" to an ordinance passed on this day provided for the appointment of twelve lieutenants of the watch, or policemen, "to preserve the peace, maintain the laws and advance the good government of the city." These lieutenants were required by the Mayor to reside in certain specific districts, and to have conspicuous signs on their homes bearing their names and office. In addition to their police duties, they were required to act as city bailiffs. Their compensation was fixed at $20 a month for their night work as lieutenants of the watch, with an additional sum of $220 a year for the other services mentioned.

1835 – **The Middle District** – April, 1835 – Also known as the Central District, the Middle District was located at Saratoga and Holliday streets. This station had a belfry atop it, while the Western District (on Green Street between Baltimore and Belvidere Street) did not. In April 1835, an appropriation was made for a belfry addition to the Green street watch house.

1835 – Mayor Jesse Hunt took occasion to call to the attention of the councils to the "lamentably defective" police arrangements of the city.

1836 – March 1836 – The **compensation** of the watchmen was increased to $1.00 for each night they served.

1837 – 17 May 1837 – The inaugural issue of the **Baltimore Sun** is printed – The first article in the Baltimore Sun that referenced our police officer is titled *Rioting*, and as we would expect it is a negative report. Even when the Department explained to the Sun that the article was incorrect, the paper still ran the story. The initial story seems to have appeared in the morning edition on the same date with the response coming in the evening edition.

1838 – 22 May, 1838 – The council substantially re-enacted the ordinance of 1835, providing, however, that if any watchman while in the performance of his duty should be wounded or maimed he should receive half-pay during the continuance of his disability, or for a period not exceeding two months. They were also paid for attendance at court. This ordinance provided as well for the annual appointment of three justices of the peace to receive the reports of the night watch. One of these justices was required to reside in each district. The yearly salary of each was $100.

1843 – In 1843, two cells were added to the district Western District station house, also known to most as the watch house, while in the Eastern station house there was but one. In the same year the Baltimore Sun declared that the custom of the watch calling the time notified thieves of the locality of the patrol and gave the former an opportunity of safely conducting their operations. This custom was consequently abandoned.

1845 – 18 February, 1845 – The **Southern District** was established under an ordinance. Two captains and four lieutenants were appointed for it, and the boundaries of the other districts were rearranged.

1845 – **Southern District History** – The Southern District was first located at Montgomery and Sharp Streets, where it sat from 1845 until 1896 when they moved to Ostend Street and Patapsco Street, where it remained in use from 1896 until 1985/86, when it moved to 10 Cherry Hill Road where it remains in use to the present. When it opened on 31 Aug 1959, Capt. Elmer I. Bowen was installed in command.

1848 – The Baltimore police, as constituted in 1848, consisted in the daytime of one high constable, one regular policeman for each ward, who was also lieutenant of the night-watch in his district, and the night watch men. Besides these, there were two extra policemen for each ward, who were called into service as occasion required. This system of day police was changed from time to time to keep pace with the increase in the number of wards in the city, until the wards numbered twenty. There was, however, no material alteration in the system until 1857, when a complete reorganization took place under the authority of an 1853 act of the Legislature.

1850 – (Mayor Member Ex-officio) Charles Howard, William Gatchell, Charles Hinks and John Davis became officers of the watch until 1861.

1850 – Charles Howard, became one of our Baltimore City **Police Commissioners** from 1850-1861.

1851 – 20 October, 1851 – The first known metallic badge worn by Baltimore Police Officers – also known as the **1st Issue badge**.

1853 – The State Legislature on March 16, 1853, passed a bill, "To provide for the better security for the citizens and property in the City of Baltimore." This statute provided that police officers **should be armed** and that a badge and commission be furnished each member. The former act of 1812 was repealed with the passage and enactment of this bill. No additional change in the police organization occurred until 1857.

1856 – 13 November, 1856 – We lost our Brother **Night Watchman John O'Mayer**.

1856 – 11 December, 1856 – City Council voted on, and passed a bill to **arm Baltimore Police Officers**. 1857 was a date given by the History Channel's "Tales of the Gun" – the "Police Guns" Episode, with an original air date, of 2 April, 2000, the Baltimore Sun reported, "Baltimore, having become the first Department in the nation to issue and provide each police officer with a firearm." The documentary went on to state that 'The Colt, 1849, Pocket Model,' was the weapon of choice, and was 1st issued, and used by the BPD and it's Officers. Sometimes, historical information is called into question because newer information contradicts it, and as in this case, we located two Sun Paper articles; one dated 11 December, 1856, titled "Proceeding of City Council", in which arming the individual City Police Officer was voted into law – then on 25 December, 1856 an article titled "The New Police Bill" appeared and the bill was released. While all of the actual revolvers may not have been provided in 1856, they were approved into law on 11 December, 1856.

Note: We only provide the aforementioned information about "Baltimore being first to arm their police" out of respect for the Discovery Channel and their source(s), but I suggest, at least for now, that we take their information with a grain of salt. Still, I will leave this place until we find further info. Others that read this line from a Sun Paper article dated 11 December, 1856, in which it was reported that a member of the City Council at the time, in trying to pass his bill to arm Baltimore Police said, "In New York and Philadelphia, where there is a penalty for carrying concealed weapons, the police are armed by the city authorities." This is being taken by us to mean, we may have been at least third in the issuance of firearms, but by these reports, we were not first.

1857 – 1 January, 1857 – Came the next important change under the provisions of this act; the ordinance introduced an entirely new order of things, and placed Baltimore's Department of Police on practically the same footing as those of the other large cities of this country. It declared that "after 1 March 1857, *the existing watch and police systems should be ABOLISHED, and all ordinances for the establishment and regulation of the same be*

repealed. The **new force** consisted of one marshal, one deputy marshal, eight captains, eight lieutenants, twenty-four sergeants, three hundred and fifty police officers, five detective police officers and eight turnkeys. The men were required to do duty day and night, and were given all the powers then vested by law in the city bailiffs, police officers, constables and watchmen. The city was divided into four police districts, whose stations were at the watch-houses. The Marshal, with the concurrence of the Mayor, was given authority to establish the geographic limits of the stations, dividing them into beats for each officer to walk, making allowance for a proper force to retain at the station houses. He also had power to alter at will the limits of the districts and beats. At this time, the Detective Bureau was established, and the City was again divided into four police districts: Middle/Central, Eastern, Western and Southern.

1857 – 15 August, 1857 – 200 **Revolvers** were purchased for issuance to Baltimore's Police Officers.

1857 – 17 Sept, 1857 – City Council approves spending $3,845.95 on 200 **Revolvers**.

1857 – 11 Oct, 1857 – Possibly the First **Police Involved Shooting** with issued firearms. The officers involved were Deputy Marshall Manly, along with Officers G.H.E. Bailey, Nicholson, Saville, Lee, George Bailey, Andrew, Presto, Chapman, and Englar. Shot was Deputy Marshall Manly, and Suspect Andrew Hesslinger was killed, as was an African American named Ramsey. The shooting took place at a bar called Seager's Lager Beer Brewery at 7 o'clock on that Sunday, at the establishment situated upon the Frederick Road at its intersection with West Pratt Street.

1857 – 14 October, 1857 – We lost our Brother **Sergeant William Jourdan**.

1857 – In this year the department compelled Patrolmen (as they were then known) to wear **uniforms**, both on and off duty. Several additional rules were established:

- Winter uniforms were made up of a black cap bearing the policemen's number; a dark blue overcoat and trousers with a patent leather belt, and the word "Police" prevalently stamped upon its buckle.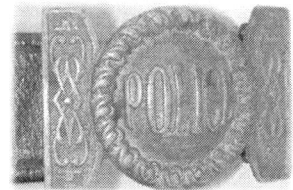

- Summer uniforms were the same minus the overcoat. Policemen were required to wear standing collars, summer or winter.

- The badge of their authority was a 3-inch star, worn on the left breast of their coat. The star was often sewn on to avoid all chances of an officer being without his badge. In the old days, our brothers would occasionally leave their

badges home, so having them sewn on alleviated that situation. Taking away an excuse used by thugs that would use a badgeless officer as an excuse to assault him and then claim he didn't know his victim was an officer.

- The final piece to the officer's uniform was his "Billy Club," known in Baltimore as an "Espantoon." It was recognizable and it was often carried in the officer's hand, spun on a leather strap, or tucked under the officer's arm. While in the station or when both hands were needed otherwise, the Espantoon might be seen hanging from a ring on officers' belts.

- Due to the increasing incidence where scofflaws carried guns, the officers' were also armed with pistols.

1857 – **First Detective Squad** – On 1 March 1857, the first squad of detectives was appointed by the mayor, under the new Police Bill in Dec of 1856 - By this time the city's chief executive again controlled the force. There were five Detectives in the first squad and they wore civilian clothes. As was mentioned above Patrolman were compelled to wear uniforms both on and off duty. In winter the uniform was a black cap with the policemen's number on it, a dark blue overcoat, trousers with a patent leather belt and the word police printed on it. These first five appointed Detectives were - Detective Thomas W. German, Detective Christian Barnes, Detective William Stevens, Detective Wm. L. Tayman, and Detective Jerome Airey.

1858 – 16 March, 1858 – The Legislature of the State took memorable action in passing a bill to "provide for the better security for life and property in the City of Baltimore." This enactment empowered the Mayor and the City Councils to increase, and in every way strengthen the police, whether with officers, bailiffs, night-watchmen, or others in any way connected with the organization of the force. When any of these guardians of the peace were injured either in person or in apparel, while in the discharge of his duties, the act required that he be fairly indemnified. This statute also provided that the police force should be armed, that a commission and badge be furnished each member, and that it should be no defense for anyone who resisted or assaulted an officer to claim that his commission or badge was not exhibited. This statute repealed the act of 1812.

1858 – 22 September, 1858 – We lost our Brother **Police Officer Benjamin Benton**.

1858 – 5 November, 1858 – We lost our Brother **Police Officer Robert M. Rigdon**.

1859 – 27 June, 1859 – A Police and fire-alarm telegraph system was put into place on 27 June, 1858.

1860 – 2 Feb, 1860 – Baltimore Police force placed back under **State control**.

1860 – Other innovations of the time was the inception of the **Marine Unit** in 1860 – The Harbor Patrol would begin patrolling the harbor based on wording in legislation that decreed had a large portion of the waters of Baltimore City, and therefor had to be protected by City Police. The budget appropriated at the time would not allow for steam or other motor-based boats. Marshal Jacob Fray was called in to figure out what could be done about the problem. An 1886 sun article said of the times, "They hadn't the funds to buy a patrol boat. What then? Well Marshal Frey conceived of the idea of placing rowboats at advantaged positions, using points where the various districts touched the harbor waters. Four boats total, two for Eastern, one for Central and one for Southern." (NOTE: There was no "Southeast" at the time, Southeast didn't come until 1958.) A second article from 1958 went on to say, "It would then be a simple matter of jumping in the boats at the required time, of pushing out from land and then of rowing over the regulated beats. It was all somewhat surprising, efficient and a novelty that worked for 31 years."

1860 – 1 May, 1860, we switched our badges to the **2nd issue badge**. It was a new "Metropolitan Police" force under a Board of Police Commissioner's (BOC), state-appointed civilians. This signaled the retirement of the "Corporation Police force," and the new badge was authorized at that time.

1861 – 19 April, 1861 – was a fateful day for Baltimore police, who had to stop rioting by citizens intent on stopping **Union Soldiers** from passing through the city headed south to the first battlefields of the Civil War.

1861 – 27 June, 1861 to 29 March, 1862 – Under control of the United States Military authorities, ten **Police Commissioners** were appointed by the Military authorities – they were Columbus O'Donnell, Archibald Sterling Jr., Thomas Kelso, John R Kelso, John W Randolph, Peter Sauerwein, John B Seidenstricker, Joseph Roberts, and Michael Warner – the name of the tenth Police Commissioner being lost to history.

1861/62 – In March of 1862, the military authorities who had taken control of the Department on June 27, 1861, turned the Police Department back to the **authority of the state.**

1862 – In 1862 Baltimore's Police commissioner suggested they form a **Park Police**; the purpose of the Park Police was to police the new Druid Hill Park, which at that time was wholly beyond the city limits and thus beyond the authority of city Police. The city's Park Commission was first granted the right to preserve peace in parklands by the City Charter of 1862.

Note: The **Park Police** Department were disbanded in 1959, with its members becoming members of the Baltimore City Police Department.

1862 – 22 June, 1862, a newly formed Baltimore Police force appeared in a completely **new uniform** with a new series of badges. The badge known as the **3rd Issue** had the same center section from the first badge, and returned the designation of "City Police," surrounded by twenty small points encircled by a narrow rim.

Note: The 20 pointer was replaced by an order from the Commissioner. He said, "too many were in the hands of the citizens." (This was according to an article in the Sun newspaper, circa 1890.)

1862 – 29 March, 1862 to 15 Nov 1866 - (Mayor's Members named were known as Ex-officio officers Samuel Hindes, and Nicholas L Wood.)

1862 – Nicholas L. Wood became Baltimore City **Police Commissioner** from 1862-1864.

1864 – Samuel Hindes became Baltimore City **Police Commissioner** from 1864-1866.

1866 – 15 Nov, 1866 to March 1867 – (Mayor member Ex-officio William T Valiant, and James Young). James Young, became Baltimore City **Police Commissioner** from 1866-1867.

1867 – The first State agency to exercise police powers was the Baltimore City Police Force. Established in 1867 under a Board of Police Commissioners, the Force was elected by the General Assembly (Chapter 367, Acts of 1867). Baltimore's police force, from 1867, was governed by a State board although jurisdiction was limited to the City.

1867 – March 1867 Lefebvre Jarrett, James E Carr, and William H B Fusselbaugh became Baltimore City **Police Commissioners**.

1867 – LeFevre Jarrett became Baltimore City **Police Commissioner** from 1867-1870.

1868 – 24 July, 1868 (Friday) – The **Baltimore Flood** overtook the city. In a crisis, the bravery of Commissioner Carr in rescuing the victims of the catastrophe became a matter of national fame. Harper's Weekly, at the time, in a long article on the floods, quoted the following editorial notice from the Baltimore Sunday Telegram, of July 26, 1868: "It is a true saying, that in times of great public calamities, some men rise to the position of a greatness, and such was the case with Police Commissioner James E. Carr.

1870 – 5 July, 1870 - We lost our Brother **Police Officer James Murphy**

1870 – 14 March, 1870 - John W Davis, James E Carr, and William H B Fusselbaugh were our **Police Commissioners**.

1870 – John W. Davis became Baltimore City **Police Commissioner** from 1870 – 1871.

1871 – 12 January, 1871 – We lost our Brother **Police Officer Charles J Walsh**.

1871 – 22 May, 1871 – We lost our Brother **Police Officer Joseph Clark**.

1871 – 14 September, 1871 – We lost our Brother **Detective John H. Richards**.

1871 – 15 March, 1871 – William H B Fusselbaugh, James E Carr, and Thomas W Morse were **our Police Commissioners**.

1871 – William H. B. Fusselbaugh, became Baltimore City **Police Commissioner** from 1871-1881.

1872 – 18 August 1872 – We lost our Brother **Police Officer John Christopher**.

1872 – 22 Nov 1872 – We lost our Brother **Patrolman Franklin Fullum**.

1873 – 12 January 1873 – We lost our Brother **Patrolman John H. Dames**.

1873 – 12 January 1873 – We lost our Brother **Patrolman James T. Harvey**.

1874 – **Northwestern District History** – 1874 - The Northwestern District was first at Pennsylvania Ave and Lambert Street where it remained until 1958/9 when they moved to their present district on Reisterstown Rd.

1874 – **Northeastern District History** – 1874 – The Northeastern District was first opened at Ashland and Chew Streets (Durham Street) where it remained until 1958/59 when they moved to their present district building at 1900 Argonne Drive.

1875 – 15 March, 1875 – William H B Fusselbaugh, Harry Gilmor, and John Milroy were our **Police Commissioners**.

1876 – Baltimore switched from the **Colt** "Model 1849" Pocket Model to the **Smith & Wesson** "Baby Russian" nickel plated revolver. These remained in service until approx. 1910 when various models were purchased for field trials. Flip flipping back and forth over the years from Colt to Smith and Wesson, Smith and Wesson to Colt and so on, up until 1990 when the Department began phasing in the **Glock** "Model 17" 9mm Semi-Automatic.

1877 – 15 March, 1877 – William H B Fusselbaugh, Harry Gilmor, and James R Herbert were our **Police Commissioners**.

1878 – 12 April, 1878 – William H B Fusselbaugh, James R Herbert, and John Milroy were our **Police Commissioners**.

1880 – 9 November, 1880 – The **Motto** for the department began in the Central District and was displayed on a plaque on the gymnasium wall, *"Ever on the Watch"* written in English, under the Latin words *"Semper Paratus"* and *"Semper Fideles"* - *"Semper"* can either mean, *"Always"* or *"Ever"* - so it could read either *"Ever Ready / Ever Faithful / Ever on the Watch"* or *"Always Ready / Always Faithful / Ever on the Watch"*. Throughout history, *"Semper Paratus"* and *"Semper Fideles"* have consistently been read as *"Always"*. However, in Baltimore using *"Ever on the Watch"* over *"Always on the Watch"* leads us to believe in this case "Semper" stood for "Ever" - Giving us *"Semper Paratus - Semper Fideles - Semper Alapa Buris Pervigil"* or *"Ever Ready - Ever Faithful - Ever on the Watch"*

1881 – 15 March, 1881 - George Colton, James R Herbert, and John Milroy were our **Police Commissioners**.

1883 – Mourning for fallen officers, and the passing of officers, was ordered upon the death of **Capt. Franklin Kenney** of the Eastern District. The mourning time was established, and set for a period of 10 days for fallen officers and 5 days for passing officers.

1883 – 15 March, 1883 - George Colton, James R Herbert, and John Milroy were our **Police Commissioners**.

1884 – 5 Aug, 1884 – George Colton, John Milroy, and J D Ferguson were our **Police Commissioners**.

1884 – 6 January, 1884 – We lost our Brother **Police Officer Charles W. Fisher**.

1884 – **Southwestern District History** - 1884 – 17 July 1884 The Southwestern District was first opened at Calhoun and Pratt Streets (200 S Calhoun St) where it remained until 11 July 1958 when they moved to their present location at 424 Font Hill Ave.

1884 – **Central District** takes on this new title, from it's former *"Middle District"* as was reported in a 1905 Sun paper report in which the author wrote of a library of police docket books "A single glance along the long row of frayed and weak back books is interesting, as it shows exactly when the old *"Middle District"* changed its name to the more dignified title of *"Central District"*. The record for 1884 is the first book bearing the name *"Central District"* Maintenance.

1885 – 15 Oct 1885, Jacob Frey begins his term as **Marshal** from Oct 15 1885 – 12 July 1897

1885 – 17 October, 1885 – The first **Patrol Wagon** went into service on October 17, 1885 - and is believed to make Baltimore the second to use patrol wagons in the country, behind Chicago. The story goes; One day Deputy-Marshal Jacob Frey was reading an illustrated magazine while in the gymnasium of Central's Station when he saw facts on Patrol Wagons being used in Chicago. He brought the idea before the board of police commissioners and they were only mildly interested. Frey didn't give up on ideas that he believed in so he called the board's attention to the matter again some weeks later. They had forgotten about it, but promised to look into it. Wagons and Police Telegraph Box Systems were the future in Frey's eyes, so after the board failed to act, "Marshal Frey" took matters into its own hands. He sent one of the members of the "Board" and Marshal Gray to Chicago to see how the "New Fanged" patrol wagons worked. They "Were Charmed" an old record states. In addition, while there they saw Chicago's new police telegraph box system, known as the call box, result was both innovations were in use in Baltimore by the fall of 1885. According to Gamewell's records, Chicago was the first to use the **Police Telegraph System**, and Baltimore was the second in this country to use this system.

1885 – 17 October, 1885 – On the same day the wagons went into effect Baltimore Police Department also began using the Police Telegraph Boxes (Call boxes) – the pilot program was begun in the Central District, but would quickly spread to use in all Districts, and on all posts.

1885 – The **Harbor Patrol** was established in 1885.

1886 – The **Police Helmet**, (Bobby Cap) worn in other cities, most notably in London England, where they are still worn today. The Bobby cap/helmet was made part of the uniform in Baltimore, introduced by Commissioner Alford J. Carr. Taking the place of the derby, or bell cap (Bell caps are still worn today, by high-ranking Baltimore Fire Department personnel), these hats were formerly worn by Baltimore police. Commissioner Carr specified that the black helmet was worn during the winter, and the pearl/gray helmet would be worn during summer months. The helmet at that time was significant of rank, only Patrolman, and Sergeants wore it. The Marshal, and his Deputy Marshal, along with all Captains and Lieutenants wore the regular cap of the period (The Bell Cap).

1886 – 25 Feb, 1886 – George Colton, John Q A Robson, and John Milroy were our **Police Commissioners**.

1887 – 15 March, 1887 – Edson M Schryver, Alfred J Carr, and John Q A Robson were our **Police Commissioners**.

1888 – The **Mounted Patrol** was established.

1888 – 23 Jan, 1888 – Edson M Schryver, John Gill Jr, and John Q A Robson were our **Police Commissioners**.

1889 – 28 March, 1889 – Ten **incandescent electric lights** which will illuminate the heretofore gloomy pathway in Druid Hill Park leading from the Clipper gate to the walk from the Mansion House to the main entrance on Madison Ave, were lighted last night (28 Mar 1889) for the first time. The lamps were mounted on cedar posts about the height of a street gas lamp, and are lighted simultaneously by the turning of a lever in the gatekeeper's house at the Druid Hill's Entrance to the park. **Street lamps** were initially began in this country at the suggestion of the Baltimore Police Department when they used oil lamps that would be lit, extinguished and maintained by Baltimore's Police in the year 1784. It was not so obvious to the public as it were to the panel of commissioners, and to the council of city hall, but the lighted streets in Baltimore were a deterrent that prevented, and decreased crime, in and around "*Mob Town.*" While at first many of the ideas and/or theories of the Board of Commissioners, and/or our Marshals were often shot down, or put off until they either died in committee or were funded privately. Many of these ideas would go on to become the norm in law enforcement throughout the country, and around the world. Furthermore, these concepts would eventually become widely approved, authorized and funded by our state legislatures.

1889 – 4 July, 1889 – We lost our Brother **Police Officer John T. Lloyd**.

1890 – 27 May, 1890 – What came to be known as the **4th issue badge** was worn with a **uniform by** all members of the force. This is a shield-shaped badge with the word "POLICE" across the top, Maryland seal in the center and a ribbon with the officer's number across the bottom. Sergeants and above had an eagle on top of their shield. Lieutenants and above wore a badge similar to the Sergeant but was gold in color. The eagle on the badges had a ribbon in its beak denoting the rank of the officer. These were worn from 1890 until 1976.

1891 – 15 July, 1891 – We lost our Brother **Police Officer Jacob Zapp**.

1891 – 10 August 1891 – The little steamer is the harbor police cruiser *Lannan* named in honor of former Deputy Marshal John Lannan, deceased, who had charge of her construction. The *Lannan* was built in 1891 by James Clark & Co., from plans kindly loaned the Department by the United States Government. The harbor patrol boat was completed on August 10, 1891, and after a very successful trial trip was accepted and immediately put into commission.

1894 – 20 June, 1894 – We lost our Brother **Police Officer James T. Dunn**.

1894 – 20 June, 1894 – We lost our Brother **Police Officer Michael Neary**.

1894 – 1 Dec, 1894 – Edson M Schryver, John Gill Jr, and John C Legg were our **Police Commissioners**.

1895 – 17 October, 1895 – We lost our Brother **Police Officer John J. Dailey**.

1896 – The **Bertillon Bureau** was established to take photographs and measurements of prisoners. The Bertillon system was used for identifying persons by means of a detailed record of body measurements, physical description and photographs. The Bertillon system was later superseded by the much more accurate procedure of fingerprinting.

1896 – 27 March, 1896 – Daniel C Heddinger, John Gill Jr, and Edson M Schryver were our **Police Commissioners**.

1897 – 15 March, 1897 – Daniel C Heddinger, William W Johnson, and Edson M Schryver were our **Police Commissioners**.

1897 – 13 July, 1897 – Thomas F Garnan, was **Deputy Marshal** / Acting Marshal from July 13 1897 - Oct 6 1897.

1897 – 7 Oct, 1897 – Samuel T Hamilton was **Marshal** from Oct 7 1897 - Oct 7 1901.

1897 – 12 July, 1897 – The active connection of Marshal Jacob Frey with the Police Department ceased. On October 7, 1897, Capt. Samuel T. Hamilton was elected **Marshal of Police** to succeed Marshal Frey. Marshal Hamilton was a veteran officer of the Civil War and a man of indisputable courage and integrity. For many years following the great civil conflict he had served on the Western frontier and took part in the unremitting campaigns against the Sioux and other Indian tribes, who were constantly waging war upon the settlers and pioneers as they pushed their way toward the setting sun, building towns and railroads and trying to conquer the wilderness and its natural dwellers. In the Sioux campaign of 1876, when Gen. George A. Custer and his gallant command, outnumbered ten to one by the Indians in the valley of the Little Big Horn were annihilated, Captain Hamilton and his troop rode day and night in a vain effort to re-enforce Custer and his sorely pressed men. It was on June 26, 1876, the Seventh United States Cavalry rode and fought to their deaths, and on June 27, the day following, the reinforcements arrived, exhausted from their terrific ride across the country. Captain Hamilton and his troop fought through the rest of the campaign, which resulted in Sitting Bull, the great Indian war chief, being driven across the Canadian frontier.

1897 – Daniel C. Heddinger became Baltimore City **Police Commissioner** from 1897-1900.

1898 – Fall of 1898 – ground was broken on the new **Northern District**. What was being built on a piece of land purchased by the City, at Cedar and 2nd was called Northern annex to be commanded by Capt. Thomas W Morris.

1899 – 29 August, 1899 – We lost our Brother **Police Officer Alonzo B. Bishop**.

1900's

1900 – **Northern District History** - The Northern District was first opened at Keswick and 34th Street on, 1 February, 1900, commanded by Capt. Gittings, Lieutenants Henry and Dempsey; Round Sergeants, Warden for Day Duty and Moxley for Night Duty. At the time, they began with 50 officers. It remained at the Keswick location until 2001 when it moved to its new building at the current location at 2201 W. Coldspring Lane.

1900 – The interesting thing about the Board of **Police Commissioners** and eventual single Commissioner is that the Commissioner(s) for the City of Baltimore were chosen and appointed by the Governor for the State of Maryland and not the Mayor.

1900 – 7 May, 1900 – George M. Upsher, Edward H. Fowler, and John T. Morris were our **Police Commissioners**.

1900 – George M. Upsher became Baltimore City **Police Commissioner** from 1900-1904.

1901

1901 – 8 Oct 1901 – Thomas F. Farnan Deputy Marshal was **Acting Marshal** from Oct 8 1901 - Aug 7 1902

1902

1902 – 20 May, 1902 – We lost our Brother **Police Officer John A. McIntyre**

1902 – 30 July, 1902 – We lost our Brother **Police Officer Charles J. Donohue**

1902 – 21 August, 1902 – "1000 members of Police Department to re-take Oath" - The entire department was forced to **re-take their oath of office**, as prior to this day, they had been improperly and illegally sworn in, and this was the case for 35 years.

1902 – 8 Oct, 1902 – Thomas F. Farnan, was appointed **Marshal** of our department from Oct 8 1902 – 8 Aug 1914

1904

1904 – 8 Feb 1904 – **The Great Baltimore Fire** raged in Baltimore on Sun, Feb 7 and Mon, Feb 8, 1904. 1,231 firefighters were required to bring the blaze under control, both professional paid truck and engine companies from the Baltimore City Fire Department, Baltimore County Fire Department and volunteer fire companies from the surrounding counties, along with some out of state units that came in on local railways. The fire destroyed a major portion of central Baltimore City, to include over 1,500 buildings covering an area of some 140 acres. It spread from North Howard Street on the west, north to the retail shopping areas on Fayette Street and began moving eastward as it was pushed by prevailing winds. Baltimore Police not only helped to fight the fires, and evacuate buildings, but they also performed extensive crowd control and fought crime associated with this type of disaster and chaos, in which looting almost always begins.

1904 – 23 March, 1904 – George M. Upsher, John T. Morris, and Thomas J. Shryock were our **Police Commissioners**.

1904 – 2 May, 1904 – George R. Willis, James H. Preston, and Thomas J. Shryock were our **Police Commissioners**.

1904 – James H. Preston became Baltimore City **Police Commissioner** from 1904-1908 (Gov. Warfield made him a member of the Board of Police Commissioners for Baltimore City, 1904-08) He went on to become Baltimore's Mayor in 1915.

1904 – George R. Willis became Baltimore City **Police Commissioner** from 1904-1908

1904 – 7 Dec 1904 – **Fingerprint Identification Section** - Baltimore Police Department becomes the first police agency in the country to use the new Fingerprint System of identification when on 26 November, 1904 they finger printed John Randles to be held over on a theft charge. Fingerprint Identification was brought to Baltimore by Marshal Farnan, who after attending a seminar himself on the subject came back to Baltimore and sent Sgt. John A. Casey to St. Louis to learn the system, and immediately put the technique into place, eventually taking the place of the aforementioned Bertillon system. The department would go on to use 7 Dec 1904 as the inauguration date of the Finger Print system.

1905

1905 – 26 January, 1905 – We lost our Brother **Police Officer Mathew Boone**.

1905 – 25 December, 1905 – We lost our Brother **Police Officer Charles Spitznagle**.

1907

1907 – 1 August 1907 – The Department was to receive a Columbia **Electric Automobile** when the completed machine was put to use in the Central District as an Ambulance and Patrol (Paddy) Wagon. It was said to have been easy to run and easily made 16 miles an hour.

1908

1908 – The **Traffic Division** was established.

1908 – May 4 1908 Sherlock Swann, John B. A. Wheltle, and Peter E. Tome were our **Police Commissioners**.

1908 - Sherlock Swann became Baltimore City **Police Commissioner** from 1908-1910.

1908 – Nov 7, 1908 – After 22 years, The Baltimore Police Department stopped using the Police Helmet, (Bobby Cap), and goes to a more modern **round, or oval top, police hat**.

From the Baltimore Sun – *The Baltimore Police go from the Bobby Type Helmet to the more modern cap and Officers donned new uniforms, veteran Captains returned to old Districts, caps supplant helmets and Espantoons are in use once again.*

1909

1909 – 4 March, 1909 – We lost our Brother **Police Officer Thomas H. Worthington**.

1910

1910 – 2 May, 1910 – John B. A. Wheltle, Peter E. Tome, and C. Baker Clotworthy were our **Police Commissioners**.

1910 – The State of Maryland started making our own Motor Vehicle Tag Plates at the

Maryland State Penitentiary (Find the rest of this story from the 22 April, 1934 reports in the day-to-day timeline)

1912

1912 – 25 November, 1912 – We lost our Brother **Officer John McGrain**.

1912 – 19 June, 1912 – The first female police officer was hired under the title of **Policewoman** was Mary S. Harvey, EOD of June 19, 1912. Her hiring was followed by that of Margaret B. Eagleston July 22, 1912 (interesting side note: on March 28, 1925 the Baltimore Sun reports - Two female members of department given first lesson in **pistol shooting**. They were Miss Margaret B. Eagleston and Mrs. Mary J. Bruff - A few days later Mrs. Mary Harvey, Miss Eva Aldridge and Ms. Mildred Campbell were also trained. So basically the first two woman officers hired by the BPD weren't trained in firearms until they had been on the force for 13 years!)

1912 – 4 April, 1912 John B. A. Wheltle, Peter E. Tome, and Morris A. Soper were our **Police Commissioners**.

1912 – 6 May, 1912 Morris A. Soper, Daniel C. Ammidon, and Alfred S. Niles were our **Police Commissioners**.

1912 – The Baltimore police goes from Horse Drawn "Paddy" Wagons to **motorized paddy wagons**. Oddly enough our first motorized wagons were manufactured by the same builder.

1913

1913 – What later became known as our **Police Academy**, then called "The Baltimore City Police Department – School of Instruction" was established – From a 1934 newspaper article referencing this "School of Instruction", it talks about the effect on its young police, initially they wrote, "It's not long, this eight week course that they put the newcomers through, up on the filth floor of the Police Building at Fallsway and Fayette, but it is both thorough, and exacting. And since its founding fourteen years ago [an indication that it was moved from its initial location to the new headquarters in 1920] by Commissioner Gaither; the school has served as something of a guide, and model for virtually every big city in the country," Departmental officials said.

1913 – 31 Dec, 1913 James McEvoy, Daniel C. Ammidon, and Alfred S. Niles were our

Police Commissioners.

1913 – James McEvoy, became Baltimore City **Police Commissioner** from 1913-1914

1914

1914 – 29 May, 1914 – The **Motor Unit** was organized on May 29, 1914 - It began with just five members, Officers, Schleigh, Bateman, Pepersack, Vocke and Louis.

1914 – 17 October, 1914 – The first female officer **shot in the line of duty** was Policewoman Elizabeth Faber. As she and her partner, Patrolman George W. Popp were attempting to arrest a pick pocket on the Edmondson Avenue Bridge they were both shot. (Note: the first women police hired by the Baltimore Police department were hired two years earlier in June and July of 1912, and none of the women hired received firearms training until 1925.)

1914 – 28 Dec, 1914 – Daniel C. Ammidon, Clarendon I .T. Gould, and Alfred S. Niles were our **Police Commissioners**.

1914 – 14 Aug 1914 – Robert D Carter Appointed **Marshal** Aug 14 1914 - until 1917

1914 – Daniel C. Ammidon became Baltimore City **Police Commissioner** from 1914-1916

1914 – "*Luxe*" and "*Morpheus*" became Baltimore's **first K-9**. A little known fact – while not an official unit, Baltimore had two Police Dogs at their call when two Airedale Terriers from London came to enroll as members of the Police Force – one belonging to Mr. Jere Wheelright, and the other to Dr. Henry Barton Jacobs. *Luxe*, Mr. Wheelright's dog was a superb example of a highly trained canine aristocrat, big, powerful and intelligent to a degree that was truly remarkable. *Morpheus*, Dr. Henry Barton Jacobs' dog was also a superb example of a highly trained K-9. It would be 42 years before we would have an official K-9 Unit, but off and on since 1914, we Police Dogs used in both a private and an official capacity. But not until 1956 did we establish an official K-9 unit, with an official methodology that would go on to become world known as the best K-9 unit.

1915

1915 – 18 April, 1915 - We lost our Brother **Police Officer George C. Sauer**.

1915 – 21 September, 1915 – We lost our Brother **Police Officer Herbert Bitzel**.

1915 – 15 Feb, 1915 – Baltimore begins its first ever **Bike Squads**. From four booths throughout the city, they worked two shifts, 4x12 and 12x8, they rode in 2 hour rotations, splitting time with officers in the booth. Dispatch phoned the booth, and calls were sent forward from there to the units on their bikes. The concept was to provide better police service to the rural homes in the city.

1916

1916 – 22 March, 1916 Lawrason Riggs, Daniel C. Ammidon, and Alfred S. Niles were our **Police Commissioners**.

1916 – 1 May, 1916 Lawrason Riggs, Edward F. Burke, and Daniel C. Ammidon were our **Police Commissioners**.

1917

1917 – 22 January, 1917 We lost our Brother **Patrolman Michael Burns**.

1917 – The title Chief became **Marshal** in Baltimore City.

1918

1918 – 19 March, 1918 – We lost our Sister **Police Matron Teresa Foll**.

1919

1919 – 3 July 3, 1919 – We lost our Brother **Police Officer John J. Lanahan**.

1919 – 5 January 1919 – 33 former members of the **Baltimore County Police Department** were accepted by BPD as the Annexation Act provided 60 men to patrol the 50 square miles of the Annexed area – areas such as "Canton" and "Highlandtown," which were formerly Baltimore County became part of Baltimore City.

1920

1920 – 2 October, 1920 – We lost our Brother **Police Officer Michael J. Egan**.

1920 – In 1920 the **Board of Police Commissioners** was abolished and General Charles D.Gaither was appointed as our first Police Commissioner. Charles D. Gaither was Baltimore City Police Commissioner from 1920-1937.

1921

1921 – Early in the year of 1921 we tested the first signal light (aka **Recall Light**) on a call box that was located on the southeast corner of Baltimore and Charles Street. The signal (Recall Light) was made up of an electric lightbulb, a washbasin type shade and a Marine lens. The mechanism for the operation of this light was located in the old Central Police Station House on Saratoga Street near Charles Street – it consisted of an alarm clock for the flashing apparatus. This method of notifying the officer that he was wanted proved very successful. Every uniformed man from the inspector to the patrolman was enthusiastic over the results, and by the end of first week of this *"Magic Blinker"* there was a demand for more from the other districts.

1922

1922 – 17 Sept, 1922 – The 1921 **Recall Light** experiment was so successful that we would put them in every district and on nearly every call box in the city. This would be the first time anything like this had been done anywhere in the country, and just as the experiment caused excitement in getting this program expanded to the entire city, it wouldn't be long before other jurisdictions also had this system installed. By 1945 Baltimore had 269 recall lights throughout the city on a much better model recall light than that first experimental model from 1921. Note: the first light was the idea of Gen Gaither, and was made by in-house maintenance, from spare parts, in fact they used an alarm clock for the flashing apparatus.

1923

1923 – We lost our Brother **Police Officer John Edward Swift**.

1924

1924 – 2 March, 1924 We lost our Brother **Police Officer Frank L. Latham**.

1924 – 20 June, 1924 – We lost our Brother **Police Officer Charles S. Frank**.

1925

1925 – 2 January, 1925 We lost our Brother **Police Officer George D. Hart**.

1925 – 17 May, 1925 – We lost our Brother **Police Officer Patrick J. Coniffee**.

1925 – 1 November, 1925 We lost our Brother **Police Officer Roy L. Mitchell**.

1925 – 3 July, 1925 – We lost our Brother **Patrolman John E. Harris**.

1926

1926 – 09-12-1926 – The **Baltimore Police Headquarters and Central District** station house opened at Fallsway and Fayette Street, where they remained until 09-12-1977 when Central moved to a new building at 500 E. Baltimore St. The old HQ/Central District building was demolished in 1984. The **Tactical Unit** was also housed here.

1926 – 9 February, 1926 We lost our Brother **Police Officer Milton Heckwolf**.

1926 – June 29, 1926 We lost our Brother **Police Officer Webster E. Schumann**.

1926 – July 12, 1926 We lost our Brother **Police Clerk Thomas J. Dillon**.

1927

1927 – 5 August, 1927 – We lost our Brother **Police Officer William F. Doehler**.

1928

1928 – 12 February, 1928 – We lost our Brother **Sergeant George M. J. May.**

1928 – February 22, 1928 – The first **vehicle actuated traffic light** was tested in Baltimore. (To the best of our knowledge, this was the first vehicle actuated signal installation in the world.) This was an automatic control with a switch attachment and two poles placed on the right-hand side of the cross street, ordinary telephone transmitters being installed inside the control boxes. These transmitters being connected to the sound relay, which when disturbed by noise for example, the tooting of horns, blowing of whistles, or the sound of voices would actuate the sound relay, breaking the circuit's automatic control permitting the motor to run. This would change the signal which had been green on the main street to amber, then to red, permitting the side street traffic to move out on the green. It would automatically reset to red. This device was invented here in Baltimore. - This control would always restore itself back to the main street green, then the break would set and the signal would remain green on the main street, until disturbed again by sound. Several of this type were installed, one being at Charles Street and Coldspring Lane, another at Charles and Belvedere Avenue.

1928 – 19 November, 1928 – We lost our Brother **Sergeant Joseph F. Carroll**.

1929

1929 – 26 July, 1929 – We lost our Brother **Patrolman James M. Moore**.

1931

1931 – 7 January, 1931 – We lost our Brother **Police Officer John P. Burns**.

1932

1932 – 2 January, 1932 We lost our Brother **Police Officer William A. Bell**.

1932 – 4 October, 1932 We lost our Brother **Police Officer Thomas F. Steinacker**.

1933

1933 – 21 April, 1933 We lost our Brother **Police Officer John R. J. Block**.

1933 – 4 March 1933 – **Radio Communications Division Established**. The First radio communications system between Patrol Vehicles and a Central Dispatcher went into service on March 4, 1933. Note Commissioner Gaither first suggested this system to the Board of Estimates in September of 1931. It took nearly 2 years to fund and implement the system.

1934

1934 – 12 February, 1934 We lost our Brother **Police Officer John Blank**.

1934 – 2 November, 1934 We lost our Brother **Police Officer John A. Stapf**.

1934 – 20 December, 1934 We lost our Brother **Police Officer Henry W. Sudmeier**.

1935

1935 – 14 February, 1935 We lost our Brother **Police Officer Max Hirsh**.

1935 – 31 October, 1935 We lost our Brother **Police Officer Arthur H. Malinofski**.

1936

1936 – 9 October, 1936 We lost our Brother **Police Officer Leo Bacon**.

1936 – 29 October, 1936 We lost our Brother **Police Officer Carroll Hanley**.

1936 – 28 December, 1936 We lost our Brother **Police Officer John T. King, Jr**.

1937

1937 – 31 December, 1937 We lost our Brother **Police Officer Thomas J. Barlow**.

1937 – 17 November, 1937 We lost our Brother **Capt. Charles A. Kahler**.

1937 – **First African American Officer** Violet Hill Whyte, became Baltimore Police Department's first African American officer. She worked out of the Western District for her 30 year career with the department.

1937 – William Lawson became Baltimore City **Police Commissioner** from 1937-1938.

1937 – 28 May 1937 – For the first time in the history of the Baltimore Police Department, **women were advanced to the rank of Sergeant** – *"Mrs. Cronin and Misses Lillie, Lynch and Ryan Promoted. The women, four in number, joined the force during or immediately after the World War, when there was a shortage of men, and functioned for a time as telephone and signal operators. Under terms of a bill signed Friday (28 May 1937) by Governor Nice, they will hereafter enjoy the rank and the pay – which is $46.50 a week – as against their previous $40.00 a week."*

1938

1938 – 1 November, 1938 – We lost our Brother **Chief Engineer Joseph Edward Keene**.

1938 – Robert F. Stanton became Baltimore City **Police Commissioner** from 1938-1943.

1938 – 21 Feb, 1938 – **Accident Investigation Unit established**.

1938 – The **first African American male officers hired**, Walter T. Eubanks Jr., Harry S. Scott, Milton Gardner, and J. Hiram Butler Jr. were hired in 1938, all of whom were assigned to plainclothes.

1938 – 5 July 1938 - Baltimore Police initiate the "**Vice Squad**" a name for the unit was going to be the "Clean-up Squad" set up under the concept of preventing or reducing STDs – The unit began within hours of a report made to the Grand Jury. Newspapers of the times speculated that there was an underlying reason for this squad, and that it had more to do with combating organized crime, and that it resulted from two tavern bombings, on Druid Hill Ave and Whitelock St. The other was on Woodyear St.

1939

1939 – 5 May, 1939 – We lost our Brother **Patrolman Charles W. Frizzell**.

1940

1940 – 13 June, 1940 – We lost our Brother **Patrolman William L. Ryan**.

1941

1941 – 11 Jan 1941 – We lost our Brother **Capt. Havey Von Harten**.

1941 – **Auxiliary Police Force established**. In December 1941, after Pearl Harbor,0 our Police Commissioner (Robert F. Stanton) realized he would be losing a lot of his men to the war effort, so he quickly organized an "Auxiliary Police Force – a unit of a Civilian Defence Organization, which now has a membership of approximately two thousand persons, whose services are on a strictly voluntary basis without remuneration of any sort. These men were selected from owners of big business, and executives – men in all walks of life, including laborers and the unemployed (if you met the requirements it didn't matter what you did for a living, your help was welcome).

In 1941 they originally provided, at their own expense, uniforms and patrol box keys, etc. The department furnished badges, whistles and night sticks. They received ten hours training in first-aid, two hours instructions in handling of bombs, and at least six hours instruction in police work, during which period they were assigned to work with the regular uniformed patrolmen. They were required to report to various districts and to perform two hours actual police duty assigned them by our District Captains. The purpose which the Auxiliary Police were serving and the manner in which its members have discharged their duties are worthy of the highest commendation, for it has been a most effective instrument in aiding in the preservation of law and order. Cooperation between this unit and the regular uniform force were the basis for the progress made in combating crime. After the war there was a bit of dissension among the Auxiliary Police Force and the regular force."

1943

1943 – 13 June, 1943 – We lost our Brother **Police Officer William J. Woodcock**.

1943 – 7 November, 1943 – We lost our Brother **Police Officer William S. Knight**.

1943 – **African American officers finally allowed to wear police uniforms**, and by 1950, there were fifty African American officers in the department.

1943 – Hamilton R. Atkinson became Baltimore City **Police Commissioner** from 1943-1949

1944

1944 – 29 January 1944 We lost our Brother **Police Officer Joseph Waldsachs**.

1944 – 7 Oct 1944 The Baltimore police switched from the round, or oval top police caps that were worn for a little more than 30 years subsequent to the "**Bobby Cap**" type helmet, to the current "**Octagonal**" or "**Eight point**" hat we wear today.

1945

1945 – "Miss Ada F. Bresnan, **Chief of Policewomen** of the Baltimore Police Department, yesterday was appointed to **Sergeant**, by Hamilton R. Atkinson, Commissioner of the Police Department. She was the first woman elevated to the rank of sergeant. Miss Bresnan was appointed to the force in November, 1929, and on October 10, 1944, was placed in charge of policewomen on an interim basis after the retirement of Miss Eva Eldridge, who held the post for 15 years. The staff now consists of six women."

1945 – 10 September, 1945 We lost our Brother **Police Officer John B. Bealefeld**.

1946

1946 – 1 March 1946 We lost our Brother **Patrolman George H. Weichert**.

1946 – 27 June, 1946 We lost our Brother **Patrolman James M Shamer**.

1946 – 20 November, 1946 We lost our Brother **Police Officer Elmer A. Noon**.

1947

1947 – 13 January, 1947 We lost our Brother **Police Officer Fred R. Unger**.

1947 – 13 October, 1947 – We lost our Brother **Police Officer Charles Hart**.

1947 – 25 January, 1947 – The Baltimore Police Department promotes one of the Department's First African American Officers to become the Department's **first African American Police Sergeant**. Patrolman James H. Butler Jr., now Sergeant Butler was formerly a College Football Player until hired by Commissioner William P Lawson, on 28 July 1938, as he was among the first three African American males hired by the Department.

1948

1948 – 13 February, 1948 We lost our Brother **Police Officer Joseph Daniel Benedict**.

1948 – 1 October, 1948 We lost our Brother **Police Officer Thomas J. Burns**.

1948 – 30 December, 1948 We lost our Brother **Police Officer John W. Arnold**.

1948 – **Crime Lab established**. The Baltimore Police Department's 1st Crime Lab.

1949

1949 – 4 April, 1949 We lost our Brother **Police Officer James L. Joyce**.

1949 – 16 October, 1949 We lost our Brother **Police Officer Thomas J. O'Neill**.

1949 – Beverly Ober became Baltimore City **Police Commissioner** from 1949-1955.

1950

1950 – 4 August, 1950 We lost our Brother **Police Officer Charles M. Hilbert**.

1951

1951 – 6 January, 1951 We lost our Brother **Police Officer Roland W. Morgan**.

1951 – 7 August, 1951 – The **Central Records Division was established**.

1952

1952 – **Armory established in 1952**. The Gun-shop (now called the Armory) was established.

1952 – In the department started using a **Single Rocker-style Shoulder Patch**, it was black with yellow trim, and yellow letters that read, "Baltimore City Police" and was worn on the left shoulder of the officers' coat, or jacket.

1953

1953 – 1 August, 1953 We lost our Brother **Police Officer James L. Scholl**.

1954

1954 – 14 February, 1954 – We lost our Brother **Police Officer Alfred P. Bobelis**.

1954 – 19 April, 1954 – We lost our Brother **Police Officer Aubrey L. Lowman**.

1954 – 1 July, 1954 – We lost our Brother **Police Officer Walter D. Davis**.

1954 – **Mobile Crime Lab established**. In May of 1954 The Mobile Crime Lab Unit was established.

1955

1955 – 24 October, 1955 – We lost our Brother **Sergeant James J. Purcell**.

1955 – 28 Nov 1955 – **Polygraph Unit established**. "First in the State, Commissioner Hepbron brings the machine to help build a polygraph unit within the Rackets Division of the department." In 1966, this unit would be transferred to the Crime Lab unit - Before the move to the Crime Lab this little machine will cause headaches for the commissioner that brought it to Baltimore.

1955 – James M. Hepbron became Baltimore City **Police Commissioner** from 1955-1961.

1956

1956 – 27 May, 1956 – We lost our Brother **Police Lieutenant William P. Thompson**.

1956 – 29 September, 1956 – We lost our Brother **Police Officer John R. Phelan**.

1956 – **K-9 Unit established** – On Tuesday, December 11, 1956, an article was published in one of our local newspapers, one of a series of articles written by one Martin Millspaugh pertaining to Scotland Yard. This article, the last of the series, was devoted to the use of police dogs in London. As a result of the letters and inquiries made by Commissioner James M. Hepbron, an article appeared in the Morning Sun on December 17, 1956, which briefly stated that Commissioner Hepbron was interested and saw the possibilities of using dogs in the department.

On December 18, 1956, two dogs (Turk & Major Von-Gruntz) that had had previous training were offered to the department. Two officers, Patrolmen Thomas McGinn and Irvan Marders, who each had previous dog experience, were assigned to the program, which was put into place on an "experimental basis." By the middle of January 1957, fourteen dogs had been acquired as potential candidates and fourteen men were selected and assigned to the K-9 Corps. These men were chosen as a result of a questionnaire which was sent to all members of the department asking for volunteers. These men and dogs were trained daily until March 1, 1957. At that time, they were put on the street on Friday and Saturday nights, working the areas where crime was most prevalent. Shortly after this, on April 17, 1957, Commissioner Hepbron, considering the experiment a success, went before the Mayor and City Council and appropriations were made through the Board of Estimates which resulted in the K-9 Corps becoming a permanent part of the Baltimore City Police Department.

(Note: - 1914 - Baltimore was using private dogs, one such dog, the first ever recorded was "Luxe" a privately owned dog protecting Baltimore's citizens through canine power.)

1956 – 30 December, 1956 – **K-9 officer makes their first arrests**, James Diggs, B/M 23. Major and Turk apprehend a suspect for breaking into a motor vehicle, and stealing contents. James Diggs, thought briefly about fleeing but quickly changed his mind while in the 400 Blk. of W. Franklin St. as he saw the sharp teeth, and fast legs of Turk, and Major Von-Gruntz (aka Major). Diggs changed his mind, giving the dogs their first arrest. The handlers at the time were Officers Irvin Marders, William Kerbe, and Robert Johnson. In Central District Court Diggs was sentenced to 30 days for theft from a parked Motor Vehicle.

1957

1957 – 9 October, 1957 – We lost our Brother **Police Officer John F. Andrews**.

1958

1958 – 19 September, 1958 – We lost our Brother **Police Officer Robert K. Nelson**.

1958/59 – **Southeastern District History** – 1958/59 – The Southeastern District building is the youngest of all of our districts, and was built in 1958/59 at its present location of 5710 Eastern Ave.

1959

1959 – 11 January, 1959 – We lost our Brother **Police Officer Richard H. Duvall**, Jr.

1959 – **Baltimore's Park Police** would disband, most members to go to the Baltimore Police Department where they retained their rank, their time, and their pension. The unit was originally founded in 1862 to cover parks that fell outside Baltimore city.

1960

1960 – 16 November, 1960 – We lost our Brother **Police Officer Warren V. Eckert**.

1961

1961 – In January of 1961, the Baltimore Police Department **merged with The Park Police**, to make one big police force that covered the city and its outlying property. This type of annexation of agencies would happen numerous times throughout the department's history, including the Housing Police and now (2016) talks of taking on the Baltimore School Police.

1961 – Bernard Schmidt became Baltimore City **Police Commissioner** from 1961-1966.

1961/66 – Commissioner Schmidt approaches an officer who when he saw the commissioner approaching, failed to show proper respect to a commanding officer. At some point the

Commissioner asked the officer if he knew who he [the Commissioner] was. The Officer apologized, saying he did not. The Commissioner introduced himself to the officer, and again the officer excused himself explaining he doesn't get downtown often so he had no way of knowing who he was. The Commissioner introduced himself and that was what seemed like the end of that. Until a week or so later, when photos of the commissioner were hung in roll call rooms behind the podiums of all nine districts. A tradition started by Bernard Schmidt while he served as Police Commissioner from 1961 to 1966 just before Donald Pomerleau took over the helm.

1962

1962 – 7 April, 1962 We lost our Brother **Police Officer Henry Smith, Jr**.

1962 – 26 May, 1962 We lost our Brother **Police Officer Richard D. Seebo**.

1962 – 26 May, 1962 We lost our Brother **Police Officer Edward J. Kowalewski**.

1964

1964 – 10 January, 1964 We lost our Brother **Police** Officer **Francis R. Stransky**.

1964 – 6 February, 1964 We lost our Brother **Police Officer Claude J. Profili**.

1964 – 11 September, 1964 We lost our Brother **Police Officer Walter Patrick Matthys**.

1964 – 15 October, 1964 We lost our Brother **Police Officer Teddy L. Bafford**.

1964 – 25 December, 1964 We lost our Brother **Sergeant Jack Lee Cooper**.

1965

1965 – 20 January, 1965 We lost our Brother **Police Officer Charles R. Ernest**.

1965 – 22 July, 1965 We lost our Brother **Police Officer Robert Henry Kuhn**.

1966

1966 – 29 April, 1966 – The **Name Plate** was first worn by City Police. Interim Police Commissioner George M. Gelston ordered all officers to begin wearing a name plate for identification. An idea the State Police started 7 years earlier to the day on 29 April, 1959. At the time Commissioner Gelston felt it would improve the image of the police department. As a side note, Patrolman Edward Campbell would be the first City Officer to wear such name plate as he posed for the Baltimore Sun a day earlier.

1966 – 24 Aug, 1946 We lost our Brother **Honorary Police Officer Simon Fried**.

1966 – The department itself had **not fully integrated** until 1966. Prior to 1966, African American officers were limited to foot patrols and they were barred from the use of squad cars. These officers were quarantined in rank, barred from patrolling in white neighborhoods, and would often only be given specialty assignments in positions in the Narcotics division or as undercover plainclothes officers.

1966 – Police Commissioner **Donald D Pomerleau** was appointed to the first of three six year terms as our Commissioner, that's 18 years of the same Police Commissioner.

1966 – Along with Commissioner Pomerleau came the idea of "Police, policing the Police." Internal Affairs (or Internal Investigations, IID... IAD... call it what you like), was the result, and **IID was initiated**. Pomerleau said, "Things will change. You may have been on the take yesterday, but you will not be on the take tomorrow, and if you are, you will be arrested just like any other criminal in Baltimore!" Some officers were smart and yielded to his advice, others were not so smart and ended up someplace with bars, "Their place is in a perp walk, 1966 style."

1966 – In May of 1966 the **Inspectional Services Division** was initiated.

1966 – The **FOP Lodge #3** Baltimore City Police was founded by Sgt. Richard Simmons, Earl Kratch and several others.

1966 – Was the first year that we had what is known today as **"In-service training,"** where time is taken off from the street to learn about new laws, rules and regulations, other new techniques, equipment and operations within the department.

1967

1967 – In August of 1967 the **Fleet Safety Program** was initiated.

1967 – **Operations Units** were formed. These special units, one in each of the nine districts, would go where the action is. Operations Units were the special groups for fighting crime, each be commanded by Lieutenant, who will deploy the men as they are needed throughout the district.

1967 – February 1967, the Baltimore Police Department instituted a **tuition reimbursement** program for personnel pursuing college degrees.

1967 – June 22, 1967, the **Public Information Division** was formed. The Division consisted of a Director, two full time police officers and two civilian stenographers. The duties of the Director and his staff consisted of preparing and disseminating all news information and releases to the news media and the public. Preparation of the Annual Report as required by law and the bi-weekly Newsletter are also part of the responsibilities of this Division.

1967 – July 1967, the first of four **Community Relations Store Front Operations** was implemented. The purpose of these centers was to reach out to the community on an intimate basis. This was the first such project in the Northeastern region of the United States.

1967 – 25 January, 1967 We lost our Brother **Police Officer William J. Baumer**.

1967 – 10 February, 1967 We lost our Brother **Police Officer Frederick K. Kontner**.

1967 – 21 August, 1967 We lost our Brother **Police Officer John C. Williams**.

1967 – Baltimore Police opens it's first "**Safety City**" to teach kids how to safely cross streets.

1967/68 – Was the last year for the **Rocker style shoulder patch**. (At this stage Baltimore was still wearing a single shoulder patch on their left arm.) This was the first year for the blue Baltimore "City" Police style shoulder patch.

1968

1968 – Due to the number of auto accidents involving patrol vehicles, Police Commissioner Donald Pomerleau decided to **remove Sirens** from two thirds of the department's fleet. This action was frowned upon by City Hall, and the MVA. The MVA pointed out that it was illegal – it would take years for the commissioner to reverse his decision.

1968 – 18 April, 1968 – We lost our Brother **Detective Richard F. Bosak**.

1968 – We lost our Brother **Sergeant Frant Ankrom**.

1968 – As a National First – Baltimore Police Department begins **In-service training** - The education and training program expanded well beyond the traditional entrance level training for recruits to a forty hour annual In-Service Training course attended by all personnel from the rank of Patrolman through Captain.

1968 – September 1968 – The department of education and training center, itself relatively new, evolved into a modern version of the Baltimore police academy and became the first fully accredited academy of its type in the country. The American University in Washington recognized portions of the training program and offered up to 12 credits for completion of specified courses in a program that combined 14 weeks of classroom work, and 6 weeks of Field Training. Three of the credits could be earned at Morgan State University. The **course for credit** function was later transferred to the University of Baltimore, where it has remained. From time to time officers are sent to the **FBI National Academy** at Quantico Virginia for courses.

1968 – 16 May, 1968, the department installed a **National Crime Information Center** (NCIC) terminal permitting direct access to the storehouse of information on wanted persons, stolen vehicles, stolen weapons, and identifiable stolen property at the Federal Bureau of Investigation headquarters in Washington, D. C. This system enabled inquiries from officer on patrol to be answered within seconds.

1968 – 23 September, 1968 – The department officially took possession of its **IBM System 360 mainframe computer** system

1968 – 4 November, 1968, - As a National First – Baltimore Police Department launched **In-service training** - The education and training program expanded beyond the traditional entrance level training for recruits to a forty hour annual In-Service Training course attended by all personnel from the rank of Patrolman through Captain - Forty Hour In-Service Training course, designed to indoctrinate our police officers in the latest developments and techniques in professional law enforcement.. The concept of In-Service Training demonstrates the department's goal in development of an officer's capabilities to function amid the complexities of an ever changing society. This coupled with **Roll Call training** kept our Officers up to date on the most current of police procedures.

1969

1969 – In May of 1969 – We have our **first father/daughter** in the department. Officer James F. Stevens and Police woman Patricia A. Loveless.

1969 – In October of 1969 – We have our first female officer honored by the Criminal Justice Commission, **Police Woman Mercedes Rankin**.

1969 – 10 Oct, 1969 – Lt. Dennis P. Mello is promoted, making him Baltimore Police Department's **first African American Captain**, a new rank, and new position, and he took command at Baltimore's Western Police District.

1970

1970 – 16 January, 1970 We lost our Brother **Police Officer George F. Heim**.

1970 – 24 March, 1970 We lost our Brother **Police Officer Henry M. Mickey**.

1970 – 24 April, 1970 We lost our Brother **Police Officer Donald W. Sager**.

1970 – The **Arson Unit** was initiated in February of 1970.

1970 – **Fox Trot** was established. The Department Aviation Unit "Fox Trot" was officially formed and began flights.

1970 – 1 July, 1970 Baltimore Police went to an all **Blue light** emergency signalling system on their patrol cars and emergency vehicles, abandoning the traditional red lights atop their patrol cars.

1970 – Aug 1970 – Police Cars are **De-Flagged** - If you have ever wondered why Baltimore Police cars lack the American Flag, it goes back to Aug 1970 when Police Commissioner Donald D. Pomerleau ordered the removal of all American flag insignias from Baltimore city police cars. The reason was said to be due to their wearing out quickly, becoming dull and looking torn and tattered. The Commissioner, however, did rule that city officers would be able to continue wearing American flag lapel pins on their uniforms.

Note: this scheme would remain unchanged until the mid-1990's

1970 – 3 December, 1970 – Police Commissioner Donald D. Pomerleau introduced the Department's first **Police Flag**... it has remained the same flag since that time with no changes ever since. The flag cost $180 at the time, and now the same quality flag would cost more

than $700.

1971

1971 – 12 June, 1971 We lost our Brother **Police Officer Carl Peterson, Jr.**

1971 – 3 August, 1971 – We lost our Brother **Lieutenant Martin Webb**.

1971 – 26 March, 1971 – Two **Hughes 300-C helicopters** were formally accepted and registered for the department. The two new helicopters raised to three the number of such craft available for tactical deployment in the department's continuing efforts to combat crime. Purchased under a Federal grant of $100,000, the Hughes 300-C models represent a maximum combination of utility and modernization for aiding the department's crime fighting efforts.

1971 – In June of 1971 – We had our first **K-9 Dog killed** in the Line of Duty, "Shane" RIP.

1971 – 27 July, 1971 – The Community Relations and Youth Divisions were combined into a new division known as the **Community Services Division**. The creation of this division and the resulting centralization of Administrative functions provided an effective channel of communication between the Police Officer and the community he served. The major thrust of our expanded Community Services function was aimed at our young people. The accomplishment of this mission was aided by the division's two **Summer Camp** operations located at Camp Perkins and Camp Ritchie. Also, our **Officer Friendly Program** geared for its first full year of operation.

1971 – The department begins its **Bomb Squad** Unit under the supervision of Lt. Karner – Before starting our own Bomb Squad, bomb-dismantling missions were handled by Army experts. A member of this unit invented a device used to more safely detonate bombs. It was made from a shotgun shell, a product of his own design, made right here in Baltimore, and would eventually go on to be used worldwide (Another Baltimore First).

1971 – 30 Sept 1971 – The police building-based **Cell Block and District Court function closed** after 12 years in operation. The courtrooms and the 24 adjoining cells in the Northeast district building was converted into a **Women's & Juvenile detention center** for women and offenders under the age of 16. The replacement facility replaced the present women's block and juvenile cells on Pine Street, which had been condemned.

Note: The court closed without ceremony at the end of a typical day's business, during which 18 Defendants faced 52 charges ranging from shoplifting to disorderly conduct, false pretense to indecent exposure and assault to violation of probation. The last case heard in the NE Court Room was against Donald F. Goetz, who was charged with burglarizing a house in the 1600 block of East Coldspring Lane.

1971 – 22 October, 1971 – The Charles D. Gaither **police boat is retired** from the Police Department and starts a new career as a fire boat.

1972

1972 – 26 July, 1972 – We lost our Brother **Police Officer Lorenzo Arnest Gray**.

1972 – 1 March, 1972 – The department initiated the experimental and innovative program of bicycle patrol. It was learned that the bicycle patrol possesses all of the advantages of foot patrol with an added advantage of mobility. Also, the use of the bicycle provided great potential for more citizen-police contact, a new dimension in establishing good community relations.

1972 – 1 April, 1972 – This may sound like a joke but it's real, and it works – On April Fool's day 1972 **Operation Identification** was formally initiated by the department. The Operation, encourages citizens to mark their property with an electro-engraver and record the make and serial numbers on a property sheet supplied by the department.

1972 – 11 August, 1972 – **Flex Squads** were initiated, and the department began hiring sworn personnel to create nine highly flexible **Crime Control Teams**. These federally funded five man teams operated within the "total police officer" concept, performing all the activities and functions found within a law enforcement agency. The project's goal was to establish stability within the community based upon freedom from criminal activity and closer rapport between police and the citizen. Interestingly, the police vehicles also purchased for these officer's use were equipped with sirens, per federal regulations – the first and only siren-equipped patrol vehicles since 1968.

1972 – 30 August, 1972 – The conversion of the department's mobile communications system to more versatile portable transceivers and to incorporate 450 MHZ channels. These portable transceivers (**walkie-talkies**) greatly increase police service to the citizenry by reducing response time for emergency calls, by providing a uniform communications system for command personnel to direct officers in emergency situations across district boundaries, and by promoting a more efficient and safer foot patrol coverage. The incorporation of 450MHZ channels created an even more efficient communications system by allowing more practical frequency allocations.

1972 – The present **Headquarters Building** of the Police Department was opened.

1972 – Baltimore Police Department's **Honor Guard** is formed.

1972 – 8 March, 1972 – The Baltimore **Police Bike Patrol** is started for a second time.

1972 – In November of 1972 – The **Baltimore Police Museum** is opened in the lobby of Headquarters.

1973

1973 – 29 March, 1973 – We lost our Brother **Police Officer Robert M. Hurley**.

1973 – 1 December 1973 – We lost our Brother **Detective Wiley M. Owens**, Jr.

1973 – 6 April, 1973 – We lost our Brother **Police Officer Norman Frederick Buchman**.

1973 – 22 September, 1973 – We lost our Brother **Police Officer Calvin M. Rodwell**.

1973 – 11 June 1973 – The Civil Service Commission authorized the single classification of "police Officer" to replace the dual designation of "Policeman/Patrolman" and "Policewoman/Patrolwoman. This reclassification was a continuation of the department's efforts in the area of equal employment opportunity. Female "Police Officers" now had the same prerogatives and responsibilities as their male counterparts. Now only one competitive test for promotions is necessary. Thus, a single career ladder was established for all sworn members.

1973 – 12 July, 1973 – **Unlimited Medical ended** – It provided that all employees, both civilian and sworn, who entered on duty prior to 16 July 1973, were entitled to sick leave benefits in keeping with the existing Baltimore Police Department's policy of unlimited sick leave. All civilian employees hired after this date were entitled to one day of sick leave for each month of completed service. For these employees, a maximum of 150 days could be accumulated. If the employee so desired, one of each four unused sick leave days (maximum 3 days) accumulated during each year could be converted to cash.

1973 – 23 October 1973 – The **Evidence Control Unit** became the central evidence repository within the department. This unit has the sole responsibility for safeguarding, accounting for, and disposing of evidence and non-departmental property which has come into the department's custody.

1974

1974 – 5 May, 1974 We lost our Brother **Police Officer Frank Warren Whitby, Jr**.

1974 – 1 August, 1974 We lost our Brother **Detective Sergeant Frank William Grunder, Jr**.

1974 – 5 August, 1974 – We lost our Brother **Police Officer Milton I. Spell**.

1974 – 10 December, 1974 – We lost our Brother **Police Officer Martin Joseph Greiner**.

1974 – 25 August 1974 – Baltimore's first **Gun Buyback program** (then called a Gun Bounty) was held on this date. The idea came to Police Commissioner Pomerleau as he stood graveside by Officer Milton Spell who was shot and killed in the line of duty on 15 August 1974. PC Pomerleau offered $30 for each surrendered gun. The surprisingly large response, more like a metallic flood, to the Commissioner's offer of money for guns was an indication of how many weapons were and still are at large in the community, each with its crime and possible death potential. Budget considerations rather quickly required the Police Department to eliminate rifles and shotguns from its bounty program and to limit its offer to city residents only.

The program would last nearly a month - The city Gun Bounty program (as it was known) was being declared a success by police spokesmen, but criminologists challenge that appraisal because the program has not been in effect long enough to produce solid evidence, and they insisted that only strong federal gun control measures can significantly limit the availability of firearms. There have been a number of gun bounty, buyback programs since, some sponsored by the Baltimore Housing Authority Police Department, area Churches, and occasionally the Private Individual/Politician. A buyback in West Baltimore once recovered 750 guns in one day, and another in June of 2005 recovered hundreds more along with several high-powered assault weapons." If only the city would have been more proactive instead of reactive, we might not have had as many police funerals to attend.

1974 – 23 March 1974 – House panel passes, "**Law Enforcement Officer Bill of Rights**" in 1974, and Maryland became the first state in the nation to enact a "law enforcement officers' bill of rights."

1974 – 11 July, 1974 – **Baltimore's Police Strike** began, after a 7 July, campaign of intentional misbehavior, and silliness. The strike would last four long days, during which looting in several parts of the city began to occur daily, ending only on 15 July when officers went back to work when union officials negotiated an end to the strike, based on the city's promise to provide police officers a wage increase in the following year. It should be noted that the previously bargained for raises were not increased due to this agreement, and amnesty was refused for the strikers. Varying degrees of punishment were meted out to striking officers, from termination to a number of lesser punishments.

1974 – May, 1974 – **Field Training** was initiated, considered an innovative change to the training format by the department. After 11 weeks of recruit training probationary officers were assigned to a Field Training Officer. The FTO's, specially selected experienced patrol officers, trained and evaluated the recruit officer. This new training format effectively blended field training with classroom instruction.

1974 – In the latter part of 1974, a study of the various types of bullet resistant **body armor** began. The culmination of an exhaustive testing program and the Federal Grant process was the issuance in January, 1976 to all sworn personnel, of a **ballistic vest** made from Kevlar 29, a synthetic cloth-like fiber stronger and lighter than ballistic nylon and steel mesh. The vest will stop the penetration of the most common types of weapons and ammunition found on the street today.

1974/75 – The Departmental Vehicle phased out the old **Blue and White paint scheme** with the old Gold Badge on the door to an all-white car with a Blue Shoulder Patch on the door, and Red under Blue Stripes.

1974/75 – Under Commissioner Donald D. Pomerleau the **Word "City"** was dropped from our large blue shoulder patch.

1974/75 – **Ammo change**, after one of our brother Officers (Lorenzo Gray) was killed in the line of duty (1972) the department was forced to change our ammo from the round nose to the **semi-wad cutter**.

(Note: This change came about because Officer Gray's shot, though striking him in the torso, merely spun the suspect around allowing him to discharge a round from his shotgun at Officer Gray, killing him. Officers wanted something they knew would save them if they needed it, and requested a hollow point bullet. However, the department rejected that idea, stating they felt that the Semi-Wad cutter round was more appropriate for use in an urban environment. The new rounds were issued in late 1974 to early 75. We were recently told this change was a big part of negotiations that lead to the 1974 Police Strike. Incidentally, while the city and the Department were not happy with the strike, current members and their families are thankful. The changes made as a result of those strikes made things better for all of us today, albeit the department fired some great men and women; men and women that made a sacrifice for us.

1975

1975 – January of 1975, our **Quick Response Teams** were formed. Quick Response Team members are specially trained to handle the most vexing and complex situations confronting law enforcement officers. Their primary objectives were to conclude a situation without gunfire or injury to anyone. These teams were analogous to the SWAT teams inaugurated in other jurisdiction throughout the country.

1975 – 1 August, 1975, the department began the implementation of its **on-line booking system**. Computer terminal units, located in the booking areas of the various districts, were linked to the department's computerized criminal history files and provided the booking districts prior criminal histories of recidivistic arrestees.

1975 – 19 September, 1975, the department in cooperation with the State's Attorney's Office and various taxicab companies became part of the "**Civilian Radio Taxi Patrol**" in an effort to increase police service to the citizens of Baltimore. If, while on duty, a cab driver, whose vehicles are identified by a "Civilian Radio Taxi Patrol" shield on the right and left rear-quarter panels, observe anything demanding immediate police attention, he notifies his dispatcher, who in turn calls the Communication Division via a special Hotline. This program is another example of the department's efforts to involve the citizens of Baltimore in a united fight against crime.

1975 – 4 June, 1975 – In May of 1974 the Baltimore City Council proposed providing **bullet proof vests** for all of its police officers. Finally in 1975 city Police would get that protection and on 4 June, 1975 the City government authorized a $288,379 expenditure for more than 3,000 bullet-proof vests for Baltimore's police officers. Baltimore was 2nd in the nation to receive vests for all of its officers, behind San Francisco - Vests would actually be issued 1 January 1976.

1975 – 13 September, 1975 We lost our Brother **Police Officer Edward S. Sherman**.

1975 – 27 October, 1975 We lost our Brother **Police Officer Timothy B. Ridenour**.

1975 – 25 June, 1975 Police Agent Lynn A. Allison becomes the department's **first female Police Agent**.

1975 – September of 1975 The **Gunpowder Range** is opened to the Baltimore Police Department for training purposes.

1976

1976 – 4 April, 1976 – The **5th Issue badge** came along and is the badge worn by Baltimore Police Officers to this day. With the exception of the 2nd Issue badge the word Baltimore did not appear on any other official Police badge. The fifth issue badge is similar to the fourth issue "Supervisor's" badge, but with a new colorful central seal that is the same as worn on the large shoulder patch.

1976 – 16 April, 1976 We lost our Brother **Police Officer Jimmy Dale Halcomb**.

1976 – In April of 1976 the **Youth Division** of Baltimore Police was implemented.

1976 – August 1976 Mounted Section was given a **mascot** named Preakness by the President of the Maryland Jockeys Club. Mr. Herman Cole. Rookie was the mascot for the 10 years

1976 – 15 July, 1976 – Baltimore has some of its first ever academy class **layoffs** - affected were classes 76-2 and 76-3, most of the members of which were eventually rehired by the department on 14 January, 1977 and 31 January, 1977. Class 76-2 had 29 of the 34 come back and 76-3 had 27 of the original 31 trainees come back

1976 – In 1976, **QRT** (Quick Response Teams) began training; it was formed out of members of Tactical Section including several of the EVU members as they had been trained in use of high power rifles and were already departmental Marksmen. In the beginning, The "New" Tactical Section, circa 1975/76, formed a "Special Weapons and Tactics" team in the BPD. The department however wouldn't let it be called SWAT. They felt SWAT was a negative of term. Lt. Joe Key has been given credit for naming QRT, which is the same kind of team as the better known SWAT teams, but with a kinder gentler name. When they finally obtained the body bunkers, and Kevlar helmets, they also purchased black ballistic face shields.

However, the department didn't want members of the team wearing the masks because "it made them look evil". So the masks stayed in the box. By 1999, the department finally gave in and let the team be called SWAT. Up until this point EVU were the primary snipers for the city. The original members of that first QRT team each had to buy their own equipment; many shopped Sunny's Surplus, and/or H&H Outdoor Supply. Today, the SWAT teams are well equipped, as they should have been all along. I'm sure all they can do is shake their heads at how poorly they were equipped in the beginning, but at the same time, I know how proud each of these men are to have paved the way. Not to mention the number of lives they saved, while putting their own lives on the line. The General Order authorizing QRT wasn't signed until after Lt Joe Key left QRT in Oct. of 1977.

1977

1977 – 9 March, 1977 – The **Auxiliary Police Unit** was formed within the Community Services Division. After training and certification, members were assigned, without compensation, to support the force. Members are assigned to various events as an addition to the normal manpower deployment.

1977 – 9 to 12 September, 1977 – The new **Central District/Youth Section/Women's Detention Center Complex** located at 500 E Baltimore St opened. Moving from the Fallsway and Fayette St. building, built in 1926, to the 500 E. Fayette St. location where it currently stands.

1977 – 20 Dec 1977 – Colonel Bishop Robinson, as Chief of Patrol, was already the highest ranking black officer in the history of the Baltimore Police Department. His new title will be Deputy Commissioner of the Services Division, one of three Deputy Commissioners. The **Deputy Commissioner** rank is immediately under the Police Commissioner. The next step for this man is Commissioner, and that would happen in 1984 making him not only the first Black Deputy Commissioner, but also the first Black Commissioner of the Baltimore Police Department.

1978

1978 – 15 February, 1978 We lost our Brother **Police Officer Edgar J. Rumpf**.

1978 – 23 April, 1978 We lost our Brother **Sergeant Robert John Barlow**.

1978 – 27 October, 1978 We lost our Brother **Police Officer Nelson F. Bell, Jr**.

1978 – 24 October 1978 – The department promoted the **first female Police Major**, Lt. Patricia Mullen, elevated two grades as she became a Major, promoted from Lieutenant of the Homicide Unit. Major Mullen was put in charge of Youth Section.

1978 – The department remained under State governance until 1978, when the **Mayor began to appoint the Police Commissioner**, subject to confirmation by the City Council (Chapter 920, Acts of 1976). – [From the Maryland State Police website.]

1978 – 23 June, 1978, The Shot Tower Park and **Police Memorial** on the southeast corner of President Street and Fayette Street were dedicated. In addition to the Memorial Trees surrounding the area, an attractive plaque is prominently displayed on a granite stone with the inscription: "This living memorial is dedicated by the Department to all members, past and present, who have served with honor, dedication, and loyalty, many of whom have made the supreme sacrifice." It was rededicated with Statues, lighting and flags in 1999.

1978 – 2 October, 1978 – A long time goal of the Department's Education and Training Division was realized with the opening of a **Police Library** specializing in law enforcement material. The facility provides entrance level sworn personnel in the E&T Center with a location to study, apply required research work and exposure to supplemental text material, and offers other personnel many unique features to meet a number of scholarship needs.

1979

1979 – The **Video Production Unit** of the Education and Training Division began producing and distributing videotaped Roll Call Training productions designed to carry specific training messages to the Department's Officers.

1979 – 2 March, 1979 We lost our Brother **Police Officer John H. Spencer**.

1979 – 7 April, 1979 – Police Officer Michael P. Dunn was the first City officer to be **saved by his Kevlar vest** after being shot in the chest.

1979 – 19 August, 1979 – We lost our Brother **Police Officer William D. Albers**.

1981

1981 – 20 July, 1981 We lost our Brother **Police Officer Ronald L. Tracey**.

1981 – 5 Aug, 1981 – The original five digit sequence numbers were assigned alphabetically. The lower the number, the lower in the alphabet your last name. The numbers were often re-issued after an officer left the department. The "new" Short Number, **sequence number** system began late in 1981. The change came about from a district court requirement for a unique number to identify officers.

1981 – Frank Battaglia, became Baltimore City **Police Commissioner** from 1981-1984.

1982

1982 – 20 January, 1982 – The Baltimore Police Department began working side by side and hand in hand with the Checker Cab Company on a project to form the TOP - **Taxi On Patrol** program. What began here in Baltimore went on to become a national program, to report and help solve crimes all over the country.

1982 – Kathy Adams became the **first female member of QRT** (Baltimore's SWAT Team).

1983

1983 – 15 January 1983 – **The First Woman Promoted to District Commander** - Major Bessie R Norris, was promoted to Major and assumed her duties as Commander of the Southwestern District.

1983 – June of 1983 the department initiates it's **Hostage Negotiation Team** (HNT).

1983 – 30 July, 1983 – The first **female K9 officer** is assigned. Officer Charlene M. Jenkins is handler to Max.

1984

1984 – 3 December, 1984 – We lost our Brother **Detective Marcellus Ward**.

1984 – The Latent Print Unit began the use of **Printrak**. Printrak enabled the department to use computerized fingerprint searches to assist examiners with responses for potential latent print identifications.

1984 – Bishop Robinson became Baltimore City Police Commissioner from 1984-1987. He was the **first black Police Commissioner**.

1985

1985 – 1 March 1985 – The new **911 emergency system** was adopted state-wide, and the new Baltimore City Police Department opens its new 911/Communications Emergency Call Center. Prior to the inception of the 911 system, emergency calls to the police department were called into the department's traditional numbers: 222-3333 for emergencies and 396-

1111 for non-emergency calls.

1985 – 6 March 1985 – a senior at Johns Hopkins University by the name of Michael Patrick Sullivan, 22 years of age at the time and a resident in the 300 Blk. of East University Parkway, was arrested for making a false call to Baltimore Police Department's newly formed 911 Emergency Call Center. This made him the first person arrested on the charge since the inception of Baltimore's Emergency Call Number/911 system just 6 days earlier.

1985 – 8 October, 1985 We lost our Brother **Police Officer Richard J. Lear**.

1985 – 18 November, 1985 We lost our Brother **Police Officer Vincent J. Adolfo**.

1985 – BPD adopted a **computerized booking** system for prisoners.

1986

1986 – 21 July, 1986 We lost our Brother **Police Officer Richard Thomas Miller**.

1986 – 20 September, 1986 We lost our Brother **Police Officer Robert Alexander**.

1987

1987 – Edward J. Tilghman became Baltimore City **Police Commissioner** from 1987-1989.

1987 – 24 Oct, 1987 – Baltimore Public Housing Projects, were first patrolled by the "**Baltimore Housing Authority Police**" on this date. This police agency was State funded and took over private security in the projects of Baltimore city. It initially was patrolled by 15 officers and 6 supervisors. It was part of REACT (Responsible Enforcement and Aggressive Community Training), and was designed to eliminate drug trafficking at the 53 public housing projects. These officers trained with City Police, under Maryland Training Commission guidelines.

1989

1989 – 10 October, 1989 We lost our Brother **Police Officer William J. Martin**.

1989 – Edward V. Woods, became Baltimore City **Police Commissioner** from 1989-1993.

1990

1990 – In 1990 the range switched from the NRA-B27 target to the FBI-Q target. The reason stated at the time was that the NRA-B27 was a silhouette target, a black figure of a man with a white background, while the FBI-Q was a grey and white target; some describe as a bottle, or bowling pin. There were two justifications for the switch, one was that some felt we were training to shoot black men, and that the FBI-Q target being grey and white eliminated any misrepresentation of race. The other reason for the switch was the size of the targets, and that had a twofold justification. One, the Q target was smaller which would help improve our accuracy in shooting; the other was that the smaller targets cost half as much, which significantly reduced budget and operating costs at the range. In any case it was a move that had to be made.

1990 – The Department begins phasing in the **Glock model 17** – 9mm semi-automatic handgun, to replace the S&W model 19 / model 64 - .38 cal. pistol. This transition took approximately 3 years to complete. (The first academy class to use the Glock's were 90-2 and 90-3).

1991

1991 – **Gunshot Residue Analysis** (GSR) using Scanning Electron Microscopy began in 1991.

1992

1992 – The Baltimore Police Department re-initiated their **Bicycle unit**, a unit that was brought back after nearly 20 years as it was formerly used in 1972 and even as many as 70 or more years earlier.

1992 – 21 September, 1992 We lost our Brother **Police Officer Ira Neil Weiner**.

1993

1993 – 26 May, 1993 We lost our Brother **Police Officer Herman A. Jones, Sr.**

1993 – The Breathalyzer was replaced with a computerized version, a unit called "**The Intoximeter.**"

1994

1994 – Construction began on the **Police Annex Building** in October to be completed by late 1996. In 2007 it would be renamed after former Police Commissioner Bishop L. Robinson.

1994 – 28 May 1994 – While awaiting their identifying marks Baltimore Police cruisers hit the street with no decals, and unlike the previous 24 years of Baltimore Police cars, these would feature both **red and blue emergency lights** (in July of 1970 Police vehicles started using only blue emergency lights). In 1994 however, as they retired the Ford Taurus' and brought in 162 new Chevy Caprice Police cars, all white, with light bars, but no decals.

1994 – 16 November, 1994 – The department ended authorized use of the **Slap Jack**.

1994 – The **Polygraph Unit** began using a computerized polygraph instrument for conducting polygraph examinations.

1994 – **SCAN** (Scientific Content ANalysis) was brought to Central District's Major Crime Unit. SCAN is a Linguistic Polygraph technique that helps pinpoint deception in written or spoken words. At the time it was introduced to the department it was so new the department refused to pay for the training course. However, within a few years Detective Kenny Driscoll was familiar enough with the system that he was requested to show the technique to and to analyse statements for units throughout the department. Likewise, he evaluated statements for the Baltimore State's Attorney's Office and various outside agencies. Before retiring from the department in 2001 due to a line of duty injury, Detective Driscoll was asked to teach the technique to the Homicide Unit. His introductory course was authorized by the developer, Avinoam Sapir, from LSI. Avinoam Sapir developed and refined statement analysis, to the point where it became widely used throughout the department. Because of Detective Driscoll's ability to use the technique and close cases, Mr. Sapir called Driscoll a Guru on the subject. Driscoll was also credited with the discovery of two linguistic observations, his favorite having to do with, "Point-of-View" or "Point-of-Perspective" [Where the writer is in his written statement vs. where the writer is in his verbal statement.] Often a person will tell where they stand in a statement, using "here" or "there" and when the "here" and the "there" don't match, that part of the statement is further investigated.

1994 – Thomas C. Frazier, was Baltimore City **Police Commissioner** from 1994-1999

1994 – June 8, 1994 – Juan Rodriguez and Linda Rodriquez became the first **husband and wife** to be promoted to the rank of Sergeant on the same day in the history of the department.

1994/95 –Baltimore City Police officers had traditionally worn wearing dark blue pants, white shirts, and black ties, with a dark blue blouse (jacket) and black shoes. In 1994, the department changed its uniform standard to **dark blue shirts** that matched the pants, phasing in the change over the next year.

1995

1995 – April 1991 – **Regional Auto Theft Taskforce** - Having your car stolen off the streets of Baltimore in the 1990's was far from unusual. Baltimore City, Baltimore County and the Maryland State Police departments all knew that something had to change, so they joined forces and formed RATT (Regional Auto Theft Taskforce). **Note**: by 2005 they had made scores of arrests, and cut auto thefts in Baltimore by about 50%.

1995 – 28 November, 1995 – **CBIF** (the Central Booking Intake Facility) opened, replacing the nine individual cellblocks (one in each police district) all over the city. Moving court proceeding from the nine police districts to the newly built Eastside Court was the next step in taking prisoners and booking out of the districts.

1995 – Under Police Commissioner Thomas Frasier comes another of Baltimore's many **shoulder patch changes**. Until 1995, BPD officers had worn a single patch on the left shoulder of their uniform shirts and coats. Commissioner Frasier changed that when he ordered patches be worn on both shoulders.

1996

1996 – The Mobile Crime Unit began using a **CAD (computer aided design)** program to do computerized crime scene sketches.

1996 –**Identikit** sketches replaced with a computerized version called **E-Fit**. The Identikit equipment was located only in the Headquarters building. E-Fit was adopted by the department because it could be used on any computer in any location by the investigating Detective, enabling them to more quickly obtain a sketch of a suspect.

1996 – Baltimore Police Officers lose their **Espantoon** when it was replaced with the **Koga Baton** in Mid-August, of 1996. According to an 11 August, 1996 Sun report, Peter Herman reports this change explaining in detail, Police Commissioner Thomas C. Frazier thoughts, and reasoning for the change. That report can be found in an article entitled, "Police Get Rid of an Old Weapon - Baton Training Aims to Supplant use of Traditional Nightstick" on the Espantoon pages of the BPD history website.

1996 – Aug, 1996 – The Baltimore Police Department became the first ever with a **non-emergency 311 system**. If the pilot program worked, the number would be used in other cities to offer residents an alternative way of getting assistance from their local police without tying up lines designed to quickly handle life-threatening emergency situations. The initial news reports began in July of 1996 and the program went into testing by August of the same year. By the year 2010, the 311 System (and phone number) had been pre-empted by city government, and is now used by the Department of Public Works and other city agencies to receive and distribute citizen concerns and complaints (i.e., pot holes, streets that were still snowbound and were impassable, street lights or traffic lights being out, etc.). Emergency calls received by the 311 system are re-routed to the 911 system.

1997

1997 – Less than lethal **Bean Bag** rounds were issued, along with green-handled Remington 870 shotguns.

1997 – 7 May, 1997 – We lost our Brother **Lieutenant Owen Eugene Sweeney, Jr**.

1997/98 – Headquarters had major improvements and modifications subsequent to the addition of the **Annex Building**.

1998

1998 – 30 October, 1998 We lost our Brother **Police Officer Harold Jerome Carey**.

1998 – 4 November, 1998 – We lost our Brother **Flight Officer Barry Winston Wood** to the first fatality from a **Foxtrot (helicopter) crash**.

2000's

2000 – 8 March, 2000 – We lost our Brother **Police Officer Jamie Allen Roussey**,

2000 – 21 April, 2000 – We lost our Brother **Police Officer Kevon Malik Gavin**.

2000 – 14 October, 2000 – We lost our Brother **Sergeant John David Platt** and our Brother Police **Officer Kevin Joseph McCarthy**.

2000 – It was mentioned earlier that in 1996 Police Commissioner Thomas Frasier banned the use of Baltimore's traditional Espantoon in favor of a west-coast substitute, the "Koga" stick. In 2000 Police Commissioner Edward Norris learned of our tradition and **brought the Espantoon back**. There were a lot of thankful police, to have had been given back one of our favorite tools. Many don't understand that the Espantoon wasn't so much used for hitting suspects as it was to avoid hitting them. It was also used in many arm-bar type holds, and the spinning/twirling of the Nightstick kept distance between an officer and those that might try to invade their personal space.

2000 – Ronald L. Daniel became Baltimore City **Police Commissioner** from 2000 – 2000. He served only fifty-seven days before resigning.

2000 – Edward Norris became Baltimore City **Police Commissioner** from 2000-2002.

2001

2001 – March 13, 2001 – We lost our Brother **Agent Michael Joseph Cowdery, Jr**.

2002

2002 – 22 August, 2002 We lost our Sister **Police Officer Crystal Deneen Sheffield**.

2002 – 23 November, 2002 – We lost our Brother **Detective Thomas G. Newman**.

2002 - The **Firearms Unit obtained a NIBIN** system, which performs both fired cartridge cases and bullet comparisons as a part of a nationwide network. This is similar to NCIC, but is focused on guns, cartridge cases and projectiles, and will recognize if a gun used in Baltimore to shoot or kill someone also matches a gun used anywhere else in the US.

2003

2003 – The Annex building was re-named in **dedication to Commissioner Bishop Robinson**.

2003 – Kevin Clark became Baltimore City **Police Commissioner** from 2003-2004.

2004

2004 – 3 July, 2004 We lost our Brother **Police Officer Brian Donte Winder**.

2004 – Leonard Hamm became Baltimore City **Police Commissioner** from 2004-2007.

2005

2005 – In 2005, the **Baltimore Housing Authority Police were disbanded** and its operations taken over by the BDP. Housing Authority officers were allowed to apply for BPD positions if they desired, and their officers, formerly working for the state, were offered the opportunity to maintain their time and seniority from their previous state employment as they moved into the retirement system of Baltimore City.

2006

2006 – 19 May, 2006 – We lost our Brother Police **Officer Anthony A. Byrd**.

2006 – 20 May 2006 – The **Underwater Recovery Unit** becomes official and fully equipped. On 7 December 2005 Sgt. Kurt Roepcke of the Marine unit was able to start the process of getting it up and running with help from Col. Scott Williams, and Sgt George McClaskey; on this day 20 May 2006 the team was fully equipped and operational.

2006 – QRT (Quick Response Team) is renamed **SWAT** (Special Weapons and Tactics) after 32 years the department finally changes the name of this highly trained, elite team. (Initially in 1974 while forming the team the department resisted using the name SWAT because it was felt the name was too harsh for the department's image – Political correctness circa 1974.) As of 2006, the Baltimore Police Department has had 38 Commissioners, starting in 1850 with Charles Howard, until 2015 with Kevin Davis. This information was altered from reports written by BPD's Public Affairs Office on Monday, March 17, 2008.

2006 – In 2006, President George W. Bush signed the Law Enforcement Officers Safety Act (**LEOSA**) bill. Among many other things, this new law allowed retired police officers to carry a firearm anywhere in the United States. As a result, a number of police departments around the country set up training programs for retired officers to be able to carry firearms.

2007

2007 – 9 January, 2007 – We lost our Brother **Detective Troy Lamont Chesley, Sr**.

2007 – Frederick Bealefeld III became Baltimore City **Police Commissioner** from 2007-2012.

2010

2010 – 27 September, 2010 We lost our Brother **Police Officer James Earl Fowler III**.

2010 – 20 October, 2010 We lost our Brother **Police Officer Thomas Russell "Tommy" Portz, Jr**.

2011

2011 – 9 January, 2011 We lost our Brother **Police Officer William Henry Torbit, Jr**.

2011/2012 – **X26 Taser** – Baltimore Police are armed with Tasers - They issued the X26 Taser to some officers in 2011 and then all remaining officers by 2012.

2012

2012 – 29 August, 2012 We lost our Brother **Police Officer Forrest "Dino" Taylor**.

2012 – Anthony W. Batts served as Baltimore City **Police Commissioner** from 2012-2014.

2013

2013 – 5 April 2013 – Retroactive **"Citation of Valor"** program is approved and initiated. Commissioner Batts listened to the concept submitted by Mrs. Patricia Driscoll, of the MD Adopt-a-Cop organization, to allow disabled retired officers that were permanently disabled in the line of duty to apply retroactively for the "Citation of Valor". This is done through Mrs. Driscoll's Adopt a Cop program, and can be submitted to her either by the retired officer, another officer with information on the case, or the officer's family. Mrs. Driscoll began working on this program in 2004. After many attempts, and a lot of hard work, she finally got her program approved. To date, ten officers' names have been submitted. Mrs. Driscoll is thankful to Commissioner Batts, Sgt. Stephanie Lansey, and Officer Robert Brown for their assistance and support. Anyone wishing to nominate an officer for this award can write Mrs. Driscoll at the department's address, or on the Baltimore Police History website.

2013 – The BPD converts from a **six pack photo spread**, in which the victim or witness of a crime is shown a photo spread containing six photos – one of the suspect, and five fill-in's of similar looking males or females. The new concept would be to show six pictures as they did in the past, five fill-ins and the actual suspect in random order, but now one at a time. Prior to the 1980's when the six-pack photo spread was initiated, BPD used physical line-ups, in which we normally used the suspect and five fill in plain clothes officers, or civilians; so that the victim/witness could make an identification. This court-ordered change seems to most police to be inconsequential. In the end does it really matter, if evidence points to the suspect and the victim/witness picks a suspect, be it through a physical line up, six-pack of photo's, or individual photo's. It should be noted that we never charge the person picked if the pick is a fill-in and not the suspect. Still, if it helps in any way to catch a bad actor and close a case – then more power to them.

2013 – Baltimore Police begins its **LEOSA** program based on the following - Baltimore City Fraternal Order of Police (FOP) Lodge 3. Trustee Detective Ed Wagner took it upon himself to convince the Baltimore Police Department to change course. He worked on implementing the program with Sam Walters, a member of the Baltimore Retired Police Benevolent Association (BRPBA) Board of Directors at the time, for 7 years, through several Police Commissioners. Baltimore City FOP Lodge 3 also committed to funding the start-up and equipment necessary to implement the LEOSA program. This is part of Baltimore Police History, and a great job by members of both our FOP and our BRPBA.

2014

2014 – The Baltimore Police Department says it will begin to post a **log of its internal investigations** into serious use of force by officers online, and for the first time will ask the city's civilian review board to look at shootings involving its officers, and deaths of people in custody.

2014/2015 – The Baltimore Police Department begins the process of changing the **markings on its marked patrol** vehicles via attrition. The new design matches that of the new Fox Trot Helicopters, and several other portions of the department, such as the command unit vehicle and the really rough S.W.A.T. truck. They use both a white base and a back base color over which the new graphics are applied.

2015

2015 – 2 January 2015 – Taking a page from the Baltimore City Police History Web Site, BPD begins **tweeting** memorial notifications about our fallen brothers when they posted a memorial tweet: "We will always remember Police Officers George D. Hart (01/02/25) & William A. Bell (EOW 01/02/32)." We hope this becomes a long-lived tradition.

2015 – 9 January, 2015 – We lost our Brother **Police Officer Craig Chandler**.

2015 – 11 January, 2015 – Baltimore City police change tactics in how they schedule patrol officers **work schedule**, which had been in place since the 1960's. In an effort to make officers' jobs more efficient and city streets safer, officers begin to work 4 days per week, 10 hour days.

2015 – January, 2015 – Officers began to wear "**Service Hashes**" on their sleeve to indicate their years of service.

2015 – In April, an in-custody death of **Freddie Grey** caused civil unrest, and the arrest of six officers and led the State's Attorney, and Mayor to ignore the law by ordering BPD and assisting officers NOT to arrest, or at least stop, the illegal activities of the many riotous protesters. This leads to a Mayor giving protesters "Room to Destroy", ordering police to stand-down (or similar words that prevented the police from taking any action as looting and burning stores and homes. Officers were also ordered to ignore and take no action as bottles, bricks, and rocks were thrown at them and disorderly protesters shouted threats and obscenities at them. Finally, BPD officers were not allowed to protect themselves by wearing offensive-looking protective gear.

2015 – 30 May 2015 – A BPD **FaceBook** page was started to show support for police officers and operations. A rally was held on this date with a turnout of about 200 to 250 people showing their support of police, countered by 15 to 20 police haters, chanting their hate for police and all things American. Again, no arrests were made.

2015 – 5 June 2015 – Apparently as a result of public distrust as a result of April's riots, BPD Commissioner Anthony W. Batts announced the creation of a new unit to oversee internal affairs, audits and the writing of police procedures, a move he hopes will strengthen public confidence in his agency. The unit was named the "**Bureau of Professional Standards**" and is commanded by Deputy Commissioner Jeronimo "Jerry" Rodriguez.

2016

2016 – Police **Commissioner Anthony Batts was relieved of duty** by the Mayor and replaced by Interim Police **Commissioner Kevin Davis**, whose interim title was later eliminated and his six-year term as Police Commissioner was approved by the city council.

Baltimore Police History

A Detailed Day-by-Day Look Through Our Past

1 January - 1857

Today in Baltimore Police History came a number of significant and long-lasting changes under the provisions of an act of the Maryland State Legislature. The ordinance introduced an entirely new order of things, and placed Baltimore's Police Department on practically the same footing as those of other large cities around the country. It declared that after March 1st the existing watch and police systems should be "abolished" and all ordinances for the establishment and regulation of the same were to be repealed. The new force would consist of one Marshal, one Deputy Marshal, eight Captains, eight Lieutenants, twenty-four Sergeants, three hundred and fifty Police Officers, five Detective Police Officers and eight Turnkeys. The men were required to do duty day and night, and were given all the powers then vested by law in the city Bailiffs, Police Officers, Constables and Watchmen. The city was divided into four police districts, whose stations were at the watch-houses. The Marshal, with the concurrence of the Mayor, was empowered to:

- Establish and modify the geographical limits of the four districts as needed;
- Divide them into "beats" allowing for a proper force distribution;
- To alter at will the limits of the these districts/beats, and;
- To establish a Detective Bureau of five detectives.
- The City's four districts would be known as: Middle/Central, Eastern, Western and Southern. It would take until 1959 before we would have the nine districts as we know them today.

1 January - 1960

Today in Baltimore Police History, Baltimore's Park Police merged with the Baltimore Police Department was approved, as reported in the following:

Newspaper report: Mar 31, 1960 - *Tawes Approves Merger of Park Police, City Force:*

"Governor Tawes has 'given his blessing' to the proposed merger of the Baltimore Park police with the Baltimore City police force, city officials said yesterday. Dr. Frank C Marino, president of the Park board, reports that development after he and other officials conferred with the governor at his Baltimore office. 'The governor has agreed to take administrative steps that city legal aids have said are necessary in order to bring about the merger,' Dr. Marino said. He reported that BPD Commissioner James Hepbron has agreed to assign one of his inspectors to survey the Park police force and arrange for its integration into the city's police department. The inspector will spend part of his time with the Park police to determine which duties each member is best suited for and to determine which members need further training. Dr. Marino said that governor Tawes is 'with us 100%' on the city plan to merge the two police forces by January 1 of next year."

"Agreement by the governor is necessary for several reasons, according to an opinion issued by Harrison Winter, City Solicitor. Since the city police, which operate under the jurisdiction of the state government, are very near their authorized strength, the written consent of both Governor Tawes and Mayor Grady must be granted before the park officers can be hired. Mr. Winter points out that the Park police derive their authority on park property outside the city through special commissions given them by the governor. Similar commissions would have to be given to some city policeman so they could patrol those parks."

"City officials will confer shortly with officials of Baltimore County and Anne Arundel County to obtain their consent to use the city police to patrol city parks in their territories. Dr. Marino repeated his determination to merge the 126-man Park police force, which has been an arm of the City Park board, with the city police department by January 1. That date was selected because it is the beginning of the next city fiscal year. In outlining the administrative steps that he said could accomplish the merger, Mr. Winter recommended that the city seek legislation in the General Assembly next year confirming the actions."

Newspaper report: 3 March 1960 - *January 1 Is Ruled O.K. As Date Of Police Merger*

"The merger of Park police into the Baltimore Police Department can be accomplished by January 1, 1961, the city solicitor ruled yesterday. This dispelled widely held beliefs that the merger might take a year or two. The city chief law officers said no state or city legislation must be passed before affecting the change. Several items of legislation, including an amendment to the city charter, are proposed to be made later. However, the law officers said the merger could go ahead before passage of the legislation. The merger of the Park police into the city force has been talked about for many years, but gathered new steam last fall when Mayor Grady and Dr. Frank Marino endorsed it."

"Since it appears that Park policeman exercise their authority within parks outside the city limits by means of special commissions from the governor, Mr. Winter said, similar authority should be obtained for some city policeman. He said an amendment to the charter should be submitted immediately to the Council for passage in time for ratification in the general election next November simply as a matter of "good legal housekeeping."

"Since some city parkland, like Fort Smallwood, is located outside its borders, the city police will need authority to take over the duties of Park policeman in those areas."

"The basic question of the authority of Park police to act as conservatories of the peace has never been conclusively resolved . . . and our inquiries have disclosed that Park police act as conservatories of the peace in park areas outside the city only by virtue of commissions issued by the governor as special police, rather than by virtue of their being Park police."

1 January - 1976

Bullet Proof Vests were issued to Baltimore Police Officers beginning on this day in 1976, after a long history of our police seeking this protection. It all started in May of 1954 when the City Council proposed bulletproof vests for its police. Finally, on 4 June 1975 it was agreed our police would get the protection they deserved when city government authorized the $288,379 expenditure for more than

2 January - 1925

On this day in Baltimore Police History we lost our brother Police **Officer George D. Hart** to a motor vehicle accident. The following newspaper account from 1925:

2 January 1925 – Patrolman George D. Hart Dies of Injuries

"Patrolman George D. Hart died early this morning at Union Memorial Hospital from injuries he received on 16 November 1924, when his motorcycle collided with an automobile at University Parkway and Charles Street. That Automobile was being operated by Henry Rogers, Jr. Mr. Rodgers would be arrested at the time, but was later released pending the outcome of Patrolman Hart's injuries. Officer Hart received a fractured skull, and numerous internal and external injuries in the collision. The suspect in this case, Mr. Rogers lives in the Carolina apartments."

As his brother and sister members of the Baltimore Police Department we will not let him be forgotten. His service honored the City of Baltimore and the Baltimore Police Department. May he rest in peace, and may God bless him.

2 January - 1932

On this day in Baltimore Police history, we lost our brother **Officer William A. Bell.** Officer Bell was shot and killed instantly on 2 January, 1932, while in the process of arresting robbery suspect Willie Wright in a 3rd floor apartment of 1709 Madison Avenue. The suspect was wanted on warrants for a series of burglaries in the Northwestern District. He was apprehended two days later in Washington, D.C. Officer Bell was 52 years old and unmarried. He joined the department on 1 October, 1908.

The following are more detailed newspaper accounts as to what transpired on that day:

"The suspect, Willie Wright, produced a handgun and opened fire on the officer attempting to arrest him, hitting him two times in the upper body and killing him instantly. The suspect then jumped over Officer Bell's lifeless body and made his

escape down a back stairwell. On hearing the shots, Officer Bell's partner, Patrolman William Sempeck rushed in, but was slowed as he briefly stopped pursuing suspect Wright to aid Officer Bell. It was only after he realized the fate of his partner that he continued on in his chase for suspect Walter Wright. Due to unfamiliar, steep, long winding stairwell, Officer Sempeck would lose his suspect that night; he was quoted as saying, 'He must've leaped down them, he got away so fast!'"

The following are headlines and stories from newspaper articles dated 3 January, 1932, and 26 January, 1932. They wrote a little differently back then; so some words were changed to represent a more modern, and less epithetical and offensive way of expressing those events and the people involved:

"Patrolman William a Bell, 52, was shot and instantly killed shortly before 9 o'clock last night (2 January, 1932) by a black male believed by the police to a been Wilbert Wright. - William Bell and Patrolman William Sempeck were about to make the arrest in the third floor apartment at 1709 Madison Avenue."

"The black male shot, then jumped over the lifeless body of Policeman William A. Bell as Patrolman Sempeck chased him down three flights of narrow, winding stairs. He escaped before his pursuer had a chance to fire a single shot."

"Wright, the suspect in a series of holdups and robberies in the northern section of the city, is said to have killed Officer Bell as the patrolman was standing guard at one of the doors to the apartment in which detectives asserted they had learned the suspect (Wright) was visiting."

"Patrolman Sempeck had gone to a door about 20 feet from the stair landing in the hall and Officer Bell had stationed himself at another door to the apartment near the stairway. Sempeck said he entered the apartment, and was walking through a dark room when he heard a shot. He said he then ran to the living room in the apartment, and saw Officer Bell falling to the floor in the doorway. A black male was leaping over Officer Bell's body, while two black females, and a man stood huddled in a corner."

"I tried to catch Bell as he was falling," Sempeck said, "Then I laid him on the floor, and started after Wright who was already running down the rear stairs. He must've leaped down them, he got away so fast."

"In a short time a score of policemen from the Northwest District Station, and a Detective detailed from Headquarters had reached the scene. Every police station

in the city was notified of the killing and a police dragnet was spread in an effort to capture the killer. Police headquarters in Washington D.C. and other nearby cities also were told of the shooting and asked to watch for the fleeing suspect. Policemen also looked for the fugitive at railway stations and area wharfs. Charles Gaither, Police Commissioner, announced that he personally would give a $250 reward for information leading to the arrest of the killer."

"The three occupants of the apartment at which the shooting occurred were arrested and held as state's witnesses – they were Dorothy Paulson, 29, who lived in the building, Andrew Walker, 29, who also lived in the building, and Katherine Dobson, 23, from the 1500 block of McCulloch Street."

"Detectives found two guns – a .45 caliber semi-automatic and a .45 caliber Army Revolver – in a white paper bag within the apartment. The residents of the neighborhood described Wright as a 'bad man,' and said he usually carried two pistols."

"The police said they had been holding numerous warrants for Wright's arrest during the last few months. And that patrolman Bell had learned from an informant that Wright could be found in the Madison Avenue apartment house. The policeman had a warrant last night for Wright's arrest in connection with a burglary in the 300 block of E. 25th St."

"Wright has served five years in the penitentiary. He was arrested for the first time September 27, 1918, for the theft of a bicycle and was paroled by Judge John J. Dobler. In April 1919, he was sentenced to six months in the house of corrections for purse snatching. He was sentenced to the pen in 1923 on charges of burglary, larceny and carrying concealed weapons. He received five years on each count, to be served concurrently. He appears in police records under various aliases – Walter Brian, James Wheatley, PD right and William Taylor."

"The shooting attracted hundreds of persons, and the police were originally hampered in their investigation by the milling crowd."

"Wright, a light-skinned black man, is about 5'5" tall and weighs about 135 pounds. Patrolman Sempeck said the Black Male who fled the shooting was wearing light trousers, but had no coat or hat, when he fled. Norbert Norris, 26, a taxicab driver living in the 2200 block of E. Fayette St., said he picked up a black man who answered Wright's description at McCulloch and Mosher streets about 15 minutes after the shooting – this black man, however was wearing a hat and coat. Norris

said he took him to Madison and Bond Streets."

"In announcing the reward for Wright's capture, Commissioner Gaither said, 'This is a case of another policeman shot down in the performance of his duty, and just goes to show the Baltimore police are ready to make the supreme sacrifice at any time. Officer Bell was one of the Boy Scouts.' Patrolman Bell recently had been assigned to the day shift, but last night was on a special detail because of a large number of robberies and holdups on the northern end of the city in the last few months."

"Patrolman Bell was appointed to the police force on October 1, 1908. He is survived by his mother, Mrs. Emma Bell, and his sister, Mrs. Jeanette McGeoch. All lived at 2949 Clifton Ave. Patrolman Bell is also survived by two daughters and a son. They are Mrs. Ruth King, of New York, and Miss Naomi Bell and Edward Bell of this city."

"Five Northwestern district policemen have been fatally shot by black men since the summer of 1926. Patrolman Webster E. Schuman and Thomas Dillon, a clerk at the station house, were fatally injured by a crazed black man at Lafayette and Argyle Avenues on June 28, 1926. Seven other persons were injured at that time."

"On 5 August, 1927, Patrolman William F. Doehler was shot and killed by David Berry, a black man, as the officer, with the suspect in custody, waited for the patrol wagon at the corner of Pennsylvania Avenue and Biddle Street. The suspect in that case never was caught."

"Patrolman John P. Burns was shot over the heart by Willie Smith, a black male, on January 26, 1931, as Patrolman Burns, accompanied by another officer, attempted to arrest him in a house in the 500 block of St. Mary Street. Patrolman Burns died the following day. The suspect in that case was riddled with bullets as he fled the scene. Last week Mrs. Margaret Burns was the recipient of the Honor Award intended for her husband. Gov. Ritchie made the presentation."

The following is from the 2nd article:

"Walter F. Wright, a black man who shot and killed patrolman William A. Bell, of the Northwestern District, was found guilty of murder in the first degree late yesterday by Chief Judge Samuel K. Dennis and Judge Duke Bond. The verdict was announced following the trial of Wright in criminal court."

"Sentencing was suspended to enable Wright to confer with his court-appointed

counsel, Welford F. Coyle Jr. Under Maryland law, the verdict makes either the Death Penalty or Life imprisonment mandatory. Unless a motion for a new trial is requested, sentence will be imposed before the end of the week. Wright, who had listened intently to the witnesses and the attorneys during the closing arguments without displaying any emotions, was affected visibly by the verdict. Wright did not testify, but in a confession read into the record by the state, he said that Patrolman Bell fired first, apparently, however, without intending to hit anyone and that he (Wright) then fired over Patrolman Bell's head. Then patrolman Bell fired a shot at him, and he then fired two more shots in the direction of the patrolman."

"The defence contended that the facts as presented by the state failed to show premeditation, and that the patrolmen illegally entered the Madison Street home and did not actually have the warrant for Wrights arrest in their possession."

"Charles C. G. Evans and William Carswell Baxter, assistant state's attorneys, argued for the prosecution that Wright, who lives in Washington, knew he was wanted by the police here and that he came to Baltimore armed with an automatic pistol and two revolvers. The shooting was done by Wright in an attempt to escape justice, the prosecution held, and asked for a verdict of first degree murder. The weapon used by Wright had been stolen from the home of a Washington, D.C., Patrolman."

As his brothers and sisters of the Baltimore Police Department we will not let him be forgotten. His service honored the City of Baltimore and the Baltimore Police Department. May he rest in peace, and may God bless him.

6 January - 1884

On this day in Baltimore Police History we lost our brother, Police **Officer Charles W. Fisher**, who drowned to death when he fell into the freezing water from a pier at the end of South Street. At approximately 0130 hours, Officer Fisher was making his rounds when it is believed he was either chasing a suspect, or investigating suspicious activity and fell from the pier, through the ice of the basin and into the harbor's waters. A harbor officer nearby heard his screams and the sound of ice breaking, at which time he immediately started searching the area with the assistance of a private watchman. The two were unable to find anything, and alerted another officer who was walking by. A short time later, the searchers located Officer Fisher's hat and Espantoon next to a hole in the ice. Additional officers were called to the scene and started dredging the water for Officer Fisher's body which was recovered a short time later.

Officer Fisher was a Confederate Army veteran of the Civil War. He had served with the Baltimore Police Department for just under 10 years and was assigned to the Eastern District. He was survived by his wife and five children.

As his brothers and sisters of the Baltimore Police department we will not let him be forgotten, on this day we'll take time to remember him and thank him for his service and sacrifice.

6 January - 1951

On this day in Baltimore Police History we lost our brother **Officer Ronald W. Morgan** - Officer Morgan was struck and killed while getting out of his patrol car to use a call box for his hourly call-in at 11 pm.

Investigation showed that he was struck by a car driven by John Caskie, Jr. – Caskie was arrested at a nightclub several hours later, and was charged with manslaughter, driving under the influence, and failure to stop after an accident.

Officer Morgan was married and the father of three children. Having been appointed on 5 September 44, he served with the department for 6 years.

As his brothers and sisters of the Baltimore Police department we will not let him be forgotten, on this day we'll take time to remember him and thank him for his service and sacrifice.

6 January - 2014

Today in Baltimore Police History 6 January, 2014, we lost our brother former police **Commissioner Bishop Robinson.**

BALTIMORE - (4:30 pm) – The first African-American Police Commissioner in the history of the Baltimore Police Department died Monday, 6 January 2014, a Department spokesman said.

"I'm so sorry that he died," Baltimore City Councilwoman Mary Pat Clarke said in a statement. "He broke the racial barriers in the police department, and he did it with strength and great dignity. He was a very strong leader in that department, and very highly respected. He went on to be involved in many other areas of civic life as well. He will be truly missed."

Bishop L. Robinson died at the age of 86. He served as commissioner from 1984 to 1987 and later served as Secretary of the Maryland Department of Public Safety, and Correctional Services from 1987 to 1997. "When Commissioner Robinson joined the police department in 1952 the role and scope of African American officers was severely restricted," Baltimore police spokesman Lt. Eric Kowalczyck wrote in a release. "African American officers were not allowed to patrol white neighborhoods, or use patrol cars. During his career the United States saw the advancement of the Civil Rights movement, opening the door for Commissioner Robinson to advance in rank."

"His ascendancy to command the Baltimore Police Department is a testament to his perseverance, character, and dedication to duty," the release continued. "Fighting through a culture that was in the midst of changing, Commissioner Robinson gained the respect and admiration of his peers and subordinates."

Robinson was one of the founding members of the National Organization of Black Law Enforcement Executives. The Annex Headquarters Building at Fayette and Presidents streets is named in his honor.

"We are saddened by the loss of Commissioner Bishop Robinson, he was our Jackie Robinson." said retired Baltimore police Det. Kenny Driscoll. Driscoll runs the website *www.BaltimoreCityPoliceHistory.com*

"He broke color barriers in one of America's toughest careers, for one of America's best police forces, the Baltimore Police Department, we were all proud to have served for him, and sorry to see him go," Driscoll said.

Baltimore officials expressed their condolences to the Robinson family, toasting his service to the city. "Commissioner Robinson was a pioneer in the field of public safety and Baltimoreans benefited from his tireless efforts to improve our city," City Council President Bernard "Jack" Young said in a statement. "His successes inspired countless men and women to dedicate their lives to public service. I enjoyed the privilege of working alongside Mr. Robinson and I was extremely proud of his career of service, which was showcased last February during a dedication ceremony for a public justice institute at Coppin State University that bears his name," the statement continued. "The institute stands as a tribute to his enduring legacy."

Councilman Carl Stokes added, "Although he led a lengthy career representing Baltimore's finest, the fact that he was an African American leader meant he faced many barriers, adapted and overcame. We have lost an able statesman whose wisdom, experience and proactive leadership will be dearly missed at a time when cities like ours could benefit from his wisdom and expertise," Stokes said in a statement to the media.

7 January - 1931

On this day in Baltimore Police History we lost our brother, Police **Officer John P. Burns** to gunfire, after his arrival to a domestic violence call in which he was lead into a home at 382 St. Mary St. When Officer Burns and his partner entered the living room, the suspect, [Willie Smith] came down stairs from the second floor with a pistol in each hand. As Smith made eye contact with Officer Burns he began firing on him, and while there were numerous shots fired, it was the first shot that took the life of Officer Burns.

The following is an account of the events that took place:

Patrolman John P. Burns and Sergeant Alfred Plitt were patrolling in the area of St. Mary's Street when Molly Aims asked for their protection from her live-in boyfriend, Willie Smith, who she said had been beating her all day in the house they live in at 382 St. Mary St. Officer Burns was quick to lead the way, closely followed by Sgt. Plitt. When they entered the house, Smith was nowhere to be seen as they began searching the first floor.

Their eyes were still adjusting from the outside light coming into the darker house, while Smith's eyes had been perfectly adjusted to the limited light in the house giving him the upper hand. He waited on the upper stairs of the house until the officers reached a point that had them at a disadvantage. Smith began descending the stairs, firing from both guns simultaneously. Officer Burns was closer to Smith, and therefore was first to be struck by the rounds. Taking one or two rounds to the upper torso, and a round nearer to his heart put him immediately on the floor.

Following a brief exchange of gunfire, a hand-to-hand fight broke out between the two, and Sgt. Plitt, who was buffaloed across the back of his head with one of the heavy revolvers, was knocked to the floor. Sgt. Plitt knew he had to continue fighting, despite being dazed. With his partner wounded, and quite possibly dead, and the suspect still standing, Plitt managed to get back to his feet just as Smith headed for the back door of the house. Plitt fired at Smith until he emptied his pistol, as Smith exited and began to run up the street. We don't know if he was hit or missed, but we do know Smith was slowed down. As Smith made his way up the street, he could only go a few houses away when he jumped under a neighbor's rear steps at 547 Orchard Street. As he did, he inexplicably placed the still fully loaded service revolver he'd taken from a stricken Patrolman Burns' holster on top the steps.

As Smith barricaded himself under the steps with two weapons – both possibly empty – Mr. Edward T. McIntyre, a civilian employed by the Baltimore Gas & Electric Co., aided the still-stunned Sgt. Plitt and the two set out after Smith, who was still in sight as he ducked under the steps. Mr. McIntyre took Plitt's gun, but found it empty as he tried to fire on Smith. With Plitt's now useless weapon, McIntyre rushed the barricaded suspect, seizing Burns' gun from atop the steps, and shooting Smith in the head. Almost simultaneously Patrolman David S. Weed of the Northwestern District came upon the scene and also began firing at Smith. Now shot by both Mr. McIntyre, Officer Weed and possibly Sgt. Plitt, Smith was taken to University hospital where he was pronounced dead on arrival.

Meantime, Patrolman Burns was fighting for his life at University Hospital, and a call went out across the city asking officers to give blood. A pint of blood was given by Lieutenant Henry Kriss of the Eastern District, as well as many other officers from east to west, and north to south – if you wore a Baltimore City Police Officer's badge, you offered your blood to help your brother. Sadly, on this day in 1931 Officer Burns, who had joined the department only ten years and one day earlier, would succumb to his injuries.

As his brothers and sisters of the Baltimore Police Department we will not let Officer Burns be forgotten, and we will take this time to remember him, think of him and thank him for his service and sacrifice.

9 January - 2007

On This day in Baltimore Police History 2007, we lost our brother, **Detective Troy Chesley** to gunfire as he was returning home from a busy day of serving and protecting Baltimore's citizens. As Detective Chesley, wearing plain clothes, began to insert his key in the front door of his girlfriend's north Baltimore home, one of those from whom Chesley had spent the day protecting us, came up behind him, stuck a 9mm handgun in the Detective's back and ordered his attention. The Detective quickly turned toward the suspect and was immediately shot in the chest and upper arm. Detective Chesley was able to draw his firearm, a .40 caliber Glock, and fire six rounds at the fleeing suspect, striking him at least once in his rear right calf. Detective Chesley would soon collapse on those front steps, where he was pronounced dead less than half an hour later.

The wounded suspect, Brandon Michael Grimes, left a trail of blood that led to a waiting van that was driven by his girlfriend. Once inside the back of the van, the girlfriend drove him to St. Agnes hospital to be treated for the gunshot wound inflicted by Det. Chesley. Following protocol, the hospital reported the newly admitted gunshot victim to Baltimore Police. Upon investigating, detectives were able to match blood at the scene to blood on Grimes, quickly linking him to the killing of Detective Chesley. Grimes was subsequently arrested and charged with murder. He was eventually convicted and sentenced to life in prison without parole.

Troy was an outstanding detective, often solving cases that others couldn't. As Sgt. Richard Purtnell, who investigated the case, was quoted as saying, "Troy ultimately caught his own killer by being able to shoot him even after being mortally wounded." Sgt. Purtnell pointed out that without that shot, leaving Grimes blood trail to the van, Grimes might not have so easily linked to this crime.

Further investigation revealed that the murder weapon, a Sig Sauer belonging to Mustafa R. Alif, had been used two months earlier in another shooting/attempted murder. The weapon had originally been purchased by Mr. Alif, who bought it Nov. 29, 1997, from the A&D Pawn Shop in Glen Burnie. Despite the gun being used to murder a police officer and an earlier attempted murder, the courts ordered it given back to Alif – and it ended up again in police hands as part of a Baltimore crime investigation.

Mustafa R. Alif, an unlucky sole, worked for 20 years for a Baltimore dairy, where he loaded milk trucks. The continuing investigation showed that Alif had purchased at least 13 firearms since 1997, seven of which were recovered by police investigating crimes by other people, including two drug offenses, an assault and robbery, and a concealed weapon violation. In March 2001, Mustafa Alif was convicted in the District of Columbia of misdemeanor possession of an unregistered firearm after he shot and wounded a man who he said tried to rob him while he was delivering milk in D.C. He was sentenced in that case to six months unsupervised probation, and five months later, on 21 August, 2001, Baltimore police raided Alif's house and confiscated eight guns, including an Egyptian-made AK-47 assault rifle, and the Sig Sauer used to kill Det. Chesley. Police had obtained that search warrant after a routine check revealed that Alif had bought ammunition at a sporting goods store in Towson. Authorities knew that his misdemeanor conviction prevented him from owning guns. Alif's conviction in the District did not prevent him from purchasing and possessing guns under Maryland law, according to an internal memo from Doug Ludwig of the Baltimore state's attorney's office.

Detective Chesley served the Baltimore City Police Department for 13 years. He was a widower, and is survived by his three daughters, two sons, his parents, and a brother. As his brothers and sisters of the Baltimore Police Department, we will not let him be forgotten, and we will take this time to remember him, think of him and thank him for his service and sacrifice.

9 January - 2011

On this day in Baltimore Police history we lost our brother Police **Officer William H. Torbit, Junior**, to a tragic case of friendly fire. At the time of his death, Officer Torbit was on duty and working a plain clothes detail. At approximately 0115 hours he responded to a report of an officer in distress at the *Select Lounge Nightclub* on North Paca Street. When Officer Torbit arrived he encountered a large group of people spilling out onto the street and fighting. Officer Torbit was a good, aggressive police officer who took pride in and loved doing his job. When this fight broke out he just looked at it as another day at the office. He identified himself to the people struggling in the street in an attempt to persuade them to stop fighting, settle down and leave the area. After identifying himself to the crowd, he was suddenly assaulted by several members of the rowdy group, punched, kicked and thrown to the ground. Being the fighter that he was, he popped back up, and in the struggle that ensued, he was assaulted several more times by even more members of the crowd. The badge that he wore on a chain around his neck was ripped away from him, and from that point on he basically lost all identifiable markings that would identify him to let citizens, or other police, know he was a working Baltimore Police Officer.

Shortly after his badge was stripped away from him, other officers began to arrive and converge on what would soon turn out to be one of the saddest, ugliest and most chaotic scenes ever in Baltimore Police History. It was as the responding officers were arriving on the scene that Officer Torbit felt sufficiently at risk that he withdrew his service weapon to defend himself against the already armed assailants that had by that point already fired upon him and others in the crowd. These arriving officers were unaware that a police officer was already on the scene and under attack – they saw only an unknown and bloodied black man drawing a gun in the midst of a large street fight where several shots had previously been fired. They reacted appropriately by drawing their own weapons and focusing their attention on the biggest threat they saw – the unfortunate Officer Torbit.

Several of the newly arriving officers mistook Officer Torbit for a threat, and quickly discharged an onslaught of rounds in his direction, many of which struck home, killing the unknown man and neutralizing the biggest threat. What they didn't see was a uniform, a badge, a radio or anything else that would tell them that the man with the gun was one of their own.

By the time the bullets stopped flying, Officer Torbit and a man by the name of Sean Gamble lay dead in the street. One of the responding officers had also been shot, as well three female bystanders. The shooting immediately raised questions about the appropriateness of the police response. Among the many issues raised by this incident were whether officers are adequately trained to handle such situations, whether the department should revise its policies on the use of plainclothes officers, and whether the officers who participated in the shooting used good judgment in firing so many rounds into an armed and violent crowd.

But this is not about pointing fingers or Monday morning quarterbacking our officers. This is about remembering our brother Police Officer William H. Torbit Jr. for the hero that he was. The media enjoys making these tug of war battles, us against them, white hats and black hats, yin and yang, but what they don't realize is that there was little else that could have been done under the circumstances. The department, on the other hand, must learn from this and find a way to prevent the possibility of future calamities.

As it turned out, this wasn't the first time a BPD officer had been shot by a brother officer - years earlier Officer Aaron Perkins had been shot in the hand under similar circumstances. He survived his injuries and was able to return to active duty, and eventually retire. And as a result of Officer Perkins' shooting, the department reacted by issuing bright yellow "Bumble Bee Raid Jackets" to plainclothes officers. They didn't last long – after all, an undercover officer or a plain clothes officer is no longer "plain" or "undercover" wearing such a jacket announcing his presence and identifying him immediately, even from a distance, as a police officer.

The department did properly react this time by dictating that all non-uniformed personnel conducting a raid or a search warrant would utilize as an outer garment a "raid jacket" which clearly identified them as police. That might have saved Officer Torbit if he had had such a jacket and the time to don it, but it wasn't to be.

William Torbit was our brother. He had two families; the Torbit family, and his Baltimore Police family. Will Torbit loved being a police officer, and as most police officers was honored to be a Baltimore City Police cop. For police officer was a title he took pride in. Let us never forget he was police, a proud, honored and loved Baltimore Police Officer.

Officer Torbit served with the Baltimore Police Department for eight years, and we all know the media wants a Torbit Family vs. Baltimore Police war, but as his police family, we will mourn our brother's death, learn from it and will never let him be forgotten. William Torbit had a love for the department that we will not let the media take away… We stand alongside anyone, in any vigil to honor his name. Let's not let anyone take away or muddy the waters as to what he stood for, what he was trying to do at the time of his death. Let's not forget the hours he put in, his dedication, and the sacrifices he made. Like the old saying goes, it is not how a man dies that makes him a hero, but how he lived, and Officer William Torbit lived his life for the job.

As his brothers and sisters of the Baltimore Police Department we will not let him be forgotten, and we will take this time to remember him, think of him and thank him for his service and sacrifice.

9 January - 2015

On this day in Baltimore Police History, 1915, we lost our Brother Police **Officer Craig Chandler** to injuries stemming from an auto accident which occurred in November 2014 while he and his partner were in pursuit of a fleeing suspect on a moped. Initially, news of Chandler's passing were announced not through a press release, but through a series of cryptic Tweets and Facebook messages. For instance, a tweet posted on Saturday 10 January, 2015, read;

"We will always remember Officer Craig Chandler #EOW 1/9/15 due to injuries in a LOD car accident. #BPDNeverForget" To those of us who follow tweets, that was the first sign telling us that our brother, Officer Craig Chandler, had died as a result of injuries sustained in the November accident. No details, no explanation. Just an obscure tweet.

In fact, the details of the fatal incident were as follows: The crash occurred in the 2200 block of Kirk Ave. in East Baltimore and left Chandler "fighting for his life." The accident was briefly reported in a November newspaper article. Neither Officer Chandler nor his partner that day were identified at the time, but on Christmas Eve an FOP representative provided Chandler's name and condition to the media – at that time he was in stable condition at the University of Maryland Shock Trauma Center. Officer Chandler and his partner were injured when the patrol car his partner was driving struck a telephone pole while pursuing a moped that had picked up a man fleeing from a gathering of dirt bike riders, police said at the time. Police also reported that commanders tried via the police radio to call the pursuit off just before the accident occurred, which also left the moped driver, Deonta Winston, hospitalized.

What is unclear is whether Chandler or his partner heard the order to end the pursuit. The order to "call off the pursuit" could have been missed by them under the sound of their siren, but in any event, the pursuit ended tragically moments after the call to end it was eventually broadcast.

Officer Chandler had been with the Police Department since 2008. "We are very saddened by the loss of BPD Officer Craig Chandler on 1/9/15," the Fraternal Order of Police Lodge No. 3, the city's police union, tweeted on 10 January 2015. "He succumbed to injuries from a LOD MVA. We will never forget our Brother!" (Note: LOD MVA means *Line of Duty Motor Vehicle Accident*.)

City Councilman Brandon Scott, who knew Officer Chandler personally, also posted about the death on Twitter when he wrote: "Rest in Peace Officer Chandler, You will suffer no longer. It has been a pleasure knowing you and watching you serve." Scott wrote.

The driver of the patrol car involved in the accident was Officer Brandon Bolt, who was treated and released the day of the accident. Officer Bolt had been with the department for approximately one year at the time of the accident.

We take this time to remember Officer Craig Chandler, and thank him for his service and sacrifice. We his brothers and sisters of the Baltimore Police Department will not let him be forgotten. God Bless and Rest in Peace.

10 January - 1964

On this day in Baltimore Police History, 1964, we lost our brother, **Officer Francis Stransky** to injury/illness.

1964 would become one of the most violent years in Baltimore Police history. By year's end five police officer's lives would end in the line of duty, and on this day in 1964 we would lose the first of those five officers.

Officer Stransky was a five year veteran and an aggressive officer. ("Aggressive" in this context is a term used to describe officers who simply do their job well, not that they are particularly aggressive with the public, or in any negative way, but that they are aggressively pursuing crime, and protecting the public from those that would do them harm.) He worked his beat, knew everyone, and did his job by the book. It was coming up on 1800 hours, maybe quarter of, when Officer Stransky, while in the 500 block of Ensor St, came across a 22 year old wise-guy by the name of Larry G. Wadsworth. Wadsworth was acting disorderly, and refused to cease his actions and move on. When told he was being placed under arrest, he felt it was up to him to resist that arrest, and that the officer wouldn't be able to subdue him.

What Wadsworth didn't know was that Stransky was tough, and he knew the laws, so he used just the amount force he was allowed to use by law, an amount of force determined by the amount of resistance shown by Wadsworth. So Officer Stransky followed the rules to the letter, and when he tried to subdue Wadsworth and found he was no match for the bigger man, he followed the progression of force going from hand-to-hand, to the introduction of his Espantoon. A few jabs, and a strike or two from the stick, and Wadsworth tapped out. Wadsworth was ready to stop by Mercy Hospital on the way to Men's detention, and that's just where he was taken. While at Mercy he was quickly treated for the lumps he took and off the two men walked to the Central District Police Station where Wadsworth would be booked on disorderly conduct, assault, and resisting arrest charges.

While Wadsworth was waiting in one of the holding cells and Stransky was in the roll call room, he began feeling odd, something between dizzy and lightheaded, and before he could call for help he would collapse to the floor.

Officer Stransky would die there on the floor before anyone really understood what was happening to him. The 22-year-old Wadsworth was brought in on what would have been relatively minor charges. But before he knew what was going on, because of the fight he decided to put up against his arrest, it would have him catching another charge much more serious than those charges – it would make him a murderer. Because in addition to a simple disturbance of the peace, minor assault and resisting arrest charges, Wadsworth was now being charged with manslaughter, in the incident which caused this patrolman's death from a heart attack.

Francis R. Stransky was a 39-year-old husband and father of two. A policeman in the Central District for five years, Francis enjoyed patrolling the area around Cicero's and the Belair market. He liked the people in the area, and he liked seeing the rich history of Baltimore. And he liked to grab a quick bite to eat in the Belair Market and the brotherhood he would find in the Baltimore Police Department.

We take this time to remember him, and thank him for his service and sacrifice. We, his brothers and sisters of the Baltimore Police Department, will not let him be forgotten. God Bless him and may he rest in Peace.

Following Stransky's death, there would be four more fallen officers by years end: officers Claude Profili, Walter Matthys, Teddy Brafford and Sgt. Jack Cooper. From an officer with less than a week on the streets, to an officer with 17-years on the streets, each was a man of valor, each was a loss that to this day is felt deeply by their families, friends and co-workers.

11 January - 1959

On this day in Baltimore Police History we lost our brother, **Patrolman Richard H. Duvall** to accidental gunfire after a high speed car chase and the recovery of a stolen vehicle.

Sixteen year old Ulbis Buiva, of the 1100 block Roland Heights Avenue and an 11th grade student at Baltimore Polytech Institute where he is taking the "A" courses, entered a car dealership lot off Mt. Royal Avenue and stole a black 1957 Thunderbird. Moments later he and his newly stolen T-Bird were involved in a hit-and-run accident at Mt. Royal and North Avenue, at which time the Thunderbird was reported as having Pennsylvania tags. Subsequent investigation revealed that the tags were stolen from a parking lot not far from Mt. Royal Ave. A short time later Patrolman Robert B. Leutbecker spotted the vehicle at Park and North

Avenues. He reported it by telephone (remember, it was 1959) and the radio alert was broadcast to all cars.

At the time Leutbecker spied the car he reported that it was occupied by several persons. After racing around the Druid Hill Park roads for a time, the sports car sped from the park using the Gwen Falls Parkway exit. This is where patrolman Howell and Duvall became involved in the chase. These partners were in one of about a dozen police cars chasing the speeding Thunderbird, when it cornered too hard, overcompensating for the turn, and struck an embankment before everyone bailed out and ran. Howell and Duvall gave foot chase to the driver, and each fired their revolvers at the youth as he ran up the alley (don't try that today folks). They would eventually capture the youth after a short foot chase.

When the officers caught Buiva, they were confronted with a "terrific struggle" as the suspect put up quite a fight. It was during that struggle that "one of the officers' guns discharged." Since both guns were fired numerous times during the chase, it was unclear at first which officer's gun fired the fatal shot that took Patrolman Duvall's life. But in any event, during the struggle one of the two guns discharged and Patrolman Duvall was shot in the left chest. The bullet passed down through his chest, cutting his main artery before exiting through his right hip.

Patrolman Howell became hysterical at the hospital when he learned of his partner's death – in fact he was so shaken by it that he had to be kept at the hospital under sedation for the night. Sadly, the next day, ballistics would show that the round which took Officer Duvall's life was indeed fired from Patrolman Howell's .38 cal. revolver.

Patrolman Richard H. Duvall Jr, 28, served the Baltimore Police department for more than 6 years. He was survived by his wife, Charlotte Duvall, and two daughters, two-year-old Suzan and three-month-old Cheryl.

From newspaper reports at the time:

"A young policeman was fatally wounded yesterday at the climax of a high-speed stolen car chase through the northern part of the city. Patrolman Richard H. Duvall Jr., 28, was shot in the chest by a bullet from his own pistol or that of his partner, Patrolman Melvin H. Howell, 29, while they were attempting to arrest the driver of a stolen sports car. Ballistics tests will be conducted to determine which pistol the bullet came from, investigators said."

"The shooting occurred in the 3800 block of Greenspring Avenue at the end of a

five-mile chase late in the afternoon. It began on Greenmount Avenue and raised it's be the river 75 miles an hour through Druid Hill Park to Northwest Baltimore. Patrolman Howell and Duvall in one of about 18 police cars chasing the speeding Thunderbird, cornered the youth driving it after it struck an embankment opposite the Children's Hospital school. They each fired their revolvers at the youth as he ran up the alley, and captured him after a short foot chase."

"Police officials who were investigating the shooting said that the youth was captured with a "terrific struggle" and that "one of the officer's guns discharged" during the fight. When asked whether the officers were clubbing the suspect with their pistol butts, Inspector Leo T. Kelly replied, "no doubt he did get hit with one of the guns." Patrolman Duvall, married and the father of two children, died at Union Memorial Hospital about half an hour after the shooting."

"Patrolman Duvall was shot in the left chest, and the bullet passed downwards as it entered his body, cutting the main artery and exiting over the right hip. Patrolman Howell broke down at the hospital when he learned that his partner had died, and was kept there under sedation overnight. Patrolman Duvall, who lived at 942 Imperial Court, Lansdowne, was on the force for only seven years. Patrolman Howell has been on the force a year and a half longer. Inspector Kelly, who conducted the investigation with inspector Bernard J. Schmidt, said the driver of the stolen car was being held at the Northern Police District for questioning about the theft and the subsequent shooting."

"The driver, who gave his age at the hospital as 15 but appeared much older, was treated at Union Memorial hospital for scalp cuts, which he apparently received while he was being captured. Inspector Kelly said that the Thunderbird was wanted by police for involvement is several crimes. It had been reported stolen from an automobile dealer Saturday and was displaying Pennsylvania tags that had been reported lost or stolen here earlier. The black 1957 Thunderbird was involved in a hit-and-run accident Saturday at Mt. Royal and North Avenue, at which time both the cars description and its Pennsylvania tags were spotted."

"Late yesterday afternoon a policeman saw it at Park and North avenues. He reported it by telephone and the radio alert was broadcast to all cars. At the time there were several persons in the car. Another officer spotted the car minutes later at 25th Street and Greenmount Avenue, touching off the chase which proceeded to North Avenue, west on Madison Avenue, and north on the Druid Hill Park Drive. After racing around the park roads, the sports car sped out of the Gwen Falls

Parkway exit from the park, where patrolman Howell became involved in the chase."

"The train of cars raced to Park Circle and up Park Heights Avenue. According to patrolman Wilbur Baldwin, one of the pursuing officers, the cars were hitting 75 miles an hour and more. They cut off Violet Ave., up Cottage Avenue and across Oswego Avenue, where the sports car turned South on Greenspring Avenue. As the sports car twisted down the hill outside the Children's Hospital school, it turned suddenly to the right into an alley, apparently in an attempt to lose the oncoming group of police cars."

"The chase continued until the T-Bird hit a slope along the side of the southernmost house in the 3800 block. Inspector Kelly said the two policemen were the only ones at the spot where and when patrolman Duvall was shot. Both of their pistols had been fired, he said."

"The inspector said the other persons reported to have been in the car when it was first seen had apparently been dropped off somewhere before the high-speed chase, although it was possible one of the riders was still in the car when it crashed. A total of three shots were fired by the two pistols, inspector Kelly said. It was the inspector who said, 'There was a terrific struggle' in arresting the youth."

"A Northwest district patrolman was charged yesterday with causing the death of his radio car partner Sunday as the two struggled with a youth at the end of a five-mile high-speed car chase. The technical charge was placed against Patrolman Melvin E Howell, 29 of 1800 block of Swansea road, after a ballistic test showed that a bullet from his gun killed his partner, Patrolman Richard H. Duvall. A total of three shots had been fired from his gun and the .38 caliber service revolver of patrolman Officer Melvin E. Howell."

As police continued their investigation of the car theft and the wild chase that led to its recovery, there were these other developments:

"The 15-year-old driver who was arrested at the climax of the chase underwent surgery at Union Memorial Hospital, where he was being treated for a skull fracture. Inspector Leo T. Kelly said Sunday he had been hit with the policeman's revolvers. Car theft charges were placed against another youth, 16, who is alleged to have had a part in taking the 1957 Thunderbird from the automobile dealer on Saturday. The hearing of the charges was held February 9 when the driver of the stolen car, one Ulbis Buiva, a native of Latvia, appeared before magistrate James

F. Fanseen in Northern district court. He lives with his parents in the 1100 block Roland Heights avenue. Bail was set at $750 on the car theft charge and a $250 on the second count, alleging that Buiva was involved in stealing a set of Pennsylvania license plates from a car in a parking lot. The Pennsylvania tags were on the stolen car which police chased through the Midtown, and Midwest sections of Baltimore."

<u>Spotted Sunday</u>

The stolen car was spotted Sunday afternoon parked in the 600 block of W. North Ave. by Patrolman Robert B Leutbecker. He said he went over to the shiny black car and asked the youthful driver for his operator's license and registration card. The officers said the youth replied the credentials were in the glove compartment, but that he would get them. He got into the car, which was occupied by three young women and another young man and they roared away. By the time the car had gone three blocks, police said, the passengers were demanding to be let out. The driver stopped and allowed all four to leave the car. The four later were questioned by police, who said yesterday that no charges will be brought against them.

As we take this time to remember him, and thank him for his service and sacrifice. We his brothers and sisters of the Baltimore Police Department will not let him be forgotten. God Bless and rest in Peace.

11 January - 2015

Baltimore City Police changed their uniformed patrol officers' work schedule. The stated purpose is to make officers' jobs more efficient and city streets safer. Henceforward, uniformed patrol officers will work 10 hours per day, 4 days a week.

12 January - 1871

On this day in Baltimore Police History we lost our brother, Police **Officer Charles J. Walsh** to gunfire. This is a strange one, folks – Officer Walsh died while on duty protecting the citizens of Baltimore, but we don't know if it was an accident that came about while he was drawing his pistol for something he may have heard or seen. We don't know if it was an accident that occurred while he was double checking his weapon to make sure he had it, or to make sure it was loaded, as he had taken it out of his possession during an initiation earlier that evening.

Here's what we know. He was excited about life, he was earlier that day accepted into a lodge (The Order of Heptasophs) that he had been trying to get into for years, he was already a member of a second lodge that he was excited about, he had moved into a new boarding house that day. He was apparently loving life. Officer Walsh's partner and friend, Officer Ross, gave a statement indicating that he had been with Walsh during the early part of the night, and that Walsh had been initiated into a lodge (The Order of Heptasophs) that night, after which Ross went with him to his boarding house, and then to dinner with him.

While headed to the station house (Western) that evening, Ross remarked to Walsh that he (Ross) thought he had forgotten his pistol (they often carried a single shot pistol in their pocket), which prompted Walsh to feel his own overcoat pocket, and feeling the shape of a gun said that he (Walsh) definitely he had his; but something about his having left it in the ante-room while being initiated, and that he did it out of fear of an accident (showing the officer was somewhat safety conscious, and not careless or suicidal – but worried about an accident): the last thing Ross stated was that Walsh 'appeared to be in good spirits' that day."

We will never know what caused these events to unfold. During a time when holsters were often not used, and carrying a gun in a pocket was common among Baltimore Police Officers, it could be an unfortunate accident that came about from the unsafe way our brothers carried their weapons, and part of the reason we use holsters today – holsters that have evolved over the years to help keep our guns, and our officers, safe. Remember the widow maker holsters (and that wasn't that long ago)?

From all that we don't know, we can more easily look at the things we do know. Officer Charles J. Walsh was a Baltimore Police Officer who liked and was good at his job. He took pride in his sense of brotherhood, as is apparent by his joining the Police Department, the Beptasophs Lodge and the Howard Lodge Number Eight Independent Order of Mechanics. And we believe that based on what we know about him, for him to have brought harm to himself was out of the question.

So we have to ask ourselves, was he checking his gun to make sure it was loaded from earlier in the night when it was out of his possession? Did he hear something and try to draw from his pocket, got tangled up and caused a misfire? Sgt Zimmerman heard a single wrap of his nightstick, just before hearing the report of his pistol, perhaps he was calling for backup? Again we don't know, but we do know he was on duty; in fact back in the 1800 officers wore their uniforms both on, and off duty. This officer loved life; he was excited about his new endeavors, laughing and joking with other officers and somehow had an accidental discharged of his weapon that night that killed him.

Whether it occurred while drawing from his pocket to check something out, or just to make sure he was armed with a loaded pistol, we know it happen while he was on duty and this is based on information found in the following Newspaper articles about Patrolman Walsh. It happened within 5 minutes of his going on duty that night, and just a few blocks from the Pine Street Station House:

These are the newspaper reports from the time:

<u>Local Matters – 13 January, 1871</u> *– Policeman accidentally shot by his own pistol*

"Coroner's inquest – Yesterday (12 January 1871) morning about 1:30 o'clock, just about five minutes after police Division C, had left the Western stationhouse, the officers in charge of the station heard the report of a pistol, apparently coming from Baltimore Street in the direction of Pearl Street. Sgt. Zimmerman and policeman Burkins, Earhart and McKee quickly ran to the spot from which the sound emanated, and there found Policeman Charles J. Walsh (who had just arrived upon his beat) lying upon the pavement, his head resting in a pool of blood, with his pistol under him, with one barrel discharged, and his Espantoon and belt lying alongside him. He was conveyed to the station-house, and Prof. Baxter summoned, who discovered that the ball had penetrated the center of his forehead and passed into the brain, causing a fatal wound. The unfortunate man lingered in an unconscious state until about a quarter past 3 o'clock when he expired."

"Dr. Spicer, city coroner, yesterday morning summonsed the following jury of inquest: - Dr. E. R. Baer, (Foreman) John Williams, E. R. Riddell, John Turnbull Junior, A. C. Pracht, T. Kearngood, Charles Stewart, E. T. Schultz, William T. Toles, Alex Towson, E. S. Parish, and James Maddox, before whom the following testimony was elicited: Policeman William Burkins testified that he was passing along Baltimore Street, coming toward Green and at that time he looked across the street and saw the deceased passing. Directly afterwards he heard the deceased drop his espantoon and his attention was particularly attracted to look toward the deceased; a moment afterwards witness saw the flash, and heard the report of the pistol: ran across the street towards him, but before he could reach him, the deceased spun around and fell: witness immediately rapped his Espantoon for assistance and Sgt. Zimmerman and other officers came up in a few moments and

on raising the deceased did they find his pistol under him, and his belt and stick lying near him; there was no person nearer him than witness himself."

"Sgt. Zimmerman testified to having heard a single wrap of a stick, and a moment afterward seeing a flash, and heard a report of a pistol. He was at the time with his squad on Baltimore Street near Pine: went back and found that the deceased was lying on the sidewalk: on raising him up found blood streaming from a wound in his forehead, and his revolver lying under him: witness, policemen Burkins, Earhart, Smith and McKee."

"Policeman Ross testified that he had been with policeman Walsh starting the early part of the night: deceased had been that night initiated into a lodge, after which witness went with him to his boarding house and took a lunch with him: when about to start to the station house remarked to him that he (witness) thought he had forgotten his pistol, the deceased felt in his own overcoat pocket and said that he (deceased) had his, and that he had left it in the ante-room while being initiated for fear of an accident: deceased appeared to be in good spirits."

"Policeman McKee testified that he parted with the deceased at the southeast corner Baltimore and Greene streets, after leaving the station house at one o'clock in the morning – as deceased left witness he said he would see him again: witness asked when: deceased in a joking manner said about the Fourth of July, a few minutes afterwards he heard the report of the pistol: went back and found the deceased lying on the pavement."

"The jury after hearing the evidence rendered a verdict that the deceased came to his death by accidental discharge of his own pistol. The deceased was 27 years of age and unmarried."

"The body was taken in charge of by a brother of the deceased, and removed to the residence of the former, number 4 Decker St., from which place to the funeral will be placed this afternoon, at 2 o'clock. It will be attended by a delegation of Police Department and by members of the order of Beptesephe."

As we take this time to remember him, and thank him for his service and sacrifice. We his brothers and sisters of the Baltimore Police Department will not let him be forgotten. God Bless and Rest in Peace

It should be noted that Officer Walsh's name will not appear on any wall, any book, or read at any candlelight vigil… but on 12 January, 1871, officer Welsh died while on duty protecting the citizens of Baltimore.

12 January - 1873

On this day in Baltimore Police History, 1873, we lost our brother, **Policeman John H. Dames** to duty related illness. The remains of Policeman Dames (who died from the smallpox on Sunday morning, 12 January 1873) were interred yesterday. He would be the third officer to die from the illness in a short time.

As we take this time to remember him, and thank him for his service and sacrifice – we his brothers and sisters of the Baltimore Police Department will not let him be forgotten. God Bless and Rest in Peace.

12 January - 1873

On this day in Baltimore Police History, 1873, we lost our brother, **Policeman James T. Harvey** to duty related illness. He contracted Smallpox while on duty, as did two other officers during that time period. He was buried in the Western Cemetery. Newspaper reports from the time said:

"The death to another policeman from smallpox – James T. Harvey, another member of the Western District police force, died at his residence 415 Lexington St. at about 2330 hours on Sunday night 12 January 1873, from smallpox, contracted while in the discharge of his duty. He was in the 28th year of his age and leaves a wife, but no children. He was regarded as a faithful conservatory of the peace."

As his brothers and sisters of the Baltimore Police Department we will not let him be forgotten, and we will take this time to remember him, think of him and thank him for his service and sacrifice.

13 January - 1947

On this day in Baltimore Police History, 1947, we lost our brother, Police **Officer Fred R. Unger** to gunfire:

Crime back then was normal Baltimore crime; they had their burglars, their drug dealers, their thieves and their stick up men. On this particular day there was a punk by the name of Milford E. Davis, who had found his niche in the crime world sticking up cab drivers and taking their hard earned cash. On this night he had committed one such hold up already from a cab driver on the corner of Saratoga St. near Gay St. After that stick-up, he quickly made his way into the Central District.

He was nearing the 900 Blk. of Brevard Alley, where he was on the hunt for another cab to hit. By now his description had been given to all police in the area, and two of Central's long time partners, Officer George Pfaff, and Fred Unger were on a different hunt, instead of looking for someone to steal from, they were on the lookout for someone about to rob a cab, and it wouldn't take long for Officer Unger to spot a potential suspect, a fellow matching the description given out earlier, running in the alley.

Pointing the suspect out to his partner, Officer Unger called out to the suspect, asking him, "Hey! Hey, you there! What are you running from?" and the suspect, looking toward them, pointed to his chest as if to ask if they were talking to him. Unger confirmed that they were, and asked him to come to their vehicle. He sauntered over toward their car, calm and collected as he was catching his breath… he acted as if he had nothing to hide, not a worry in the world. His apparent calm took the officers off their normal guard, and they didn't even exit their vehicle to interview him – they thought perhaps this was not the right guy after all. Still, they decided to try to talk to him, as he may have seen something, he may have had some information to lead them in the right direction. They motioned to him and told him to come over to passenger side of their car so they could talk to him.

The suspect continued walking calmly toward the passenger door, pausing momentarily to listen to Officer Unger's questions through the passenger door window. Then, without saying anything or answering their questions, the officers watched as he calmly began walking again, still without saying a word. As he passed the rear door and situated himself slightly behind the officers (who were still seated in their car), he suddenly turned and drew a .25 caliber semi-automatic pistol from his waist band and fired several shots into the car, striking Officer Unger several times.

Officer Pfaff quickly bailed of the car, trying to take a safe vantage point at the front of their car while drawing his weapon. As he came up to find his target, he saw the suspect was running away. Pfaff began chasing the suspect past the east side of the Armory into an alley beside a warehouse near Dolphin St. Then suddenly he was gone; Pfaff lost the visual he had on the suspect when they were someplace near Dolphin Street and Linden Green. Then suddenly Pfaff was being fired on by Davis from around the corner of a building. Pfaff reacquired the suspect and might have had a chance to return fire, but he saw that the suspect was running toward a group of people, and did not fire, out of fear that had he missed it could have led to one or more of the bystanders being shot. So he did the next best thing – he armed himself with a description and ran back to his vehicle to check on his partner and broadcast his description so the other officers in the area could look for him.

Once back to his car he found his partner, Officer Frederick R. Unger had been struck in the head, the face, and several times in his upper body… Pfaff, somewhat in shock quickly called for medical attention, giving the description of the suspect with warnings of his danger and a direction of travel. Now armed with a clothing description and direction of travel, soon another pair of Central District Officers, Joseph Levin and John Griffin were on his trail. At the corner of Morris Alley and Dolphin Street, they met the gunman coming toward them with the same weapon in hand. Officers Levin and Griffin were ready for what might be coming, so they drew their service revolvers and called out to the suspect to stop. However, Davis, instead of doing what he was told, did what he thought was his best chance for escape – he stopped, spun around and fired on the officers, who returned fire, killing the suspect. They recovered the gun he used to kill Officer Unger, as well as the money stolen in the earlier cab robbery.

Officer Unger died that night trying to make Baltimore a safer place for all of us. Officers Levin and Griffin fired their guns and killed a man, while bullets were being fired in their direction from the gun of a guy that didn't care who he hurt, he didn't care about his backdrop, which brings us to Officer Pfaff, who refused to shoot at a fleeing felon, while he himself was being fired on, so that he wouldn't accidently shoot someone in the background. He put public safety ahead of his own safety and ran back to their car to call for help and to check on his partner. These are the brave men of the Baltimore Police department.

Officer Unger was married and the father of 2 daughters, Carol (eight) and Gail Patricia (eighteen months). Officer Fred R. Unger was 38 years of age and a 3 year veteran of the force.

We his brothers and sisters of the Baltimore Police department will not let him be forgotten as we take this time to remember him, and thank him for his service and sacrifice.

14 January - 1941

On this day in Baltimore Police History, 14 Jan 1941, we lost our brother, **Captain Harvey Von Harten**, who died of a heart attack after a hard day's work at the Marine unit.

From newspaper reports at the time – this one actually worth reading:

"Police Capt. Harvey Von Harten, chief of the Baltimore harbor police, died of a heart attack yesterday afternoon. At the age of 61, he was the oldest member of the department's marine division. He was said to be the only man on the force who was raised to the rank of lieutenant from that of patrolman. He received the promotion in February of 1921, two years after he joined the harbor patrol."

"He was elevated to the captaincy of the harbor police ten years later, in December of 1931. Captain Von Harten was born and bred in the tradition of seafaring. The son of George Von Harten, proprietor of a seaman's hotel on Pratt Street, near Gay, Von Harten as a youth often listened to sailors from all parts or the world as they spun their tales in the little lobby of the hotel."

These stories and a love of the sea he inherited from his family had their effect on him. While still a young man he went to sea, making trips to Europe as an ordinary seaman. When he returned to Baltimore and before he was appointed to the police force, he acted as skipper of the Sunbeam.

He was appointed to the force in June 1911, and was assigned to the Southern District. In March 1919, he was transferred to the police boat. Captain Von Harten saw five police boats come and go and he command three of them. The police boats Marshall Farnan and the Lannan were sold by the department long ago. Within the last year the new Charles D. Gaither was put in commission to take the place of the George G. Henry. The Robert D. Carter still is in service.

One of Captain Von Harten's favorite stories about policing came out of the Longshoremen's strike here about six years ago. The strikers formed picket lines with boats along the harbor and it was the job of the water-front police to patrol these lines. One afternoon a group of longshoremen landed on a company dock. This was private property, the act was trespassing and Captain Von Harten knew there was sure to be trouble. He ordered his men to drag out the fire hose. In a few minutes the dock was clear and trouble averted.

Early in his career, while .he was patrolling a beat in the Southern district, a storekeeper called to Von Harten as he walked past the establishment. He ran inside, and the proprietor screamed he was being robbed, and a large man who was standing in front of the counter offered no resistance as he was arrested.

However, Von Harten took him to a call box, and while they were waiting for a patrol wagon, the suspect whipped a butcher knife out of his sleeve. In the struggle that followed, the man stabbed himself died. Von Harten was uninjured.

For several months he had been under physician's care for a heart ailment. He went on sick leave last November 14, but returned to duty December 9 and had been working regularly since that time.

Yesterday, he died at 4.20 P. M., a few minutes after he left the police boat dock at the foot of Willis street. There he had told Lieutenant Timothy Welsh, "I never felt better in my Life." Patrolman Edward J. Travers drove the captain to his home at 3814 Echodale Avenue. Just as the automobile pulled up in front of the house, Captain Von Harten was stricken. Travers drove to the St. Joseph's Hospital, where efforts to revive his superior failed.

Twice during his career as a policeman, Captain Von Harten was commended for highly meritorious service of the department. He received numerous other awards. He is survived by his mother, Mrs. Ida Von Harten, of 1626 St. Paul Street, his wife, Mrs. Lottie Von Harten, and one son, Harvey, Jr.

We his brothers and sisters of the Baltimore Police department will not let him be forgotten as we take this time to remember him, and thank him for his service and sacrifice.

15 January - 1983

Today in Baltimore Police History, 1983, the first woman to be named District Commander –Bessie R. Norris – was promoted to Major and assumed her duties as Commander of the Southwestern District

16 January - 1905

Today in Baltimore Police History, 1905, we remember what might have been the department's first recorded attempt at the maintenance of our Police History, when

Patrolman William Burgess of the Central District began his new job in the newly established office of *Librarian* and *Keeper of the Archives* of the Central District.

The following is from a Sun paper report that day:

"Patrolman William Burgess, of the Central District, is now busy with his new office as librarian and keeper of the archives of the Central Police Station. All of the musty old records of the police station, dating back to before the Civil War, are being resurrected from the dark, dusty closet in the rear of the Capt.'s office and arranged in their proper order on neat shelves in a little room on the second floor."

"Patrolman Burgess, who was an expert stage carpenter before he laid aside the saw and hammer for the Espantoon and "Billy," erected the shelves and is now busy arranging the record books in rows upon them. A single glance along the long row of frayed and weak back books is interesting, as it shows exactly when the old Middle District changed its name to the more dignified title of Central District. The record for 1884 is the first book bearing the name Central District".

"Held together by their fellows supporting them on either side, the worn and dilapidated volumes present a pitiable spectacle of a departed usefulness. Could they but speak to stories of crime, and blood, and misery, and man's inhumanity to man, that be hidden within their musty pages, they would a tale unfold that would make a weird offspring of Poe's erratic genius seems commonplace."

16 January - 1970

On this day in Baltimore Police History, 1970 we lost our brother, Police **Officer George F. Heim** in the line of duty. While directing traffic around a disabled vehicle on O'Donnell Street, Officer Heim was struck by Robert Bryant's vehicle as it approached the accident scene.

The following from the Sunpapers at the time:

"It was at 9 o'clock on the morning of 16 January, 1970. When Police Officer George F. Heim was called for assistance in dealing with heavy traffic, around an accident scene on O'Donnell Street, Patrolman George Heim was quick to answer the call, and make his way through a nearly blinding snowstorm to the 500 block of O'Donnell Street. Dealing with drivers that can't handle a snow flake, much less the whiteout mess Baltimore Police Department's Traffic and Patrol Division had

to deal with on the waterfront streets of Canton, and other parts of the city that cold winter day."

"Officer Heim was a seasoned veteran, well aware of the dangers that surrounded him and his fellow officers that day, trying to handle an accident scene, heavy snow, and still protect the public. He had the family of this disabled car wait inside the vehicle as he worked to keep them protected by directing oncoming traffic away from them."

"In order to appropriately guard against other vehicles traveling in the area, Officer Heim went to the trunk of his patrol car and grabbed some road flares, wisely thinking if he could alert oncoming traffic, he might prevent further incident this morning with the use of a simple road flare."

"Like all police, he had officer safety in mind, but was also concerned for the lives he was assigned to protect and on this day, and this call it was the family inside that car."

"With the events that were about to unfold Officer Heim never had a chance, he wasn't even given time to so much as light a single flare from the handful he had just grabbed from his trunk."

"Robert Bryant, was a man in way too much of a hurry to allow the city salt trucks, and snow ploughs time to clear the streets for him. In fact, his hurry was too much to even allow himself time to completely clear the snow from his own windshield. Instead, he removed little more than a tiny peek hole from the ice and snow that had gathered there, a hole that he could barely peek through, with just one eye. Still it was the only view point he had from inside of his vehicle as he drove down the street in what were already dangerous icy road conditions. With his eye pressed to the inside of his windshield, glancing up and down and from side to side, he quickly scanned the streets he was racing through to get to work. Every once in a while Bryant would wipe the fog on his windshield from his breath, from the inside of his windshield, from where his face was pressed so tight to that tiny hole he had cleared in the ice.

"Worse, he couldn't use his rear window at all, and to clear the ice, and snow from his side windows he simply did a quick job of rolling them down, and then back up again. Nothing was cleared from the roof, or back widows, and every time he stopped the icy snow build up would slide forward creating a snow buildup hood scoop for Bryant to have to look over and around and through as he drove. Like a snowball rolling down hill, the further he drove the more he added to the piles of snow on his car's trunk, roof, and hood.

"Every so often he would slam on his brakes, and if he was lucky, the car would stop fast enough to cause the snow from the hood, roof, and trunk to clear itself. If he were even luckier, he could do this and get to work without killing anyone.

"Too bad, Officer George F. Heim's life was riding on the luck of one man; one man too lazy, and in too much of a hurry to stop and take a minute to clear the snow from his car, to clear more than a 4x7 inch ice window from his windshield."

"The mess Robert Bryant had created was headed down O'Donnell Street at near 20-25 miles an hour toward our Brother officer, and he had no time in these conditions to so much as light a single flare from the handful he had grabbed from his trunk, before he would hear, then see Bryant's snow covered heap coming in his direction, a tiny eye could be seen peering through that ice carved hole in the windshield."

"Officer Heim knew he couldn't be seen by the driver, because he couldn't see in… other than a single eye peeking from that hole in the ice, an eye that was frantically scanning the area, making contact with everything, everything that is… except Officer Heim's eyes; it seemed he would not look at the officer, the two could not make eye contact, and officer Heim knew he couldn't run in either direction in time to avoid being struck."

"It was more than ice banks that prevented his escape, more than the snow that was too high, or that everything was too slippery; we may have for a moment in our reading forgotten, but Officer Heim, never forget… there was still a family under his protection, and that when he knew he couldn't save himself, he did everything to save theirs."

"Witnesses said, it happened fast yet it seemed to be moving in slow motion… too fast to help but so slow I'll never forget having seen ever part of it… said one witness, it seemed Officer Heim saw Bryant coming and knew he could do nothing for himself, so he did everything he could to save and protect that family. Imagine knowing you are going to die, protecting a family, knowing there was nowhere to go, and standing there watching yourself about to be run over. Still, his primary concern was protecting the family in that car."

"Witnesses said it was both the saddest, and bravest thing they had ever seen, a man standing out there in that weather, in that traffic, on that day… knowing he *was about to die to help a family he didn't know. Risking his life was nothing new for him, he was a police officer, they do it every day, but to knowingly give your life to help others from being killed by not a gun, or a knife, but from a guy too lazy to clean his windshield after or during a snowstorm."*

"The speed of Robert Bryant's approaching automobile, combined with the weather preventing any chance of Officer Heim's escape would claim his life. Bryant was driving entirely too fast for conditions, conditions created partially by the weather, but mostly by himself and that tiny ice window he was peeking through. Barely able to see in front of him, Bryant's car slid into the helpless policeman, inflicting the fatal internal injuries that would take his life."

"Investigation determined that Bryant was operating his car with gross negligence, in terrible conditions, and he was charged with causing the death of our brother officer George Heim."

"Officer Heim's supervisors and co-workers described him as both honest, and trustworthy adding that he was pleasant to be around, and had a special knack for police work. George F. Heim was 41 years old when he died, and behind him he left his wife Rosemary, daughter Miss Rosemary Goodnow, & Son George Heim Jr."

As we take this time to remember him and his family on this day, we also take the time to thank him for his service and sacrifice. And as his brothers and sisters of the Baltimore Police Department we will not let him be forgotten. God Bless and Rest in Peace.

20 January - 1965

On this day in Baltimore Police History, 1965, we lost our Brother Police **Officer Charles R. Ernest** to a pedestrian related auto accident that occurred at the intersection of Pearl and Saratoga Streets. From the Sun paper the following:

"At the intersection of Pearl and Saratoga St., Mr. Ferman Simmon and Mr. Louis Owens were involved in a minor traffic accident. Mr. Simmon was sitting in traffic when he was struck from behind. Mr. Owens had failed to stop for a stop sign, (he was driving a 1959 Chevy) when he slammed into the rear of Mr. Simmon's 1953 Ford. Even though their cars were operable the two drivers failed to remove their cars from the street causing a traffic back-up.

"It was approx. 11:15 am on the morning of June 13, 1964. Patrolman Ernest and his partner Officer Joseph Keirle arrived to handle what in terms of Baltimore City Police Department's calls, would be considered as "routine". More modern times it would be called a Sig 30. Patrolman Ernest examined the licenses, and other paperwork that Mr. Simmons and Mr. Owens had provided, while he and Mr. Simmons stood at the rear of the heavily damaged 53 Ford owned by Mr. Simmons.

"Mr. Owens was told to back his car away so Officer Keirle could better direct traffic around the scene and free up some of the traffic from the intersection. Mr. Owens jumped in behind the steering wheel, started the engine, and nervously put the car in the gear. As most people are around Police, Owens was nervous, his anxiety as it was, he did not get the car into reverse, but instead found first gear, and as he let up off the clutch while peering through the back window, his car lunged forward. Realizing his mistake, he quickly went to push the brake, but again his nerves got the best of him, and he pushed the pedal to the floor... had it been the brake, he may have saved a life, but as it was the gas, and instead of saving a life, he crushed the hips of two men between the cars.

"Mr. Fermon Simmons and Officer Charles Ernest were powerless to stop the two vehicles from crushing them between the two, and in an instant the pair were pinned between the cars. Mr. Owens immediately switched the car from 1st gear to reverse and backed his car away; but it was too late, the damage had already been done. When released from the massive trap of mangled steel and chrome, Patrolman Charles R Ernest could do nothing but fall to the ground in horrific, unbearable pain.

"The collision had shattered the hips, pelvis and entire lower spine of both men. Patrolman Keirle immediately called for an ambulance and did his best to comfort his partner. The crew of Medic #1 rushed to the scene and took the two men to University Hospital."

"The hospital summoned Dr. John A. O'Conner, the official Departmental Doctor, to care for Officer Ernest. After a week in the hospital, and several surgeries, Doctor O'Connor determined Officer Ernest would need long-term care, and assigned Dr. Edward Wenzlaff as his primary doctor. When the immediate danger to his health had passed, Officer Ernest was taken from the hospital to his home with hopes of a full recovery."

"At home, his wife Dorothy and daughter Mary provided care for him constantly, and he seemed to be doing better. There was never a shortage of visitors.

Unfortunately, things took a turn for the worse, and hopes would soon wane as there was a steady decline in his condition."

"Though he had the benefits of the assigned physician to care for him, he did not progress the way Dr. O'Conner had originally hoped he would. On January 20, 1965, after multiple surgeries, numerous therapies and 221 days of bed rest at his home, Officer Charles R. Ernest suffered a severe heart attack and died as a result of the initial injuries."

"Officer Charles R. Ernest served the department for 18 years and one month, and was a well-respected Police Officer. During World War II he was a Sergeant in the Army and faced the dangers of combat for a little more than two years. In Baltimore he spent almost half his life in the Western District facing its dangers every day. In 1960, he was awarded the Silver Star after confronting an armed suspect and trading shots with him. A brave officer, he was never cavalier about dangerous situations. Ironically, it was his keen sense of area awareness that kept him safe, a sense of awareness that was caught off guard by the usual routineness of a call like this. He could have never suspected that call for a simple traffic accident would take his life. Which went on to teach future generations of police that there is no such thing as a routine call."

As his brothers and sisters of the Baltimore Police Department we will not let him be forgotten, and we will take this time to remember him, think of him and thank him for his service and sacrifice.

20 January - 1982

Today in Baltimore City Police History, 1982 - The Baltimore Police Department began working side-by-side and hand-in-hand with the Checker Cab Company on a project to form the TOP - Taxi on Patrol program. What began here in Baltimore went on to become a national program, for radio-equipped cab to report and help solve crimes all over the country.

22 January - 1917

On this day in Baltimore Police History, 1917 we lost our brother, **Patrolman Burns** came along on his bicycle on his way to the unit's sub-station at Parklake

Avenue and Reisterstown Road. His attention was called to an unlit lamp by a passer-by, and Officer Burns, always helpful, answered the call saying that he could make the light come on again to its normal power by tapping on the wire that leads from the pavement about 6 feet up the pole to the lamp itself. Upon doing this he was struck by a jolt of electricity that knocked him to the ground, where he was soon pronounced dead by Dr. James S. Akehurst, who lived hearby at nearby 4012 Parklake Avenue, who reached the side of the patrolman's body only a few minutes after he was electrocuted.

As his brothers and sisters of the Baltimore Police Department we will not let him be forgotten. His service honored the City of Baltimore and the Baltimore Police Department. May he rest in peace, and may God bless him.

25 January - 1947

Today in Baltimore Police History, 1947, The Baltimore Police Department promoted one of the Department's first African American officers to the rank of Sergeant. Patrolman James H. Butler Jr., now Sergeant Butler, was a College Football Player until hired by Commissioner William P Lawson. Sergeant James H. Butler Jr. was among the first three African American males hired by the Department on 28 July 1938.

25 January - 1967

On this day in Baltimore Police History, 1967 we lost our brother, Patrolman **William J. Baumer** to a heart attack on the job during a struggle. From newspaper accounts at the time:

"Officer Baumer suffered a fatal heart attack early yesterday, 25 January, 1967, as he attempted to arrest a 21 year-old man after a disturbance at a sandwich shop on the corner of Orleans Street and Patterson Park Avenue. While struggling with the suspect he was arresting, Baumer felt pain in his chest and collapsed to the sidewalk."

"It happened during the struggle when Patrolman Baumer was taking the young man to a police call-box about a block and a half away. The suspect broke free during the brief struggle, and when Patrolman Baumer started to give chase he

collapsed and crumpled to the sidewalk. He was dead on arrival at Church Home and Hospital. An Autopsy showed that a heart attack was the cause of death."

"Patrolman William Baumer was 49 years of age at the time of his death - A requiem mass was offered for him, at 9 am Saturday at the Sacred Heart Catholic Church, 600 South Conkling Street. A veteran of twenty years on the force, he was born and raised in East Baltimore, and graduated from Patterson Park High School."

"Patrolman Baumer joined the Baltimore Police Department in 1947 after service in the Army, which included duty in Europe during World War II."

Patrolman Baumer's survivors include two sisters: Mrs. Margaret Punte and Miss Barbara Baumer, and two brothers; John Baumer and Germanus Baumer, Jr., all of Baltimore.

We his brothers and sisters of the Baltimore Police Department will not let him be forgotten. God Bless and rest in Peace.

26 January - 1905

On this day in Baltimore Police History, 1905, we lost our brother, Patrolman **Mathew Boone**, to a line of duty illness. While we won't find his name engraved on any memorial walls or hear his name at candlelight vigils, make no mistake Officer Boone died of an illness brought on by his service to the citizens of Baltimore, as you will see in this Sun Paper article dated 27 Jan 1905.

"Patrolman Boone was found in the neighborhood of Lafayette Square about 5 o'clock yesterday morning, numb with the cold, and sent to his home, at 1402 Argyle Avenue, where he died a short time later. Death was due to heart disease, believed to have been super-induced by the intense cold. Patrolman Boone, who was considered one of the most efficient officers in the department, was a member of the C division and reported for duty at 3.45 o'clock yesterday morning. Before leaving the station house he complained to several of the officers of feeling bad. He left with the squad of Sergeant Foster and his "beat" was in the vicinity of Lafayette Square. This is considered one of the most exposed sections of the city. For nearly two hours the faithful policeman patrolled his post, while the heavy wind caught up the snow and drove it into his body and face. At about 5 o'clock he was met by Sergeant Foster, a Rounds Sergeant that was making his rounds and Boone's

superior officer immediately noticed his Officer wore a distressed look. He inquired as to what was wrong, and Boone said, he was feeling ill and was very much affected by the cold. Sergeant Foster thereupon sent him home with Patrolman Thomas Clark as escort."

"On reaching the house Patrolman Boone begun to warm himself beside a stove, while a hot cup of coffee was prepared by Patrolman Clark. After drinking the coffee Patrolman Boone, remarked to his fellow officer that he "felt as if he was going to die." Patrolman Clark immediately had medical assistance summoned. But Boone lapsed into unconsciousness and expired a few minutes later."

"The death of Patrolman Boone was a great shock to all the officers of the Northwestern District, where he had been assigned since the organization of the district, in 1874. Patrolman Boone was very popular among the men of his district. He was 62 years old, and was appointed to the police force on 14 October, 1870, Patrolman Boone was sent to the Western district four years later in 1874 and was detailed to the Northwestern District. He had an excellent record. He was a member of the Odd Fellows, and the Heptasophs."

"Patrolman Boone is survived by his widow, who was formerly Miss Mary Doud, of Richmond, Va., and seven children – Mrs. Harry L. Amoss, of Pittsburg; Mrs. Frank M. Beckwith, of New London, Connecticut, Misses Ella and Gertrude Boone, of Baltimore; Messrs. William Boone, of the United States Navy, and Edward and Jas A. Boone, both of this city."

We his brothers and sisters of the Baltimore Police department will not let him be forgotten, as we take this time to remember him and thank him for his service and sacrifice. RIP and God Bless Brother Patrolman Mathew Boone.

<u>Author's Note</u>: *I had the good fortune of reading one of our old roll books from the Northwestern dated 1877-1878, which contained records of the many arrests young Officer Boone had made or taken part in by assisting other officers. Before learning of his death, I noticed Officer Boone was an aggressive officer, and often listed alongside his signature were his many arrests and assistance to his fellow officers with their arrests. The name stuck out to me at the time because of all the years I worked with another great Officer Boone; everyone's favorite, Officer Paul Boone of the Central District. As I read the logs of more than 100 years before my service as a Baltimore Police Officer, I couldn't help but think of how things had not changed much – backing-up your brother officer was as important back then as it was nearly 30 years ago when I walked the beat.*

29 January - 1944

On this day in Baltimore Police History, 1944 we lost our brother, Patrolman **Joseph Waldsachs** after a serious fall in which his neck was broken. Again, with this officer, we won't find his name engraved on any of our walls, or hear his name at the candlelight vigils, but that doesn't make him any less a hero.

From newspaper accounts of the time:

"Patrolman Joseph Waldsachs, who had been a member of the Police Department for 25 years, was killed late yesterday afternoon when he tripped in the balcony of a dark motion picture theater and fell down the stairs, breaking his neck."

"Police reported that Patrolman Waldsachs, who was assigned to the Northwestern district, was making a routine inspection of the theater, located in the 1400 block West Lafayette Ave. where he was leaving the projection booth. He had just been talking with the theater manager when he stepped from the booth and took his fall."

"The policeman, who was 54, and lived at 2023 Wheeler Ave., was taken to the West Baltimore General Hospital, where he was pronounced dead."

"Patrolman Waldsachs was the beloved husband of Bessie Hughes Waldsachs."

As his brothers and sisters of the Baltimore Police Department, we will not let him be forgotten. His service honored the City of Baltimore and the Baltimore Police Department. May he rest in peace, and may God bless him.

29 January - 2014

Today in Baltimore Police History, we lost our brother Officer **Jim Mitchell**, who passed away at his home in Hanover PA. He was good police officer, a good man, and a good friend, and he will always be missed. If ever we need to remember the meaning of brother as in brotherhood, all we need to do is think of Jim, as he is, and always will be our brother in blue… God Bless, Rest in Peace.

1 February - 1900

Today in Baltimore Police History 1 February, 1900 - The Northern District was opened at Keswick and 34th Street. This district consisted of Captain Gittings;

Lieutenants Henry and Dempsey; Round Sergeants Worden for Day Duty and Moxley for Night Duty; and a total of 50 officers. The station house remained at the Keswick location until 2001, when it moved to its new building located at 2201 W. Coldspring Lane.

The new Northern District boundaries were established, and all other districts' boundaries were re-aligned on this date in the year 1900, according to newspaper accounts at the time (note that some of the streets mentioned in this account from 1900 no longer exist or many have had their names changed, making some of the references quite confusing):

The police Commissioner yesterday issued an order that the new northern district will be opened at 8 o'clock the morning of 1 February 1900, and that at the same time the changes in the boundary lines of all the old districts shall go into effect. These changes were authorized by the Board of Police Commissioners in August of 1899.

Capt. Gittings will take charge of the new district this morning, will make a short address to the members of the force under him and will begin arranging divisions and squads, assigning sergeants and laying out posts for patrolman. Lieutenants Henry and Dempsey will also begin their duties in the new district. Of the round sergeants Capt. Gittings will probably assign Ward to day duty and Moxley to night duty. For the present there will be 50 patrolmen in the district.

In changing boundary lines of the seven old districts, the members of the force working in any area taken from one district and added to another will be transferred with that area to the district to which it is added. Considerable work will be required to change the connections of patrol telephone boxes that are transferred from one district to another. At present the boxes in each district are connected with the station house according to the old boundary lines, and Marshal Hamilton said yesterday that it will take a few months to get everything changed and in good working order. The connection of the telephone boxes transferred will have to be cut out from one district and connected with another, according to Hamilton. Until this is done men will have to make calls to their new station houses by way of their former station.

<u>*The other seven station house locations are as follows*</u>*:*

Eastern District Stationhouse – Bank Street near Broadway

Northeastern District stationhouse – corner of Cedar and Second Avenue

Western District stationhouse – Pine Street near Lexington Street

Northwestern District stationhouse – corner of Pennsylvania Avenue and Lombard Street

Southern District stationhouse – corner of Patapsco and Ostend Streets

Southwestern District stationhouse – corner of Pratt and Calhoun

Central District Stationhouse – North Street near Lexington Street

<u>*The new district boundary lines are as follows:*</u>

<u>*Northern District*</u> *– Boundary begins at the intersection of Hillen road and northern city limits, runs along the west side of the Hillen road to Harford road, then along the Northwest side of Harford Road to Jackson Street, then along the northeast side of Jackson Street to Taylor Avenue, then along the west side of Taylor Street along the north side of Gorsuch Avenue to Montebello Avenue, then along the west side of Montebello to 22nd Street, then along the north side of 22nd St. to York road, then along the west side of York road to North Avenue then along North Avenue side of North Avenue the Pennsylvania Avenue then along the northeast side of Pennsylvania Avenue to liberty road, then along the northeast side of liberty road to the Western city limit, then along the Western city limit to northern city limits and then along the northern city limits to the place of beginning.*

<u>*Central District*</u> *– The boundary begins at the intersection of Greenmount and North Avenue, then runs along the west side of Greenmount Avenue to fourth Street, then along the west side of Four Street to Orleans Street, then along the south side of Orleans Street to Asquith Street, then along the west side of Asquith Street to Baltimore Street, then along the north side of Baltimore Street to Jones falls, then along the west side of the Jones falls to the waterfront, then along the waterfront to Pratt Street and Light Street, then along the north side of Pratt Street to Howard Street, then along the east side of Howard Street to Liberty Street, then along the east side of Liberty Street to Park Avenue, then along the east side of Park Avenue to Preston Street, then along the south side of Preston Street to Maryland Avenue, then along the east side of Marilyn Avenue to the Jones falls, then along the east side of the Jones falls to North Avenue, then along the south side of North Avenue to the place of beginning.*

<u>*Western District*</u> *– The boundary begins at the intersection of Park Avenue and Franklin Street, then runs along the west side of Park Avenue to liberty Street, then*

along the west side of Liberty Street to Howard Street, then along the west side of Howard Street to Barre Street, then along the north side of Barre Street to Ridgely Avenue along the west side of Ridgely Avenue to the Baltimore and Ohio railroad crossing, then along the Baltimore and Ohio railroad crossing to Scott Street along the east side of Scott Street to Pratt Street, then along the north side of Pratt Street to Schroeder Street along the east side of Schroeder to Franklin Street along the south side of Franklin Street to the place of beginning.

<u>Northwestern District</u> – *The boundary begins at the intersection of Park Avenue and Franklin Street, then runs along the west side of Park Avenue to Preston Street, then along the north side of Preston Street to Maryland Avenue, then along the west side of Marilyn Avenue to Jones falls, then along the west side of the Jones falls to North Avenue, then along the south side of North Avenue, then Pennsylvania Avenue along the Southwest side of Pennsylvania Avenue to Liberty Road, then along the southwest side of Liberty Road to the Western city limit, then along the Western city limits to Edmondson Avenue, then along the north side of Edmondson Avenue to Baltimore and Potomac railroad tracks, then along the east side of the Baltimore and Potomac railroad tracks to Franklin Street and along the north side of Franklin Street to the place of beginning.*

<u>Southern District</u> – *The boundaries begin at the intersection of Light and Pratt Street, then run along the south side of Pratt Street to Howard Street, then along the east side of Howard Street to Barre Street, then along the south side of Barre Street to Ridgely Street, then along the east side of Ridgely Street to Gwynn's Falls, then along the Gwynn's Falls to the waterfront, then along the waterfront to the place of beginning.*

<u>Southwestern District</u> – *The boundary begins at the intersection of Schroeder and Franklin streets, then along the south side of Franklin Street to the Baltimore and Potomac railroad tracks, then along the west side of the Baltimore and Potomac railroad tracks to Edmondson Avenue, then along the south side of Edmondson Avenue to the Western city limits, then along the western city limits to the southern city limits and along the southern city limits to the Gwynns Falls, then along the Gwynns Falls to Ridgely Street, then along the Northwest side of Ridgely Street to the Baltimore Ohio railroad tracks, then along the Baltimore and Ohio railroad tracks to Scott Street, then along the west side of Scott Street to Pratt Street, then along the south side of Pratt Street to Schroeder Street and along the west side of Schroeder Street to the place of beginning.*

"We have tried to divide the districts to where they will work to the best possible advantage with a small force we have," said the president yesterday. "We need about 300 more men on the force and will have to get along as best we can until the next legislature meeting. There only 750 men on our force, while Boston a city nearly the same size as Baltimore has over 1,400."

2 February - 1860 - 2nd Issue Badge

Today in Baltimore Police History, the department was taken out of City control and placed under State control. By 1 May, 1860 we would switch our badges to the **2nd issue badge**.

We became a new "Metropolitan Police" force under a Board of Police Commissioner's (BOC) comprised of state-appointed civilians. This signalled the retirement of the "Corporation Police force" with the authorization of a new badge. The 2nd Issue Badge was issued May 1, 1860, a large oval badge with Roman "Fasces", an axe bound by wooden rods as its central symbol. Across the top and sides of the "Fasces" is a banner with the words "Baltimore Police" in raised letters.

The Baltimore City Police Department remained under State governance until 1978, when the Mayor again began to appoint the Police Commissioner, subject to confirmation by the City Council (Chapter 920, Acts of 1976).

From the Maryland State Police website:

"Baltimore City Police Force. The first State agency to exercise police powers was the Baltimore City Police Force. Established in 1867 under a Board of Police Commissioners, the Force was elected by the General Assembly (Chapter 367, Acts of 1867). Baltimore had been developing a police force since the formation in 1784 of a night watch "very necessary to prevent fires, burglaries, and other outrages and disorders" (Chapter 69, Acts of 1784). Its police force, from 1867, was governed by a State board although jurisdiction was limited to the City."

From 1900 to 1920, the Board of Police Commissioners was appointed by the Governor. After 1920, a single Police Commissioner of Baltimore City was chosen and also served on the Governor's Advisory Council.

The Baltimore City Police Department remained under State governance until 1978, when the Mayor again began to appoint the Police Commissioner, subject to confirmation by the City Council (Chapter 920, Acts of 1976).

In 1909, the Board of Police Commissioners of Baltimore City urged the creation of a State detective force since the Governor, the Fire Marshal, and State's Attorneys in the counties frequently sought help from Baltimore City's expert investigators.

The first tentative step towards a state-wide police force, however, was taken in 1914 as a corps of motorcycle officers under the Commissioner of Motor Vehicles began to enforce motor vehicle laws throughout Maryland (Chapter 564, Acts of 1914).

4 February - 1929

Charles Adler installed a pedestrian push button at the intersection of Charles Street and Cold Spring Lane in Baltimore to control the traffic lights. It was the first pedestrian-actuated signal in the country. Charles Adler, Jr. (June 20, 1899 – October 23, 1980) was an American inventor. An engineer, he invented a number of safety signals, some of which are still in common usage. He was a lifelong resident of Baltimore, Maryland. At age 14, he formally started his career as an inventor when he received a patent on an electric automotive brake. After high school, he attended Johns Hopkins University and during World War I served briefly in the US Army. In 1919, Adler became associated with the Maryland and Pennsylvania Railroad (better known as the "Ma and Pa") and developed a series of safety and signaling devices.

On February 22, 1928 Adler installed a device he had invented to control automotive traffic at the intersection of Falls Road and Belvedere Avenue (now Northern Parkway) in Baltimore. It was the first modern traffic light.

In 1937, Adler changed railroads and became a consultant to the Baltimore and Ohio Railroad. He had his office and laboratory at the north end of one of the B&O's Mount Royal Station, where he continued to invent safety and signal devices for pedestrians, automobiles, trains and airplanes. In the end, Charles Adler, Jr. was granted over 60 U.S. patents for devices in general use today. He was also a licensed pilot and donated ten aircraft device patents to the U.S. Government. One of these was his patent for an "External lighting system for airplanes" – the familiar flashing lights on planes.

6 February - 1964

On this day in Baltimore Police History, we lost our brother, Police Officer Claude J. Profili to gunfire. After several area armed robberies had taken place over several weeks, a call was broadcast to Franklintown Road and Franklin Street for a robbery in progress at the Maryland National Bank branch – a bank known for false hold-up alarms. Officer Profili answered that call, and as he entered the bank, the teller nodded his head at the officer, and one of four suspects immediately turned and fired on Officer Profili, striking him in the head.

Background – Nine days earlier, a Chevy Sedan was stolen from the Bowie Race track. That car, bearing a stolen license plate from a separate offense and location would be used in the robbery of that Maryland National Bank branch.

Investigation revealed that Henry Haggard, the attendant at a service station a few doors down from the bank, said that the day before the robbery, and again shortly before the day and time of the robbery, a man pushed a 1953 Studebaker, grey two-door sedan with Maryland tags (turned upside down) onto his lot. The attendant at the time, 23-year-old Haggard said the man he saw was described as being a white male between 24 and 26, dressed nice, wearing a coat and tie with a tan top coat. He was said to have stopped the car near the station, and then pushed it the last few feet up onto the lot. Haggard said the guy walked down the street toward the bank, peering over toward the bank when for no reason, he came running back, jumped in the car, started it with no issues and peeled wheels off the lot and up the street west on Franklin Street. Haggard went on to say, the man told him it was not his car, but one which a dealer had loaned him for a test drive.

The following day, four men would rob that Maryland National Bank branch. As they entered the bank, three of the men, armed with an automatic pistol, a revolver and a rifle ordered the tellers all face away from them and look at the wall behind them. Likewise, all customers were forced to face the wall opposite the wall the tellers would be facing. One of the bandits stood at the door, and as new customers came in they were put against the wall, and robbed of their property and monies. A customer, Ms. Grace Mullingar, 25 of the 3600 block of Greenvale Road, said a teller put bundles of money into a brown paper shopping bag and gave it to the suspects.

Shortly after the robbery began a call went out for a 10-31 (in-progress) robbery; Patrolman Claude J. Profili heard the radio call at 1:37 pm broadcast to a two man car to respond to the bank – a bank known for false alarms. Patrolman Profili was in the area, driving through. He pulled up to the bank, got out and entered. According to witnesses, an assistant cashier, Mr. Walter Haney saw the policeman enter the bank and nodded his head at the robber.

With that nod toward Officer Profili, the robbery suspect turned and fired on the patrolman, mortally injuring him. Initially the shot would land Officer Profili in the hospital with a bullet lodged against his brain. That bullet would take it's time, tormenting the officer and his family, giving them hope, but also sadness in seeing their loved one in such pain. Then 8 days later on 6 February, 1964, it would end the pain and suffering, when it took the life of our brother for nothing more than responding to a call of a bank alarm, a bank that had become known for numerous false hold-up alarms in the past.

There were those at the time that thought the teller (Mr. Haney) was warning the suspect of the officer, and not the other way around – however, Mr. Haney was never formally accused of being in on the robbery. We've all experienced victims getting a little stupid when we arrive, either from relief or all of a sudden they feel empowered, knowing we are there and on their side.

In either case, that bank teller's ignorance caused a good man to be shot, and within 2 weeks it took that officer's life. When Officer Profili approached the bank, which had two sets of double doors in the front, he had his pistol drawn. Upon entering the first set of doors, the suspect opened the second set of doors and fired a single shot. That shot would strike Officer Profili in the forehead just above his left eye. Officer Profili fell backward, and down the steps out to the street. The four suspects fled the scene with $23,466. Officer Profili was rushed to the Lutheran Hospital where he died eight days later from that wound.

Investigators were able to trace the license plate on the auto to Vincent Lee Sirbert, 32, a Maryland-born man to his residence in Virginia. He was already wanted for unlawful flight to avoid prosecution from Virginia on a grand larceny charge. That suspect was caught within 48 hours. As is sometimes the case, he gave information about the identity of the others, and they were apprehended several days later by FBI agents. One was captured in Las Vegas, Nevada, another in Ozark, Arkansas, and the third in Denver, Colorado.

Patrolman Claude J. Profili was survived by his wife the former Clara Lejsiak, his mother Mrs. Alain Digenio two children Cynthia, and Claude Profili Junior, along with three brothers John B, Bernard, the Louis G Profili. Burial was held at the Holy Redeemer Cemetery.

Three of the suspects were convicted in Officer Profili's murder and sentenced to life on 2 July, 1964. Officer Profili had been with the agency for 12 years at the time of his death.

As we take this time to remember our brother, and thank him for his service and sacrifice. We his brothers and sisters of the Baltimore Police Department will not let him be forgotten. God Bless and rest in Peace.

7 February - 1904 - Great Baltimore Fire

Today in Baltimore City History was the start of the Great Baltimore Fire – one of this country's worst fires of all time (it has since been determined to be the 3rd worst). The Great Baltimore Fire raged in Baltimore, Maryland, on Sunday, Feb 7 and Monday, Feb 8, 1904. At least 1,231 firefighters were required to bring the blaze under control, both professional and volunteer truck and engine companies from the Baltimore City Fire Department and fire companies from the surrounding counties. Along with that some out-of-state units came in on local railroad cars.

The fire destroyed a major portion of the center of the city, including over 1,500 buildings and covering an area of some 140 acres. It spread from North Howard Street on the west, north to the retail shopping areas on Fayette Street, and eastward to the edge of Jones Falls, as it was pushed by prevailing winds. Had the fire not been stopped at the water's edge, it is likely the fire would have continued to burn in the residential areas of the south-eastern portion of the city.

Baltimore Police not only helped to fight the fires and evacuate buildings, but they also had to deal with the crime associated with this type of chaos, during which looting almost always begins – even way back then, crimes of opportunity occurred when they presented themselves.

A newspaper story dated Feb 29, 1920, included a lengthy and minutely detailed memoir written by Wilbur F. Coyle, who was at the time of the fire the City Librarian. He described the destruction of Baltimore some sixteen years earlier, as seen from the unique vantage point of the inside of the City Hall dome – the removal of the city land records and other important documents, the plan to cut irreplaceable historical portraits of mayors from their frames to save them from the flames, and many other unknown details. These are the comprehensive personal Chronicles, recounted in their entirety, from a man who watched Baltimore burn:

"One black night from inside the dome of City Hall I saw Baltimore burn. I will never forget that sight. Few people have ever been obliged to look down upon their prosperous city and watch as its very heart was eaten. It was a terrible experience – to watch and know that there was no force to stay the flames; that thousands of human beings must stand impotent and hopeless while myriads of hot, red tongues of flames withered everything in their path."

"It was as a memorable night, 7 February, 1904 – the night of black despair – to which I refer: when Baltimore was swept by a conflagration almost without equal in the history of American cities: when modern building after modern building, theretofore assumed to be fireproof, succumbed that night with amazing rapidity. Fireproof – alas, the term refers to something that does not exist. I saw Baltimore burn – yes, that was a terrible day followed by a more terrible night. The city was stunned as thousands of individuals – exhausted by fruitless efforts to rescue their goods and merchandise, their livelihoods, their homes and their hopes and dreams – abandoned all hope."

"Late that night, utterly fatigued, I was at my post in the library at City Hall. Suddenly, I remembered that hanging upon a hook within reach was the key to the dome. I was dead tired, but I realized that never again would I have an opportunity to see such a spectacle. What time it was I do not know – because I did not know then. I took no note of time in its flight. With the key to the dome, I went from the third to the fourth floor where in the west corridor there was a door barring the way to the dome. There I encountered two men from York, Pennsylvania, who had come on a special train that brought fire apparatus and men from that city to our city. I invited those strangers to go along. The little door blocking our path responded readily and we began to gradually ascend through the halls of solid masonry, just where the dome shows above the roof that covers the rest of City Hall."

"The passage was so contracted that we had to go single file and with great caution. As we slowly rounded the curvature of the dome, approaching the point of exit above, we noticed through the narrow aperture the reflection of the flames. It seemed almost that the City Hall itself was on fire. This strange, uncanny staircase,

which upon that particular night had all the unpleasantness suggested of a dungeon, was the connecting link between the lower regions of City Hall and the large circular mid-dome compartment into which we emerged. This is in reality a great barrel fifty or more feet from its stone floor to its ceiling. The view in all directions is unobstructed through immense, oblong vertical windows extending almost from top to bottom facilitating unhampered observation."

"The view from the Crystal Room of the dome – it may be so designated because of the number and character of its windows – there extends a long spiral staircase which brings the traveler to the section of the dome where the clock and the apparatus that run it are installed. I had intended to climb those precipitous stairs and keep going, but I did not do so. The spectacle from those long windows of the Crystal Room were almost paralyzing in their effect. One's power of locomotion seemed affected. I was utterly tired. I wanted to curl up. To have gone higher would have added nothing to the view. It was all laid out before me – splendid old Baltimore was ablaze. It seemed that the whole of the lower part of the city had caught fire, so near had the flames crept, and the sweeping glance to the south showed that the entire section between City Hall and the waterfront was red. Great columns of fire viciously stabbed at the darkness; flames passed from building to building, from block to block. Leaving nothing but gaunt, gutted buildings and desolation in the wake."

"Mere words can convey no adequate idea of the terrible scene: any description must fail. It was maddening to realize that dear old Baltimore was burning like tinder and that no human power could render effectual aid. This strange room for the time being sheltered me from the dense smoke and flying embers sent over the dome, the inside of which was brilliantly and spasmodically illuminated. The effect of the fire was startling. Flash after flash being accompanied by dull booms of explosions, which concussions mingled with countless other unwanted disturbances incident to the fire."

"I really do not think the extent of Baltimore's catastrophe is now appreciated. I watched that night as flames ate their way through the city's heart. I did not see how the city could ever recover. Think of the vastness of the destruction: from Liberty Street on the west, Jones falls on the East, Charles and Lexington streets on the north, with all the buildings on the south side of Lexington Street to St. Paul Street, either going or gone, and a great battle staged on St. Paul Street to save the courthouse, which was next in the path of the destroyer – that was the appalling

situation that night. It is beyond mere imagination to picture 140 acres of a compact city like Baltimore burning or wrecked. It was terrifying to realize that there was practically no limit to which the fiend, now unharnessed, might go. It seemed to look down upon it that the fire would take its course to the whole of East Baltimore to the waterfront and burn until open country was reached. And so I am convinced it would, had not its course been stayed by that filthy stream, the Jones falls."

"A grand total of 1,526 buildings, many modern, and in addition to lumber yards were the fuel for that disastrous combustion. Truly an appalling panorama it was as viewed by the awe struck watchers way up in the dome of the City Hall. Acres blazing or in ruin, and no relief in sight. How long I was in the dome I have no means of estimating. But suddenly I heard faint shouts. Which noises I knew could come only through the narrow channel through which we had climbed. I knew, too, the call was a warning, and although I felt there was no immediate danger, we lost no time in retreating through the tunnel and were soon back in the corridor on the fourth floor. It developed that a watchman, no doubt making his rounds, found the door of the dome open and, suspecting that someone was up there, had reported the discovery to the custodian of the building. The latter wisely decided to make an investigation, and as the searchers ascended it was their shouts which I heard and answered."

"At that moment the City Hall was in no danger, but it wasn't long before its doom seemed sealed. Only those who were in the building that night realized what a close call it was. True, to the westward, whence the fire earlier came, the Hall was protected by the courthouse (one side of which was badly damaged) on St. Paul Street and also by the granite post office; the stone structures acted as a screen for the Municipal building and both would have succumbed before the City Hall was attacked from the West. The threatened assault, however, did not come from that direction at all but from the southeast. I cannot recall the variations of the wind that fiery night nor the phenomenon that occurred. However, it is a fact that the flames having swept from west to east and seeming well beyond City Hall, slowly worked back from the south and southeast. Coming steadily toward the big structure; this was the situation when I returned from my venture into the dome."

"The flames continue to approach. From the first Council chamber, a good view of the approach of the fire would be obtained when I went there, and I found a number of persons assembled. The fine Chamber of Commerce building a few blocks away to the southeast was ablaze midst a score of others in sight and the destroyer was

beating back with seeming deliberate purpose of getting the smaller structures along Fayette Street, opposite the exposed southern wall of the City Hall. It wasn't long before all the buildings across narrow Fayette Street were ablaze and all but one, the Giddings bank building at the southeast corner of Fayette and Guilford Avenue, were utterly burned, and collapsed. Through the balance of the night a determined fight was put up to save this antiquated bank and strange to say this effort was successful. With blazing structures across the street it seemed for a period that the City Hall must certainly catch. The heavy window glass was hot and with myriads of sparks in the air seeking lodgment in the edifice there seemed little chance of escape."

"*The catastrophe was so widespread and appalling that the senses were actually deadened or numb and a building more or less did not seem of great moment. I glanced about the sumptuous chamber luxurious in its heavy draperies, its walnut furnishings and costly carpets and I wondered whether the time had come to put into execution a plan I had to save the most valuable objects in sight – the portraits of the past mayors of Baltimore. Although many of these paintings have since been removed and distributed throughout City Hall, a score or more at present hanging in the mayor's suite, they were at the time of the fire all in the two chambers of the Council. The great wall space in each branch was covered, the rooms in fact were each a portrait gallery of great consequence, containing as they did effigies of the mayors from James Calhoun, 1797, to Thomas G. Hayes, 1903. There were other fine paintings in the group, particularly of the men – including Gen. Samuel Smith – who took part in the defense of Baltimore in 1814. Such artists as Charles Wilson Peale, Rembrandt Peale, Thomas Sully and others of lesser reputation were represented. The canvases, some of which were very large and heavily framed and of great intrinsic value were historically and sentimentally priceless."*

"*Earlier in the night I had labored to get all the records in my custody out of City Hall when it seemed the building was directly in the path of the fire, and it was almost a personal disaster to have to abandon the portraits of those fine men who had in a sense been the builders of Baltimore. I determined these paintings should not be abandoned. I would cut them from their frames!*"

"*This I could do quickly. For I had a trusty knife ready, and with the assistance of the others present it would not be a difficult job, I could roll the canvases up and escape with them under my arm – but when should I begin to cut?*"

"That was in reality a burning question. From the other side of Fayette St., south to the waterfront, the city was ablaze. The City Hall would be next. Nothing was now between it and the fire. Was it the time to strike? I waited. I waited. The structures across the street were gone. Somehow, the blistering heat did not burst the heavy window glass and ignite the hall. The showers of sparks passed harmlessly by. A miracle had been wrought. Daybreak, with the terrifying spectacle it revealed, was at hand. The little party in the Council chamber broke up. Such were the culminating incidents of the night spent in the City Hall while ruin reigned without. A night that followed a day into which had been crowded gloom, dismay, and fear amounting almost to terror."

"Early in the day when it was noised all over town that a great fire was spreading to unwanted proportions involving a considerable area, no one dreamed of the impending danger. I went downtown in the early afternoon and called at a newspaper office to obtain information concerning the conflagration. I was asked by the editor to procure a plat of the South Library Street section where the fire was raging, the purpose being to reproduce the chart immediately in connection with the story of the conflagration. I went to the City Hall to get the map and brought forth a large atlas containing, among other charts, the plat requested. Some persons on the sidewalk seeing me emerge from the hall with a mammoth atlas twitted me, assuming I was taking the record to a place of safety because of the fire then still half a mile or so distant. Those gawkers must later have credited me with supernatural wisdom or discernment. Only a few hours elapsed ere not only myself but other city officials were nervously hurrying wagon loads of records from the City Hall. I did not let my atlas get out of sight and before it could be used, the newspaper office was in flames. By that time, the volume was back in city hall's library. I saw to that personally."

"Sometime later the big Continental building at the corner of Baltimore and Calvert Street became luminous: flames streaming from every window. I thought the City Hall and post office doomed. Therefore, for I and others, there would be no further delay; we must move. I had engaged some teams [so I thought] to meet the emergency but who could hold conveyances under such conditions? People were frantic and offering fabulous sums to have their goods moved, in front of almost every establishment along Baltimore, Lombard, South, Calvert and scores of streets where wagons were backed up, loaded in hustle to drive away and deposit their burdens in another building, which surely would fall prey to the flames. This unfortunately was the experience of very many."

"There were few officials at the City Hall that memorable Sunday. Mayor Robert M. McLean, clad in a fireman's outfit, was on the fire line with the superintendent of buildings and his force on St. Paul Street assisting in saving the then new courthouse. However, I recall three persons I met momentarily at the hall – Mr. William A. Larkins, then deputy Commissioner of Street cleaning; deputy city solicitor Hartman, now judge of the appeal Tax Court; and Mr. Frank J. Murphy, clerk of the same court. To Mr. Larkins and Mr. Murphy I feel I owe a debt of gratitude. They voluntarily sent me a detail from his cleaning forces to assist in removing invaluable records from the city library. Mr. Murphy suggested that I share the wagon he had managed to commandeer, which with the one I seized enabled me to clear the city library of many official street plats, books and other records, the loss of which would have been irreparable."

"Quite a force of men were carrying out these archives. The drivers were instructed not to unload the wagons under any conditions. I think the records were sent to Union Station. At any event, they were taken to a place of safety and returned immediately after the fire. Though several times we were taking out, this did not make a great impression on the whole inventory. Many, many books were left in the cases, but the rarest of the collection was sent away. In addition, I loaded myself down in my arms, including first records of Baltimore town in Jonestown: the first directory of Baltimore town and Fell's point, and such. As a final choice I would have turned the crowd on the streets into the library rather than see the books destroyed, on the chance of getting some back again. Many merchants did this in an effort to salvage their stock."

"While stirring around the city hall I ran into Mr. Hartman, deputy collector. We passed each other in a rush, but I reminded him that in a large attic room where the accumulated tax records of over a century which were doomed if the building caught. It was the work of days under ordinary conditions to remove these. And Mr. Hartman said the books would have to be abandoned. He was desperately intent upon getting the "live" records of his department out of harm's way since these showed what money was due the city from taxpayers, and the loss of the volumes meant not only chaos and irreparable confusion, but the loss to the municipality of millions of dollars."

"All the strenuous physical effort. Mental strain and sustained excitement was very exhausting, and having done my utmost in the circumstances to protect the city *property and records in my custody, I went back to the city library. Where the key to the dome suggested a trip, heretofore described, to that point."*

"I remained downtown in the fire zone or at my office until 6 o'clock that evening – Monday, 8 February 1904. I was as black as a minor when I got home and so tired I seemed in a trance – yet I was but one of many thousands in the same plight. Some were half crazed by their losses; demoralization and disorganization were complete. Everyone had been laboring under intense excitement, accompanied by a depressing sense of irreparable loss. The city was shocked beyond measure. As I write all this seems an occurrence of yesterday rather than of 1904. It is almost impossible to conceive that a new generation has risen which has no personal knowledge of that moment of this occurrence. Oft has the statement been made that Baltimore is better because of that fire. I made that statement myself, and it is true – but I always make a sentimental reservation. It did make possible the building of a splendid system of municipal docks; it did give the opportunity to widen streets, and there is no question that in many physical respects this city has splendidly advanced. It, too, waked the people and they have since been more alive to their opportunities. The spirit abroad is an evidence of this – yet even to this day it makes me sick to think how building after building, landmark after landmark went up in a flash of flame and a puff of smoke."

"As to chance – well possibly it is necessary to make all Baltimore look like new; to get away from the original surveys; to turn Cow paths into boulevards, to revamp, rebuild and beautify from time to time but how much of the old city individuality, or personality, was destroyed in the process?"

"Is it better that Baltimore look new and bright and smart and modern and right up to the minute – rather than an orderly, enterprising, populous city with a dash of quaintness, and suggestions of historical associations in its buildings and streets? Has a city like Boston lost anything by adhering its old areas to early surveys, and accentuating, rather than destroying and obscuring evidence of its antiquity? Well, well, I'm getting over my head now, – let's get back to the fire, for a brief period."

"It started at 10:48 am [the time registered by thermostat alarm] in the six story brick building occupied by the J. E. Hurst company, wholesale dry goods and notion house, in German Street [now Redwood] and Liberty Street and Hopkins place. In his report Chief Engineer Horton said, 'The fire raged until 11:30 AM Monday, 8 February 1904,' but this does not mean necessarily that it was then extinguished.

In fact, it loomed and burned brightly along the eastern extremity of the area until much later, an estimated 36 hours in all. There is no way of accurately computing the loss, but $125 million is the generally accepted estimate, taking all elements in the consideration. This figure is, however, more or less arbitrarily set."

No one was killed during the fire, though some firemen sustained injuries, and there were for a time wild rumors of many fatalities. After the fire, Mayor MacLean refused all outside financial aid and he announced to the world that Baltimore would rebuild through her own efforts, which it did with amazing rapidity.

The United States has, it is said, a record of destruction by fire not equaled by any other country. The greatest, of course, was "The Great Chicago Fire," which swept that city in 1871, burning over 2,124 acres covered by buildings, causing the loss of a great many lives and a property loss of more than $100,000,000.

The greatest fires Baltimore had ever known up to this time were the Clay street fire of July 25, 1875, and the Hopkins Place fire of Sunday, September 2, 1888, both of which are described elsewhere in this book.

Two little girls (at the time of the fire) living in Baltimore during those fateful days provided further descriptions of the Great Baltimore Fire of 1904. A newspaper story written by Sun reporter Isaac Rehert appeared on 7 February, 1979 (the 75th anniversary of the fire). It reported the following recollections of that fire, from the perspective of these two young neighborhood girls, now well into their 80's. They still well recall the fear, the danger and the excitement of those two days, when the destruction of the whole city, and their whole world, seemed imminent.

One of the girls, Rosa Kohler Eichelberger, has written a book about it for children and young adults called "*The Big Fire in Baltimore*," published by Steiner House, a local firm. In the 1950's (she was by then approaching the age of 60), Mrs. Eichelberger took a course at the New York University in writing for children, and shortly afterwards published her first book. On the strength of that success, she went to a New York publisher and asked if he would be interested in a projected book about the Baltimore fire. He was not.

"He said to me, 'but you know, Mrs. Eichelberger, every little town in America has had its big fire.' That made me so mad."

Therefore, she decided to write the book first and see if she could peddle it afterwards.

"I wanted children see the fire as it actually happened. So in the book I centered it around a 12-year-old boy named Todd, who wanted to become a Western union telegrapher – he learned the Morse code by practicing it on his gate latch – and he carried information to everyone about the fire."

"I got up every morning at 5 o'clock and worked on this book. Later in the day, I had my regular job and my housework to do. Getting up that early, I've wondered often how many millions of talented women writers have been smothered under housework. I finished that manuscript, then I rewrote it, and then I rewrote again, and then again.

"Then I began talking to publishers, but nobody in New York was interested.

"It never occurred to me that there might be a publisher in Baltimore until one day I attended a reunion of book dealers in Washington, and a friend of mine from Baltimore was there, and she told me about Barbara Holdbridge and Steiner House. So I wrote to Barbara and she was interested right away.

"And that's how it happened"

From her book:

The fire began at Hopkins place and German (now Redwood) Street, in the warehouse of the J. Hurst Company; from there it quickly spread to surrounding buildings. For 2½ days it raged, eating its way eastward in a roaring, hissing sheet of red flames across the half-mile front reaching from Fayette Street to the harbor.

Before it was contained at the Jones falls, it consumed an area of more than 140 acres, destroying 1,500 prime office and manufacturing buildings, leaving Baltimore's entire business district a graveyard of smoking black embers. Financial losses were estimated at between 100 million and $150 million.

It was a bitter cold Sunday morning, about 10 or 11 o'clock, and what first got my attention were the fire engines, shrieking by every minute, with their sirens and their bells. We knew there had to be a big fire somewhere.

We were living at 329 North Carrollton Ave. – one of those three-story houses with white marble steps. It was a beautiful neighborhood in those days with lots of teachers and doctors living in our block.

I was eight years old. Daddy was a telegrapher for Western Union. His office was in the equitable building, but that was one of the first buildings to go and later they

set up a transmission office in the attic of Welch's restaurant, which survived the fire.

There weren't any telephones or radios, so we didn't know about the fire – until the clanging of the fire engines. With so many of them passing, we all ran outside and then we could see the sky to the east all lit up with flames, and the dark black smoke gathering and blowing in the distance.

That, for the little girl, was the beginning of three of the longest and most event packed days of a long active life – days of anxiety, of furious chasing around town, of our ordered world turned suddenly to chaos, of events that seared themselves permanently into her mind. She never forgot them, and she could never imagine how any Baltimorean – whether they lived through the fire or not – could ever forget them.

"Later, when I was grown, I worked with children in the playground athletic league, and I would ask them what they knew about the Baltimore fire. It burned me up that they didn't know a thing. I told them about it and they were shocked. I said to myself that someday I was going to have to write that story. One reason the children hadn't heard was because of the immediate, far-flung, effective action in the city to rebuild.

There was a brief mood of pessimism; but then Mayor Clay Timanus created a "district commission," and public officials, merchants and financiers got together with plans and activities.

By the time Rosa Kohler's playground children came along, memories of the fire were lost in the pink glow of Baltimore's first Renaissance. But she didn't intend that it should be lost forever. She went on:

Later, I lived in New York, and we would have a dinner party and I would tell people I was from Baltimore and I would bring up the subject to the fire. "They looked at me with eyes full of doubt and it asked, "Oh, did Baltimore once have a fire?

I had always loved to talk about Baltimore, but remarks like that – they started my inner fires raging and I began to think again about writing my book.

Her head was still full of memories, but the first night, when her mother disappeared, was the worst.

Nobody knew where she was, nobody could call or wire, we were getting information about the fire, but only through the neighborhood grapevine. And there was no word about my mother.

Everyone was frantic, we imagined the worst, and nobody slept.

The fire was spreading the other way, but embers were blowing back in our direction, and we never knew whether our house might catch fire.

Men wore celluloid collars in those days. And I remember one man — an ember landed on his collar and set fire to him. They had to douse him with a bucket of water to put the flames out.

That night, in every block, they set up bucket brigades on the rooftops keeping watch in case the roofs of houses should catch fire.

Next morning mother showed up. She had spent the night with a friend on Biddle Street, helping her pack and move in case the wind would turn and flames eat up that part of the city.

She still recalled what the Fire did to her Grandfather:

He was in the shoe business. He had a factory on Water Street and three retail shoe stores. One was in the old Sun building on Baltimore Street. I remember it so well, on the same floor was a shop selling Minsk badges and another for the Warner Hat Company. I used to ask myself, how does the company make out selling nothing but badges?

Daddy couldn't go to work Monday, so he went with my grandfather to see if they could save the factory. There were hordes of people downtown. They came to go to work, just as they always did. They had heard there was a fire, but it was a workday, so they knew they had to get up and go to work.

The military was out, keeping the spectators away from the danger zones. People standing around watching got so excited that sometimes when a wind came up, it would scatter some paper money that somehow wasn't burnt up. However, nobody would bother chasing it.

"They couldn't save grandfather's factory. It was completely gone. Everything stank and burned up. Later, they found a foot of water on the floor, and they were sloshing around, trying to find what might be left when my mother showed up.

Nobody was supposed to get through the military lines. However, mother was good-looking and somehow she got through. When she appeared, she looked at my father's wet feet and smiled. She said she knew it would be that way and she had brought him a pair of dry socks.

Grandfather never rebuilt his factory; he was too old. He did reopen some stores, but he could never get used to selling shoes made by someone else. It was never the same.

After those kids, I personally told the story of the Baltimore fire to. I'm glad now that finally it'll be available to them all.

My next book? I'm thinking about tackling my memoirs.

The other girl, Esther Wilner Hillman, in an interview related her own perspective of that stirring piece of Baltimore history. From that interview:

There's a Messiah on the door jam, and on the window, little decals about Israel. The walls are hung with pictures of children and grandchildren and great-grandchildren. And there's a big homemade greeting card tacked on the kitchen door from someone who I would say loves her.

Esther Wilner Hillman, 82 years old but looking nowhere near that age, is animatedly talking on the telephone, and the soap operas playing on the TV behind her.

But when you tell her you've come to hear her reminiscence about the Baltimore fire, everything stops.

Hastily she tells her friend, "I'll call you back," hangs up and leaves the instrument off the hook. She quickly turns off the TV. She explains that people are often here because she collects clothing to forward to poor people in Israel. And that today is her 82nd birthday, so she's getting lots of calls. However, right now, first things first:

I've been waiting over 50 years to tell the story about what our Jewish people did in the Baltimore fire. Now that I've got a chance to do it, everything else is going to wait, even my birthday calls."

First, though, a cup of tea and a cookie – you cannot drink tea without a cookie. It is hot enough? If it isn't hot enough, so warm it up. Now that she is sure that you're comfortable, she begins her intimate tale:

I've tried to tell the story before, but they weren't interested. Nobody has ever written what our Jewish people did. It was this way:

It was bitter cold, just like today. We were living on Sharp Street, at Camden.

Sharp Street, she explains is the old name for Hopkins place. [It's still Called Sharp St., South of Pratt Street]

That's where the fire began, at Johnny Hearst's place, right near the corner of German [Now Redwood] and Sharp.

She narrows her eyes and looks off into the distance, the better to see the exact corner in her mind's eye. She looks solicitously into the teacup to be sure it isn't yet empty, then continues her story:

Johnny was in the Drygoods and Notions business.

In those days, South Baltimore was a Jewish ghetto from Baltimore Street down to about the Cross Street Market.

On the Shabbats, everything shut down because everybody went to shul.

But Sundays, they worked. Half a day, from 8 o'clock till two. Other days, they worked 12 hours. And they had to put in six days. Otherwise, they didn't get their full pay. It was four dollars a week. Imagine, and today they get more than four dollars an hour.

Anyway, my father worked for Sol Ginsberg, whose factory was across the street from the Heinz factory.

He's going to work that morning as usual, at about 10 o'clock he came hurrying home carrying these enormous books, weighed down with them. I'd never seen him look so intense and burdened. They were the ledgers from Ginsberg. He slapped them on the chair and told my mother, not to let the children bother them. Tseppenin, that's the word he used. Then he ran back for more ledgers, and then he took my older brother, Sam, with him, back to the plant, to help them carry out bolts of cloth. Sam was nine years old. I was only seven. The bolts were so heavy; it took three of them to carry each one. But they kept running back and forth bringing more bolts, until the police wouldn't let them go back anymore.

Then my father told everybody what happened. He had smelled fire and smoke, and a sent some of the workers to break the fire alarm. And then to stand at the corner until fireman came. Remember, they were horse-drawn engines in those days.

They saved all they could. What made it so sad was that there was a hardware store next door, and they kept barrels of gasoline and coal oil out on the sidewalk – they weren't allowed to keep them indoors.

In addition, when the fire reached them they exploded. It was terrible, after that, nobody was allowed to go back in, and the police went house to house throughout the road, telling us to get ready to move out, in case the winds shift toward the south. We ran upstairs and carried down all our perenes [eiderdown quilts]. What else do people have in those days? And then boys ran around and notified everybody who had a wagon to stay on alert – in case we had to move. But thank God, the wind didn't shift to the south.

That night we children all slept downstairs on the perenes while our parents poured buckets of water on the roof, in case a spark should kindle them.

I remember father on the roof. And mother on the sidewalk down below, filling the bucket and tying a rope to it so the men could pull it up."

She interrupts to refill the plate holding the cookies. Not homemade, she apologizes. But she can't get around as well as she used to.

Now where was I? Oh, yes, sleeping on the perenes downstairs. You know, I'll never forget that. Ask me what happened yesterday, and I won't be able to tell you. But those days of the fire, I'll never forget.

You know, after just a couple of hours it was clear that the fire was so big that our firemen couldn't handle it alone. So they sent help from other cities – from Washington, from Philadelphia, from Norfolk, from Richmond. Of course, the firemen from out of town couldn't go home, and even the Baltimore firemen couldn't go home. They would work for four hours, and then they were exhausted and needed some rest, but in four hours they had to start again. So the police came to our neighborhood and asked us to help. The firemen needed hot coffee, could we keep a pot always going on the stove? And could do firemen come in and sleep in our houses? Ordinarily we never use the parlor in winter, so it was always cold. We ate all meals in the kitchen. But my father filled the big Latrobe stove with wood and coal, and we dragged the perenes in there on the floor, and that's where the firemen slept. Of course you couldn't just give a man coffee without a bun. So my mother, like all the other women, began baking bread to feed the firemen. I remember an old man, his name was Singer, he was very pious, and he kept a strict kosher grocery store. He sent over so many things. Without charge, naturally. On Camden Street a family named Surasky kept the department store. It wasn't like a department store today, but in those days it seemed very large to us. They sold everything. They sent boots for the firemen, and woolen socks, woolen caps, earmuffs, mittens. Whatever they had they sent, and everything was free of charge.

My mother worked day and night, the only rest she got was on the couch in the kitchen. Moreover, my father and Sam were busy keeping the stove going day and night. For us children it was terribly exciting, what with strange men sleeping and eating in our house. Since they slept around the clock, the house had to stay quiet, and my job was to watch the smaller children so they shouldn't make any noise.

Of course, the firemen were all black from the soot, and they would wash and dry themselves on our towels – and the towels turned all black. I remember my mother standing all day over the washboard, scrubbing them clean. My father strung lines around the kitchen which were full of drying towels.

Our toilet in those days was outdoors, and we didn't want to ask tired firemen to use that, so my father provided them buckets. I remember him, and my mother carrying the full buckets out, dumping them and carrying the empty buckets back in.

Only the following Sunday, after it was all over, my father took us up there. What used to be such nice buildings were now all open fields. You couldn't even tell where the streets had been."

Everything was smoldering. I remember picking up a piece of black cinder. As I held it, it still smoked.

Back in the house, now the firemen were gone. Everything was so quiet. I remember how I missed the excitement. But now we had to clean up. We had no linoleums or rugs on our floors — everything was bare wood. And all the boards were black from soot. The floors now had to be scrubbed clean. What a job that was!

Downtown eventually was rebuilt, and the story the fire has been written and told hundreds of times. However, nobody ever told the part our South Baltimore Jewish community played in it.

I've always said that before I died, I want to tell the world that story. Now, thank God, I've told it so the people will know."

Newspaper report – Feb 4, 1973:

84-year-old Forrest Griffith recalls the most famous fire in Baltimore city history happening 69 years prior when he was just 15 years old. As he tells the story:

I remember the Baltimore fire of 1904... Sundays were quiet family affairs on N. Carey St. when I was a boy of 15. Some families devoted mornings to church, some to browsing through the Sunday paper, and there was the usual huge dinner, which

was even at midday. The rest of the afternoon, the adults had time for a nap and the children did their homework.

A certain Sunday 69 years ago began as calmly as ever at our house at 904 N. Carey, but before noon Joseph came home from Sunday school, having been told by their teachers to go directly home and stay off the streets. There was a big fire downtown.

By noon, most of Baltimore knew the story. For this particular Sunday was February 7, 1904 and "the big fire downtown" was what is still known in Baltimore as the Fire, the biggest in local history.

The fire raged out of control for two days, and flared up again and again in scattered spots for several more. At the end, 140 acres of downtown Baltimore had been reduced to smoldering ashes, 1500 buildings were destroyed. And the loss was estimated at hundred and fifty million dollars.

All the boys and men ran to the fire in those days, the men to help, the boys to watch. There was a sort of detached fascination in watching firemen fighting a fire in somebody else's neighborhood. However, watching the fire your own neighborhood, seeing something close and familiar burned, gave you an added tingle of apprehension. So it was with the fire on this day. We lived 10 or 12 blocks – a mile or more – from this fire. It was somebody else's neighborhood in the matter of distance. But from our street we could see the clouds of black smoke, shot through the sky of flying sparks. We could smell the smoke, and we could hear the distant clanging of the horse drawn fire engines.

My father and I wanted to go right away. My mother didn't want us to, afraid we might be in danger. There was a sort of compromise. Dinner was almost ready. In those days, meals weren't prepared by defrosting, heating and serving. It took an efficient housewife all of a busy morning to put a good meal together. And when she called the family in to dinner, it was unthinkable that anybody would let it sit there and get cold, earthquake, flood or fire notwithstanding. So after we had our dinner – my father and I went to the fire.

We walked, and our steps quickened with every block. The closer we got the louder the noise. There were the noises of shouting men, the clattering of steel horseshoes on the cobblestones, the rattling fire engines, the shouts of the firemen. Moreover, over it all, the frightening roar of the fire itself, a wild and angry, unleashed

invincible sound that I haven't forgotten. We got so close that the smoke made us cough and we had to beat out the flying sparks falling on our clothing.

I drew a picture late that afternoon when we got home. It was my first glimpse of the fire. The scene is the intersection of Mulberry and St. Paul Street. Looking West on Mulberry Street. My father was a salesman for the Heinz Company, and when we got home, I turned over one of his business letters and sketched the picture with a pencil. I can't explain my compulsion to draw the scene, except that I k new I had seen something terribly important. Later I outlined the pencil lines with a pen. I finished the drawing with watercolors.

After the picture was done, I lost interest in it. There was too much going on. While the fire burned, and for many days afterward, nobody could think of anything else. At that time, I was a student at the high school at Howard and Center streets. It later became City College. Classes at our school, and I presume and many other schools, were dismissed for two weeks.

I assumed my picture had been thrown away. Then a few years later, my sister India, found it in a drawer somewhere. "I like this picture," she said, "I think it should be preserved." So she took it out had it framed and later gave it to me as a birthday present. I'm glad she did, now I wouldn't part with it for anything.

In later years, I learned to draw much better. I went to the Maryland Institute when it was located at marketplace – and graduated in 1912 as a gold-medal student in mechanical arts, which is to say I held the highest average in my class for my four years there. But my crude version of the great fire still brings back the feeling I had that day when I first drew it.

The picture is now a pattern of smudged browns, blacks and grays, for the bright colors I applied on that Sunday in 1904 have long since faded to everyone except me.

By Forrest Griffith Sr. circa 1904
I Remember ... The Baltimore Fire Of 1904

8 February - 1904

Millions Lost in a Few Blocks – Newspaper Report, Feb 8, 1904

A careful and conservative estimate of the loss in the wholesale business district in which the Great Baltimore Fire originated places it at something over $11 million. This affected area is bounded by Baltimore, Liberty and Lombard Streets and contained many of the largest dry goods, clothing and shoe houses in the city, as well as two prominent banks – the National Exchange and the Hopkins Place Savings Bank. Mr. George E. Taylor, of the insurance firm of Jennise and Taylor,

made this estimate for the Sun last night. Mr. Taylor dictated to a reporter of the Sun until it was discovered that the fire was only a few doors away, when he found it necessary to remove himself and the valuables and papers from his office.

The estimate is for each building lost, the loss given representing each building and its contents. According to Mr. Taylor the heaviest losers were John E. Hearst and Company, R. M. Sutton and Company and the Daniel Miller Company, all of which were heavily stocked with dry goods, and in each case the loss in building and content was placed at 1½ million dollars. The Armstrong and the Cator and Company's loss is estimated at half a million dollars, and the great majority were estimated to be one hundred thousand dollars or more each. This district contained about 125 buildings, among them some of the finest business structures in town, which were occupied by more than 150 firms.

Signs of Abating

Mayor McLane and Dr. Geer have just returned from a circuit of the fire, the mayor said; "I feel the conflagration shows some signs of abating. I have received a telegram from New York stating that the fire department of that city has sent over six engines, six carriages, six trucks and horses. These will probably reach Baltimore between six and 7:00 AM" police Marshall Farnan said: "I think the fire is practically under control."

Flames Sweep Southward

Archibald McAllister, a fire patrolman, discovered the blaze. Smoke was coming from the basement of the John E Hurst and Company building. The automatic alarm registered and McAllister turned in the alarm from box 447. When chief Burkart arrived the flames were going out through the roof, and in 10 minutes, it is said, the roof and the floors of the Hurst building had fallen. The sound of the collapse could be heard for miles.

From the Hurst building the fire jumped northwesterly across Liberty Street and attacked the building of Carr, Owens and Hindman, drugs, on the northwest corner of Liberty and German streets. Then the national exchange bank, on the northeast corner, caught and the fire was on its way to Baltimore Street. In less than an hour Hopkins place, Liberty Street and the south side of Baltimore Street between Liberty and Hanover Street was devastated. Sparks fell in a shower almost impossible to walk through as far as Charles Street, and every building within these limits was on fire before 1 o'clock.

Daniel Miller and Company's establishment, adjoining that of Hurst and Company, caught in less than half an hour later. Mr. J. Albert Hughes, the manager, carried out a few books, but the important papers and holdings of the company, which were in a vault on the first floor, were unreachable as the smoke and heat drove out Mr. Hughes and a few employees who had forced their way inside. The Miller building was burned from bottom to top by 1 o'clock, and the fire had jumped across Hopkins place and into the upper floors of the R. M. Sutton and Company warehouse, 33 and 35 Hopkins Pl. The Stanley Brown drug company building at 31 Hopkins Pl., had burned slightly, but not until Suttons was almost destroyed did the fire burst through the roof of the drug house.

<u>Twenty-Four Blocks Burned In Heart of Baltimore – Losses estimated at from $50 million to $80 million – Blaze Still Sprinting Eastward and Southward at 3:30 AM</u>

Starting in John E. Hurst building the fires sweep South to Lombard, East to Holliday and North to Lexington, destroying wholesale business houses, banks, and the Continental, Equitable, Calvert, B&O, Central the Sun and other large buildings. The fire started at 10:50 o'clock yesterday morning, and devastated practically the entire central business district of Baltimore. At midnight the flames were still raging with as much fury as at the beginning. Many of the principal banking institutions, all the leading trust companies, all the largest wholesale houses, all the newspaper offices, many of the principal retail stores and thousands of small establishes went up in flames, and in most cases the contents were completely destroyed.

What the loss will be in dollars no man can even estimate, but the sum will be so gigantic that it is hard for the average minded to grasp its magnitude. In addition to the pecuniary loss, will be the immense amount of business lost by the necessary interruption to business while the many firms whose places are destroyed or making arrangements for resuming business.

There is little doubt that many men, formerly prosperous, will be ruined by the events of the last 24 hours. Many of them carry little or no insurance, and it is doubtful if many of the insurance companies will be able to pay their losses dollar for dollar, and those that do will probably require time in which to arrange for the payments.

Appalled at the Silence

All day and all night throngs crowded the streets, blocking every Avenue to the fire district, moving back out of danger only when forced to do so by the police on duty, or by the heat from the fire. Many of the spectators saw their futures in flames before their eyes, and there were men with hopeless faces and the mournful expressions seen on every hand. In fact, the throng seemed stunned with the magnitude of the disaster and scarcely seemed to realize the extent of it all.

They stood around usually in dazed silence, and not occasionally was the word of despair to be heard. That they were almost disheartened was apparent to the casual observer, and there is little wonder, for the crushing stroke fell with the suddenness and lightning from the cloudless sky.

Gasoline Explodes

After burning fiercely for perhaps 10 minutes there was a loud explosion from the interior of the Hurst building as the gasoline tanks used for the engines in the building let go. Instantly the immense structure collapsed and the flying burning debris and the breeze caused the flames to be communicated to the adjacent buildings on all four corners.

By this time, the first of the fire apparatus had reached the scene and was quickly put to work, but the fire had already gone beyond control and swept with irreversible and irresistible force and swiftness on its devastating way. The conflagration would prove vastly destructive, but not one of those who witnessed it at this time imagined for an instant the terrible results which would ensue.

Chief Horton Disabled

Chief engineer Horton of the fire department was quickly on the ground, but scarcely had he begun to direct the force of firemen when a live trolley wire fell on him at the corner of Liberty and Baltimore streets, knocking him senseless, and he had to be carried to his home and placed in bed. By this accident the city was deprived of the services of its most experienced and trusted firefighter, and although district chief Emerich, who succeeded Chief Horton in command on the ground, did apparently all that was possible, those present could not but regret that chief Horton was not there.

Mayor McLane arrived and was on the ground until a late hour in the night. He walked around the burning district and conferred with various officials as to the steps necessary to be taken and various stages of the fire.

Aid from Washington

Within half an hour after the first alarm every piece of fire apparatus in Baltimore was on the ground and at work. Realizing the gravity of the peril a telegram was sent to Washington for aid and two engines from that city were placed on a special train and hurried to the city via the B&O Railroad in record-breaking time. It was said that the trip was made in 37 minutes.

It was an awe aspiring sight to witness the progress of the flames. A building eight or ten stories in height would suddenly break into flames from top to bottom almost in an instant and wood burning fiercely until with a crash that would be heard for blocks the walls would collapse and the spot be marked only by a heap blazing ruin. The crash of falling walls is almost incessant and now and then could be heard the muffled roar of an explosion as some gasoline tank or chemical substance became ignited by the heat and let go with a terrific force.

Many Firemen Injured

Every minute the lives of the firemen were in imminent danger from falling walls or leaping flames, and more than fifty of them were carried from the ground severely burned, and all were dismayed by the danger and hopelessness of the task. Still they continued the unequal struggle, and took the hoses into narrow alleys, where the flames roared menacingly overhead on both sides of them, and directed streams of water where it was thought some affect could be produced.

Long ladders were placed against the walls of fiercely burning buildings and brave firemen climbed up, broke windows and turned streams of water into the doomed buildings until the walls weighed and rocked and the crowd of onlookers shouted to them to come down, and many turned away their eyes in momentary anticipation of a fatal calamity.

Apparently, every person in Baltimore was in the vicinity of the fire, and the various streets leading to the fire district were full during the entire day. The entire police force, in charge of Marshal Farnan and Deputy Marshal Manning, was on the ground and with ropes succeeded in keeping the crowds back from the most dangerous points. As the fire spread further and further the ropes were shifted and the crowds moved back one block at a time.

Great Buildings Gone – A Block by Block and Building by Building Description, Written in the Lofty Rhetoric of the Time

The section of the city most devastated contains the largest and most modern buildings in the city, and this renders the calamity the more appalling. Immense office buildings, ten and twenty stories high and large modern wholesale houses made of brick and steel all disappeared as if built of the flimsiest material.

The exact origin of the fire is not known, but the explosion which started spread of the flames to other buildings is said to have been caused by gasoline tanks in the Hurst building. Mr. S. F. Ball, who was standing on the corner of Sharp in Baltimore Street when the fire first broke out, said that in less than ten minutes the entire Hurst building was a burning mass of flames from top to bottom. When the explosion occurred Mr. Ball was cut on both hands and a hole was cut through his hat by flying fragments of glass.

From German Street fire spread rapidly to Lombard Street, leaping from building to building, and sometimes skipping two or three buildings at a time and in this way a block would become ignited in a remarkably short space of time. At Lombard Street the fire paused for some time and the large building of Guggenheimer, Will and Company stood for a time apparently undamaged. It was eventually doomed, however, and all arrangements were made for dynamiting it in order to save the Lloyd L. Jackson building, just across Lombard Street. However, the Guggenheimer building suddenly burst into flame and in a very short time the floors began falling in with a crash, the heaviness of graphing machinery causing a detonation that made many think the place was really being dynamited. The walls quickly followed the floors and the Jackson building was saved after a hard struggle.

A number of other buildings on the south side of Lombard Street became ignited, however, and both sides of that street from Liberty to Charles are practically ruined, the houses on the north side being completely destroyed and those on the south side, with the exception of the Jackson building, badly damaged.

Across Sharp Street

Meantime the flames swept through the block to the east and quickly began destruction of the buildings on the west side of Sharp Street. With scarcely a pause they jumped over to the east side of Sharp Street and the large buildings on that side of the street began to sparkle and burn. Hardly had a piece of the fire apparatus

been shifted to meet the new danger when the fire swept madly across to the west side of Hanover Street, and there the scene was repeated. Almost before the firemen realized the fact the buildings on the east side of Hanover Street were blazing.

To Baltimore Street

At this time the scene in this portion of the burning district was magnificent in its spectacular grandeur. Looking up Hanover Street to Baltimore nothing but a seething burning mass of flames, mingled with dense smoke, could be seen. Baltimore Street itself was a furnace. On every side were flying cinders, the war of the flame was broken at frequent intervals by the crash of falling walls and now and again the detonation of some explosive sounded with other sounds of destruction.

Dynamite Used

After crossing Hanover Street there was little to oppose the onrushing flames and the blaze continued its destructive course without check to Charles Street. Prior to this time there had been much talk of dynamiting buildings in the path of the fire to try and slow its progress and Mr. Roy C. Lafferty, a government expert, came especially to take charge of the work of dynamiting the buildings. By that time it was realized that the flames were completely beyond control and only desperate measures could be expected to relieve the situation. City Engineer Sindall and Mr. Lafferty placed charges in the building adjoining the Armstrong, Cator and Company on the west and set it off. The building fell with a crash but the blazing ruins ignited the Armstrong building and the situation was, if anything made worse. The Armstrong building burned rapidly. A large charged dynamite was set off in it, but the structure failed to collapse and the idea of destroying it with dynamite was abandoned.

The flames by this time were raging fiercely all along German Street to Charles Street and it was then that Mr. Lafferty set off six charges of dynamite, each charge containing 100 pounds of explosives, in the building at the southwest corner of Charles and German Streets. The tremendous force of the explosion tore out massive granite columns that supported the building and left it with apparently almost no support, but those walls failed to collapse and stood until the flames had crossed Charles Street and were eating into the block between Charles and Light streets.

The Carrollton Goes

The fire had meantime been communicating to a row of buildings on South Charles Street, between German and Lombard streets, and all those places, occupied principally by wholesale produce and grain dealers, were in flames.

Shortly before midnight the Carrollton hotel was in flames and the fire was sweeping toward Calvert Street with irresistible fury.

The firemen working on the south side had succeeded in checking the flames at Lombard Street, and as the wind was blowing toward the Northwest there was little danger of it spreading further in that direction. The western limit had also been reached at Howard Street, and the danger was now on the east and north.

The progress of the flames toward the north had in the meantime been so rapid as to be simply appalling. From structure to structure the blue, looking up the massive buildings as if they were composed of paper. In the block between German and Baltimore Street they flew along, and almost before it could be realized the building along Baltimore Street were blazing from roof the basement.

Mullins in Ruins

For a time it was hoped the fire could be kept from crossing to the north side of Baltimore Street and the firemen made a desperate effort to prevent it. The effort was useless however, and soon the tall, narrow structures of Mullin's Hotel began to dart out tongues of flames from several stories and in a few minutes, the entire building was an immense flaming torch. At almost the same time the remainder of the building between Sharp and Liberty streets were ablaze and the fire began its march to the North. The small two and three-story buildings on little Sharp Street burned comparatively slowly in this narrow space and the Washington companies fought a plucky battle with the devouring element. They were hemmed in on both sides by fire as they directed streams of water at the buildings from which smoke and flames were pouring, at a distance of only two or three yards away.

Across Charles Street to the Pots Building

It was utterly, heartbreakingly useless. The flames darted rapidly from place to place, and soon the entire south side of Fayette Street was in the grasp of the flames. Down Fayette Street to Charles Street they swept, and in a space of time that seemed incredibly short the building occupied by J. W. Pots and Company was essentially doomed.

Seeing that nothing could save it Mr. Fendall, acting under instruction from chief Emerich, decided to destroy the building with dynamite, in the hope of preventing the fire from crossing Charles Street. The explosion was successful in accomplishing that object, and the entire corner collapsed instantly, but this had apparently no effect upon the progress of the fire, for almost before the sound of the falling walls had died away the building on the east side of Charles Street began to blaze, and it was evident that the entire block was doomed.

Calvert and Equitable Company

Desperate, but futile, efforts to prevent the fire from going any further to the east, building after building was dynamited in this block, but it was all to no avail and the fire proceeded steadily forward. The daily record building was soon in flames, and not many minutes later the fire had leapt over St. Paul Street and the lofty, massive Calvert building began to admit smoke and flame. The Equitable building, just over a narrow alley, quickly followed, and these two immense buildings gave forth a glare that lighted the city for miles around.

It was thought that the fire could be prevented from crossing to the north side of Fayette Street and here again a desperate stand was made by firemen. Again it was useless, and soon the large building of Hall, Haddington and Company, on the northwest corner of Charles and Fayette Street, was blazing brightly. With scarcely a pause the fire darted across to the east side of Charles Street and began to lap up the handsome building of the Union Trust Company, while at the same time the large buildings to the west of Hall, Haddington and Company, occupied by Wise Brothers and Oppenheim, Oberndorf and Company, were of flames throughout.

On Philpott Street – Business Heart of City a Scene of Desolation

After 30 hours defiance of all human agencies, the fire which began before 11 o'clock Sunday morning was officially declared under control at 5 o'clock tonight. In the burned district extending from Liberty Street on the west, Philpott Street on the East, and from Pratt Street on the south to Lexington Street on the north small bands of fire continue in a desolate wasteland, but they have all but ceased to menace adjoining property.

Up to last night the loss was conservatively estimated by Mr. Alexander Brown and various prominent real estate and insurance men at from $75 million to $250 million. These estimates are of course rough and not intended to be accurate for there is as yet no way of arriving at a definite estimate.

It is impossible for the human mind to conceive the magnitude of the disaster and it is utterly beyond the power of man to approximately depict the extent of the ruin and the far reaching and disastrous consequences of the calamity.

Imagine a beautiful modern city of over 600,000 souls, with all the building needs to house the population and the thousands of buildings needed to provide for its material prosperity and enterprise. Wholesale houses, built with all the massive stability that modern architectural ingenuity can suggest, elaborate financial establishments constructed with an eye to substantial richness and ornate design, lofty skyscrapers of handsome finish and magnificence of detail soaring far above the earth, elaborate retail stores fitted in the expensive and artistic manner necessary to attract 20th century buyers, immense buildings containing all the latest and most expensive machinery for supplying the critical needs of the present generation in the shortest possible time and in the least expensive manner. All of these and many more buildings, occupying block after block of busy streets and comprising the very center of commercial life, from which the entire population must draw its sustenance, either directly or indirectly.

The men of wealth were dependent solely upon this section for their annual income, and the humble toiler was equally dependent upon it for his daily bread. The small merchant and artisan looked to the workers of this district for his patrons and prosperity and one and all of the city inhabitants must derive their support from the products and profits of this section.

All this essential portion of Baltimore's property is gone like the mists of morning, wiped out in a day, and in magnificent array of buildings the visible sign of our greatness and place among the cities of the land is tumbled around the ears of the citizens like a house of cards knocked over as if in a wanton sport by the titanic hand of the giant fire.

<u>Ruin and Devastation</u>

The erstwhile busy streets which had echoed to the rumble of traffic are now choked and blocked from curb to curb by half burnt bricks, tangled masses of wires and long electric poles, and the citizens who trod them almost daily for years fail to recognize them. On each side, where formerly the vision was bounded by solid rows of bricks, the eye passes through the dismantled shells of towering walls or forms unobstructed views to more distant scenes of ruin and devastation. Where 48 hours ago the trolley cars plied unceasingly and the vehicles in traffic wound in and out and the prosperous, happy pedestrians thronged on business or pleasure intent, the

monopoly of desolation is relieved only by the sight of two or three workmen making their way slowly and tiresomely over piles of debris in an effort to cut away the tangled wires or by placing dynamite under tottering walls which threaten to topple on the heads of passersby and causing more destruction, clear the way for the Phoenix of the new Baltimore to rise from the ashes of her old self by the indomitable pluck and ingenuity of her people.

The Zone of Ruin

Starting at the corner of Lombard and Liberty streets, the fire zone extends in a rectangular five blocks in width to Calvert Street. At this point the varying winds caused the path of destruction to wind by devious and eccentric ways down to Jones's falls, taking in the territory as far South as the North side of Pratt Street. At the falls a branch of the flames by some strange fatality of the wind, switch back and traversed the south side of Pratt Street to Light Street, destroying every building along both sides of Pratt Street to the waterfront. Thence apparently taking the waterfront as a boundary, the flames swept down toward the east, consuming everything in their track and leaving only heaps of blackened and worthless ruins to mark their path.

Help from Other Cities

Early Sunday it was realized that the fire department of this city was totally inadequate to cope with the conflagration and requests for assistance were sent to Washington, Philadelphia, New York, Wilmington, Annapolis and other nearby towns. The responses were prompt and generous. Washington sent three companies with apparatus, New York sent seven companies, Philadelphia responded with several companies, Wilmington sent one company, Annapolis sent almost her entire force, Chester Pennsylvania sent one company, all the suburban towns around Baltimore sent in their quotas and yesterday afternoon a small army of firemen finally baffled the flames.

Errors of Judgment

Many experienced firefighters expressed the opinion that, in the exigencies of the tremendous battle with the flames Sunday, when the fire first started, serious mistakes in judgment were made by those in charge. It is said that the men of the engine companies were placed in many instances where the danger to their own lives was greatest and the chance of any beneficial result was almost non-existent. It was remarked that almost the entire by aim of water used was directed at

buildings that were either already burning fiercely or hopelessly doomed. By this method it is said, the firemen were placed in imminent danger of being crushed by falling walls or suffocated by the densely growing smoke. Repeatedly a lofty wall would totter and tremble for an instant and with an ominous rumble fall on the narrow street, while the members of the fire company who had been placed directly under it would barely escaped destruction by a precipitate flight.

Many thought the available streams of water could have been used to much better advantage and the lives of the brave firemen better safeguarded if the streams had been directed principally to the buildings in the pathway of and not immediately contiguous to the flames. By thoroughly drenching these buildings in advance of the fire, it is said, there would have been a much better chance for effective results.

Why Dynamite Failed

The same complaint was made of the use to which the hundreds of pounds of dynamite were put. The general opinion was that its use was too long delayed, and when it was decided to use it those in charge placed the charges in buildings too close to the flames and in such small quantities as to be entirely inadequate for the purpose designed.

The case of the Armstrong, Cator and Company building was cited as proof of this idea. It was pointed out that the dynamite was placed in an adjoining building already ignited and the ensuing explosion merely caused the flames to scatter, causing the fire to spread with accelerated rapidity.

It was said that the use of dynamite was advised as early as 3 o'clock Sunday afternoon, and it was at that time pointed out that nothing else could be expected to halt the flames. But city officials and those in charge of the fire, it is said, declined to take the responsibility of ordering the use of explosives and precious time was lost.

When the dynamite was finally used, it is said, the charges should have been placed in buildings at some distance from the fire and entire blocks should have been demolished, thus providing a wide space over which the flames would have been compelled to leap in order to proceed onward. Much is allowed for the pressure under which the officials were working and stupendous nature of the unaccustomed responsibility which was thrust upon them but many persons cannot help sighing as they recall the fate of the brave firemen and think that he might have been spared had a different and bolder policy been used in fighting the fire.

Peril from Gasoline

Many expressions of wonder were also heard at the immensity of the lesson that Baltimore had been taught about the danger of the indiscriminate use and storage of gasoline in the city. For several years, the Sun has persistently and repeatedly pointed out the dangers of this treacherous and powerful explosive and has published case after case of loss of life or serious injury caused by this means, but the authorities have procrastinated until this awful calamity seemed inevitable.

As surely as the kicking over a small lamp by the cow of Miss Leary started the conflagration which practically destroyed Chicago thirty years earlier, so surely did the gasoline storage tanks in the John E. Hurst and Company building place in motion the muddy engine of destruction which has devastated Baltimore. But for the fact that this subtle, but tremendous, force was caged within the building, the fire would have undoubtedly resolved itself into an ordinary one, such as the local fire department has frequently handled effectively.

Once the mighty force within the insignificant looking tanks was let loose, however, the proposition became different altogether. Instead of one building there were four or five burning fiercely and communicating the flames to still others, and the firemen faced a situation when they arrived on the scene that totally exceeded their limitations of power.

Chief Engineer Horton of the fire department was quoted in the Sun not long since as saying that a dish of gasoline placed in a small closed room could be allowed to evaporate and if a lighted match were applied to the keyhole the explosion which would follow would wreck the largest most substantial building in Baltimore, and the recent experience proves that Chief Horton did not underestimate the power of the stuff.

"Fireproof" a Delusion

Another fact that is claimed as emphasized by the fire is the utter failure of so-called fireproof buildings to resist the power of intense heat. The Continental Trust building, which on completion was heralded throughout the country as an absolutely fireproof building, was an easy prey to the flames Sunday night and now only the charred and dismantled remains of the sixteen story structure marks the position of the much vaunted fireproof structure. The Equitable building is cited as another "perfectly fireproof" building and when the menacing flames drew nearer and nearer to the building Sunday night the manager of the Western Union

telegraph company is said to have laughed at those who advised him to get out of the building.

"This building is fireproof," he is said to have responded. "There is no danger of it catching fire."

Yet a few minutes later the manager and his corps of assistance were compelled to flee for their lives from the blazing structure. Instances of much heralded fireproof buildings which went up in flames and smoke on that direful Sunday could be multiplied almost without limit and the conclusion is clearly drawn that only by using proper precautions and protecting their buildings from the influence of fire and owners and occupants hope to escape disaster.

Baltimore Under Military Control

Baltimore was placed under military control yesterday. Brig. Gen. Lawson Riggs and his staff established headquarters at the courthouse. The fourth and fifth troop regiments guarded every Avenue of approach to the burned district and orders issued were to allow no one to pass without a military pass signed by Gen. Riggs.

In addition to the military, almost the entire police force of Baltimore, reinforced by the numbers of officers sent over from Washington, Wilmington, Philadelphia and other cities, assisted the military in guarding the lines, and a detachment of regulars from Fort McHenry oversaw the post office, custom house and other government property.

All these precautions were taken to prevent looting which is almost universal when some dire calamity causes the human birds of prey to flock to the scene for purposes of plunder, pillage and perhaps even murder. Due undoubtedly to the prompt and effective measures taken Baltimore has been signally free from this gruesome addition to her other calamities, and so far as can be ascertained at this time not a case of looting or violence has been discovered. Indeed, it has been prevented.

Crowds View Ruins

All day yesterday thousands of people congregated in the outskirts of the fire district to view the scene of desolation. The burning of the Pratt Street powerhouse had tied up nearly all the cars of the United Railway and Electric Company and only the York Road, Maryland Avenue and one or two other lines were operated at all – and these could not reach the center of the city. For this reason, a vast majority of the curious crowds which visited the scene of the fire were compelled to make their way

on foot, and the sidewalks of the streets leading to the fire were thronged with pedestrians during the day and early evening.

Wagons in Place of Cars

The tying up of the trolley line was an "ill wind" which was apparently "good" to the proprietors of vehicles of every description and they practically made their own terms. At whatever price charged every vehicle that will carry passengers was kept busy taking people to and from their homes and carrying passengers back and forth between the various depots.

In this connection it is recalled that a novel sight was witnessed Sunday night and one which, but for its extreme paths, might in many instances have been much worse.

Suspension of Business

All business was suspended yesterday [February 8], as there was little left in Baltimore's wholesale district to do business with. Most of the merchants will call their salesmen off the road, having no stock to deliver to buyers. Others are arranging with out of state Jobbers in similar line to take care of their trade pending arrangements for the resumption of business. What is true of the jobbing trade was true in all markets. Commission trade was at a standstill. Many of these houses were destroyed, and those who escaped the flames were prevented from doing business by the impassable condition of the streets and by the rigid military guard which was maintained throughout the whole center of the city. Accommodations could not be obtained at the banks, and without credit, business is necessarily paralyzed. There was little heart for trade, however, and it will be many weeks before matters in this line will go along in their accustomed groove.

The Aftermath of the Fire

The Great Baltimore Fire raged in Baltimore on Sunday, February 7, and Monday, February 8, 1904. At least 1,231 firefighters were required to bring the blaze under control, both professional paid Truck and Engine companies from the city's B.C.F.D. and volunteers from the surrounding counties and outlying towns of Maryland, as well as out-of-state units that arrived on the major railroads. It destroyed a major part of central Baltimore, including more than 1,500 buildings covering an area of some 140 acres. From North Howard Street in the west and southwest, the flames spread north through the retail shopping area as far as Fayette Street and began moving eastward, pushed along by the prevailing winds.

Narrowly missing the new Circuit Courthouse [now the Clarence M. Mitchell, Jr. Courthouse], passed the historic Battle Monument Square from 1815-27 North Calvert Street, and the quarter-century old Baltimore City Hall (of 1875) on Holliday Street; and finally further east to the Jones Falls stream which divided the downtown business district from the old East Baltimore tightly-packed residential neighborhoods of Jonestown (also known as Old Town) and newly named "Little Italy". The wide swath of the fire burned as far south to the wharves and piers lining the north side of the old "Basin" [today's "Inner Harbor"] of the Northwest Branch of the Baltimore Harbor and Patapsco River facing along Pratt Street. It is believed to be the third worst conflagration to affect an American city in history, surpassed only by the Great Chicago Fire of 1871, and the San Francisco Earthquake and Fire of 1906. Other major urban disasters that were comparable (but not fires) were the Galveston Hurricane of 1900, the San Francisco earthquake and most recently, Hurricane Katrina that hit New Orleans and the Gulf of Mexico coast in August 2005.

Among the reasons for the fire's long duration was the lack adequate building codes, and the lack of national standards in firefighting equipment. Although fire engines from nearby cities (such as Philadelphia and Washington, D.C. as well as units from New York City, Virginia, Wilmington, and Atlantic City) responded, with horse-drawn pumpers, wagons and other equipment [primitive by today's standards] carried by the railroads on flat cars and box cars, many could not help because their hose couplings could not fit Baltimore's hydrants. Very few, if any, were motorized in those early years except for steam engines.

Much of the destroyed area was rebuilt in relatively short order, and the city adopted a building code, stressing fireproof materials. Perhaps the greatest legacy of the fire was the impetus it gave to efforts to standardize firefighting equipment in the United States, especially hose couplings

<u>Background</u>

Almost forgotten in these days of strict fire codes is that in centuries past, fires regularly swept through cities, frequently destroying large areas of them. Close living quarters, lax, unenforced, or non-existent building codes; and a widespread dearth of firefighting services all contributed to both the frequency and the extent of city fires. The rapid growth of American cities in the nineteenth century contributed to the danger.

In addition, firefighting practices and equipment were largely unstandardized: each city had its own system. As time passed, these cities invested more in the systems they already had, increasing the cost of any conversion. In addition, early equipment was often patented by its manufacturer, making such standardization problematic. By 1903, there were over 600 sizes and variations of fire hose couplings in the United States. Although efforts to establish standards had been made since the 1870s, they had come to little: no city wanted to abandon its system, few saw any reason to adopt standards, and equipment manufacturers did not want competition.

<u>Progression of the Fire</u>

Fire was reported first at the John Hurst and Company building on West German Street at Hopkins Place (modern site at the southwest corner of the Baltimore Civic Center of 1962, later the 1st Mariner Arena) in the western part of downtown Baltimore at 10:48 am on Sunday, February 7, and quickly spread. Soon, it became apparent that the fire was outstripping the ability of the city's firefighting resources to fight it, and calls for help were telegraphed to other cities. By 1:30 pm, units from Washington, D.C. were arriving on the Baltimore and Ohio Railroad at Camden Street Station. To halt the fire, officials decided to use a firebreak, and dynamited buildings around the existing fire. This tactic, however, was not well executed and was unsuccessful. Not until 5:00 pm the next day was the fire brought under control, after burning for thirty hours.

One reason for the fire's duration was the lack of national standards in firefighting equipment. Fire crews and fire engines came from as far away as Philadelphia and Washington that day (units from New York City were on the way, but were blocked by a train accident – they arrived the next day – Monday, February 8). The crews brought their own equipment. Most could only watch helplessly when they discovered that their hoses could not fit Baltimore's gauge size of water hydrants. High winds and freezing temperatures added to the difficulty for firefighters and further contributed to the severity of the fire. As a result, the fire burned for more than 30 hours, destroying 1,545 buildings spanning 70 city blocks—amounting to over 140 acres.

While Baltimore was criticized for its hydrants, this was a problem that was not unique to Baltimore. During the time of the Great Fire "American cities had more than six hundred different sizes and variations of fire hose couplings." It is known that as outside firefighters returned to their home cities they gave interviews to newspapers that condemned Baltimore and talked up their own actions during the crisis. In addition, many newspapers were guilty of taking for truth the word of travelers who, in actuality, had only seen the fire as their trains passed through the area. All of this aside, the responding agencies and their equipment did prove useful as their hoses only represented a small part of the equipment brought with them. One benefit to this tragedy was the standardization of hydrants nationwide.

In addition to firefighters, outside police officers, as well as the Maryland National Guard and the Naval Brigade, were utilized during the fire to maintain order and protect the city. Officers from Philadelphia and New York were sent to assist the City Police Department. Police and soldiers were used to keep looters away and keep the fire zone free of civilians. The Naval Brigade secured the waterfront and waterways to keep spectators away.

Thomas Albert Lurz (b. January 9, 1874), a Baltimore native, made a career as a letter carrier with the U. S. Post Office. He was honored by the U. S. Post Office for his efforts in rescuing tons of mail from the burning Central Post Office on the east side of Battle Monument Square, on North Calvert Street, between East Lexington and Fayette Streets. Thomas gathered a group of men who loaded bags of mail onto horse–drawn wagons and directed it by wagon and on foot to North and Pennsylvania Avenues. They stood guard while the mail sat on the sidewalk until it could be protected by the Maryland National Guard when it was called out. Back at the General Post Office, employees kept spraying on water on the sides and roof of the building and were able to keep the damage to a minimum and saved the 1889 Italian Renaissance pile with its nine towers and central tall clock tower (later razed and replaced by the current 1932 building, later owned by the city as Courthouse East).

Aftermath

Over $150,000,000 worth of damage was done. Immediately after the fire, Mayor Robert McLane was quoted in The Baltimore News as saying, "To suppose that the spirit of our people will not rise to the occasion is to suppose that our people are not genuine Americans. We shall make the fire of 1904 a landmark not of decline but of progress." He then refused assistance, stating, "As head of this municipality, I cannot help but feel gratified by the sympathy and the offers of practical assistance which have been tendered to us. To them I have in general terms replied, 'Baltimore will take care of its own, thank you.'" Two years later, on September 10, 1906, the

The Sun reported that the city had risen from the ashes and that "One of the great disasters of modern time had been converted into a blessing."

Most of the books written on "The Great Fire" stated that no deaths occurred as a direct relation to the fire. A bronze historical marker located next to the main western entrance of the old "Wholesale Fish Market" from 1907 commemorates "The Great Fire." This major commemorative tablet of the disaster also reads "Lives Lost: None." However, a recently rediscovered newspaper story from The Sun of the time tells of the charred remains of a "colored man" being pulled, almost two weeks after the fire, from the harbor basin. This was near the modern area of the Inner Harbor at Constellation Dock (old Pier 2), where the historic Civil War-era sailing frigate USS Constellation is currently docked.

Five lives lost later were also attributed indirectly to the fire. Two members of the 4th Regiment of the Maryland National Guard, Private John Undutch of Company 'F', and Second Lieutenant John V. Richardson of Company 'E', both fell ill and died as a result of pneumonia. Firefighter Mark Kelly and Fire Lieutenant John A. McKnew also died of pneumonia and tuberculosis due to exposure during the Great Fire. The fifth person who died because of the fire was Martin Mullin, the proprietor of Mullin's Hotel. Located on the northwest corner of West Baltimore and North Liberty Streets (above Hopkins Place), the hotel was a block away to the north from the John E. Hurst Building where the fire started.

In the aftermath, 35,000 people were left unemployed. After the fire, the city's downtown "Burnt District" was rebuilt using more fireproof materials, such as granite pavers.

Legacy

Because of the fire, a city building code was finally adopted. Public pressure, coupled with demands of companies insuring the newly re-built buildings, spurred the effort. The process took seventeen nights of hearings and multiple City Council reviews. A national standard for fire hydrant and hose connections was adopted by the National Fire Protection Association. However, inertia remained, and conversion was slow for many cities; and it remains incomplete. One hundred years after the Baltimore Fire, only 18 of the 48 most populous American cities were reported to have installed national standard fire hydrants. Hose incompatibility contributed to the Oakland Firestorm of 1991: although the standard hose coupling has a diameter of 2.5 inches (64 mm), Oakland's hydrants had 3-inch (76 mm) couplings.

H. L. Mencken, future famed columnist/commentator/author and linguist at the beginning of his blossoming journalism and literary career, survived the fire. However, the offices of his newspaper, the Baltimore Herald, at the northwest corner of St. Paul and East Fayette Streets, were destroyed on the northern edge of the "Burnt District." But the City's massive new Circuit Courthouse just to the east, across St. Paul Street and completed just four years earlier, survived untouched. The Herald printed an edition the first night of the fire on the press of The Washington Post, in exchange for providing photographs to The Post, but could not continue this arrangement as The Post had a long-standing agreement with the Baltimore Evening News.

For the next five weeks The Herald was printed nightly on the press of the Philadelphia Evening Telegraph and transported 100 miles (160 km) to Baltimore on a special train, provided free of charge by the B&O Railroad. In addition, the other major newspapers of the city were also devastated, including The Sun with its famous "Iron Building," considered the forerunner of modern steel skyscrapers, built 1851 at East Baltimore Street. Across the intersecting South Street/Guilford Avenue was the publishing headquarters of The Sun's main competitor, The Baltimore News, founded 1871 and built in 1873 with its mansard roof and corner clock tower. This intersection, the information center of town for most of the later 19th century, was the site of many "newspaper wars" with the mounted bulletin boards and chalk boards on the front of the buildings, posters and hawking "newsies" (newspaper delivery boys—made famous in the 1990s by the Broadway musical and later Disney movie *Newsies*). The Baltimore American, the town's oldest news publication, dating back to 1796 and traditionally further back to 1773, owned and published by local civic titan, General Felix Agnus, was also burnt out of its offices and so out-of-town arrangements had to be made to have papers printed and shipped back into the city by train.

Mencken relates the fire and its aftermath in the penultimate chapter of Newspaper Days: 1899-1906, the second volume of his autobiographical trilogy, published in 1941. He writes:

"When I came out of it [the Fire] at last I was a settled and indeed almost a middle-aged man, spavined by responsibility and aching in every sinew, but I went into it a boy, and it was the hot gas of youth that kept me going."

The "*Box 414 Association*", which has assisted the Baltimore City Fire Department for many years, acts like a local American Red Cross or United Service

Organization (USO) for the military, sending refreshments and break-time trucks to the sites of major alarms and fires to provide exhausted firefighters some comfort and snacks. "Box 414" was so-named because it was the first alarm box pulled on the morning of Sunday, February 7, 1904. Ceremonies of the BCFD are held annually at the bronze statue of a firefighter at the old headquarters of the Department, facing City Hall, the War Memorial Building and the broad ceremonial plaza in between at East Lexington and North Gay Streets.

Observances are also held at the closest street corner to the Great Fire's beginnings at South Howard and West Lombard Streets alongside the old Civic Center/Arena. On the Centennial observances in February 2004, an exhibition was mounted at the Maryland Historical Society with an accompanying internet website, and a number of other events, lectures, and tours through the auspices of the Fire Museum of Maryland on York Road in Lutherville-Timonium-Cockeysville in Baltimore County.

Several commemorative stories and special sections were published during the month in Baltimore's only remaining daily newspaper, The Baltimore Sun, and coverage was televised on the four local television stations' local news programs, along with several documentaries and interviews/discussion programs on the city's public radio network (NPR) station, WYPR-FM. An additional commemorative "coffee-table" style illustrated book *The Great Baltimore Fire* by Peter B. Petersen, was published through the Maryland Historical Society to supplement the earlier, well-known historical tome and authority *Baltimore Afire!* by Harold Williams of The Baltimore Sun, with additional photos, information and stories, and some more recent historical scholarship and research.

9 February - 1904

On this day in Baltimore City Police History, 1926 we lost our Brother, Police Officer **Milton Heckwolf** to what may or may not have been a Line of Duty illness, based on the following:

Mrs. Heckwolf wrote the following letter to the Baltimore sun to report the loss of her husband Officer Milton Heckwolf;

Newspaper Article - July 7, 1926 – *Limitations of the Police Pension Fund Explained by Commissioner Gaither*

To the Editor of the Sun – Sir: my husband was an officer of the Central Police Station from August 7, 1922 until February 9, 1926, this being the date of his death. A great many people think that I am well provided for by the Police Department of the City of Baltimore. But all that I've received is the paltry sum of $770 to rear and educate three children, the oldest one only 12 years old. Also, I've had to work from the time my husband entered the police force until the present time. I asked about his pension or an allowance for my children, and received the cold reply that there is no provision for such in the state of Maryland, that my husband died a natural death.

This much I do know —my husband contracted his illness while on duty helping the firemen while fighting a fire at the Ainslee Apartments. A firehose burst, and he caught his death of cold by getting dripping wet and continued to patrol his post for the balance of the night.

From the severe cold, he developed the flu; then double pneumonia, and pleurisy followed. It was mighty heartbreaking to stand by and watch and administer to his every want in vain.

Now I am left a burden to the old folk, for most of this death benefit has been devoured by the funeral expenses and doctor bills.

I have been told that my husband was always on the job, had been cited for bravery and was well thought of at the Central Station. And that he had many friends on his post, but of all the friends he had there isn't one of them that has been to see me since he has been buried to ask me how I am getting along, or if there is anything they could do. Not that I want anything for myself! With the help of God, no: but something should be done for my children.

I also extended my sympathy to the wives of those officers that have been shot, and I am glad to know that they are being given more consideration than was given me, but it only proves that an officer must meet a tragic death in some way while on duty before the widow and children are provided for after the husband's death.

I am sure there are more widows of police officers who will reason with me on this point.

Mrs. Milton Heckwolf

In response:

Police Commissioner Charles D. Gaither said in reference to the above letter that there is nothing in the records of the Police Department to show that patrolman Heckwolf died from anything other than natural causes. This being the case, Mrs. Heckwolf will not receive a pension, because the law provides a life pension only for the widows of a policeman who was killed, or died from injuries received in the performance of their public duty. The $770 which Mrs. Heckwolf received was provided by the Police Benefit Association, which raises its funds by appropriating weekly amounts from the salaries of its members in the department. A new insurance proposition went into effect on 1 July, 1926, that provides $1,500 to the beneficiaries at the time of death of those policeman who elect to become policyholders.

10 February - 1967

On this day in Baltimore Police History, 1967, we lost our brother, Police Officer **Frederick K. Kontner** to gunfire. Officer Kontner, who was 27, died at Union Memorial Hospital of an infection, resulting from three gunshot wounds received from a fleeing suspect on January 25.

Newspaper Article; Feb 11, 1967:

Patrolman Kontner was shot in the left arm, chest and abdomen by a former patient of the Patuxent Institute, whom police were questioning about narcotics. The suspect, Donald Leo Sabutas, was killed shortly afterward in a barrage of police gunfire.

A native of Baltimore, Officer Kontner graduated from City College in 1957. He also studied pre-law for a year in Baltimore. He was a former member of the Marine Corp reserves. After joining the Police Force on 29 December, 1960, he was assigned briefly to the traffic division. He was transferred to the Northern District 16 March, 1961, where he remained for six years. He was assigned to a paddy wagon which patrols the entire District but concentrates particularly in an area bounded by Greenmount, Pennsylvania, and North Avenues and 33rd Street.

He received official commendations in 1962, 1963, 1964 and 1967. The commendations were for his work in arresting three school burglary suspects, three suspects later convicted of assault and robbery, and three home burglary suspects.

His wife, the former Mary Lou Moniewski, worked as a police clerk in the Central Records Bureau from 25 February, 1960, until 6 October of 1966. He was a

member of the Zion United Church of Christ

The bullet wounds which led to Patrolman Kontner's death came after police saw a transaction at North Avenue and Calvert Street which made them suspect narcotics. The patrol car in which Patrolman Kontner was riding followed the suspects as they ran north at about 8:30 pm 25 January, 1967. After the suspects were stopped, and while police were taking the suspects names, Sabutas suddenly fled, with Patrolman Kontner in pursuit. As he chased the suspect behind the old Department of Motor Vehicles building, now the State Office Building, Patrolman Kontner was shot.

Sabutas was cornered, and gunned down by police after he sought refuge in a stopped car carrying eight passengers, on 23rd St. near Guilford Avenue.

The Patuxent Institute later revealed that Sabutas had been released from its treatment program against the recommendations of the staff psychiatrist.

Besides his wife, Patrolman Kontner is survived by his parents, Mr. and Mrs. Frederick H Kontner, of Baltimore, and his grandmother, Mrs. Robert Davis of Bishop of Maryland.

We take this time to remember him, and thank him for his service and sacrifice. We his brothers and sisters of the Baltimore Police Department will not let him be forgotten. God Bless and Rest in Peace.

12 February - 1928

On this day in Baltimore Police History, 1928 we lost our brother, Police Sergeant **George M. J. May** – Sergeant May was killed in the line of duty when he and another officer were struck by a streetcar near the Hanover Street Bridge. The accident involved a police patrol car, a delivery truck, and a street car. Sergeant May was driving his patrol car along the bridge, when due to another accident started to turn around in the middle of the structure to pull up in front of a police booth there. According to reports, a Curtis Bay Street car then struck his machine [vehicle]. Patrolman John Peters, witnessed the accident, started to provide assistance only to be struck by a delivery truck that was being operated by John Fuchs of the 2000 block Aiken Street. Patrolman Peters suffered a broken leg. Sergeant May received a head wound from which he later died at South Baltimore General Hospital.

As we take this time to remember Sergeant May, and thank him for his service and sacrifice, we his brothers and sisters of the Baltimore Police Department want him to know he will not be forgotten. God Bless and Rest in Peace.

12 February - 1934

On this day in Baltimore Police History, 1934 we lost our brother, Police Officer **John Blank** – Officer Blank had less than five minutes remaining before the end of his shift in the Northeastern District, when he was shot and killed by three safe crackers making their escape from H. L. Carpel, Inc., a mayonnaise manufacturer in the 1400 block of North Central Avenue.

It all began when another officer noticed something suspicious at the factory and called for back-up units. Officer Blank responded and secured the rear of the establishment. As other officers went into the building through the front entrance, three men ran out of the back. On their way out they began shooting at Officer Blank. One of their shots found its way to Officer Blank, striking him in the temple, killing him instantly.

As we take this time to remember Officer John Blank, and thank him for his service and sacrifice. We his brothers, and sisters of the Baltimore Police Department want him to know will not let him be forgotten. God Bless and rest in Peace.

13 February - 1948

On this day in Baltimore Police History, 1948 we lost our brother, Patrolman **Joseph D. Benedict** to gunfire after a series of cab hold ups. Sgt. Mann of the Northern District was making a routine cab check, pulling alongside the cab. He called out to the cabbie to see if everything was alright, and it just so happened that cabbie Michael J Kozak had in his car as a passenger the suspect police were looking for concerning previous cab robberies. Twenty-four year old Roy Arnold Wood was sitting alongside Kozak with a gun to his ribs, and he ordered Kozak to refuse cooperation with the Police Sergeant, and to "Keep Going… Keep Going!!!" The cabbie bravely double clutched causing his cab to stall, Officer Benedict quickly exited his car and approached the cab on the side away from the driver, the suspect threw open the door and fired one shot which struck the policeman just below his badge. The gunman then jumped out of the cab and fled as Sgt. Fred Mann, the Patrolman's companion, fired three shots at the fleeing suspect.

Police believe that the gunman was the same man who had robbed Howard Profft, another cab driver, of the 1500 block of E. Baltimore St. of his cab and $16 at about 3:30 o'clock that same morning. He had freedom for a few days, but as you will read in the following news articles, he was eventually captured:

The murder of Patrolman Joseph D. Benedict is something far more than the personal tragedy of his bereaved family and his intimate friends. It is a tragedy the entire community shares. That is because Patrolman Benedict, as he performed his fatal duty in the early morning of Friday 13 Feb 1948, embodied the law. And the law is the set of rules by which a civilized community, lives-without which, by definition; it cannot deserve the description "civilized." The murder of Patrolman Benedict was a direct attack on the embodiment of the law. Such an attack cannot go unpunished, because it is a direct challenge to society. The police, we may be sure, will do their utmost to capture the murderer. They have a right to expect aid from any member of the community who is in a position to give it. It is to encourage such aid by the community at large that the Sun paper has offered a reward of $1,000 for the person or persons who may be responsible for the apprehension of the murderer.

16 February 1948 - *Man Quizzed in Killing of Policeman - Caught in elaborate police trap as girl gives tip; found armed*

Police last night overpowered and arrested a 24-year-old armed man in connection with the slaying of Officer Joseph D. Benedict. The man was taken into custody at Broadway and Pratt Street at 8:30 pm as he left on a date with his girlfriend. Although he had not been entered on the police docket early this morning, he was being questioned at the detective Bureau where he was taken immediately after his arrest.

Leading the squad of 30 men which participated in the capture were Hamilton R. Atkinson the Police Commissioner; Chief Inspector M. Joseph Wallace; Capt. Henry J. Kriss, Commander of Detectives, Capt. I. Forrest, Commander of the Northern District.

The key figure in elaborately arranged trap, however, was the girlfriend, who gave a prearranged signal when the man approached and spoke to her.

Crowd Gathers

Immediately the police converged and grappled with the struggling man. A crowd of several hundred gathered almost immediately to watch as the police disarmed the man and rusting away in a private automobile. Plans for the arrest began to unfold at 6 pm when the police detectives assembled and Capt. Kriss's office for instructions. Participating was the entire homicide squad, led by Lieutenant George Brian, approximate 20 detectives and several plainclothes in the northern district.

Waited in Doorways

After being briefed, they took their post shortly after 6 o'clock. Twelve automobiles were stationed strategically around the intersection, eight of them being placed at and near the corners and the others at the far end of the block. In order to be inconspicuous, the automobiles were all privately owned by individual policeman, and each was occupied by two men. Other men in the detail waited inside doorways or paced up and down the street.

She Waited on the Corner

The man the police had been told was to meet the girl at 8:30 o'clock. At 8:15 the girl, whose identity police declined to reveal, appeared at the corner. She took up the vigil, with her back to the Goodwill industries. Capt. Kriss stood waiting in the doorway, and three other detectives the loitered on each of the other corners.

At precisely 8:30, a young man appeared, walking south on Broadway. He was dressed in a tan gabardine topcoat, dark felt hat, brown shoes, brown pants, and red socks.

Captain Kriss Dove

The young man crossed Pratt Street to the Southeast corner. There he stopped in front of the young girl. They spoke a few words. The girl then gave the prearranged signal. Capt. Kriss dove from the doorway while other police rushed from their positions of concealment and from the opposite corners.

Police on Top of Him

In a moment they were grappling and then the man was on the sidewalk with at least eight police piled on top of him.

A woman pedestrian on the other side of the street screamed. Commissioner Atkinson himself rushed up to help collar the man and disarmed him of a .38 caliber

pistol. The captive was rushed to the nearest sedan, pushed into the back seat with Capt. Kriss and Commissioner Atkinson and driven away.

Suitcase at Station

At police headquarters he was searched and police took from his pockets a number of .38 caliber cartridges, and a baggage check from the Mt. Royal Station. Detectives took the check to the station where they recovered a cheap cardboard suitcase which contained a number of freshly laundered shirts, and unpressed suit, six dice, a blank notebook and a slip of paper, bearing three telephone numbers. Capt. Kriss and Inspector Wallace were still questioning the man in Capt. Kriss' office at an early hour this morning.

Meanwhile, police revealed that they had been covering a house on 33rd St. since Saturday morning. The man taken into custody was said to have occupied a room there. Commissioner Atkinson said that a discharged .38 caliber shell was found in the room which had been occupied by the tenant.

Northern District police early this morning were still holding a 25-year-old man who had been arrested Saturday morning at his Mosher Street home. His 17-year-old wife, arrested at the same time, had been released a few hours after the arrest.

Threw Open Door

Patrolman Benedict was shot about 4:30 am Friday on 33rd St. near the Alameda by a passenger in a taxicab which was approaching to investigate, a short time after another cab had been held up in the same general vicinity. As the patrolman approached the cab on the side away from the driver, the passenger – who was sitting in the front seat – threw open the door and fired one shot which struck the policeman just below his badge. The gunman jumped out of the cab and fled as Sgt Fred Mann, the patrolman's companion, fired three shots. Police believe that the gunman was the same man who had robbed Howard Prough, a cab driver, of the 1500 blk. of E. Baltimore St. of his cab and $16 at about 3:30 o'clock that same morning.

Forced From Cab

Prough picked the bandit up at St. Paul and Center Streets and at St. Paul and Mt. Royal Avenue felt the gun pressed into the back of his neck. After driving the bandit around for some time in the Guilford area the cab driver was forced from the cab at Calvert and 13th Streets. The abandoned cab was recovered at Guilford Avenue and 20th St.

"*Keep Going, Keep Going*"

At about 4 o'clock that same morning, a man hailed a cab driven by Michael J. Kuczak at North and Guilford Avenues, and asked to be driven to Loch Raven Boulevard and 33rd St. As the cab reached 33rd and the Alameda the police car drew alongside it and the Sgt. Mann called: "Is everything all right cabbie?" At that point Kuczak said the passenger forced a hard object in his ribs and told him to "Keep Going... Keep Going!!!"

By alternatively engaging and disengaging the clutch, Kuczak was able to stall his cab, and Patrolman Benedict got out of the police car and approached the cab. As he approached the door the gunman removed his pistol from the cabbie's ribs and, threw open the door and fired three shots at the Patrolman.

Patrolman Benedict was appointed to the Police Department in 1941 and had received four commendations from the Meritorious Service Board. In addition to his wife, he is survived by three children, Donald 14, Thomas 11, and Robert 3. His wife is expecting another child.

As we take this time to remember him, and thank him for his service and sacrifice. We his brothers and sisters of the Baltimore Police Department will not let him be forgotten. God Bless you and Rest in Peace Officer Joseph Daniel Benedict.

14 February - 1935

On this day in Baltimore Police History 1935, we lost our brother, Police **Officer Max Hirsch** to an on the job injury based on the following:

Patrolman Max Hirsch of the Southern District was still unconscious at South Baltimore General Hospital on 14 February, 1935, more than 16 hours after he had been injured in a fall at a garage in the rear of 614 Light St. during a commercial burglary investigation.

While patrolling his post, Officer Hirsh received information of a burglary in progress, and upon arrival at the location he found an open door. During a meticulous search of the property he made his way up to the second floor and continued his search. This part of the building was cluttered, unstable and unsafe;

as he searched he came upon a suspect in hiding. This part of the events become blurred, some say the suspect may and struggled with Officer Hirsch and pushed him, which caused his fall.

Others says the man startled Officer Hirsch as he jumped up and ran, Officer Hirsch gave chase apparently forgetting where he was, and fell through the already weakened floor. In either case the suspect was never seen, or heard from again, as he made his escape and was never captured.

Because the witness that gave Officer Hirsch the info on-view was anonymous too; for all we know it could have been a set-up, and we will never know. There were no leads to follow, no clues, nowhere for the detectives to go for leads. The case was cold before it ever got hot.

Physicians said he had a "Probable Skull Fracture" as he staggered into a Fire House located at Light and Montgomery Streets for help; it was 6am, his hat was missing, and in asking for help all he said was, "I fell." Authorities at the time were able to learn more from him, and they ascertained that he climbed to the second floor of the garage as part of an on-view/in-progress burglary investigation that he stumbled upon while working his post.

He was able to explain that he fell through the second floor landing, to a concrete floor below. Before getting to his feet and making his way to the Fire House for medical attention, and before being taken to South Baltimore General where he would later succumb to his injuries, he wasn't clear in describing his confrontation with the suspect before slipping into what would become more than 16 hours of unconsciousness. He would eventually succumb to his injuries.

The location of the incident was later learned when the home owner located his cap and hat device in his garage located behind 614 Light St.

As we take this time to remember him, and thank him for his service and sacrifice. We his brothers and sisters of the Baltimore Police Department will not let him be forgotten. God Bless and rest in Peace.

14 February - 1966

Nearly 20 years earlier on 24 August, 1946, Simon Fried, at 38 years of age, a Tailor by trade from the 100 block Aisquith Street, was shot and seriously wounded by an assailant who resisted arrest, and then assaulted with the intent of murdering

Patrolman Edwin J. Humphries.

As Officer Humphries attempted to arrest a young man that had been following two young women threatening them with a brick, the suspect pulled a gun, and buffaloed the Officer across the top of his head knocking him to the ground, Officer Humphries was falling to the ground as he drew his own pistol but dropped same. Now unarmed, and partially unconscious the officer was no threat to anyone, still the suspect began taking aim at the officer's head ready to assassinate him simply for wearing a badge.

Seeing a young man ready to kill a police officer, a 38 year old tailor by the name of Simon Fried, residing in the 100 block Aisquith street, ran toward the scene and picked the officer's gun up from the street. Pointing it at the young man, he yelled, "Drop that Gun!!!" The suspect redirected his attention to Mr. Fried, took aim and fired three shots; the Mr. Fried returned fire, but apparently missed. Still, the round put the fear of God into the suspect, causing him to turn and run away.

Patrolman Edwin J. Humphries' life was saved that night, other than a minor head injury Patrolman Humphries would heal up fine. The unfortunate Mr. Fried, on the other hand would never walk again. This hero took one round to his spinal cord and would be paralyzed and wheelchair bound for the rest of his life.

While Mr. Fried never applied to become a police officer, was never sworn in, and never told the golden rule of backing up your partner, on that day in August, of 1943… he was all police, and he knew what it meant to lay his own life on the line for another.

He was made an Honorary Officer by many of the Police Unions and, Police Originations of the time. He was awarded Bronze Stars, along with several other Commendations for his bravery.

The assailant was later caught and sentenced to 22 years for assault with intent to murder.

Sadly on 14 February, 1966, the Tailor, Mr. Simon Fried died from complication that came about as a result of the injuries he received on that day. He may not have been an actual trained, Sworn Police Officer that day, but he put his self on duty, risking, and ultimately giving his life, to save the life of one of our brothers, and for that reason, we will put him on our website as a, "Fallen 'Honorary' Baltimore City Police Officer".

As we take this time to remember him, and thank him for his service and sacrifice. We his brothers and sisters of the Baltimore Police Department will not let him be forgotten. God Bless and Rest in Peace.

14 February - 1954

On this day in Baltimore Police History we lost our brother. Police **Officer Alfred Bobelis** to an auto accident based on the following;

On that fateful day, Officers Alfred Bobelis, and Marvin March were dispatched to an accident at the intersection of Hanover and Randall Streets. Upon arrival to the scene one of the drivers of the vehicles (Calvin Lucky) fled the scene for lack of a driver's license, and Officer Marvin gave chase. Officer Bobelis stayed back to handle the accident and to direct traffic due to the inclement weather and poor visibility.

While directing traffic at that intersection Officer Bobelis was struck by an automobile operated by Earl L. Kirkley Sr. a 46-year Baltimore florist living in the 3400 block of Greenmount Avenue. Officer Bobelis was struck hard enough to throw him through the air with such force that when he landed in the street, the impact fractured his skull and broke both legs.

Officer March succeeded in catching, and arresting Calvin Lucky, and was on his way back to the accident scene when he saw that his partner had been struck and mortally wounded. Knowing his partner was probably dead and there was little he could do, he rushed him to South Baltimore General Hospital where he would be pronounced dead on arrival.

Kirkley would eventually be convicted of manslaughter, and numerous other traffic violations. He was sentenced to three years in prison. Over the next few months he would lose several appeals to overturn his conviction, but in December of 1954, Judge Michael J Manley in criminal court noted that he had received a number of letters attesting to Kirkley's good character, and that defence attorneys had disclosed a civil settlement approaching $50,000 had been made to the Bobelis' family. With this, Judge Manley reduced Earl L. Kirkley's sentence to time served, and a $1,000 fine with court costs for vehicular manslaughter in the death of Patrolman Alfred Bobelis.

Officer Bobelis was survived by his wife Emma Bobelis, and their daughters, 21-

year-old Constance, and six-year-old Emily.

We his brothers and sisters of the Baltimore Police Department will not let him be forgotten. God Bless and rest in Peace.

15 February - 1915

Today in Baltimore Police History Baltimore initiated its first ever, "Bike Squads." From four booths throughout the city, the assigned officers worked two shifts, 4x12 and 12x8. They rode in 2 hour rotations, splitting time with officers in the booth. To dispatch calls for service, dispatchers phoned the booth and calls were sent forward from there to the units on their bikes. The concept was to provide better police service to the rural homes in the city

18 February - 1845

Today in Police History the Southern District was established under a city ordinance. Two captains and four lieutenants were appointed for it, and the boundaries of the other districts were rearranged to accommodate this new area.

21 February - 1938

Today in Police History, the Accident Investigation Unit was established.

22 February - 1928

Today in Baltimore Police History the first vehicle actuated traffic control light was tested in Baltimore. To the best of our knowledge, and based on the news reports from that year, this may have been the first vehicle actuated signal installation in the world.

According to news reports, the inventor of the device, Charles Adler, Jr. lived in Baltimore. This device was an automatic control with a red/orange/green light attachment. Two funnels were placed on poles on the right-hand side of the cross street, with telephone transmitters installed inside the funnels. These transmitters were connected to a sound relay, which when disturbed by noise such as the tooting of horns, blowing of whistles, or the sound of voices would actuate the sound relay, causing the automatic control to run a motor. This would change the signal which had been green on the main street to amber, then to red, permitting the side street traffic to move out on the green. It would automatically reset to red. The device was invented right here in Baltimore.

This control would always restore itself back to green on the main street. Then the switch would set, and the signal would remain green on the main street until disturbed again by sound. Several of this type were installed, one being at Charles Street and Coldspring Lane, another at Charles and Belvedere Avenue. The issue they had was with area residents complaining about horns blowing all day long, and worse, they would blow late at night. For more info on Charles Adler, Jr. see 4 February, 1929 above, where Adler installed a pedestrian push button at the intersection of Charles Street and Cold Spring Lane in Baltimore. It was the first pedestrian-actuated signal in the world.

26 February - 1799

Today in Baltimore Police History – An authorization for the appointment of a city constable in each ward was issued. This ward constable was a policeman, and the term of city constable was not properly his, although his duties were defined by the ordinance to be the same as those of the city, or high constable.

More than a hundred years later, in a report by Baltimore's James Hepbron regarding The Royal Irish Constabulary that the London Metropolitan Police Department was patterned after, he pointed out that *the London department was a great success, and paved the way for the passage of the "Peel Act" in England. The report of the House of Commons committee of 1828 sounded the death knell of the previous system of "Runners."*

It was found that these runners were compromising robberies on a regular basis, and that they were concerning themselves more with the recovery of stolen property (for their own personal use) than with the arrest of the thieves. Crime was found to have increased 41% in seven years (and that there was one criminal to every 822 persons in London). Fully 30,000 people were living solely by crime, and the annual toll was close to $10 million. It was the following year that saw London's Modern Police System inaugurated. Strange as it may seem, the Baltimore Police

Department is older than the London Metropolitan organization, since 1784 marks the beginning of the regularly constituted Police Department of Baltimore city.

Like London, Baltimore went through the experience with volunteer watchmen, then constables, and finally Patrolman, or police.

1 March - 1857

Today in Baltimore Police History, the first squad of **Detectives** was appointed by the mayor, under a New Police Bill of December, of 1856 - By this time the city's chief executive again controlled the force. There were five Detectives in the first squad, and they wore civilian clothes. (As was mentioned elsewhere in these pages, Patrolmen were compelled to wear uniforms both on, and off duty. In winter the uniform patrolmen wore was a black cap with the policemen's number on it, a dark blue overcoat and trousers and a patent leather belt with the word police printed on it). The first five appointed Detectives were - Detective Thomas W. German, Detective Christian Barnes, Detective William Stevens, Detective Wm. L. Tayman, and Detective Jerome Airey.

1 March - 1972

Today in Baltimore Police History the department re-initiated an experimental, if not new, bicycle patrol initiative. It was learned that the bicycle patrol possesses all of the advantages of foot patrol with an added advantage of mobility. Also, the use of the bicycle provided great potential for more citizen-police contact, a new dimension in establishing good community relations. This was the 2nd attempt at a bike unit, and this one would also fail, only to be attempted a third time twenty years later, in 1992. This third time may be the charm, since the program is still in operation.

1 March - 1946

On this day in Baltimore Police History we lost our Brother **Patrolman George H. Weichert** to a heart attack while on duty.

While working yesterday Patrolman George Weichert, a 51 year old father of seven, collapsed on the street and died before he could be taken to University hospital. Once at the hospital, physicians pronounced him dead and tentatively attributed his death to a heart attack.

Patrolman Weichert, a veteran of World War I, joined the Police Department in the spring of 1924. He served in the Eastern and Western Districts, and in 1939 was commended for outstanding service.

He lived at 5816 Greenhill Avenue, and was survived by his wife, Mrs. May Weichert; a son, Private Adrian Weichert USMC, who was stationed in Japan; and six daughters, Lucille, Georgette, Catherine, Mrs. Leonard Greig, Mrs. Irving Sweeting and Mrs. Michael Thurfield, all of Baltimore.

We his brothers, and sisters of the Baltimore Police Department will not let him be forgotten – RIP Patrolman George Weichert and God Bless, for your service honored the City of Baltimore, and the Baltimore Police Department

1 March - 1957

Today in Baltimore Police History the Baltimore Police Department's K9 Unit was introduced. Months earlier, on 11 December, 1956, an article was published in one of our local newspapers which piqued the interest of then-Commissioner James M. Hepbron. One of a series of articles written by Martin Millspaugh pertaining to Scotland Yard, this article was, significantly, devoted to the use of police dogs in London. According to an article which appeared in the Morning Sun on December 17, 1956, Commissioner Hepbron was interested in the idea, and saw the possible benefits of using dogs in the Baltimore City Police Department.

On December 18, 1956, two dogs (Turk & Major Gruntz) that had had previous training were offered to the Baltimore City Police Department and, with two officers (Patrolman Thomas McGinn and Irvan Marders) also with previous dog experience, the program was put into effect on an "experimental basis". By the middle of January 1957, fourteen dogs had been acquired as potential candidates and fourteen men were selected and assigned to the K9 Corps. These men were chosen as a result of a questionnaire which was sent to all members of the department asking for volunteers.

These men and dogs were trained daily until March 1, 1957. At that time, they were put on the street working Friday and Saturday nights, assigned to the areas where

crime was most prevalent.

Shortly after this, on April 17, 1957, Commissioner Hepbron announced that the experiment was a success. He then went before the Mayor and City Council to request funding for such a unit, and appropriations were made through the Board of Estimates which resulted in the K9 Corps becoming a permanent and valuable part of the Baltimore City Police Department.

2 March - 1924

On this day in Baltimore Police History we lost our brother, Patrolman **Frank L. Latham** to gunfire. Police and detectives working on the case were roused by the news to greater vigor in the search for the killer.

Mrs. Ethel Latham, the murdered patrolman's wife, and Mrs. Sophia Latham, his mother, were at his bedside at Johns Hopkins Hospital when the end came. The night before physicians had pronounced the patient out of danger, following a blood transfusion from Motor-Cycle Patrolman Louis Zulauf.

Informed of her husband's death, Mrs. Latham fainted. Latham's mother, who is ill herself, was present against her physician's advice, seemed stunned. An internal hemorrhage of the wound near the heart set in early yesterday. Patrolman Latham then lapsed into a coma and died some hours later without regaining consciousness.

From Newspapers Dated 3 March 1924:

The murderer, police say, is Leon Schmidt, of 511 South Collington Avenue. No trace of him has been found. It was believed at first that he had escaped the city in his automobile. However, Lieutenant Michael Ward and Sgt. Charles Bavis located the machine yesterday at the auto shop of C. V. Weller, 2016 East Madison Street. Weller, according to the police, said Schmidt had left the machine there a few days before the shooting to be repaired.

Harry Wirth, 418 North Gay Street, went to the Eastern Police Station yesterday and told detectives, "I was approached Friday night at Patterson Park Avenue and Baltimore Street by a policeman who asked me to drive him to 511 South Collington Avenue. He said there was some trouble there." Wirth said he then drove Latham to Schmidt's home on the night of the shooting. He told police he would have come forward sooner, but did not think his statement was of any importance. After hearing Wirth's account of the shooting, detectives told him he would in fact be one

of the most important witnesses in the prosecution when Schmidt is caught and charged with the shooting.

Wirth gave a statement that revealed the following details about the shooting: *Once at the Collington Avenue address, the first thing they noticed was that the house was dark – no interior lights on. They exited the car and approached the house. "We went through a side alley and up the back. The officer entered the dark house and I followed close behind him. With the aid of his flashlight the policeman and I went through the front room and then the back room, but found nothing. In the middle room, which was also unlit, a man stepped out of the darkness as the officer opened the door to enter the room. The officer apparently recognized the man and told him he was wanted. 'You don't want me,' the man said, and with these words the man partly closed the door between where they were and where I was in the hallway. Then I heard four successive shots, and then a fifth round went off before someone shouted, 'You would have done the same for me.' I did not have a pistol or a light and I felt I was in danger, so I groped my way down the stairs and out front."*

According to Mr. Weller, about an hour after the shooting, Schmidt came to the garage and tried to get his car. At that time he was dressed in a ragged coat and appeared excited.

After further investigation, detectives developed information that led them to believe that Schmidt was hiding on a farm near Wilmington, Delaware. Based on that, a party of four headquarters detectives, armed with riot guns and wearing bullet proof vests, left Baltimore in an automobile yesterday morning for the farm. Those who made up the party were Detectives Robert Bradley, Frederick Carroll, Charles Burnham and Frank Coleman.

Failing to find any trace of Schmidt on or near the Wilmington farm, the party went to Hillsboro, in Caroline county, Maryland, where they searched the farm of Alexander Kartinski. They returned last night empty handed, after a trip of 375 miles. Based on my research, I've been unable to determine whether or not Schmidt was ever arrested and tried for the crime.

We his brothers and sisters of the Baltimore Police Department will not let him be forgotten – RIP Police Officer Frank L. Latham and God Bless - For your service honored the City of Baltimore, and the Baltimore Police Department"

4 March - 1909

On this day in Baltimore Police History, 1909, we lost our brother, Patrolman **John H. Spencer** to gunfire. The following newspaper account of the shooting:

The Baltimore Sun: An off-duty Northwestern district policeman was found shot to death beside his parked car at Pennsylvania Avenue and School Street last night, homicide investigators reported. The fifteen-year Police Department veteran, assigned to the Northwestern district, was found dead beside his car after a neighbor called police about gunshots in the vicinity, the reports said. The officer, identified as John H. Spencer, 40 years old, was pronounced dead on arrival at Provident hospital shortly after 10 pm.

Officer Spencer had been wearing civilian clothes when apparently accosted that Friday night by two persons at Pennsylvania Avenue and School Street, police reports said. He had been shot once in the chest, according to Dennis S. Hill, the Police Department's chief spokesman. The dead police officer's badge and gun were missing from his body, Mr. Hill said. Police officer are required to carry their service revolvers for use in emergencies, even when they are off-duty, according to the detectives on the case. No witnesses to the shooting had been found early today, according to Mr. Hill. The sling was discovered after a resident of a house nearby heard a single gunshot and called police. Detectives did not identify the caller and would not even say it was a man or woman

The motive for the shooting was not known, he said, nor was it known if Officer Spencer, although not on duty, was following up on a case he'd been investigating earlier, as he was wont to do. Colleagues at the Northwestern said early this morning that Officer Spencer was married and had two children.

According to a story in the Baltimore Sun on March 4, 1979, page B8: City police last night arrested a 23-year-old man and a teenager sought in the slaying of police officer John H. Spencer, 40, who was shot to death in an apparent robbery while off duty Friday night.

Acting on an anonymous tip, seven homicide detectives and two uniformed officers went to an apartment in the first block S. Exeter St., "kicked in the door and caught [the suspects] by surprise," said Dennis S. Hill, the police department spokesman. He said the raid occurred on the seventh floor of a high-rise apartment building.

Arrested and charged with murder last night were Joseph Lee Roy L. Wood, 23, of the 500 block of Gold Street, and Cedric Eugene Scott, 17, of the 2100 Block Ettings St., police said.

Neither suspect resisted arrest, and police found no firearms in the apartment, Mr. Hill said. He was unable to say in whose name the apartment was rented. The men were held last night at Western district lockup pending a bail hearing today, detectives said.

Mr. Hill said the location of the suspects was learned "through a continuous investigation" since the slaying Friday night and "an anonymous phone call" to detectives late yesterday afternoon.

Recovery of the slain officer's badge, which had been stolen along with his .38 caliber service revolver yesterday morning, was a great help to the investigation, leading to the issuance of arrest warrants for the two suspects, Mr. Hill said.

The warrant naming Mr. Allen listed his address as the same property were a child reported finding Officer Spencer's badge yesterday, he said. The child, whose age was not given and who was not identified, discovered the badge "in the grass" outside of a building in the 500 Block Gold St., he said.

Police had no details about why Officer Spencer had been in the neighborhood, and Mr. Hill was unable to say if the officer had been following up an earlier police case.

The officer was pronounced dead on arrival at Provident hospital shortly after 10 pm Friday. Police said he received a gunshot wound to the chest.

Mr. Hill said robbery was the likely motive for the killing. He declined to elaborate on the evidence detectives collected that led them to issue the two arrest warrants.

<u>The Baltimore Sun</u> *Mar 5, 1979; pg. A8: Officer Spencer was slain while off duty Friday during an apparent robbery at Pennsylvania Avenue and School Street. Two suspects were charged with homicide last night. Officer Spencer was 40 and lived in Randallstown. Mr. Hill said the officer's home address would not be made public, but added that he did not live in the area where the shooting occurred.*

His supervisor, Lieutenant Bessie Norris, of the Northwestern district, said yesterday that throughout Officer Spencer's nine years with the district operations unit, his specialty had been working with youngsters.

On his own time, Lieutenant Norris said, Officer Spencer worked with youths at the Towanda recreation center at Park Heights Avenue and Garrison Boulevard, and earned their respect. In the summer, he also recruited young people for Little League and recreation programs. He also enlisted the urchins to attend the police Boy's Club Summer Camp. Aside from his interest in kids in particular and people in general, the Lieutenant said, Officer Spencer was a dedicated professional who when on-duty was assigned to special crime-prevention patrols in high-crime areas. Those areas included the Park Heights Avenue corridor from Garrison South to Virginia Avenue, as well as the area around Liberty Heights and Gwynn Oak Avenue.

Lieutenant Norris said her colleague was "a quiet guy who never flew off at the mouth," and that this quality was reflected in his personnel file, which contained no citizen complaints in his 15 years of service in the district and on narcotic and vice squads.

She said Officer Spencer had been urged to study for the sergeants and lieutenants exams, but always rebuffed those suggestions, saying, "There is a place for everybody – my place is as a patrolman." His supervisor at the time, she said she felt officer Spencer may have had a premonition about "his time," since only Friday had he introduced his mother to people on his post for the first time. Recently he also had gotten some of his things "in shape," Lieutenant Norris said, "Because I think John somehow knew he was going."

Spencer was born here and was a 1956 graduate of St. John's College, a military high school, in Washington. He had been a worker at the Boy's Village in Cheltenham, Maryland, a post-office worker and a merchant seaman before becoming a police officer. He was a member of the Saint Mary the Virgin Episcopal Church.

Survivors include his wife, the former Nancy Burke, and three sons, Scott H. Spencer, Brian S. Spencer and John H. Spencer, Junior, all of Randallstown. His mother, Freda Spencer, of Randallstown, and his father, John T. Spencer, of Glen Burnie, were also left bereaved.

<u>*The Baltimore Sun*</u>*; Jul 19, 1979; pg. C2: Judge Mary Arabian cleared the way yesterday for the trial of two men charged with the murder of an off-duty police officer, ruling that the police service revolver was properly seized in a raid on an Exeter Street apartment.*

Today, Cedric E. Scott, 17, of the 2100 block of Etting Street, and Joseph L. Owens, 23, of the 500 Block Gold St., will face trial on murder and robbery charges in the death of officer John H. Spencer, of the Northwestern district.

According to arguments by Richard Karceski and Thomas E. Klug, defense lawyers, police improperly searched the Exeter Street apartment, where neither of the defendants lived, a day after the shooting occurred. However, Judge Arabian agreed with Leslie Stein, an assistant state's attorney, that the police had obtained a proper warrant for the search of the apartment after a group of seven persons had been taken into custody.

<u>The Baltimore Sun</u>*; Jul 24, 1979; pg. C3: A .38 caliber police service revolver was identified yesterday in criminal court as the weapon that killed Officer John H. Spencer, an off-duty police Officer who was shot to death in March 1979 in the 600 block of School Street.*

The identification of the weapon, which belonged Officer Spencer, was the last testimony offered by the prosecution in the murder trial of John L. Owens, 23, of the 500 block of Gold Street, and Cedric E. Scott, 19, of the 2100 block of Etting Street.

Both defendants are charged with killing Officer Spencer after robbing him of his gun, and two wallets [badge wallet/money wallet] as he fumbled for the keys to his car, which was parked on School Street.

Before closing his case, Leslie Stein, an assistant state's attorney, told the jury that the defense had stipulated to the testimony of the ballistics expert, which showed that Officer Spencer was killed by a bullet from his own gun.

A witness, Ralph Willett, testified he saw Mr. Owens fire several shots from Officer Spencer's gun after he [Willett] watched Mr. Owens and Mr. Scott yoke the Officer near the front door of his car. Mr. Owens said in a statement given to police that Mr. Scott found the police officer's service revolver after knocking him to the ground and searching him. Mr. Scott in his statement said that Mr. Owens had the gun.

Despite the conflict in their testimony, JoAnn Chester, who lives on School Street, testified both Mr. Owens and Mr. Scott were visiting her when they saw officer Spencer stagger to his car in a way they felt showed he had been drinking.

Ms. Chester said she recalled telling the two defendants: "don't you mess with that man." Mr. Owens and Mr. Scott left her house, the witness said, and then she heard a noise "that sounded like three or four firecrackers."

Mr. Willett, who also was visiting Ms. Chester, said he saw both defendants grab Officer Spencer and throw him to the ground. The witness said Mr. Owens stood up with the gun and said. "This is my lucky day." Owens fired one shot into the air and then he leveled the revolver and fired at Officer Spencer, who had gotten up off the ground, Mr. Willett said.

Police arrested the defendants the next day after obtaining information they were at a seventh floor apartment of an apartment building in the first block of S. Exeter St.

Detectives testified that a search of the apartment discovered Officer Spencer's revolver in a paper bag in a drawer of the coffee table in that apartment.

One of Officer Spencer's wallets was found at Gold and Etting Streets. His badge was given to another police officer by a young boy who said he found it in the area but was unable to say exactly where, testimony disclosed.

<u>Newspaper Reports</u>, Jul 25, 1979: Two men were found guilty last night of what a prosecutor called a "senseless and stupid" murder of an off-duty police officer who was attempting to get into his car on March 1979, in the 600 block of School Street.

Convicted of felony murder charges in the death of Officer John H. Spencer, 44, were Joseph Lee Roy Owens, 23, and Cedric Eugene Scott, now 19. Held on $260,000 bail, they face sentences of life imprisonment. A jury under Judge Mary Arabian deliberated for six hours before handing down the verdict.

Spencer was shot once through the heart with his .38 caliber service revolver, which the witness said Owens took from him after knocking him to the street.

<u>Newspaper reports</u>; Sep 6, 1979; pg. C20 - Joseph L. Owens was sentenced to life imprisonment +15 years yesterday for the felony murder of an off-duty policeman who was shot with his own service revolver as he was making fumbling attempts while intoxicated to get into his car.

A codefendant, Cedric Eugene Scott was also sentenced to life imprisonment but an additional 15 year sentence in his case was made to run consecutive with a life term.

Judge Mary Arabian, in criminal court, commented that evidence showed the victim, officer John H. Spencer, 44, was "vulnerable and apparently helpless" at the time he was shot because he had been drinking.

Both defendants were convicted 24 July, for the fatal shooting of the 15 year veteran policeman, which occurred to March 1979 in the 600 block of school Street, officer Spencer was shot once in the chest with his own 38 caliber service revolver.

Owens, 23, of the 500 block of Gold Street, was identified as the gunman during the trial of the case. Owens and Scott, now 19, of the 2100 block of Etting Street, had just left the house in the 600 block of School Street when they saw the policeman trying to get into his private car.

After Spencer was knocked down and searched by the two defendants, Owen found the police officer's service revolver and shouted out, "This is my lucky day," the witness, Ralph Willett, said.

<u>Newspaper reports</u>; *Jun 5, 1981; pg. C3: Annapolis – two men, convicted of killing an off-duty Baltimore city police officer during a robbery, yesterday lost in their efforts to have their convictions overturned. The court of special appeals found no error in the trial of Lewis L. Owens, 25, and Cedric E. Scott, now 21 that would justify sending the case back for a new trial. Both men are serving lifetime terms in prison. Each man admitted participation in the robbery but blamed his companion for the murder.*

4 March - 1909

On this day in Baltimore Police History, 1909, we lost our brother, **Patrolman Thomas H. Worthington** in the line of duty to electrocution. On that night in March, 1909, many people were killed or injured as a result of loose electric wires due to a powerful storm in the area. One woman was struck in the face by a falling wire. As she was falling to the ground, she became tangled in more wires, and was fully electrocuted by the time she completed her fall and hit the ground.

At the time of the storm, the Canton area was covered by the Baltimore County Police. During the storm, a Baltimore County officer by the name of Michael Moore – one of the best-known members of Baltimore County's department at the time – stepped on a live wire as he worked his post in Canton. He received a severe shock but extricated himself before receiving the full strength of the current. He was burned about the side, and slightly bruised.

Patrolman Thomas Worthington wasn't so lucky. He was first struck by a falling live wire while trying to save others from danger or possible death from the same live wires. Patrolman Worthington, who was out of the Northwest District, was killed shortly after midnight. It was a Wednesday night and he was in the intersection of McMechen St. and Mt. Royal Ave., where he had just cleared a tangled mass of telephone wires from the street and was fastening them to a nearby pole to prevent danger to pedestrians in the area, as well as any teams of horses. At the time, horses were commonly killed by loose wires.

As Officer Worthington was clearing the area a charged electric wire fell from an above pole striking him. Charles Harvey, a watchman to United Railways, and George Bartholomew a Fire Patrolman, ran to Officer Worthington's assistance and hurried him into the car barn. The Northwestern police wagon was summoned and he was taken to Maryland General Hospital, where Dr. M. A. V. Smith pronounced him dead. Coroner Solace W. Baldwin decided an inquest unnecessary as it was obvious why he had died. The patrolman was 50 years old, he been on the force about 12 years always being stationed at the Northwestern District, and for more than 10 years on the post where he met his death. He leaves behind a widow, Caroline Ogle Worthington, four sons and two daughters.

It is said that patrolman Worthington, while on his way to report for duty that Wednesday night met a friend a few blocks from the police station and because of the weather (storms with wires down) he remarked, "It's a tough night, and it's going to cost a few lives before it's over." Who knew his would be one of those lives?

May he never be forgotten as his service honored the City of Baltimore and the Police Department" God bless and RIP.

4 March - 1933

Today in Baltimore Police History 1933, the **Radio Communications Division** was established. The first radio communications system between Patrol Vehicles and a Central Dispatcher went into service on this date in 1933. Commissioner Gaither first suggested this system to the Board of Estimates in September of 1931.

5 March - 1989

Today in Baltimore Police History, 1989, Retired **Officer Calvin McCleese** died while effecting an arrest in his neighborhood.

For years, a toll bridge at the end of Dundalk Ave in Baltimore County was closed. It sat unused and inoperable. Even longer than that it was under the watchful eye of one of our Department's finest; Southeast District's Officer Calvin McCleese, who lived on the corner of Dundalk Avenue and Bullneck Road, just across the street from the bridge and Watersedge Park. For all the years the toll bridge operated, the ladies and gentlemen who collected tolls were safe from anyone trying to bring them harm because, even though it's located in Baltimore County, Officer McCleese protected his neighborhood – just like he protected his family when he was off-duty, and his post when he was working. He had two sons, Michael and Jeff, who would also grow up to be police officers.

Calvin McCleese worked his entire career in the same area of southeastern Baltimore City, after joining the department in 1957. He started out working in the Eastern District's Southeast Substation, until 1959 when the Southeast District stationhouse on Eastern Avenue opened.

Here's the kind of police officer that Calvin was; on 22 Jan 1970 while patrolling in Highlandtown, he observed and grew suspicious of a car parked around the corner from the Chesapeake Federal Savings and Loan. Officer McCleese approached the car just as the car's tag number was broadcast over the police radio in connection with an in-progress bank robbery at Chesapeake. Officer McCleese drew his weapon and was able to singlehandedly capture the two bank-robbers in the car, one of whom was armed with a sawed-off shotgun. But that was 1970, and that was the way Officer McCleese worked his entire career.

He retired from the department in 1985, and went on to become the typical retired police officer – he still looked out for his family and his neighborhood. Then one day in 1989 a vehicle being operated by a drunk driver hit the bridge embankment near the toll booth and burst into flames, with the unconscious driver still inside. Hearing the accident, Officer McCleese immediately ran to the driver's aid. At obvious risk to his own life and limb, he broke out the driver's window, opened the door and pulled the nearly comatose driver out of the burning car.

As he did so, the driver woke up. Apparently fearing he would be arrested for DWI, or on an out of state arrest warrant for which he was wanted, the drunken driver decided he would fight the man who had just come to his aid and saved his life, and try to flee.

Having just fought his way into a burning car and getting get an intoxicated man out, and realizing the man was drunk, Officer McCleese wasn't about to just let him get away, so he fought back, subduing the individual until Baltimore County Police arrived on scene and took over the arrest. Immediately after the arrival of the Baltimore County officers, Calvin McCleese suffered a fatal heart attack; he had held on as long as he could. His last action in life was to first save a life, and then effect the arrest of a drunk driver and wanted fugitive.

Those knew him, knew how much he loved being a Baltimore Police Officer, knew the pride he had in wearing our badge and while he had already been retired for a few years, he died on this day in 1989 doing what he loved best… serving his community.

May he never be forgotten, as his service honored the City of Baltimore and the Police Department. God bless and RIP.

8 March - 2000

On this day in Baltimore Police History, 2000 we lost our brother, Police Officer **Jamie Allen Roussey** to a departmental accident based on the following:

Officer Roussey died from injuries he sustained when his Jeep Cherokee patrol vehicle collided with a car at an intersection in West Baltimore. Jamie was responding to help an officer involved in a foot pursuit. As he travelled northbound in the unit block of N. Fulton Ave, he collided with a Dodge Neon at the 1700 block of W. Fayette St. The driver's side of the Jeep was forced by the collision into a utility pole. Officer Roussey was transported to the hospital where he succumbed to his injuries. Officer Roussey's father, brother, uncle and a cousin were also members of the force.

Newspaper Reports – March 10, 2000 – *Jamie A. Roussey had one career and one family, and the two were indistinguishable.*

His father, brother, uncle and cousin doubled as colleagues in the Baltimore Police Department, a proud lineage that makes the Roussey name synonymous with law enforcement for virtually anyone who wears a badge in the city.

The close ties were evident Wednesday, when Roussey sped to help three fellow officers and died when his cruiser collided with another car in West Baltimore. His cousin, Seth Roussey, was the first officer on the scene.

"That's a very proud police family," said Mayor Martin O'Malley, who has Roussey's uncle, Officer Vincent Roussey, on his security detail. "He was a young, bright, dedicated kid who has the toughest job in this great city."

O'Malley ordered flags flown at half-staff until Monday's funeral at the family church in Catonsville. Roussey, 22, is the third officer in two years to die in the line of duty and the 100th since the department was formed in 1870.

He graduated from the police academy four months ago. He lived with his mother and father, Frederick, a police sergeant, who often brought his young son to work in the Western District.

"He knew he was going to be a Baltimore City police officer," said Rob Tomback, Roussey's principal at Catonsville High School. "There was no doubt. He had his sights set on that, and that is what he achieved."

Grief-stricken family members did not make public statements yesterday but indicated they might meet with reporters today. Two years ago, Roussey's parents took out a full-page ad in his high school yearbook to showcase their son's achievements.

"Your sparkling personality and sense of humor have brightened many days," they wrote under a photo spread showing Roussey in his football uniform, standing beside his pickup truck and smiling like a baby.

"Nothing is beyond your reach," they added. "We love you and we'll always be there to support you."

Roussey was killed as he sped through an intersection at North Fulton Avenue and West Fayette Street at about 5:45 pm Wednesday. He was trying to reach officers chasing a man suspected of possessing marijuana. The suspect was later arrested.

A Dodge Neon broadsided the passenger side of the police Jeep, sending it hurtling into a utility pole and crushing the driver's side of the vehicle.

The cause of the accident remains under investigation. Maj. Michael Bass, a police spokesman, said witnesses reported that Roussey had his emergency lights and siren activated, but that he may have gone through a red light.

Police vehicles are allowed to go through red lights only after coming to a complete stop, to make sure the intersection is clear of traffic. Bass said investigators have not determined whether that was done in this case.

The driver and passenger of the Neon, who were not seriously injured, have not been charged or cited in connection with the crash. But police said they found a Glock 9 mm gun in the Neon's trunk and suspected drug paraphernalia with a trace amount of suspected marijuana. As a result, Calvin Thompson Jr., 20, of the 4100 block of Mountwood Road, and Robert Scott, 28, of the 100 block of Palormo Ave., were charged with handgun and drug possession and were being held in the Central Booking and Intake Center last night.

Accidents involving police cars occur frequently, though the numbers have declined since 1995, when 554 were reported. That year, 186 were listed as the officer's fault. In 1998 – the most recent year for which numbers were available – 255 departmental accidents occurred, with 95 listed as the officer's fault. As an extreme example, Officer Harold A. Carey was killed in 1998 when his cruiser collided with another patrol car – both speeding to the same emergency. One went through a red light.

Roussey's death hit the Western District station hard. Though new to the police force, the young officer was well-liked. He wanted to patrol the Western, in one of the city's toughest neighborhoods, and teased his cousin, Seth, assigned to the more sedate Southern, officers there said.

"My learning experiences will be a lot greater than yours," he told his cousin, recalled Sgt. Andre O. Monroe. "He used to always come up to me, and he used to tell me how excited he was to come into the Western District."

The mood was somber during yesterday's roll call for Roussey's 4 pm to midnight shift. Lt. John Mack told officers that Roussey would want them to continue to make the city safer. Business as usual was easier said than done yesterday. "Behind this blue uniform, there are definitely hurt souls," Mack said.

Roussey grew up in Catonsville, across the street from the high school – a center of neighborhood activity in the close-knit community. The response to a call to the school and a request for someone who knows the Rousseys tells how well the name is known there. "That would be everybody," said an administrator.

In high school, Roussey excelled as a student and participated in lacrosse, football and wrestling. His principal, Tomback, remembers the 6-foot-2, 215-pound lineman

motivating his teammates to rally for a come-from-behind victory that at "one point just seemed hopeless."

The five active-duty Roussey's made up one of the largest family contingents in the Police Department. His father, Sgt. Frederick Roussey, is assigned to the sex offense unit. His brother, Frederick Roussey Jr., patrols the Southern District, along with his cousin, Seth. His uncle, Vincent, is a member of the mayor's security detail.

It's one of those names that is synonymous with law enforcement in Baltimore City," said Officer Gary McLhinney, the police union president. Added Bass: "Their friends are in the hundreds in this agency."

Lt. Susan Young has known Roussey since he was 10. Not only is she a family friend -- she was at their home Wednesday night to help them grieve -- she helped train the young man at the academy. "He had the potential to be one of the best," Young said. Unlike his father, who was outgoing, she said Roussey was "one of those quiet ones that maybe you didn't think was listening, but if you asked him a question, he had the answer."

Young said she kept her friendship with young Roussey a secret at the academy, to avoid any appearance of favoritism. But they had their own hidden game during inspections, where Roussey tried to be serious. "I would crack a smile, give him a wink, and he couldn't keep a straight face," Young said. "I purposely did it to him, just to make him laugh."

At his Nov. 5 graduation, Roussey joined 46 of the department's newest officers at the War Memorial Building, where they heard a top police commander tell them, "The quality of life on the streets is still rotten," and it was their job to make it better.

Roussey's friends said he took those words to heart. His father had worked the drug-torn streets of the Western District, and that was where he wanted to be.

McLhinney described Roussey's father, whom he spoke to Wednesday night, as proud but devastated. "Most fathers want their sons to follow in their footsteps," the union president said. "He was such a young guy who really wanted to make a difference."

<u>Sun staff writer Stacey Hirsh contributed to this article</u>

The family has set up the Jamie A. Roussey Scholarship Fund. Donations can be sent to Baltimore City Fraternal Order of Police, Lodge 3, – 3920 Buena Vista Ave., Baltimore 21211.

We his brothers and sisters of the Baltimore Police Department will not let him be forgotten. God Bless and Rest in Peace as, "His service honored the City of Baltimore and the Police Department."

9 March - 1807

A general ordinance was passed defining the duties of the city commissioners. They were given large powers. Among other things, with the Mayor they were authorized to employ as many captains, officers and watchmen as they might, from time to time, find necessary, but the expense should not exceed the annual appropriation for the service. The board was also required to make regulations and define the hours of duty of the watch; see that they attended to their duties with punctuality, receive their reports and cause them to be returned to the Mayor's office.

9 March - 1826

The Mayor was given control of the police. The power given the Mayor was unlimited. The ordinance provided that the Mayor should appoint annually two Captains, two Lieutenants for the Eastern District; two Captains, four Lieutenants for the Middle District; two Captains, two Lieutenants for the Western District. He could also appoint any number of watchmen.

9 March - 1826

Central/Middle District History – Holiday and Saratoga Streets, established 03-09-1826, building that housed it was built in 1802 and was in use until 1870. 202 N. Guilford Avenue, (North Street) built in 1870 used until 1908. Saratoga and St. Paul Streets, renovated school, March 4, 1908 until 1926. Fallsway and Fayette St. built in 1926 and used until 09-12-1977 when they moved to 500 E Baltimore St. from 12 Sept 1977 until present.

9 March - 1826

Eastern District History – 1621 Bank Street built around 1822, still stands. Used until the summer of 1959, when the station was moved to the old Northeastern station house at Ashland and Chew St. (Durham) in the summer of 1959 where they stayed until 1960. In December 1960 they moved to their current location 1620 Edison Highway.

9 March - 1826

Western District History - Green St between Baltimore St, and Belvidere St. Used from 1826 until 1876 when they moved to their new location, Pine Street, (still stands today and is used by the Maryland University Police). Baltimore Police used it from 1876 until 1959 when they built their new station house at 1034 N Mount St, which is the current site of the Western District.

9 March - 1835

A "Supplement" to this ordinance, which was passed on this day, 1835 provided for the appointment of twelve lieutenants of the watch, established policemen "to preserve the peace, maintain the laws, and advance the good government of the city." These lieutenants were required to reside in certain districts by the Mayor, and have conspicuous signs on their houses bearing their names, and office. In addition to their police duties, they were required to act as city bailiffs about the markets, their compensation was a fixed $20 a month for the night work lieutenants of the watch, and they received an additional sum of $220 a year for the services mentioned by the ordinance.

9 March - 1977

The Auxiliary Police Unit was formed within the Community Services Division. After training and certification, members were assigned, without compensation, to support the force. They are assigned to various events as an addition to the normal manpower deployment.

9 March - 1963

My big brother, **Dennis Bruce Driscoll** was born... Happy Birthday Bro

12 March - 2001

On this day in Baltimore Police History, 2001 we lost our brother, Police Agent **Michael Joseph Cowdery, Jr.** to gunfire. The gunman who killed Baltimore Police Agent Michael J. Cowdery, Jr. last week first shot the officer in the leg and then grabbed him and shot him in the head as he lay disabled on the sidewalk, according to documents filed in Baltimore courts 21 March, 2001.

From Newspaper Reports: 21 March, 2001: The shooting that took place on 12 March of this year, in which Agent Michael J. Cowdery Jr., 31, in the 2300 block of Harford Road was shot, happened so quickly that by the time one of his partners shouted "gun!" it was too late to react, according to court documents. Charging documents filed in District Court referring to this killing say that as Officer Cowdery – who was wearing plainclothes but had his badge prominently displayed around his neck – lay wounded on the street, the shooter stood over him, grabbed him by his collar, pulled him up a little and shot him "in the head at close range." The suspect, Howard T. Whitworth, 26, was later shot and wounded during an ensuing gun battle between him and two Baltimore officers.

Whitworth was released from Maryland Shock Trauma Medical Center to the City's Detention Center Monday, 19 March 2001, and 20 March 2001 he made his first court appearance, during which his court-appointed lawyer, Assistant Public Defender John P. Markus, waived the bail hearing. Whitworth was ordered back to the Detention Center, where he awaited indictment by the Circuit Court, which is the usual procedure and would have happened within the following month. Markus could not be reached for comment yesterday. His client, with no permanent address, is charged with first-degree murder, attempted first-degree murder, reckless endangerment, using a handgun in the commission of a felony and possession of a handgun within city limits. Whitworth was facing the death penalty. The Police Commissioner at the time, Edward T. Norris said he plans to discuss that issue with the state's attorney's office. The charging documents filed on that 21st day of March 2001 provided details but did not offer a solid motive. Even the surrender of a key witness, William A. "Mookie" Houston, 20, who was sought for several days before turning himself in to be questioned, was of no help. Houston was released.

On 21 March 2001, Norris said, "Interviews with witnesses 'haven't' shed any light on the motive in this case." Police said they believe Officer Cowdery may have entered an open air drug market and was mistaken for a rival dealer that had been harassing the crew. It was said that the suspect had recently purchased a .357 Magnum handgun because he had been held up. Police say when arrested Whitworth had 40 vials of crack cocaine on him. While Police say they are not sure if Whitworth knew Officer Cowdery was an officer, the badge around his neck was visible and obvious. Agent Cowdery and three of his colleagues - also in plainclothes with their badges around their necks – had stopped to question two men outside a carryout on Harford Road about 10:15 pm Officers Robert L. Jackson and Ronald A. Beverly chatted with the two people as Cowdery talked with a woman leaving the carryout. Police said a gunman turned the corner at Cliftview Avenue and ran up to the officers, whose back was turned to him, and pulled a gun – determined to be a .357 Magnum.

Court documents say Officer Tiffany D. Walker saw the gunman approach and yelled, "Gun" just as the man opened fire, hitting Cowdery in the leg. The second shot, was fired as Whitworth grabbed officer Cowdery's shirt pulled him from the ground and fired a shot directly into his head. That shot was fired seconds after the first.

Officer Walker ducked into a carryout and hid on the floor behind a counter, while Officers Jackson and Beverly "moved to other areas of cover," and exchanged fire with Whitworth. Officer Beverly, was struck in the leg and ankle, but still managed to return fire and hit the gunman, said a police spokesman.

The suspect was convicted of Agent Cowdery's murder and sentenced to life in prison. Agent Cowdery had been employed with the Baltimore City Police Department for four and a half years, and is survived by his parents, sister, and son.

We his brothers and sisters of the Baltimore Police Department will not let him be forgotten. God Bless and may he rest in Peace.

15 March - 1808

On this day in Baltimore Police History, 1808 we lost our brother, Night Watchman

George Workner. Officer Workner was stabbed to death during the jail break of nine inmates from the Baltimore Jail. The inmates made a set of keys, and picked the locks to their cell doors. Then they attacked the guards with a small knife one of the inmates had obtained. Watchman Workner was stabbed in the side during the escape, and died from the wound the following day.

Four of the nine inmates were apprehended and sentenced to death for Watchman Workner's murder. Their execution date was set for April 22, 1808, but they again attempted to escape two days beforehand. That escape attempt failed, and they were hung in the jail's courtyard at noon on April 22, 1808.

We his brothers and sisters of the Baltimore Police Department will not let him be forgotten – RIP Officer George Workner

15 March - 1875 – Marshal Gilmor

Harry W. Gilmor (January 24, 1838 – March 4, 1883) served as Baltimore City Marshal starting on 15 March, 1875, but he was most noted as a Confederate cavalry officer during the American Civil War. Gilmor's daring raids, such as *The Magnolia Station Raid* gained his partisans fame as "Gilmor's Raiders."

Gilmor was born at "Glen Ellen," the family estate in Baltimore County, Maryland, but after the war he moved to New Orleans, where he and his wife had three children. Gilmor later wrote his war memoirs, entitled *Four Years in the Saddle* (New York, Harper & Bros., 1866). He soon thereafter returned to Maryland and was appointed colonel of the cavalry in the Maryland National Guard. He also served as the Baltimore City Police Commissioner from 1874 to 1879. Gilmor died in Baltimore, plagued by complications from a war injury to his jaw. He was buried in Loudon Park Cemetery in an area now known as "Confederate Hill." At his death, Baltimore police stations flew their flags at half-staff. Gilmor's funeral was a large local event with many dignitaries present to honor this war hero.

Civil War

During the American Civil War, as a member of Captain Charles Ridgely's Baltimore County Horse Guards, Gilmor was arrested and imprisoned in Fort McHenry following the occupation of Baltimore by Federal troops. Upon his release, he traveled south and eventually rejoined the fighting serving, for a while, under General Turner Ashby. He was again captured during the Maryland

Campaign and spent five months in prison. During the Gettysburg Campaign, Major Gilmor was assigned command of the First Maryland Cavalry and Second Maryland Cavalry, supporting Brig. Gen. George Stuart's infantry brigade. Gilmor was the provost marshal of the town of Gettysburg while it was occupied by the Confederates July 1–4.

The Magnolia Station Raid

After the Battle of Monocacy on July 9, 1864, Colonel Gilmor's command, along with Brig. Gen. Bradley T. Johnson's infantry, made a series of raids around Baltimore going as far east as Magnolia Station in Harford County, Maryland and Fork, Maryland. On July 10, 1864 Major Harry Gilmor of the 2nd Maryland Cavalry was given 135 men of the 1st and 2nd Maryland, and directed to cross Baltimore County into Harford County at Jerusalem Mill, and destroy the railroad bridge of the Philadelphia, Wilmington and Baltimore Railroad at Magnolia Station, northeast of the city. Early on the morning of July 11, Gilmor's cavalrymen reached Magnolia Station, located just off present-day I-95 near Joppa. There they proceeded to wreck two trains, one northbound and one southbound. After first evacuating the passengers and looting the cars, the troopers set fire to one of the trains and backed it over the trestle, thus partially destroying the bridge. To further sweeten the pot, aboard the northbound train was an unexpected prize—convalescing Union Maj. Gen. William B. Franklin. This raid was always regarded as one of the most daring ever attempted by detached cavalry on either side during the war.

Later in the day on July 11, 1864, Gilmore's advance group were passing the home of Ishmael Day on Sunshine Avenue in Fork, Maryland. Day was a Union sympathizer, and knowing Gilmor's troops were passing through, hung a large Union flag across the road. In the advance guard unit, Confederate color bearer and Ordnance Sergeant Eugene Fields told Day to take the flag down. After Day refused, an argument followed and Ishmael Day shot Sgt. Field at close range with a shotgun. In retaliation, Gilmor's men burned Day's home and Day immediately fled, cowering under a cider press for days until the passing troops were gone. The mortally wounded Sgt. Field was taken, accompanied by Gilmor, to Wright's Hotel operated by W. Wright on Harford Road, where Field later died.

15 March - 2012

Today in Baltimore Police History, 2012, we lost our brother Retired Police **Officer William "Bill" Hackley**.

Ret. Officer Bill Hackley passed away on 15 March, 2012 - An avid historian, Bill started the BaltimorePoliceHistory.com website. Bill started an outstanding tradition in his creation of the History website (since taken over by this writer, Retired Detective Kenny Driscoll). We think the work that Bill has done, along with the assistance of Bobby Brown, David Eastman, and tons of others have provided in a way of information, and donations of so much. Others have also gone a long way toward helping to keep the site up and running again through donation, from retired officers like Mark Frank, John Heiderman, Jim Mitchell, and way too many others to mention, some of whom insist on not being mentioned, and enough others that create a list that is so long it is amazing.

At the time of this writing it has been nearly 5 years since Bill's passing, he left me with his website, 90 pages of some of the most informative history on any Police history site anywhere on the web. Since then it has been rebuilt twice, first we took the 90 pages to more than 200, and now we are well over 500. We hope to continue Bill's dream of showing just how hard all of the men and women of the Baltimore Police Department work, and how serious we all take, and or took the oath we swore to serve and protect the citizens of Baltimore. The site can be found at www.BaltimoreCityPoliceHistory.com and we think you will like it as much Bill and I had hoped you would. While maintaining the memory of those that have fallen or become disabled in the line of duty, we also want to remember the dedication Bill had to their memories and the history of our department. RIP Officer, William, "Bill" Hackley, and may God Bless you, and your project – As we work to make sure none of it, or you, are forgotten.

16 March - 1853

Today in Baltimore Police History 1853 - The State Legislature on March 16, 1853, passed a bill, "To provide for the better security for the citizens, and property in the City of Baltimore." This statute provided that police **officers should be armed**, and that a badge and commission be furnished each member. The former act of 1812 was repealed with the passage and enactment of this bill. No additional changes occurred in the police organization until 1857.

16 March - 1858

Today in Baltimore Police History, the State Legislature took memorable action in passing a bill to "provide for the better security for life and property in the City of Baltimore." This enactment empowered the Mayor and the City Council to increase, and in every way strengthen the police, whether they were called officers, bailiffs, night-watchmen, or in any way connected with law enforcement. When any of these guardians of the peace were injured, either in person or apparel, while in the discharge of his duties, the act required that he be fairly indemnified. This statute also provided that the police force should be armed, that a commission and badge be furnished each member, and that it should be no defence for anyone who resisted or assaulted an officer to claim that his commission or badge was not exhibited. This statute repealed the act of 1812.

17 March - 2006

The QRT (Quick Response Team) is renamed **SWAT** (Special Weapons and Tactics) after 32 years the department finally changed the name of this highly trained, elite team. (In 1974, while forming the team the department was against using the name SWAT because they felt the name was too harsh for the department's image – Political correctness circa 1974.) Since its inception, the Baltimore Police Department has had 38 Police Commissioners, starting in 1850 with Charles Howard, until 2015 with Kevin Davis, the current Police Commissioner.

19 March - 1798

Today in Baltimore Police History, 1798 - An officer at the time was known simply as "The City" or "High Constable," a position created by an ordinance of March 19, 1798. His duty was *"To walk through the streets, lanes and alleys of the city daily, with mace* in hand, taking such rounds, that within a reasonable time he shall visit all parts of the city, and give information to the Mayor or other Magistrate, of all*

nuisances within the city, and all obstructions and impediments in the streets, lanes, and alleys, and of all offences committed against the laws and ordinances." He was also required to report the names of the offenders against any ordinance and the names of the witnesses who could sustain the prosecutions against them, and regard the mayor as his chief. The yearly salary of the city constable was fixed at $350, and he was required to give a bond for the performance of his duty.

*Mace – A "Mace" typically consists of a strong, heavy, wooden or metal shaft, often reinforced with metal (the modern Mace of 1798 were all wood, no metal was allowed). In short a mace is a stick, or pole type weapon. Making this the first time, the Nightstick/Espantoon was mentioned as one of our tools. For many years, it was considered a badge of authority, and was used to defend ourselves, or to communicate with other officers. In Baltimore, police were known to tap their Espantoon on the curbs, sidewalks, cobble stone streets or copper down spouts, and having formerly used what was called a "Rattle," police already had codes worked out, and would use these taps and raps to communicate with other nearby officers.

19 March - 1918

On this day in Baltimore Police History, 1918, we lost our sister Police **Matron Teresa Foll**, as she died in her chair, in her office while working – Miss Teresa Foll served two years at the Southern District stationhouse – Officers and other employees of the Southern Police Station were shocked that evening by the sudden death of Mrs. Foll. Mrs. Foll lived at 3124 O'Donnell Street, and had served as the substitute Matron of the Southern District for more than two years.

Newspapers reported: Patrolman Harvey Romner was passing Mrs. Foll's office on the second floor of the station house at about 5:30 o'clock pm when he noticed her sitting limply in a chair. Thinking she had either fallen asleep, or may have taken ill he stepped into her office, and in a playful tone told her to wake up. Receiving no response, he reached out and touched her on the side of her face, at which time he found she was dead.

Coroner Reinhardt was summonsed and pronounced death due to heart disease. She was survived by her daughter, a Miss Regina Foll. On this day, we'll take a moment to remember her service to the city of Baltimore and our Police Department, as we pray she may rest in peace.

21 March - 2002

Today in Baltimore Police History we lost our brother, retired Officer **Richard Mioduszewski Sr.**, 56, a police officer who helped end a 1971 shooting spree.

<u>Newspapers</u> reported: *that on March 21, Richard B. Mioduszewski Sr., a highly decorated Baltimore Police Officer who earned the department's highest honor for helping end a 1971 shooting spree that killed five people, died Saturday 21 March of liver failure while a patient at Johns Hopkins Hospital.*

The former long-time Millersville resident had lived in New Freedom, Pa., since 1996. Born in Baltimore and raised in Brooklyn, Mr. Mioduszewski was a 1964 graduate of Southern High School, where he played tackle on the high school football team. After graduating from the Baltimore Police Academy in 1966, he was assigned as a Patrolman in the Southwestern District.

On Nov. 22, 1971, while on his way to begin his shift, he arrived at a shooting. Raymond D. Ferrell, 29, an Army veteran dressed in camouflage clothing, had carried a carbine and a .30-caliber hunting rifle into the PPG Industries brush manufacturing plant in the 3200 block of Frederick Ave., where he was employed dipping brush handles in vats of lacquer.

Once inside, Mr. Ferrell, a former teacher's aide in Baltimore public schools, began shooting, killing five co-workers and wounding another.

"The killer was `yelling as he shot, laughing wild hysterical laughter,' an officer said," the Sun reported. "But the gunman calmly asked one witness to help him get out of the plant with his rifles."

After leaving the building, he crossed Frederick Avenue and was standing near a fire station reloading one of his weapons when police arrived. Patrolman Kenneth Hayden approached, and Mr. Ferrell opened fire, wounding him in the left knee. Mr. Mioduszewski "was late for work and was zipping down an alley when he arrived at the crime scene," said his wife of 25 years, the former Margaret L. Keeney. "He quickly realized it was a bad situation. He saw the wounded officer and was afraid that Ferrell was going to shoot him again, so he shot him. It was the only time in his career that he ever drew his weapon."

The gunman was wounded in the stomach and fell to the ground. After recovering, he was found innocent by reason of insanity and committed to the state's Clifton T. Perkins mental hospital.

In 1972, Mr. Mioduszewski was awarded the Police Medal of Honor, the department's highest decoration, for his role in responding to the shooting.

"He seldom talked about the incident, and was a very quiet and modest man who took the job of protecting people's lives and property very seriously," said Mrs. Mioduszewski. After resigning from the Police Department in 1978, he joined the University of Maryland campus police and was a patrol officer on the school's Baltimore campus until retiring in 1996.

23 March - 1974

The House panel passed the *"Law Enforcement Officer Bill of Rights."* With **LEOBR**, Maryland became the first state in the nation to enact such a law intended to protect officers from legal entanglements based on their legal actions or conduct.

This bill has recently come under fire, but what people lose sight of is that the bill is not there to protect the *bad* cop… it's intended primarily to protect the innocent hard working police from being wrongfully prosecuted. With or without the bill, officers would still have their constitutional rights and they can still invoke their 5th amendment rights. If forced to give a statement, that statement might be considered coerced. Therefore, it might be best to leave that bill alone, and work harder to seek out bad cops, than to just through a blanket over all police and assume they are all criminal – that's a form of profiling, based on prejudging a person based on his membership in a group. Anytime we do that, profile, or assume we know the facts based on the way a person dresses, or looks, we enter a slippery slope of prejudice. This risks punishing the good for things they did not do, which in turn will make other good cops fear doing what is right, because they have no voice, as their voice was removed because of prejudices. In many ways, those who persecute all police, for misdeeds of a few police, are becoming what they hate about the bad police that took the lazy route of instead of looking for criminals in a neighborhood, and assumed everyone in a high crime area was a criminal.

24 March - 1970

On this day in Baltimore Police History 1970, we lost our brother **Officer Henry Mickey** to gunfire during a drug raid.

Officer Mickey, a member of the Central District plainclothes unit, was part of a team of three officers serving a narcotics warrant at a second-story apartment in the 1800 block of Pennsylvania Avenue. Officer Mickey, 28, was killed by a single rifle shot to the chest fired by James Stewart, the subject of the warrant, who lived in the apartment. Stewart was then shot and killed by Officer Vincent Cole, who returned fire.

Officer Mickey was pronounced dead on arrival at Providence Hospital. Stewart was DOA at the same hospital. Stewart's roommate and partner in crime, Dick Tune, age 37, was arrested; Tune shared the apartment with Stewart, and was taken into police custody as both a potential partner in the drug trade, but more importantly as a material witness to the shootings. Tune would go on to testify that he was in the apartment at the time of the shootings and observed as Stewart opened fire on and killed Officer Mickey, before he himself was killed by Officer Cole.

A police spokesman said, "The officers climbed a rear stairway entrance to the apartment before announcing their presence. Stewart, apparently realizing there was no way out, opened the door and immediately opened fire on the officers. The apartment, located above a shoe store, had a single rear entrance virtually trapping the suspect and his roommate in the apartment.

Officer Mickey, of the 5200 Blk. of Eastbury Avenue, had been on the Baltimore Police force since May, 1969. The third officer in this squad of three was Sergeant Victor Dennis. The warrant being served was for drug dealing from the apartment.

Some background on Officer Mickey shows the character of a leader, the character of a Baltimore Police Officer, and what it is in most of police officers that give them the pride they hold in having served alongside such quality of life as guys like Officer Mickey, Officer Cole, and Sergeant Dennis.

Before joining the police department Officer Mickey worked at a Baltimore Hospital. He left Dunbar Junior High School during the 9th grade to go to work and help support his family. Taking a job at Montebello State Hospital as a food-service employee, he did more than just bring in some extra cash to help his family. He also learned at a young age how to deal with people; people who didn't always want the help they so desperately needed. He also learned that he enjoyed helping people, he enjoyed a regimented lifestyle, and he wanted to make that kind of thing his life's work.

When he was of age, he left the hospital and enlisted in the United States Navy in

1963, where he trained at the Great Lakes Naval Training Center. Because of the leadership ability he demonstrated during training, he was named one of the class platoon leaders. He studied hard in the Navy and served aboard the USS Rankin, a cargo ship, where he served as a diesel mechanic foreman. He completed his high school education while in the Navy, and was discharged in 1967 as a non-commissioned officer. After the Navy, he went on to drive a bus for the Baltimore Transit Company, until May of 1969 when he joined the Baltimore City Police Department.

Officer Mickey had been working as a plainclothes Officer for just several weeks at the time of his death. His father, Henry Mickey, Sr. said of his son, "Henry enjoyed his work, and had requested the assignment to Pennsylvania Avenue" and went on to say that his son tried to help the kids whenever he could. Officer Mickey was survived by his wife, his parents, a stepson, two sisters and four brothers.

We his brothers and sisters of the Baltimore Police Department will not let him be forgotten – RIP Officer Henry M. Mickey and God Bless - For your service honored the City of Baltimore, and the Baltimore Police Department.

26 March - 1971

Two **Hughes 300-C helicopters** were formally accepted and registered for the department. The two new helicopters raised to three the number of such craft available for tactical deployment in the department's continuing efforts to combat crime. Purchased under a Federal grant of $100,000, the Hughes 300-C models represented a maximum combination of utility and modernization in the department's ongoing crime fighting efforts.

28 March - 1889

Ten electric incandescent lights were lighted last night for the first time in Druid Hill Park. The lights will illuminate the theretofore gloomy pathway in Druid Hill Park leading from the Clipper Gate, to the walk from the Mansion House and to the main entrance on Madison Avenue. The lamps are mounted on cedar posts about the height of a street gas lamp, and are lit simultaneously by the turning of a lever in the gatekeeper's house at the Druid Hill Drive entrance to the park.

Electric street lamps were introduced in this country at the suggestion of the Baltimore Police Department when oil lamps were still being used for street lighting. The Baltimore Sun newspaper claimed credit for this suggestion as a way to curb crime. The oil street lamps had been lit, extinguished and maintained by Baltimore's Police Department since 1784.

It may not have been as obvious to the public as it was to the panel of commissioners and to the council of city hall, but lighted streets in Baltimore were an undisputed deterrent that prevented and decreased crime in and around "*Mob Town.*" While at first many of the ideas and theories of the Panel of Commissioners, were often shot down, or put off until they either died in committee, or were funded privately. Many of these ideas would go on to become the norm in law enforcement, and not just here in Baltimore, but throughout the country, and in some cases around the world. Furthermore, these concepts would eventually become widely approved or, paid for, and authorized by our state legislatures.

28 March - 1925

Today in Baltimore Police History, two female members of the Baltimore Police Department would become the first female Baltimore police officers to receive firearms training. They were Miss Margaret B. Eagleston, and Mrs. Mary J. Bruff. Lieutenant James O. Downes, expert marksman and instructor of the Department's Pistol Team, explained the use of pistols to the policewomen, A few days later Mrs. Mary Harvey, Miss Eva Aldridge, and Ms. Mildred Campbell were also trained in firearms use and safety.

Two interesting side notes about this that will show the dedication of our women in law enforcement.

First: 13 years before they were trained with firearms Policewoman Mary S. Harvey, EOD [Entered on Duty] 19 June, 1912, and Policewoman Margaret B. Eagleston EOD 22 July, 1912 became the first women to be hired by the Baltimore Police Department as police officers.

Second: 17 October, 1914, we had our first female officer shot in the line of duty. Her name was Patrol Woman Elaibeth Faber, and she was shot on the Edmonston Ave Bridge, alongside her partner Patrolman Popp who was also shot, and still it would take 11 years before women would be trained, and armed

29 March - 1973

On this day in Baltimore Police History we lost our brother, **Officer Robert M. Hurley** to a heart attack. Officer Hurley was involved in a car chase one day earlier. More than a simple chase, this went on for longer than normal, it went through more than one district, resulted in a bailout, a foot chase, and a struggle before the suspect was taken into custody. Officer Hurley told others after the chase, the accident and the struggle, he didn't feel right, he felt excited, anxious and different from normal.

He went home from work not feeling well. He told his wife about the car chase, the foot chase, and the struggle. He told her how he was a little tired, sore, and as he put it, "I just don't feel right!" This coming from a guy who never complained.

The next day, while driving to work in his nearly brand new 1972 Chevy Impala, he felt a tightness in his chest, then all of a sudden Officer Hurley grabbed his chest in in severe pain. His car began swerving back and forth in the street, and concerned for those around him and their safety he worked to bring the car under control. At one point witnesses said they could see he was having trouble, and that he was in pain. A store owner who knew him realized he was having an attack of some kind, as he was heading the wrong way into traffic. Nevertheless, despite his obvious distress he somehow managed to prevent a head-on collision, and he brought his car to a stop, resting against a pole and parked car, with little damage to either. A witness that was taking his wife to a nearby banquet (but running late) saw the start of these events as Officer Hurley first began grabbing his chest at a red light. The witness went on to drop his wife off at the banquet and came back to the scene, to tell how heroic it was for a man in desperate pain to still avoid an accident, bringing the car to rest without injuring anyone.

This was a minor traffic accident, but it could have been a lot worse. The heart attack took Officer Hurley from us that day. It came on as a result of the excitement and an unacknowledged injury Officer Hurley had while working the night before. He was injured in a way no one understood, and no one knew what he was going through, even though he had told everyone he didn't quite feel right; but there were no visible injuries so he and everyone else dismissed it. And that was probably when the heart attack occurred. One day after that, with severe chest pains he suffered throughout the night, he would die. But even then he would die a hero, with more concern for the safety of those around him than for the safety of himself.

Officer Hurley, 46 years of age, was born in Baltimore, attended city schools and once worked at Bethlehem Steel Corporation as a welder. In 1944, he joined the Navy and served as a gunner's mate 3rd class in the Pacific. He was a charter member the Baltimore City Police Union and was on the personnel board. He was 2nd vice president of the Union at the time of his death. Patrolman Hurley was also a co-founder, and charter member of the Police Council #27. He was survived by his wife Angelina Hurley; and their three sons, as well as three daughters. He also left behind two granddaughters. Also surviving him was his brother Edgar Hurley and his sister Joan Hurley. All are of Baltimore.

We his brothers and sisters of the Baltimore Police Department will not let him be forgotten – RIP Officer Robert M. Hurley and God Bless - For your service honored the City of Baltimore, and the Baltimore Police Department"

1 April - 1972

This may sound like a joke but it is real, and it actually works to everyone's benefit – except for the thieves. On April Fool's day, *Operation Identification* was formally initiated by the department. The Operation encourages citizens to mark their property with an electro-engraver and record the make, model and serial numbers on a property sheet supplied by the department. This information is invaluable in the case of theft, and enables the department to reconnect recovered property with its rightful owners.

1 April - 1979

Police Officer Michael P. Dunn was the first City officer to be saved by his Kevlar vest after being shot in the chest. Truly a signal moment in the department's history.

3 April - 1797

Today in Baltimore Police History, 1797 – Happy Birthday to us… on 3 April, 1797 the City Council passed the first ordinance affecting the Baltimore police Department. It directed that three persons were to be appointed Commissioners of the watch. They could employ for one year as many Captains and watchmen as had been employed in the night watch the year past for the same remuneration. While we were actually police well before this day in 1797 – since August 8, 1729, to be exact, this day we became official. The Commissioners prescribed regulations and hours of duty and pay for its members.

4 April - 1938

Today in Baltimore Police history was the inauguration of the **Accident Investigation Bureau** (AIB). Finding the "why" of automobile accidents before the inauguration of AIB was a guesswork proposition for the Baltimore Police Department. Three "crash cars" were used by the few members, who all received comprehensive and specialized training involving the use of physics, mathematics, chemistry and bio-chemistry, psychology, medicine and even human anatomy. For good measure, he'll throw in a smattering of law, engineering and art – all replacing the snap judgement and intuition of the past.

The officers got received their intensive and varied schooling at two schools – the University of Maryland and an rigorous course of training at police headquarters under the tutelage of Sergeant Clarence O. Forrester, who then commanded the new division. It was that exhaustive training which resulted in the squad's being commended for the thoroughness of their investigation, testimony and evidence by all three Traffic Court magistrates at the time. For the men had more than merely a passing acquaintance with the sciences they used in their investigations.

Under the subject of bio-chemistry, for instance, they learned how to collect and preserve human tissue, blood and saliva samples for further scientific evaluation. The officer in the crash car knew his mathematics – especially trigonometry - and he used it in determining the relative positions and paths of the cars involved in an accident after he made his tape-measure readings. He used a decelerometer to test the brakes of cars in a crash, and with its readings along with his mathematical calculations, his knowledge of the laws of moving bodies, of negative acceleration, of force and of gravity, the officer could often reconstruct the accident without even asking any information of the drivers of the vehicles.

Psychology helped the men to more easily approach and question drivers and witnesses, and to begin to evaluate the truthfulness of their information, which was often more self-serving than accurate. They also benefited from the rudiments of human anatomy, as taught to them by doctors and other medical experts, and the different types of bone breaks and other injuries in order that they could better understand the kind and amount of forces applied by the collision.

They were taught how to most effectively evaluate injuries and administer first aid to accident victims. Art and engineering entered the equation with the diagramming of the accident. Moulage work – the casting of impressions – was often necessary to preserve tire tread marks in hit-run cases. And they became experts in the workings of "modern" photography, and the chemistry used to develop pictures from accident scenes.

He knew a good deal of law in order to properly present his case in court, and he was taught the sometimes subtle differences between the legal and illegal collection of evidence and testimony. Besides this training, two members of the squad had bachelor's degrees in the sciences, according to Sergeant Forrester. And he concluded, "I could talk all afternoon about the things my officers studied. It was an exhaustive and demanding training course - I didn't let up on them for even one minute." The sergeant himself attended the prestigious Northwestern University traffic school in 1935 and again in 1937. This training resulted in a commendation on the thoroughness of the squad's court testimony and evidence presentation by the three Traffic Court Magistrates at the time – William F. Laukaitis, William J. Stocksdale and George Eckhard.

With three crash cars at his command at the time, Sergeant Forrester hoped to eventually expand that number to ten. As it was, one car covered an area extending from Pratt Street to North Avenue between Charles street and Patterson Park Avenue, the, second covered an equal area west of Charles Street and the third took11 the territory north of North Avenue between Belair Road and Charles Street. The cars were sent out of their areas of primary responsibility frequently and when necessary to handle the always growing volume of serious accident calls. The sergeant averred one of his officers could be at the scene of any accident in the city within ten minutes of receiving a call. There were sixteen men in the division, who worked eight-hour shifts day and night.

4 April - 1949

On this day in Baltimore Police History we lost our brother, Police **Officer James L. Joyce**, to an auto accident. Officer Joyce, 42 years of age, was stopped on Falls Road near the city line in his patrol car. Another vehicle, driven by Frank Love, 21 years of age hit the railing on the Falls Road Bridge over the Pennsylvania Railroad tracks causing it to go out of control. Love's vehicle struck the left side of Officer Joyce's radio car pushing it over the curb and up an embankment. Richard Farace, a passenger in Love's car, was killed instantly. Officer Joyce received broken ribs, punctured lungs, and internal injuries, and was transported to Union Memorial Hospital where he died of his injuries.

We his brothers and sisters of the Baltimore Police Department will not let him be forgotten – RIP Officer Robert M. Hurley and God Bless – for your service honored the City of Baltimore, and the Baltimore Police Department"

4 April - 1976 - 5th Issue Badge

Today in Baltimore Police history the **5th issue badge** was issued. It is the badge worn by Baltimore Police Officers to this day.

With the exception of the series two badge, the word, "Baltimore" did not appear on any previous official police badges. The series five badge is similar to the series four supervisors badge with a new center colorful seal that is the same as shown on the BPD shoulder patch. Police Officers and supervisors wear the same badge, with the ribbon in the eagle's beak denoting the rank of the officer wearing the badge. Lieutenants and above wear the same badge as everyone else, but theirs is gold in color.

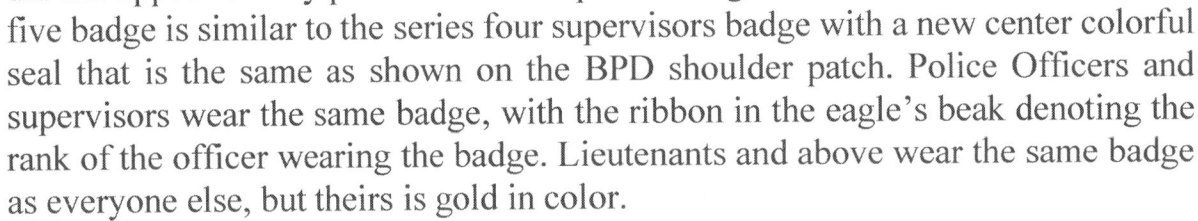

The 5th issue badge was designed by then-Major Robert DiStefano, since retired. He made a pair of drawings that were submitted to the committee for approval, only one of which was subsequently given to the manufacturer. Police Commissioner Donald D. Pomerleau was given two different designs by Major DiStefano – one was more of an Oval Badge, and the one that he [Maj DiStefano] himself personally liked better – a design he said was intended to be somewhat "different" than the classic *Eagle on Shield* design.

He has said that he purposely made the eagle's wings too high in proportion on that badge, and squared off, sort of boxy, because he wanted the committee to choose the larger oval – but he lost that battle. Police Commissioner Pomerleau liked the more traditional *Eagle on a Shield* design, and that's how "we lost a really nice looking, more modern badge," according to DiStefano. However, he says the chosen design has "grown on him."

5 April - 2013

Today in Baltimore Police History a retroactive *Citation of Valor* program was approved by Commissioner Anthony Batts, who listened to the concept conceived and submitted by my wife, Mrs. Patricia Driscoll. The Maryland "**Adopt-a-Cop**" program, doing business as **D.A.L.E.** – Disabled American Law Enforcement – was intended to allow officers who were permanently disabled in the line of duty a chance to apply for the department's *Citation of Valor* commendation. Commissioner Batts approved of the idea, which is coordinated by Mrs. Driscoll's Adopt a Cop (D.A.L.E.) program. Applications for the *Citation of Valor* commendation can be submitted to her either by the officer, another officer with information on the case, or the officer's family. Mrs. Driscoll began working on this program back in 2004, and after many attempts, and a lot of hard work; she finally got her program approved. To date (at the time of this writing) twelve officers' names have been submitted and all have been awarded – a listing of the names can be found on the BPD History site under the *Citation of Valor* link.

Mrs. Driscoll is thankful to Commissioner Batts, Sgt Stephanie Lansey, Officer Robert Brown and several others for their help on this project. Anyone wishing to submit an officer for this award should contact her through either the Kenny@BaltimoreCityPoliceHistory.com e-mail address, or at her e-mail address at Patty@BaltimoreCityPoliceHistory.com

6 April - 1968

Today in Baltimore Police history was a black day for the city of Baltimore. It was the start of the Baltimore Riots.

In reaction to the assassination/murder of Dr. Martin Luther King in Memphis, Tennessee, on 4 April, 1968, rioting broke out in 125 cities across the country. In Baltimore, Maryland however, the trouble didn't start until two days later, on this Saturday in April, 1968. When rioting did break out the Governor of Maryland, Spiro T. Agnew, called out thousands of National Guard troops, and 500 Maryland State Police to help quell the disturbance. When it was determined that the state forces could not control the riot, Agnew requested Federal troops from President Lyndon B. Johnson.

By Sunday evening, 7 April, 5,000 paratroopers, combat engineers, and

artillerymen from the XVIII Airborne Corps in Fort Bragg, North Carolina, specially trained in riot control tactics – including sniper school – were on the streets of Baltimore with fixed bayonets, and equipped with chemical (CS) disperser backpacks. Two days later, they were joined by a Light Infantry Brigade from Fort Benning, Georgia. With all the police and troops on the streets, things began to calm down. The FBI reported that H. Rap Brown was in Baltimore driving a Ford Mustang with Broward County, Florida tags, and was assembling large groups of angry protesters and agitating them to escalate the rioting. In several instances, these disturbances were rapidly quelled through the skillful use of bayonets and chemical dispersers by the XVIII Airborne units. That unit did not fire a single round of ammunition and arrested more than 3,000 detainees, who were identified, tagged with ID bracelets, and delivered in cattle trucks to the Baltimore police precincts.

By the time the riot was over, 6 people would be dead, 700 injured, 4,500 arrested and over a thousand fires set. More than a thousand businesses had been looted or burned, many of which never reopened. Total property damage was estimated at 13.5 million in 1968 dollars.

One of the major outcomes of the riot was the attention Spiro Agnew received when he criticized local black leaders for not doing enough to help stop the disturbance. While this angered blacks and white liberals, it caught the attention of Richard Nixon who was looking for someone on his ticket who could counter George Wallace's American Independent Party third party campaign. Agnew became Nixon's Vice Presidential running mate in 1968.

For additional information and photos, visit our Baltimore Police History Site.

6 April - 1973

On this day in Baltimore Police history we lost our brother Patrolman **Norman F. Buchman** of the Northwest District to gunfire. Officer Buchman, 24, was slain on a Friday as he investigated the man now charged with his murder, Sean Garland, 23.

The Monday before he shot and killed Officer Buchman, Garland had been arrested for a marijuana violation. A check of police department records revealed that Garland was driving the same car when arrested last Monday as he was driving when he was pursued by officers before the fatal shooting Friday afternoon.

Garland's older Brother, Elvin Garland alleged that Officer Buchman had "picked up" his brother three times recently, taking him to the northwest police station each time for narcotics violations.

Police officials said that they could confirm only one recent marijuana arrest, and that they could not find any information to support Elvin Garland's allegation that his brother had recently been arrested or taken to the station three times by the Officer Buchman. Records did indicate that the prior to arrest on Monday he had been arrested 27 times since 1968. His record included charges ranging from disorderly conduct to assault by shooting with intent to murder. According to police records, nine of the 27 cases resulted in convictions. In 1969, he was arrested, charged and convicted of assault on a police officer, for which he received a suspended sentence of 18 month. Police officials refused to locate or turn over reports in that case. At the time a spokesman said they will examine the case in the future and turn records over then. That has not yet happened.

Police said Officer Buchman was apparently making a routine "ownership check" when he attempted to stop the 1970 Lincoln Continental that Garland was operating on Friday. Police said that Officer Buchman notified communications that he was in pursuit of a vehicle when moments later, officers in the area heard gunshots, which led them to Officer Buchman, who was found shot in the head, lying on the sidewalk in the 2500 block Quantico Avenue, in the Park Heights-Pimlico area of the city. Suspect Sean Garland was arrested at the scene, police said, and the Lincoln he had been driving four days earlier was determined to be the car Officer Buchman had apparently been chasing. An autopsy report released the day after the murder indicated that Officer Buchman had been shot in the head six times with his own revolver; twice in the front of his head and four times in the back of his head. He was found lying face down on the sidewalk.

Police officials conceded yesterday that the reason Patrolman Buchman had attempted to stop the car is unknown. "We don't know why he stopped it," said police spokesman Dennis Hill. "I don't know what was in his mind." Hill said one theory was that police were investigating a group of people, including Garland, who were allegedly "switching driver's licenses," and then carrying false identification for "various activities." Hill did not elaborate.

Elvin Garland said that Patrolman Buchman had arrested his brother the prior Monday in the 4400 block Park Heights Avenue, several blocks from the Friday shooting, for an "unpaid" traffic ticket. Police records showed that he was indeed

arrested on that Monday and charged with a minor narcotics offense. A search of the Lincoln that day uncovered a small amount of suspected marijuana in the ashtray and a suspected marijuana cigarette elsewhere in the vehicle.

After that arrest, Garland was released on a $500 bail after paying a bondsman 10% of the bond amount. The brother claimed he saw Patrolman Buchman searching the car and when he approached." Elvin Garland said, his mother prevented his being arrested when she "grabbed me by the back of my neck and put me in her car." The murder of Officer Garland occurred almost in front of the home of Mr. Garland's mother, Dorothy L Garland, who claimed that Friday police "arrested" her son. Ms. Garland said her son had just been released from jail, and that he was in and out of jail frequently because of harassment. (it had nothing to do with the crimes he had committed - in fact, if police would ignore the crime he would've gone to jail at all).

Patrolman Buchman was eulogized at his funeral by his district commander, Captain Ted Weintraub, who said that Officer Buchman was, "A kid that didn't just do his job, but that he cared. He became involved in the community in a helpful and positive way." The Captain went on to say, "rather than just chastise the kids, he [Buchman] tried to work with them...To follow-up on their cases. He made it his business to go back and say, 'Hey, how are you doing? Staying out of trouble?'" Captain Weintraub added that Officer Buchman was a former army combat photographer who was wounded in Vietnam, and that he was a good officer who became involved in his cases "on a human basis."

The captain was bitter over reports that Garland had only a "minor" police record. He noted Garland's conviction for assaulting a police officer in 1969, as well as his eight other convictions (and 18 other arrests with no disposition) within a five year span. "Look at the crimes," he said, indicating that the punishment for Garland's nine convictions were "garbage. The most time he ever got was 30 days for filing a false report to the police department."

Officer Buchman was survived by his wife, a two year old daughter, his mother, a sister, two brothers and a stepbrother.

We his brothers and sisters of the Baltimore Police Department will not let him be forgotten – RIP Officer Norman F. Buchman, and God bless you for your service, which honored the City of Baltimore, and the Baltimore Police Department.

<u>Note</u>: Shortly after Officer Buchman's funeral, city comptroller Hyman Pressman

said he had ordered his "crime commission" to investigate the slaying of Officer Buchman to determine whether the leniency of the courts was in any way responsible for Buchman's death. "I want to know all the circumstances behind the non-prosecution of Garland on the charge of assault with intent to murder, and the reason for the mere fines given in various other charges involving assaults and other crimes."

"I want to know whether anyone who should have been behind bars was out on the streets free to shoot a policeman" Mr. Pressman said. The chairman of the comptroller's self-appointed committee is weighing pulling in a former deputy police commissioner, Mr. Pressman said.

We his brothers and sisters of the Baltimore Police Department will not let him be forgotten – RIP Officer Norman F. Buchman and God Bless - For your service honored the City of Baltimore, and the Baltimore Police Department"

From newspaper reports: Contempt Bid Made in Probe of Police Killing

William H. Murphy, Jr., a Baltimore attorney, yesterday was given until May 4 to show-cause why he should not be adjudged in contempt of the grand jury for allegedly preventing four witnesses from appearing before that jury in a case involving the fatal shooting of a policeman. The contempt citation was sought by Robert Veith, grand jury foreman, in a petition that accused Mr. Murphy of causing "interference with the grand jury process and proceedings and with the due administration of justice." Judge Marshall A. Levin signed the order giving the attorney until May 4 to respond to the allegations, and assigned the case for a hearing before Judge William J. O'Donnell in Criminal Court. Continuing investigation the actions alleged in the petition occurred in the ongoing investigation of the shooting of Patrolman Norman Buchman, 24, on April 6, which ultimately resulted in the April 9 indictment for murder of Michael Sean Garland, 23, of the 4900 block Queensberry Avenue.

The Grand jury alleged that on 9 April, it issued subpoenas for the personal appearance of four witnesses the next day. These four were identified as Dorothy Garland, mother of the accused; Beverly Garland, his sister-in-law; Nancy Dorsey, a girl friend of the accused and James Hughes, a friend of the accused.

The petition alleged "that after each had been served with the summons as aforesaid, they all failed to appear as required." However on April 11th the four were questioned by the Grand Jury concerning their failure to appear on the 10th

and each of the charged gave the same answer. The jurors said were told that all four of the witnesses went to Billy Murphy's office at approx. 9:30 am on the 10th of April where they handed their subpoenas to Billy Murphy at his request, and were told by him to, "wait here!" and then he left and did not return, until after the Grand Jury had adjourned for the day. Each witness was interviewed separately and each gave a similar account as to what Billy Murphy said and what he did.

The petition charged that Billy Murphy the son of a District Court Judge "Did not disclose the whereabouts of said witnesses to anyone connected with the case before the grand jury until after the grand jury had adjourned for the day!"

The Jury panel said it learned that on 10 April Mr. Murphy "had statements taken from said witnesses concerning their knowledge in the matter of a case pending before them and about which they were to testify."

Further it was charged that on April, 11th before the appearance of the witnesses to the grand jury Billy Murphy entered into an attorney client relationship with each of the witnesses in connection with their anticipated appearances before the grand jury, at least two by his own solicitation. There were no newspaper reports of the disposition of the case against Mr. Murphy.

7 April - 1962

On this day in Baltimore Police History, 1962 we lost our brother Police Officer **Henry Smith Jr**. to gunfire

<u>From Baltimore newspapers</u>, dated 8 April, 1962

Two Guarded in Officer Slaying Case – Wounded Men Hospital as Police Probe Street Shooting

Two wounded men remained under guard at University Hospital yesterday as Police investigated the murder of then off-duty Central District Officer Henry Smith.

The slain officer, 35 year old Officer Henry Smith, Jr. was the father of five and a five year veteran of the force. He was shot to death early on this date outside a tavern in the 700 block West Lexington Street. Police said bullets extracted from the officer and the two wounded men will be sent to the crime lab for ballistics examination.

The service weapons of Officer Smith and the two officers who came to his aid have also been sent to the laboratory for comparison according to police officials. Police believe Officer Smith may have been slain with his own weapon. His holster was empty and his revolver was found later in an areaway next to 702 West Fayette Street.

Plainclothes and uniformed officers canvased the area throughout the day seeking possible witnesses to the slaying which occurred shortly before 2 am. Police said they have not been able to question the wounded men. One was a 30 year old resident of the 500 Blk. North Freemont Ave. He is listed in serious condition with gunshot wounds. The second subject, 39, who lives in the 200 Blk. of North Freemont Avenue, was shot five times and was listed in satisfactory condition, the hospital said.

Officer James Thompson of the Western District said he was a block away when he heard gunfire and upon investigation found the mortally wounded Officer Smith on the sidewalk.

Evidence at the scene included a stack of bills and a pair of dice, which led police to theorize, the off-duty Officer Smith came upon a dice game outside the saloon and was shot to death when he went to break it up.

<u>*Newspaper Follow-up Story*</u> *- On 10 April 1962, Police had not found the gun used to kill their brother officer - Officer Henry Smith Jr. They had at first felt he may have been killed with his own departmentally issued handgun, as his gun had been found after the shooting in the 700 Blk. of West Fayette Street, loaded with six empty shell casings. Another officer had witnessed the two men standing over Patrolman Smith apparently emptying a gun into his body. That officer emptied his revolver into the two men.*

We his brothers and sisters of the Baltimore Police Department will not let him be forgotten – RIP Officer Henry Smith and God Bless - Your service honored the City of Baltimore, and the Baltimore Police Department.

7 April - 1994 - SCAN

SCAN (Scientific Content ANalysis) was introduced to the Central District's Major Crime Unit. SCAN is a Linguistic Polygraph technique that at the time was so new the department refused to pay for the training received by Detective Kenny Driscoll.

Within a few years Detective Driscoll had demonstrated the technique to different units throughout the department and used it to analyse statements in just about every unit or division within the department; everything from Homicide, to Sex Offence, to Robbery, to Missing Persons to Theft units. He was soon analysing statements not just within the department, but also for the State's Attorney's Office and various outside agencies. Before leaving department in 2001, for a surgery due to a LOD injury Detective Driscoll was asked to teach his introductory course to Baltimore's Homicide Unit.

The course was authorized by Avinoam Sapir, from LSI, the company for which Avinoam Sapir developed and refined Statement Analysis, and because Det. Driscoll took it so seriously and made several observations that had not yet been discovered, Avinoam called him a Guru on the subject. A technique he called *"Point of Perspective"* - *"Here vs. There"* was just one of Kenny's many observations that were eventually included in LSI's training after Detective Driscoll brought it to Mr. Sapir's attention. Detective Driscoll still uses the technique, and practices reading statements even though he has been retired for more than 12 years.

One of the more well known cases he was involved in was the Laci Peterson case, about which he contacted the Modesto, California Police to offer his assistance providing observations on Scott Peterson's words.

These observations came within five days of Laci's going missing. Based on a verbal statement Peterson gave to the local media about his wife's disappearance, Detective Driscoll determined Laci was dead, and not missing as Peterson was reporting. To Detective Driscoll the conclusion was pretty easy; if Scott Peterson knew Laci was dead, when everyone else only suspected she was missing, then he must have killed her.

At the time the Modesto, California Police detectives decided it was too early to file charges, saying they didn't want to accuse him of anything too early. But within a year they asked Retired Detective Driscoll for a complete write up of his observations. Detective Driscoll was able to tell them what room she was killed in, and what time she was killed, all based on Scott Peterson's video recorded words. Within a year Laci's body was recovered, and Scott Peterson was later arrested, tried and convicted for her murder.

Other cases he assisted with included Haleigh Cummings, in which police were told to look more closely at the girlfriend A few years later, it was determined the girl was indeed taken from the girlfriend over money she may have owed them for drugs. The technique is very strong in the right hands, and has been used to solve many cases throughout this country and internationally.

16 April - 1976

On this day in Baltimore Police History we lost our brother Police **Officer Jimmy Dale Holcomb** to gunfire on Good Friday near the intersection of Lombard and Carey Streets in west Baltimore. As shots rang out from a high-powered rifle it was determined that a sniper was firing rounds out onto the street from inside a 3rd floor apartment of 1303 West Lombard Street. Responding to the sniper call were units from several districts, including the Southern, Southwest, Western and Tactical sections.

Officer Halcomb, 31, was assigned to the Operations Unit of the Western District and was one of the first to arrive on the scene. On arrival he sought cover behind his car as he surveyed the scene looking for the sniper. As Officer Halcomb crouched behind his car, the sniper fired a single round from a third floor window which penetrated the automobile Officer Halcomb was using for cover, striking him. Mortally wounded, Officer Halcomb lost consciousness immediately and unfortunately never regained it, dying on the scene from his injuries before he could be extricated and taken to a hospital.

Throughout the forty-five minute incident, the deranged suspect would shoot several more responding police officers and a nearby civilian. Among them were twenty-five year old Officer James A. Brennan of the Western District as he crouched behind a van a few feet south on Carey Street. He went down severely wounded. Officer Roland W. Miller, 23 of the Western District, sustained a minor wound to his left arm.

Officers Neal C. Splain, 28, Calvin R. Mencken, 33, and Arthur E. Kennell, Jr., 27, all of the Southern District, were hit by a shotgun blast that came from the rear of the building. A civilian was also wounded. It took nearly 45 minutes for the situation to be resolved. The suspect, an 18 year old male was using not only a high-powered rifle, but also armour piercing ammunition, which flew through police vehicles like a hot knife through butter. The suspect eventually surrendered to officers without incident after telephoning his intentions to the Communications Division of the Department.

Officer Halcomb had served with the Baltimore Police Department for 8 years at the time of his death. He was survived by his expectant wife and two daughters. The suspect, who won't be named here, was convicted of first degree murder and a number of other related charges and sentenced to life plus 60 years in prison on July 1, 1977.

It has been 38 years since this nightmare began - Taking our brother Jimmy Halcomb, and while he is gone he will never be forgotten by us, his brothers and sisters of the Baltimore Police Department. RIP and God bless Jimmy, you are truly missed

17 April - 1957

On this date, Police Commissioner Hepbron put into place his plan to use **K-9 dogs** in a variety of roles in Baltimore City law enforcement by appearing before the Mayor and City Council and testifying on behalf of the idea, presenting the highly positive results from a several month's long experiment. As a result, appropriations were made through the Board of Estimates that resulted in the new K-9 Unit becoming a permanent part of the Baltimore City Police.

Commissioner Hepbron had first become interested in the idea based on reading a local newspaper article written December 11, 1956, by Martin Millspaugh, pertaining to Scotland Yard's use of police dogs in London. Intrigued by the idea, he communicated back and forth with officials from Scotland Yard about how they were using their dog/officer teams, and he became convinced the idea had merit and great potential. Despite a lack of specific funding and a tight budget, within a week, according to a Morning Sun report on December 17, he had created a small unit with the purpose of putting together two such teams to be used in Baltimore on an experimental basis.

The next day, on December 18, 1956, two dogs (Turk & Major Gruntz) that had had previous training were offered to the Baltimore City Police Department and, with two officers (Thomas McGinn and Irvan Marders) who had previous experience training dogs, the program was put into effect on an "experimental basis." By the middle of January 1957, fourteen dogs had been acquired as potential candidates and fourteen men were selected and assigned to the K-9 Corps. These men were chosen because of a questionnaire that was sent to all members of the department asking for volunteers. These men and dogs were trained daily until April

1, 1957. During that time, they worked the streets on Friday and Saturday nights, working the areas where crime was most prevalent.

18 April - 1915

On this day in Baltimore Police History we lost our brother **Patrolman George C. Sauer** to gunfire.

Patrolman George C. Sauer, of the Eastern District, was shot in the stomach by gunmen yesterday morning, following a running battle between the gunmen and a gang from Highlandtown, in which more than a dozen shots were fired. Officer Sauer was unconscious for eight hours, and when revived he was found to be too weak to allow a deposition to be taken.

Three hours after the encounter three men had been rounded up on the charge of shooting Officer Sauer, and a confession was obtained from one of them that he was the shooter, and specifically that he shot Officer Sauer.

The prisoners were:

- David Bender, alias Daniel Martell, alias Kid Bender, 22 years old, 344 S. 3rd St., New York.
- James Miller, alias Slim, alias Harry Martin, 23 years old, 1722 N. 8th St., Philadelphia
- Joseph Grose, 25 years old, 2543 Jessop St., Philadelphia.

Newspaper Report at the time: *Bender Admits Shooting*
Bender and Miller are directly charged with the shooting. Grose is held as a state's witness. Bender admitted shooting the patrolman. He said he fired at Sauer, thinking he was one of the gang from Highlandtown which was chasing them.

Within 30 minutes after Bender and Miller were arraigned on the shooting charge, they were identified by Charles M. Budd, 1314 N. Broadway, as the pair who held him up near his home early Thursday morning, as told exclusively in the Sunpaper yesterday. A watch bearing the initials "C. M. B." Led to the summoning of Budd to the station. The watch was found in their room at O'Hara's hotel, N. Liberty St. Bender readily admitted he and Miller held up Mr. Budd.

Sauer was wounded soon after he had gone on duty, at 4 am He was at Baltimore

Street and Milton Avenue when he heard shots beyond the east end of Patterson Park. Sauer hailed a passing taxicab, which had just come from Highlandtown, and ordered the chauffeur to take him to the scene.

He stood on the running board as the auto sped East, and at Decker Avenue he saw three men run to the corner.

The men fled as the taxi stopped, and Sauer leaped from the running board in pursuit. They turned into a small alley running east and west from Decker Avenue, and as Sauer ran after them two of the three swung around in their steps and fired. Three shots were fired.

One of the balls struck Sauer in the stomach, but did not hold him, for he ran forward about 8 feet and seized one of the men. It was only then that he realize he had been shot and, crying for assistance, he pressed down on his prisoner and bore him to the ground, with his knee jammed on the man's chest. The taxi chauffeur, Larry Purcell, 204 North Pine St. ran to his aid.

<u>Chauffeur Helps Sauer</u>

"Oh, I'm shot! I'm shot; hold him!" shouted Sauer. And Purcell did.

Joseph Jasckoliski, a park patrolman, ran from his home to Sauer's side, but when he saw Purcell helping hold the prisoner he started after the fleeing pair. They disappeared around the corner of the second alley, and Jasckoliski emptied his pistol to attract other policeman.

Detective Lawrence King, of headquarters, ran from his home nearby a moment later, and also Frank Link a former wrestler, 20 North Decker Ave. They hurried to Sauer, and the policeman was placed in Purcell's taxi and taken to St. Joseph hospital.

A report of the shooting of Sauer was telephoned to Detective's headquarters, thence to all the stations, and detectives Hogan and Kahler went to Highlandtown to pick up the lines of the case. They found the Eastern neighborhood for a mile around aroused by the shooting, and there were wild stories of a running gunfight in Highlandtown that preceded Sauer's wounding and drew him to the scene.

This brought them to a saloon at Eighth Street and Lombard Street in Highlandtown, where they learned that three men had been ejected from the place about 20 minutes before Sauer was shot. Descriptions were obtained, one of which tallied with the man captured by Sauer. This was Grose.

These descriptions were wired around the city to the entire force, and within two hours Sergeants Wortman and Kelly and patrolman Sedicum of the Western district had arrested Bender and Miller in their room at the O'Hara hotel.

The pair were furious over their arrest, and expressed their regret that they hadn't finished "the other guy," Sauer.

They told the sergeant that he was lucky they had not seen him first when the detectives approached their room. Two loaded pistols were found under the pillows of Bender and Miller's bed and when the two were about to be taken from the patrol to the station a black mask was found on the patrol floor, where one of the pair had dropped it.

Met Grose in City

In effect, Bender's statement was that he and Miller met Grose at the Raleigh Hotel at about 8 o'clock Thursday night. Grose was in town to see the show of Thurston, the magician. They spent the evening together in the city until about 1 AM when they went to "Scotty" Pugh's saloon, 1 South 8th Street, Highlandtown.

Shortly after 3 o'clock they left Pugh's and went to the club next door, where an altercation arose between them and the club employees, and they were hustled out into the street. Bender said a mob of nearly 20 men followed them, and a volley of bricks and bottles were hurled at them.

Benny Franklin, proprietor of the club, said the three came into the place sometime before 4 o'clock and ordered drinks.

"I can't give you any drinks," said the waiter, "you're under age." Bender, while heavy-set, has an extremely youthful face.

"What's that?" cried Bender. "Do you know who I am? I'm 'Kid Bender."

"Well, you can't have any drinks, the boss says," replied the waiter.

"Well, tell your boss to bite his neck," cried Bender. "Tell him I'll give him one of these pills." At which point, "Bender pulled out a .38 caliber revolver" said Franklin, "and shoved it under my waiter's nose. A couple of the men in the bar came up just then and grabbed this Bender and the others and threw them down the steps."

Stolen Watch in Room

Bender and Miller declared to the police that they had come in from Philadelphia

"to look things over on a chance." A search of the room where they were arrested resulted in the finding of Mr. Budd's watch, and later information was obtained that the two had police records. Twenty-two additional cartridges were also found in the room. Bender, known to the Philadelphia police as a pickpocket, served time for highway robbery there, while Miller served time for shoplifting.

Patrolman Sauer was 55 years old. He had been on the police force since 1898 and bears an excellent reputation. He has a wife and four children – three daughters and a son.

<u>Hope for Policeman - Newspaper Article</u>; Apr 11, 1915

Bender, one of the Men Held for Shooting Patrolman Sauer, had been paroled in Baltimore and his parole had just expired.

Patrolman George C. Sauer, of the Eastern district, who was shot in the stomach by gunmen early Friday morning in the Eastern city limits, was reported yesterday to be holding his own at St. Joseph's hospital.

Dr. Frank C Kirby, of the hospital staff, has expressed the opinion that he may be able to save his life.

One Sauer regained consciousness Friday afternoon an effort was made by Capt. Zellers, of Eastern district, to have Dr. Kirby grant permission to allow a deposition to be gotten from the wounded patrolman, and also to have Sauer identify Kid Bender and Slim Miller, the gunmen. The surgeon said it would be perilous. "It would likely excite Sauer," said Dr. Kirby.

<u>Promises Statement Later</u>

Dr. Kirby however promised that the Capt. that if Sauer should lose strength again and reached the point where he was doomed he would immediately notify the police that the necessary deposition and identification could be obtained

Bender and Miller were put through a strenuous gruelling at the Eastern district police station late Friday night by state's attorney Broening in a move to ascertain the real records of the two. One result was the identification of Bender as a paroled prisoner from Judge Elliott's court. The parole expired last month. The charge was larceny.

The two men showed the result of their growing and their increasing anxiety yesterday when they were taken to headquarters to be "mugged" and Bertillonized. Bender had lost something in his jauntiness. Which amazed everyone Friday.

Sends for His Father

This jauntiness apparently remained with the boy till the state's attorneys' siege began, and was evidenced in a telegram he sent to his mother. The message read:

"Am in trouble; have pop come on as soon as possible. 2nd degree. But don't worry. Here's a kiss."

Pending the outcome of patrolman Sauer's wound, Miller and Bender were arraigned before justice Smith on the charge of attacking and holding up Charles M. Budd, 1314 N. Broadway, Thursday morning, a day previous to the shooting. Budd was seized by the throat by Bender and struck in the face while the other seized his watch and chain and diamond stickpin.

Both Held on $5000 Bail

Bender admitted the charge and the magistrate held each man on $5000 bail on that count. Both men will be kept in jail without bail on the charge of suiting patrolman Sauer a tentative hearing has come granola mortality get that been set for April 23

Patrolman Sauer Sinking - Newspaper Article - Apr 12, 1915; pg. 12

Patrolman George C. Sauer, of the Eastern district, who was shot by gunmen following a running street fight between the gunmen and a Highlandtown gang early Friday morning, developed an infection and suffered a severe vomiting spell last night and the surgeons feared that he would not live through the night. An effort was made to have the two gunmen, "Kid" Bender and "Slim" Miller, released from jail temporarily that they might be taken before Sauer for identification, but it was found impossible to get the prisoners before this morning. Sauer passed a good night Saturday and seemed to have gained slightly in strength during the day. Detective C. A. Kahler received a telephone message from Robert D. Cameron chief of detectives of Philadelphia, that Bender is not only wanted there for shooting a man in a poolroom brawl but that he attacked a policeman who interfered, taking from him his pistol after a stiff fight. It is believed that one of the pistols that Bender and his alleged pals used here is that taken from the Philadelphia policeman. Arthur Keller, 21 years old is the Philadelphian Bender is alleged to have shot through the mouth during the brawl in the poolroom. He is in a serious condition in a hospital.

Marshal Carter said he did not expect to deliver Bender to the Philadelphia authorities on warrants that they will bring here today for him on charging that he shot Keller and pocketed the policeman's pistol. "We have obtained a confession from Bender that it was he who fired the shot that wounded Patrolman Sauer and we will try him here as soon as the officer is able to leave the hospital and appear in court against him. It will be the same with the other two men under arrest. We will try them here unless we find more serious charges are being held against them in other cities."

<u>Gunman's Shot Fatal - Newspaper Article</u> - Apr 19, 1915

Patrolman George C. Sauer, of the Eastern district, shot by a gunman on 9 April, died last night at St. Joseph's Hospital.

His death came suddenly. A rapid turn for the worse was noticed about 8 o'clock and a hurry call was sent to the police. Captain Zellers, with Sergeant Roche and Justice Smith, hurried to the hospital to obtain Sauer's deposition, but the patrolman had become unconscious in the meantime. He died at 9.30 - Mrs. Sauer and Sauer's four children were with their father when he expired. One of the daughters collapsed and was carried from the room. Sauer had a previous sinking "spell last Tuesday and the gunmen, "Kid" Bender and "Slim" Miller, of New York City, together with the companion of the gunmen, David Grose, New York where hurried to Sauer's bedside for identification. He refused, however to make a dying deposition", declaring stoutly and persistently that he would recover, and it was unnecessary for him to make such a statement.

<u>Pension for Policeman's Widow - Newspaper Article</u> - Apr 30, 1915

The Police Board on Wednesday awarded a pension of $10 a week to the wife of Patrolman George C. Sauer, of the Eastern district, who was shot and killed by an out-of-town gunman. On 9 April 1914, Sauer died from the wound at St. Joseph's Hospital. It was on the recommendation of Deputy Marshal Samuel W. House that the pension was awarded for life to the patrolman's Widow.

<u>Two Slayers Sentenced - Newspaper Article</u> - Oct 8, 1915

Men who killed patrolman Sauer confined for 18 years. Bender's mother collapses as he and McQuaid are led away to lock up.

David Bender and James McQuaid, whose correct name is said to be Miller, charged with the murder of patrolman George C Sauer, who was shot early on the morning of 9 April 1915, were both convicted of murder in the 2nd degree. They were each sentenced to 18 years in the penitentiary, the maximum penalty. The

verdict was rendered and the sentences imposed by Judge Bond, before whom the case was tried this week without a jury.

"For a while," the judge said in rendering the verdict, "I was rather of the impression that this murder must be held one of 1st. I see the difficulty on this point with the state's attorney seems to experience. There is a margin of doubt which in my opinion saves the prisoner from a verdict of murder in the 1st, but it seems to be a very wide margin. With men of this age I'm especially relieved to find that the verdict of a lesser degree. I find each of the prisoners guilty of murder in the 2nd."

Harry B. Wolf, attorney for the defence, called the court's attention to the fact that his client had been in jail six months awaiting trial.

"I think," the judge replied, "This is a very sad case. Each prisoner will be sentenced to 18 years in the penitentiary."

Instantly there was excitement in the courtroom. As Bender and McQuaid were started toward the courtroom lockup, Bender exclaimed: "I want my case taken to the court of appeals." In reply, Judge Bond said he had a lawyer who could attend to that.

Bender's parents, who were in the courtroom, added to the excitement. Mrs. Bender began to scream, and continued her lamentations until taken outside. There she collapsed - but was revived and went away sobbing. In the lockup Bender raved and threatened, while McQuaid was silent. Bender was the only one of the two who testified. He said that Bender was his correct name. That he belonged in Brooklyn, New York and that he was just 18 years old. He is fat and chubby, with an exceptionally clear complexion and a bushy mass of black hair. McQuaid, or Miller, is about the same age as Bender, but is the opposite in appearance, being lean and lanky. Both have criminal records.

Denies Signing Confession

Bender denied that he signed a typed written confession that he fired the fatal shot. He also denied Sgt. Kelly's testimony. He said he and his companions were chased by a gang from Highlandtown, and that he fired at them when they fired at him. Denying that he saw patrolman Sauer, he said he only shot at the men who were shooting at him. Just 24 hours before the shooting Bender and his companion held up Charles Budd on Broadway and robbed him of a scarf pin and a watch.

Grose, who had been held as a witness for the state, was released when the other *two were sentenced.*

18 April - 1968

On this day in Baltimore Police History, 1968 we lost out brother, Detective **Richard F. Bosak** to gunfire.

From a Newspaper Article - 19 April 1968

A convicted drug user shot a homicide Detective killing him after the policeman wrestled him to the floor of a Eutaw street bar. The gunman died of a bullet wound in the head minutes after he killed the policeman. The convict had escaped Wednesday from a jail guard escorting him to City Hospital for treatment. The slain policeman, Detective Patrolman Richard F. Bosak, 40, was shot three times as he wrestled on the floor of the Golden Glow Restaurant in the Unit block North Eutaw Street. The convict, James V. Gallaird, 29, died minutes later, less than a half a block away after the slain policeman's partner had cornered him in the Hecht Company parking lot. A parking lot attendant said Gallaird shot himself.

Gallaird shot his way temporary to freedom Wednesday with a pistol slipped to him by a young woman who brushed by him and an armed guard as they were leaving City Hospital. The City Jail inmate fired several times at the pursuing guard and one bullet harmlessly pierced the guard's pants. Police said that yesterday shortly before 6 pm Patrolman Bosak and his partner in the Criminal Investigation Division's crimes against persons section went to the Golden Glow Restaurant to check out a tip that Galliard was to meet a friend there... As the policeman and the bar owner emerged from the kitchen, Galliard and his companion broke for the door... The policeman tackled Galliard. The detective and the convict fell heavily to the floor and continued struggling. Suddenly, shots rang out. The policeman slumped down dying on the floor of that restaurant.

Galliard freed himself, holding a long-nosed revolver in one hand and grabbing the Policeman's .38 caliber service revolver with the other, he would run less than a block where he was blocked into a parking lot with no exit. With no way out, Galliard turned the gun on himself taking what some might say was the easy way out.

We his brothers and sisters of the Baltimore Police Department will not let him be forgotten – RIP Detective Bosak, and God Bless - For your service honored the City of Baltimore, and the Baltimore Police Department

19 April - 1861

The most significant Civil War action in Baltimore took place during the Pratt Street riots on Friday, 19 April, 1861 which directly caused 17 known deaths, and at least 50 injuries and seven recorded arrests

Most of the fighting took place along President Street from near Harbor North, to Pratt Street along Pratt St., west to Light Street. The violent action lasted from about 11 am to 12:45 pm and mostly involved 220 New England Militiamen, some of whom carried and fired muskets, and a mob of Baltimore civilians reported to number anywhere between 250 and 1,000, a few of which fired pistols, but fought mainly by grappling, and or hurling paving stones.

Of the 700 or so officers and men of the 6th Massachusetts Infantry Regiment, a volunteer militia, who passed from the President Street Station to Camden Station on their way to Washington, D.C., four were killed and about 35 wounded. The dead soldiers, all of enlisted rank, were Addison O. Whitney, Luther C. Ladd, Charles A. Taylor, and Sumner H. Needham. The last named died with little resistance in a Baltimore Hospital about a week after the riots during a 19th Century style operation on his fractured skull.

Of the 700 unarmed Pennsylvania Militiamen and the 100 additional members of the sixth Massachusetts – including the Regiment Band – who arrived at the same time none made it through the mob around President Street Station on this journey but only one died of injuries sustained here. He was George Leisenring, who succumbed about a week later, after being returned to Philadelphia.

Many Baltimoreans were wounded, and 12 were killed – James Carr, William R. Clark, Robert W. Davis, Sebastian Gill, Patrick Griffiths, John McCann, John McMahon, Francis Maloney, William Maloney, Philip S. Miles, Michael Murphy, and William Reid.

Leading Baltimoreans were most outraged by the death of Mr. Davis, a 36-year-old dry goods merchant and semi-innocent bystander - he may have cheered for the Confederacy, but he did not join the fighting, and was shot by someone on the 6th Massachusetts train as it later left Camden Station. He cried, "I am killed!" as he fell. The next day a Baltimore coroner's jury decided that he had been ruthlessly murdered by one of the military. Mr. Davis's funeral was elaborate but his murderer, if that term is strictly accurate, was never named, charged, or prosecuted.

Two of the dead civilians, Patrick Griffiths and William Reid, were described as boys (which at the time might have meant that they were black, that they were adult males white or black with low wage jobs, or that they may have been very young males, probably poor whites – such was the language of the time). Patrick Griffith was employed on an Oyster's Sloop that was tied up near Pratt and Light Street. William Reid was employed by a Pratt Street establishment described only as "The Greenhouse" and was shot through the bowels while looking on from the business door.

The ages, addresses, occupations and specifically the circumstances of death of the other Baltimore casualties have apparently never been recorded, although those who fell in the Pratt Street riots turned out to be the first fatalities of a hostile action in the Civil War (no one was killed during another action which had ended four days earlier at Fort Sumter, South Carolina).

The most thorough contemporary accounts of the riots in Baltimore newspapers state that the police arrested "great numbers" afterward. Only seven were apparently ever named anywhere though – Mark Hagan and Andrew Eisenbreeht, charged with "assaulting an officer with a brick," Richard Brown and Patrick Collins for "throwing bricks creating a riot," William Reid for "severely injuring a man with a brick," J. Friedenwald for "assaulting an unknown man," and Lawrence T. Erwin, for "throwing a brick on Pratt Street." These seven constituted another Civil War first.

The troops from Massachusetts and Pennsylvania were responding to Abraham Lincoln's April 15 call for volunteers, and many Baltimoreans in slave-holding Maryland interpreted that to be an effort to recruit an army to invade such seceding "sister states" as Virginia. A Confederate Army recruitment office flourished at Marsh Market: a pro-secession mob of about 800 had roamed Charles Street on the night of 18 April, and more than one of the suspects had recently been flogged for daring to cheer the Republican President in public. So the Baltimoreans in the Pratt Street riots were as much pro-Southern as they were simply pro-Maryland and simply outraged by the so-called violation of State sovereignty by another state's Militia (An idea suggested in "Maryland! My Maryland!" the official Maryland state song that was inspired by and written shortly after the riots by a writer named Randall, a native Baltimore English teacher then in New Orleans)!

And so the seven Baltimoreans arrested were the first Civil War partisans of either side who suffered official legal action for their pains. Of them, only Lawrence T. Erwin was convicted and "held for sentence," so far as contemporary accounts, histories and memories revealed. His sentence, if any, is unrecorded.

One history of Baltimore Police Department explains that "it was useless to arrest men when not an officer could be spared to put them in jail." It seemed too, that although the department had been reorganized about a year earlier under Marshal George P. Kane to rid it of corrupt "Know Nothing" political elements, it had no patrol wagons in 1861. And since the main body of police detailed to maintain order during the militia's passage was either a half mile away at Camden Station or in route to the scene of the fighting during most of the combat, it is perhaps remarkable that as many as seven arrests were made.

Why the main body of police was at the end of the troop's projected route, instead of at its beginning, is still something of a mystery. The recollection of the riots that was published 19 years after the events by George William Brown, who had been Mayor of Baltimore in 1861, lays part of the blame on the management of the Pennsylvania, Wilmington & Baltimore (PW&B) railroad company's failure to answer marshal Kane's repeated telegrams that asked how many troops were in route to the President Street location. So when by 10:30 on the morning of April 19, the police could do nothing better than send their main body – "a strong force" – to the Camden Station.

Such action was proper, one infers from Mayor Brown's account, even though a large crowd had assembled at both stations as early as 9 AM and even though the secessionist flag – a circle of white stars on a field of blue – was displayed by the throng at the President Street station. Passengers to arrive from the north on the PW&B bound for Washington then customarily stayed on the cars at President Street station and the cars were then hauled one by one by four-horse teams to Camden station, where the passengers got off and boarded Baltimore and Ohio (B&O) trains to continue to the national capital. "As the change of cars occurred at this point," a Police Department history published in 1888 remarks, "it was here that the attack was feared."

But why at Camden station, to which the troops would have been pulled more than a mile through angry spectators who had already been criticizing Jefferson Davis, President of the new Confederacy, and cheering president Lincoln for an hour and a half?

Only the day before, a lesser riot (resulting in no deaths) began near the Bolton station when another troop of Pennsylvania Militiamen detrained in North Baltimore and was stoned by a mob as it marched south to board a train for Washington (it should be noted that the tracks of the different railroad companies did not meet anywhere in Baltimore at the time.) The police applied more but less effective protection for the first defenders while they were afoot in Baltimore on April 18. Why then did marshal Kane apparently reverse strategy on April 19 and decide that the 6th Massachusetts would be safe while on the cars as they were pulled from the President Street station to Camden station? Mayor Brown later decided (as he wrote in his memoirs of the riot, published in 1887) *"that the 6th Massachusetts would have been more imposing, and therefore safer, if they had marched as a body of 1,700 men from one station to the other."*

The logic of hindsight suggests that the main body of police should have met the train at President Street station and that adequate details of officers should have escorted each horse-drawn car of soldiers to Camden station. As it happened the first nine cars of the thirty-five-car troop train hauled Col. Jones and seven of his eleven Massachusetts companies off President Street, across Pratt Street and down Howard Street to Camden station with little, if any police escort – and still they made the trip without serious mishap. The crowd hissed but threw stones at only the last car, and Mayor Brown, who by this time had arrived to Camden station from his law office, thought that maybe the nine cars he saw were the lot of them.

The 10th car was halted at the Pratt Street bridge over Jones falls by a wagon load of sand that the mob dumped in its path, some anchors that seamen from nearby ships drew across the tracks, and a motley barricade of lumber and paving stones that were handy because the street was by chance under repair at that point.

Unable to pass, the 10th car returned to the President Street station, where the mob had swelled to about 2,000 and where some police arrived (from outlying districts, apparently not from the main body at Camden station) as the 220 or so soldiers detrained and lined up in single file. Their effort to March to Camden station in this unlikely formation was blocked by a knot of men flying the "Succession Flag" so they were reformed into double file, about faced, and marched in the opposite direction, (i.e. retreat) conceivably to be inspired to dive into the harbor and *swim* west to Light Street. The mob having savagely choked a Union sympathizer who tried to tear down the "Succession Flag", circled the soldiers and halted the de facto retreat. The troopers then fell in by platoons, four abreast, and with police help wedged a path north on President Street. The gang with the "Succession Flag" then marched ahead of them and savagely beat two or more union sympathizers who tried to tear down the banner, then ran along the militia ranks. Part of the crowd behind the 6th Massachusetts columns then began to throw stones, one of which felled a trooper named William Patch, who was then beaten with his own musket.

The four companies – C, D, I and L – then began either "to run" or march "at double quick," presumably on orders from one or all of their captains, who were named Follansbee, Hart, Pickering and Dike. Two more soldiers were knocked down at President and Styles streets – possibly by a flatiron or one of the "queer missiles" (meaning chamber pots) that were thrown by Baltimore women in the mob, according to the 1936 reminiscence of Aaron J. Fletcher, the last survivor of the Civil War 6th Massachusetts.

Mr. Fletcher's is the only direct account that even suggests that any women were involved in the riots. (A romantic story, written in 1865, alleges that a Baltimore prostitute named Manley saved the 6th Massachusetts Regiment Band by guiding them away from President Street station by back alleys – but most accounts state that the police protected the musicians) at about the time the troops turned the corner into Pratt Street – at any rate, someone fired the first shot.

E. W. Beatty of Baltimore fired that shot from the crowd, according to the opinion that seemed to be based on the reports of Confederate officers with whom he later served before he was killed in action. On the other hand, one of the 6th Massachusetts soldiers fired that first shot, according to contemporary newspaper accounts that attributed the information to a policeman identified only as "number 71." By that time Mayor Brown had heard that the mob had poured up Pratt Street and had hastened to the bridge, where he met then and joined them in their March at the head of the column as far back toward Camden station as Light Street.

Mayor Brown's account states that he slowed the soldiers pace (they also had to pick their way through the haphazard barricade at the bridge). Capt. Follansbee said: "We have been attacked without provocations" and that Mayor Brown replied "you must defend yourselves."

The troopers, of whom about 60 carried muskets, then began to fire in earnest – in volleys, according to the newspaper; over their shoulders as they ran and helter-skelter, according to Mayor Brown; definitely not in volleys, according to Captain Fletcher's recollection (although he was with Company E, which had passed safely through in one of the nine cars). The first Baltimorean hit (in the groin) was supposed to be Francis X. Ward.

A Unionist newspaper in Washington quoted Col. Jones the next day as saying that Mayor Brown had seized a musket and shot a man during the march. Mr. Brown wrote later that a boy had handed him a smoking musket which a soldier had dropped and that he had immediately handed it to a policeman, without firing at anyone.

The Mayor must have found the Pratt Street riots greatly embarrassing. Then 48 years old he had been elected in October, 1860, on the reform ticket dedicated to absolving Baltimore of its nickname "Mobtown" and he helped put down the Bank of Maryland riots in 1835. He believed in freeing the slaves gradually, but felt that slavery was allowed by the Constitution and that the South should be allowed to secede in peace.

He was early arrested by the federal military in September 1861 and imprisoned until November 1862. From 1872 until 1890, the year before his death, he served as chief judge of the supreme bench of Baltimore city. He was defeated in a campaign for mayor in 1885.

When Mayor Brown left the Massachusetts infantrymen, near Pratt and Light Street, most of the casualties had fallen, the fighting having been heaviest near South Street. The Baltimore dead and wounded were mostly bystanders, according to most Baltimore accounts, because the running soldiers allegedly fired to the front and sides and not at the hostile mob behind them which may have been as small as 250 men, according to the "Tercentenary History of Maryland."

A historian who took notable exception to the bystander-only version was J. Thomas Clark, author of the "Chronicles of Baltimore" which describes an "immense concourse of people" that to a man threw paving stones at the troopers from in front of them.

Before the column reached Charles Street, Marshal Kane and about 40 policemen finally arrived from Camden station and threw a cordon around the soldiers. "Halt men, or I'll shoot!" the Marshall is supposed to have cried as he and his men brandished revolvers. The mob halted.

At some point, Marshal Kane telegraphed friends to immediately recruit Virginia rifleman to defend Baltimore further from invasion by union militia. In June, after General Benjamin Butler "occupied" Baltimore with other Massachusetts troops, at which time Marshall Kane was arrested and imprisoned. Released in 1862, he went to Richmond apparently by informal agreement, and apparently served in the Confederacy during the war. He died at the age of 58 in 1878, seven months after he was elected Baltimore's Mayor.

The 6th Massachusetts had left Baltimore by 1 pm on April 19, 1861 – short of its Regimental Band, its dead and some of its wounded, who were cared for in Baltimore hospitals or temporarily buried in Greenmount Cemetery. Thereafter, their Regimental bandsmen, along with 1,000 unarmed Pennsylvania volunteers, were more effectively protected by the police from two attacks at President Street station by mobs which may have increased to 10,000 persons, according to Mr. Scarf's Chronicle.

The Pratt Street riots occurred on the anniversary of the revolutionary war battle of Lexington, a coincidence of which both northern and southern propagandists made note. Much of the city might protest that its sovereignty had been violated, the riots appeared to the North to be a pro-Confederate outrage, and it is not difficult to understand why the federal government soon decided to clamp down on the city.

Note: At the time of these incidents, Marshal George P. Kane was Baltimore's police Commissioner (called Marshall) and George W. Brown was the city's mayor.

Newspaper reports of the times; Mar 22, 1887; pg. 6

Interesting Historical Incidents that occurred during the Civil War:

The following extracts are from Judge Brown's book describing the events and concerning Baltimore prior to the opening of the war of secession. The first of interest is the supposed plot to assassinate President Abraham Lincoln, and his midnight ride in the streets through Baltimore in February 1861. Several other writings, some contradictory, are also presented in contrast to one another. It is up to the reader to determine which are the more accurate.

The Alleged Plot and the Midnight Ride

In February 1861 – when Abraham Lincoln was on his way to Washington to prepare for his inauguration as president of United States – an unfortunate incident occurred which was a sinister influence on the state of Maryland, and especially the city of Baltimore. Some persons, carried away no doubt by their own imaginations and perhaps in part stimulated by the temptations of getting up a sensation of the first class, succeeded in persuading Mr. Lincoln that a formidable conspiracy existed to assassinate him on his way through Maryland.

It was announced publicly that he was to come from Philadelphia, not by the usual route – through Wilmington – but by a circuitous journey through Harrisburg, and then by the Northern Central Railroad to Baltimore. Misled by this statement, I, as mayor of the city of Baltimore, accompanied by the police Commissioner [KANE] and supported by a strong force of police, was at the Camden Street station on Saturday morning, 3 February 1861, at 11:30 o'clock, the appointed time of arrival, ready to receive with due respect the incoming president. An open carriage was in waiting, in which I was to have the honor of escorting Mr. Lincoln through the city to the Washington station, and of sharing in any danger that he might encounter. Though it is hardly necessary to say, I apprehended none. When the train came in it appeared, to my great astonishment, that Mrs. Lincoln and her three sons had arrived safely and without hindrance or molestation of any kind, but that Mr. Lincoln could not be found. It was then announced that he had passed through the city incognito in the night train by the Philadelphia, Wilmington and Baltimore railroad, and did reach Washington at the usual hour in the morning. For the signaled deliverance from an imaginary peril, those who devised the ingenious plan were of course devoutly thankful, and they accordingly took to themselves no little amount of credit for its success.

Mr. Lincoln had later arrived in Baltimore at the time expected, and spoken a few words to the people who had gathered to hear him, expressing the kind feelings which were in his heart with the simple elegance of which he was so great a master. He could've not failed to make a very different impression from that with which he produced, not only by the tone of confidence and respect manifested toward the city of Baltimore by the plan pursued, but still more in the manner by which it was carried out. On such an occasion as this even trifles are of importance, and this incident was not a trifle. The emotional part of human nature is its strongest side, and soonest leads to action. It was so with the people of Baltimore. Fearful accounts of the conspiracy flew all over the country, creating a hostile feeling against the city, from which it afterward suffered. A single specimen of the news that spread will suffice. A dispatch from Harrisburg, Pennsylvania, to the New York Times, dated 23 February, 8 AM said: "Abraham Lincoln, the President-elect of the United States, is safe in the capable hands of the nation." Then, after describing the dreadful nature of the conspiracy, it added, "the list of names of the conspirators presented a most astonishing array of persons high in southern confidence, and some whose fame is not confined to this country alone."

Of course the list of names was never furnished, and the men in buccal vanished in the air. This is all the notice the matter would require, except for the extraordinary narrative contributed by Mr. Samuel M. Felton, at the time president of the Philadelphia, Wilmington and Baltimore Railroad Company, to the volume entitled "A History of Massachusetts in the Civil War," published in 1868. In 1861, Mr. Felton had made, as he supposed, a remarkable discovery of "the lead conspiracy to capture Washington and break up the government."

Soon afterwards, a philanthropist came to his office on a Saturday afternoon, stating that she had an important communication to make him personally, and then, with closed doors, and for more than an hour, she poured into his ear a thrilling tale, to which he listened tentatively. "The sum of all was (I quote the language of Mr. Felton) that there was then an extensive and organized conspiracy throughout the South to seize upon Washington, with its archives and records, and then declare the southern conspirators the de facto government of the states. The whole was to be a coup d'etat. At the same time, they were to cut off all modes of communication between Washington and the north, east or west, and thus prevent the transportation of troops to wrest the capital from the hands of the insurgents. Mr. Lincoln's inauguration was thus to be prevented, for his life was to fall a sacrifice to the attempt at inauguration. In fact, troops were then drilling on the lines of our railroad, and the Washington and Annapolis lines and other lines."

It was clear that the knowledge of the treasonable conspiracy of such vast proportions, which is already begun its operations, ought not to be confined solely to the keeping's of Mr. Felton and Miss Dix. Mr. P. N. Trist, an officer of the road, was accordingly admitted into the secret, and was dispatched in haste to Washington, to lay all the facts before Gen. Scott, the commander and chief. The general, however, would give no assurance except that he would do all he could to bring sufficient troops to Washington to make it secure. The matter stood in unsatisfactory condition for some time until a new rumor reached the ears of Mr. Felton.

A gentleman from Baltimore, he says, came out to Back River bridge, about 5 miles east of the city, and told the bridge keeper that he had information which had come to his knowledge of vital importance to the railroad, which he wished communicated to Mr. Felton. The nature of his communication was that a party was then organized in Baltimore to burn the bridge in case Mr. Lincoln came over the road, or in case an attempt was made to carry troops for the defense of Washington.

The party at that time had combustible materials prepared for the bridge, and were to disguise themselves as African Americans, and be at the bridge just for the train in which Mr. Lincoln traveled had arrived. The bridge was then to be burned, the train attacked and Mr. Lincoln to be put out of the way. The man appeared several times, always, it seemed, to the bridge keeper, and he always communicated new information about the conspirators, but he would never give his name nor place of abode, and both remain a mystery still. The chief of police in Baltimore, with the assurance that he was a perfectly reliable person, Marshal Kane was accordingly seen, but he scoffed the at idea that there was any such thing afoot as a conspiracy to burn the bridges and cut off Washington, and said he thoroughly investigated all matters and there was not the slightest foundation for such rumors. Mr. Felton was not satisfied, but he would have nothing more to do with Marshal Kane. Felton next sent for a celebrated detective in the west, whose name is not given, and through his chief and his subordinates, every nook and corner of the railroad and its vicinity was explored. They further reported that they had joined the society of conspirators in Baltimore and got into their secrets, and then the secret working of succession was laid bare, with all its midnight plotting and daily consulting. The conspiracy being thus proved to Mr. Felton satisfactory, he at once organized and armed a force of 200 men and scattered them along the line of the railroad between the Susquehanna near Baltimore, principally at the bridge. Strange to say, all that was accomplished by this formidable body was an enormous job of whitewashing."

The narrative proceeds: "these men were drilled secretly and regularly by drill masters, and were apparently employed in whitewashing the bridges, putting on some six or seven coats of whitewash saturated with salt and alum, to make the outside of the bridges as nearly fireproof as possible. This whitewashing, so extensive in its application, became (continues Mr. Felton) that days' wonder of the neighborhood." And well it might. After the lapse of 25 years, the wonder over this feat of strategy can hardly yet have ceased in that moral and peaceful neighborhood. However, fortunately for Mr. Felton's peace of mind, the program of Mr. Lincoln's journey was suddenly changed. He had selected a different route. He had decided to go to Harrisburg from Philadelphia, and thence by day to Baltimore over another rival railroad, known as the Northern Central. Then the chief detective discovered that the intention of the conspirators had suddenly turned to the Northern Central railroad. The mysterious unknown gentleman of Baltimore appeared again on the scene and confirmed this statement. He gave warning that

Mr. Lincoln would be waylaid and his life sacrificed on the railroad on which no whitewash had been used, and where there were no armed men to protect him.

Mr. Felton hurried to Philadelphia, and there in a hotel joined his chief detective, who was registered under a foreign name. Mr. Lincoln, cheered by the dense crowd, was at the moment passing through the streets of Philadelphia. A sub detective was sent to bring in Mr. Judd, who was in procession with Mr. Lincoln, and the emergencies admitted no delay. The eagerness of the sub detective to meet Mr. Judd was so great that he was three times arrested and carried out of the crowd by the police before he could finally reach Mr. Judd. The fourth succeeded and Mr. Judd was at last brought to the hotel, where he met both Mr. Felton and his chief detective. The narrative then proceeds in the words of Mr. Felton: "we lost no time in making known to him [Mr. Judd] all the facts which had come to our knowledge in reference to the conspiracy, and I most certainly advised that Mr. Lincoln should go to Washington privately in the sleeping car. Mr. Judd fully entered into the plan, and said he would urge Mr. Lincoln to adopt it. On his communicating with Mr. Lincoln after the services of the evening were over, he [Mr. Lincoln] answered that he had engaged to go to Harrisburg to speak the next day, and that he would not break his engagement, even in the face of such a peril, but that after he had fulfilled his engagement he would follow such advice as we might give him in reference to his journey to Washington."

Mr. Lincoln accordingly went to Harrisburg the next day and made an address. After that, the arrangements for the journey were made with the profoundest mystery. It was given out that he was to go to Govenor Curtin's house for the night, but he was, instead, conducted to a point about 2 miles out of Harrisburg, where he waited to take him to Philadelphia. The telegraph lines east, west, north and south of Harrisburg were quiet and said that new messages as to his movement could be sent in any direction. All this caused a contention, and the night train from Philadelphia to Baltimore had to be held back until the arrival of Mr. Lincoln at the former place. If, however, the delay proved to be considerable, when Mr. Lincoln reached Baltimore the connecting train to Washington might leave without him. But Mr. Felton was equal to the occasion. He devised a plan that was communicated to only those on the railroad. A messenger was sent to Baltimore to say to the officials of the Washington railroad that a very important package must be delivered in Washington early in the morning, and requested them to wait for the night train from Philadelphia. To give color to this statement, a package of old railroad reports done up with great care, and with a large seal attached, marked

by Mr. Felton "very important," was sent in the train which carried Mr. Lincoln on his famous night ride from Philadelphia to Maryland and Baltimore. The only remarkable incident of the journey was the mysterious behavior of the few officials who were trusted with this crucial secret.

I do not know how others may be affected by this narrative, but I confess now a feeling of indignation that Mr. Lincoln, who was no coward, but proved himself on many an occasion to be a brave man, was thus prevented from carrying out his original intention of journeying to Baltimore in the light of day in a company with his wife and children, relying, as he always did, on the honor and manhood of the American people. It is true we have, to our sorrow, learned by the manner of his death, as well as by debate of still another president, that no one occupying so high a place can be absolutely safe, even in this country, from the danger of assassination, but it is still true that as a rule the best way to meet such danger is boldly to defy it.

Mr. C. C. Felton, son of Mr. Samuel M. Felton, in an article entitled, "The Baltimore Plot," published in December, 1885, in the Harvard monthly, attempted to revive his observed story. He repeats the account of whitewashing the bridges and of the astonishment created among the good people of the neighborhood. He has faith in the "unknown Baltimorean" who visits the bridge keeper, but would never give his name, and in the spies employed, who, he tells us, were "The well-known detective Pinkerton and eight assistants," and he leaves his readers to infer that Mr. Lincoln's life was saved by an extraordinarily complicated strategy which had been exercised, and the ingenious plan which had been devised, but, alas! "The earth has bubbles, just as the water has," and this was one of them.

Col. Lamon, a close friend of President Lincoln, and the only person who will come to him on his night ride to Washington, has written his biography, a very careful and concise work, which unfortunately was left unfinished, and he, of course, had the strongest reasons for carefully examining the subject. Asked for examination of the documents, Col. Lamon pronounces the conspiracy to be of mere fiction, and adds in confirmation the mature opinion of Mr. Lincoln himself.

Col. Lamon says, "Mr. Lincoln soon learned to regret the midnight ride. He had committed a grave mistake in yielding to the solicitations of a professional spy and of friends too easily alarmed. He says that he had fled from the danger purely imaginary, and felt the shame and mortification natural to a brave man under such circumstances. But he was not opposed to take all the responsibility on himself"

The Riot of 19 April 1861

"The 6th Massachusetts Regiment had the honor of being the first to March in obedience to the call of the president, completely equipped and organized. It had a full band and Regimental staff. Mustered at Lowell on the morning of the 16th, the day after the proclamation was issued, four companies from Lowell presented themselves, and to these were added two from Lawrence, one from Groton, one from Acton, and one from Worcester. Moreover, when the Regiment reached Boston, at 1 o'clock, an additional company was added from that city and one from Stoneham – about 700 men. It was addressed by the governor of the state, in front of the state house. In the city along the lines of the railroad, on the 17th, everywhere ovations attended them. In the march down Broadway, in New York, on the 18th similar scenes occurred in the progress through New Jersey into the city of Philadelphia. At midnight on the 18th reports reached Philadelphia that the passage of the Regiment through Baltimore would be disrupted.

By way of a response, an unarmed and un-uniformed Pennsylvania regiment, under Col. Small, was added to the train in either Philadelphia or when the train reached the Susquehanna – it has been stated both ways, and I am not sure what to account as accurate – and the regiments made the force of about 1,700 men.

The proper course for the Philadelphia, Wilmington and Baltimore Railroad Company was to have given immediate notice to the Baltimore Mayor and board of police commissioners of the number of troops and the time when they were expected to arrive in the city, so the preparation might have been made to receive them, but no such notice was given. On the contrary, it was purposely withheld, and no information could be obtained from the office of the company, although Marshal Kane of the police repeatedly telegraphed to Philadelphia to learn when the troops were to be expected. No news was received until from a half hour to an hour of the time in which they were to arrive. Whatever was the reason that no notice of the approach of the troops was given, it was not because they had no apprehensions of trouble. Mr. Felton, president of the railroad company, says when the troops left Philadelphia he called the Col. and principal officers into his office and told them of the dangers they would probably encounter, and advised that each soldier should load his musket before leaving and be ready for any emergency. Col. Jones official report, which is dated, "capital, Washington, 22 April – 1861," says: "after Philadelphia I received information that passage through the city of Baltimore would be resisted. I caused ammunition to be distributed and arms to be noted, and went personally through the cars, and issued the following orders: "the Regiment will march through Baltimore in columns of sections, arms at the ready. You will undoubtedly be insulted, abused, and perhaps assaulted, to which you must pay no attention whatever, but march with your faces square to the front, paying no attention to the mob, even if they throw stones, bricks or other missiles, but if you are fired upon, and any of you are hit, your officers will order you to fire. Do not fire into any promiscuous crowds, but select any man that may be seen aiming at you, and be sure you drop them."

If this order had been carried out, the danger of the serious disturbance would have been greatly diminished. The plainest dictates of prudence require the Massachusetts and Pennsylvania regiments to march through the city in a body. The Massachusetts regiment was armed with muskets, could have defended itself, and would have had aid from the police, and although the Pennsylvania troops were unarmed, they would have been protected by the police just as troops from the same state had been protected on the day before. The Mayor and police commissioners would have been present, adding the sanction and authority of their official positions. But the plan adopted laid the troops open to be attacked in detail when they were least able to defend themselves, and were out of the reach of assistance from the police. The plan was that when the train reached President Street station, in the southeastern part of Baltimore, each car should, according to custom, be detached from the engine and be drawn through the city by four horses for the distance of more than a mile to the Camden Street or Washington station, in the southwestern part of the city, someone had blundered.

The train of 35 cars arrived at President Street station at about 11 o'clock. The course with the troops to take was first northerly on the President Street for squares [blocks] to Pratt Street, a crowded thoroughfare leading along the heads of the docks, then along Pratt St., west for nearly a mile to Howard Street, and then south on Howard Street one square to Camden station.

Drawn by horses across the city at a rapid pace, about nine cars, containing seven companies of the 6th Massachusetts, reached the Camden Street station, the first carload having been assaulted only with jeers and hisses: but the last car, containing company K and Maj. Watson, was delayed on its passage – according to one account was thrown off the track by obstructions, and had to be replaced with the help of a passing team: paving stones and other missiles were thrown, the windows were broken and some of the soldiers were struck. Col. Jones was in one *of the cars that passed through. Near Gay Street it happened that a number of laborers were at work repaving Pratt Street, and taking cobblestones for re-laying them. As the troops passed, the crowd of bystanders grew larger, the excitement and – among many – the feelings of indignation grew more intense; each new aggressive act was the signal an example for further aggression. A car coming by with a load of sand, the track was blocked by dumping the cartload of sand upon it. I have been told that this was the act of some merchants and clerks of the neighborhood; and then, as a more effective means of obstruction, some anchors line near the head of the Gay Street dock were dragged up to and placed upon the track.*

The next car being stopped by these obstructions, the driver attached to horses to the rear end of the car, and drove it back to the President Street station, the rest of the cars also, of course having to turn back, or – if any of them had, not yet started – to remain where they were at the depot. In the cars stopped and turned back there were four companies, "C," "D," "I" and "L," under Captain's Follansbee, Hart, Pickering and Dike; also the band, which, I believe, did not leave the depot, and which remained there with the unarmed Pennsylvania Regiment. These four companies, in all about 220 men, formed on President Street, in the midst of a dense and angry crowd, which threatened and pressed upon the troops, uttering cheers for Jefferson Davis and the Southern Confederacy, and groans for Lincoln and the North, with much abusive language. As the soldiers advanced along President Street, the commotion increased; one of the band of rioters appeared bearing a Confederate flag and it was carried a considerable distance before it was torn from its staff by citizens. Stones were thrown in great numbers, and at the corner of Bond Street, two soldiers were knocked down by stones and seriously injured. In crossing the Pratt Street Bridge, the troops had to pick their way over joists and scantling, which by this time had been placed on the bridge to obstruct their passage.

Col. Jones' official report, from which I have already quoted, thus describes what happened after the four companies left the cars. As Col. Jones was not present during the march, but obtained the particulars of others, is not surprising that his account contains errors. These will be pointed out and corrected later;

"They proceeded to march in accordance with orders, and had proceeded for a short distance before they were furiously assaulted by a shower of missiles, which came in faster as they advanced. They increased their step, which seemed to infuriate the mob, as it eventually impressed the mob with the idea that the soldiers

did not fire for they had no ammunition, and pistol shots were numerously fired into the ranks, and no one soldier fell dead. The order to "fire!" was given, and was executed; in consequence, several of the mob fell, and the soldiers again advanced hastily. The Mayor of Baltimore placed himself at the head of the column beside Capt. Follansbee, assuring the captain that he would protect them, and begging him not to let the men fire. However, the mayor's patience was soon exhausted, and he seized a musket from the hands of one soldier and killed a man in the mob therewith, and a policeman, who was in advance of the column also shot a man with a revolver.

"They had at last reached the cars, and they started immediately for Washington. On going through the train I found there was about 130 men missing, including the band. Our baggage was seized, and we have not yet been able to recover any of it. I have found it very difficult to get reliable information about the killed and wounded, but believe there was only three killed. As the men went into the cars [meaning the men who had marched through the city to Camden Station] I caused the blinds to the cars to be closed, and took every precaution to prevent any shadow of offense to the people of Baltimore, but still the stones flew thick and fast into the train, and it was with the utmost difficulty that I could prevent the troops from leaving the cars and revenging the deaths of their comrades. After a volley of stones someone of the soldiers fired and killed a Mr. Davis, who, I ascertained by reliable witnesses, threw a stone into the car."

"It is proper and right that I should now go back and take up the narration from my own point of view: "On the morning of 19 April 1861 I was at my law office, on St. Paul Street, after 10 o'clock, when three members of the city Council came to me with a message from Marshal Kane informing me that he had just received intelligence that troops were about to arrive. I did not learn how many, and that he apprehended a disturbance, and I immediately hastened to the office of the board of police and found that they had received a similar notice. Counselor of the city, Mr. George M. Gill, and myself drove rapidly, in a carriage, to the Camden Street station. The Board of Police Commissioners followed, and on reaching the station, we found Marshal Kane already on the ground, and the police coming in, in squads. A large and angry crowd had assembled, restrained by the police from committing any serious breach of the peace. After considerable delay, seven of the 11 companies of the Massachusetts Regiment arrived at the station, as already mentioned, and I saw that the windows of the last car were badly broken. No one I applied to could inform me whether more troops were expected or not. At this time

an alarm was given that the mob was about to tear up the rails in advance of the train on the Washington road, and Marshal Kane ordered some of the men to go out to the road, as far as necessary, to protect the track. Soon afterward, and when I was about to leave Camden Street station, supposing all danger to be over, news was brought to police Board Commissioner Davis and myself, who were standing together, that some troops had been left behind, and that the mob was tearing up the tracks on Pratt Street, so as to obstruct the progress of the cars, which were still coming to the Camden Street station. Mr. Davis immediately ran to summon the Marshal, who was at the station with the body of police, to be sent to the point of danger. I hastened alone in the same direction. On arriving at the foot of Gay Street, I found that anchors had been placed on the track, and as Sgt. McComas and four policemen who were with him were not allowed by the group to remove the obstruction. I at once ordered that the anchors were to be removed, and my authority was not resisted. I hurried on, and approaching Pratt Street Bridge, I saw a Battalion, which proved to be four companies of the Massachusetts Regiment, which had crossed the bridge, coming toward me in double-quick time. They were firing wildly, sometimes backward, over their shoulders. So rapid was the march that they could not stop to take aim. The mob, which was now very large, as it seemed to me, was pursuing with shouts and stone, and, I think, an occasional pistol shot. The uproar was furious. I ran at once to the head of the column, some persons in the crowd shouting, "Here comes the Mayor." I shook hands with the officer in command, Capt. Follansbee, saying as I did so, "I am the Mayor of Baltimore." The captain greeted me cordially. I at once objected to the double-quick, which was immediately stopped. I placed myself at his side, and marched with him. He said, "We have been attacked without provocation," or words to that effect. I replied, "You must defend yourself." I expected that he would face men to the rear, and, after giving warning, would fire if necessary. However, I said no more, for I immediately felt that, as mayor of the city, it was not my province to volunteer such place. Once before in my life I had taken part in opposing a formidable riot, and then learned by experience that the safest and most humane manner of quelling a mob is to meet it at the beginning with armed resistance.

The column continued its march. There was no concert of action organized among the rioters. They were armed only with such stones and missiles as they could pick up and a few pistols. My presence for a short time had some affect, but very soon the attack was renewed with greater violence. The mob grew bolder. Stones flew thick and fast. Rioters rushed the soldiers and attempted to snatch their muskets.

And at least one to occasions succeeded. With one of these a soldier was killed... Men fell on both sides. A young lawyer, then, now known as a quiet citizen, sees the flag of one of the companies, and nearly tore it from its staff. He was shot through the thigh and was carried home apparently a dying man, but he survived entered the Army of the Confederacy, where he rose to the rank of Capt., and he afterwards returned to Baltimore, where he still lives. The soldiers fired at will. There was no firing by platoon, and I heard the order given to fire. I remember that at the corner of South Street several citizens standing in a group fell, either killed or wounded. It was impossible for the troops to discriminate between rioters and bystanders. But the latter seemed to suffer the most, because, as the main attack was from the mob pursuing the soldiers from the rear, they, in their March, could not easily face backwards and fire, but could shoot at those who they passed on the street. Near the corner of Light Street a soldier was severely wounded, who afterwards died, and a boy on a vessel lying in the dock was killed, and about the same place three soldiers, leveled their muskets and fired into a group standing on the sidewalk, who, as far as I can see, were taking no active part. The shots looked to be perfect, but I cannot say how many fell. I cried out, waving my umbrella to emphasize my words, "for God's sake, don't shoot!" However, it was too late. The statement that I begged Capt. Follansbee not to let the men fire is incorrect, although on this occasion I did say, "Don't shoot." It then seemed to me that I was in the wrong place, for my presence did not protect either the soldiers or the citizens, and I stepped out from the column. Just at this moment, a boy ran forward and handed me a discharged musket which had fallen from one of the soldiers. I took it from him and hastened into the nearest shop, asking the person in charge to keep it safely, and returned immediately to the street. The boy was far from being alone in his sympathy for the troops, but their friends powerless except to care for the wounded and remove the dead. The statement in Col. Jones's report that I seized a musket and killed one of the rioters is entirely incorrect. The smoking musket seen in my hand was no doubt a foundation for it. There is no foundation for the other statement that one of the police shot a man with a revolver. At the moment when I returned to the street Marshal Kane, with about 50 policeman (as I'd supposed, but have since ascertained that there were not so many) came at a run from the direction of the Camden Street station, and throwing themselves in the rear of the troops, they formed a line in front of the mob, and with drawn revolvers kept it back. When at Light and Charles Streets, Marshal Kane's voice shouted to the mob, "Keep back, men, or I'll shoot!" This, which I saw myself, was gallantly executed,

and was perfectly successful. The mob recoiled like water from a rock. One of the leading rioters, then a young man, now a peaceful gentleman, tried, as he himself has told me, to pass the line, but the Marshal seized him and shouted that he would shoot if the attempt was made. This nearly ended the fight, and the column passed on under the direction of the police, without serious molestation, to Camden station. I had accompanied the troops for more than a third of a mile, and regarded the danger to be now over. At the Camden Street station there was rioting and confusion. Commissioner Davis assisted in placing the soldiers in cars from Washington. Some muskets were pointed out the Windows by the soldiers.

He earnestly objected as likely to bring on a renewal of the fight, and he advised the blinds to be pulled closed. The muskets without withdrawal, and the blinds closed by military order, as stated by Col. Jones. At last, about a quarter before 1 o'clock, the train, consisting of 13 cars filled with troops, moved out of Camden station, amid the hisses and groans of the multitude, and passed safely on to Washington. At the outskirts of the city, half a mile or more on from the station, occurred the unfortunate incident of the killing of Robert W Davis. This gentleman, a well-known dry goods merchant, was standing on a vacant lot near the track with two friends, and as the train went by they raised to cheer for Jefferson Davis and the South, when he was immediately shot dead by one of the soldiers from the car window, several firing at once. They did not know that the troops had been attacked on their March through the city, and there was no "volley of stones" thrown just before Mr. Davis was killed.

This was the last of the casualties of that day, and was by far the most serious and unfortunate in its consequences, for it was not unnaturally made the most of to inflame the minds of the people against the northern troops. Had it not been for this incident, there would perhaps have been among many of our people a keener sense of blame attaching to themselves as the aggressors. Four of the Massachusetts Regiment were killed. Twelve citizens were killed, including Mr. Davis. The number of wounded among the latter was never ascertained.

As the fighting was close quarters, the small number of casualties shows that it was not as severe as has generally been supposed.

But peace, even for the day, had not come. The unarmed Pennsylvanians and the band of the Massachusetts Regiment were still at the President-Street station, where a mob had assembled, and the police at that point were not sufficient to protect them. Stones were thrown, and not a few of the Pennsylvania troops were hurt, not

seriously, I believe. A good many of them were, not unnaturally, seized with panic, scattered through the city in different directions. Marshal Kane again appeared on the scene, with an adequate force, and arrangements were made with the railroad company by which the troops were sent back in the direction of Philadelphia. During the afternoon and night a number of stragglers sought the aid of the police and were cared for at once and taken to one of district station houses.

April 19 - 1861

The First Official Casualty of the Civil War was a 65-year-old **Escaped Slave**.

The first man to shed blood during the Civil war was an escaped slave by the name of Nicholas Biddle from Pottsville, PA. Due his having escaped a life of slavey very little is known of Mr. Biddle's life. From what we have learned he was born to slave parents in Delaware circa 1796. At some point he escaped slavery and settled in Pennsylvania. It was common practice for escaped slaves to change their names to avoid capture, two stories told of Nicholas Biddle.

According to one historian's findings; Biddle escaped to Philadelphia and got a job as a servant for **Nicholas Biddle**, the wealthy financier and president of the Second Bank of the United States. In this story, the former slave and the financier traveled to Pottsville for a dinner meeting of entrepreneurs and industrialists at nearby Mount Carbon to celebrate the first successful operation of an anthracite-fueled blast furnace in America. The servant remained in Pottsville to live. Another account is that Biddle relocated from Delaware directly to Pottsville and became a servant at the hotel where the aforementioned celebratory dinner was held, at which he met the famous Biddle.

In any event, we know that he adopted the name of the prominent Philadelphian, and by 1840 Nicholas Biddle was residing in Pottsville. He worked odd jobs to earn a living, including street vending, selling oysters in the winter and ice cream in the summer. The 1860 U.S. census lists his occupation as "porter."

Biddle befriended members of a local militia company, the Washington Artillerists, and attended their drills and excursions for the next 20 years. The company members were fond of Biddle and treated him as one of their own, and although African Americans were not permitted to serve in the militia, they gave him a uniform to wear.

At the outbreak of the Civil War and the fall of Fort Sumter on April 15, 1861, President Lincoln issued a call for 75,000 volunteers to serve for three months to suppress the insurrection in the South. Unlike other antebellum militia units, the Washington Artillery had maintained a state of readiness and was among the first companies to respond to Lincoln's call to arms.

Two days later, the Washington Artillerists departed Pottsville by train to enter the war, along with 65-year-old Nicholas Biddle, who served as an aide to the company's commanding officer, Captain James Wren.

On April 18, five companies, numbering some 475 men, were sworn in at Harrisburg and mustered into the service of the United States. That is, all except for Nicholas Biddle, who as an African American was prohibited from serving in the U.S. Army.

The soldiers left on an emergency order to defend Washington, DC against a rumored Confederate attack. But in 1861, there was no continuous passenger rail service through Baltimore, and when the soldiers detrained in the largest city in the slave state of Maryland, they encountered a hostile mob of pro-Southern sympathizers.

As the companies marched to meet their trains, members of the mob taunted the soldiers and hurled bricks and stones. Biddle, a black man in uniform, was an easy target. Someone threw a brick at his head that knocked him to the ground, making him the first casualty caused by hostile action in the Civil War.

The wound was grave enough that it exposed his bone. It was reportedly the first and most serious injury suffered that day, and he bore the scar the rest of his life.

An anxious President Lincoln learned of the arrival of the five Pennsylvania companies and of their treacherous passage through the mob at Baltimore. The morning after they arrived in Washington, Lincoln personally thanked each member of the five companies, and singled out the wounded for special recognition.

After his military service, Biddle returned to relative obscurity in Pottsville, where he eked out a living performing odd jobs. In the summer of 1864, he appeared at the Great Central Fair in Philadelphia, where photographs of him in a Washington Artillerists uniform, captioned "the first man wounded in the Great American Rebellion," were sold to raise funds for the relief of Union soldiers. In the end, however, Biddle was forced to solicit alms to make ends meet. He died destitute in 1876 without even enough money to cover his burial expenses. Surviving members of the Washington Artillerists and the National Light Infantry each donated a dollar to purchase a simple headstone for him, and they had it inscribed: "In Memory of Nicholas Biddle, Died August 2 1876, aged 80 years. His was the Proud Distinction of Shedding the First Blood in the Late War for the Union, Being Wounded while marching through Baltimore with the First Volunteers from Schuylkill County, 18 April 1861. Erected by his Friends in Pottsville."

Throughout the remainder of his life, Biddle retained unpleasant memories of his perilous journey with the Washington Artillerists through Baltimore. Although it garnered him the "proud distinction of shedding the first blood," he was often heard to remark "that he would go through the infernal regions with the artillery, but would never again go through Baltimore."

<u>Nicholas Biddle and the First Defenders</u> - By **Ronald S. Coddington**

April 18, 2011 10:00 pm

On the afternoon of April 19, 1861, Nick Biddle was quietly helping his unit, the Washington Artillery from Pottsville, Pa., set up camp inside the north wing of the Capitol building. The day before, he was almost killed.

Biddle was a black servant to Capt. James Wren, who oversaw the company of about 100 men. On April 18 the Washington Artillery had been one of several Army outfits, totaling about 475 men, heading through Baltimore in route to Washington, D.C., in response to President Lincoln's call for 75,000 troops to put down the Southern rebellion.

Collection of Thomas Harris Nicholas "Nick" Biddle by William R. Mortimer of Pottsville, Pa., circa 1861 - Thousands of pro-Confederate Baltimoreans turned out to meet them at the city's northern train station. (Another group, 45 regular Army soldiers from the Fourth Artillery in route from St. Paul, Minn., to Fort McHenry, also disembarked.) The crowd expressed disappointment in the non-military look of some of the volunteers, who hailed from eastern Pennsylvania coal-mining country. They "were not more than half uniformed and armed, and presented some as hard-looking specimens of humanity as could be found anywhere," reported the Baltimore Sun. Most of the men carried their own revolvers, while a few toted antiquated flintlocks. A select group carried state-issued modern muskets, but had no gunpowder for them.

Captain Wren, Biddle and the others were aware of Baltimore's pro-secession sentiment and expected trouble. One volunteer reportedly asked Biddle if he was

afraid to face rowdy "plug-uglies" and jokingly warned, "They may catch you and sell you down in Georgia." Biddle replied in dead earnest that he was going to Washington trusting in the Lord, and that he wouldn't be scared away by the devil himself — or a bunch of thugs.

The Pennsylvanians formed a line and prepared to march through Baltimore to another station, where they could catch a Washington-bound train. The regulars would lead the way. The line started and moved rapidly, shielded from the abusive mobs by policemen stretched 10 paces apart. A private recalled the "Roughs and toughs, 'longshoremen, gamblers, floaters, idlers, red-hot secessionists, as well as men ordinarily sober and steady, crowded upon, pushed and hustled the little band and made every effort to break the thin line."

The mob derided the volunteers and cheered for Jefferson Davis and the Confederacy. Some aimed their abuse at Biddle. Capt. Wren remembered, "The crowd raised the cry, 'Nigger in uniform!' and poor old Nick had to take it."

Around the halfway point of the journey, the regular troops split off and marched to Fort McHenry, leaving the Pennsylvanians alone. "At this juncture the mob were excited to a perfect frenzy, breaking the line of the police and pushing through the files of men, in an attempt to break the column," wrote one historian. The boldest in the crowd spit, kicked, punched and grabbed at the coattails of the volunteers.

As the Pennsylvanians neared the station, rioters chucked cobblestones and jagged pieces of broken brick. The bombardment intensified as the volunteers arrived at the station and began to board the cars. Suddenly a chunk of brick struck Biddle in the head and left a deep, profusely bleeding cut. He managed to get on the train as the mob climbed on top of the cars and jumped up and down on the roofs. Biddle found a comfortable spot, wrapped his head in a handkerchief, and then pulled his fatigue cap close over the wound.

When the Pennsylvanians finally arrived in Washington that evening, they received a very different reception, as enthusiastic crowds welcomed them as saviors. They occupied temporary barracks in the north wing of the Capitol. One officer remembered that, when Biddle entered the rotunda of the building, "He looked up and around as if he felt that he had reached a place of safety, and then took his cap and the bloody handkerchief from his head and carried them in his hand. The blood dropped as he passed through the rotunda on the stone pavement."

"From Heber S. Thompson's The First Defenders, scanned by openlibrary.org Front and back of a commemorative medal approved by an act of the Pennsylvania legislature in 1891 and issued to surviving members of the First Defenders.

A grateful President Lincoln later greeted the Pennsylvanians. He reportedly shook hands with Biddle and encouraged him to seek medical attention. But Biddle refused. He preferred to remain with the company. At the time some considered Biddle's blood the first shed in hostility during the Civil War.

The House of Representatives later passed a resolution thanking the Pennsylvanians for their role in defense of the capital. The volunteers came to be known as the "First Defenders" in honor of their early response to Lincoln's call to arms.

21 April - 1933

On this day in Baltimore Police History, 1933, we lost our brother, Police **Officer John R. J. Block** to gunfire. Although there were no witnesses to his shooting, and no way of ever knowing exactly what happened or who shot Officer Block, deft investigation of a number of seemingly (at the time) unrelated incidents and reports led to the following conclusions:

Fact: Late on the night of April 21, 1933, two young men robbed a pair of United Bus drivers. According to the drivers, they were held up at their northern terminal at Charles and Thirty-ninth Streets by two men who had boarded the bus driven by William Hoffmaster, at Charles and Franklin streets. The two had ridden to the end of the line, and once there, *they produced a handgun and told Hoffmaster, "Let's have the change rack, and whatever bills you've got!"*

Fact: *As Hoffmaster handed over the money the shorter of the two men said to his partner, "You get the other driver. I can take care of this fellow!" The taller man returned to the bus in a moment with Huster, who had been sitting in his parked bus waiting to start his run. He was forced at gunpoint into Hoffmaster's bus. After stripping them of their money – they took $34 from Huster and $29 from Hoffmaster – the pair stepped to the pavement and, turning to the frightened drivers, said, "You stay right there. We're coming back in five minutes - if either of you has moved, we'll kill you deader than hell!"*

Fact: *The two escaped on foot, running north on Charles Street. Unbeknownst to*

anyone at the time, this was to be the beginning of the end for Officer Block.

Fact: Shortly after the bus drivers had been forced at pistol point to hand over their day's receipts, Patrolman Robert L. Campbell, Northern district, arrived on the scene, and while listening to the bus drivers' troubles, observed a machine with three men in it shoot past them at a high rate of speed and with its headlights doused, heading south on Charles Street. The alert Patrolman Campbell jotted down the license number of the speeding, unlit car bearing Florida license number 115345, but at the time didn't connect it with the bus hold-up he was investigating.

Fact: A few minutes later Patrolman Campbell notified headquarters of the bus robbery, and of the Florida tag number that was on the car he'd seen speeding past him, which at the time he thought was a separate occurrence entirely, having no idea at the time of the connection between the speeding machine and the robbery he was investigating.

Fact: Soon, at Roll Calls throughout the districts, every policeman in the city was put on the lookout for the bus robbers, and for the fast moving machine with Florida tags. Still no connection was made between the two incidents. Officer Block took notice of the information on the robbery and of the speeding Florida car, writing it down in his lookout book.

Fact: Shortly after hitting the street following Roll Call, Officer Block was met by Sergeant Edward Pansuka. He said that he had talked to Patrolman Block only ten minutes before the shooting occurred. Block told him, he said, that he was going to the Hanover Street and Belle Grove Road intersection and watch for the speeding Florida car. He also intended, according to the Sergeant, to turn off the traffic light at the intersection, apparently a routine procedure for the night shift officers.

Fact: Soon thereafter, Officer Block was found lying on the ground next to his police car, which was parked facing south; he died at 1:34 am at the South Baltimore General Hospital.

Fact: The final piece of the puzzle came from a concerned taxi driver, who rushed into the Southwestern district stationhouse with a story that proved pivotal. The excited taxi driver reported a mysterious journey he had just completed. The driver, Louis Boyle, reported that he had picked up two fares, bearing three suitcases, on Charles Street at about midnight. Rather than giving him a destination address, one of the men pointed to a small sedan waiting at the curb, and told Boyle to just follow it, and the two cars set out, southbound on Charles Street. The rest of Boyle's story

was chilling, and provided the link between both earlier reports and his recent fare.

Fact: On the way to an unknown destination, Boyle said a Kentucky license plate dropped from the rear of the sedan he was following, revealing underneath it a Florida license tag, No. 115345. He felt then, he said, that there was something queer about the whole business, but continued on his way.

Fact: As they reached Hanover Street and Belle Grove road, Boyle said, the Florida car was halted by a police car – which later developed to have been that of Patrolman Block. The men in his cab told him to just go around the stopped police car and sedan and to keep going, and he obeyed. A short distance farther on, he said, they told him to "stop and wait." The point at which the cab waited for the Florida car was at Audrey street and Annapolis Boulevard, about eight' blocks beyond the scene of the shooting.

Fact: Ten minutes later the Florida car came up and stopped behind the taxi. His fares immediately got out and clambered into the other machine. Then somebody in the car asked him the way to Annapolis, Boyle said, and the machine sped away, heading south. The taxi driver drove immediately to the Southwestern district police station and reported the incident - at the time not knowing anything at all of the shooting.

<u>Supposition and Conclusions Reached</u>:

The pieces of the puzzle were now complete, and it was only for the Homicide detectives to fit them together. Soon they did, the key being the sedan with Florida license number 115345, which was now believed to be headed for Annapolis. Baltimore police were put on guard at all points where the car might leave the city, while State police were guarding all the highways to the south. They hoped to capture the automobile before daylight.

It now seemed apparent that Officer Block stopped the car with the Florida plates, presumably based on the description and tag number he had noted at roll call, and that he then approached the car he'd stopped, whereupon he was shot and killed, thought the exact circumstances of the car stop and shooting remain unknown.

Fact: Further investigation made sometime later revealed that the three men being sought in the case were thought to have registered at an apartment house in the 600 block North Charles Street on Monday of the same week, using the names Buck Slade, Bill Drake and Joe Green, all of St. Augustine, Florida. According to their landlady, Mrs. Howard R. Yourtee, they paid a week's rent in advance, were

especially well dressed and rather quiet, but "had a serious look for such young men."

The three suspects escaped and a two state manhunt began, including the District of Columbia. Law enforcement agencies from surrounding counties, the city, and the FBI joined efforts to locate the assailants, but they were never found.

22 April - 1934 - Md. Tags

On this date in 1934, the State began for the first time making its own metal license plates at the Maryland Penitentiary, rather than purchasing them from metal stamping companies in New York and Kentucky.

Maryland Auto Tags in Historical Review

The first written history of automobiles of any kind in Maryland dates from 1904. At the time a fee of one dollar was required to be paid by the car's owner to the Secretary of State. That year in Annapolis, 644 applications for license numbers were received and the first issued, on 28 May 1904, was to Earl MacNeill Shannahan, of Easton, Talbot County. The records do not show the make of his car, but it was registered as having 8 hp.

There were no actual physical license tags issued – the license number issued had to be painted somewhere on the vehicle, preferably on the side glass of the two carriage-like lamps with which some vehicles were equipped.

Many "Autoists" (as automobile enthusiasts of the time were often known) who had no vehicle lights (for these were not obligatory on vehicles then, and were only needed by the more daring and adventurous souls who dared drive at night) went to one of the shops of those days, and purchased and installed these lights themselves.

Many also purchased a black patent leather flap with the allotted license number on it in large aluminum figures similar to those used for numbering houses.

<u>Newspapers</u> of the times; Apr 22, 1934; as written at the time (remember, folks, they wrote very differently back then, and these accounts are related as written at the time, so bear with us and try to keep up):

With this tag attached to the rear axle of the chariot, complaints were registered by auto owners that the tag was too large and conspicuous. The automobile Commissioner's reply to this protest was that it was needed visible proof of the

operator's privilege to rush around on the county roads at the maximum legal speed of 1 mile in six minutes, or 10 miles an hour (provided his vehicle could make it to that speed).

Other troubles perturbed some drivers more at the time. For one, he was allowed only 6 miles an hour in Druid Hill Park, and was apt to be chased and caught by any bicycle club who thought he was exceeding that rate; for there were no speedometers on either motor vehicles or peddling vehicles at the time, although the law said the fine was $12. In many of the parks of other cities during the same era, notably in Central Park, New York City, motorized vehicles would not be allowed at all, but as his automobile required the aid of a freight car to reach such distant proportions of the country, most Maryland motorists only knew of this ban by hearsay and so derives a little consolation therefrom.

In 1908, Governor Crothers advocated the creation of the office of an Automobile Commissioner – he admitted that, while the fees so collected would probably not be sufficient to pay the salary of such an official for the first year, possibly as much as $100,000 might be raised by it annually in the future

Fiscal Conservative

In proof that the governor was what might be termed a fiscal conservative, it may be mentioned in passing that a little over 9½ million dollars was the total revenue derived from automobiles in Maryland in 1933.

Official metal license plates for automobiles in Maryland date from 1910, or about two years after the appointment of John E. George, the first Commissioner of motor vehicles. The tags that year were of the same color, only reversed, as those used this year of grace 1934, that is, gold and black. They were slightly shorter than those of today because they were required to allow for only four numbers.

In addition, Maryland auto enthusiasts were required to have District of Columbia plates and an operator's license card for Washington in order to enter that city. Finally, through the organized efforts of the automobile club of Maryland, which was founded as early as 1901, full reciprocity between Maryland and the District, eliminating this necessity, was established, but this was achieved only in 1924.

Made First Plates

An automobile war existed for a short time between Maryland and Delaware, when it was obligatory for the Maryland car to have attached the plates of Delaware in

order to cross the line into the state.

The first Maryland plates were made by a metal ceiling company in New York – a few years later by a firm in Kentucky. In 1918, just at the close of the world war, production of all the tags were restricted and delayed, and it was not until 12 o'clock midnight of December 31 that those for solid-tired vehicles arrived from the manufacturer.

Resulting from the late delivery, soldiers were rushed from one of the military camps and they assisted in unloading the freight car containing them, getting the tags to the office of distribution just in time to issue them on the very morning that they were required.

It was in 1918, too, that the only color dye obtainable was so poor for the black background used that year, that, like the foliage of the trees, it turned green in the spring and to a sickly grey in winter. Indian dyes have been adopted since and the colors are now more permanent.

Stamper a "Lifer"

In 1918, which was a couple of years after Col. Claude E. Sweezy assumed charge of the penitentiary, the manufacture of the auto license plate was begun in that place and they have been made by convict labor ever since. The shop in which this is done is located at one end of the large courtyard of the penitentiary and occupies two floors, the first one devoted to the cutting off of metal sheets into the proper size, punching holes, stamping the numbers and trimming; the second floor to the enameling process.

Work in the auto license shop of the penitentiary is agreeable and greatly sought after by the men.

The man who manipulates one of the die stamps is a "lifer," other shorter-term men attend to the two drippings of the background color, done by means of slowly ravelling, hanging racks, and to the operation of the inked wells by means of which the raised portion of the plate are colored. Fire engine tags are red and police car tags of blue are painted by hand, but run mechanically through the same baking ovens as the others.

Maryland was one of the pioneer states to put its prisoners to making auto license plates. Formerly Maryland also made the tags for several other states, but nowadays most of the Commonwealth have introduced this work into their own

penal institutions.

Complete Set Rare

A complete set of all the tags of any state is extremely rare, and, in consequence, of considerable value to collectors of such things. One set for Maryland happened to be owned by a chauffeur in the family of the present Commissioner of motor vehicles, who year after year had nailed them up in the garage after they became outdated. It was from these originals that the early specimens were reproduced in the penitentiary for the full set of Maryland tags which now adorn the south end wall of the lobby of the automobile Commissioner's building at Guilford Avenue and 22nd St.

Special blocks of numbers and tags are assigned to electric autos, of which there are now comparatively few, to commercial vehicles for hire, to motor trucks, motorcycles, sidecars and trailers, solid-tired vehicles, used cars, buses and dealers. Latest of all are tags to employers, giving them the right to haul workmen for pay to and from their office or shop.

Private car numbers in the city of Baltimore begin nominally with 30,000, but the first 2,000 of these, that is all those beginning with 30,000 itself and 31,000 are what is known as gratis tags and are reserved for official use. The actual city numbers, therefore, for private cars begin with 32,001 this year up to 149,000.

From 150,000 to 199,000 is for commercial trucks. From 200,000 and up is allotted to the privately owned cars in the counties.

Even Numbers Sought

The request for even numbers, numbers in sequence, "full-houses" and other unique combinations, has always been so great, that lately an effort has been made to turn this desire on the part of the motoring public to good use by making the granting of them an incentive to extra carefulness in driving. Such numbers as are available are assigned and the following notice stamped on the registration card;

"This is a special number – issued to you as a symbol of good faith to respect the motor vehicle laws and set a good example to other motorists. The department reserves the right to recall the special plates for any reason and issue other plates in lieu thereof."

Shriners, the Tall Cedars and several other fraternal organizations, are also issued numbers within certain blocks so that the members may the more easily recognize

one another. The automobile club for instance is a lot of those numbers that are within the 60,000 block.

The tags for 1935 – in production at present, will be blue on white, which was the color combination scheduled for 1934, when the state colors were substituted on account of the Tercentenary celebration. The slightly thinner grade of steel was also used for 1934 – 22 gauge instead of the customary 20 gauge – on account of the additional lead lettering necessary to be pressed into it.

A dozen or more grades and shades of enamel of white on black, which will be the color combination for 1936, are being tested out now on plates exposed up on the roof of the penitentiary shop, where they are still to remain for months. Those pigments that best withstand this test will be the ones selected. The numerals of the year and the MD (for Maryland) which since 1922 has been written out in full to avoid confusion with the MO abbreviation for Missouri, have alternated top and bottom on your license plates. In odd years the name of the state appears above the large license numerals and then even years below them. This current year, however, violated that rule in order to embody the word Tercentenary.

Tags returned to the automobile Commissioner's office for a refund, or for any other reason, were formerly cut up and thrown on the city dumps. But several years ago an enterprising though not overly scrupulous Autoist, laboriously riveted some of the small pieces he found thus thrown away into a pair of matching plates and drove for some time under these matched up, false colors, until hauled into the traffic court for some other offense, when his money-saving scheme was discovered.

Since which time discarded auto tags have been turned over to a local salvage company – where they are melted down and put to raising windows instead of taxes.

24 April - 1970

On this Day in Baltimore Police History, 1970, we lost our Brother **Officer Donald W. Sager**, to gunfire. Officer Sager, assigned to the Central District, was shot and killed on Friday, 24 April, 1970, while working in the 1200 block of Myrtle Avenue, while doing nothing more offensive that sitting in his parked radio car.

In Officer Sager's car with him at the time was his partner Officer Stanley Sierakowski, who was also shot and seriously wounded. As Officers Sager and Sierakowski were seated in their car, a suspect [a member of the Black Panther

Party] snuck behind the car and shot through the back window, striking Officer Sager in the back of the head, killing him instantly. Officer Sierakowski was then shot 5 times with a .45 caliber pistol. The suspect's sole motivation was to ambush and kill police officers.

Officer Sager had served with the department for 12 years. He was survived by his wife, and one child. Though he is no longer with us, as his brothers and sisters of the Baltimore Police Department we won't let him be forgotten.

From newspaper reports at the time:

On 24 April, 1970, Police Officer Donald W Sager was shot and killed, while working the 1200 block of Myrtle Avenue. He and his partner, Officer Stanley Sierakowski, were seated in their radio car, when without provocation or warning, a member of the Black Panthers snuck up to the rear of their car and began shooting through the back window at them. The first rounds struck Officer Sager in the back of the head, killing him.

Officer Sierakowski rolled out his door in an attempt to escape the attack, and to gain a vantage point from which he might be able to return fire on the suspect; however, he was also shot. In fact when the smoke cleared it was learned Officer Sierakowski ended up taking 5 rounds from a .45 caliber pistol. A coward by the name of Marshall Eddie Conway, whose sole motivation was to ambush and kill police officers, was arrested, tried and convicted for the crime.

During the early 70's, the heat of the 1968 Baltimore riots was still festering, and was far from cooled, or cooling – African American groups like the Black Panther Party and other groups were killing police, or involved in shootouts with police, at an alarming rate, most often totally unprovoked. Either through fake calls to calls for the police, thereby drawing officers to areas where they were set up to be ambushed, or just by following officers waiting for them to let their guard down, stop for a bite to eat, make a car stop, or even to help someone faking distress.

When an officer wasn't looking, or least expecting it; he would be attacked. And it wasn't just white police, the Panthers considered anyone wearing a badge to be their mortal enemy, and they would shoot a black officer as quick as they would a white officer – in fact during that time in Baltimore Police history, black officers had it pretty rough; they were not accepted by the white community, and they were shunned by most of the black community.

It was a confusing time, a time when a man could be shot for no other reason that wearing a uniform. Conway, the Black Panther in question wasn't being chased, wasn't wanted by the police... had never been arrested by either of these partners... They just happened to have been wearing the uniform of a Baltimore Police Officer at a time when the Baltimore's Black Panthers wanted to shoot and kill Baltimore Police Officers – and Sager and Sierakowski were in the wrong place at the wrong time.

In the year 2014, after 44 years the filth that took the life of a Baltimore Police officer on this day in 1970 was freed - After being behind bars for 40 years, a man who killed one police officer and tried mightily to kill another, is a free man. Marshall "Eddie" Conway – a former member of the Black Panther Party – was released from prison Tuesday. Civil rights activists say it's a big win – in what universe is it acceptable that a man who kills wantonly be let back out on the public street amidst an civilized, unsuspecting public a "win?" Fortunately, others are upset that he's walking free, considering it a strike against civil society, where rules are supposed to have real meaning, and evil deeds real, lasting consequences.

As your brothers and sisters of the Baltimore Police Department we will not let you be forgotten – RIP - Officer Donald W. Sager and God Bless - For your service honored the City of Baltimore, and the Baltimore Police Department.

Newspaper reports from the time; May 25, 1972; pg. D24

Murder case defended, citing party orders

Jack Ivory Johnson Jr., the third Black Panther Party member to go on trial for the ambush slaying of one policeman and the wounding of another, told police in a statement admitted into evidence in criminal court yesterday that he was sent on the killing mission on orders of the Party. "When Black Panthers are told they are to do a job, no questions are ever asked; they just have to go and do it," Mr. Johnson was quoted as saying by Detective Lieutenant Thomas J. McKew of the police department's Homicide Division.

Two other party members already have been convicted and sentenced to life in prison, plus consecutive terms in the slaying of Officer Donald Sager, 35, and the near fatal wounding of Sgt. Stanley Sierakowski, at the time a fellow officer, in April, 1970.

Fourth man mentioned

For the first time since the trials began, it was revealed that a fourth assailant was mentioned in a signed, written statement made by Mr. Johnson. The fourth man, Mr. Johnson had said, carried a sawed-off shotgun, but apparently did not fire it.

Johnson, of the 1700 block of N. Asquith St., told Lieutenant McKew that his role in the shootings was to make sure that the policeman nearest the microphone in a departmental cruiser did not call for assistance.

Johnson declared that he himself had merely fired two shots in the air from his .32 caliber pistol, because after he had seen all the shots fired at the officer by the Conway, he "did not have the heart to just kill the pig," the jurors and Judge J. Harold Grady were told in the courtroom.

Testimony disclosed that patrolman Sager was killed by bullets that struck him in the head and chest and that Sgt. Sierakowski received five .45 caliber gunshot wounds, from which he recovered. The two officers were sitting in a parked police car in the 1200 block of Myrtle Avenue writing a report on a domestic complaint when they were felled by a barrage of shots from behind their car.

Lieutenant McKew quoted Mr. Johnson as saying at before his written statement started, "you're not going to get me for killing anybody because I fired my gun in the air. If I had did what I was supposed to do you would never have caught me," Mr. Johnson was further quoted as saying. Asked just exactly what he was 'supposed' to do, Mr. Johnson replied that, "it was my job to see that the police officer did not get to the mic," the Lieutenant testified.

The defended in his statement averred that he and James E. Powell, 35, who already has been convicted, were on the east side of the city when they received a call to come to the west side, where they were notified they had a "job to do" and to make sure they had gloves and firearms.

26 April - 2006

Today in Baltimore Police History, 2006 we lost our brother, Police **Officer Norman Stamp** to an off-duty case of friendly fire.

On the night of his 44th anniversary as a Baltimore police officer, Norman Stamp drank beer at a strip club on Haven Street with members of a motorcycle club that he helped found — a tight fraternity called the Chosen Sons.

Shortly after midnight, a dispute with another group led to harsh words and then punches. A brawl spilled out into the parking lot and drew three uniformed police officers. Stamp, brass knuckles on his fist, rushed out a side door. He apparently did not hear or notice the uniformed Officer John Torres or his orders to stop.

Torres, a five-year veteran, felled Stamp with an electric jolt from a Taser, and the off-duty officer pulled out his service weapon. In response, Torres fired his service revolver twice, hitting Stamp at least once in the chest. The 65-year-old struggled to his feet and said, "I didn't know you were a cop," before collapsing, according to a person familiar with the investigation.

Stamp died at Maryland Shock Trauma Center about 1:30 am, leaving police stunned at how one of their colleagues — a person with more than four decades of police experience — challenged a fellow officer and ended up fatally wounded on a grimy lot.

"The Norm Stamp that I know would not have pulled a gun on police," said Paul Blair, the police union president. "Maybe it was tunnel vision and he didn't realize they were officers. It is an unbelievable way to end a career. It is a hell of a way to end a career."

Blair defended the officer who shot Stamp, saying, "Officer Torres did everything by the book. That officer was devastated by what happened."

Bleary-eyed police commanders stood at a morning news conference and concurred, saying it appeared that Torres followed department policy when he fired. "Torres was issuing commands," said Police Commissioner Frederick H. Bealefeld III. "He deployed his Taser. He followed his training; he did what he was taught to do in terms of dealing with these types of situations."

City police officers have shot 10 people this year, killing seven. Last year, they shot 33, killing 13.

About Stamp, the commissioner said, "He was a mentor to some and a friend to many."

Bealefeld said one man involved in the incident broke his leg while resisting police and that person was arrested. Police had not released his name or affiliation yesterday.

"This is an incredibly difficult time," Bealefeld said. "But the men and women of your Police Department will remain focused, vigilant and undaunted."

Men from the Chosen Sons, the other brotherhood that defined Stamp's life, shed quiet tears. They put on a pot of coffee and sat around their clubhouse, smoking cigarettes and telling stories about the man who they said founded their organization with other police officers and firefighters in 1969.

"He's a survivor," said Paul "Nitro" Treash, the sergeant-of-arms of the club. "This [biker] lifestyle, it isn't for everybody. These guys will fight and die for each other." As Treash talked about his friend, he was frequently interrupted by phone calls. "Norm's dead," he told a caller. "I know, I know. They are going to try to cover this up," he said, shaking his head.

Like the police, none of the bikers could believe Stamp would pull a weapon on an officer. "That is stuff that he has preached to us. When a cop gives an order, you should comply. We're just beside ourselves right now." They said that the night began with an initiation. Stamp, as a founding member of the club, played a key role. The members, as part of a hazing, told a new guy he had been rejected and ordered him to leave the clubhouse.

But Stamp, 65, ran out after him, saying: "Get back here and tell those guys to [expletive] off," then tossed him a wadded-up jacket with the club's colors — or patch — emblazoned on the back, said Michael Privett, who became the newest member of the club.

The men celebrated at the club for a while. Some went home. Others walked two blocks to Haven Place, a strip club that bills itself as "a gentleman's tavern" with "go-go girls." That is where the fight broke out. Police, who interviewed many of the people in the bar, said the fracas started over women. Members of the motorcycle club interviewed by The Baltimore Sun did not mention the women.

Treash, who was not there but spoke to many of the club members yesterday, said Stamp had tried to stop the fight in the bar.

Outside, police Officers Raymond Buda, a 27-year veteran, and Jason J. Rivera, who has seven years on the force, tried to break up the fight. One person was brandishing a broken bottle, police said, and as the officers were trying to arrest people, Torres positioned himself by the bar's side door to keep others from joining the fight.

It was then that Stamp emerged from the club with brass knuckles, Bealefeld said.

Treash said he thought Stamp knew that police had been called and intended to mediate the situation. However, he also noted that his friend always liked a good fight.

Torres commanded Stamp to stop and he did not, said the police commissioner. There was "no indication" that Stamp identified himself as an officer, Bealefeld said.

Charles Thrasher, owner of the Haven Place, said he has worked hard over the years to keep the club free of trouble. He inherited the business from his father in 1980. Three years before, a 35-year-old Sparrows Point man was stabbed to death outside the bar with a broken bottle, in what police suspected was a robbery.

One of two suspects was a man on a motorcycle, according to an article in The Evening Sun at the time. *"I think I've settled it down quite a bit over the years,"* said Thrasher, who said he was a friend of Stamp's and had known him for 30 years.

Yesterday, a white rubber glove and an unused oxygen mask lay on the parking lot near pools of blood. A police field interview card also lay on the ground with a bloodstain. The parking lot where Stamp was shot is isolated, surrounded by a BGE transmission station. Gang graffiti are sprayed on a back wall.

Several cars stopped by in the morning. People said they had heard about what happened and were curious to see the place where a city police officer killed his off-duty colleague.

Stamp Upheld Two Loyalties – April 25, 2008

For decades, Norman M. Stamp belonged to two brotherhoods.

The 65-year-old was one of the city's longest-serving active-duty officers, who on Wednesday had celebrated his 44th year with the Baltimore Police Department.

He also belonged to the Chosen Sons - a gritty motorcycle club that Stamp helped found in the 1960s, with a tight-knit membership that didn't shy from a fight.

Stamp looked out for his fellow bikers, according to his friends in the club. To his colleagues on the force, Stamp was a loyal officer who would never knowingly harm

a colleague. He was killed early yesterday in a confrontation with fellow officers in southeast Baltimore, one of whom fatally shot him as they tried to quell a brawl outside a strip club.

For decades, Stamp combined his passion for motorcycles with his job. He joined the department in 1964 and, five years later, was assigned to the motorcycle unit, where he served for 28 years, covering traffic duty and special events. In 1974, he broke his arm when he was struck by a patrol car while riding his departmental motorcycle.

"He did his job - he was no-nonsense," said Gary L. McLhinney, a former police union president. "If you were in a car and he was directing traffic, you went the way he told you to go. There's just a handful of guys like Norman left in this department."

In 1969, the year Stamp was transferred to the department's motorcycle unit, he helped form the Chosen Sons. It was a motorcycle club that started out consisting mostly of police and firefighters.

Paul "Nitro" Treash, the club's sergeant-at-arms, said Stamp liked to ride to Ocean City and smoke cigars with his biker friends. More than 40 years after its founding, the club and its traditions remained important to Stamp, Treash said.

"He was always the first to enter a fight and the last to leave," said Treash, who noted that he never saw Stamp draw his gun.

In 1997, Stamp was one of scores of officers caught up in a widespread staff shake-up in the Police Department. He eventually landed in the department's special operations section: cruising the harbor in a police boat for the marine unit.

Many who knew him said that Stamp initially resented being forced out onto the water after cruising the streets of Baltimore for decades on a motorcycle. But his friends said that he grew to like the assignment.

"To get a biker on a boat is like getting him to church," said the Haven Place strip club's owner, Charles Thrasher, who knew Stamp for 30 years. "I think he believed he wouldn't like it. He loved it. "Thrasher, who wasn't working when Stamp was shot, called his friend "'one of those unforgettable characters'" that one would encounter in Reader's Digest.

He said Stamp and the Chosen Sons would stop in his club every week after their meetings, have a few drinks and then leave - and Wednesday was no different.

"They've been coming here a while," said Thrasher. "They sort of think it's their bar."

Stamp, who was divorced and remarried, had a grown daughter and lived in Essex.

Officer Daniel J. Fickus, a former police union president who works in the marine unit, said Stamp had "a couple of loves in his life, and this job is one of them. He will be sorely missed, that is a fact. His family has 3,000 members - we'll be there for him and his family. We will be."

Bearing bruises, man says slain officer did not intervene - April 26, 2008

For Nick Roros, Wednesday night started when he went to Haven Place, had a couple of drinks and watched the dancers. It ended in the wee hours of the morning at the city's homicide unit. Roros said that he became involved in a bar brawl Wednesday evening that ultimately led to the fatal shooting of off-duty Baltimore City Police Officer Norman Stamp by another member of the force.

Roros, 43, gave his account during an interview yesterday morning at his Highlandtown home, where he showed the bruises and scrapes he said he got from fighting with members of the Chosen Sons, a close-knit motorcycle club that frequented the strip club. Stamp was a founding member of that club. Roros said he told his story to dispute news accounts suggesting that the off-duty officer tried to defuse the fight. "They act like they are all innocent like they were trying to break up the fight," Roros said. "They didn't try to break up [expletive]." During the interview, Roros asked, over and over, why nobody called police. He wanted to know why Stamp, a 44-year veteran of the force, didn't intervene on his behalf.

Members of the Chosen Sons say that Stamp tried to defuse the fight. Paul Treash, a sergeant-at-arms of the group, said that some of the bikers were fighting but maintains that Stamp was a peacemaker - he tried to calm people down.

However, police say that when Stamp emerged from the bar, he was wearing brass knuckles.

A group of uniformed police officers was attempting to break up a fight involving some members of the gang in front of the bar when Stamp came out the side door. An officer who was watching that exit hit him with a Taser, and Stamp fell down. When he rose and drew his gun, police say, [the uniformed officer] pulled his gun and shot Stamp at least once in the chest.

Police Commissioner Frederick H. Bealefeld III said at a news conference Thursday that the fight in the bar started over a woman. Police have said that it was someone outside the bar who called for help. A Police Department source familiar with the investigation confirmed that Roros was at the bar, was beaten and was interviewed by homicide detectives. But the person could not confirm all of the details of Roros' account.

Roros said that he got to the strip club around 10:30 pm - his wife was working, so he decided to go out. "The whole bar was full of bikers," he said. "They were dressed like bikers. They had the Chosen Sons patch and all that."

He struck up a conversation with a woman who came to the bar looking for a job. But, he said, one of the Chosen Sons wanted to talk to the same woman. "I was talking to some girl, and he was talking to the same girl," Roros said.

"He said, 'That's my girl,'" Roros said. In response, Roros said as a joke: "That is my wife."

Tensions rose. Roros used his cell phone and called his brother-in-law asking him to come to the bar. Roros didn't say why he didn't just leave. While he was on the phone, Roros said, one of the Chosen Sons punched him in the face.

"Once he hit me, I hit him," Roros said. "I got him on the ground." Roros said he had the upper hand, but then others joined in the fight. Next thing he knew, he said, he was on the ground. "I just felt everyone kicking me and just getting stomped," Roros said. He showed his one black eye yesterday. The other eye was filled with blood. He said that he doesn't have health insurance but is worried about his chest, which he said hurts when he breathes in.

"I was getting kicked from everywhere once they had me on the ground," he said. "After that I curled up and they just kept kicking and kicking. They were acting like . . ." He didn't finish his sentence.

"Why didn't he stop it?" Roros said, talking about Stamp. Roros told The Sun yesterday that he was dragged down to the end of the bar and then thrown out the side door. Bikers, he said, kept beating him in the parking lot. But a police source said multiple fights eventually broke out and Roros was never outside the bar.

Either way, Roros said that after being beaten he went back into the bar and was inside, standing near the side door, when he heard the gunshots that killed Officer

Stamp. "By that time I was all dazed," Roros said. "I don't know when the cops came what happened."

Slain Officer's Chosen Sons Not Known to Run From Fight - April 28, 2008

The one-story clubhouse in Southeast Baltimore has wood floors and framed photographs of members who have died. It feels like a chapter of an Elks Club, the American Legion or Veterans of Foreign Wars.

But the members are big beefy men who wear red crosses on their backs. Many are covered in tattoos, and some grow long pointed beards. They belong to the Chosen Sons - a motorcycle club started by city police officers in 1969 that bills itself as the largest in the state. For decades, the Chosen Sons has been an insular group, wary of outsiders and little known except in the East Baltimore neighborhoods where they gather.

That changed early Thursday morning when one of its founding members, Norman Stamp, an off-duty police officer, burst out of a North Haven Street strip club, brass knuckles on his hand, heading toward a brawl that had spilled from the bar into the street. Before he got there, Stamp was stopped by a uniformed officer sent to quell the fight. In the confusion, Stamp drew his gun, and the other officer shot and killed him, according to police accounts. He had been on the force for 44 years.

The unusual fit between the public and private sides of Stamp's life will be on full display at his funeral today. Because his death is not considered to have come in the line of duty, he will not get full police services.

Even so, Mayor Sheila Dixon and Police Commissioner Frederick H. Bealefeld III plan to attend. They will sit in a 100-seat Essex funeral home alongside members of the Chosen Sons and other motorcycle clubs from around the state "You will see guys from clubs that feud with each other," said Paul "Nitro" Treash, the sergeant-at-arms of the Chosen Sons. "Norm [Stamp] was the most likable guy."

Little is known about how Stamp balanced his job on the force - for the past decade, he served in the maritime unit, and for years before that, he was a motorcycle officer - with his off-duty activities. Some of his acquaintances from the world of the Chosen Sons say Stamp was always eager for a fight, but current members aren't saying much, other than to offer a relatively wholesome, if tattooed and leather-clad, vision of the club's activities.

Treash said members of the Chosen Sons organized rides to places like Myrtle Beach in South Carolina. Stamp, he said, participated in the club's last "poker run" - an outing on which members of the crew ride together to other clubhouses in the city or state. At each clubhouse they pick up playing cards - the person with the best poker hand by the end of the night is the winner.

But there was an air of paranoia at the clubhouse Thursday morning when news of Stamp's death spread. Members wondered out loud about a Verizon truck that had been sitting outside the building for a few hours. When a man drove up in a car and sat outside, a junior member of the club was dispatched to determine whether the person in the car was the same person who caused a fight with the club members the evening before.

Treash would not answer most questions about the club for this article and would not make any of the members available to comment. Current members declined to talk about the group. Treash did say that the club is the largest in the state, but he declined to give a number of total membership. A photograph of some members on the wall inside the club showed about 100 men gathered for an event. Treash would not say how many members are police officers.

Initially, the club was open only to public service employees, said William Council, a retired police officer who knew Stamp and was in the club in the late 1970s. At that point there were 15 to 20 members, he said, including one member who repaired motorcycles for the Baltimore city garage.

"We'd take group rides," Council said. "We'd pick a place where we wanted to go and go bar hopping. It wasn't a threatening group or anything like that." Council said that the name came from being chosen for the club. "You had to have somebody represent you to get in," he said. "They bring you in, they ask you some questions. Now I don't know how they do it."

According to the Chosen Sons Motorcycle Club Web site, prospective members still need to be tapped: "The C.S.M.C. does not solicit for members or accept any unknowns. All prospects must be sponsored by a member in good standing."

A fictional version of the club was featured in a January 1995 episode of Homicide: Life on the Streets. In the show, the club was called the Deacons, and some members who appeared in it put a Deacons insignia over the red crosses on backs of their jackets. The insignia from one of those jackets is hanging, framed, on the Chosen Sons clubhouse wall.

The group was started in 1969 and grew in the 1970s and 1980s, a macho time when motorcycle clubs like the Hells Angels and the Pagans would fight for territory and respect. Unlike those clubs, the Chosen Sons is not viewed as a criminal organization, according to a city police source who is not authorized to speak to the news media.

In fact, in the very early days, the club had to combat the perception that they would always run from a fight because its members - all public service employees - could lose their jobs if they got in trouble, said Richard C. Fahlteich, a retired major from the city's homicide unit who knew Stamp and talked to him recently about the club. That was a perception the club would not abide by.

"If someone was going to attempt to start a big fight, they were not going to run away from it," Fahlteich said. "That is where the tough guy thing came from. They did not go out looking for trouble, but they were not going to bow to trouble either. They were going to stand up for themselves."

The penchant for standing up for themselves was viewed differently in the neighborhood. Steve Fugate, the president of the city's fire officers' union, grew up in the same Highlandtown area where the club members would ride. "It was a bunch of bad asses," Fugate said. "From an outside perspective, they were the local version of the Hells Angels. That was anecdotal neighborhood gossip that was going around." Fugate, 54, said that he would never pick a fight with them. "Because I'd get my ass kicked," he said. "Been there, done that. It's not fun."

<u>*Cops and Bikers – Baltimore Police Officer Killed Outside a Bar Gets an Unusual Sendoff from His Buddies*</u> - April 29, 2008

Two rows of men, police officers and bikers, faced each other yesterday morning - lining the edges of Old Eastern Avenue as bagpipes played and city police carried the casket of Norman Stamp to a waiting hearse.

The police wore their dress uniforms to honor the death of the man who spent the past 44 years working for the city's Police Department.

The motorcycle riders wore the red cross of the Chosen Sons on their backs to signal their association with the motorcycle club that Stamp helped to found 39 years ago.

It was an unusual sendoff for a man who was one of the city's longest-serving police officers. Bikers from various clubs around the state outnumbered the uniformed

police officers. Photographs on display showed Stamp doing daredevil stunts on police motorcycles, posing with various police weapons and drinking beer with a woman clad in a leather bikini.

The police commissioner and mayor listened as the audience cheered for a speaker who disputed the official account of how Stamp came to be shot by a fellow officer early Thursday. Stamp was shot in the chest after police were called to quell a bar brawl at an East Baltimore strip club. Police say Stamp burst out of the bar, with brass knuckles on his fist, and failed to comply with verbal orders to stop from a uniformed officer.

The officer used a stun gun on Stamp, who then drew his gun, police said. The uniformed officer, John Torres, drew his own weapon and shot Stamp twice, hitting him at least once in the chest. But Rick Mueller, a member of a pleasure club called Fat Boys, stood in front of Stamp's open casket and said: "Hopefully, with the help of the witnesses who were there that night, the truth will come out." Applause from the audience lasted 15 seconds. When it died down, he continued: "Procedure wasn't followed, but it was not Norm that failed."

Stamp's widow, Suzanne, sobbed as those words were spoken. Over the weekend she enlisted the help of two attorneys and a private investigator, Michael Van Nostrand Sr., to conduct an independent probe of the shooting. Van Nostrand, reached by phone, had questions about that account: "Did he have the brass knuckles on as they say? How do you reach for a gun if you have knuckles on?" Police recovered brass knuckles from the parking lot where the fight occurred.

Dozens of bouquets of flowers lined the inside of the funeral home. One was shaped like a motorcycle, another like a police shield and another like a heart. Stamp's black leather biker boots and his wooden nightstick stood next to his coffin. Two cigars, his motorcycle colors and his police motorcycle helmet rested near his body.

At the service, Police Commissioner Frederick H. Bealefeld III praised Stamp's 44-year career with the city but appeared to choose his words carefully. "All of us have a spiritual calling to service and responsibility to service," he said. "How that manifests itself, what that looks like ... takes on many dimensions. Norm's calling was police service. "He dedicated himself to that for 44 years. In that time, I'm absolutely convinced, he helped many, many people," Bealefeld said.

Paul Blair, president of the city's police union, knew Stamp and called him a good officer. Though Blair usually wears business suits to police events to signal his role

as the union chief, this time he put on his dress uniform. "I said, I had to wear my colors," Blair said, making reference to the many bikers in the audience who use colors to refer to the patches they wear on their backs. "We call it the thin blue line," Blair said, adding that Stamp's police family holds him just as dear as Stamp's biker family. The audience laughed when Blair referred to Stamp's time at the city police marine unit as Stamp's "private navy."

The ceremony was led by Sgt. Don Helms, a police chaplain, and was organized loosely, with various speakers telling stories about Stamp's life. Timothy J. Haefner, a police officer in the Southeastern District, had trouble getting though his speech without crying. "There were so many words that described Norm," he said. As his voice cracked, some of the women in the audience asked for tissues. "Norm lived his life to the fullest," Haefner said. "My heart is truly broken."

The first biker to speak was Reds Sullivan, president of the Chosen Sons, who thanked Stamp for starting the club and called him a mediator. "Call Stamp and he'd fix it," Sullivan said. Then, becoming emotional, Sullivan said: "I'm going to get out of here before I begin to cry."

Mueller, who spoke last, recalled one of Stamp's favorite police stories. He said Stamp pulled over a man in East Baltimore and the man, not realizing to whom he was talking, tried to get out of the ticket by saying he was a close friend of Norm Stamp.

Because Stamp's death was not considered to have been in the line of duty, he did not receive the full police honors afforded many officers who are killed. Those funerals usually tie up city streets for hours as processions of police cars roll to Dulaney Memorial Gardens. Instead, mourners yesterday were invited to the Chosen Sons' headquarters - a clubhouse that is about two blocks north from the strip club where Stamp was shot.

Civil Trial Begins In Wrongful Death Case of Officer Shot by Police - October 07, 2010

Police said that in April 2008, off-duty officer Norman Stamp burst out of a Southeast Baltimore strip club with brass knuckles on his hand, barreling toward a brawl involving members of his motorcycle club that had spilled into the street.

That's when, according to police, the 44-year-veteran got into a confrontation with a uniformed officer sent to quell the fight, pulled his service weapon and was fatally shot.

An attorney for Stamp's widow said Thursday — the first day of trial in a wrongful-death civil suit brought against Officer John Torres — that there's a different story that the Police Department wanted to suppress.

In opening statements, attorney Peter T. McDowell said Stamp was shot by Torres as he exited the Haven Place club to leave for the night, a hasty decision that McDowell said was made by an officer who had "wrongly prejudged" the situation.

He plans to call witnesses who were at the bar — tracked down by a private investigator hired by Stamp's wife of four years, Suzanne — and a forensic expert to counter the Police Department's findings. "Police investigating [the shooting] just didn't want to uncover the truth," McDowell told jurors.

However, attorney Troy A. Priest said Torres was separating Stamp from another man when Stamp fell down some stairs. Stamp then came at Torres, shaking off a three-second Taser jolt and drawing his gun. As Priest described the officer's account of the events, Torres put his head down and appeared emotional. Priest said Torres now suffers from post-traumatic stress disorder. "He was in fear for his life, and took actions necessary not only to save his life but the others there," Priest said.

Stamp had not been involved in the initial fight inside the bar, which prompted the club operators to turn on the lights and cut off the music. Nick Roros, who had been injured in the brawl, called his brother-in-law, a Fells Point bar owner, who in turn called the personal cell phone of Officer Raymond Buda, who was patrolling the area with Torres and another officer. McDowell said that Stamp, unaware of a situation brewing outside, said good night to a bartender, then exchanged brief words with a dancer near the back door. A moment later, the dancer heard two gunshots, McDowell said, adding that she never heard any commotion or commands to drop a weapon.

Torres' attorney said that Roros had charged Stamp, and they had to be separated by Torres. Stamp was shot after stumbling down the steps and pulling his weapon on Torres, who shot downward from the top of the stairs. He said brass knuckles were recovered from the scene.

"The decision [to shoot] was reasonable, and consistent with his training and experience," Priest said.

But McDowell said a man who was in the parking lot and heard the gunshots wheeled around to see Stamp falling down the steps, where he remained until

medics arrived. McDowell said the trajectory of the bullets that struck Stamp suggest that he was shot by someone who was below him.

The lawsuit initially alleged that Torres was hired as part of a Baltimore Police Department policy to "hire untrained Puerto Rican applicants to assist with the Spanish-speaking community within Baltimore City." It said the applicants were hired with "blatant disregard for the safety of the public" and kept in order to maintain a quota of Spanish-speaking officers.

The department and the city were removed as defendants in the case, and no such claims were made in McDowell's opening statements.

The two witnesses called to testify Thursday appeared to be an effort to counter the image of Stamp as a brawling biker and strip club patron.

Zeinab Rabold, a former Baltimore police colonel who oversaw internal affairs until she was forced to retire in 2004, said she knew Stamp for years and described him as a "mellow" officer who was deft at defusing tense situations. He worked mainly in the traffic and marine units, and took pride in being a police officer, she said.

His motorcycle club, called the Chosen Sons, was formed by a group of five law enforcement officers in the 1960s, said friend and former prosecutor Robert Donadio, who was a member of the group for about 10 years. The group, in those early days at least, was open exclusively to those in law enforcement, and they did charity events for children. Donadio, 78, said Stamp would dress up as Santa Claus. "Officer Stamp was a peacemaker," Donadio testified.

Baltimore jury finds in favor of officer in shooting death - October 21, 2010

A Baltimore jury found Thursday that a city officer acted reasonably when he killed an off-duty member of the force while responding to a fight at a Southeast Baltimore strip club. The widow of Officer Norman Stamp, a 44-year veteran who was fatally shot in April 2008, sued Officer John Torres, alleging that he "wrongly prejudged" the situation and that the Police Department didn't aggressively investigate the circumstances of the shooting.

The trial lasted about two weeks, during which jurors visited the Haven Place club where the shooting occurred. Jurors took only a few hours to decide in favor of Torres, the Daily Record reported on its website Thursday afternoon. Police have said that Stamp, 65, who was hanging out with members of his motorcycle club, *rushed out of the bar with brass knuckles. Torres struck him with a Taser, then fired two shots when Stamp reached for his service weapon, police said. As he lay dying, Stamp identified himself as an officer.*

In opening statements, Peter McDowell, an attorney for Stamp's widow, Suzanne Stamp, said that the police account did not mesh with descriptions from witnesses and forensic experts gathered by a private investigator. For example, McDowell claimed that Stamp was shot while standing at the top of stairs leading out of the club, though Torres said he was at the top of the stairs and had shot downward at Stamp. McDowell said that Torres impulsively shot Stamp as he left the strip club for the night unaware of the police action outside.

But Torres' attorney, Troy A. Priest, dismissed those claims and said the officer was in fear for his life and followed his training. McDowell said Thursday that Suzanne Stamp was "obviously disappointed in the jury's verdict," but said she was content that the other accounts of the night were "now part of the public record." Priest did not return a message seeking comment

The lawsuit initially alleged that Torres was hired as part of a Baltimore Police Department policy to "hire untrained Puerto Rican applicants to assist with the Spanish-speaking community within Baltimore City." It said the applicants were hired with "blatant disregard for the safety of the public" and kept to maintain a quota of Spanish-speaking officers.

Testimony included how the shooting had affected both sides; friends of Stamp said his wife was devastated and still talks about Stamp as if he is alive. Torres' attorney said his client suffers from post-traumatic stress disorder.

29 April - 1966

Today in Baltimore Police History, **name plates** were first issued to and worn by City Police Officers - Effective 9 am, Interim Police Commissioner George M. Gelston ordered all officers to begin wearing a name plate for identification purposes. An idea the State Police started 7 years earlier to the day, on 29 April, 1959. At the time, Commissioner Gelston felt it would improve the image of the police department, and initiate some sort of transparency.

Note: the first officer to wear a nameplate was Patrolman Edward Campbell. Officer Campbell, would affix his name plate to his uniform one day earlier when he acted as a model to wear his name plate as he posed for the Baltimore Sun Paper on 28 April 1966, making Officer Campbell the first Baltimore Officer to officially wear his nameplate.

30 April - 1800

Today in Baltimore Police History, a meeting took place forming a committee of three persons from each of 20 wards, to plan a reorganization of the Police Department's "Nightwatch." At a subsequent assembly, this committee advised that the patrol should be increased. After a vote, that recommendation was approved and at a later assembly of this group, it was learned that by the vigilance of the Nightwatchmen, disorder for a time in Baltimore, was suppressed.

1 May - 1860 - 2nd Issue Badge

Today in Baltimore Police History the **2nd issue badge** was issued, replacing the original badge (a large six pointed star) worn by Baltimore Police officers since 20 October 1851. This signalled the creation of a new "Metropolitan Police" force, under a newly created Board of Police Commissioners (made up of state-appointed civilians) and the retirement of the "Corporation Police" force. This new badge had a large oval Roman "fasces," an axe bound by wooden rods, as its central symbol. Across the top and sides of the "fasces" was a banner with the words "Baltimore Police" in raised letters. Absent from the new badge was the official city seal (the War of 1812 Battle Monument) that had been the centerpiece of the first badge.

5 May - 1974

On this date in Baltimore Police History, 1974, we lost our brother, Police Officer **Frank Warren Whitby, Jr.** to gunfire. Shortly after 1:00 pm Officers Frank Whitby and William Nowakowski were working 311 post in the Eastern District, when they received a call to back-up another unit that was handling a call for an armed person in the 1900 Blk. of E. Lanvale Street.

On arrival, Officer Whitby took the shotgun from the trunk of his patrol car and approached the door of the house with his fellow officers. The officers spoke to the woman who had answered the door, and she assured them that the suspect was in the house, and that he was unarmed. She had no explanation for why the call was dispatched as an armed person.

Still, the officers entered the location with great care, Officer Whitby in the lead. Suddenly, gunshots rang out from the far end of the hallway. Officer Whitby was struck three times, and fell to the floor. His fellow officers sought cover, while returning fire. A volley of rounds were exchanged with the suspect as Officer Whitby crawled from the hallway back to the safety of the street. Additional back-up units arrived, and the business of getting the suspect out of the house began. Once out of, or low on ammo, the 42-year-old suspect surrendered to Police Officers after several minutes of negotiations.

Taken to Johns Hopkins Hospital, Officer Frank Warren Whitby, Jr., a 22-year-old father of two young daughters, would succumb to massive abdominal wounds brought about when he was shot by a coward who lay in wait in the dark, just apparently waiting for officers to walk into his line of sight. Only after killing our brother and running low on ammo, would this suspect negotiate for his own life, because as usual, as with most cold blooded killers, they are only tough when they have the upper hand. After that, the testosterone shrinks, and their willingness to die for their cause shrivels up with it.

While he is no longer with us, he is still our brother, and as such we his brothers and sisters of the Baltimore Police Department will not let him be forgotten.

5 May - 1939

On this day in Baltimore Police History 1939, we lost our brother Patrolman **Charles W. Frizzell** due to injuries from a line of duty assault approximately one year earlier.

The Baltimore Sun - May 6, 1939; pg. 17

Patrolman Frizzell – Succumbs in Hospital – Was Operated on Several Days Ago – Injured a Year ago When Attacked By Prisoner

Patrolman Charles W. Frizzell, of the Eastern District, died last night [Friday – 5 May 1939] at University Hospital. His condition had been serious after an

operation. Several emergency calls for blood donors had been issued within the last two days. No further information concerning the Patrolman's injuries or death are available, probably because his death is not listed as a Line of Duty fatality.

Patrolman Frizzell was assaulted about a year ago as he was taking a prisoner to a police call box. His fellow – officers said the injuries that led to his death appeared at the time of that arrest.

Eastern District police said, however they have not definitely connected the assault with Patrolman Frizzell's Death. An investigation will begin today.

Patrolman Frizzell was 41. He was appointed to the force and assigned to the Eastern district in October, 1932. He had been commended at least once and was injured several times in the line of duty.

While he is no longer with us, he is still our brother, and as such we his brothers and sisters of the Baltimore Police Department will not let him be forgotten.

7 May - 1997

On this day in Baltimore Police History, 1997 we lost our brother **Lieutenant Owen Eugene Sweeney**, Jr. to gun fire in the line of duty. Twenty-eight year veteran Lt. Owen E. Sweeney's death underscores the dangers police face daily.

Lt. Owen Sweeney, 47, was doing paperwork from a safe location inside the district's station house on that Wednesday, 7 May, 1997 when he heard a call come across the police radio for a mental case. He could have stayed at his safe desk, in his safe chair, and let his officers handle the call they'd been dispatched on their own – after all, that was their job. But he was known as a working lieutenant, and he always felt his place was to be on the scene with his officers. So away he went, arriving at the home with his officers.

Every bit the compassionate officer, he took it upon himself to try to pacify the mental patient, believing that it is always better to calm a suspect and take them in without a struggle or injury to anyone – on either side. So as he tried to negotiate with the subject through the door of his home, he and the officer with him heard the racking of a shotgun, the sound coming less than a second before they heard the blast from the same gun. The blast came through the wall and door, killing the 28-

year police veteran before he had any kind of real time to react.

In some ways, the Northeast Baltimore confrontation was an uncanny reminder of an incident that took place some sixteen months earlier. At that time, a mentally ill woman, distraught and armed with a large kitchen knife, was shot and killed as she lunged at officers. Advocates for the mentally ill attacked police behavior unmercifully, saying that despite her knife, she was outnumbered by officers who should have been able to overpower her or defuse the crisis with the aid of psychiatrists.

According to accounts that emerged yesterday, neither Lieutenant Sweeney nor other officers on the scene of the 7 May, 1997, incident knew the accused killer, Baron Michael Cherry, 41, had a shotgun.

His wife did not say he was armed. Mr. Cherry had stopped taking the medicine that controlled his disruptive behavior three weeks earlier. His wife correctly telephoned 311, the number reserved for non-urgent, non-emergency police matters.

Under those circumstances, Lieutenant Sweeney thought his intervention could help. He was not wearing protective armor at the time – since it was the end of his shift and he was already at the stationhouse waiting for his shift's officers to come in at the end of their tour of duty, he had already shed the body armor at the station.

He had his back to the door as he was in the process of walking away from the locked door when the shotgun's sound, and then the blast through the closed door occurred, hitting him in the back.

At the time of Lieutenant Sweeney's killing he was the first Baltimore City Officer to be killed in the line of duty in almost 5 years. The last before him came about on 21 September, 1992 with the murder of Officer Ira Neil Weiner.

Lieutenant Sweeneys' death underscores the risks law enforcement officers take, in putting their lives on the line every time they put on their uniform and head out the door to serve and protect the public.

There was a common thread in the Northeast Baltimore shooting of Lt. Sweeney and the case mentioned earlier. One in which officers killed a mentally ill patient, the other where a mentally disturbed patient killed an officer. In both cases, prescribed medications kept the patient's violent tendencies and abusive behavior at bay, and in both cases the patients had decided on their own to terminate the use of the prescribed medications. While it is all too common, and obviously all too easy, for such patients to discontinue the use of their medications, it underscores the current lack of treatment facilities which can administer the needed medications to the patient while also treating their conditions psychologically. These are situations over which the police have no control, leading to all too many such deadly confrontations. And in too many cases, it's all too easy to blame the police.

We can no longer continue to regularly ask police, or other innocent citizens to give their lives for the sake of someone who while on their meds might be the perfect citizen, but while off those same meds is homicidal. Perhaps police commanders should endeavor to promulgate and implement procedures for involving medical resources and specialists in such cases as soon as a confrontation develops. The job of policing the streets is tough enough. Law-enforcement officers should be able to turn to psychiatric professionals for help immediately after a problem occurs.

While he is no longer with us, we his brothers and sisters of the Baltimore Police Department will not let Lieutenant Owen Sweeney be forgotten. RIP Brother.

9 May - 2013

Today in Baltimore Police History, 2013, we lost our brother, retired **Police Officer Gary Dresser.**

While on the force Officer Dresser was a Medal of Honor recipient. He received his Medal of Honor after effecting the rescue of four other officers who were also wounded in a gun battle on October 31, 1974. What follows tells the story of that gun battle and Officer Dresser's heroism:

The streets of West Baltimore were almost deserted as Officer Alric K. Moore, of the Western District began trying-up doors on his post in the early morning hours of Thursday, 31 October, 1974. While approaching a bar in the 1600 block of West Baltimore Street he noticed that the side door was slightly ajar. Closer examination revealed fresh pry marks and he immediately called for back-up units.

When other officers arrived they discovered that the juke box and other items from the bar had been removed. Further investigation revealed a trail of scuff and drag marks left by the heavy juke box being wrestled along the alley. These marks led down the alley to the rear porch of a house on Fayette Street. There on the back porch sat the stolen juke box in plain view. With the front of the house covered by other back-up officers, Officer Gary Dresser and Officer Moore approached the closed door that was partly blocked by the stolen juke box. As they got onto the porch of the darkened house rapid-fire gun shots rang out from inside striking Officer Moore in the right shoulder and wounding Officer Dresser in the hand as he dove for cover.

As Officer Dresser helped the wounded Officer out of the line of fire Officer Glenn D. Hauze was hit in the right shoulder by a second burst of gunfire as he rushed to their aid. Back-up units responded quickly and tightly sealed off the area. The gunman moved from one window to firing more short bursts from his semi-automatic .45 caliber rifle, as the officers returned fire and Officers Hauze and Moore were extricated and rushed to the hospital. One of the bursts struck Officer Joseph E. Hlafka wounding him in the jaw, back shoulder and both arms as he took up a position in a near-by yard. Officer Hlafka was removed and rushed to an area hospital as the officers returned fire and attempted to talk the suspect out of the house.

The suspect moved to the front of the house and officers continued to ask him to surrender and throw his weapon out. Soon the semi-automatic was dropped from a second floor window. It rested on the front steps as officers cautiously approached the front door. As they edged towards the entrance the suspect came partially out of the front door and yelled, "Put your guns away and I'll give up." Officer Charles Thrush holstered his service revolver and advised the suspect that he was going to handcuff him. As Officer Thrush walked towards him, the gunman suddenly bent over and grabbed the semi-automatic rifle lying next to the steps. Sergeant Anthony Sarro, of the Southwestern District, warned Officer Thrush, who dove for cover, and as the suspect began to raise the weapon, Sergeant Sarro fired one round from his shotgun, striking the suspect who then dropped his weapon and quickly retreated back into the house.

After the other occupants of the dwelling came out, officers cautiously entered the premises, guns drawn. The suspect was found dead in the hallway on the third floor. A search of the house revealed a recently stolen .357 magnum handgun, which had been taken in a robbery the day before, in the 2000 block of W. Pratt Street.

Officers Dresser and Hauze were treated at area hospitals and released. Officers Moore and Hlafka were admitted to Bon Secours Hospital, but fully recovered. God Bless them all…And on this day, let us take a moment to remember our brother, Retired Officer Gary Dresser.

16 May - 1968

The department installed its first National Crime Information Center (NCIC) computer terminal, permitting direct access to the storehouse of information on wanted persons, stolen vehicles, stolen weapons, and identifiable stolen property at the Federal Bureau of Investigation headquarters in Washington, D. C. This system enabled wanted/stolen inquiries from officers on patrol to be answered within a few short minutes, rather than the twenty minutes or more such inquiries previously took.

17 May - 1837

The first issue of the Baltimore Sun was printed - The first article in the Baltimore Sun that referenced our police was titled "Rioting" and it was a negative report. Even when the Department pointed out factual errors in the report, the paper still ran the story.

17 May - 1925

On this day in Baltimore Police History, 1925, we lost our brother, **Patrolman Patrick J. Coniffee** in the line of duty.

Patrolman Patrick J. Coniffee of the Central District died Monday night at St. Joseph Hospital from injuries he received when he was struck by a streetcar while walking his beat at Fleet Street and Patterson Park Avenue a day earlier. An inquest will be held on 18 May, 1925, by Dr. J.S.H. Potter, coroner for the Northeast district of Baltimore.

Immediately after the accident, the streetcar stopped, and the motorman and conductor picked up the injured officer up. He was taken to St. Joseph's Hospital the hospital in the automobile of William Longe, of the 600 block S. Bond St. It was thought that the patrolman was suffering from a fractured skull and other possible internal injuries.

The motorman operating the streetcar, David E. Miles of 811 South Calhoun Street was arrested, but later released to appear at the inquest tomorrow. The conductor was Frank Walters, of the 800 block of Scott Street. Mr. Walters will also appear at the inquest.

The patrolman was 44 years old and lived at 720 Mura St. - The policeman was crossing the street when he was struck by a car about 11 pm. Officer Coniffee has been on the Baltimore police force since June, 1913 and prior to that time he was a special officer for the B&O Railroad Company.

19 May - 2006

On this day in Baltimore Police History, 2006, we lost our brother, **Officer Anthony A. Byrd** to a departmental vehicle collision with another radio car, operated by Officer Raymond E. Cook Jr., who was listed in serious condition at Maryland Shock Trauma Center immediately after the accident.

The collision occurred at the stop sign-controlled intersection leading to the Southwestern District stationhouse. Neither officer was in route to an emergency call, and which officer was at fault has not, to your writer's knowledge, been released to the public.

While he is gone, he will not be forgotten, as we his brothers and sisters of the Baltimore Police Department will not allow that. He stood tall, and made us proud to call him our brother. RIP Officer Byrd, and God Bless.

20 May - 1902

On this day in Baltimore Police History, 1902, we lost our brother **Patrolman Charles J. Donohue**, of the Northwestern police district to Gunfire.

From newspaper reports at the time – 20 May, 1902

Patrolman Donohue was shot behind the left ear by John Prewvines, aka Charles Wilson; a colored man, in the latter's house at 1332 Whatcoat Street. The shooting was done with Patrolman Donohue's own revolver. Prewvines made his escape after firing the fatal shot, and at an early hour this morning had not been captured.

Patrolman Donohue had been called in to the house by Mary Jones, Prewvines' common-law wife, to arrest Prewvines, the couple having had trouble about money. It was said the trouble between Prewvines and the Jones' woman started over 50 cents he is alleged to have gotten from her by claiming a friend had been arrested,

and that he wanted money to help pay the fine. When the woman learned that the story was false, she demanded the return of the money.

The Dispute Grew Warm, and the Woman Called in Officer Donohue

According to Mary Jones, as Donohue entered a rear room in search of Prewvines, he was struck over the head by the man with a beer bottle. While dazed from the blow Donohue attempted to draw his revolver. Prewvines grabbed it, and knock the half conscious officer to the floor, then aimed the pistol and deliberately fired into Donohue's head, the ball entering just behind the left ear. The report of the pistol attracted Sergeant Plum, who was in the area. When Plum arrived at the house he found Patrolman Donahue bleeding on the floor, but his assailant had fled through a rear yard.

Patrolman Donahue died last evening, at 8.40 o'clock, at the Maryland Homeopathic Hospital, to which he was removed after the shooting. He did not regain consciousness, and therefore no dying deposition could be taken. No hope of Patrolman Donohue's recovery was entertained at any time at the hospital. Doctors found that the bullet had lodged at the base of the brain and could not be extracted. Probing for the bullet had to be discontinued because of the great flow of blood from the wound. The doctors realized the patrolman's condition was hopeless, and all that they attempted to do was to make him as comfortable as possible.

Once Officer Donohue was taken to the hospital, a general alarm was sent out for Prewvines. According to the description sent out that morning, Prewvines was 30 to 35 years old, about 5'6" to 5'7" inches tall, moderately stout, of dark brown skin color, has a small mustache and an upper front tooth is missing. He wore a dark coat and vest, had plaid trousers, with light flat soft hat. As far as can be determined, Prewvines was never caught or charged with the crime.

Patrolman Charles J. Donohue was appointed on 20 August, 1901, and was 27 years of age when this occurred. His home address was 704 North Fremont Ave. His father was Mr. John Donohue, a well-known liveryman. Miss Margaret Donohue, a sister of the dead patrolman, spent the whole day at his bedside. His father and his other brothers and sisters were present when he drew his last breath.

20 May - 2006

The **Underwater Recovery Unit** becomes an official unit of the department. It is as of this date fully equipped and operational. On 7 December 2005, Sgt Kurt Roepcke of the Marine unit was able to start to process of getting it up and running, with the backing and assistance of Col. Scott Williams and Sgt. George McClaskey

22 May - 1838

The council substantially re-enacted the ordinance of 1835, providing that if any watchman while in the performance of his duty should be wounded or maimed he should receive half-pay during the continuance of his disability, or for a period not exceeding two months. They were also paid for attendance at court. This ordinance provided as well for the annual appointment of three justices of the peace to receive the reports of the night watch. One of these justices was required to reside in each district. The yearly salary of each was $100.

22 May - 1871

On this day in Baltimore Police History, we lost our brother, **Patrolman Joseph C. Clarke** to gunfire.

From newspaper reports at the time:

The wanton and cold-blooded shooting of Patrolman Joseph C. Clarke on Monday night by Frederick M. Kusey as reported in the Tuesday night May 23rd SunPaper yesterday gave rise to considerable feelings during the day in the community. The body of the deceased was at an early hour removed to his late residence. Policeman Clarke was a very worthy citizen, and a good officer.

He leaves a wife, nine children as well as many grandchildren. The alleged murderer, Frederick M. Kusey is said to belong to Philadelphia. He was arrested about 6 am yesterday by policemen Bradley, McGuire, and Chew on the warrant of Coroner Spacer. Kusey was committed to jail to await the selection of the grand jury.

Kusey is a young man about 23 years of age, rather spare, and about 5'8" in height.

It appeared that on Monday night after committing the deed he escaped from the premise number 28 Center St. by a gate leading out to Holliday Street without his hat. He first went to the labor house by Voechell on the corner of Franklin and North Streets where he procured a hat, and about midnight when all the spare men of the police force were searching for him, he appeared at the Lighter beer saloon of Mr. Johnson, under the mansion house corner of St. Paul and Fayette Streets and asked for and obtained a drink.

Here he said that he had gotten himself into a scrape, and that he had shot a policeman. He then displayed the pistol with which he alleged the shooting was committed. He complained of being tired, and having no money, borrowing $.50 with which to pay for a bed at the mansion house. Mr. Johnson had not learned of the policeman's murder, and was disposed not to believe Kusey. At an early hour yesterday morning on reading the account of the affair in the Sun paper he at once gave information to Policeman Bradley, who calling to his assistance of McGuire, and Chew proceeded to the room of Kusey and arrested him as he was about leaving the bed.

As his brothers and sisters of the Baltimore Police Department we will not allow him to be forgotten. May he Rest in Peace and May God Bless him.

26 May - 1956

On this day in Baltimore Police History, 1956 we lost our brother, Police **Lieutenant William P. Thompson** to a Heart Attack based on the following newspaper reporting at the time:

<u>W. P. Thompson, Policeman, Dies</u> - Newspaper Report; May 28, 1956; pg. 13

Police Lieutenant William P. Thompson, 48, of 372 Marydell Rd., died early yesterday, [Sunday, 26 May, 1956] apparently of heart trouble, while on duty, and in a patrol car within the Southwest District.

He was slumped over the steering wheel when found at 3:35 am by Sgt. Walker Jasper, at Fayette and Stricker Streets. Police said Lieutenant Thompson had been receiving treatment for a heart condition but was cleared for duty.

He had left the Southwestern Station House (Located at Calhoun Street and Pratt Streets) at about 3:30 am after helping a patrolman make an arrest, police said.

Native of Baltimore Maryland

A native of Baltimore, Lieutenant Thompson lived here all his life, joining the Police Department 17 May, 1933. He was promoted to Sgt. on 10 February, 1948, and then to Lieutenant on 28 December, 1950.

He was assigned to the Eastern district after his appointment and to the Northeast district when promoted to Lieutenant. He had been at the southwestern district for about four years, police said.

Lieutenant Thompson is survived by his wife, Mrs. Doris M. Thompson: a daughter, Mrs. Frederick Glover: a brother, Joseph P. Thompson, and three sisters, Mrs. Anna Rivers, Mrs. Margaret Headle and Mrs. Marie Rann. All lived in Baltimore.

The body is at the Walters Funeral Home, Pratt and Stricker Streets. The Requiem Mass will be offered tomorrow at 10:00 am at St. Joseph Monastery Church, Loudoun Street and Old Frederick Road. Burial will be in Loudon Park Cemetery.

While he is no longer with us, he will never be forgotten, by us; his brothers and sisters of the Baltimore Police Department. RIP and God Bless, as we take this time to remember you on this day.

26 May - 1962

On this day in Baltimore Police History, 1962 we lost our brother, Police **Officer Richard D. Seebo** to gunfire.

Officer Seebo stopped a vehicle in the 300 Block of E. 20th Street for traffic violations. As he pulled his motorcycle to the rear of the vehicle, the driver put his car in reverse backed into the officer, throwing him to the ground. Getting up Officer Seebo went to the driver's side window to confront the motorist. When he approached the vehicle, the driver withdrew a pistol and shot officer Seebo in the chest. Officer Seebo fell to the ground and the assailant shot him again in the back as he stood over top of him.

The occupants of the car, Henry Ben Huff, 18, and Wallace Creighton were later arrested in South Carolina and charged with the murder of the Officer Seebo.

Officer Seebo was married, and the father of two children. He served in the U.S. Navy from August 15, 1955 to August 23, 1957.

While he is no longer with us, he will never be forgotten, by us; his brothers and sisters of the Baltimore Police Department. RIP and God Bless, as we take this time to remember you on this day.

26 May - 1993

On this day in Baltimore Police History, 1993, we lost our brother, Police **Officer Herman A. Jones, Sr**. to gunfire. Officer Jones had just finished his shift as a footman in Central Districts Operations unit when he stopped at his favorite carry-out on his way home, where he was shot and killed as he waited for his order.

Three teenagers entered the restaurant with intent on robbing the business and occupants, at some point they grabbed Officer Jones, who was off-duty, but wearing his officer pants, navy blue with black piping down the seams. As a result of his pants, it could be that he was recognized as police, and as such one of the teenagers drew a .38 caliber handgun and shot Officer Jones twice. Officer Jones was able to return fire, striking two of the three suspects.

All three suspects were later apprehended and arrested. Officer Jones had served with the agency for 24 years. He was survived by his wife and two children.

While he is no longer with us, he will never be forgotten, by us; his brothers and sisters of the Baltimore Police Department. RIP and God Bless, as we take this time to remember you on this day.

Here are some additional news reports

Three youths charged with slaying officer - May 27, 1993

Three teen-agers were charged with first-degree murder in the death yesterday of an off-duty Baltimore Police Officer who was gunned down during a shootout inside a carryout restaurant, police said. Investigators said the youths had already "cased" the Jung Hing Carryout in the 1500 block of N. Gay St. and were waiting for a customer to rob as well when 50-year-old Officer Herman A. Jones Sr. entered the restaurant. "We believe the officer was the intended victim," police spokesman Sam Ringgold said. "I'm not sure if they knew he was an officer, but they found out very quickly." The 23-year veteran had just gotten off his 4-to-midnight shift and was still in his police uniform, partially covered by a blue wind breaker. He was still wearing his bulletproof vest, police said.

Two youths were in the carryout pretending to read a wall menu when they grabbed the officer and pushed him into a corner, police said. The third youth then entered the carryout and pointed a .38-caliber pistol at Officer Jones, police said. Either accidentally, or in an attempt to distract the youths, the officer dropped several personal items, including his key rings, money clip, a pen knife and two packs of Tic-Tacs, police said. When the youths began picking them up, Officer Jones pulled out his gun. In an exchange of gunfire, Officer Jones shot two of his assailants, and was himself shot twice. One bullet struck his left knee and another entered his left thigh, ripped through his femoral artery and came out his right hip, police said. The officer got off five shots before being felled, police said.

As the mortally wounded man lay on the ground, one of the youths took Officer Jones' 9-mm Glock pistol and ran from the store with the other two youths, police said. The officer died two hours later in surgery at Johns Hopkins Hospital. Charged yesterday as adults with murder and handgun violations were Herbert "Squeaky" Wilson, 17, of the 2100 block of E. Biddle St.; Clifton "Chip" Price, 17, of the 1600 block of N. Montford Ave.; and Derrick N. Broadway, 16, of the 1800 block of Aiken St. The Broadway youth was arrested after police followed a trail of blood for four blocks. The Wilson, and Price youths were arrested at their homes at about 6 am yesterday, police said. They were being held on no bail at the Eastern District. Police said the Wilson youth was thought to have been the shooter. They said he was shot in the right thigh and treated, and released at Hopkins. Derrick Broadway, shot in the shoulder and upper chest, was in stable condition at Hopkins, police said.

Detectives interviewed Herbert Wilson and Clifton Price, who told them the three had been "prowling the streets looking for victims, they had cased a nearby pizza shop, when they noticed Officer Jones... and decided to rob [him]," a police report said.

Officer Jones, a Central District officer who walked foot patrols in an increasingly heavy crime area of downtown, grew up in East Baltimore and often stopped by the Jung Hing carryout in his old neighborhood, family and friends said. "That was one of his favorite stops after work," said Clinton Stewart, 50, a fellow Central District officer and a friend who had known Officer Jones for 23 years. "He worked in one of the roughest areas of town, but this happened after work, when he went to his old neighborhood to just get something to eat."

Officer Stewart, a member of the Vanguard Justice Society Inc., which represents

about 550 black officers, said Officer Jones was a founding member of the group in 1971. A former football player at Baltimore City College, Officer Jones was a soft-spoken man who spent most of his spare time either at home or on an occasional fishing trip, said his wife of 26 years, Linda Jones. The couple lived in the Hamilton section of Northeast Baltimore. Both their children are grown. "He was a quiet kind of guy, he really was," she said. "In the last three years, he said he was considering retiring. It might have been because it was getting rough [on the street] but those are my words, not his. He was quiet about that."

Officer Jones regularly walked his beat around Eutaw and Howard streets downtown, making regular contact with merchants who he said recently were growing more and more fearful of crime. "He preferred the street. He was the type of policeman they're trying to model neighborhood policing after," Officer Stewart said. "It was important to him to walk his beat. He grew up here. He was part of the Baltimore community." Officer Jones is Baltimore's 134th homicide victim of 1993, compared with 118 at this time last year, the city's worst year ever for murder.

<u>*Two teens plead guilty in police officer's murder*</u> *– January 07, 1994*

Two East Baltimore teenagers each could be sentenced to 50 years in prison after pleading guilty yesterday to participating the murder of an off-duty city police officer last May. Derrick N. Broadway, and Clifton "Chip" Price, both 17, plead guilty to second-degree murder, attempted armed robbery, and use of a handgun in a crime of violence in connection with the May 26, 1993, shooting death of Baltimore police Officer Herman A. Jones Sr. Officer Jones, 50, was killed when he stopped at a Chinese food carryout in East Baltimore after completing a 4 pm - to-midnight shift.

Under the terms of the plea agreement, neither teen-ager will be sentenced to more than 30 years, the maximum, for second-degree murder and 20 years, to be served consecutively, for attempted armed robbery. For the handgun violations, each would receive a five-year, no-parole sentence to be served concurrently. As part of the plea bargain, the teenagers agreed to testify against 18-year-old Herbert "Squeaky" Wilson, who allegedly fired the shots. In return, prosecutors dropped felony murder charges – which carry life sentences – against Broadway and Price. Mr. Wilson is scheduled to stand trial on first-degree murder and related charges Thursday.

Broadway and Price are to be sentenced Feb. 24 by Judge Richard T. Rombro. Both

teenagers stood with heads bowed as Bridget Shepherd, an assistant public defender representing Price, explained to them that Maryland law holds that those who participate in a crime such as an attempted robbery can be held responsible for the outcome, even if they didn't actually fire any shots. Broadway, who was 16 when Officer Jones was killed, appeared to have recovered from two shots to the chest sustained when Officer Jones exchanged shots with his would-be robbers. An autopsy showed that the officer was shot in the thigh, and knee and bled to death.

In presenting a statement of facts to the court, prosecutor Mark P. Cohen began by saying the three teen-agers were drinking together in a house in East Baltimore the night of the shooting when they decided to commit a robbery. He said they obtained a .38-caliber revolver from another man and headed to a pizza carryout but found no one to rob. From there, they went to the Jung Hing Chinese Carryout in the 1500 block of N. Gay St., where they crossed paths with Officer Jones, Mr. Cohen said. The prosecutor said Mr. Wilson announced a robbery and ordered the officer to his knees, but Officer Jones reached for his gun and the shoot-out began. Mr. Wilson was shot in the thigh. The teen-agers fled – with his chest wounds, Broadway made it only about four blocks before collapsing – and the revolver was given to a man with the street name "Dirty Butt Cheeks," Mr. Cohen said. That gun was later recovered, and ballistics tests linked it to the bullets taken from Officer Jones' body.

Ms. Shepherd, the defense lawyer, said that the men were not only drinking but were smoking marijuana before the botched robbery. She also said the officer's 9-mm semiautomatic service weapon, which has never been recovered, probably was stolen by "bystanders." Alexander R. Martick, a lawyer representing Broadway, said his client was not aware that the victim, who was wearing a windbreaker over his uniform, was a police officer. Mr. Martick also said Broadway at first regarded the discussed plans to go out and rob someone as "a joke," Ms. Shepherd said, "As far as I know, it was their first effort, and they just happened to hit someone who was armed."

When the events surrounding the shooting were described in court, Karen Smith, the slain officer's niece, began to dab at her tears. Later, she said, "Everybody loses. We've lost an uncle, and society has lost two more young men." In that vein, the officer's sister, Grace Neal, said, "They get with the wrong crowd. I feel sorry for their mothers today, and I feel sorry for me because I lost my brother." After the hearing, the officer's relatives and Broadway's mother exchanged condolences. Broadway's mother could be heard telling the officer's relatives, "I grieve for

Officer Jones and this whole situation." Ms. Smith replied, "I know you do."

27 May - 1890 - 4th Issue Badge

Today in Police History, the 4th issue badge was worn with an entirely new uniform by all members of the force. This a shield "I" shaped badge with the word "POLICE" across the top, Maryland seal in the center and a ribbon with the officers number across the bottom. Sergeant's and above had an eagle on top of their shield. Lieutenants and above wore a badge similar to the Sergeant but was gold in color. The eagle on the badges had a ribbon in its beak denoting the rank of the officer. These were worn from 1890 until 1976 until replaced with the current badge.

The 4th issue badge serves to replace the 3rd issue badge which was worn from 22 June, 1862 until 27 May, 1890 and is described as follows: On 22 June, 1862, a newly formed Police force appeared in a completely new uniform with a new series of badges. The badges having the same center section of the first badge, and returning the designation of "City Police" surrounded by twenty small points encircled by a narrow rim, the 20 pointer was replaced by an order from the Commissioner as he said, "Too many were in the hands of the citizens." (Stated in an article in the Sun paper from 1890.)

Note: The 20 point badge had meaning, as in Baltimore from 1846 to 1887 we had 20 Wards, there was a point on this badge for each of the 20 Wards, and the thin band around that badge, served to represent the police that protected those 20 wards and held it all together.

28 May - 1937

For the first time in the history of the Baltimore Police Department, women have been advanced to the rank of Sergeant - Mrs. Cronin and Misses Lillie, Lynch and Ryan were all promoted. The women, four in number, joined the force during or immediately after the World War, when there was a shortage of men, and functioned for a time as telephone and signal operators. Under terms of a bill signed

Friday (28 May 1937) by Governor Nice, they will hereafter enjoy the rank and the pay, which is $46.50 a week as against their previous $40 a week as patrolmen.

28 May - 1994

While awaiting their identifying marks, Baltimore Police cruisers hit the street with no decals or police graphics. Unlike the previous 24 years (from 1 July 1970 until this day 28 May, 1994) when Baltimore Police cars used an all blue emergency light bar system in which the emergency light bar had no red lights, the new light bars featured both blue and red lights, similar to other departments throughout the country. The following article described the reasoning behind the 1970 abandonment of the then nearly universal use of red lights exclusively.

Newspaper Article; 30 June, 1970 - City Police Cars Get Blue Emergency Lights

More Visibility and penetration than red ones – mainly to help reduce the large number of departmental accidents, according to a Police Department spokesman. The spokesman said it is hoped the blue light will get a better public response when police cars are rushing to an emergency.

Donald D. Pomerleau, who complained last year that the city's police cars had been involved in a "horrendous" number of accidents, said yesterday "a blue light has better visibility and penetration qualities." Many of the departmental accidents of last year involved police cars crashing into each other while in route to the same call, according to a Police Department spokesman.

29 May - 1914

Today in Baltimore City Police History, 1914, The Motors Unit was organized and introduced. It began with just five Officers, Patrolman Schleigh, Bateman, Pepersack, Vocke and Louis. They had five Indian twin cylinder motor cycles, until an enterprising Harley Dealer opened a shop in Baltimore, and invited Baltimore Police to make a change.

The main duty back then was to chase down speeding horse drawn vehicles, but that quickly changed with the growing number of automobiles in Baltimore. Our Motors unit has been in continuous operation since this day 29 May, 1914.

Likewise it has seen continuous in growth, picking up new responsibilities, and new members over the years, going from five members in 1914, to more than double in 1916… and by the mid to late 1920's they doubled yet again. Starting with Indians in 1914, they were obliged to switch to Harley Davidson throughout the years.

Two things forced that change: First, Indian went out of business, and second Harley was the best bike going at the time, and some say it still is. Harley's were by then being used by the military, fire departments and police departments throughout the country.

In the beginning Motors Officers worked out of the Districts, but in the 1930's they were centralized and reassigned from patrol to the newly formed Traffic Division, and were designated as part of the "Traffic Enforcement Section". The "Motors Unit" or "Motorcycle Unit" (the division also handled, parking control, Foot Traffic that directed traffic downtown, and were part of the "Accident Investigation Unit". The number of officers has risen, and fallen several times over the course of our department's history due to finances, safety, and political issues. But it is alive and well today, with some of the best motor men it has seen in years. Recent Commissioners supported the Motor Unit and have promised to keep them running strong.

Harley Davidson is currently the only brand used, and has been since 1920 when a Harley shop opened in Baltimore. The Department has been known to use Cushman's, small Hondas, and other mini bike/moped type scooters, but nothing other than Harley has been ridden by our Motors Officers since those initial Indians.

Cushman, Hondas and lesser bikes were used by special operations, and footmen to get to their posts. You might see some dirt bikes ridden today by special operations officers throughout the city, some rooster tails in city parks coming off the rear tire of a dirt bike, whatever it takes to catch the bad guy and keep our public safe.

2 June - 1945

Today in Baltimore Police History, Sgt. Ada F. Bresnan become first female officer promoted to Sergeant based on the following:

Woman Appointed Sergeant of Police - Jun 3, 1945; pg. 10

Miss Ada F. Bresnan, Chief of Policewomen of the Baltimore Police Department, yesterday was appointed to the rank of Sergeant by Hamilton R. Atkinson, Commissioner of the Police Department.

The first woman elevated to the rank of Sergeant, Miss Bresnan was appointed to the force in November, 1929, and on October 10, 1944, was placed in charge of policewomen after the retirement of Miss Eva Eldridge, who held the post for 15 years.

The staff now [in 1945] consists of six women.

4 June - 1975

In May of 1954 city Council proposed bulletproof vests for all of its police… Finally, in 1975, twenty-one years later, the city Police would get the protection they should have had all along. As on 4 June, 1975 City government authorized a $288,379 expenditure for more than 3,000 Bullet-proof vests for Baltimore's police officers. Baltimore was 2nd in the nation to receive vests for all of its officers, behind San Francisco - Vests would actually be issued, 1 January, 1976.

8 June - 1994

Juan Rodriguez and Linda Rodriquez became the first husband and wife to be promoted to the rank of Sergeant on the same day in the history of the Baltimore City Police Department.

11 June - 1973

The Civil Service Commission authorized the single classification of "Police Officer" to replace the dual designation "Policeman/Patrolman" and "Policewoman/Patrolwoman." This reclassification was a continuation of the department's efforts in the area of equal employment opportunity. Female "Police Officers" now had the same pay, prerogatives and responsibilities as their male counterparts. Now only one competitive test for promotions is necessary. Thus, a single career ladder was established for all sworn members.

12 June - 1943

On this day in Baltimore Police History, 1943 we lost our Brother Police **Officer William Woodcock**, as he was beaten to death while attempting to effect an arrest based on the following:

At approximately 10:37 pm on this date, Officer Woodcock responded to 1004 Brentwood Avenue to investigate an assault, or threat thereof. During the investigation, Officer Woodcock took the suspect into custody and was responding back to the victim's house when the suspect, Ronald Harris, attacked the officer, taking his Espantoon and using it to knock Officer Woodcock unconscious, still while on the ground the officer was kicked, punched and stomped. Some witnesses say, Harris had three friends join him in the beating.

Witnesses said Harris (39) first struck Officer Woodcock in the face, and knocked him to the ground. Harris then used Officer Woodcock's Espantoon against him. Officer Woodcock was taken to the ER, where he later died. I tend to think he may have told investigators he was struck with his stick, as we know he came to, and gave a statement to Captain Joseph Itzel, in which he gave an account of events to the Captain while naming suspect Harris. Others say Harris was joined by three of his friends who also took part in beating Officer Woodcock about the head, while kicking and punching him as he lay unconscious and defenceless on the ground.

From the newspaper – *"Reports say Officer Woodcock regained consciousness at the hospital just long enough to identify one of suspects to Captain Joseph Itzel. Identified was Ronald Harris, 39, who at the time was held without bail for grand jury action on a charge of murdering Patrolman William J. Woodcock." This verse from the papers using the quote "long enough to identify one of suspects" let us know there was more than one suspect. That is all dropped as the case goes on. A hearing was held before magistrate Elmer J. Hammer in Central Police Court. Harris was held in $1,000 bail on each of two charges of assaulting two men who lived near his home in the 400 block East Eager Street. The assault charges were brought by John J. Mulgrew, of the 1000 block Brentwood Avenue, and Salvalor Costa, of the 600 block East Eager Street.*

Arrested On June 12, Harris was on the front steps of his home about 9.30 P. M. His Attorneys were James E. Tippett, and Bernard S. Melnicove, who asked for a jury trial on the assault charges, didn't really need a trail, there are three attorneys in a courtroom, aside from the Prosecuting attorney, and the Defense Attorney, there is the Judge, he is supposed to be impartial but this judge (Eugene O'Dunne) was pro-defense, he already had a disliking for police, and what he believed to be, "a willingness to use their Espantoon", or as he said to "over use it," so of all cases he to make a point, O'Dunne, picked this one. To make his point, he let a Police Killer go free, a case of an officer killed in the line of duty, would make headlines and get his point across... 5 Oct 1943, Judge Eugene O'Dunne acquitted Ronald Harris, the so called "maniac bandit," of a charge of Murdering Patrolman William J. Woodcock, holding that Woodcock's attempt to arrest Harris was illegal, and that the defendant did not use "unreasonable" force to repel the arrest. Judge O'Dunne contended that the officer's attempt to arrest Harris without a warrant for a mere misdemeanor, which the officer did not observe in progress was illegal. He pointed out the attempted arrest was based on the complaint of a mother who was not the victim, reported Harris threatened to beat her son.

<u>Note</u>: If Harris would have admitted to this misdemeanor to Officer Woodcock, the arrest would have been legal, and his resisting wouldn't have been justified. That said, the judge in this case was still wrong, because the resisting should have only been enough to escape the arrest. As with resisting a legal arrest, the officer can't continue beating them once they have been apprehended and restrained with the resistance abated. Likewise, to resist arrest is to fight to escape, but to continue once free Harris should have left, but by coming back or continuing the assault, was the same as an officer that uses excessive force, (the judge even eluded to it when he said, "the defendant did not use "unreasonable" force to repel the arrest." But he did, Woodcock made a statement, he told who his killer was, and that while, "down he was hit, kicked and stomped" by the defendant and three of the defendant's friends. We already know a suspect is guilty of a crime if more force is used than is needed to resist that arrest, and if that crime leads to death, he should have been found guilty of manslaughter at the very least. I have read a lot of the judge's words, and it was obvious he was not a fan of police, and it seems he used his powers and dislike of police in general to free a Cop Killer.

The day after being acquitted Harris was arrested for being drunk and disorderly. When taken before an afternoon judge, (he was still too drunk for morning sessions) he was asked by the judge if he had ever been arrested for drunk and disorderly, he answered, "I don't think so," so he was fined and given no jail time. In December (the 11th 1943) he was involved in a fight where he would be arrested and charged with assault, the courts again were lenient giving him just 60 days. In March of

1944 Harris was arrested with three friends for Theft and Burglary charge. Harris wasn't in court as he was too ill, so he was taken to the hospital, but his partners were sentenced to 4 and 5 years for their part in the crimes. Those arrested were Vince Bateman 21, Winthrow Thompson 22, and Joe Williams 25… All three signed affidavits saying they refused to assist Harris on a Robbery scheme he cooked up for an area Tavern owner, who was crippled. Harris called all three "Chicken Hearted" and told them, "when you go in to rob a man, rob him, and get it over quick!" a soldier who was AWOL was also arrested with Harris, but he was turned over to the military (He will probably be getting out of the brig sometime within the next few years)

In March 1944, Harris was accused of theft of auto twice, the first February 24th and then again on the 28th - they stole a third vehicle from reliable Motors on the 27th of February. Ronald Harris was sentenced last night to ten years in the Penitentiary after his conviction by a Criminal Court jury on charges of larceny, receiving stolen goods and unauthorized use of an automobile. "Your record is extremely bad. Superlatives hardly describe it," Judge John T. Tucker told the 40-year-old defendant in imposing sentence. "As soon as you get out of one difficulty, it seems you are in another." Convicted on Four Counts, Judge Tucker imposed four-year terms on each of the two automobile larceny charges, and one-year terms on charges of receiving stolen goods and unauthorized use of an automobile. The sentences were to be served consecutively.

Three other men indicted jointly with Harris on one or more of the charges received sentences ranging from four, to five years when tried before Judge Tucker several weeks ago. They were Vincent Bateman and Withrow F. Thompson, each given five years, and Joseph F. Williams, who received a four-year term.

According to statements by Joseph G. Finnerty, Assistant State's Attorney, Harris was the "ring leader" of a gang which rode the streets of Baltimore in stolen automobiles seeking places to "stick up."

The evidence disclosed that the defendants began operations last February 20, when Thompson stole the automobile of Robert Farnell Jr., of the 5400 block Jonquil Avenue, parked it on a side street in Westport and then joined the others in a West Fayette Street tavern.

Their witnesses said that Harris told them of a man in the tavern who had $500, describing the owner of the money as a "good man to roll." Harris added that an automobile would be necessary before the robbery could be committed, and

Thompson then informed the group of the stolen car in Westport and they went there by taxicab to get it, it was testified. When they returned to the tavern, the man had left. So the group rode around the city and nearby counties looking for places to stage holdups, the court and jury were told.

Famell's car was recovered on February 26, but prior to that time the gang had gone to a lot in the rear or the 300 block Monastery Avenue and stolen the high powered automobile of Newton Dale Johnson, the evidence disclosed.

Witnesses said Mr. Johnson's automobile was recovered on February 27 from a location where it had been parked by the defendants, but the next day they returned to the lot and again stole Johnson's automobile. Mr. Finnerty contended they wanted the car because of its high speed capability. Harris also was convicted of receiving property stolen from the third-floor apartment of Randolph Hoffman and his wife in the 200 block North Greene Street. Mr. Finnerty read Harris' criminal record to the court. It follows:

1918- One year In St. Mary's Industrial School for Larceny.

1923- Nine months in Wilmington, Del., for breaking and entering.

1923- Six months for receiving stolen goods

1924- Three years on six burglary charges

1925- Committed to Spring Grove State Hospital

1925- Escaped Spring Grove State Hospital

1925- Ten years for shooting at four policeman, burglary, assault and robbery, larceny and receiving stolen goods

1925- Committed to Spring Grove State Hospital

1925- Escaped Spring Grove State Hospital (Apprehended In South Carolina.)

1928- Committed to Spring Grove State Hospital where he remained until 1933

1934- Two to five years in a Philadelphia prison for breaking and entering.

1938- $25 and costs for assault.

1940- Suspended sentence for assault.

1940- Eighteen months on two assault charges.

1942- Eighteen months for assault and robbery.

1943- Sixty days for disorderly conduct and assault.

1943 – September, Judge Eugene O'Dunne acquitted Harris of a charge of murdering a policeman after ruling that Harris was justified in resisting arrest because the arrest was illegal. What a sick SOB and worthless judge. He went on to make a statement during another trial to try to explain his verdict, and he came across as liberal judge with a dislike of police, who wanted to make a statement.

Judge O'Dunne, in the course of his statement, mentioned his recent acquittal of Ronald Harris, charged with the murder of a policeman, on the grounds that the defendant had been justified in resisting arrest because the arrest was unlawful. The case attracted widespread public interest. "May I take advantage of this occasion," the jurist said yesterday, "to say a few words. Baltimore has just cause to be proud of its Police Department. It is headed by Commissioner Hamilton R. Atkinson, a man risen from the ranks to the head of the department, a man beloved by his force and enjoying the confidence and respect of the community."

O'Dunne Puts Police in Two Classes

"I would like the commissioner and the Police Department as a whole to feel that the Criminal Court is disposed to stand behind the department in the just enforcement of law and order, and to compel respect for its members as the representatives of law and order and to promote a feeling that the uniform is a badge of authority and entitled to be respected, and its officers obeyed - when acting within their legal rights. I am equally anxious to have them know and realize, that the courts will not protect them in illegal arrests, begotten either of ignorance or arrogance; nor will it tolerate them building up a case in court to warrant their illegal action, by the use or false and perjured testimony."

Judge O'Dunne stated that from his experience he has observed that police officers fall into two classes, which are: "One: There are those who are conscious of their power and of its corresponding responsibility; men who are self-poised, self-restrained and disposed to be firm but polite in the exercise of official duty.

"The other class of policemen may be described as those conscientious in the discharge of their duty, zealous in its performance, anxious to make arrests on all possible occasions, ignorant of the law of when arrests may be legally made without a warrant, fresh and arrogant in the exercise of their authority, utterly oblivious as to what constitutes a disturbance of the peace, men who regard themselves as the public peace, and in their minds, any disturbance of the police, or any question of

their authority, is in itself, a crime - the "I am the law" type. "What they call 'back talk,' to such an officer, warrants slapping them in the face, white or colored. They feel free themselves to use any kind of opprobrious language to the victim, and goad him into loss of temper, then they assault or arrest him without warrant of law, and charge him with assault on an officer at the slightest resistance and then come to court and lie about the facts so as to justify their conduct."

"There are comparatively few men on the police force, even from the higher rank down, who know what constitute disturbing the public peace. They fail to put the accent on public. Too many are infused with the idea that cursing the police under any circumstance, at any time or place, is not only a greater sin than cursing God, but mounts up to a public crime

When Judge Eugene O'Dunne acquitted Ronald Harris, the so-called "maniac bandit," of a charge of murdering Patrolman William J. Woodcock, holding that "Woodcock's attempt to arrest Harris was illegal and that the defendant did not use unreasonable force to repel the arrest."

Judge O'Dunne contended that the officer attempted to arrest Harris without a warrant for a mere misdemeanor which he did not see. He pointed out the attempted arrest was based on the complaint of a mother who reported Harris threatened to beat her son.

We all saw Harris' record, and know he was arrested at least four times within the year after being released of killing Officer Woodcock, and on the last case of robberies, theft's etc. he was given 10 years. I was unable to find anything further. Some records indicate he may have gone back into Spring Grove State Hospital, but it is unclear if it is the same Ronald Harris.

Officer Woodcock is no longer with us, but he will never be forgotten. May he rest in Peace, and May God Bless Him.

12 June - 1971

On this day in Baltimore City Police History 1971, we lost our brother Police **Officer Carl Peterson, Jr.** to gunfire. On 12 June, 1971, about 2155 hours, in front of Pine Street Station, Officer Bruce Green, operating 128 car, received information from Gwendolyn Jeanette Carter, 17, that a man was holding her mother, Mrs. Katherine White and her daughter Leisa Carter, age 2 ½, at gun point, at 250 Pearl

Street. The officer proceeded south on Pine Street to Lexington Street and East on Lexington to Pearl Street.

At this point, he was stopped and approached by Alvin Lee Gill, who reported that an officer had been shot on the corner at Lexington and Pearl Street. Officer Green observed Officer Carl Peterson lying on the sidewalk at that location. He observed that the officer's revolver was missing and the officer was bleeding from the left side of the face. Municipal Ambulance #1 responded to the scene and removed Officer Peterson to University Hospital. Officer Peterson was treated for a gunshot wound of the head and died as a result of this wound at 2345 hours on June 12, 1971, pronounced dead by Dr. Daniel Cook of the neurological staff.

Officer Kenneth Burke assigned to Unit 122 received a call from Communications at 2155 hours, 12 June 1971, to 239 N. Pearl Street, for a man with a gun and a two year old hostage on the second floor. Officer Arnold Adams, Unit 112 responded to the scene as a back-up unit. On arrival at 239 N. Pearl Street, the officers were advised that a person had kicked open the front door and entered the house. This person was carrying a baby in one hand and a revolver in the other hand. Officer Adams removed the departmental shotgun from 112 car and in company with Officer Burke proceeded to the house. The officers entered that house through the kicked-in front door and heard footsteps on the second floor. They made their way up the staircase and commanded the person in the room to show himself with his hands stretched out. The person in the room came out and identified himself and advised them that the person they wanted was on the third floor. The officers proceeded to the third floor calling commands to release the girl and come out with his hands up.

Once on the third floor and Officer Adams kicked in a door. At this point he observed the suspect standing to the left of the door and the 2 ½ year old girl just to his right. The suspect pointed the revolver at Officer Adam's face. He stepped back and pointed the shotgun around the door. The suspect grabbed the barrel of the shotgun. Officer Adams did not fire for fear of hitting the child. A struggle then ensued for the shotgun. The suspect then released it and pointed the gun he was carrying around the door at Officer Burke. Officer Burke grabbed the suspect's gun hand and pulled his own revolver and fired a shot. Officer Burke then rushed into the room and struggled with the suspect. Officer Adams quickly removed the child from the room then went to Officer Burke's assistance. The officers attempted to bring him down the stairs. The suspect fell down several steps but was restrained by the officers.

Both suspect and officers were treated at Mercy Hospital for injuries received as a result of effecting the arrest. The arrested person was identified as Roland Leroy Jackson of 209 Myrtle Avenue. The revolver taken from Jackson was the service revolver of Officer Carl Peterson.

Investigation revealed that Officer Carl Peterson was at the call box at Lexington and Green Streets when a man fitting Jackson's description knocked him down. The person then removed Officer Peterson's revolver and shot him above the left eye and fled the scene. Officer Adams and Officer Burke were unaware that a police officer had been shot when taking Roland Jackson into custody. Roland Jackson made a "res gestae statement" to Officer Anthony Lamartina while at Mercy Hospital. Jackson blurted out "I don't know why I did it, I was trying to find myself." Officer Lamartina immediately advised Jackson of his rights. Jackson again stated "I don't know why I did it. Officer Pete has given my daughter and others' children in the area candy and other goodies." Jackson made no further statements.

Res gestae (**Latin** "things done") is a term found in substantive and procedural American jurisprudence and English law. In English substantive law, it refers to the start-to-end period of a felony. In American procedural law, it refers to an exception to the hearsay rule for statements made spontaneously or as part of an act. The English version of res gestae is similar. (It used to be anything *spontaneously blurted* out)

13 June - 1940

On this day in Baltimore Police History, 1940 we lost our brother, **Patrolman William L. Ryan** to knife wounds based on the following:

Accused Slayer Faces Mind Test - Newspaper Articles dated; 14 June, 1940

Man held as attacker of policeman slated for quiz today - Witnesses say the victim was stabbed to death without warning. Mental examinations are expected today for Joseph Abata, 37, who was being held for investigation at the Central District police station in connection with the fatal stabbing yesterday of Patrolman William L. Ryan. A hearing is scheduled for 9 AM tomorrow at which the results of an autopsy performed yesterday are expected to be disclosed. Patrolman Ryan, police

said, was stabbed several times with a butcher knife as he approached the accused in front of the mission house (Grace and Hope Mission) in the first block of S. Gay St. to investigate a complaint that Abata was brandishing a knife.

Without a word from Abata, witnesses said, Officer Ryan was stabbed in the heart. He fired two shots at the beating man before falling mortally wounded to the ground. Neither shot struck the assailant – Ryan was pronounced dead at Mercy hospital. He had been on the force since March 11, 1921. He was 44 years old, and is survived by his wife Margaret, a son William L. Ryan, Jr., 4, and a daughter Patricia Margaret, 18 months old.

Abata, who was captured by several firemen and citizens, lives in the 1400 block of Gough Street. He told police that he was born in Sicily, came to this country at the age of four, served in the Army and has a wife and young child somewhere in New York.

Could Judge O'Dunne have some involvement in this case, too? In a previous item in this tome, Judge O'Dunne set free a suspect who killed our Brother William Woodcock, and the news reports dated 1 October, 1940 entitled - "Judge O'Dunne to Help - Speed Criminal Cases - To Devote Next Week to Hearings - Will Try Hollins Market Stall Keepers." It is reported as follows;

As there are more than 500 open cases on the criminal dockets and several important cases are scheduled for trial in the next week, Judge Eugene O'Dunne has consented to devote his time next week to hearing cases in a third Criminal Court. Immediately, 134 cases were assigned for trial in the third court, including seventy-one gambling cases. Next Tuesday, Judge O'Dunne will try a number of Hollins Market stall keepers charged with violating a city ordinance.

It is interesting to note that the report ends by naming other judges slated to help with these trials - Slated for trial in the two regular Sessions of the Criminal Court presided over by Judge Edwin T. Dickerson and George A. Solter are Neil Grant, former deputy city solicitor, and Albert E. Schmidt, former city cashier, both charged with larceny and embezzlement, members of the Communist party charged with perjury, and John Joseph Abata, accused of killing a policeman.

Could it be, could the same Judge that would free a Police Killer four years later in the Woodcock case, free this killer… while the above reports make it appear as though this would be the case, the following reports say, "NO!" Judge Edwin T. Dickerson, heard this case and freed this defendant, or at least it would seem as though he was freed, he was sent to Shepard Pratt, and then off to a New York Mental Institution.

Note: For the record, I did a little research on nut houses of the 40's… which while it may sound like a category on Jeopardy, they were no game… more like horror houses. It may have been best for a police Killer to have spent the rest of his life in one of these places. After all our brother did nothing more than answer a call for service, a call made by concerned citizens, citizens concerned for their safety. Officer Ryan wanted to make the streets safer, rid them of people like Abata, and he did… Adata was never able to walk the streets or harm anyone again, what follows are the final reports on this case in which it says, "*Abata Acquitted in Knife Slaying.*" And continues, Man Who Killed Policeman Is Declared Insane and Likely to Remain So - Described as Suffering from Delusions, Believing People Are "Out To Get Him" Reported 9 October, 1940; Joseph John Abata, 38, yesterday was acquitted, by reason of insanity of the charge of fatally stabbing patrolman William L. Ryan last June 13, at Baltimore and Gay Street.

Judge Edwin T. Dickerson who rendered the verdict, said he based his conclusion on the testimony of two mental experts who testified that in their opinion Abata was insane at the time of the crime, insane now and likely to remain insane.

Taken To Spring Grove

Abata immediately was taken to the Spring Grove state hospital pending efforts to have the defendant placed in a mental institution in New York where Abata was a resident until shortly before the murder. Dr. Manfred S Guttmacher, medical advisor to the supreme bench, said it is customary to put mental patients in an institution in the state where they maintained residence. The stabbing occurred when patrolman Ryan, who was investigating a report of a man who was wielding a knife was attacked and stabbed several times by Abata.

Delusion Described

Patrolman Ryan was unable to defend himself, the attack was so sudden and violent, but he succeeded in drawing his revolver and firing two wild shots after Abata threw him to the ground. He was pronounced dead shortly afterward.

Dr. Guttmacher and Dr. Arthur A. Luttrell assistant superintendent of the Shepherd Pratt Hospital, testified that Abata suffered from delusions and thought that people were "out to get him." It was because of this delusion that he carried a knife, they said.

Served in the Army

Dr. Guttmacher said the defendant had served several Army enlistments and acted in an orderly manner before the stabbing, when he began to suffer from mental disorders. He said Abata believed himself an inventor and thought people were attempting to steal his inventions. Abata was represented by Charles C. DiPaola, attorney appointed by the court.

Our Brother William Ryan was survived by his wife, 4 year old son and 18 month old daughter. He is gone, but will never be forgotten. Killed at a time when his family was only given one years salary to bring up those kids, his wife was quite the hero too. God Bless him, and may he Rest in Peace.

17 June - 1965

The **Cadet program** was started to help bring better quality police to Baltimore, it gave us a chance to give younger men a chance to see if they wanted to be police, as it also gave us a chance to grab them before they found other career paths, or before other police agencies did.

Another benefit was that it allowed more police to work the streets, while cadets handled some of their work, answering phones, filing or finding reports, as we'll find in the following news reports.

Police Cadet Plan Urged - The Baltimore News; Jun 21, 1964

Pressman sites training program in County

Baltimore's Police Department should institute a police cadet program similar to the one used in Baltimore County, Hyman A. Pressman suggested yesterday.

Mr. Pressman, the city Comptroller, said a cadet program might be one method of helping fill the vacancies in the city force's ranks. According to Mr. Pressman, there are no vacancies in the counties force, whereas there are more than 100 in the city's.

Aimed at high schools

Cadets in the county may begin at age 18, and become eligible for the rank of patrolman at age 21. He said recruiting is directed to high schools. Cadets receive a beginning salary of $3,995, and work up to $4796.

The cadets go to the police academy with a considerable knowledge and also already know whether they like police work. Mr. Pressman said.

This program should reduce some of the expense in turn-over that plagues the Baltimore force.

Their on-the-job training includes clerical work, checking parking meters, working on the switchboard and relieving crossing guards. All of this allows patrolman to be used for the harder types of law enforcement, Mr. Pressman said, "it would be well for Baltimore city to profit from the favorable experiences [of the county]," Mr. Pressman said, "thereby enabling us not only to fill our vacancies but also to recruit better policeman."

48 Police Cadets in Courses - Baltimore News; Sep 22, 1967

Forty-eight city police Cadets have begun mandatory classes in law enforcement, at Baltimore Junior College under a department-financed program which could lead to an associate of arts degree for each cadet.

The plan requires that each of the department's cadets take six semester hours of courses during the fall and spring semesters and at least three hours during the summer months.

In addition to the 48 cadets starting the program an additional 11 Cadets have already been taking courses at the Junior College or at Morgan State College. Six men now on the police academy who began as Cadets are also taking college courses under the program. From departmental training funds, each student tuition and book expenses will be paid, making the total costs to the department for each semester of about $5,200 per cadet.

The police cadet program was initiated in the city in 1965. As it is currently structured, a youth can become a cadet at the age of 18 and then enter the police Academy at age 21 and upon graduation become a full-fledged patrolman.

Under the present schedule, a cadet who begins the college program at the age of 18 can earn about two thirds of the credits needed for an associate of arts degree in law enforcement by the time they leave the Academy. In order to remain a cadet, the use must maintain passing grades in his classes.

Starting courses

Cadets just starting the classes will take courses in English and sociology.

Donald D. Pomerleau, police Commissioner, said he feels "education and training and mandatory college programs for the cadets will ensure that we have a constant flow of intelligent young men entering the department."

He said, "if we're to get the very most out of our cadet program, it is necessary that we make it mandatory for them to enroll in a police administration course."

Under the program, the Cadets have been divided into two groups, half of which will take classes on Monday and Wednesday nights and the other half will attend on Tuesday and Thursday nights.

As we see from the articles of the time, the concept of the program was to get and retain quality men for the Baltimore City Police Department. And as you'll will see from the following information pertaining to the first cadet hired, Edmond Bossle, hired to the program on, 17 June, 1965, the day it was initiated. Cadet Bossle was issued badge number 101, from Cadet he would go on to become a sworn Patrolman, then on to Detective, from there he would be promoted to Sergeant, and finally he would make Lieutenant. When he started, the program, the program was so new they did not even have a shoulder patch, in fact, and he would already have been advanced to the rank of patrolman, when in 1968, they came out with the first shoulder patch, a grey and blue "rocker" patch.

Probably the biggest success of the program was a cadet named Timothy Longo, who achieved the rank of Colonel in a surprisingly short number of years, while continuing his education and earning a law degree. The department benefited from his knowledge and experience in many different positions, as he served in a variety of different capacities, finally retiring to become the long-time Chief of Police in Charlottesville, Virginia, where he remains today. There, he came to national attention in 2014 for his and his department's role in identifying and charging a suspect in a nationally known kidnapping/rape/murder case involving a young University of Virginia student.

19 June - 1912

Today in Baltimore Police History, 1912, the first **Female Officer** was hired under the title of Policewomen. She was Ms. Mary S. Harvey, EOD of 19 June, 1912. Her hiring was followed by that of Margaret B. Eagleston EOD 22 July, 1912.

(Note: It is interesting to note on March 28, 1925, the Baltimore Sun reported that two female members of department were being given their first lesson in pistol shooting. They were Miss Margaret B. Eagleston and Mrs. Mary J. Bruff - A few days later Mrs. Mary Harvey, Miss Eva Aldridge and Ms. Mildred Campbell were also trained. So the first two woman officers hired by the BPD were not trained in the use of firearms until they had been on the force for 13 years!)

20 June - 1894

On this day in 1894, we lost our brothers **Policeman Michael Neary**, and **Policeman James T. Dunn**, of the Central District as they were both instantly killed at 8:25 pm when they were struck by a locomotive of the Northern Central Railway at the bridge between Chase and Eager Streets.

Policeman Neary's head was severed from his body, and the two parts were picked up separately. Policeman Dunn was hit on the right side of the head. His skull was fractured in several places and his body was knocked from the railroad bridge into Jones's Falls. The two bodies were recovered immediately after the accident by Captain Frank Toner of the Central District, and were carried some time later into Calvert Station on a private car furnished by the railway company, from where they were taken to the City Hospital.

The accident occurred while the policemen were attempting to arrest a number of boys who were bathing in Jones's Falls. Boys have been accustomed to take off their clothes and get into the waters of the Falls at this point almost daily. Their antics in the water caused many of the people who lived in the neighborhood to become indignant. A complaint was made to the police and an effort was being made to break up the practice. About an hour and a half before the accident happened, Policeman Dunn had arrested one boy, and sent him to the station house. Returning to his beat he saw other boys in the water, and set about to capture them.

Policeman Neary was off duty at the time and at his home on Guilford Avenue in citizen's dress. Appreciating the difficulty that Dunn would have in arresting the boys, or restraining them when and if caught, he put on his coat, and went to Dunn's assistance. The two officers crossed to the east side of Chase Street Bridge and descended the high bank to the railroad tracks. They walked over the railroad and getting close to the boys called to them to come out of the water. Captain Toner was an interested spectator of the scene, and remained to see how the officers would capture the boys.

A small crowd had collected on the street above, two of the boys voluntarily came out of the water toward the officers, and Captain Toner says that when he saw one boy in Dunn's charge, he left the bridge and went up Guilford Avenue toward Biddle Street. At that time Neary and Dunn were going up the bank on the west side of the railroad bridge with their captive. This was the last the captain saw of his men alive.

Soon afterward a larger crowd of people gathering on the Chase Street Bridge caught Captain Toner's attention, and he hastened back to find out what the trouble was. Then he learned of the fatal accident. After getting up the bank the policemen got on the bridge to walk over to the point where they could get out of the railroad yard onto Chase Street. The train that struck them was the Parkton accommodation, which had left Union Station on its way into Calvert Station. It is supposed the policemen did not see or hear the train until it was too late for them to get out of the way. When the men saw the locomotive upon them, they made a desperate run for their lives. But it was too late. The fatal blow was struck at the north end of the railroad bridge.

Policeman Neary was born in Ireland. He came to Baltimore when he was sixteen years of age. On October, 15, 1877 he was appointed a policeman and patrolled the section between Exeter, and Forrest Streets and from Gay to Monument Street. He was a member of "A Division" and was assigned to day duty. Officer Neary leaves behind a widow and nine children – six boys and three girls ranging from several months old to nineteen years.

Policeman Dunn was six feet tall and weighed 220 pounds. He was thirty-four years old and was born at Long Green, Baltimore County. He was appointed a probationary patrolman December 18, 1890 and was promoted to the regular force May 5, 1891. He was married nearly three years ago, and had a baby boy six months old.

They are gone but will never be forgotten by us his brothers and sisters of the Baltimore Police Department. RIP Brothers and God Bless

20 June - 1896

On this day in Baltimore Police History, 1896 we lost our brother, Police **Officer**

William Wilder in the line of duty.

During a struggle Officer Wilder suffered a heart attack and died. Officer Wilder was off duty when he responded to a family disturbance involving teenagers in his neighborhood, a struggle ensued, it was during that struggle that Officer Wilder suffered a massive heart attack and died. Due to circumstances of his being off duty and placing himself on duty it took nearly a year for his death to be determined a line of duty death. But in the end because he came to the aid of one of his neighbors, his death was confirmed to be a line of duty related death.

We his brothers and Sisters of the Baltimore Police Department won't let him be forgotten, RIP Officer Wilder - May you never be forgotten - "Your service honored the City of Baltimore, and the Baltimore Police Department"

20 June - 1924

On this day in Baltimore police history, 1924 we lost our brother, **Patrolman Charles L. Frank** of the Southern District to gunfire.

From Newspaper Articles: dated 21 June, 1924

Patrolman Charles L. Frank of the Southern District, was shot early yesterday (20 June, 1924) when he entered a dwelling at 1619 Marshall St. to quell a dispute between Harry C. Jones and his wife. The patrolman died of his injuries at 9 o'clock last night.

Though there was much conflicting information forthcoming from Mrs. Jones and Harry Jones, this is the best summary of the incident, as taken from a deposition taken at the South Baltimore General Hospital by Magistrate Joseph O'Donnell, five hours before Frank died. He had remained unconscious from the time of the shooting until he awoke and gave his statement. He accused Harry Jones of firing the unprovoked fatal shot, under the following circumstances:

Patrolman Frank said he walked past the Jones home at 1 am and though he could hear quarrelling from the house, he believed that nothing serious was amiss, and he did not stop, but continued on his rounds. An hour later he again approached the house. The quarrel had become violent. He entered the yard and Mrs. Jones appeared at the rear door and asked him to come inside, presumably to mediate the ongoing dispute.

Patrolman Frank climbed the steps to the porch hoping to be able to pacify the man and his wife. As he stepped across the threshold, Harry Jones produced a pistol from underneath a hat on the table, aimed at Patrolman Frank and fired twice. The first bullet missed its mark. The second entered Frank's stomach.

Frank staggered outside and fired his pistol several times to summons assistance. He then collapsed and remembered nothing more until he regained consciousness in the hospital some 15 hours later.

Patrolman Arthur McCloskey reported that he heard the shots and hastened to the scene. He found Frank unconscious in the back yard and summoned the police ambulance and had Frank taken to the hospital. McCloskey then entered the house and arrested Jones.

An operation was performed on Frank, and throughout the day physicians said he had an even chance for life. He regained consciousness at 5 pm and made a deposition. From that time he remained conscious until 8 pm. His stepfather, John T. Kennedy and patrolman Albert C. Mont were at his bedside when he died, but Frank gave no further statement.

Arraigned in the southern police court in the afternoon, Jones was committed to jail without bail for a hearing July 20 on a charge of shooting patrolman Frank. The date was set because it was believed Frank would have recovered sufficiently to testify at that time.

Frank's death meant that the inquest would be held within a few days, before Dr. Otto Reinhardt, Southern District coroner, and the charge against Jones would be changed from shooting Frank to murder, causing the death of Patrolman Frank.

Frank was 33 years old and he had been a member the Police Department for only six months. During the war he served in the Army but was not sent overseas. He lived at 53 South Carrollton Ave. with his mother Mrs. Annie Kennedy, his stepfather and a brother, George Frank. Patrolman Frank will not be forgotten by us, his brothers and sisters of the Baltimore Police Department. God Bless him, and may he rest in peace.

22 June - 1860 - 2nd Issue Badge

In 1860 there was a uniform change, which included a new badge (Roman Fasces), new head gear, and redesigned coat buttons, which were documented in a newspaper article as having for the first time the inscription "B.C.P."

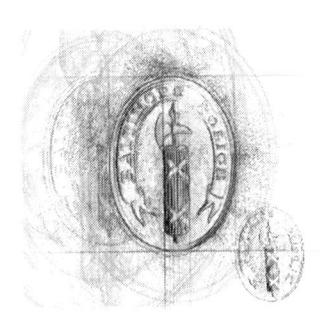

22 June - 1967

The Public Information Division was formed. The Division consisted of a Director, two full time police officers and two civilian stenographers. The duties of the Director and his staff consisted of preparing and disseminating all news information and releases to the news media, and the public. Preparation of the Annual Report as required by law and the bi-weekly Newsletter are also part of the responsibilities of this Division.

23 June - 1978

On this day, the Shot Tower Park and the Baltimore Police Memorial were dedicated. In addition to the Memorial Trees surrounding the area, an appropriate plaque is prominently displayed on a granite stone with the inscription: "This living memorial is dedicated by the Department to all members, past and present, who have served with honor, dedication, and loyalty, many of whom have made the supreme sacrifice." Located at the corner of President and Fayette, next to the famous Baltimore Shot Tower, it was rededicated with statues, lighting and flags added in 1999.

26 June - 1946

On this date in Baltimore City Police History, 1946 we lost our brother, **Patrolman James M. Shamer** to an on-duty illness.

Patrolman James M. Shamer suddenly became ill last night while on duty in a Northern District radio car, and died a short time later at Union Memorial Hospital.

Northern District officers said Patrolman Shamer slumped in the seat of the car shortly after he complained of feeling badly. His partner in the car was Patrolman William Ellinghaus, who immediately drove him to the nearest hospital, where he was pronounced dead.

Patrolman Shamer is survived by a wife and one child. He lived at 5508 Frederick Avenue. Patrolman Shamer won't be found on the Baltimore Police Fallen Officer Wall, or ODMP.com but he was one of ours and he die while working a radio car.

As such he will always be remembered by us, his brothers and sisters of the Baltimore Police Department. RIP Patrolman Shamer and may God Bless him.

27 June - 1861 - Fed Takeover

27 June, 1861 – Today in Baltimore Police History, 27 June 1861, the department was taken over by the federal military authorities The Federal military took control of Baltimore in July, 1861 which did not include martial law but was just a takeover of some municipal functions. It would returned to the control of the State nine months later on 29 March 1862.

Once it ended, the local authorities so despised the "Federal police" that the uniform, including the badge, was changed. This change included the buttons that were changed to a simple "P". By the late 1880's to the early 1890's the Maryland seal was made a part of the button, with only minor changes since then.

This makes sense when we think of the 20 August 1886 Baltimore Police captain's badge. The "Seeing Eye" or "Ever on the Watch" Badge. The badge had an eye on the top part of the artwork, but we should more concern ourselves with the Maryland Seal, as Marshal Frey says, "The force being a state institution, I thought it appropriate to have placed the Maryland coat of arms upon the badge!" an indication that this has not been done before, and if it wasn't on the badge, it wasn't on the buttons.

New Badge Article from Newspaper of the time – 20 August, 1886

New badges for the police captains – today the captains of the police force of the city will appear with new badges. The police board having issued an order to that effect. For some time past, Marshall Frey states, the captains have complained that their old badges were identical with the badges worn by nearly every private

detective or watchman in the city. The old badges were simply a star within a circle, with the words "Capt. of police" on the rim. The new badges are much more elaborate, and are very handsome. The form is a shield, about 2 ½ inches long and 2 inches wide. Of silver. The Maryland Coat of Arms is and blazoned on the face. An "eye" is engraved over the coat of arms. The word "Capt." appears below. The new badges were made by Mr. John W. Torsch. Marshall Fray says that the force being a state institution, he thought it appropriate to have placed the Maryland coat of arms upon the badge. He further says that the "eye" is intended to remind the captains that their duty is to be always on the alert.

22 June - 1862 - 3rd Issue Badge

Today in Baltimore Police History, 1862, a newly formed Police force appeared in a completely new uniform with a new badge series (the Federal takeover had ended three months earlier, in March 1862). Known as the **3rd Issue badge**, it had the same center section as the first badge, and returned the designation of "City Police" – surrounded by twenty small points encircled by a narrow rim.

29 June - 1926

On this day in Baltimore Police History, 1926 we lost our brother Police Officer **Webster E. Schuman**, and **Thomas Dillon**, a Police Clerk at the Northwestern Police Station, as a result of a running gun battle which took place near Argyle and Lafayette Avenues. Two other patrolmen and a police chauffer were also shot during the efforts to capture the gunman, identified only as 'Mr. Lee' in newspaper reports of the time.

Lee, according to witnesses, originally ran amuck in a lunchroom where the first shooting occurred, not far from Argyle and Lafayette Avenues. After quarrelling with Arthur Redding, the lunchroom proprietor, Lee ran out onto the sidewalk. Redding followed and struck Lee, witnesses said. Lee then drew a pistol and shot Redding in the neck.

Lee then ran home to 635 West Lafayette Avenue, but soon reappeared armed with

a rifle and another pistol. Sitting on the steps in front of his home, with the rifle across his knees and his pistols nearby, Lee calmly smoked a cigar, witnesses declared.

Meantime, residents had notified Rex Moore, telephone operator at the Northwestern Police Station that a crazy man had shot another man and was terrorizing the neighborhood. The police of the Western district were asked to send the patrol, and Police Clerk Thomas Dillon, Patrolman Schuman and Patrolman Howard Collins set out for the scene of the shooting in a Police Department automobile.

First on the scene, Patrolman Schuman jumped from the automobile and found cover in the doorway of a grocery store, as bullets from Lee's weapons struck the glass front of the store. A bullet from Lee's rifle penetrated two large plate glass windows and wounded Patrolman Schuman in the mouth. As Police Clerk Dillon, unarmed, ran to Patrolman Schuman's side he was shot in the chest and killed. The patrolman later was rescued by other patrolmen and sent to the hospital, where he died.

Lee was eventually shot and killed by responding patrolmen after he had been driven from behind parked automobiles, but not before shooting and wounding several other innocent people.

Col. Rufus E. Longan, superintendent of the Baltimore City Hospitals, said yesterday that the failure of the State of Maryland to provide adequate quarters and facilities for the care of mentally deficient persons in Baltimore was responsible for the pistol battle in the Northwestern District. He added that Mr. Lee was once an inmate of the insane ward in Baltimore City Hospitals.

Charles D. Gaither, Police Commissioner, highly commended the courage and actions of the police at the scene, and particularly praised the efforts of those who were shot. "The patrolmen did everything possible under the circumstances," Gaither said. "It especially unfortunate that Mr. Dillon was shot, since he was unprepared for such action. Mr. Dillon volunteered when the call for reserves went out, even though the work called for was not in direct line of duty for him."

The others shot were:

- Patrolman Ignatius Benesch, Northwestern District. Shot in the right hip; skull probably fractured by blow struck by Lee with empty pistol during hand to hand combat;

- Police Chauffeur Leroy E. Lentz, Western District. Shot in the ankle.
- Patrolman Howard L. Collins, Northwestern District. Shot in the right hand.
- William H. Kammerer, druggist, Lafayette and Fremont avenues, shot in the right leg.
- Arthur Redding, 34 years old, shot in the neck; condition serious.
- Calvin Howard, 16 years old, shot in the hand; treated at the University Hospital.
- Mildred Duncan, 11 years old. Shot in the abdomen; condition serious; at Colonial Hospital.

We their brothers and sisters of the Baltimore Police Department will not let them be forgotten. God Bless, and rest in Peace. Their service honored the City of Baltimore and the Police Department - RIP Patrolman Schuman and Clerk Dillon.

1 July - 1891

Today in Baltimore City History, 1891 - Baltimore experienced the first Courthouse/Political scandal when the City began to widen and straighten Fayette Street, between Calvert Street and Liberty Street. The City sold all of the unused lots at auction, including the land where the current Courthouse sits. In all, 49 lots were sold for between $1,000 to $4,000 per lot to local citizens.

When the auctioneer got to the five lots located between St. Paul Street and Calvert Street (the lots where the current Courthouse stands) an unknown person by the name of John T. Carter purchased all five for $132,000, outbidding all others for this group of lots. His five lots were later purchased for twice the cost of all of the other 44 lots combined! Citizens immediately began to suspect that Mr. Carter was brought in to secretly purchase this land on behalf of several friends of the Mayor. The Mayor emphatically denied any such arrangement, but less than four years later the City re-purchased all such land on Fayette Street between St. Paul Street and Calvert Street for much more than they were originally sold for, for the construction of the new Courthouse. The mysterious Mr. Carter, only four years later, made a pretty penny on those investments. What do you think?

1 July - 1954

On this day in Baltimore Police History, 1952 we lost our brother, **Police Officer Walter Davis** to a line of duty accident.

On 16 October, 1952, Walter Davis' dream of becoming a Police Officer came true. He entered the academy on that day, then passed all of the required classes and graduated. Upon graduation he was assigned to the Northeast District. He was an aggressive officer, showed up for work on time, handled his calls, and understood and practiced sector and post integrity.

On 1 July, 1954, one year and nine months after his hiring he was working 431 car and was in the 4400 block of Harford Road responding to a call that the lights on all the safety pylons between the Harford Road Car Barn and Cold Spring Lane were out. Officer Walter Davis was killed when his departmental vehicle crashed into one of those dark pylons that he apparently didn't see in time.

He will forever be missed, but never will he be forgotten by us his brothers and sisters of the Baltimore Police Department... God Bless and Rest in Peace.

1 July - 1970

Baltimore Police went to an all **blue emergency light** signalling system on their patrol cars, motor cycles and all emergency vehicles, eliminating the previous red lights entirely. This would remain in practice, until 28 May, 1994, when we converted to the Red and Blue light bars seen today.

2 July - 1962

2 July, 1962 – On this day in Baltimore Police History, 1962 we lost our brother **Police Officer Edward J. Kowalewski** to Gunfire based on the following:

While attempting to assist a cab driver who was being robbed, Patrolman Kowalewski was shot and killed, and became the third Baltimore City Police Officer to be killed in 1962.

The following *Newspaper Article* best tells the events of 2 July, 1962

Suspect to be Charged in Slaying of Policeman – 3 July, 1962 – Police said last night [2 July 1962] they will charge a suspect today [3 July 1962) in connection with the slaying of a city policeman who was shot when he attempted to help a wounded cab driver at North Avenue and Charles street yesterday.

The deceased officer, is the third policeman killed in the line of duty this year. He was Patrolman Edward J. Kowalewski a 35 year-old father of four children, and an eight years veteran of the department.

He died after receiving treatment for a bullet wound of the lower back at Maryland General Hospital.

Mr. Rich had driven the suspect to Baltimore from Washington after a shooting that had taken place there during a failed robbery attempt. Washington police knowing of the incident had issued a lookout for a fugitive in an armed robbery that closely resembled the man in custody, police said. The suspect, fleeing in another cab, and pursued by a third cab, was captured by Patrolman Stanley Zawadski, a boyhood friend of slain officer at Orleans and Gay streets.

Police said he was reloading his gun when taken into custody. Witnesses including a hold-up victim and the victim of an attempted hold-up, each from Washington, viewed the suspect in lineups at Police Headquarters yesterday [2 July, 1962]. Police identified the man as Ray Allen Nixt, 40, a waiter with no fixed address. Officers said he was paroled recently from Folsom Prison in California after serving ten years to life sentence for armed robbery.

Cab drivers credited with aiding to the capture, were Zonnie Wisc. 34, who chased the fugitive and picked up Patrolman Zawadski on the way. Charles L Wise, who was forced at gunpoint to drive him alway from the shooting scene, and later disarmed him. And, Charles H. Miller, 33, who saw the flashing light alarm on the commandeered vehicle, and forced it to the curb.

Patrolman Kowalewski whose home was at 1231 Church Street, Curtis Bay, will be given an inspector's funeral.

We his brothers and sisters of the Baltimore Police Department will not let him be forgotten. God Bless and rest in Peace.

3 July - 1919

On this day in Baltimore Police History, 1919 we lost our brother, **Patrolman John J. Lanahan** to gunfire at the Central Police Station while he was searching a prisoner incident to an arrest for theft.

Turnkey John J. Lanahan, 57, of the Central Police Station, whose home was located at 2028 Robb Street, Northeast Baltimore, was shot to death at 8:55 am on 3 July, 1919, by arrestee Frank Wozniak, 31 years old, an un-naturalized Russian Pole, who the night before burglarized the office of the American Railway Express Company's office at Sudbrook, on the Western Maryland railroad.

The murder of Turnkey Lanahan happened before the eyes of Lieutenant W. F. Klinefelter, Patrolman Crass and Patrolman Traupe, of the Central District. A few minutes after Crass and Traupe brought Wozniak to the police station for investigation concerning his possession of watches and jewelry suspected of being stolen, which when apprehended he was trying to sell to two Harrison Street second-hand dealers. Patrolman Crass arrested him, but did not call for a patrol wagon, as the prisoner offered no resistance, and it was quicker and simpler for Crass to just walk Wozniak to the police station. Wozniak stood before the desk in the usual manner and there was nothing in his attitude to indicate that he contemplated either escape or attack. He freely gave his name and address as 1637 Eastern Avenue.

The apparently cooperative prisoner was questioned yesterday afternoon by Capt. A. L. League and Lieutenant Klinfelter of the Central District, and Wozniak admitted that for several weeks he had gone on thieving expeditions. He confessed that he went to Sudbrook Station Wednesday night, broke into the office and rifled express packages, seeking money and jewelry. He made his escape with two boxes containing watches and when he attempted to sell the watches yesterday, he was arrested by Patrolman Crass.

At the end of the questioning, Lieutenant Klinfelter called Turnkey Lanahan to come take charge of the prisoner, and Lanahan, in his usual jovial and sympathetic manner approached the prisoner. "Come, my boy, let me see what you've got," said the turnkey as he raised Wozniak's hands and started to feel the pockets of his coat. At this juncture Patrolman Crass was standing a few feet from the prisoner and Patrolman Traupe was standing at the entrance to the corridor leading to the lock-up. Patrolmen Kerns and Kelly, housemen, were behind the desk and Captain League was at his desk.

As Turnkey Lanahan raised Wozniak's hands, Wozniak suddenly backed away a pace, drew a pistol from his right hip pocket and fired two shots. Of two shots fired by Wozniak, one entered Turnkey Lanahan's chest, and the other went through the open window of a partition, lodging in the plastered wall of the signal operator's office. Crass and Traupe immediately pounced upon Wozniak while Captain League, with pistol drawn, ran from his desk. The prisoner was beaten into helplessness and was dragged away. His arms were held by four policemen. The pistol was taken from his hand and a second weapon was taken from his pocket. Twenty bullets were found in another pocket.

The Central ambulance was on-call, but no time was lost getting Turnkey Lanahan to Mercy Hospital. Patrolmen carried him to the automobile of Frank H. Cook, 318 North Charles Street, and Mr. Cook sped to Mercy Hospital with the mortally wounded Lanahan. At Mercy Hospital, Dr. Eustace H. Allen, of the surgical staff, pronounced Turnkey Lanahan dead. The bullet, he said, penetrated his heart, causing internal hemorrhage.

Headquarters Detective J. F. Dougherty, of the homicide squad, in making his investigation of the shooting, obtained information from Wozniak indicating that Wozniak fired the shots with the idea of effecting his escape after realizing that imprisonment was inevitable. According to the statement made by Wozniak, "… I can't say why I shot the man and don't know why I pulled the pistol from my pocket."

Turnkey Lanahan was regarded as one of the most efficient turnkeys in the department. He was known particularly because of his kindness and consideration for prisoners, and he always tried to cheer them while in his custody. He was appointed to the department 19 years ago. He had been one of the alternating turnkeys at the Central Police Station for seven years.

He was survived by his widow, Mrs. Mary Lanahan, two sons, who are in the armed forces of the United States, and two daughters.

We his brothers and sisters of the Baltimore Police Department will not let him be forgotten. God Bless and rest in Peace. His service honored the City of Baltimore and the Police Department - RIP Officer Lanahan.

3 July - 1925

On this day in Baltimore City Police History, 1925 we lost our Brother **Patrolman John E. Harris** of the Druid Hill Park Police to a line of duty illness. Patrolman Harris died yesterday in West Baltimore General Hospital from pneumonia, which is said to have been caused by injuries Harris received last Monday when he was struck by an automobile operated by a 73 year old student driver.

Student driver Harry Siegel, 2366 McCulloch Street, was under the tutelage of Alley Applestein, 6 North Bond Street, and was operating the machine which is said to have struck the patrolman. He was released into the custody of his attorney at the Northwestern police station, pending the action of Dr. J. Terrell Hennessey, coroner. Siegel was charged with causing Patrolman Harris's death. The police said Applestein also may be arrested, but no immediate action against him has been taken.

We his brothers and sisters of the Baltimore Police Department will not let him be forgotten. God Bless and rest in Peace. His service honored the City of Baltimore and the Police Department - RIP Officer Harris.

3 July - 2004

On this day in Baltimore Police History, 2004 we lost our brother, **Police Officer Brian Donte Winder** to gunfire. Officer Winder was shot and killed by two men, one of whom he had arrested earlier in the week for selling illegal copies of pirated CDs and DVDs.

The events that led to the fatal encounter began at 2048 hours with a 911 call about a domestic incident from a West Baltimore woman who said she wanted a man out of her house. When Officer Winder arrived, he was told there were two men involved, both of whom had just left her home. She warned the officer that one of the men was armed. She identified the armed subject as Jermaine Gaines, with whom she had just had a domestic dispute. She provided the descriptions of the two men, pointed out their direction of travel and Officer Winder went in search of them.

Shortly, he spotted two people outside the G&G Village Liquor store who fit the descriptions given and called out to them. In response, both suspects fled into the liquor store on Edmondson Avenue, where they were cornered in the roughly 100-

square-foot area where customers place orders through a security barrier.

As the men entered the store, Winder made a radio call requesting a back-up officer. As another officer arrived, Winder approached the store, and as he entered the suspect(s) opened fire from within, striking Officer Winder twice in the legs and once in the chest just above his vest. Winder called on his radio to report shots had been fired, staggered from the store and collapsed on the pavement outside. He never had a chance to fire his weapon.

Just as the first shooting was ending, Officer Ed Lane arrived on the scene and began firing at the two men. Gaines ran back inside the store, unhurt, police said, while the other man escaped. It was unknown at the time whether the 2nd suspect was wounded.

Gaines, trapped again, this time chose to surrender to Officer Lane. A 9mm handgun was recovered inside the store. Officer Winder was transported to University of Maryland Shock Trauma Center, where he died.

After several days of intensive investigation, the suspect who escaped was identified and located in a Baltimore motel on the morning of July 7. He committed suicide as the Baltimore Police Department's Quick Response Team armed with an arrest warrant entered his room.

Winder, a 1985 graduate of Carver High School, joined the police force in 1994 and spent most of his career patrolling the streets in the Southwestern District, which included the Edmondson Village area where he was raised. He served a brief stint in the department's internal affairs unit, returning to his home district in June 2003, saying that he needed to be on the street – the street that would kill him.

Officer Winder had served with the Baltimore City Police Department for 10 years, and was assigned to the Southwest District. He was survived by his wife, two sons, and a stepdaughter.

We his brothers and sisters of the Baltimore Police Department will not let him be forgotten. God Bless him and may he rest in Peace. His service honored the City of Baltimore and the Police Department - RIP Officer Winder.

4 July - 1889

On this day in Baltimore Police History, 1889 we lost our Brother **Police Officer John T. Lloyd** to Gunfire. Officer Lloyd of the Southern police district, was shot at 1:30 am at the Northeast corner of Light and West Streets.

Prior to succumbing to his injuries, Lloyd gave the following account to Justice Donovan: He said, "In patrolling my beat I went up Light Street to West Street and I found Samuel Cooper with three or four others standing on the corner. I said to Cooper 'Don't make so much noise, the proprietor of the drug store will come down and complain.' Cooper replied, 'What are you talking about?' and without further provocation or conversation pulled out a pistol and fired three shots. Then he and Ed Doyle, who I recognized, and two or three others whom I did not recognize, jumped on me." A witness confirmed the officers' statement and stated after the first shot was fired, Cooper ran into the middle of the street before being grabbed by Officer Lloyd. Another shot was fired and then a third, and the policeman fell to the ground. The witness said that three or four men jumped on the downed officer, who was somehow able to hold onto his prisoner. Several officers arrived at this time and placed Cooper, Edward Doyle and James Reynolds under arrest. Lloyd was shot in the abdomen and the upper part of his leg. The wounded patrolman lay in pain all day at his home, before dying at 8:40 pm Lloyd was just 30 years of age.

Newspaper article dated 5 July 1889:

On 4 July, while clearing a corner, Officer Lloyd was attacked by for men, one of whom shot him three times at close range, so close in fact that the muzzle flash from the gun set fire to Officer Lloyd's jacket. Shot three times, severely beaten, and nearly unconscious Patrolman Lloyd still managed to not only survive his injuries for several hours, long enough to give a deposition as to what happened, and not only to identify his killer but to hold onto to that attacker until back-up had arrived.

The present year has been a remarkable one for the Baltimore Police Department on account of the unusual number of deaths by violence that have occurred. The latest victim was patrolman John T. Lloyd of the southern district, who was shot about 1:30 o'clock yesterday, 4 July, 1889, at the northeast corner of Light and West Street.

Complaint had been made at the southern district police station of men loafing and disturbing the peace at that corner, and Patrolman Lloyd had been ordered to give it his attention. A crowd of men were there, and when the patrolman ordered them to keep quiet and they did not obey him he attempted to arrest one of their number. Resistance was made to this action, and he was shot and then beaten. The patrolman's clothing was set on fire by the shots, which indicated that the assailant stood close to him at the time. Samuel Cooper, Edward Doyle, James Reynolds, James Toole, and Thomas H. Hudson were arrested in connection with the shooting. Cooper is charged with being the man who fired the shots and the others are accused of being accessories. They were committed to jail by Justice Donovan. The police are also looking for other men who were supposed to have been connected with the assault.

Patrolman Lloyd was carried into the drugstore on the corner and afterword taken to his home at 18 Conway Street in a patrol wagon. He was attended to by Dr. George Strauss and Dr. John Blake, who found that he had been shot twice. One of the bullets entered his abdomen about 2½ inches to the right of the naval and ranged downward. The second bullet passed straight through the thigh. Dr. Strauss says that in addition to these there was a glancing wound in the abdomen in close proximity to the first wound. The doctor says the wounds in the abdomen both had a downward course. The coat, shirt and undershirt were burned, which clearly indicates the shots were fired at close range. The doctor recovered in the clothing of the wounded patrolman a bullet of .38 caliber, which was the one that caused the glancing wound spoken of. Death was caused by shock and internal hemorrhage.

Sgt. Chailou was standing at the corner of Light and Cross streets when he heard three or four shots. He ran to the corner of Light and West streets, and was the first officer to arrive on the scene. The Sergeant saw two men struggling on the ground, and in pulling the top man off, he recognized him as Cooper. He did not recognize the other man as patrolman Lloyd at first. Cooper said to the Sgt., "Let me go. I've not done anything." The patrolman was able to say, "I'm shot," and pointed out Cooper as the man who shot him, whereupon Cooper was arrested.

<u>Picking up The Others</u>

Patrolman Ludwig was standing at the corner of Light and Hamburg Streets and heard four shots. He ran to the scene and saw Sgt. Chailou with Cooper under arrest and helped to take the prisoner to the patrol box. The officers then carried the wounded patrolman into the drugstore. In response to inquiry from Patrolman Ludwig as to who had shot him, patrolman Lloyd said Cooper had done it. The officers afterwards arrested Edward Doyle and James Reynolds. The two men were

in the crowd when the officers arrived. Bread walked away when Cooper was arrested. They were caught several blocks away. Tool and Hudson were arrested later in the day, being known as two of the crowd that had traveled around that night.

What Mr. Strauss Saw

William Strauss, jeweler at 1128 Light St., was looking out his shop window when the shooting occurred. He heard the patrolman warn the men, and says that when the first shot was fired he saw one man, whom he believed to be Cooper, run into the middle of the street and caught by the officer, who exclaimed, "I'm shot!" Another shot was fired, and patrolman fell to the ground when the third shot was fired. Three or four men then jumped on the patrolman, who had hold of one of the men. Mr. Strauss was hastening to the assistance of Patrolman Lloyd when the other officers arrived.

The wounded patrolman lay in great agony all day. Patrolman Lloyd was 30 years of age and unmarried. He was a native of Baltimore, and the nephew of William J. Lloyd of Lloyd's Hotel, and of Edward Lloyd of the Peabody house. His father was John Lloyd contractor and miller. He resided with his parents. He was appointed to the police force as a probationer 24 August, 1888, and was promoted to be a regular officer in November of the same year. Previous to his appointment on the police force he was a truck driver and also worked with his father for a time.

Since the organization of the present Metropolitan police force one detective and three policemen and have been killed while in the discharge of their duty.

We his brothers and sisters of the Baltimore Police Department will not let him be forgotten. God Bless and rest in Peace. His service honored the City of Baltimore and the Police Department - RIP Officer Lloyd.

5 July - 1870

On this day in Baltimore City Police History, 1870 we lost our brother, **Police Officer James Murphy** to an assault based on the following:

About 3 o'clock on the afternoon of the 4th of July, the attention of Patrolman James Murphy, while passing through the Lexington Market, was attracted to three young brothers named James, John and David Duering, who were acting in a riotous manner. The officer remonstrated with them and told them if they did not behave themselves he would take them to the station house. James Duering commenced verbally abusing the Policeman and as a result the latter took him into custody. The brothers told James not to go to the station house, whereupon James began resisting his arrest.

At that point the other two brothers joined the resistance and one of them struck the officer upon his head with his fist as hard as he could. Officer Murphy pulled out his Billy, but in the scuffle that ensued he lost it to one of the brothers. James succeeded in getting away and all three ran up Paca Street. The officer followed and succeeded in taking James back into custody when the other brothers again surrounded the officer and struck him in the head with his own Billy.

Policeman Murphy, however, succeeded in holding onto his prisoner long enough for Policeman Mantle to come to his aid, chasing David and catching him hiding in an outhouse in the rear of Paca Street. Policeman Engle afterwards arrested John at his mother's house on Orchard Street.

They were all taken to the Western stationhouse and arraigned for the charge of assaulting the officer. They were all released upon giving bail, the policeman at the time not appearing to be severely injured. Soon after the release of the accused, Officer Murphy was taken with convulsions in the yard of the stationhouse. Help was summoned but the officer continued to grow worse. A priest was called in to administer the last rites of the Catholic Church. Murphy lingered in convulsions until about half past one o'clock on this morning (5 July, 1870) when he expired, having remained unconscious up to the time of his death. Warrants were at once issued for the re-arrest of the Duering brothers and all three were arrested again.

Officer Murphy was 23 years of age and single. He was appointed to the force on the 4th of April last. We his brothers and sisters of the Baltimore Police Department will not let him be forgotten. God Bless, and rest in Peace. His service honored the City of Baltimore and the Police Department - RIP Officer Murphy.

5 July - 1938 - Vice Squad Creation

Commissioner Lawson Plans Special Squad to Battle Vice

Newspaper reports of the Times; 5 July, 1938

Commissioner Lawson will name his new group this week to attack prostitution and gambling. A special cleanup squad of police whose sole duty will be to ferret out vice and gambling in all forms will be appointed this week by police Commissioner Lawson.

The Commissioner announced this yesterday [4 July, 1938], and at the same time disclosed that about 20 members of the department will appear shortly before medical examiners to determine their fitness to continue on duty.

The Commissioner's statement came 24 hours after J. Bernard Wells, State's Attorney, had made public a report showing that vice is widespread in this city, and which indicated a close association between vice activities and some members of the Police Department.

No definite evidence of police protection of vice was obtained, however, by the investigators who compiled the report for the American Social Hygiene Association. Copies of the report, which was made by a citizen committee headed by Dr. J. M. T. Finney, Senior, were given to Commissioner Lawson and Mr. Wells on Friday.

Dr. Finney last night said he was delighted to hear that Commissioner Lawson had decided to set up a cleanup squad

"But the citizens committee are not reformers." Dr. Finney said. "They are an interested group of citizens trying to cooperate with the police to make Baltimore a better place to live. We are not after anybody's scalp. A report was made and that report was submitted to the proper authorities."

Commissioner Lawson declined to say how large the new cleanup squad would be or how it would be recruited. He explained it would be under his direct supervision, and that the personnel would include some of the most efficient men in the department. The squad, he added, would be on duty 24 hours a day.

Commissioner Lawson disclosed that he is carefully studying the report submitted by the Finney committee. Although the copy of the report released by Mr. Wells

abbreviated names and locations, the copies given to Mr. Wells and Commissioner Lawson were accompanied by a key.

This key gave the full names of nightclub, tavern, grill and saloon proprietors investigated; the names of their employees; what the employees earn in salaries and commissions; what many waitresses earn by "sitting" and soliciting; the names of prostitutes, their ages, addresses and other details about them, including places they visit; taxicab drivers names, numbers and their interests in certain parts of the vice racket; perverts and where they practice; the names and addresses of hotels and apartments were prostitutes and perverts live or temporary quarters, and many other details.

Commissioner Lawson's announcement was a surprise to executive officers of the police department. No mention of the creation of such a squad, it was said, was made by the Commissioner when he conferenced yesterday morning with the inspectors and captains at police headquarters.

The move has been urged lately on several occasions by representatives of the criminal justice commission and others.

The Vice Report

Newspaper reports of the Times; Jul 5, 1938;

Judging by the published summary of the vice report prepared at the behest of a committee of citizens, the most disturbing feature of the whole business is the hint, repeated constantly, that open prostitution is possible in Baltimore because the police themselves "protect" it.

Prostitution is an evil that has existed in all communities. No effort to eradicate it has ever been successful. None of the laws passed against it, some harsh and inhumane, some wiser and more intelligently framed, has ever more than temporarily driven it to cover. In all probability, the most that can be hoped for is to keep it in reasonable bounds and to prevent it from flaunting itself to the shame of honest men and women.

But even this most modest result cannot be attained if there is any sort of alliance between prostitution and its beneficiaries on one hand and the police force on the other. That such alliances do tend to grow up we know by recent experience. That the existence of the alliance breaks down the morale of the force is self-evident. That a lowered morale in the force is an invitation to gangsters, and racketeers, to practice their trade is proved by recent outbreak in Baltimore of bombings and other violent crimes.

Baltimore's problem at the present time arises out of the fact that its police force is headed by a man is clearly unfit for his job. An invasive, ambiguous man, willing to leave the public in general doubt as to his connection with the whiskey business, cannot by any means persuade either the people of the city or the policemen serving under him that he knows how to attack his problem and how to solve it.

For this particular point of view, the vice report may serve a good purpose. Mr. Wells, the State's Attorney, who made the decision that resulted in the publication of the report, will doubtless lay its findings before the grand jury. Indeed, considering its implication, he could hardly do less. If Commissioner Lawson himself cannot see how important it is for Baltimore city to have the police commissioner who has the confidence of the police and of the community, then perhaps the jury, using this report as a basis, may be able to make the point clearer to him.

One thing is certain; the people of Baltimore will not long endure a condition which is so ominous as to have brought some of our reputable citizens to believe that the police force, far from being engaged in an active war against vice and crime, is actually in partnership with these evils.

<u>New Vice Squad Acts Swiftly – Makes Two Raids</u>

<u>Newspaper reports</u> of the Times; Jul 6, 1938; pg. 20

Less than 12 hours after Commissioner William Lawson, had named the new vice squad the squad made two raids and three arrests.

Capt. Joseph H. Itzel, temporarily detached from command of the central district, sent his hand-picked squad of seven men to investigate three places during the evening, and disorderly house charges resulted in each instance.

The Grand Jury, in the meantime, interrupted its inquiry into the Whitelock Street bombing case the year Dr. Finney, Senior, chairman of the citizens committee responsible for the vice investigation.

Carrying two bulky envelopes, Dr. Finney went before the a Grand Jury impaneled for the purpose of investigating the issue, and emerged 15 minutes later without the papers. One package was said to contain an all-important "key" to the names of persons figuring in the vice report.

The cases of law violations described by investigators for the American Social Hygiene Society, which conducted the vice survey, identified persons only by initials, and it is said that their true identity is contained in this "key."

The vice situation was called to the attention of the jury by Jay Bernard Wells, State's Attorney. After Dr. Finney had been before the body, Mr. Wells carried into the chamber a copy of the report.

In the first raid last night, Jeanette Allen, 37 was taken in the custody in a house in the first block of E. Biddle St. A patrolman named Owen Smallwood gained admission to the apartment and shortly advised the woman she was under arrest.

Then, he said, she resisted him and called a large dog. After a scuffle with both the woman and the dog, Smallwood reported, he admitted the other policemen.

The dog also was taken to the central police station.

In the second raid, Patrolman Henry Seybold, a rookie policeman, went to the second floor of a house in the 800 block of Eutaw Street and told the woman she was under arrest and admitted the other patrolman.

Miss Louise B. Cole, 34, and Wilbert Smith, 65, were docketed at the police station on charges of conducting a disorderly house.

The bombing inquiry was resumed last night, at the first night session of the grand jury since the 1937 investigation into vice conditions. Julius (Blinky) Fink is held on $10,000 bail on charges arising from the bombing.

The jurors met at 6:30 PM and interrogated about a dozen witnesses in the bombing case until a few minutes before 11 o'clock.

It was reported last night that routine matters would be discussed before the last of the witnesses in the bombing case was heard today. There was little likelihood, it was said, that the jurors would call witnesses in connection with the vice report, although it was thought that they would continue their joint study of it for part of the day.

In Capt. Itzel's absence, the central district will be commanded by three lieutenants, James Kane, Michael McKew, and Albert Hanssen.

The officers who will work under Capt. Itzel are Sgt. Ralph Amekin, Sgt. James Santmyer, Patrolman William Stone, Patrolman John Delaney, Patrolman Owen Smallwood, Patrolman Philip Germack

Capt. Itzel revealed yesterday that he might enlist the aid of the public service commission and the liquor license board in his activities, the first to revoke licenses of taxicab drivers involved in vice and the second to do the same in the case of tavern owners.

The liquor license board will meet at 11 AM today, it was learned last night, for a thorough discussion of the entire tavern situation.

Dr. John J. McGinity, chairman, and his colleagues, Louise Wellfeld and Harry Lay Duer, will study a report on the raid conducted Saturday night by central district police, it was said.

Vice Squad History

<u>Newspaper reports</u> of the Times; Jul 6, 1938

A certain number of policemen will be told to check up on reports about prostitution and gambling, keep the Commissioner informed as to the activities of those engaged in these pursuits and, when possible, to make court cases against them.

The project has an engaging sound, and, if it were new and untried, it might be possible to await the outcome with some hope. However, the vice squad idea is not new. In fact, the appointment of such a squad is almost a regular step in police departments in the process of demoralization.

They used to have a vice squad in Chicago in the days of big rackets. Public opinion finally forced its abandonment. They had a vice squad in New York for years. What investigation finally showed was that the vice squad was an integral part of the vice racket. The police were working not for the public but for the racketeers. Like the pimps and procurers, they were supposed to track down those who lived off the women of the streets. Lucky Luciano, the head of the vice ring in New York, never showed up in the record as cool, callous or sadistic as some of the policemen on the vice squad.

The reason for this development is not hard to seek. Your ordinary policeman is very much like your ordinary citizen in other walks of life. He knows that vice and prostitution exist and he has little hope that they can ever be eradicated. His duty as an officer of the law makes it incumbent upon him, however, to see that they are kept in balance, and usually, when the morale of the Police Department is good, he is willing to do his bit toward that end. On the whole, he would rather be catching burglars or tripping up pickpockets. The idea of spending his life spying on scarlet

women is repulsive to him. Given his choice he would almost certainly decline the assignment.

But in police departments, as in other departments of life, some men do enjoy pursuing women, and all too often these men, because of the reluctance of their betters, tend to get the vice squad appointments. That is what happened in Chicago, and it is what happened in New York.

It may be that Baltimore is going to be luckier than these cities. It may be that the original squad will do its distasteful work and that it will never be possible to level against it the charge that it is persecuting its victims and getting some sort of perverse pleasure out of hounding them about when they don't pay up. However, that outcome is not likely. In all probability what we are seeing is the usual recourse of a politically minded police Commissioner anxious to silence a public outcry.

The vice squad idea is an exploded idea. A way to get good policing, which means not only keeping vice within bounds but also the suppression of rackets and the prevention of major crimes - is to raise the morale of the whole department. Men who take pride in their work and who have a wholesome respect for their commander will do their work for them.

Tavern Blast Feared Sign of Racket Raid

Newspaper reports of the Times; Jun 14, 1938; pg. 22

Bombing is regarded as effort to extract tribute from a business operator. But terrorism, similar to that used by big-time racketeers in other cities, apparently has invaded Baltimore, it was feared last night by police.

One of the strongest theories on which police were working yesterday was that at least one of the two bombs which exploded over the weekend with heavy property damage into widely separate sections of the city was used in an effort to force a tavern keeper to pay tribute.

Such a method was well known in the pre-repeal days of Chicago, where business firms, reluctant to pay slices of profits to gangsters, were bombed into submission. Such a method, with accompanying gunplay, was well known in New York and was the main strong-armed persuasion used in the Rackets exposed by the present district attorney, Thomas Dewey.

That such methods would be attempted in this city has been predicted several times by those conversant with criminal trends. Just how deep the racketeer intrusion has *penetrated in the city the police don't know, but they are inclined to view the present situation with concern.*

There have been six other bombings in Baltimore since 1907. No one ever was convicted for placing any of them. Of the six, two bombs were aimed at the homes of incumbent Mayor's Broening, in 1927, and Jackson two years ago in 1936. Another bomb exploded at the city's sewage pumping station at East Falls and Eastern Avenues. The remaining bombing cases apparently were the result of individual hatred. No reasons ever were assigned to the bombings of the mayors homes.

More than Revenge

In each of the previous instances, there was nothing to lead police to attribute the bombings to organize crime. The bombing of the Whitelock Street and Druid Hill Avenue taverns, on the other hand, had earmarks of more than individual revenge.

After a hearing yesterday afternoon in the Northern Police Court, Julius Fink, 42, of the 400 block of Andrus Street, was held by magistrate Harry Allers, for a further hearing Thursday morning on a charge of "assault with intent to murder one William Adams, by placing a bomb on premises at 2340 Druid Hill Avenue…"

Police were so much concerned about the bombing that they asked for an extension of time in which to follow up several angles. Fink was held at the Northern police station instead of being sent to City Jail, as is the usual practice in similar cases. Police would not comment on rumors that there was fear of possible attack if the prisoner were sent to jail.

Testimony Meager

Testimony given at the hearing was so meager that magistrate Allers had to request additional information. Detective Lieut. William Feehly, one of the police assigned to the case, informed the magistrate that the case might be injured if extensive testimony were given.

Counsel for Fink, C. Morton Goldstein, associate judge of the people's court and an associate of Harry O. Levin, chairman of the state tax commission, told the magistrate that his client would deny any connection with the bombing. Lieut. Feehly informed the magistrate that there was a possibility of connection between the Tavern bombing and the one in the 300 block of Woodyear Street. Magistrate Allers was asked, despite the reluctance of the police to testify, to hold Fink.

"We have reason to believe that the same people did both jobs and we need a postponement of the case in order to further investigate the job on Woodyear Street." Lieut. Feehly said. "This man's freedom will jeopardize our investigation, we believe."

Held at Police Station

Magistrate Allers then ordered Fink held, not in jail, but in the Northern district police station.

Meanwhile, city officials entered the probe, at least by recognizing its importance. Mayor Jackson conferred with Commissioner Lawson. One result was an order by the Commissioner that every available man be placed on the case under supervision of chief inspector Stephen G. Nelson.

J. Bernard Wells, States Attorney, as far as any official action was concerned left the matter in the hands of the police.

Fink was arrested by Sgt. Wilbur Martindale and patrolman Edgar F. Wilson as a result of what they called a "lucky break." A short time before the Tavern bombing, the two were cruising in that vicinity when they saw an automobile, without lights, pulled away from the curb and drive past the boulevard stop sign.

Actions Recalled

The officers gave chase, caught the car and gave the driver traffic ticket. It was not long before the bomb exploded. After the explosion, the officers recalled the action of the driver and went to his home. They said the driver was Fink.

Damage done by the Tavern bomb was much more extensive than that wrought on Woodyear Street. In the latter section, numerous windows were shattered, metal slugs were driven through shutters, ceilings and floors, but the effect was scattered along both sides of the street and was spread over a wide area.

The Tavern, at Druid Hill Ave. and Whitelock Street, however, took the brunt of the second bombing. Placed by a side door, the bomb tore it from its hinges and shattered the sill, the brick frame, and the stone doorstep. The interior of the Tavern was also extensively damaged by flying debris and metal slugs.

5 July - 1938

Those Patrolmen over 70 Years of Age to be Examined for Fitness.

Police Commissioner Lawson's actions on this date in naming a vice squad to work out of his office coincided, perhaps coincidentally, with his decision to call before the board of police physicians and surgeons 17 policemen who are over the age of 70 to face medical tests on their fitness for duty.

The officers will be examined for their fitness to continue on active duty. The move was said at police headquarters to be the first of several contemplated by the Commissioner, all looking toward the greater efficiency of the department. Commissioner Lawson insisted that the medical examinations should not be interpreted as a general shakeup in the department. Such examinations, he said, are held periodically. Any vacancies caused by those examinations must be filled, he added, and this may cause some changes in assignments.

11 July - 1958

Today in Baltimore Police History the **Southwestern District** moved from Calhoun and Pratt Streets (200 S. Calhoun St) to their present location at 424 Font Hill Avenue.

11 July - 1974 - Police Strike

Today in Baltimore City Police History, 1974, an unknown but large number of Baltimore Police officers and supervisors went on **Strike**. The unionized officers of the Baltimore Police Department who went on strike did so for better wages ("*We Won't Die, for Five point Five*" was the police union's slogan at the time, referring to the city's pending offer of a 5.5% wage hike over three years), joining many other municipal workers of the city at the time. Maryland State Troopers were brought in the next day to help keep the peace, along with non-striking Baltimore officers, supervisors and detectives.

Despite these reinforcements, rioting, burning and looting broke out all over the city the first night the police went on strike, particularly in the Southwestern and Northwestern districts where the union was the strongest and the work stoppage and picketing had originated. The rioting, burning and looting continued for the first three days and nights of the strike, until many striking officers began to cross the picket lines and go back to work, re-enforcing the overwhelmed non-strikers little by little as order was restored.

During the five-day strike, working police officers, supervisors, detectives and State Police troopers were considered scabs. The non-strikers were routinely subjected to officer vs. officer confrontations, spitting, name-calling and even rock and bottle throwing by the striking officers as the working officers crossed the angry picket lines to go to work to protect and serve Baltimore's citizens.

The strike ended five days later, when most of the strikers went back to work, side-by-side with the "enemy scabs." While many other municipal workers staging work stoppages at the same time were given an increase in their wages, the police officers were given only the already offered 5.5% increase (over three years) to begin the next year. The scars of that strike on the city itself, her citizens, businesses, and on the relationships and futures of her police officers were felt for an entire generation of city police.

The Police Commissioner eventually fired many of the officers involved, and revoked the union's bargaining rights. That was the end of public sector unionization for the Baltimore City Police Department, and enabled the Fraternal Order of Police (FOP) to assume the bargaining rights abdicated by the union.

12 July - 1973

Unlimited Medical Leave – The previous Medical Leave policy had provided that all employees, both civilian and sworn, who entered on duty prior to 12 July 1973, were entitled to sick leave benefits in keeping with the existing Baltimore Police Department's policy of unlimited sick leave. However, all civilian employees hired after this date were entitled only to one day of sick leave for each month of completed service. A maximum of 150 days could be accumulated. If the employee so desired, one of each four unused sick leave days (maximum 3 days) accumulated during each year could be converted to cash. Sworn members were still covered under the traditional unlimited sick leave police.

12 July - 1897 - Frey Retires

Today in Baltimore Police History, 1897, Marshal Jacob Frey Retired.

Newspapers of the time reported on that on this date, 12 July, 1897, the active connection of Marshal Jacob Frey, with the Police Department ceased.

From a September 28, 1901 *newspaper article:*

Former Marshal of Police Frey was dismissed by the preceding Board of Police Commissioners on July 12, 1897, and he was replaced at that time by Marshall Hamilton, who was not appointed until October 7, 1897. In the meanwhile, Deputy Marshal Farnan performed the duties of Marshal.

15 July - 1891

On this day in Baltimore City Police History, 1891, we lost our brother Police **Officer Jacob Zapp**. Officer Zapp of the Southern District was struck and run over by a Baltimore and Ohio locomotive on Ostend St. near China Street in South Baltimore, killing him instantly. The officer was walking near the track during a thunderstorm and stepped across the rails to avoid a puddle of water. Locomotive 634 was backing down the track at the time, and the rush of rain and the thunder prevented the patrolman from hearing the locomotive, and as his head was bowed to avoid the downpour he did not see it approaching until the locomotive was too close to him for him to avoid.

When he raised his hand instinctively as if he could somehow stop the locomotive, it was the last of him. Witnesses of the accident ran to the spot where it had occurred, and were horrified at what they saw. The body had been so mangled that all of the remains gathered together could fit in a two-foot soapbox and a wooden cigar box. Patrolman Zapp was fifty-seven years of age and had been on the force since August 27, 1872.

We his brothers and sisters of the Baltimore Police Department will not let him be forgotten. God Bless, and rest in Peace. His service honored the City of Baltimore and the Police Department - RIP Officer Zapp.

15 July - 1976

Today in Baltimore Police History, 1976, the Baltimore Police department recorded its first academy class **layoffs** in the history of the department – Affected were classes 76-2, and 76-3. Both of which were eventually rehired, by the department on 14 January 1977, and 31 January 1977. Class 76-2 had 29 of the original 34 come back, and 76-3 had 27 of the original 31 come back.

16 July - 1877

An incident that highlighted the abilities of the Baltimore police force occurred during the **railroad riots** of July 1877 – abilities making Baltimore's Police shine. Monday, 16, July 1877, the firemen of B&O Railroad's freight engine team left their jobs. It was a time when the policemen in Baltimore and Deputy Marshal Jacob Frey in particular, remained cool, were brave, and were strongminded. The strike was brought about by a 10% reduction in their wages. These men had loudly complained well before the cuts that they were working at a pauper's wage, but that with the cuts, they would not be able to afford to live the life of a vagrant. The Railroad, however, declared that a downward spiral in the overall business interests of the country, had compelled the pay cuts, and made them unable to pay a higher wage.

There were about one hundred of them at first. In many instances, they went out on their trains a few miles from the city, and when the engines stopped to take on coal, they left their places, refusing to go any farther. At first, the strike seemed easy to manage, but as the first day wore on, and news came that the trouble had reached Martinsburg, further that the militia had been called out, and things became more serious. The police were promptly on hand. They were stationed in twos and threes, at various points between Baltimore, the Relay House, and a squad of twelve that were at Camden Junction.

Like many times of tension in the city of Baltimore, both before this riot and in many riots since, the first day passed rather quietly, although in this case few of the freight trains left the city. On the second day however, 17 July 1877, (Tuesday) the excitement began. A freight train of eighteen loaded cars from the West; bound for Locust Point, was partly wrecked by means of a misplaced switch at a trestle near the foot of Leaden Hall Street, Spring Garden, the engine and several cars were thrown into a gulley. News arrived of a fight at Martinsburg, in which two railroad firemen were shot. At first light, the employees of the Baltimore and Ohio Company held a meeting, they decided to support the strikers, but first, they would try seeking conciliation with the company.

The conciliation failed, and the strike went on. It was Wednesday, 18 July, 1877 the third day of troubles for B&O, when the West Virginia authorities called on President Hayes for troops, and a proclamation was issued at once by the President. Troops were promptly sent. Of course, all this had its effect in Baltimore, but on that day, there were no hostile demonstrations here. The freight business amounted practically to nothing, but the passenger trains arrived and departed as usual.

The Company decided not to recede from its position, and a reward of $500 was offered by it for the arrest of the person, or persons who caused the Spring Garden wreck. On the fourth day, 19 July 1877, the troubles continued in Martinsburg, but there was no outbreak here in Baltimore. It took nearly a full five days for any excitement to take place here. However, when it arrived, Baltimore was more excited than it had been since the war.

About 3 o'clock in the afternoon of Friday, when the news had been received that the strike at Cumberland threatened to assume general proportions, Governor Carroll held a consultation with the officers of the Baltimore and Ohio Company, and became convinced that the presence of the military at Cumberland was necessary for the preservation of peace and order. A half hour later, he issued an order to Brigadier General Herbert, commanding the First Brigade, Maryland National Guard, ordering him to proceed to Cumberland. Simultaneously he issued a proclamation calling upon the rioters to desist. Soon afterwards, General Herbert held another consultation with Governor Carroll to consider whether the military should be summoned to their respective armories by a "military call" from the bells. Governor Carroll objected to this, and General Herbert tried to get the men at the armories by the ordinary means, but not succeeding very well, again asked the Governor that the bells be rung. This was done, and a great misfortune was proven.

At twenty minutes to 6:00, the emergency call was sounded from the fire bells at City Hall. The people knew what it meant, and in a very short time, the streets around the armories were filled with men and boys of all ages who sympathized with the strikers. It was about the time that work in the factories was over, and all the workmen helped to swell the crowds. In front of the armory of the Sixth Regiment, at Fayette and Front streets, the mob numbered at least 2,000. Strangely enough, the officers of the regiment sent word to the police headquarters, asking that policemen be sent to clear the way, so that the regiment could march on to Camden station.

The old system then in vogue scattered the policemen, so that not enough of them could be collected in time for the work, and in two hours the crowd was so large that no force was able to handle it.

The troubles at the Sixth Regiment Armory began at about seven o'clock. A brickbat was thrown into one of the windows.

Four policemen, Officers Albert Whitely, James Jamison, Oliver Kenly, and Roberts-were stationed at the door, and in spite of the volleys of stones, missiles and jeers that followed they manfully stood their dangerous guard, although the four militia men who had been with the policemen had been called in. The hour set for marching was 8:15 o'clock, and the crowd had become maddened and aggressive. The companies, however, determined to resist the rioters. When they appeared on the street, there was a riot so general that it drove the men back again into the building. The next time they came out, they had orders to fire. The first company fired high, but the attack became so heavy on the following companies that they discharged their weapons into the crowd. From that instant all along the march to Camden station the firing was continuous and general, resulting in the killing of about a dozen people and the serious wounding of as many more.

The Fifth regiment did not use its guns, although it was severely attacked and had every provocation to fire. The men marched admirably through showers of stones and other missiles. There were 250 of them. At the junction of Camden and Eutaw Streets, a solid mass of rough-looking men blocked their passage. They came to a halt for a moment, and although the bricks were falling fast, Captain Zollinger counselled his men NOT to fire.

Then he ordered them to prepare to double-quick with their fixed bayonets into the depot. Drawing his sword, Captain Zollinger shouted to the mob to give way that the command might pass. A brawny man opposed the Captain, who promptly knocked him down, and amid the hoots and yells, came several shots from the crowd, inviting the regiment to charge the depot. Soon after the regiment had reached the station the building was set to fire, the rioters attempted to interfere with the firemen, but fortunately their attempts had failed, and the flames were knocked to embers, and then ashes.

The fearless service of the police during these rebel-rousing times has never been properly recognized bar a few brief passages in the newspapers. In every instance, they awed the mob, while the soldiers exasperated the situation.

One policeman was equal to a dozen soldiers. Until long after midnight, the police protected the military, and guarded all the depot buildings. And it was our police who protected the firemen, their fire engines, and the hoses they used, and therefore it was our police who saved the buildings. They were fired upon by the mob, and some were wounded, but they wounded a number of the mob in return, and in addition, they made many arrests.

The result of this great excitement was that the order sending the soldiers to Cumberland was withdrawn, and a proclamation to that effect was issued by Mayor Latrobe.

During these days the efficiency of the police department was tested, and proven. Deputy-Marshal Jacob Frey had command of those around Camden station. While for nearly seventy hours, he went without sleep, as he single-handedly maintained control of the mob. Long before any of his officers could assemble, on that Friday and before the arrival of the military, Frey had cleared the platform and front pavement of several hundred excited and unruly men. However, reinforcements arrived, and without hesitation Deputy-Marshal Frey waded into the crowd, where he in short order arrested two of the agitators. Without incident, they were taken into his custody, and transported to the Southern District Station House where Frey himself, booked the pair.

On Saturday night, crowds again collected around Camden station. About 9 P. M. a fire-alarm excited the rioters so that they rushed towards the lines that the police had formed. Shots were fired by the rioters, and 'several officers fell wounded. Then it was that Deputy-Marshal Frey told the men to keep steady, and a moment afterwards, their pistols being drawn, the command of "Take aim - Fire" was given. The police fired low, and as they fired they rushed forward, and each officer grabbed a prisoner. Fifty arrests were made; several men were killed and a number wounded. There was another outbreak at 11 o'clock and fifty three more arrests were made.

On Sunday morning, large crowds again collected around the Camden Station, and they were closely pressing upon the picket lines of the Fifth regiment. Deputy-Marshal Frey, not liking the looks of things, sent for a squad of twenty policemen. When they arrived, the Deputy-Marshal took charge of them in person. He told the crowd that he was going to "clear that street" and he advised all peaceably disposed persons to go home. Many of them did so, but many more remained. Turning to his men, the Marshal gave orders to "Move Forward," and in a very short time, the rioters were driven away. They knew the Deputy-Marshal, and they were afraid of him.

When the riot had assumed such threatening proportions, every effort was made to protect the city. United States soldiers from New York and other cities were promptly ordered to Baltimore. General W. S. Hancock arrived with eight companies of troops from New York harbor, and two war vessels with 560 men, fully equipped, anchored in the Patapsco. Several hundred special policemen were sworn in by the Police Board. Among them were such well-known citizens as William M. Pegram, Alexander M. Green, C. Morton Stewart, Frank Frick, E. Wyatt Blanchard, James H. Barney, J. L. Hoffman, Robert G. Hoffman, W. Gilmore Hoffman, John Donnell Smith, William A. Fisher, Frederick von Kapff, and Washington B. Hanson. They were supplied with the regular badges, and they did good work.

The regular policemen were unfaltering in their duty, and most of them did not sleep during more than fifty hours. The great show of strength by the police and troops overawed the rioters, and the troubles were gradually quieted. The following Saturday freight trains, each guarded by ten soldiers, moved out on the road.

The strikes in other cities continued, more or less, but within two weeks, they were over. Trouble on the Northern Central road was happily averted. The jury of inquest which sat in judgement of the man killed by the Sixth Regiment was very thorough in its investigations, and after several days consumed in taking testimony it rendered a verdict which found the rioters guilty of the troubles, but charged the regiment with shooting too hastily and too indiscriminately. It found fault because there were not more policemen on hand around the armory. This however was purely the fault of the military authorities in not giving sufficient notice to the Marshal. The part that the police force took in the memorable conflict will ever stand a monument to its courage and efficiency.

20 July - 1981

On this day in Baltimore Police History, 1981 we lost our brother, Police **Officer Ronald L. Tracey**, who was murdered as he investigated a property damage accident at Monroe and Baker Streets shortly before midnight on July 20, 1981. At about 11:15 pm he responded to that location to process an accident scene. As is normal for this type of incident on a warm summer night, a number of citizens gathered to watch as wreckers were called to the scene to remove inoperable vehicles. Those who had been involved in the accident provided Officer Tracey with the appropriate information. There was no tension and no problems.

Things remained "routine" until about 11:45 pm when a citizen came out of the crowd and snuck up behind the Officer who was concentrating on the work at hand. He suddenly jumped the officer from behind and a life and death struggle began. Officer Tracey was able to broadcast one frantic call for assistance. He did not have time to identify himself or give his location. The assailant wrestled the officer's service revolver from its holster and shot the officer in the stomach and in the head.

Witnesses later told investigating detectives that while this was occurring, the crowd retreated, with not one citizen coming to the assistance of the officer. Citizens did call Police Communications, which dispatched appropriate units. Officer Tracey was transported to Lutheran Hospital where he was pronounced dead.

Investigating officers and detectives recovered his service revolver about two blocks from the scene of the homicide. Citizens called police with information regarding the possible identity of the assailant and throughout the early morning hours, police searched for him. At 5:00 am on July 21, 1981, Northeastern District Officers located and arrested the man as he slept on the floor of a Northeast Baltimore residence. He was apprehended and detained in Baltimore City Jail. A motive for the crime was never developed, and/or never shared with the public.

Officer Tracey will forever be missed, but never will he be forgotten by us his brothers and sisters of the Baltimore Police Department. God Bless and Rest in Peace.

21 July - 1986

On this day in Baltimore Police History, 1986 we lost our Brother, Police **Officer Richard Thomas Miller** to a vehicular assault as he was run down while on duty.

Officer Richard Miller, assigned to the Traffic Division, was busy directing traffic at the west end of the parking lot at Memorial Stadium, prior to a baseball game. Officer Miller, along with others observed a 1977 Toyota which was about to drive the wrong way down a one-way street. They attempted to flag down the car, but the driver of the vehicle instead swerved towards the officers, traveled a short distance, and ran down Officer Miller, throwing him into the air and striking two parked cars. The driver of the Toyota was arrested and charged with murder and three counts of attempted murder. Officers quickly administered first aid to Officer Miller while an ambulance was summoned. He was taken to University of Maryland's Shock Trauma Unit. For several weeks he fought to live. Medical staff at the Shock Trauma Unit performed several operations to repair massive internal injuries. On July 21, 1986, Officer Miller succumbed to his injuries, one day away from his 32nd anniversary of service with the department.

Leonard P. Cirincione, 40, was convicted in 1987 of first-degree murder and related charges in the 1986 slaying of Officer Richard Miller, who was run down while directing traffic outside Memorial Stadium before an Orioles game. Cirincione is serving a sentence of life plus 20 years. Miller survived for 5 ½ weeks on life support before this death.

Cirincione, a drug abuser since high school, testified he had smoked up to eight PCP cigarettes within 12 hours of the incident and that he blacked out shortly before hitting Miller. In 1996 he began asking for a new trial, a reduced sentence – he is a new man since his arrest he says, and he has turned his life around 360 degrees. The judge basically told him to pound sand… you did the crime do the time… new trial denied for killer of city police officer

Officer Richard Miller will forever be missed, but never forgotten. God Bless him and may he Rest in Peace.

22 July - 1965

On this day in Baltimore Police History, 1965 we lost our brother, **Officer Robert Kuhn** to gunfire based on the following:

On July 22, 1965 at the intersection of North Avenue and Ellamont Street, Officer Robert Kuhn observed a car double parked. He approached the vehicle and found it to be empty. As he looked inside the car, a suspect approached him from behind. The suspect shot Kuhn six times with a pistol. The suspect then took Officer Kuhn's service revolver from his holster and shot him six more times [the account that the officer was also shot with his own weapon was later disputed by the one witness to part of the incident]. Police eventually killed the suspect. Investigation revealed that the suspect had narcotics inside his vehicle.

Officer Kuhn served in the U.S. Marine Corps from September 24, 1962 to March 23, 1963. He was active in the Marine Corps Reserves until the time of his death.

For more information we have pulled the following two news articles from the time of this incident

Two Killings Laid To David Cooper - By George J. Hiltner

David Cooper, 45, of the 2900 block Westwood Avenue, was charged by police yesterday with shooting and killing Western District Patrolman Robert H Kuhn, early Thursday morning (22 July 1965). Six other charges, including the shooting and killing of William Cooper, his own 29 year old nephew, also were placed against Cooper. All were marked "Abated by death" since the accused man also died after police arrested him for the spree. The charges included three assaults on his arresting officers, Patrolman John Hess, James Griffin and Robert Powell: one charge of possessing marijuana, and one charge of possessing three deadly weapons, .22 and .38 caliber pistols and a blackjack.

Decided at Conference

The decision to institute charges against the elder Mr. Cooper, and to accuse no one in connection with his death was made yesterday in a high-level conference attended by State's Attorney Charles E. Moylan, Capt. Wade Poole, of the Western District; Lt. Anton Glover, of the homicide squad, and Sgt. Hobert Lewis, also of homicide. Mr. Moylan stated that he also conferred with Dr. Charles S. Petty, assistant medical examiner for Maryland. The State's Attorney complimented the Police Department for the "superlative job that had been done in piecing together the narrative of what occurred in the early morning hours of Thursday. "Mr. Moylan then said: 'it appears incomprehensible that David Cooper shot officer at least five times in the body, thereby causing his death. Three pellets were recovered from the body of Officer Kuhn and a total of 15 gunshot wounds were found on his body. The attack was clearly unprovoked as Officer Kuhn was simply making a car check for double parking in the 3100 block of W. North Ave. "It also appears that David Cooper was responsible for the death of his nephew, William Cooper. Some minutes after shooting Officer Kuhn, the elder Cooper shot the nephew three times

in the right temple with a .22 caliber revolver thereby causing his death. This revolver was recovered on Cooper at the time of his arrest. No charges will be placed against anyone for the death of David Cooper himself. Dr. Petty found Cooper to be suffering from advanced case of heart disease showing both an enlarged heart and significant clogging of the arteries. "The cardiac condition was such that any excessive strain might have well brought on the heart attack.

Cooper had himself extreme exertions of energy in the shooting of the officer, the apparent struggle with his nephew, his later violent resistance to the arrest on the street in the 1600 block of St. Stephen Street, in the cruising patrol going to Lutheran hospital and in the Lutheran hospital itself where he had to be physically restrained at the request of the doctors. "Cooper also was suffering from two gunshot wounds, one in the left elbow and one in the right ankle. It appeared that the gunshot wounds were inflicted by his own .22 caliber revolver during the struggle between him and his nephew which resulted in the nephew's death. At no time did any police officer in the case even draw, let alone use his service revolver."

Blood on the blackjack

"There were also superficial abrasions about Cooper's head, some of which were certainly caused when the officers had to restrain him as he struggled to retain possession of his .22 caliber revolver and some of which may have been inflicted by his nephew who had a homemade blackjack accessible to him, which was found on the rear seat of Cooper's automobile. "It should be pointed out that when the officers first approached David Cooper on St. Stephen's Street they noticed that he already had blood on his head and shirt and the blood was also found on the blackjack in the automobile. "At any rate, the abrasions were a very minor contributing factor at most since the autopsy showed no skull fracture of any sort and no blood clotting at all in the area of the brain."

Ballistics Report

Mr. Moylan further explained that the uncle in his first contact with patrolman Kuhn used another weapon, a .38 caliber pistol. And emptied it into the body of the police victim. Then he used a .22 caliber revolver to fire at the nephew and it was this weapon with which he himself was shot during the struggle with the younger relative, the State's attorney said. This reconstruction of events is borne out by the finding of police ballistics experts yesterday that the .38 caliber bullets recovered from the body of patrolman Kuhn were fired from the empty weapon which David Cooper abandoned in the car. Ballistics findings also verified the bullets taken from *the body of William Cooper were fired from a .22 caliber gun.*

David Cooper Due Charge of Murder

Chief Inspector says only a change in facts will alter plans.

The Police Department's chief inspectors said last night that, barring new developments, the department expects to charge David Cooper with the murders of patrolman Robert Henry Kuhn and William Cooper early yesterday morning.

David Cooper died at 3:05 AM yesterday. Two hours after the shooting of the 23-year-old policeman and the discovery of William Cooper's body slumped in the back seat of a car a few blocks away.

George J Murphy, the chief inspector said he felt the facts that have been gathered so far in the case suggests David Cooper was responsible for the two shootings.

Await Ballistic Reports

He said that if no new facts come in late, the department expects to place murder charges against the elder Cooper. A definite decision on the charge could not be made yesterday. Because the results of the ballistics and fingerprint test essential to the investigation will not be available until today. The charge, if made, will be academic in any case. In technical language, it will be abated by the death of the defendant.

Inspector Murphy's statement came at the end of the day of intensive investigation of the shooting of patrolman Kuhn and the deaths that followed it. Investigation was hampered by the fact that there were no direct eyewitnesses accounting of any of the three shootings and that all of the principles are dead.

David Cooper was arrested by police less than a half-hour after the shootings. He died at Lutheran hospital at 3:05 AM following a struggle with policeman in a patrol car.

15 Bullet Holes in Officer's Body

Dr. Charles S. Petit Junior, assistant medical examiner, said yesterday afternoon that David Cooper died of a severe heart condition combined with the several injuries he had received in several struggles. Dr. Petty said patrolman Kuhn died of gunshot wounds. He said three .22 caliber bullets were found in his body, and that there were 15 bullet holes in his body. William Cooper died of bullet wounds in the head caused by three .22 caliber bullets. Dr. Petty said that the bullets that killed patrolman Kuhn might have come from the same gun with which William Cooper was shot but of that he could not be certain.

Six or Eight Shots

Only one witness was located. Firefighter Carlos A. Downs of the firehouse at North Avenue and Hellmont Street observed a part of the scene. He told police that he was sitting at the desk in the firehouse when he heard a shot, got up and went to the door. About 90 feet away on the south side of North Avenue he saw a man pointing a gun at the sidewalk in front of him, Mr. Downs told police.

He then heard six or eight shots in rapid succession. He said he thought at the time that the man was drunk and just shooting. Mr. Downs said at first he did not see what the man was shooting at. He said he saw the man with the gun get into the black and white convertible and drive east on North Avenue. Mr. Downs said patrolman Kuhn's gun was still in his holster as he lay on the ground. He said the officer was still alive when he got to him, "moaning" and "bleeding real bad."

Found Car and Body

A police dragnet was thrown around the area, and a patrol car a few minutes later found William Cooper laying in the back seat of a black and white convertible in the 1600 block of St. Stephen Street. Searching the car, police found a .38 caliber automatic and a handmade blackjack. A few minutes later, officers in another patrol car apprehended David Cooper, who was running in the 2000 Block Pressbury St. the officers reported they saw blood on his hands and shirt before they arrested him.

Officer Robert Henry Kuhn will forever be missed, but never forgotten by us his brothers and sisters of the Baltimore Police Department. God Bless and Rest in Peace.

24 July - 1868 - Great Baltimore Flood

Today in Baltimore Police History, 1868 – The **Great Baltimore Flood** - Shortly after Commissioner Carr's election to the Police Board came a most dreadful calamity, the Baltimore flood of 24 July 1868, overtaking the city. This Flood would take lives, destroy property and cause major changes to the path of the Jones falls.

In that crisis the bravery of Commissioner Carr in his rescuing of victims from this catastrophe, became a matter of local and national fame.

Harper's Weekly, at the time, in a long article on the floods, quoted the following editorial from the Baltimore Sunday Telegram, of 26 July 1868: "It is a true saying, that in times of great public calamities, some men rise to the position of a great public benefactor, and such was the case yesterday with Police Commissioner James E. Carr. He at first sight apprehended the character of the calamity, and he immediately sent for boats, and organized a sufficient force of police, to manage them.

He soon had work enough to do, as he led the search in his boat to places of great peril, as he rescued women, and children.

26 July - 1929

On this day in Baltimore Police History, 1929 we lost our Brother, Patrolman **James M. Moore** to a line of duty shooting that took place some 43 years earlier, in 1887, when a bullet left lodged in his chest at that time caused his death today; based on the following Newspaper reports:

Former Policeman Dies Of Old Wound - Newspaper Article - Jul 28, 1929;

A retired Policeman today died of a forty-three year old wound. Policeman James M. Moore was shot while making an arrest forty-three years ago.

Sensation at Time – Bullet Lodged Near Heart – Physician Feared to Remove It

While on duty in the Western Police District in 1887, James M. Moore then a patrolman was shot several times by a drink-crazed man. He was blinded in one eye, and a shot lodged near his heart, resting in such a position that doctors dared not attempt to remove it.

Mr. Moore was placed on a pension list, and died Friday night (26 July 1929) from the breast wound received 43 years ago. The shooting which ultimately caused his death was one of the newspaper sensations at that time, as Patrolman Moore was lauded for arresting his assailant although seriously wounded.

Reported for the Baltimore Sun – Apr 11, 1887 - *Shooting a Policeman*

A flurry of gunfire in Josephine Street and an Officer is wounded four times. Police

Officer James M. Moore, of the Western District, was shot and seriously injured Saturday night (9 April, 1887) at eight o'clock, by Martin Gundlach, a driver for the Standard Cab Co., and Charles P. Gundlach, box-maker, living at 722½ West Lexington St. The shooting occurred at the residence of the mother of the men, Mrs. Christiana Gundlach, 654 Josephine Street. At the hearing yesterday before Justice Benner the wounded officer's statement of the affair was read.

It is as follows:

"About 8 o'clock Saturday night, (9 April 1887) while patrolling my beat, which includes Josephine Street, I was notified by a citizen that there had been trouble at Mrs. Christiana Gundlach's. Number 654 Josephine Street, between her and her son Martin, who drives one of the Standard cabs. I went towards the house and heard some loud words, but nothing further.

"Later Martin came out and I advised him to get in his cab, which was standing at the curb, and go away. The man proceeded to get on the box of the cab, when his brother, Charles P. Gundlach, came out of the house and said, "What is the matter here?' and began to pull off his coat, and almost simultaneously Martin Gundlach stood up on his seat and called out, "You _____, you can do the niggers, but you can't do me," and began firing at me. I was struck: and felt shots in the chin and breast, and as I staggered against the horse and tried to drag my assailant from the cab he jumped down and ran into the house. I succeed in drawing my pistol and fired one shot at him as he ran into the doorway and three shots in the air to call for assistance. In the meantime his brother, Charles Gundlach, fired two shots at me, one taking effect in the calf the left leg and one grazing the right thigh. One of the shots was fired after Martin had gone into the house. I grabbed Charles, but he broke away from me, jumped on the cab and drove furiously down Josephine Street to Arch to Lexington. At the same time Martin came out of another house and ran after the cab. I followed him as well as I was able, and came up with him on Arch Street, near Lexington Street. As I grappled with him he turned and struck me, and I dealt him a blow upon the head with my pistol, which I held in my hand. At this time several officers came up and I delivered my prisoner over to them."

The officers who caught Charles Gundlach, and who relieved Officer Moore of his prisoner, Martin Gundlach, were Sergeant Tierney and policemen Berney and Graves. Sergeant Tierney and officer Berney were standing in the station-house in citizens' clothes, having gone on duty an hour before. Four pistol shots were heard, and Lieutenant Fullem, who was sitting at his desk, exclaimed, "My God, somebody has been shot!" The men ran down Josephine street to the scene of the shooting, and then to the officer's assistance, as given in his statement.

Sgt. Tierney stopped the cab and pulled Charles Gundlach from his seat, while officers Berney and Graves took charge of the other man and assisted officer Moore to the stationhouse, where Lieutenant Fullem, with the assistance of some citizens, undressed and put the wounded officer to bed in one or the upper rooms at the station, and summoned Dr. J. J. R. Crozer and Louis C. Horn, who, upon examination, found that; one bullet entered the mouth below the lip, plowed its way over the left lower jaw bone, and out under the jaw; another struck him in the left side, in the region of the heart, struck a rib and glanced off. The third struck him in the calf of the left leg, going in about one and a-half inches. Another was a glance shot, making an abrasion on the right thigh.

The fact of one the bullets entering the back of the officer's leg set Lieutenant Scott to thinking, and knowing that officer Moore had not turned his back on his assailant, he had a consultation with him, when he made out his statement, and at the hearing preferred the charge of shooting with intent to kill Officer Moore against Charles P. Gundlach, who had up until that point only been held on the charges of disorderly conduct and reckless driving. When Martin Gundlach was taken into the station house, Lieutenant Fullem said to him, "Why did you do this, Mart?" He replied, "Mr. Fullem, I'll kill that_____ yet."

When searched a large table knife was found on him, which he had picked up as he ran through the house. Marshal Frey was present at the hearing, and commended Captain Cadwallader for his activity in working up the case and for sending Lieutenant Scott after a statement from Officer Moore, it not being customary. The wounded man's face was badly burned by the powder. He showed great nerve in chasing his man and holding him, injured as he was until other officers arrived. Eleven witnesses were examined. They were: Miss Cora Tate, Wm. Schnelder. Ida Miller, colored, Charles P. Logue, Wm. Logue, Harry Turnbaugh, Sergeant Tierney, Lieutenant Fullem, Dr. L. C. Horn and Lieutenant Scott. Mr. Louis Hochhelmer has been retained to defend the prisoners, who were committed for court by Justice Benner, bail being refused.

26 July - 1972

On this day in Baltimore Police History, 1972 we lost our Brother, **Officer Lorenzo Gray** to gunfire during a hold-up at a Holiday Inn.

On Tuesday, July 25, 1972, at approximately 10:30 pm, Officer Lorenzo Gray and Officer William Heath, of the Southeastern District, received a call for a hold up in progress in the 3600 blk. of Pulaski Hwy. As they were responding to the scene at the Holiday Inn, they encountered two suspects, one of whom was armed with a sawed-off shotgun. Officer Gray pursued the suspect on foot, while Officer Heath attempted to apprehend the second suspect. After a brief chase, the first suspect wheeled around and fired his shotgun directly into Officer Gray, who then managed to fire one shot from his service revolver, slightly wounding the suspect. Agents of the Federal Bureau of Narcotics and Dangerous Drugs, who had been near the scene at the time of the shooting, apprehended the suspects. Officer Lorenzo Gray, a three year veteran of the Department, was pronounced dead of the gunshot wound at Johns Hopkins Hospital several hours after the shooting. Officer Gray was 24 years old and the father of 2 young children.

Newspaper article; Jul 26, 1972

Wounded officer dies after foiling holdup; 2 caught

A 24-year old Southeastern district patrolman was fatally shot last night as he and another officer were struggling with two armed men at the Holiday Inn, in the 3600 block Pulaski highway. Patrolman Lorenzo Gray was shot in the chest with a sawed-off shotgun as he was chasing a masked man through the motel's kitchen at 10:40 pm, police said. He died in the Johns Hopkins Hospital about 1:00 am today (26 July, 1972).

Patrolman Gray, who had been on the force for three years was the first city police officer to die on duty this year.

The shotgun-carrying man and his accomplice, who was armed with a revolver and also masked, were arrested in a scuffle at the Holiday Inn by Patrolman William Heath and other officers, who rushed to the scene after the shooting. Police gave the following account or the events that led to last night's tragedy:

The two Southeastern district patrolmen operating separate cars on Pulaski highway, looking for suspects in an earlier holdup in the area, when they were flagged down by a person who told them that he had seen two masked men enter

the motel.

After entering the inn, the officers found the gunmen in the dining room, where Patrolman Heath struggled with a man armed with a revolver and managed to subdue him, police said.

Patrolman Gray meanwhile chased the man with the shotgun to the motel kitchen, where the man suddenly turned around and shot at him, striking him in the stomach and chest. The blast knocked him 20 feet backward police said.

The patrolman was admitted in critical condition to Johns Hopkins hospital. The two suspects and four other policeman were injured during the struggle that preceded the pairs arrest officials said.

The gunmen were taken city hospital while the officers were treated and released at Mercy Hospital. The extent of their injuries was not available last night.

<u>Newspaper Article</u>; Jul 30, 1972;

Full dress police funeral services were held yesterday for Patrolman Lorenzo Gray, the Southeast district policeman who was shot Tuesday while stopping an attempted robbery at an East Baltimore motel. Patrolman Gray a Vietnam Veteran who joined the city police after his discharge from the Marine Corps in 1968. He was eulogized by the Rev. Leslie G. Metcalf, pastor of the Matthews United Methodist Church, as a man of "devotion to duty," whose death in the line of duty was the single greatest tribute to his dedication. Mr. Metcalf, long active in police affairs, remembered meeting Patrolman Gray after his assignment to the Southeastern district

"I was introduced to a young man with a pleasant smile and a desire to do the job right. I met him again on his beat on monument Street just before he was killed. He wore that same smile that day and his determination to serve the community was even greater."

More than 400 policeman were present for the 11:15 AM services, including some 350 from the Baltimore area. Only 45 of these were assigned to attend, according to the police spokesman – the rest were there on their own time.

Among the 21 police who came from out of state were representatives of departments from Plainfield, New Jersey; Washington, D.C.; Newcastle, Delaware; Philadelphia and Cherry Hill, New Jersey. One Plainfield policeman, Robert Caravan, said that he came because he has a brother on the Baltimore police force and he wanted to show his solidarity with fellow policeman. "Everybody else might *be against us, but were all together," he said.*

Other Units present were police from Maryland units in Montgomery County, Anne Arundel County, seat Pleasant Township, Howard County and Baltimore County. Federal law enforcement agencies attending the services included the United States Secret Service, US Park police and the Federal Bureau of Narcotics. The Baltimore fire department was also represented.

Gov. Mandel and police Commissioner Donald D Pomerleau were among those who filed past Officer Gray's casket. Gov. Mandel called the killing "a tragedy" and said that more cooperation between police and citizens might help avert such incidents in the future. "People should let the police know if they see someone carrying a dangerous weapon," said Mr. Mandel.

Patrolman Gray was killed with a sawed-off shotgun.

About 150 people, including 50 friends and relatives attended the half hour service, while some 300 more waited outside.

Flag Draped Casket

Patrolman Gray's flag draped casket was taken two blocks to a hearse by pallbearers through a double column of policeman who stood at attention and saluted. The six pallbearers were members of the original narcotics squad Patrolman Gray worked with when he joined the Police Department in 1969.

A motorcade of about 200 vehicles, many of them marked police cars, left the funeral establishment at noon for Harmony Memorial Park, a cemetery in Prince George's County, near Washington. There, on the hill above the gravesite, a fellow policeman and former Marine, Robert L. Domney, played taps, and the flag that had draped patrolman Gray's casket was presented to his stepfather, Milton Cross.

In addition to his stepfather, survivors include three stepsisters, Mrs. Benita Jones, Daphne Green and Delphine Green, two stepbrothers, Joseph Green and Nathaniel Green and two daughters Audrey Gray and Sandra Gray all living in Baltimore.

He will forever be missed, but never forgotten by us his brothers and sisters of the Baltimore Police Department... God Bless and Rest in Peace.

27 July - 1971

The Community Relations and Youth Divisions were combined into a new division known as The Community Services Division. The creation of this division and the resulting centralization of administrative functions provides an effective channel of communication between the Police Officers and the community they serve.

"The major thrust of our expanded Community Services function is aimed at our young people. It is the Division's priority to keep clear the channel of communication, between officers, and the community. The accomplishment of this mission is aided by the division's two Summer Camp operations located at Camp Perkins and Camp Ritchie. Also, our Officer Friendly Program geared for its first full year of operation."

29 July - 1776

Today in Baltimore City History, 29 July 1776, the **Declaration of Independence** was read to the citizens of Maryland from the Baltimore City Courthouse steps.

The next day, *the papers reported*:

"Yesterday, by order of the Committee of this Town, the Declaration of Independence of the United States of America was read at the Court House to a large and respectable body of Militia, and the company of Artillery, and other principal inhabitants of this Town and County. The Declaration was received with general applause and heartfelt satisfaction. At night, the Town was illuminated; and at the same time, the effigy of our former King was carted through the Town, and committed to the flames, amidst the acclamations of many hundreds – the just reward of a tyrant."

30 July - 1902

On this day in Baltimore Police History, 30 July, 1902, we lost our Brother, **Patrolman John A. McIntyre** to a Line of Duty Illness.

Patrolman John A. McIntire - Patrolman John a McIntyre of the Northwestern District, 1724 North Calhoun St. died yesterday morning about 11 o'clock of nervous prostration. He had not been in good health for the past two years, but was stricken on July 4 last and thereafter had not been on duty. He was born in this city 53 years ago, and was the son of the late Michael McIntyre.

He was formally employed in Druid Hill Park. He was appointed to the police force April 4, 1887. Lieut. Carter, who was acting Capt. of the district yesterday, stated that Patrolman McIntyre was a very efficient officer, and that he had made credible arrests.

On December 12, 1892, a pocketbook was snatched from the hands of Mr. Julia Eichelberger at the corner of Lyndon and Lafayette Avenue. She reported the case at once to the police, and a few hours later based only on the descriptions given, Patrolman McIntyre arrested Daniel Thomas, John Smith and James Kristen, all colored males and all matching the suspect descriptions. Thomas was sentenced to the penitentiary for 18 months, Smith for three years and Kristen for eight years. Patrolman McIntyre was a member of St. Gregory's Catholic Church. He belonged to Eutaw conclave and the Heptasophs into the Catholic benevolent Legion.

Officer McIntyre was survived by his widow Miss Katherine Fillmore, and four sons – Frank, Leo, George and Charles McIntyre.

30 July - 1983

The first female K9 officer is assigned. Officer Charlene M. Jenkins is handler to Max.

1 August - 1907

The Department received a Columbia Electric Automobile, its first. The machine was put to use in the Central District as an Ambulance and Patrol (Paddy) Wagon. It was said to have been easy to run and easily made 16 miles an hour.

1 August - 1953

On this day on Baltimore Police History, 1953, we lost our brother, **Sergeant James L. Scholl**.

Sgt. Scholl was 41 years old when he was shot on 20 July, 1953 in a pre-dawn gun battle inside an east Baltimore tavern named "Brown's Bar," located in the 1800 block of Broening Highway. One gunman was killed in the battle, another policeman was wounded and a second bandit was seized without firing a shot after twelve policemen had converged on the tavern in response to calls for help from inside.

The officers were investigating a call about a suspicious automobile, which they found sitting empty near the bar. Finding no one in the car, the officers examined the closed tavern for signs of forced entry, and found that a window on one side of the building had been jimmied. After two additional police officers arrived as backup units, Sergeant Scholl crawled through the open window to investigate further. He was followed into the building by the three additional officers. Using flashlights, Sergeant Scholl and the other policemen made their way down a narrow, dark hall to an unlit storeroom in the rear of the tavern. Sergeant Scholl entered the storeroom first and immediately faced a round of gunfire from someone inside.

The policemen returned the fire, and it was all over in a few seconds. Scholl and one of his officers were wounded and one gunman was killed in the shooting. The wounded policeman is Patrolman Thomas Alford, 25 who was shot in the shoulder. The dead suspect was identified as Beauford Saunders, a 20-year-old Cleveland man.

Newspaper Article; Aug 2, 1953; pg. 34

Eastern District Sergeant James L. Scholl, walked into a dark storeroom and a fusillade of a bandit's bullets, but was able to empty his own pistol before falling. He would go on to die nine days later, as the result of gunshot wounds to his stomach and pelvis.

Sergeant Scholl underwent a three-hour intestinal operation immediately after being shot as he was in the midst of apprehending two tavern burglars on 20 July, 1953.

Nearly 200 volunteer blood donors came to the hospital within just a few hours after officials said Sergeant Scholl would need the transfusions. Despite the operation, and the transfusions, the Sgt Scholl remained in critical condition until his passing on 1 August, 1953.

The gunman killed in the shooting was identified as Beauford Saunders, a 20-year old Cleveland man. The wounded policeman is Patrolman Thomas Alford, 25 who was shot in the shoulder. Since the shooting, the grand jury indicted, Rodger Dennis

Wyley, 20-year-old young man from Fostoria, Ohio, on charges of assault with intent to murder both suspects, and with burglary at the Broening highway tavern. Subsequent to the Sergeant's demise, Wyley was also charged with his murder.

Eastern District Captain Gribbin said, he was deeply grieved by the death of Sergeant Scholl. "I'm sure his memory will linger long as a man of outstanding courage and bravery," the Captain said, "The Eastern district, and the department as a whole have lost a real policeman, a policeman of great promise. He was very popular throughout the entire department, and deserved to be for any one of the many fine traits he possessed."

The wounded policeman is Patrolman Thomas Alford, 25 who was shot in the shoulder during the fire-fight. Since the shooting, the grand jury has again presented Rodger Dennis Wyley, of Fostoria, Ohio, with additional charges of assault with intent to murder, and with burglary at the Broening highway tavern. However, subsequent to the Sergeant's passing, Wyley was additionally charged with murder in this case.

Sgt. Scholl was survived by his wife Margaret, and two daughters, Catherine, 10, and Linda, 7. He was appointed to the force on 1 June, 1942, and served for many years in the Central District. On 9 August, 1951, he was promoted to the rank of Sergeant and assigned to the Eastern District. He received two commendations during his twelve years of service. The first was in 1943, and the second on 23 February, of this year [1953] when the Police Commissioner, Beverly Ober, cited his work in the investigation of an assault, and robbery case.

We his brothers and sisters of the Baltimore Police Department will not let him be forgotten. Sgt. James L. Scholl's service honored the City of Baltimore and the Police Department - God Bless and Rest in Peace.

1 August - 1971

On this day In Baltimore Police History, 1971 we lost our brother **Lieutenant Martin Webb** to a drowning during a freak summer storm of tropical intensity that hit the Northern and Northeastern sections of Baltimore City and County. At least sixteen persons died as a result of the storm and the flash flooding it caused. Lieutenant Martin E. Webb of the Southern District was one of those victims.

Baltimore County Police discovered Webb's personal automobile the following morning. All of the vehicle's doors were open, and no trace was found of the Lieutenant. Later, witnesses reported that they had seen the Lieutenant park and leave his vehicle in a heroic and ultimately successful attempt to rescue a woman trapped inside her overturned automobile. The Lieutenant was last seen as he was swept away by the intensity of the floodwaters that surrounded them.

A seventeen-year veteran of the Department, Martin Webb had been promoted to Lieutenant in March of this 1971. Prior to his assignment in the Southern District he had been assigned to the Laboratory Division. He had also served in the Central District and in the Motorized Section of the Traffic Division.

The Lieutenant's body was recovered on Tuesday, August 3rd, in Kahler's Run, approximately one half mile away from where he had rescued the woman. For the two days before the discovery of Lt. Webb's body, Lieutenant Donald Sutton had twelve off-duty Southern District Patrolmen searching in a futile attempt to locate him.

The Lieutenant is survived by his widow, Frances, and their two children. Lieutenant Webb did not hesitate to risk his life in order to save the life of another. His tragic death was the direct result of the compassion and concern he held for his fellow man, a dedication commensurate with the esteem in which his memory will forever be held.

We his brothers and Sisters of the Baltimore Police Department won't let him be forgotten, RIP Lieutenant Webb - May you never be forgotten - "Your service honored the City of Baltimore and the Baltimore Police Department."

1 August - 1974

On this day in Baltimore City Police History, 1974, we lost our brother **Detective Sergeant Frank W. Grunder, Jr.** to gunfire based on the following:

Sgt Gunder, head of our Escape and Apprehension Unit, had spent several weeks attempting to track down members of an elusive hold up team. On August 1, 1974, after a day of patrolling locations in the city in an attempt to find the holdup suspects with no results, a tired Sergeant Grunder finally went home.

While off duty, Sergeant Grunder was driving on Harford Road in Hamilton with his wife and three children in the back seat. As he approached Echodale Avenue, he saw a man sitting crouched on the steps leading to the play lot at St. Dominic's Roman Catholic Church. Weeks of waiting and watching had finally paid off – this was one of the suspects. He parked his car a safe distance from the church, called for a uniformed back up unit and waited. Officer Joe L. Shaw of the Northeastern District wasn't the assigned back up unit, but readily stopped when Sergeant Grunder waved him down. The 12-year veteran explained the situation to the uniformed officer as they approached the suspect who was still sitting on the steps. Sergeant Grunder was a few feet ahead of Officer Shaw as he ordered the suspect to stand and place his hands on the wall.

At this point, the suspect lurched to his feet and began running up the steps. As Sergeant Grunder reached the top step, the suspect wheeled and began firing at point blank range. Despite being hit, the Sergeant was able to fire three shots in return as he fell to the sidewalk, mortally wounded. Officer Shaw also returned fire. The suspect dropped. The Detective Sergeant was transported to Union Memorial Hospital where he was pronounced dead on arrival. The assailant, a resident of the area, was pronounced dead on the scene. Investigation into the suspect's past revealed a string of felony arrests dating back to 1960.

Newspaper Article - Aug 3, 1974

Frank W. Grunder, Jr., exemplified the best qualities of a policeman dedicated to the safety of Baltimore and its citizens. An off-duty sergeant, he was driving through Hamilton Thursday with his wife and three small children when he recognized a man suspected of bank robbery. As head of the department's unit for apprehending fugitives, Sergeant Grunder instinctively set aside personal considerations, stopped his car, and with every proper precaution approached the suspect. Upon identifying himself as police, the suspect turned and fled, with the sergeant in pursuit, it wouldn't be too far before the suspect retrieved a handgun from his waistband, turned and fired directly into the Sergeant who had advanced to within point blank range of the suspect. The Officer was fatally gunned down to the shock of the entire community. All Baltimoreans can sympathize with the anguish and sorrow his family feels.

But citizens can take pride, along with the family, in the dedication of Sergeant Grunder, and other policemen like him, who seriously and professionally go about their jobs. The only appropriate words to describe his valor came from the man

who preceded him as head of the Escapee and Apprehension Unit: "You had a damn good copper there."

<u>News Article</u> - Aug 4, 1974;

Sgt. Grunder was 33 and lived in Hamilton. A 12 year veteran of police service, he was the head of the escape and apprehension squad, and a lie detector operator. There he worked under his father, a retired police lieutenant who headed the polygraph unit.

A native Baltimorean, Sgt. Grunder was a graduate of Calvert Hall. He attended the University of Maryland, and the National Training Center of Lie Detection. He was a member of the Marine Reserve, and the Call Box 414 Association.

Sgt Grunder played quarterback on his high school football team, and was an end on the Brooklyn Broncos, a sandlot team that won the Pop Warner League Championship. He later coached amateur football.

In addition to his father and mother, both of Linthicum, his survivors include his wife, the former Beverly Eibner; two sons, Mark A. and Frank W. Grunder III, both of Baltimore; a daughter, Beth Grunder, of Baltimore; a brother, Joseph A. Grunder, of Pasadena, and a sister, Mrs. Linda M. Koch of Pasadena.

We his brothers and sisters of the Baltimore Police Department won't let him be forgotten, RIP Sgt. Grunder - May you never be forgotten - Your service honored the City of Baltimore and the Baltimore Police Department.

1 August - 1975

The department began the implementation of its on-line booking system. Display units, located at the various district booking desks, were linked to the department's computerized criminal history files and provided the booking districts with prior criminal histories of recidivistic arrestees.

4 August - 1950

On this day in Baltimore City Police History, 1950, we lost our brother, Police **Officer Charles M. Hilbert**, to a vehicular assault. Officer Hilbert, a recent appointee to the police force, was killed in the line of duty when he was struck by an automobile as he was directing traffic at the corner of Potee Street and Patapsco Avenue.

The striking vehicle was being operated by a drunk driver who was heading in the wrong direction and ignoring the officer's instructions. The impact threw Officer Hilbert into the air and up against a street pole causing need for him to be transported to South Baltimore General Hospital where he was pronounced dead from his injuries. Officer Hilbert was a US Army veteran of WWII. He had served with the Baltimore Police Department for 2 months and was survived by his wife.

We his brothers and sisters of the Baltimore Police Department won't let him be forgotten, RIP Officer Charles M. Hilbert - "Your service honored the City of Baltimore, and the Baltimore Police Department"

5 August - 1927

On this day in Baltimore City Police History, 1927, we lost our brother, Police **Officer William F. Doehler** to gunfire based on the following.

Officer Doehler arrested David Perry and took him to a call box at Pennsylvania and Biddle to call for the wagon. Doehler had arrested Perry at a pawnshop for possession of stolen goods. While at the box, the assailant pulled a gun, and shot the officer in the chest, killing him.

Officer Doehler was married, and the father of two children. He entered the department on 3 September, 1919.

We his brothers and sisters of the Baltimore Police Department won't let him be forgotten, RIP Officer William F. Doehler - "Your service honored the City of Baltimore, and the Baltimore Police Department"

5 August - 1981

The original five digit officer identification numbers were assigned alphabetically. The lower the number, the lower in the alphabet your last name. The numbers were often re-issued after an officer left the department. The new "Short Number" sequence number system began this date in 1981, replacing the old numbers, which were no longer to be used. The change came about from a district court requirement for a unique number to identify each officer.

The new system assigned unique identifiers to each officer, based on the hire date of the officer, using a leading alphabetical character to separate each chronological series. These numbers were never reissued after an officer left the department, and remained as the key by which all of an officers' personnel, payroll, and other records were organized and associated.

In this new system, the existing officer with the most time on the department was issued sequence number A001, the next officer hired was issued A002, and so on. Since this was to be a four character identifier, when the 999th officer was given his number, the next newest officer was issued the first sequence number in the "B" series (e.g. B001, then B002, and so on).

Once all officers who were members at the time of the switch had been issued their sequence number, the next officer hired was issued the next available number in the current series, and so on. Starting with the "A" series (obviously), as of this writing the department is using the "J" series (with each series representing 999 officers).

7 August - 1951

Today in Baltimore Police History, 1951 – A centralized records division was established as the single repository for all police reports, fingerprint cards and arrest records. The Central Records Division was created 7 August, 1951.

8 August - 1729

Today in Baltimore Police History, 1729, the Legislature created Baltimore Town, which was the start of a system to preserve the peace and protect property (i.e. a Police Department was established). Its officers had powers of arrest for any of the town's offenders. This had been a goal of Baltimore residents since the town was informally created years earlier. To put things into perspective, keep in mind that the Declaration of Independence was adopted by the Continental Congress of the United States of America on 4 July, 1776, some 47 years later. Refer to the year 1779 section in the Year-to-Year History section of this book for a comprehensive accounting of this portion of the department's history.

8 August - 1902 - Marshal Farnan

The Grand Master of Baltimore Cops - Marshal "Tom" Farnan

Drawn from Newspapers and Magazines of the Times; 10 October, 1909

Tom Farnan, Marshal of police of Baltimore, was one of the greatest police chiefs in the country, and his record was one that could hardly be equalled.

There were chiefs, and then there were chiefs. Some chiefs had become chief primarily by virtue of enormous and helpful political pull. Some have become chiefs merely because fortune happened to be in a sunny humor one day and blew the feather of leadership onto their caps.

Marshal Farnan became chief in his own right, because he saw two score years [40 years] of practical service in Baltimore without a single lapse of duty, because he has been through all the knotty experiences that the men under him have to go through, because there is no windy beat, or troublesome post so windy, or so troublesome that his own experience couldn't bring forth suggestions to help those under him who must tackle it. He knew his job, and his job fit him like an old shoe.

There was no fuss or hurry or glitter in Marshal Farnan's office in the courthouse. He created a thoroughly work-a-day atmosphere. There are no hidden private rooms, or solemn ante-rooms, with bell boys hopping from one to another. Everything ran as smoothly and quietly as a Swiss clock that was among the best ever made.

His Daily Routine

When Marshal Farnan came to work every morning at 8:00 prompt, he first opened his mail, and dictated his replies to his ever ready, vigilant and hyper-excellent secretary, John Swikert. The replies to communications from departments in other cities he dictates right away. If there is no special hurry for a response he saves the letter until later in the day, and turns his attention to the next matter on his docket, which was his daily reception to the police captains.

Every morning the captains from all the districts in the city make their way to the Marshal's office at about 9:00 or 9:30 am. That explained to the people in the area of those times why it was that you would see magnificent apparitions of gold lace and blue on the downtown streets in the early morning.

They head toward the courthouse like Kingfishers after snakes. Once within the sacred precincts of the Marshal's office they salute clear their throats and sit down to bring forth their daily written reports.

First off the Marshal looks over these reports. Many get ready for the regular morning captain's discussion of each of their district's current events.

A Secret Conclave

The rest of this description must be written from imagination, for that meeting was held behind closed doors, and the reader may assist in the next paragraph or two, if he or she pleases, by as many thoughts from his or her imagination as they like.

After the mob has been assembled, Marshal Farnan harangues his Captains about their individual reports and asks them for confidential tidings regarding affairs within each of their respective districts. They told him all that was going on – who was selling on Sundays, what old offenders have bobbed back up, what hand-books have been reported, how many dogs are howling at night and how many husbands were beating their wives. Marshal Farnan hears them in silence and then gives his opinion. He asks his chiefs their opinions, too, and every morning, in fact, there is a formal council of war. If there is a big case on hand the conference may last until noon.

The deliberations of this august body are never made public. They never find their way to any record. The findings of the counsel were simply repeated by the captains to their lieutenants and the men under them, who were supposed to carry out orders.

Many tales are told before this gathering. Some more pathetic, some more humorous, some more tragic, some more comic, and some merely sordid and pitiful. Many of them were filled with human nature at its rankest. There was material enough for volumes of equally rank novels, magazine stories, or theatrical plays in these incidents of real life, yet any one of them would flavor a Henry James book for 20 chapters, or 20 years.

Many Tales of Woe

So accustomed has Marshal "Tom" grown to such tales, however, that he does not think about their more appalling side. His sympathies are not hardened nor is he apathetic, and he looks at them only as problems of police work that he has to solve, and as such he did not allow himself to become excited.

At the conclusion of his captain's meeting Marshal Farnan finished as much mail as he could and began receiving callers. There are continued calls upon him and upon his tolerance. Men and women come to him with the most absurd complaints.

For instance, last week an unshorn individual who claimed that he hailed from Washington materialized himself before the Marshal's desk. The Marshal looked at him and said, "Good morning," pleasantly. "I want you to find my boy," said the unshorn individual. – "I waited two days for you to find my boy!

"Who is your boy?" asked the Marshal with a patience born out of long experience.

"I sent you a letter about him two days ago" said the ever-weary stranger gruffly. "I live in Washington."

"What makes you think that your boy came to Baltimore." asked the Marshal softly.

"He didn't have money enough to go farther away," said the stranger in a final tone, "He is here."

Then The Stranger Faded

"Did you ever stop to consider that your son might have jumped a freight train and gone further away!" asked the Marshal. "If you have good cause to believe your son came here, and is still here, I will have our police search the city once more, but we can't waste valuable time in following foolish clues."

It was at this point that the stranger went and peace brooded once more over the northeast corner of the Courthouse.

The principle offenders in the way of butting-in were women however, it must be hastily and firmly noted. They have the excuse that they didn't know much about police procedures of the times.

Their inquiries and subtleties were very, very trying. No immediate specific instances came to mind, because examples of such a kind are so frequent that they were not noted when they occurred, but it is not infrequent for a woman to ask for the personal assistance of the Marshal of the Baltimore Police Department to find a stray pet poodle.

At about noon Marshal Farnan goes out to lunch. He places a tall black derby hat above his cadaverous and melancholy countenance, dons a long coat of a somber hue and slides out of his office.

He lunches at his home on West Lombard Street, near the corner of Fremont, and he returned to work at about half after one o'clock. Then the afternoon from that time until 4 o'clock is taken up with hearing complaints of various sorts or in personnel excursions to different points in the city, and in answering letters not gotten to in the early morning session.

At 4 o'clock he goes home for supper and stays there until his return to the office at 6. There he remains until 8 o'clock, when he strolls out of the office, and if that night is fine walks home, content that one more day's work has been dispatched.

<u>Something Like Old Abe</u>

It takes a peculiar talent to handle nicely the problems that arise in the Marshal's office in a great city, but Marshal Farnan has the gift. To be a good chief of police, you must be wise and moderate, firm and harsh, kind, severe, lax, strict or stringent, pleasant and unpleasant, as occasion demands. And above all, you must have a sense of humor and a sense of proportion. If you have not this sense of proportion in a position so filled with bothersome little details, you are lost, indeed. Marshal "Tom," like Abraham Lincoln; has a sense of humor. If we look at his photos we'll even notice the resemblance between Tom Farnan and Abe Lincoln in many respects. Tom Farnan loves jokes, jokes of all kinds, big, broad jokes and little ladylike jokes. He was always ready to swap a joke at the proper time. Beyond that, he never lost his head during an emergency.

When dealing with the big situations Marshal Farnan was always calm, cool, and collected. He did not act hurriedly, though he handled matters promptly and boldly.

Marshal "Tom" simply dotes on a good, rattling, puzzling, sleuthing job that calls all of his wits into play. This side of his nature is shown very well in the fact that when he was on the force as a common, garden variety member of Baltimore's "finest" he was especially fond of burglary cases. He solicited and sought out all manner of burglary cases just for the pleasure of working the case.

Now, a burglary case, to an ordinary policeman, is a nuisance. He doesn't know how to handle it. It requires a deep thought and much diplomacy and a natural knack for untangling somebody else's tangles.

<u>A Specialist in Burglars</u>

Marshal "Tom" used to specialize in burglary cases. The more tangled they were, the better he liked them. He made himself famous for a number of clever captures

he effected among the gentleman of the jimmy and dark lantern, and he is on record as having unearthed burglary cases where burglary cases would never be thought to grow.

Then another quality besides patience and persistence that helped to make Marshal Farnan a good police officer was his ability to pick out the salient one amidst a mass of clues and run that one down. He was practical with common-sense, and he had worked among men so long that he is able to perceive by a process of divination how a man would act under given circumstances – a valuable skill in a Marshal of police.

In the office Marshal Farnan is silent with his mere acquaintances; approachable but taciturn with those who have not yet made his acquaintance, and affable and even jovial with his friends. After hours, or when there is a slackness in the rush of things at the office, he was laughing, good humored, boisterous sometimes, and they all together a good fellow made.

<u>Sometimes He Explodes</u>

Marshal Farnan usually well-controlled hot temper if allowed to get out of bounds rampages around in a very the lively matter until it cools off, which happens very shortly. It is not often that the Marshal gets fighting mad, but when he does he is red-hot. The object of his wrath goes to a cyclone cellar, or picks up his remains and escapes.

Cursing, screaming, swearing, yelling, blaspheming, cursing, cursing, and still more cursing "It was one of the Marshal's off days." Assistants of all sorts scamper out into the marble corridor like leaves blowing by a frosty autumn wind. But they don't come often these spells of wrath, and they clear away shortly and politely.

"Marshal Farnan is one of the most pleasant men in the world to work for" said John Swikert, his time-tried secretary, last week. "He doesn't hurry you, and he is always good tempered – unless you interfere with his work. I have been with him for years, and I wouldn't want to work for any other man in Baltimore." Another one of Mr. Farnan's Office family is his deputy, Mr. Manning. Deputy Manning is almost as well-known as his chief, and his duties are almost as onerous. He has been associated with Mr. Farnan for many years, and he was a brother in blue on the force with him for many years. He is ready at any minute to lookout for Marshal Farnan's interests and all the jobs in addition to his own, when Marshal Farnan, for any reason, is not at the office.

Last May a year ago, when Marshal Farnan had been 40 years a policeman, his official family, and many of his admirers in the city and State joined together in giving him a banquet and a silver service. The banquet and presentation came off at Hazazer's Hall and a large crowd was in attendance.

Governor Warfield was there, and Marshal Farnan made a speech. There were other speeches by various men prominent in Baltimore.

His Police Career

In presenting the service, President Willis, of the police board said;

"On April, 30th 1867, just 40 years ago tonight the young man, then just 21 years of age was appointed as a patrolman on the police force of Baltimore. He reported to the Southern Police Station and was assigned to duty, with the instructions to keep his post quiet. By daylight this new officer had made 25 arrests.

"On February 1, 1870, just three years later, he was promoted to the grade of Sergeant, and his rigid enforcement of discipline and as kind words of caution to his squad, some of whom are members now of the force, are well remembered and appreciated.

"On 24 April, 1871, this young man was promoted to the grade of Lieutenant; on 24 October, 1885, he was promoted again this time to the grade of Captain on 23 February, 1893, he made the grade of Deputy Marshal, and on 8 August, 1902, he was promoted to Marshal of the Baltimore City Police Department.

"Upon examination of records of the department there is nowhere to be found any entry indicating that this young man had ever been censured for neglect of his duty, or for the slightest violation of any of the rules of the department. During his long career of faithful service many incidents can be pointed out where, at the risk of his own life, he had intervened for the protection of life and property, and where violators of the law had been uncovered by him and brought to face the charges made against them.

His Record Is Clean

"Marshal Farnan occupies a most enviable position in the history of police affairs in this city. So far as can be ascertained Baltimore alone can boast one of the Chiefs who has surged 40 years in various ranks without interruption and is still vigorous and strong. That he showed, city's long years of experience, occupying from the lowest to the highest rank, come in contact with many exciting situations, *temptations, hardships and dangers, come out of all unharmed and with a record perfectly clean, and with a reputation of having faithfully performed his duties, is a great record, and should excite emulation by the members of the police force.*

"In presenting this beautiful testimonial to you on behalf of the force and your many friends, it is proper that I should say that your services have not gone unrewarded. There may be cities where a man in your position commands more money than you get, but there is no man in public service anywhere in the world who was more appreciated then you among your fellow citizens, and this testimonial should be a lasting memory to you of the esteem in which you are held by your fellow citizens.

His Duet of Vices

Marshal Farnan is common sense in his mode of life. He rarely touches liquor, but if when off-duty he wants a drink he takes one He smokes and chews tobacco and he eats very rapidly. These two points are about the only ones in the schedule of his personal economy that could be marked with black crosses: He smokes periodically outrageous cigars and then fairly bolts his food.

How He Joined the Force

The main facts of Marshal Farnan's life since he joined the police force are in President Willis' speech on the occasion of the affair at Hazazer's Hall. His life before he became a policeman can be summed up briefly.

Thomas Frank Farnan was born in Baltimore on March 15, 1846. His father was Michael F. Farnan, a labourer, who had been frugal enough to retire from work in his old age.

Young Farnan attended the public schools of Baltimore, and later Calvert Hall, from which he was graduated in 1862. His ambition had always been to become a carpenter when he should grow to manhood. From his early boyhood days he had played and worked with carpenters' tools, and soon as he finished his high school he apprenticed himself out to a carpenter.

As a carpenter he labored for about four years, when a want of work in his chosen line prompted him to turn his attention to millwrighting. He was not long a millwright before another dull season found him without work.

At this time there occurred a reorganization of significance in the Baltimore police department, and several of Farnan friends found themselves positions of influence within the new board of police commissioners. It was suggested to him that while he was without work in his own trade he try his hand at being a policeman.

Farnan was at that time just 21 – the age requirement for applicants for positions as police – and he determined to permit his friends to secure for him a place. In April, 1867, he was appointed as policemen.

In those days the police were not required to serve as probationers, as they are today, and the young officer was given a regular assignment, and that in one of the least desirable districts of the city. Four days of police duty in the Southern District decided the young officer that he had not been intended for a policeman. That day as he greeted the Lieutenant of the district it was with no cheerful face, and he frankly announced that he was tired of being a policeman and that he wished to put in his papers and resign.

"Hold on a little longer," the Lieutenant advised. "You will like it better after a while." Young Farnan, yielded his advice and held on.

His First Big Case

One of the first cases Marshal Farnan ever figured in was that of George Woods, alias George Moore, African-American male who was a desperate thief. Woods came as his first big case, and for that reason and the arrest is still green in the memory of the Marshal.

It was on the night of January 7, 1869, that he made the arrests, after having worked on the matter for nearly a year. Captain Wallace Clayton, lying at the bowery wharf was one night robbed and the thieves cut out one of his eyes when the captain tried to fight for his life. The case aroused a great deal of indignation, and though the thieves left no clues behind, young Patrolman Farnan worked steadily to unearth the crime. Finally he struck the trail, and captured Woods. Captain Clayton identified him as his assailant, and Woods went to the Maryland penitentiary for 15 years.

One of the most eventful periods of the Marshal's life was during the railroad riots of 1877. He was a Lieutenant in the Southern District working under Captain Delanty at the time, and was in charge of a squad of men at Camden Junction Station. When the fifth regiment arrived at the depot the mob threw stones at the soldiers and Lieutenant Farnan saw a big man serve one of the missiles.

Fought His Way Out

He grasped the man and his fellow officers tried to persuade him not to fight his way through the mob with the prisoner. Lieutenant Farnan said, "I've arrested this man, and I intend to take him to the Southern District Police Station!"

He started with his prisoner, and the mob made to rush for him. Women called from the windows to the officer to take refuge indoors to keep from being killed, but he shook their advice off, and continued about his path.

In a short time things became so heated, the Lieutenant saw no other choice but to go to the extreme to impress upon the crowd his determination in leaving the area, and leaving it with his prisoner I tow.

With this he withdrew his pistol, placed it against his prisoner's forehead, right at his temple, leaned in and calmly told him, "If you do not tell this mob, you are willing to go to the police station with me, I am going to blow your brain out of your head, and into the crowd!" The prisoner recognizing something in Farnan's tone that let him know Farnan wasn't bluffing became thoroughly frightened, and began yelling to the crowd, "Stand down, Stand down, I wish to accompany this officer freely and of my own will!"

With that the mob withdrew their advances on the Lieutenant, making Farnan one of the first policeman to go into the mob and come out with a prisoner.

His presence of mind and ready wit saved him upon that occasion, as it has many times since. But those things are past now, and as he looks back on them the Marshal laughs heartily, as though they were all big jokes.

He is particularly fond of telling these war stories in which he was the butt of the joke, but he also knows a good many in which he figures as the joker, for the Marshall is full of fun.

A Frenzied Irishman

He tells with great delight of a case which occurred while he was Lieutenant in the Southern District

"There was a lot of excitement down there one day," he says, "and it was all caused by a little Irishmen. He raised such a racket about his house that the neighbors complained and a nearby minister declared he could not conduct his services. I went around to the house, and there stood probably 800 persons listening to the curses and shrieks of the man. Some officers stood outside, and I ask why they did

not go in and arrest the man. "Why, he has a pistol and told us he would kill the first man who comes near the door," they said.

"I asked who had the warrant, for I knew one had been issued in the case, and when it was given me I called to the man inside, asking if he heard me."

"Yes, I hear you," he said, "and I'll blow the top of your head off if you come near me"

"I read the warrant to him and then told him to open the door. He refused and repeated his threat that he would kill the first man who tried to enter his house.

"I put my shoulder against the door, and it went in with a crash. I stepped into the room, holding a lantern in one hand, which had been provided by a woman who live nearby, my pistol was in the other, and I started to the part of the house that we had sensed he was staying. As I rounded the corner from the hallway to the great-room, there stood the little Irishman, he was in the middle of the room, we quickly locked eyes, and as I was bringing my pistol up on target he said: "Why, Mister Farnan, how do you do? If I'd known it was you I'd have opened the door long ago!"

Baltimore, the First American City to Adopt New Identification Method

Marshal Farnan is another great leader who, like Frey and Carr before him worked to make changes that would last, and that would change the way police would be done for years to come. For example; he brought fingerprinting to The Baltimore Police Department, making us the first police department in the country to use this system.

In the old days it used to be a free chase in the open with no odds given, and a scrimmage at the end between the defenders of the law and its violators. But all this is passed. Criminals are now cataloged. When they are wanted the apprehension is gone about in a matter-of-fact, systematic manner. There is nothing left to chance.

In line with this tendency in the ancient trade is the fingerprint method of identification, invented by E. R. Henry, of Scotland Yard, London, and lately tried in Baltimore for the first time in the United States. By its means a criminal is tagged and recorded without the possibility of error. His identity, once his fingerprints have been taken, can never be disputed, and his life story, with a summary of his habits and personal characteristics, is always where it can be reached at a minutes notice.

Keeping Track Of Crooks

For the last half century the constant effort in police circles has been to find some means by which a criminal's identity could be permanently fixed. The great utility of the rogue's gallery and the system of keeping a record of all persons convicted in the upper courts has made this and evidently desirable one. But a rogue's gallery or cabinet of biographies is of little use, it can be seen, if the identity of the law breaker is a matter of uncertainty. An alias or disguise is easily assumed, so if there is no other way of fixing the identity of the person than by name or photograph the rogue's gallery any criminal record might as well go to the trash pile.

To accomplish the desirable and of absolute identification various schemes have been proposed and tried. All have been based upon the principles that there are certain parts of the human body whose form cannot be changed without detection, and which are unique to that person.

First came photography. This was in the days when the art was thought to have marvelous value. At one time, for instance, it was believed that a photograph was a sure means of telling whether or not a person was going to develop an eruptive sickness, for it was said that the irruption would show on the photograph even if it had not yet made its appearance on the face. Despite its many real virtues, however, photography did not fully cover the ground desired.

Failure of Photography

It had been supposed that a series of photographs showing a criminal in various poses – full face, half face, profile and so one – would be a complete means of identification should that criminal be apprehended at any time after the photographs had been made. This idea was proved a fallacy, mainly through the cleverness of the criminals, who found that a contortion of the muscles of the features materially altered the value of the portrait.

Anyhow, the schema was wholly inadequate for the task it was at first supposed to perform. So many criminals looked like that in some notable cases their portraits were hardly distinguishable.

Photographs proved of such accessory value as a means of apprehension of criminals, however, that the gallery and camera were made a permanent adjunct to most police bureaus. Still something else than pictures was needed for an absolute means of identification.

The Bertillon Method

The Bertillon method was the next thing of consequence to make its appearance. Much has been written about the Bertillon method, and by many criminals and it is regarded with a sort of superstitious reverence, its intricacies seeming a sacred rite. It has proved very effective, but is not altogether infallible, as the case that happened in London about 10 years ago suffices to show.

At that time two criminals were measured and it was found that their records were exactly the same. This is rather a marvelous coincidence and is the only one recorded in the whole history of the system. Nevertheless, it shows that it is not absolutely infallible. Other points to be urged against the Bertillon method are that it is complicated, time-consuming, and can only be applied to adult prisoners.

The Fingerprint System

Adherents' claims for the latest arrival, the fingerprint system, are that it has none of the faults of the Bertillon method and that it has all of its virtues. This is rather a broad assertion, but to prove it they point out that the fingerprint method is simple, quick, absolutely accurate and applicable to an individual of any age. These supporters are intensely enthusiastic, but the process is rather new and votaries of any new faith are always apt to go to the extremes.

E. R. Henry Fingerprint Classification System

If the E. R. Henry fingerprint system of identification really does pan out in practical working – and its test in Baltimore seems to show that it will – palmists will be jubilant and reproved, for the principle upon which it rests is one that fortune tellers have long banked upon.

It is the theory that the lines of the fingers of every person in the universe form patterns, which have no exact duplicate, and that moreover, these lines remain unchanged in an individual's hand from his birth to his death.

It is a rather awesome reflection. Look at your fingers – and consider that there is nothing else like them in the whole universe and that probably there never will be. It reminds one of the story of the little boy who after having been told of the wonders of nature looked up at his teacher with a puzzled look and asked if the Lord didn't ever run out of ideas. It seemed too big, and too good, to be true. Still that is the principle upon which the Henry fingerprint system is based.

Taking the Prints

If the skin of the hand be destroyed and grows back again in a natural manner, its lines, after it has completed its growth, will be identical with those of the skin that was destroyed. It really seems as if fate had stamped a trademark upon the hand of each individual. At all events the only thing that will permanently destroy the tell-tale lines is a scar.

If you have ever gone to a palmist and had him (or her, as the case is more apt to be) smear your hand with black ink and press it on a piece of white paper, you will understand at once just how the fingerprint system is worked. If the palm impression is afterward examined with a magnifying glass and the palmist discovered interesting things in it you will know also how the print is classified and filed in the Henry system of criminal identification.

The making of fingerprints consists of a clever use of glass and printers ink and a bit of care. The ink is usually black, or if not that, of some intense color, and is the same as that used for printing fine cuts or engravings. The glass is a strip about 5 x 6". Upon the glass the ink is spread in a thin coating.

Then a paper form with spaces reserved for the impression of the different fingers is laid upon the table beside the ink and the glass and all is in readiness to take the prints of the fingers of the person whose record is desired.

Prisoners Are Frightened
These preparations are all very simple. They certainly don't seem to have anything in them to frighten a person. But prisoners in the Baltimore Bureau who are to be fingerprinted seem always to regard them in a respectfully timid way. They think that there is some sort of "voodoo" about them. With the colored gentry this is especially true. The idea of making a fingerprint evidently seems possessed of menace to them.

Twelve prints are made from each individual to be recorded. First each of the 10 fingers is printed separately; then the forefingers of each hand are taken together. A simple roll of the ink on the glass and a pressure upon the paper constitutes the whole mechanical part of the operation. The methodology used then is still used in the same way today, except in many agency's embrace of the natural evolution to electronic technology.

Classification and Filing

The next step in the making of the fingerprint record is classification and filing. The first term may not be understood, but the second seems simple enough. Say filing and the word instantly brings to mind a picture of cabinets with their content arranged alphabetically.

Filing a fingerprint to us seems to be very easy of comprehension. In reality, it is the most difficult part of the process. Fingerprints cannot be filed according to the alphabet. They must be put away according to fixed characteristics of their own, and this is why they must be classified before they can be filed.

Suppose a man is in custody. It is thought that he has a fingerprint record, and that this record is desired by police officials. Would it be possible to look for it under the name the man gives? Certainly not, because this is just as well as not an alias.

That is the whole point. If names were a fixed quality in life and could not be changed they would serve as a means of identification. Otherwise identity must be ascertained by means of an individual's personal characteristics. In this case a fingerprint record must be found by means of a fingerprint and not by name.

Sorting the Prints

The task of devising a means by which fingerprints could be filed was one of the greatest difficulty. By successfully carrying it through Mr. Henry gave his name to the process now standing as a monument to him. The peculiar virtues of fingerprints as a means of identification were known before his time, but there was no way to classify them, file them or find them once filed.

Through the study of several thousand fingerprints which he had collected while in service in India, where the government has long had them used for signatures among the lower castes of natives, Mr. Henry came to the conclusion that there were two great classes into which all fingerprints could be divided. In other words, he found that there were certain general designs upon which the patterns of all finger ends were based. These designs he named "arches," "loops," "whorls" and "composites." Arches or loops occur wherever no single line of the fingertip makes a complete circle. Whorls are formed wherever a line does a complete circle. Composites are a sort of hybrid pattern partaking more of the nature of the whorl than of a loop. The proportions of these three classes he found to be as follows:

Arches, 5%.

Loops, 60%.

Whorls and composites, 35%

Since the number of arches was found to be inconsiderable, Mr. Henry place them in a single class with the loops. Whorls and composites were very easily associable. Thus Mr. Henry had two great natural classes and was all fingerprints could be divided.

The 1,024 Classes

In every finger record there are 10 separate prints to be considered. Either one of these prints can be one of two classes, and there are a number of combinations that might be formed among fingers of different classes. For instance, there might be five loops and five whorls, or there might be four loops and six whorls, and so on. The point was to find out how many classes there might be. This Mr. Henry set himself to do. If he discovered exactly the number of classes in a primary classification of his fingerprints he would be able to commence a system of filing.

One of the simplest propositions is to find out the number of possible combinations among a given number of objects. A very simple formula has been worked out for this purpose. By this formula Mr. Henry ascertained that within sets of two and 10 objects there was a possibility of 1,024 combinations. Accordingly, if a cabinet should be instructed to hold 1,024 drawers, the bases of a reliable system of filing fingerprints was at hand. Since 1,024 is a square of 32, the cabinet might very conveniently be made with 32 drawers each way.

It is useless to follow the process of fingerprint record filing further. It simply becomes more complicated as one goes on. It is sufficient to say that the 1,024 primary classes can be subdivided by minor peculiarities of fingerprints, which Mr. Henry enumerates in his book dealing with the subject, and so the process is elastic and will accommodate any number of records. In an up-to-date manual print Bureau a record can be found or filed in less than two minutes time. In modern electronic systems, a record can be filed, or found, virtually instantaneously.

Originated in India

The fingerprint system originated in India and came from that country by way of the British conquest and the St. Louis exposition to Baltimore and America. In all the Eastern countries the value of finger – prints has been known from time immemorial. In China, indeed, there is a pleasing little story about an ancient

Empress whose official seal for all the coinage of her realm was her finger impression. At any rate, for many centuries before the British took possession of India fingerprints had been used as signatures among the lower castes.

After the Empire had been established governmental difficulties with natives who impersonate each other for the sake of fraudulently receiving pensions became so great that some method had to be found by which one Indian could be told from another. The fingerprint method, which had been observed among the natives themselves, was adopted as a happy solution and proved itself all that could be desired.

At first fingerprints were used only in the government departments in India in lieu of signatures. Then they were taken up by the police department also. Notably this was the case in the Bengal Bureau. Mr. E. R. Henry was then a young subaltern in the branch.

Years afterward, when Mr. Henry was appointed chief of Scotland Yard, in London, he took his Indian method with him. When he saw the immense need of a systemized use of fingerprints, he perfected his method of classification and filing alluded to above and gave his invention to the world.

<u>Scotland Yard the First</u>

Scotland Yard was – of course – the first police Bureau among civilized nations to receive the benefit of the Henry method. His introduction there took place in 1897, and it was made an adjunct to the Bertillon method. Its complete adequacy for attending to the duties of identification by itself, however, soon convinced the English officials of the superfluity of the older method, so the time tested Bertillon system was dropped.

When the St. Louis exposition was opened here in 1904 the British government sent a delegation from Scotland Yard to demonstrate the effectiveness of its new system. The national Association of Chiefs of police was in session in St. Louis at that time, and the English representative took advantage of the opportunity to address them upon the new method of identification. This is the combination of circumstances that brought the system to the United States.

Marshal Farnan of the Baltimore Police Department was one of those who heard the lecture on the fingerprint method. He was much impressed and sought an opportunity to speak personally with the lecturer. When he returned to Baltimore at the conclusion of the convention he sought out Sgt. Casey, of the Bureau of identification, confided to him his knowledge and delegated him to visit St. Louis and receive special lessons in this new system.

Sgt. Casey departed an incredulous scoffer and returned an enthusiastic convert. His zeal in the work has made the Baltimore Bureau one of the most favorably known in the country. The bureau was established here 17 December, 1904, and was followed shortly by others in other big cities of the United States.

Exit, M. Bertillon

It has been often asked of late in police circles if the fingerprint method would ever supersede the Bertillon method in the United States. In case the example of Europe be followed, it most certainly will. There is now no great nation in the old country, with a single exception of France, where the Bertillon method was born, that does not use the fingerprint system exclusively.

The advantages of the finger – print method are that it is cheaper, simpler and more reliable. The personal element of the operators of efficiency or non-efficiency does not materially alter the results. Finally the instruments of its use are neither many nor costly. In this last point especially the Bertillon method lags far behind. Special and delicate instruments of much cost have been installed before it can be successfully practiced.

An application of fingerprints that has caused much interest is in the detection of criminals. Suppose a burglar enters the house and leaves his finger mark upon the windowpane. No other clue was wanted by the enterprising police of today. The fingerprint is carefully taken and sent to the Bureau of identification. There the prints are classified.

Then someone looks into the file, turned over a few leaves and, presto! If the burglar is an old offender, his name, photograph, criminal record and habits of living are staring one in the face. It sounds like a fairy tale, but the experiment really has been tried with complete success in England.

Where Science Failed

In Baltimore not long since it was thought that this same idea could be given an application in connection with the Cunningham murder case. The search was for the murderer. In the victim's room were found a number of checks with black finger marks upon them. The police generally were jubilant and Sgt. Casey exalted. Here at last, it was thought, was a chance to throw the limelight on the fingerprint

Bureau. Finally it transpired that the marks were not those of the murder, but of an enthusiastic member of the detective corps who, in raking around among the ashes of the hearth for clues, had gotten his fingers dirty and had then picked up the bunch of checks. Science had a downfall.

10 August - 1891

The Baltimore harbor police cruiser "Lannan" was built in 1891 by James Clark & Co., from plans kindly loaned the Department by the United States Government. The harbor patrol boat was completed on August 10, 1891, and after a very successful trial trip was accepted and immediately put into commission. It was named in honor of former Deputy Marshal John Lannan, who had charge of her construction.

11 August - 1972

The department began hiring federally funded sworn personnel to create nine "highly flexible" Crime Control Teams – mostly referred to as "Flex Teams" – one for each district. The stated purpose of these five man teams was to operate within the "total police officer" concept (whatever that is), performing all the activities and functions found within a law enforcement agency. The project's goal was to establish stability within the community based upon freedom from criminal activity and closer rapport between police and the citizen.

14 August - 1914 - Marshal Carter

Today in Baltimore Police History a **new Marshal** was named. Robert D. Carter would remain the department's Marshal until 1917, when Baltimore Police stopped using Marshals, making Marshal Carter Baltimore's last.

Robert Dudley Carter was born in Gaston/Littleton, Halifax County, North Carolina, on 28 March, 1852. In 1869, he came to Baltimore at age 17, and enlisted at 67 Thames Street in Fells Point, Baltimore Maryland, and served in the U.S. Navy for 3 years. He married Dona Burkhart early in 1875 at the age of 23. In 1880, Robert and Dona bought their first house, at 1650 North Gilmore Street.

On May 12, 1884, at age 32, Robert was appointed a Baltimore Police Officer, and went to work at the Northwest District. He worked hard at being the best, and in 1888, after only four years on the force, he was promoted to Sergeant. Then in 1892, after only another four years, he was promoted to Lieutenant – a meteoric rise.

Working long 18 hour days, he showed great promise, and was promoted on August 14, 1914 to be Marshal of the Baltimore City Police Department (he skipped the rank of Captain). He was only 62 years old.

In February of 1915, Marshal Carter made his debut as a public speaker, when he told an audience of students at the Johns Hopkins Medical School what the Police Department of Baltimore City was doing in the way of seeing that the laws of the city and State were obeyed.

Marshal Carter was personally known to Police Chiefs across the country. He was a close personal friend of William A. Pinkerton of the Pinkerton Detective Agency, and at the time a well noted Private Detective.

This information was gathered and compiled by Marshal Carter's Great Grandnephew Kenneth M. Carter of Mount Airy, Maryland.

15 August - 1857

Two hundred revolvers were purchased for issuance to Baltimore's Police Officers. Previously, officers had to provide their own firearm for on-duty use.

15 August - 1974

On this day in Baltimore Police History we lost our brother Police **Officer Milton I. Spell**, in the 1600 block of North Bradford Street. Just before 9:30 pm as Officer Spell parked his radio car to begin foot patrol his attention was drawn to a vehicle weaving side to side traveling in the same block. Feeling that the driver may be intoxicated, he notified the dispatcher that he was attempting to stop the vehicle to investigate the driver.

Following normal procedures, he requested a backup unit and approached the vehicle. Moments before the backup unit arrived, while Officer Spell was speaking to the driver, shots suddenly rang out from inside the suspect's vehicle, striking Officer Spell in the chest and abdomen. The suspect and a companion fled the scene.

Officer Louis W. Michelberger was a little more than a block away when he heard the shots fired. He arrived to find more than 200 indifferent citizens standing near the fallen officer. Officer Michelberger attempted to save Officer Spell's life using CPR, and Officer Spell was transported to Johns Hopkins Hospital, where he died undergoing emergency treatment. Officer Spell had been a member of the Baltimore Police Department since 1967, and he was 27 years old at the time of his death.

May he never be forgotten, for his service honored the City of Baltimore and this Police Department.

[Author's Note: *On that fateful night, Milton was working 332 post and I was working 333 post on the 4x12 shift. He and I were talking at Luzerne and Federal St. when I received a call for "Holding a shoplifter at the A&P" on Edison Hwy. I responded to the call and left Milton there. The rest is History. I always wonder if I had waited 5 minutes or so maybe Milton would be alive today. I've always had that thought in my mind, even now, 40 years later.*]

19 August - 1979

On this day in Baltimore Police History 19 August 1979, we lost our brother Police **Officer William D. Albers**, who died this day because of a struggle and gunfire inside the Johns Hopkins Hospital emergency room sixteen days earlier.

In the early morning of the day of the shooting, Officer Albers was working part time at Johns Hopkins Hospital, stationed in the Emergency Room. Thirty-four year-old Willie Shaw checked himself into the Emergency Room, seeking psychiatric treatment. Since the man appeared to be in a highly emotional state, he was given a sedative and placed in one of two nearby psychiatric care rooms. He slept while his wife and hospital staff completed arrangements for a more permanent long-term care.

At about 10:00 am, Shaw awoke and wandered into the hallway. A nurse confronted him and instructed him to return to the room. Instead, Shaw fell to the floor in a "spread eagle" position refusing to move. The nurse summoned Hospital Security to the scene, and Officer Albers also responded to assist. As Security began picking the man up, Officer Albers joined in and hey carried him into the psych room. Shaw was placed onto a mattress. He was given an injection and staff began leaving the room to allow the sedative to take effect.

As they filed out of the room, Officer Albers stayed behind, and he followed everyone out last to make sure they would be safe with him between them and the mental patient. Before he could fully exit the room; Shaw lunged from the bed, grabbed Officer Albers' gun and ripped it, still in its holster, right off his gun belt. As quickly as he grabbed the gun, he fired it at the officer. The round passed through the bottom of the holster, through Officer Albers' arm and into his abdomen. A violent struggle then ensued during which Officer Albers was shot four more times. The suspect then removed the revolver from the holster, which he threw on the floor, and fired that sixth and final shot into his own chest, falling to the floor inside the psych room and out of sight from where Albers staggered to in the hallway and fell to the floor.

Doctors and nurses worked heroically to save the life of Officer Alders. For nearly three weeks Officer Albers fought for his life. Over the next sixteen days, Doctors performed several operations in an effort to repair several organs, fight infections and improve the chances for survival, but it was just too much; Officer Albers succumbed to his injuries on this date, 19 August, 1979. The mental patient that took Officer Albers life would never see the inside of a court room; he died in surgery from that single self-inflicted shot to his chest. In the end Officer Albers did as he had intended; he protected everyone in that room from Shaw as no one else was injured that day.

As his brothers and sisters, of the Baltimore Police Department it is up to us to make sure he is never forgotten. For his service honored the City of Baltimore, and Baltimore Police Department. May God be with him, so that he may rest in peace.

[<u>Editor's Note</u>: *At the exact moment the call for an "officer shot at JHH" was broadcast over the police radio, I was in route to meet with him, and was less than a half block away. Therefore, I was first on the scene, but too late to do anything other than stand guard over him and the nurses as they rushed to his aid. I was then able to locate the suspect in one of the two Psych rooms. The suspect had (unbeknownst to me or anyone else) shot himself in the chest with the last round in Albers' gun – I've always thought that if I had had one less red light on the way, or had decided to meet him just a few minutes earlier, he might never have been shot.*]

20 August - 1902

Today in Baltimore Police History, 1902, it was discovered that all personnel of the entire department would be required to re-take their oaths of office, as up to this point, they had all been improperly and illegally sworn. Moreover, they had been improperly sworn for the entire 35 years of the department's existence, according to the following:

<u>Sun paper article</u> dated 21 August, 1902 titled, <u>1,009 to retake Oath</u>

- *Entire police force, including Matrons, Must be Re-Sworn*
- *1,009 to retake Oath*
- *Old Form of Administration of the Oaths Declared Illegal*

Mr. Alonso Miles, Counsel for the Board, makes the discovery and change is ordered.

Is it really possible that for 35 years, or ever since the recognition of the Police Department in 1867, the members of the department have been sworn in illegally?

Is it possible that each and every member of the department, from the veteran Marshall to the greenest Probationary Patrolman and to the lowliest Matron, must file up to the courthouse, pay $.10 and be properly sworn in by the Clerk of the Superior Court before being allow to resume his duties?

These questions are not vaguely speculative, but have assumed distinct form, and already preparations have been made for the swearing in once more of the entire department, this time by the Clerk of the Superior Court. The walls of the police board sanctum will echo more oaths within the next few days than done in any other since the board was created.

News of this remarkable prospect only leaked out yesterday (Wednesday, 20 Aug, 1902), and behind it is an interesting story. Hitherto it has always been the custom for the secretary of the board of police commissioners to swear in the newly appointed or promoted policeman, rather than the Clerk of the Superior Court, as required by law. No other person is empowered to administer the oath. The system has been in vogue since the recognition of the department and its legal status has never heretofore been questioned. It is probably a relic of the old regime, when the department was a municipal organization. The discovery that the old way of administering the oath by the Secretary of the Board or the President of the Board

is illegal was due to the desire of the present board to conform to the letter of the law in all matters.

Mr. Upshur Investigates

When Marshal Farnan was appointed to his present rank on August 8 it happened that Mr. Joshua H. Kinsley, the secretary of the board, was spending his vacation at the seashore. After the appointment had been made the question arose who should administer the oath of his new office to Marshall Farnan. Present ups are for the time being by concluding that as the secretary had administered the oath in the past, the president of the board had an equal right to do so, especially as the president is empowered to administer the oath to witnesses at trials. He accordingly swore in Marshal Farnan.

Afterward, in thinking over the matter, it occurred to Mr. Upshur that, while he had as much right as a Secretary to swear in an officer, the authority of the latter official to do so was not entirely clear.

Mr. Upshur being a lawyer, the subject naturally interested him and he made a diligent search of the state and police logs, but failed to find any statue which would enlighten him. Realizing that the matter was an important one and required immediate attention, he determined to call attention to Mr. Alonso W. Miles, the Council to the board, to the subject. This was accordingly done.

Legal Counsel Miles Opinion

Mr. Miles devoted much time to the subject and, after a painstaking investigation, came to the conclusion that since its organization in 1867 no member of the Police Department had been sworn in by the Clerk of the Superior Court as specifically required by the law and the Constitution. Neither grants that right to the secretary of the Board. This option he based upon a section of the Maryland Constitution and a statue of the public general laws of Maryland.

Section 6 of article 1 of the Maryland Constitution is as follows:

"Every person elected or appointed to any office of profit or trust, under this Constitution, or under the laws made pursuant thereto, shall, before he enters upon the duties of such office, take and subscribe to the following oath or affirmation:

"I, _____, do swear (or affirm, as the case may be) that I will support the Constitution of the United States; and that I will be faithful and bear true allegiance to the State of Maryland, and support the Constitution and laws thereof; and that I *will, to the best of my skill and judgment, diligently and faithfully, without partiality or prejudice, execute the office of _____ according to the Constitution and laws of the state, and (if a governor, senator, member of the House of Delegates or judge) that I will not directly, or indirectly receive the profits of, or any part of the profits, or any other office during the term of my acting as _____."*

Article 7 of the public general laws deals with official oaths, by whom, when and where they must be taken. After describing the oath for the governor, secretary of state, judges, comptroller incorporation officers, the article section 6 says:

"All other officers elected or appointed to any office of trust or profit under the Constitution or laws of the state, including the mayor or other chief magistrates of municipal corporations, shall take and subscribe to the said oaths, in the city of Baltimore before the clerk of the Superior Court, and in several counties before the clerk of the circuit court or before one of the sworn deputies of such clerks."

Section 7 says:

"The said clerk shall each procure and keep in his office a well bound book, to be called a test book, in which shall be printed or conspicuously written the oaths aforesaid, and every person taking or subscribing the same shall annex to his signature the title of the office to which he shall have been elected or appointed, and the date of his signature."

Section 2 of the same article 6 is the fee of the clerk for administering the oaths at $.10 each.

<u>1,009 Will Swear Anew</u>

At yesterday's meeting of the board, Mr. Miles submitted to the board the result of his investigation. Immediate action was then taken. Deputy clerk Peter Stevens, of the Superior Court, was summoned to the board room and consulted about the best possible means of administering that oath to the 1,009 members of the Police Department. He was also ordered to procure a book to be used as a "test book" in which will be preserved to signatures of each officer. This announcement will probably cause an immense expenditure of ink on the part of those who signatures resembled Chinese laundry tickets and who will naturally desire to improve their penmanship.

The work of re-swearing in the membership of the department will begin at once, and will be carried on as rapidly as is consistent with the workings of the

department. Exactly how it will be done has as yet not been definitely settled. There are 1,009 members of the Police Department, including matrons and civilian employees, and at $.10 each these will net the clerk of the Superior Court about $100.

A Great Surprise to the Board

President Upshur was seen last night at the Maryland club. In answer to questions about the change in the manner of swearing in the members of the department he said:

"Yes, it has been found necessary to re-administer the oath of office to every member of the department. Mr. Miles announced to the board today that this was necessary, and the work of re-swearing in the officers will begin at once. Mr. Stevens has been ordered to procure a test book, and the swearing in of the men will probably take place in the board room.

"The discovery that the oaths as administered to the officers by the secretary of the board is illegal was a great surprise to the board. Ever since the recognition of the department in 1867 it has been the custom of the secretary to swear in the officers, and his right to do so has never, I believe, been questioned. As soon as Mr. Miles gave his opinion on the subject the board ordered that all of the men must take another oath, as prescribed by the law, and sign the Test Book, to be acquired."

Doesn't Affect Departmental Acts

Mr. Alonso W. Miles, counsel to the board, at first declined to discuss the matters, but when pressed to talk, said:

"There is no doubt that the manner in which the oath of office has been administered in the past is illegal. The law is very plain and definite as to the manner in which the oath must be administered, and the wonder is that the fact should not have been discovered years ago. The question involved, however, is one of a minor detail and does not affect anything that the department has done or any arrests that have been made. The law says that a fee of $.10 is required for each oath and the men themselves will probably have to pay this fee."

Mr. Peter Stevens, Deputy Clerk of the Superior Court, was seen, but declined to say anything about the matter. He admitted, however that he had been indeed called before the board on business.

21 August - 1967

On this day in Baltimore police history, 1967 we lost our brother, Police **Officer John C. Williams** to fire when the vehicle he was in caught fire as his partner was filling it with fuel, and Officer Williams became trapped inside.

Officer Williams had been with the agency for 19 years. As his brothers and sisters of the Baltimore police department we will keep his memory alive, thank him for his service and may God rest his soul.

[Author's Note: Robert Yamin wrote that he had just parked his unmarked car about 40 feet from the car being fueled. He said he was almost in the building when the fire erupted and the car was completely engulfed in flames. Another officer immediately notified the dispatcher requesting fire equipment. The flames and heat were so intense that from 30 to 40 feet away it was impossible to get closer. Radio cars were not equipped with fire extinguishers at the time, and nor was the area of the gas pumps. Officer Yamin ran thru the archway to the front of the building, and pulled the fire alarm, then waited to direct the first arriving fire truck to the archway. It was a horrible incident to observe, he said, and there was absolutely nothing any of them who were there could do. The fire occurred at the old Northern District, Keswick and 34th.]

22 August - 2002

On this day in Baltimore police history, 2002 we lost our sister, Police **Officer Crystal Deneen Sheffield** in an auto accident based on the following:

Officer Crystal Sheffield succumbed to injuries received approximately twelve hours earlier when her patrol car collided with another patrol car as the two units were responding to back-up another officer just before 2330 hours. The collision occurred at the intersection of Lafayette and Carey Streets. Officer Sheffield, who was assigned to the Western District, was driving a marked patrol unit and the other vehicle was an unmarked unit also assigned to the Western District. Both were responding with lights and sirens activated. Officer Sheffield was transported to a local hospital where she remained in a coma until her death. The two officers in the other unit were treated and released.

Officer Sheffield was the first female Baltimore City Police officer to be killed in the line of duty. She had been employed with the agency for three years, and is survived by her husband and 11-year-old son.

As her brothers and sisters of the Baltimore police department we will keep her memory alive, thank her for her service and may God rest her soul.

23 August - 1872

On this day in Baltimore Police History, 1872 we lost our brother, **Patrolman John Christopher**, to gunfire that occurred five days earlier, on 18 August 1872. The incident started out as nothing more than a cloud of dust being thrown up by two young men as they raced their wagon teams neck and neck down a dirt road near Catonsville's Railway Park. The drivers cursed their horses and one another in a race where friendly competition quickly ended, as both James Ford and James Dorsey cracked whips from their wagons into their animal's necks and backs in order to gain speed. Each struggled more and more to go faster, and each had nothing more in mind than to try to overtake the other and win the race.

The race had begun at "Kelly's Woods" in Catonsville, and was nearing the City/County line near the Western District when the two men finally stopped their wagons and an argument ensued. The two young men argued as they raced – they were loud, and each wanted nothing more than to win. They each wanted to win so much that their voices and actions drew the attention of Baltimore City Patrolman John Christopher.

As Patrolman Christopher neared Ford and Dorsey, they began to fight physically, each throwing blow after blow at the other. Baltimore Police have not changed much in the 150 or so years since this incident; police were strong, often relying on the use of brute strength to overcome the situations in which they find themselves. On this particular day in 1872, things were not much different, and Patrolman Christopher undertook to single handedly separate the two combatants and force them back into their wagons and on their way.

To continue to keep the peace, Patrolman Christopher climbed into James Ford's wagon with him, and rode with him toward his destination continuing his ongoing effort to maintain peace.

Despite Patrolman Christopher's best efforts, however, the two drivers resumed their argument which escalated quickly into another fight. Then Dorsey began throwing stones at Ford, and warned him that if he bumped into his wagon again, he [Dorsey] would shoot him. The fisticuffs resumed across the space between the two wagons, and Dorsey decided to live up to his promise of shooting Ford and drew a pistol.

Patrolman Christopher saw the weapon and once again gained control over the more violent of the two men by forcefully throwing him from his wagon to the ground. That momentary separation was lost when Ford dove onto Dorsey and went for Dorsey's gun. Before Patrolman Christopher could regain control over either of the men the pistol was fired one time. Even while Dorsey's anger was focused on Ford, the bullet left his weapon and found its way into the stomach of Officer Christopher, causing severe pain, and what would five days later become a fatal injury. Patrolman Christopher felt the burn in his stomach as he fell to the ground.

Patrolman Christopher was quickly taken to a nearby house where he was treated by a Dr. Worsham, who was summoned to the scene. At the same time, citizens John Young and Justice Pilot responded to the scene of the shooting and were able to apprehend both Dorsey and Ford.

Despite his wound and his extreme pain, when Dorsey and Ford were brought before him, Patrolman Christopher made a positive ID. The patrolman was then taken to his home located at 14 South Fremont St. where he was cared for by Doctor J. H. Butler. His injuries were painful and they were fatal, leaving the medical professionals in a place where no matter what they could have done they were unable to save his life. Patrolman Christopher lay in pain from the night of the shooting on 18 Aug, until the day he passed away on 23, Aug. 1872 at approx. 3:30 in the afternoon.

As his brothers and sisters, of the Baltimore Police Department it is up to us to make sure he is never forgotten. For his service honored the City of Baltimore, and the Baltimore Police Department. May God be with him, so that he may rest in peace.

25 August - 1974

Today in Baltimore Police History saw the first day of the "Gun Buy-Back" program (then called a Gun Bounty). The idea came to Police Commissioner Pomerleau as he stood graveside of Officer Milton Spell who was shot and killed in the line of duty on 15 August 1974.

Commissioner Pomerleau offered $30 each for surrendered guns. The surprisingly huge response, more like a metallic flood, to the Commissioner's offer for guns was an indication of how many weapons were and still are at large in the community, each with its crime and possible death potential. Budget considerations rather quickly required the Police Department to eliminate rifles and shotguns from its bounty program and to limit its offer to city residents. The program would last nearly a month - The city gun bounty program was declared a success by police spokesmen, but several criminologists challenged this appraisal because the program had not been in effect long enough to produce solid evidence, and they insisted that only strong federal control measures can significantly limit the availability of firearms.

There have been a number of gun bounty and buyback programs since, some sponsored by the Baltimore Housing Authority, The Police Department, Area Churches, and Occasionally Private Individuals. A buyback in West Baltimore once recovered 750 guns in one day, and another in June of 2005 recovered hundreds more along with several high-powered assault weapons."

27 August - 1926

Today in Baltimore Police History, 1926 – The Department's Height Requirement was increased by 3 inches, and weight went up by 10 pounds – Citizens under 5' 10" and 150 lbs. needn't apply to the Baltimore Police department.

29 August - 1899

On this day in Baltimore City Police History, 1899, we lost our brother, Police **Officer Alonzo B. Bishop** to the department's first ever traffic related death.

At the time Baltimore was a booming port city and accidents were a natural part of the busy streets of Baltimore. Western District's Officer Alonzo B. Bishop and Wagon Driver William Smeak were patrolling the Western, a district of heavy foot traffic, horse-drawn traffic and rumbling street cars.

The two officers were headed to answer a wagon call to call box #23 (Poppleton & Pratt) where they were to pick up a prisoner from an officer that had just made an arrest. As they began crossing Freemount Ave. they were struck by street car number #556 of the Freemount Avenue line.

Those who witnessed the collision said the wagon was hit with such force that it was lifted and thrown across the street and into a telephone pole. Officer John Delaney was nearby and witnessed the accident, and he quickly gained control of the wagon and horses (In 1899 a wagon man operated horse drawn wagons). P/O Delaney righted the wagon, and with assistance from the public loaded both men into the wagon; he then drove them to University of Maryland Hospital (some things never change).

Wagon man Smeak was treated for non-life threatening injuries. Officer Bishop however was in agony as he lay there in the hospital ER. Doctors at the time felt if they could operate they might be able to save his life, but he developed peritonitis, which is an inflammation of the thin tissue that lines the inner wall of the abdomen and covers most of the abdominal organs. Since Officer Bishop's injuries were mostly abdominal, surgery (in 1899) was impossible. He was in unbearable pain as he lay there knowing there was nothing that could be done, and that he was waiting to die. His family by his side, he said his goodbyes, and died on this day 29 August 1899.

At the time of his death Officer Bishop was 42 years old, he was married, and had two grown sons Alonzo and John, and a grown daughter Bessie, all married.

Newspaper Article; Aug 25, 1899; pg. 7

Patrol Wagon Driver William Smeak and Reserve Officer Alonzo Bishop, of the Western police district, were thrown from the patrol wagon early this morning at Lexington and Fremont streets. Officer Bishop sustained a fractured skull and was otherwise injured. Driver Smeak was injured internally. Both were taken to the Maryland University Hospital. Officer Bishop is not expected to live. The patrol wagon was crossing Fremont Street at Lexington when it was struck by car 556 of the McMechen street division of the United Railways and Electric Company.

The force of the car knocked the wagon into a telegraph post on the Southwest corner. The wagon was badly broken. The wagon was responding to a call from box 25, at Poppleton and Pratt streets. In going to this box it is customary to drive west on Lexington Street and thence south on Poppleton Street on account of the asphalt pavement. Before reaching cross streets the bell of the patrol wagon is rung to notify wagons and cars of its coming. The wagon passed over the east tracks on Fremont Street and was half way across the west tracks, when it was struck by the

car, which was bound south.

Officer Bishop was thrown out first, as the car struck the rear wheel immediately behind where he was sitting. He fell on his head and was rendered unconscious. The force of the car raised the back of the wagon from the street, hurling it against the telegraph post. Driver Smeak was thrown into the middle of the street. Patrolman John R. Delaney, who was on duty near the corner, went to the assistance of the injured men. He notified Lieutenant Kalbfielsch and then put the men in the wagon to take them to the hospital.

Driver Smeak was conscious. He was unable to tell how the wagon was struck. Deputy Marshal Farnan and Captain Cadwallader were notified and both went to the hospital. Conductor Egbert P. Maynard and Motorman Robert S. Berry had charge of the car. Neither would make a statement. The dashboard of the car was demolished. After taking the men to the hospital Patrolman Delancy answered the call at box 25, which was for a colored man charged with being drunk and disorderly.

Driver Smeak is considered one of the best hostlers in the employ of the Police Department. He is unmarried and lives at 706 West Lexington Street. He was appointed a patrolman April 2, 1887, and has been in charge of the wagon at the Western Station since the patrol system was put into use, about nine years ago. He is careful and attentive to his work. He is 43 years old. Officer Bishop was born in Baltimore in 1830. He was appointed a patrolman on August 19, 1886, and since his connection with the department figured in a number of important arrests. Of late years he has been a reserve officer at the Western Station at night, and went with the wagon on all calls. He is married and lives at 1307 North Gilmore Street.

Newspaper Article; Aug 30, 1899; pg. 7

Reserve Officer Alonzo Bishop, of the Western Police District, who was injured last Thursday night in a collusion between the patrol wagon and a car of the Fremont Avenue line, died early yesterday morning at the Maryland University Hospital. His wife and son were with him at the time of his death. Previous to Monday some slight hopes of his recovery were entertained, but peritonitis set in during that day, and the fatal result was afterward expected. It was found that he would be unable to stand an operation for peritonitis, and none was made. An inquest will be held Sunday at 1 pm at the Western Police Station. Mr. Bishop was born in Baltimore in 1837. He was reared and educated here, and went on the police force in 1886. His work as patrolman was very successful, and he was liked by all those associated *with him. His widow, two sons John W. and Alonzo, both married and a married daughter, Mrs. Bessie Haugh, survive him. Mr. Bishop's home was at 1307 North Gilmore Street.*

As his brothers and sisters of the Baltimore Police Department we will not let him be forgotten, His service Honored the City of Baltimore, and the Baltimore Police Department may he rest in peace, and may God bless him.

29 August - 2012

On this day in Baltimore City Police History, 2012, we lost our brother, **Officer Forrest "Dino" Taylor** due to a traffic accident that occurred on 12 February 2012.

Oddly enough, also on this day 1899, we lost a Brother; Officer Alonzo Bishop, Officer Bishop was our Department's first traffic related LOD death. Officer "Dino" Taylor was our Department's last traffic related LOD death. Let us all take a moment to pray that this will remain the case, and we never lose another of our brothers, or sisters in the line of duty to traffic related, or any other Line of Duty death.

On 18 February, 2012 at 5:50 am, while on the way to assist another Officer, Officer Taylor activated his lights and siren and traveled through a red light in the 600 block of Guilford Avenue in Mount Vernon, according to police spokesman Anthony Guglielmi. Taylor's vehicle was hit broadside by a sports utility vehicle driving through a green light, police said. The cruiser struck a telephone pole and came to rest in the 500 block of Guilford Ave. Officer Taylor was not found at fault for this accident as his emergency equipment had been activated. As Police we are taught to use caution when driving through red light intersections during an emergency situation, but that does not always prevent accidents. Guglielmi said, "This was just a tragic, tragic accident," he said.

A 17-year veteran of the department, Taylor worked in jobs throughout the agency, including stints as a homicide detective in 2003 and a violent crimes investigator in 2008. He received four commendations from the department, including three for his work with a task force that in 2000 served 4,500 warrants and cleared 150 percent of cases (that calculation includes cases from previous years). Taylor was best known for walking his foot post in the downtown community. He is survived by his wife and two children. "Officer Taylor backed up the quality of his service with his life." Guglielmi said. "He was responding in an emergency capacity to help a complete stranger. It's a sobering reminder of what police officers do every day."

Officer Forrest "Dino" Taylor, 44, of Annapolis, died this day 29 Aug 2012 after undergoing the latest in a series of medical procedures. He had been injured 12 February 2012 in a crash at a stoplight in Mount Vernon while responding to a call. "Each and every day Officer Forrest 'Dino' Taylor and his fellow officers place their lives on the line to make our neighborhoods safer," Police Commissioner-designee Anthony W. Batts said in a statement.

"We will never forget Officer Taylor's dedication and commitment to making Baltimore a better place to live and work." May Officer Forrest "Dino" Taylor never be forgotten - His service honored the City of Baltimore and the Police Department.

30 August - 1972

The Department began converting the department's mobile communications system to more versatile portable transceivers, and to incorporate 450 MHZ channels. The portable transceivers greatly increase police service to the citizenry by reducing response time for emergency calls, by providing a uniform communications system for command personnel to direct personnel in emergencies, and by promoting a more efficient and safer foot patrol coverage. The incorporation of 450 MHZ channels created an even more efficient communications by allowing more practical frequency allocations – no more would three districts share the same radio frequencies.

31 August - 1959

Western District moves from the famed "Pine Street Station" where they were housed from 1876 until 31 August 1959 when they moved to their then brand-new station house at Riggs Ave and Mount St. (1034 N Mount St). On opening the new district stationhouse, it was commanded by Capt. Wade H. Poole.

31 August - 1959

Southern District moves from Ostend Street and Patapsco Street, where it was in use from 1896 until 31 August, 1959, to 10 Cherry Hill Road where it remains in use to present. It first opened under the direction of Capt. Elmer I. Bowen.

9 September - 1977

The new Central District/Youth Section/Women's Detention Center Complex was completed at 500 E. Baltimore St. opened. Moving from the Fallsway, and Fayette St. building, built in 1926, to the 500 E. Fayette St. location where it currently stands.

10 September - 1945

On this day in Baltimore Police History, 10 September 1945, we lost our brother, Police **Officer John B. Bealefeld** after was sent to investigate a family disturbance in the 1500 Blk. Boyle Street. Upon arrival, he met two brothers, Thomas and Joseph Geisler. These brothers were not exactly what one would call model citizens. Even from the street, the two could be heard inside their 1526 Boyle Street home swearing, yelling and fighting at all hours. Because of their language and actions, they were menacing to the neighborhood; frightening those that lived or passed by.

Neither would listen to Officer Bealefeld's orders to quiet down and act civilly. We have all heard their senseless argument, "No one is coming into my house and telling me how to act, what to say, or how loud I can say it!" So Bealefeld did what came naturally, and told them, "I can't tell you how to act in your house? Fine. You're under arrest. I'll take you to *my* house (the stationhouse) and give you a free lesson in how to act, what to say, and how loud you can say it!" Bealefeld was a big, strong man, and after he informed them of their arrest, he led the way out of their house to escort them to the nearby call box to call for a wagon. And the three exited the building into the night.

Neither brother was handcuffed, and neither brother wanted to go to jail – Joseph in particular, so the first chance he got, he balled up his fist and struck Officer Bealefeld in the back of the head with everything he had. At this point, something else we have all experienced in Baltimore came into play that night. Those beautiful white marble steps; those white marble steps that when wet are as slippery as ice. Because of his size, the weather, and the unexpected attack, Bealefeld fell several steps to the ground below. As he fell he twisted, and turned with a force so strong the femur in his leg broke in two. While suffering pain from his broken leg, and dazed from the blow to the back of his head, he still managed to have the presence of mind to reach out and grab Joseph Geisler as Geisler attempted to run. Now with a broken leg, busted head and an arrestee in his hand, he called out for help. Other officers were arriving on scene just as Bealefeld was falling from the porch, and they took control of Joseph Geisler. Joseph and Thomas Geisler were both taken to the Southern District for processing. Officer Bealefeld was taken to South Baltimore General Hospital, where he would stay for several days before passing away on 10 September due to an embolism resulting from the fracture in his femur. Joseph Geisler was charged with his murder.

As his brothers and sisters, we will not let him be forgotten. His service honored the city of Baltimore, and the Baltimore Police Department. RIP Officer John Bealefeld, and may God bless you and your family on this day.

11 September - 1964

On this day in Baltimore City Police History, 1964, we lost our brother, Police **Officer Walter Patrick Matthys.** Officer Matthys was fresh out of the academy as he walked a foot post in Baltimore's Eastern District. He was full of pride and enthusiasm, as are most officers at that stage of their careers. Officer Matthys came on at a time when rookies learned their own way, they walked their post and were more often molded into the officers they would become by the people they met. The good folks in the community taught them compassion, the criminals taught them respect; respect for life, respect for what's right and respect for the laws. Laws that would be used as a tool to control those that were on the wrong side of it.

Officer Matthys' first day of patrol was September 7th 1964, just five days before he found himself on the corner of Central and Edythe Streets, where he met a suspect simply known in the area as "The King" – aka Cleaven Dupree.

Dupree was recently released from a mental hospital. In fact, Dupree had been in and out of jail and mental hospitals most of his life – forty-three arrests for various crimes and eleven trips to Crownsville State Mental Hospital to be exact. Dupree was called "The King," because everywhere he went he was seen wearing a crown studded with costume jewels. While he was most commonly known for the Crown he wore, has was also known for his constantly getting into trouble.

Veteran officers know who the troublemakers are on their post(s). Even a seasoned rookie will get to know whom they need to watch out for, and whom they need to get back-up for before approaching. However, five days into his career Matthys knew none of this. Times were different in 1964; no radios to call for a back-up, and some of the old timers didn't take rookies under their wing and teach them the ropes the way they did after this incident took place. In this case, the young rookie approached an unknown suspect wearing a crown, for disturbing the public peace. Matthys tried to talk to him, tried to calm him down, but the suspect only got louder and became more of a public nuisance, and the young officer had no choice but to place him under arrest. Officer Matthys proceeded to grab Dupree by his belt to take him into custody when Dupree, already agitated, came up with other ideas; he became more bellicose and began to fight Officer Matthys, in one of the most violent and vicious manner any one of the many witnesses had ever seen.

Dupree was a tall, skinny, delusional man full of anger and rage; and he quickly overtook the young inexperienced officer, taking him by surprise. Dupree grabbed him round the waist and threw him to the ground.

Storeowners and other bystanders looked on with horror as this known mental patient had an advantage over the young officer, throwing him to the ground. Once on the ground, it wasn't over. The officer was down and had no way of defeating Dupree, or even to defend himself; Dupree had won. However, it wasn't enough, and he continued assaulting Officer Matthys, punching and kicking him while he was down until he eventually reached down and ripped the young officer's gun from its holster and unloaded it into the officer's body.

During the initial fight several witnesses called the station to get help for Officer Matthys, but none of the witnesses themselves came to his aide; they all just stood in shock and watched as a young police officer was being killed while they waited for police to come do what few others have the courage to do. After firing the officer's gun into him once, and apparently killing him, Dupree stood over his lifeless body and fired repeatedly, until the gun was empty. Then he simply walked away as if nothing had happened. Police quickly swarmed the area where they had no trouble locating and arresting Dupree, who was still wearing his toy plastic crown. Officer Matthys was taken to Church Home Hospital where he was pronounced dead from his injuries.

After Dupree was captured, he was eventually taken to court, where he proved to be unable to stand trial, so he was taken to Crownsville State hospital where he would remain for the rest of his life.

Officer Walter P. Matthys served the city of Baltimore for just 5 days, and on the 5th day he taught us all a lesson that would somewhat change the way things were done, the way veterans would treat rookies. Some veterans remained hard asses but for the most part, veterans would slowly begin to give warnings to the young rookies, telling them what to look for, and what to lookout for, how to handle mental patients, trouble makers and hard core criminals. All of this was of little conciliation to Officer Walter P. Matthys' young widowed bride, for not only was 21 year old Officer Matthys new to the department, but he was also newly married to Mrs. Shirley Anne Matthys who he left behind.

12 September - 1926

Baltimore Police Headquarters and the combined Central District stationhouse opened at Fallsway and Fayette Street, where it remained until 12 September, 1977 when Central District personnel moved to a new building at 500 E. Baltimore Street. The old Central District/Headquarters building was demolished in 1984.

13 September - 1975

On this day in Baltimore City Police History, 1975 we lost our brother, Police **Officer Edward Sherman**. Southwestern District's Officer Edward S. Sherman, a 5-year veteran of the Baltimore Police Department, was found unconscious in his patrol car by two fellow officers who were on routine patrol. The following excerpts from investigative reports shed light on what caused the officer to succumb to carbon monoxide poisoning. "At about 0710 hours 09/13/1975, Officers Gary Martin and R. Gooden were working 812 car, responded to the rear of Edgewood Elementary School…to try up same. Upon arrival they found 811 car… it was parked on the rear lot with the motor running and all the windows rolled up tight…"

- "The car was butted against a chain link fence with a deep undergrowth (of weeds and grass). After attempting to rouse the officer by beating on the windows and getting no response, Officer Martin broke the right front window and pulled Officer Sherman from the vehicle. While on the scene Officer Martin checked Officer Sherman's vitals and finding none, he and Gooden rendered first aid/CPR." Investigation of Officer Sherman's vehicle revealed that a thin rubber seal was missing underneath the trunk lid. Combined with the facts that the vehicle was butted against a chain link fence with dense undergrowth and with all the windows up and the engine running caused the carbon monoxide level to become fatal.

Investigators felt that due to his working a midnight shift, Officer Sherman would have backed his car up to the curb near a chain link fence to guard against anyone approaching from the rear. At the time 1974/1975 officers were being targeted and attacked by members of the Black panthers; we lost many of our brothers to them by ambush… so he may have felt this was his best line if defence against attack. He wouldn't have known about the thick deep undergrowth of the weeds that were covering his exhaust pipes on the 1974 Plymouth Satellite he was using as his patrol car that night. He would have begun to feel drowsy, but who hasn't on a midnight shift.

He unwittingly became the victim of an odorless poison which would have given him no chance of defeating this silent killer. In most cases people under the effects of carbon monoxide poisoning just feel extra tired and think they are falling asleep. This happens while the carbon monoxide is slowly replacing the oxygen in the body, eventually taking a life. There is one positive to an ugly and tragic situation such as this, and that is that carbon monoxide poisoning is said to be painless, so we know he didn't suffer.

Officer Edward S. Sherman was a 5 year veteran Baltimore police officer, the father of two children, and husband to his beautiful wife. According to the Sun Paper of 6 Nov 1975, City Hall offered his widow and now fatherless children, just 25 per cent of his pension pending a Pension Board Hearing to determine whether she should get full benefits. I am not sure of the outcome of that hearing, I can only hope they did the right thing. Because not only was he our brother, but based on this incident, it was learned that the trunk seal on nearly all of the 1974 Plymouth Satellites in patrol were defective, allowing carbon monoxide to enter the vehicles. Many officers during that period were suffering severe headaches, and never knew why until Officer Sherman lost his life due to carbon monoxide poisoning. All of the vehicles were removed from service, inspected and repaired. Officer Sherman lost his life, but his death saved many of his brothers and sisters from serious illness, or death.

As his brothers and sisters, we will not let him be forgotten. His service honored the city of Baltimore, and the Baltimore Police Department. RIP Officer Edward Sherman and may God bless you and your family on this day.

14 September - 1871

On this day in Baltimore City Police History, 1871, we lost our brother, **Detective John H. Richards** based on the following:

On 31 August, 1871 at 7:45 pm Detective Richards was attempting to question a young man about a stolen satchel. The suspect was seen in front of a store on Franklin Street when Detective Richards called out to him. The suspect suddenly produced a revolver, causing the unarmed Detective Richards to pull out his club and close the distance between the two. One shot was fired by the suspect, striking Detective Richards' arm. A second shot was fired striking him in his upper chest.

Those in the area heard two shots from a small pistol, which resulted in seriously wounding Detective John Richards. A group of citizens observed the shooting and started to chase the suspect. The suspect attempted to shoot at the group but the gun misfired.

Witnesses are unsure of the events that followed. Some believed that after the gun misfired the suspect began to examine it to determine the cause of the misfire, and during that examination he pulled the trigger and accidentally shot himself in the head. Others said he was cornered and once he realized he had no place to go, the subject turned the gun on himself. In either case the suspect died that day from a single shot to the head.

Detective Richards was taken to his home where his condition grew increasingly worse until he succumbed to the wounds he received that day.

Detective Richards was survived by his wife. As his brothers and sisters of the Baltimore Police Department we will not let him be forgotten. His service honored the City of Baltimore and the Baltimore Police Department. May he rest in peace, and may God bless him.

14 September - 1940

Today in Baltimore Police History, 1940 - The *Charles D. Gaither* was placed in commission with the Baltimore City Police Department's Marine Unit. The police boat was named after Commissioner Charles D. Gaither, known as the General. Gaither was born in 1860, and was 60 years old when he became the first police commissioner of the modern system. Prior to Commissioner Gaither we had a panel of three commissioners who were appointed. They, in turn, appointed a Marshal of Police to actually command the force of Police. In 1920, Governor Richie abandoned the Marshal position and the three member Board of Commissions, and appointed the general to the new position of Police Commissioner of Baltimore City, a position he would hold for 17 years, from 1920 until 1937

The *Gaither* was placed into commission replacing the 1928 *George G. Henry*, which was proceeded by the 1911 *Robert D. Carter*, and the very first police boat, commissioned in 1891, the *Lannan*.

17 September - 1857

The City Council authorized the expenditure of $3,845.95 on 200 revolvers, to fulfill a bill passed on 11 December 1856, in which the City Council voted and passed a bill to arm Baltimore Police Officers. The 1850's were violent times for Baltimore Police, who were often fired on by the public in response to political issues of the times.

17 September - 1922

A program that was initiated in 1921 gets off the ground on this day in 1922. The department installed a signal light on top of a call box on the southeast corner of Baltimore and Charles Street. The signal was made up of an electric lightbulb, a washbasin to shade the bulb, and a Marine lens. The mechanism for the operation of the light was located in the old Central Police Station House on Saratoga Street near Charles Street.

This method of notifying an officer that he was wanted proved very successful and at by March of 1945, there were 269 recall lights in operation throughout the city, on a much more improved platform than the first jury-rigged system. By 1945 the recall system consisted of one commercial sign flasher in each district stationhouses, which carried 110 volts to each recall light's location on Call boxes, and were operated with a steady or a flashing light by the telephone operator in each district. The above system was used in all districts.

These Recall Lights in Baltimore were the first use of such a system in the country, initially handmade by our maintenance crew. This method of notifying the officer that he was wanted proved very successful. Every uniformed man from the inspector to the patrolman was enthusiastic over the results, and by the end of first week of this *Magic Blinker*, there was a demand for more from the other seven districts, and other jurisdictions around the country.

18 September - 1914

18 September, 1914 – "Luxe" and "Morpheus" Baltimore's first recorded K9 dogs - A little known fact, while not an official unit, until 1956 Baltimore Police had two Police Dogs at their call when two Airedale Terriers from London came to enroll as members of the Police Force. Their owners learned two dogs were already here, privately owned, one belonging to Mr. Jere Wheelright, and the other to Dr. Henry Barton Jacobs. "Luxe", Mr. Wheelright's dog was a superb example of a highly trained equine aristocrat, big, powerful and intelligent to a degree that was truly remarkable. Morpheus, Dr. Henry Barton Jacobs' dog also a superb example of a highly trained K9. It would be 42 years before we would have an official K9 Unit, but off and on from 1914, until 1956 we had, had Police Dogs used in both a private, and official capacity. But not until 1956 did we establish an official unit, with an official methodology that would go on to become world known as the best K9 unit in the country, and then in the world.

By December Marshals Carter and House decided they should have their own K9 unit within the Baltimore Police department, as is found in the following news article dated 18 Sep 1914

To Try Police Dogs - Newspaper Articles; Sep 18, 1914; pg. 12

Department Here Will Use Belgian Hounds In Suburbs. Their Job to Chase Crooks

Success in Other Cities Prompts Experiment Here For Detection and Protection

Four Belgian hounds, trained to attack a burglar or murderer or to assist anyone who needs protection, will soon be doing police duty for the Baltimore Police Department in the suburban districts. At a meeting of the Police Board Wednesday it was decided to give the police dog a tryout in Baltimore and Marshal Carter and Deputy Marshal House were instructed to create a dog squad as an aid to policemen who work extensive posts.

As soon as the dogs are bought they will be placed in the custody of four night policemen, who will care for them, being amply repaid for the care by the department.

While the board's action is one of an experiment it is believed that the dog squad will meet with favor and be an important adjunct of the police force.

The policemen who will have the dogs as aids will take them from their homes directly to their posts. Journeying with the policemen the dogs will work until 5 o'clock in the morning. The dogs will be taught to make detours around houses to detect possible marauders.

The record of police dogs in New York, Brooklyn and cities of the West is said to be a surprising one, many notable captures having been made by the animals. According to Marshal Carter and Deputy Marshal House the Belgian hounds can be trained in criminal detection as well as in protective work. As a constant colleague of the patrolman and as a detective he is considered by police as invaluable.

"When the dogs are in regular police service," declared Deputy Marshal House, "They can be put on guard at the door of a house and no one will be permitted to pass in or out. If one is rash enough to try it, the dog will knock him down and sit on him. He does this by getting between the legs of the would-be fugitive and causing him to lose his balance and fall."

Marshal Carter said last night that he would arrange immediately to get at least four dogs in the department within the next two weeks. It is expected that a Belgian bound will cost about $100. Marshal Carter was in Milwaukee several years ago and in looking over the police situation he learned of the work that the Belgian police dogs do there.

This is only one of the many new ideas that the Police Board has to better the police system. It is probable that within the next six months the department will Increase the dog squad.

19 September - 1958

On this day in Baltimore City Police History 19 September 1958, we lost our brother Police **Officer Robert Nelson**, based on the following;

On 16 Sept 1958, Motors Officer Nelson entered the intersection of Broadway and Gay Streets; at the same time Richard Bishop also entered the intersection causing a collision between the two (Bishop was operating a truck and had just moved to Baltimore from New Jersey). Officer Nelson's motorcycle was struck so hard that not only was he ejected from it, his body was thrown more than 20 feet across the intersection, with his head to hit a pole and curb upon landing. He was taken to St Josephs' Hospital where doctors worked feverously to try and save his life. His supervisor immediately sent for Officer Nelson's wife, Emma Nelson. Emma was brought to the hospital from the couple's Williams Avenue home. Upon her arrival to the hospital doctors were still working to save her husband's life; they would eventually have done everything they could, ending by putting a steel plate in his head, they were at a place where all they could do now was to wait. With Emma by his side, three days would pass before Officer Nelson would succumb to his injuries.

Richard Bishop, had only been in Baltimore for two days before he would end the life of our brother with his reckless driving and be charged with vehicular manslaughter. On 4 October, 1958, two magistrates from Baltimore County dealt leniently with the New Jersey man who would end the life of Officer Nelson.

Nelson was on the department for a year and half, having served our country in the Korean War 1950-1953. Ironically, he transferred to motors after hearing of the loss of Patrolman John Andrews of the BPD Motors Unit, who was also struck by a reckless driver and killed nearly a year earlier on Oct 9 1957.

As his brothers and sisters of the Baltimore Police Department we will not let him be forgotten, His service Honored the City of Baltimore, and the Baltimore Police Department may he rest in peace, and may God bless him.

19 September - 1975

The department in cooperation with the State's Attorney's Office and various taxicab companies became part of the "Civilian Radio Taxi Patrol" in an effort to speed police service to the citizens of Baltimore in need of help. When on duty a cab driver, whose vehicle is identified by a "Civilian Radio Taxi Patrol" shield on the right and left rear-quarter panels, observes anything demanding immediate police attention, he notifies his dispatcher, who in turn calls the Communication Division via a special Hotline. This program is another example of the department's efforts to involve the citizens of Baltimore in a united fight against crime.

20 September - 1986

On this day in Baltimore City Police History, 1986, we lost our brother, Police **Officer Robert Alexander** based on the following:

During the early morning hours of September 20, 1986, a citizen traveling home from work stopped for a red light at Frederick and Boswell Avenues, and his 1978 Dodge was rear-ended by a pick-up truck. They flagged down a motorist who offered help and went to call police to the scene. Officer Robert Alexander of the Southwest District received that call, and responded to help.

On arrival he activated his rooftop emergency lights to provide a warning to other motorists of the stopped vehicles. Officer Alexander got out of his car and began interviewing the drivers of both vehicles. Suddenly, a 1985 Nissan pickup truck came around the curve, speeding and out of control. The truck was headed toward the group, and Officer Alexander, concerned for their safety, pushed the citizens into a wooded area and out of the path of the oncoming truck. His actions were credited with saving their lives, by sacrificing his own.

The truck crossed over the centerline, hitting Officer Alexander's police car and then striking him. The truck overturned and struck the vehicles involved in the original accident. Those two drivers rushed to the aid of Officer Alexander, who just moments before had saved their lives. Another citizen traveling nearby saw the accident scene and ran to the patrol car to use the fallen officer's police radio to summon help. An off-duty officer, John W. Parrott, who was also driving by, witnessed the accident, stopped and used Officer Alexander's car radio to better notify the dispatcher of the events that had just taken place and the specific location.

Paramedics were already in route to care for the citizens involved in the initial accident, and were there within seconds. Officer Alexander's injuries were so severe that he died at the scene. The suspect/driver of the truck was arrested on the scene and charged with DWI and vehicular manslaughter, as well as a host of other charges. Officer Alexander was 22 years old, served as a Cadet, graduated in class 85-3, and had just nine months on the street.

Newspaper Article - Apr 13, 1987; pg. 12d

Barbara Harris had just a few, quiet words to say as she accepted a posthumous award for her son, Baltimore police officer Robert Alexander, who was struck and killed by a pickup truck last September after pushing two men to safety. "Nothing has to be said, because his action speaks for itself," she whispered to those nearest her Saturday evening. Then she clutched the plaque, the highest honor bestowed by the Vanguard Justice Society, a fraternity of black city police officers.

The award was presented to Ms. Hanis by the widow of Detective Marcellus Ward, Jr, for whom it is named. Detective Ward was shot to death in 1984 during an undercover narcotics operation, "We try to [honor] a police officer who has done outstanding work and put his life in jeopardy to save others. That's what Robert Alexander did when he made the supreme sacrifice," said Officer Rick Palmer, who helped coordinate the group's annual awards banquet. And "outstanding" was how the crowd of about one hundred officers, their families and friends, remembered Officer Alexander during the society's gathering at the Palladium.

"He was outstanding, his whole heart went into being a policeman," said Lt. Alvin A. Winkler, who taught Officer Alexander during his training at the police academy. Those close to 22-year-old Officer Alexander remembered him saying, often, that he would risk his life to help others without a second thought. In September, he did. While he was able to push other men to safety, the young officer – father of a 2-year-old daughter, a policeman just three months – was unable to save himself. The driver of the pickup truck, Carl E. Carpenter, 27, was sentenced to five years in prison on charges stemming from the incident.

As his brothers and sisters of the Baltimore Police Department we will not let him be forgotten. His service honored the City of Baltimore, and the Baltimore Police Department. May he rest in peace, and may God bless him.

21 September - 1915

On this day Baltimore City Police History 21 September, 1915, we lost our brother **Patrolman Herbert Bitzel** in an on-duty fall from a trolley car.

Newspaper Article; Sep 21, 1915; pg. 5

On 21 September, 1915 Patrolman Herbert Bitzel, a Policeman, was killed from a fall, as Patrolman Bitzel tumbled from front platform of trolley car. Patrolman Herbert Bitzel, of the Northwestern district was killed by the fall from the platform off an Edmondson Avenue trolley car on Edmondson Avenue near Arlington Avenue early yesterday morning. He was picked up unconscious by Frank Kapraun, the motorman, and several of his brother police officers and later died in a Western District ambulance while being taken to the Franklin Square hospital. Dr. George G. Swann, who examined him immediately upon his arrival to the hospital, cited a fracture at the base of the skull for causing his death.

A short time after 4 o'clock yesterday morning Bitzel, with round Sergeants Davis and Kaiss and several patrolman boarded the Edmondson Avenue car on their way home from duty. Bitzel, according to motorman Kapraun, announced that he was going to remain on the step of the front platform, saying he was only going to ride a short distance.

A few minutes later Kapraun called back to the policeman in the car that Bitzel had fallen off the step and into the street. The car was brought to a stop and Bitzel was found lying face downward, bleeding from wounds on his face. Bitzel was 28 years old. He was appointed a probationary officer in February, 1913 and a regular seven months ago. He patrolled the area near Lafayette market. Before entering the Police Department he was a fireman having been a member of both the number 19 Engine Company and number 10 Truck Company. He was survived by a widow and five children.

As his brothers and sisters of the Baltimore Police Department we will not let him be forgotten. His service honored the City of Baltimore and the Baltimore Police Department. May he rest in peace, and may God bless him.

21 September - 1992

On this day Baltimore City Police History 21 Sept, 1992 we lost our brother Police **Officer Ira Neil Weiner** to gunfire when he respond to a call for service at 1929 West Mulberry Street. As he approached the home, without provocation or warning, Officer Weiner was suddenly savagely attacked and stabbed repeatedly in the head with an ice pick. The suspect then grabbed Officer Weiner's pistol, ripped it from his holster and fired it into Ira as he stood over his now lifeless body. Officer Weiner was stabbed, and shot multiple times, but that was not enough; the coward then leaned down and shot him once more in the back of his head. The suspect then began an exchange of gunfire with the responding backup units. Those back-up officers would proceed to cut him down in the hail of gunfire that he deserved.

The Sun paper would report:

A drug-crazed man stabbed Officer Ira N. Weiner multiple times with an ice pick before he took the officer's pistol and shot him in the back of the head, according to the state medical examiner's office.

Officer Weiner, 28, was fatally wounded when he answered a call at a West Baltimore house on Saturday. Apparently, the Western District officer was unable to draw his 9mm Glock pistol because he was overwhelmed by his assailant. After stabbing Officer Weiner, the assailant used the officer's handgun to shoot him in the back of the left side of the head, a wound that proved fatal, Ms. Tori Leonard reported. Additional stab wounds occurred after the shot, officials said.

Ira was well known, well liked and well respected, and he will be missed. As his brothers and sisters of the Baltimore Police Department we will not let him be forgotten. His service honored the City of Baltimore and the Baltimore Police Department. May he rest in peace, and may God bless him.

Shomrim Society to Honor Fallen Officer - September 21, 2012

BALTIMORE - Twenty years ago Baltimore Police Department Officer Ira Neil Weiner was assaulted, shot and died in the line of duty. Sunday, his death will be commemorated by the Shomrim Society of Maryland.

The Shomrim Society of Maryland was organized to unite members of the Jewish faith in the field of public safety across the State of Maryland. It was founded in 1978 and has since worked to raise awareness and honor officers who pay the ultimate price for ensuring the safety of others.

22 September - 1858

On this day in Baltimore City Police History, 1858, we lost our brother, Police **Officer Benjamin Benton** to gunfire based on the following:

News reports of the time wrote:

A Police Officer is Shot Dead - The Western quarter of the city on Wednesday night was the scene of an affray, the result of which was the instant killing of police Officer Benjamin Benton, of the Western District. He was killed by a single shot from a pistol in the hands of a man named Henry Gambrill, the keeper of a public house on Franklin Street, near Howard Street. It appears that a dance or some other kind of amusement was going on in a house on Biddle Street, near Pennsylvania Avenue. A number of disorderly characters were among those present, and at about 11:30 pm Officer Burke, of that beat, apprehending a disturbance, gave the usual "Double Rap" for assistance. The term "Double Rap" refers to an officer striking his Espantoon two times in quick succession against any solid building, downspout or cobblestone street to summons other officers in the area to come help him. Basically, the "Double Rap" was 1858's version of a 10-16 (a request for a back-up officer), and just a step below a Signal 13 (officer needs immediate help).

Burk was joined by his brother Officers Benton (the deceased), Rigdon and Brown, who seized two of the party – David Houck and John Isenhart – at the request of the proprietor of the house, and attempted to take them to the stationhouse. Officers Benton and Rigdon took hold of Houck, and while they were struggling with him, Gambrill interfered.

After threatening to knock Benton down, Gambrill stepped back several paces, leveled a revolver within three feet of Benton's head, and fired. The ball entered immediately back of the left ear, and passing entirely through the neck, came out at the right ear, almost in line with its entrance. Benton released hold on Houck and fell dead, the ball having severed the spinal cord and cut the base of the brain away. Gambrill escaped, but was afterwards arrested by Captain Linaweaver, and locked up with Houck and Isenhart at the western on Pine Street station.

No other details about the incident have been unearthed. As his brothers and sisters of the Baltimore Police Department we will not let him be forgotten. His service honored the City of Baltimore and the Baltimore Police Department. May he rest in peace, and may God bless him.

22 September - 1973

On this day in Baltimore Police History, 1973 we lost our brother, **Officer Calvin Rodwell** to gunfire based on the following:

Like many officers, Officer Calvin Rodwell longed to instil a positive image of police officers to the children of Baltimore. To that end he sought assignments within the department that allowed him time to spend teaching children, and building a foundation of trust in their young minds. Officer Rodwell's dedication to children went beyond the normal eight hour workday. In addition to teaching traffic safety schools at Baltimore's "Safety City" in the Southeast District, he also volunteered as an assistant Scoutmaster at his local Scout Troop, and served with the Big Brothers of Baltimore. In his official position, he rarely confronted violent suspects; still he was a hero to many.

To make ends meet living on the income of a 1970's police officer; Officer Rodwell was forced to take a job moonlighting as a taxi driver. (That was not unusual: off-duty officers often worked as cabbies, and the department gave its blessing, because this type work for police was widely publicized, and helped decrease a trend at the time in robberies and other violent crimes against Baltimore cab drivers.)

Shortly before midnight on Friday, September 21, 1973, Officer Rodwell picked up a fare at the corner of McCollah and Wilson Streets, in Baltimore's Central District. Louis Walker got in the back of the off-duty Officer's cab, and requested a trip to Orleans and Asquith Streets. Officer Rodwell quickly drove his cab from the west side of Baltimore to the east side, when all of a sudden Walker produced a handgun and forced Officer Rodwell to pull to the curb. Complying, Officer Rodwell pulled over and stopped the cab.

Walker ordered him out of the cab, and Walker drove away with it, leaving the Officer alone on the side of the road. Unknown to Walker at the time, he drove off with more than the Officer's cab and money – Officer Rodwell's handgun was tucked under the cushion of the driver's seat. Rodwell pursued the cab on foot but quickly lost sight of his attacker. It was later determined that the gun used by Walker to rob Officer Rodwell was borrowed; Walker had borrowed the gun from another cabbie by the name of Ridgely Young, and in fact Walker was heading back to return Mr. Young's gun when he decided to rob Officer Rodwell.

Not long after losing sight of his cab, Officer Rodwell spotted another cab coming toward him and ran toward it for help. Of all the cab's in Baltimore, this one was being driven by none other than Ridgely Young, and as Rodwell neared it he had no way of knowing that Louis Walker had already met Young and returned his pistol, and that he now possessed Officer Rodwell's service weapon.

Worse, Louis Walker was now riding in the backseat of Young's cab after abandoning Rodwell's cab. Unfortunately, Walker had found Rodwell's gun between the cushion of his cab before he abandoned it. So as Young was flagged down by Rodwell, Louis Walker now knew that Officer Rodwell was more than just a cab driver; he knew that Rodwell was a police Officer. Fearing he would be arrested for the robbery, Louis Walker exited Young's cab and confronted the now unarmed Officer.

Witnesses heard Rodwell's plea to Walker for his life seconds before 3 shots were fired by Walker; two of those rounds struck their target, mortally wounding Officer Rodwell right there in the street. Officers and medics dispatched to the scene transported the wounded officer to Church Home Hospital, where he was pronounced dead just after midnight on the morning of Saturday, 22 September, 1973.

Officer Calvin Rodwell touched the lives of many during his 12 years of service with the Baltimore Police Department. Sadly he would leave behind his wife Dorsey, and their three children Kimberly, Andre and Dino. Shortly after the shooting, Walker was arrested and charged with the murder of this devoted husband, father, family man, police officer, and role model.

Newspaper Article; Jul 25, 1974; pg. C18

A 29 year old admitted dope addict was given prison terms totaling 50 years yesterday for the robbery and murder of an off-duty police officer who taught traffic safety to school children.

Judge Charles D. Harris, who imposed the sentence directed that the defendant first be sent to Patuxent Institution to determine if he was sane. After he was declared sane, Louis Walker, of the 2300 block Norfolk Avenue, pled guilty in June to second degree murder and armed robbery of Officer Calvin M Rodwell, 34, who was moonlighting as a taxicab driver when he was killed on 22 September.

In June, Ridley W. Young, 22 of the 2800 block Springhill Avenue, a taxicab driver, also pled guilty to being an accessory in the robbery that caused the death of Officer Rodwell. Young received a 10 year term from Judge Albert L. Sklar.

Other charges were not filed against Young in connection with the robbery/slaying in return for his providing evidence in the case against Walker, according to Dominic Lamele and Gerald Richman, the prosecutors in this case.

As his brothers and sisters of the Baltimore Police Department we will not let him be forgotten. His service honored the City of Baltimore, and the Police Department. RIP Officer Calvin Rodwell

23 September - 1968

The department officially took possession of its IBM System 360 mainframe computer system.

27 September - 2010

On this day in Baltimore Police History, 2010 we lost our brother, Police **Officer James Earl Fowler III** to an auto accident based on the following:

Police Officer James Fowler, a 33-year veteran of the Baltimore Police Department was killed in a single-vehicle accident in Pennsylvania while traveling to a training program. Officer Fowler, was driving through Lewistown, Pa. at about 5:25 pm when his 2002 Chevrolet truck hit a berm on U.S. 22/322 West and came to rest along a concrete barrier on the left side of the roadway, killing him.

Fowler joined the Baltimore Police Department in 1976 after he was honorably discharged from the U.S. Navy. The bulk of his career was spent in the patrol and traffic investigation divisions. Fowler received medical training in the Navy, and served as a volunteer medic with a Carroll County fire department.

As his brothers and sisters of the Baltimore Police Department we will not let him be forgotten. His service honored the City of Baltimore and the Baltimore Police Department. May he rest in peace, and may God bless him.

29 September - 1956

On this day in Baltimore Police History, 1956, we lost our brother, Police **Officer John R. Phelan** due to gunfire based on the following:

With only four months of service protecting the City of Baltimore, Officer Phelan died in the back of an ambulance, the victim of a bullet from his own service revolver. His widow, 19 year old Jacquelyn Phelan, described her late husband's love for police work as if it were a religion or another woman. She spoke of the time he would take to arrange and rearrange his uniform, clean his gun, polish his belt, his shoes and the brim of his hat. When he felt everything was perfect, he would then move on to shine his badge, a badge that he had worked so hard to earn. Sadly, Officer Phelan was killed before the birth of his first child.

The neighborhood he worked in the Northwest District lived in fear, as gangs of armed robbers on a rampage were robbing small businesses and citizens at will. Officer Phelan bravely patrolled the areas hardest hit by these robbers. In an effort to catch the robbery suspects in the act, several officers hid in nearby alleys, and the back rooms of liquor stores, and grocery stores, while patiently waiting for these criminals to strike. Hence, they were called "stake-outs."

On this night in 1956, Officer Wilbert J. Schroeder hid in the rear of the Park's Liquor Store in the 2700 blk. of W. North Ave. Late in the evening of 29 September three men burst through the front door of the liquor store brandishing handguns; they began shouting orders to the store owner, William Park, and his two employees, Gilmor Donte and James Curtis. On emerging from his hiding space, Patrolman Schroeder was met with a barrage of gunfire from less than 10 feet away. Bullets flew, shattering bottles and cases of beer, but, amazingly, not a single person was struck, and the three robbers fled to the street.

Officer Schroeder, close behind, took aim at the largest member of the group and let his final round fly. It struck Alvin Herbert Braxton, a 6 foot, 210 lb. seventeen-year-old in his leg as he ran. The shot stopped Braxton in his tracks. With news a gun battle spreading fast, requests for assistance were quickly answered. Among those who responded were Patrolman Phelan and his partner, Patrolman Theodore Weintraub. With the scene secure, the officers sent for an ambulance to take the young robber for treatment of his leg wound.

Medics Walter Robinson and Mark Rohm arrived shortly afterward and loaded the critically injured man into their ambulance. In the mid 1950's, handcuffs and leg irons were a luxury item and were not provided by the department. Those patrolman who had them spent their own money to acquire them. On this night not a single responding patrolman had a set of handcuffs to restrict the movement of the prisoner. In order to properly guard against escape, Officers Phelan and Weintraub joined the medics in the back of the ambulance for the ride to Lutheran Hospital.

Braxton saw an opportunity to escape and began to fight despite the throbbing pain in his leg. The two patrolmen fought back in a desperate struggle within the closed quarters of the ambulance. The medics stopped their vehicle in the intersection of Popular Grove and Baker Street and went to aid the officers in the back of the ambulance. Before Robinson and Rohm could help, Braxton ripped Officer Phelen's gun from his holster and began firing wildly. He managed to shoot his way to temporary freedom by fatally wounding Officer Phelan and hitting Weintraub in both legs.

The violent youth forced open the doors to the ambulance and assaulted a taxicab driver who was stopped nearby. He then took control of the cab and rammed the rear of the ambulance to keep the patrolman inside. By this time, other officers responded to the sounds of gunfire and the frightened calls from citizens. Patrolman Henry Hau was first on the scene and upon seeing Braxton armed with a weapon took careful aim and shot Braxton four times. Despite the damage to their ambulance, Robinson and Rohm sped to the hospital in an attempt to save the two patrolmen's lives.

Officer John Phelan died before he could reach the hospital, and became the youngest officer to lose his life in the service of the city of Baltimore. Officer Weintraub recovered from his wounds.

Officers Phillip Buratt and William DePaula, who were driving the paddy wagon, responded to the scene and, still without handcuffs, transported the wounded Braxton to Lutheran Hospital for much needed care. Upon arrival to the hospital Braxton would again attempt an escape – this time he would fight with all his strength despite his extensive injuries, eventually being subdued by an overwhelming number of police who finally handcuffed him.

After he had received the necessary care, Braxton revealed the names of his fellow gang members, and where they could be found. Police arrested and charged Alvin Braxton, Roger Ray, Earl Pickett, and Albert Braxton, Alvin's older brother, with eleven more robberies. The gang had stolen nearly $36,000 and three pistols. Alvin Braxton was tried convicted of murdering Officer Phelan.

If anything good could come of such a tragic moment, it was the public's outcry over the fact that officers were not properly equipped. Newspaper editorials insisted on properly funding and equipping the Baltimore Police Department. One editorial looked upon the idea as a matter of common sense, stating, "Certainly relatively small budget items should not stand in the way of maximum protective equipment for all policemen." The editor went on to suggest that taxpayers "would be far from hostile to inclusion of relatively small sums for general issuance of both handcuffs and improved holsters."

These measures did little to comfort young Jacqueline's grief at the loss of her new husband, but they did promise that in the future officers would have the added measure of safety that many officers today take for granted.

As his brothers and sisters of the Baltimore Police Department we will not let him be forgotten. His service honored the City of Baltimore and the Baltimore Police Department. May he rest in peace, and may God bless him.

31 September - 1971

The Cell Blocks and District Courtrooms housed in eight of the nine police stationhouses closed after 12 years in operation. The courthouse and the 24 adjoining cellblocks in the Northeast district building were to be converted into a detention center for women and offenders under the age of 16. The newly renovated facility replaced the current women's cellblock and the juvenile cells on Pine Street, which had been condemned.

Note: The court closed without ceremony at the end of a typical day's business, during which 18 defendants faced 52 charges ranging from shoplifting to disorderly conduct, false pretense to indecent exposure and assault to violation of probation. The last case heard in the Northeast District Court Room was against Donald F. Goetz, who was charged with burglarizing a house in the 1600 block of East Coldspring Lane.

2 October - 1920

On this day in Baltimore Police History, 1920, we lost our brother **Patrolman Michael J Egan** of the Southwest District to a heart attack brought on by back-to-back aggressive calls based on the following:

The second call was for an apparent murder/suicide, in which 20-year-old Kenneth Tucker and his 28-year-old wife both died. That is all that the police of the time were clear on; we have been unable to learn what proceeded the double shooting.

What was known was that Eunice Honeycutt, the 14-year-old daughter of the woman by a former marriage, was in the house when her stepfather (Kenneth Tucker) came to the door seeking admittance. Once inside, he sent young Eunice out of the house while he was to have a talk with her mother, his wife. Eunice called the police fearing something was amiss, and shortly after calling the stationhouse, she and a friend heard the sound of gunfire coming from inside the house.

Officer Egan had just returned to the stationhouse with a disorderly arrest, which ended in a struggle to get the arrestee to the station. Egan was tired from the struggle with the disorderly arrest when his desk sergeant sent him back out to handle the West Saratoga Street, Kenneth Tucker incident. Officer Egan had a reporter with him and the pair began to run to the location of the shots fired call from Eunice Tucker.

Officer Egan, tired from the previous arrest, became winded in route and needed a lift, so he flagged down a motorist and he and the reporter were given a ride the rest of the way to the scene at 1313 W. Saratoga St. Upon arrival at the location, Officer Egan pushed open the door and went in. Not long after when the patrol wagon from the Western District arrived and went in, they discovered Officer Egan's lifeless body lying across Tucker's just inside the door.

It was believed that the sight of Tucker caused him to collapse, but we don't know, there could have been a struggle for the gun; he may have collapsed from the long run, or the earlier struggle with the disorderly arrest that he just cleared. As we all know even without a struggle, a disorderly can get our heart rate up, but most disorderly lead to a struggle and with an already weak heart, this could have led to the death of Officer Egan

As his brothers and sisters of the Baltimore Police Department, we will not let him be forgotten. His service honored the City of Baltimore and the Baltimore Police Department. May he rest in peace, and may God bless him.

2 October - 1978

A long-time goal of the Department's Education and Training Division (then housed on the ninth and tenth floors of the Headquarters building at Fayette and Fallsway) was realized with the opening of a library specializing in law enforcement material. The facility provided entrance level sworn personnel in the E&T facility with a location to study, perform required research work and be exposed to supplemental text material. It also offered other departmental personnel many unique features to meet a number of scholarship needs.

October 3 - 1967

Today in Baltimore Police History, 1967, our Brother Retired **Officer Joseph B. Hoffman** was blinded in a gun battle.

Newspaper Article; Dec 18, 1970;

A Central District patrolman has won his fight for a 100% disability pension.

The Board of Trustees of the fire and police pension system awarded Retired Officer Joseph B. Hoffman, 43, a $10,044 a year pension for life Wednesday. It was the first full pay disability award made by the trustees under the new ordinance that was passed primarily because of efforts of Officer Hoffman.

In November of 1970, he picketed City Hall, arousing the sympathy of nearly every politician inside. The pension ordinance, which had been languishing for two years, was quickly resurrected and passed. It went into effect early this month.

Patrolman Hoffman – on full paid medical leave since he was blinded – was scheduled to be pensioned off under the old system that would have given him only about $6,000 a year – the new pension system will allow him to retire at full pay.

"My family is really happy. My family is really happy," Officer Hoffman repeated over and over again at his Glen Burnie home yesterday. "That's why I got out and walked and did what I did to have the old pension system changed."

Officer Hoffman, the father of three children, said he plans to get trained and find a job. He has yet to decide what job to take.

He was wounded in the head October 3, 1967, while trying to capture a burglary suspect. The wound forced the removal of both eyes. His plight prompted a visit and a pair of cufflinks from then Gov. Agnew, and a fund drive by the police wives association that collected $21,000. The patrolman's case gained further prominence in February a year ago when the police wives association charged that six Baltimore restaurants refused to serve him because he was accompanied by his seeing-eye dog, Ritchie.

The restaurants later apologized when informed of the state law permitting service to blind persons with seeing-eye dogs.

Firefighter Edward had tried, a pension fund board member, set a fireman and a policeman Lieutenant also are being considered for full disability pension.

Full disability under the ordinance is described as brain damage, or the loss of two arms, hands, eyes, feet, legs or any combination of the two.

At this time we remember and thank Officer Hoffman and his family for their sacrifices. May God bless them and hold them close to his heart, as we his brothers and sisters are proud of the strength shown and the sacrifices that were made.

Only sketchy details were available from *Newspaper reports* of the time.

Blinded in one eye by a police bullet during an early morning fracas which resulted in the death of a burglary suspect, a Central district officer was in danger yesterday of losing all of his eyesight. A spokesman for University Hospital said there were no complications during surgery on Officer Joseph B. Huffman, 40, but added that "prospects for his left eye are poor." He was listed in "satisfactory condition." The policeman lost his right eye, which was hit accidentally by either another officer's bullet or a ricocheting bullet from his own pistol, during a gunfight at Pratt and Paca Streets with Charles E. Dorsey, 20, of the 2900 block West North Avenue, a burglary suspect who was shot and killed by police.

4 October - 1932

On this day In Baltimore Police History, 1932 we lost our brother **Officer Stienacker** to an auto accident based on the following.

On September 29, 1932 at 9:50 am Officer Stienacker was crossing the intersection of Frederick Avenue and Willard Street. A motorist struck the officer as he crossed Frederick Avenue. As a result of being hit by the car, he was thrown against a United Railway and Electric Company streetcar. He suffered a skull fracture, lacerated head and ear. He succumbed to his injuries on this 4 October in 1932.

As his brothers and sisters of the Baltimore Police Department, we will not let him be forgotten. His service honored the City of Baltimore and the Baltimore Police Department. May he rest in peace, and may God bless him.

7 October - 1897 - Hamilton

On October 7, 1897, Capt. Samuel T. Hamilton was appointed Marshal of the Department to succeed Marshal Frey.

Note: From a *newspaper article* dated September 28, 1901:

Former Marshal of Police Frey was dismissed by the preceding Board of Police Commissioners on July 12, 1897, and his replacement, Marshal Hamilton "was not appointed until October 7, 1897. In the months between the two events, Deputy Marshal Farnan performed the duties of Marshal."

Marshal Hamilton was a veteran officer of the Civil War, and a man of indisputable courage and integrity. For many years following the great civil conflict he served on the Western frontier, and took part in the unremitting campaigns against the Sioux and other Indian tribes, who were constantly waging war upon the settlers and pioneers as they pushed their way toward the setting sun, building towns, railroads, trying to conquer the wilderness and its natural indigenous peoples.

In the Sioux campaign of 1876, when Gen. George A. Custer and his gallant command were outnumbered ten to one by the Indians in the valley of the Little Big Horn, Captain Hamilton and his troop rode day and night in a vain effort to reinforce Gen. Custer and his sorely pressed men.

On 26 June, 1876, when Custer's Seventh United States Cavalry rode and fought to their deaths, no reinforcements arrived. However, one day too late, Hamilton and his Cavalry arrived. Exhausted from their terrific ride across country, Captain Hamilton and his troop, though weakened, fought through the rest of the Indian campaign. His troops eventually drove Sitting Bull, the great Indian war chief, across the U.S. Border and into the Canadian frontier.

It would be more than twenty years after fighting Sitting Bull that Hamilton came to Baltimore and became the successor to the great Marshal Jacob Frey. Frey was no slouch, having led Baltimore Police into riots the same way he himself had gone

into battle against Indians, while helping to lead America to the Western Frontier.

If we were to list the accomplishments of Jacob Frey we could write another book. On the short list, he brought us paddy wagons, call boxes, organized the marine unit, added the Maryland Seal to our badges, and other uniform accessories. Frey was our first Medal of Honor recipient. He had great respect for our city and our police department. We invite you to surf through the BaltimorePoliceHistory.com site to learn more about the things he accomplished.

Samuel T. Hamilton was our Marshal from Oct 7, 1897 to Oct 7, 1901.

7 October - 1944 - Helmet Type Hats

Today in Baltimore Police History, 1944, Baltimore police switched from the round or oval top police caps that were worn for a little more than 30 years after the "Bobby Cap" type helmet, to the current "Octagonal" or "Eight Point" hat we wear today.

1886 – Under direction of Jacob Frey and Commissioner Carr, The Police Helmet, (Bobby Cap) worn in other cities, was made part of the uniform in Baltimore. (It was introduced by Commissioner Alford J. Carr. Taking the place of the derby formerly worn by Baltimore police. Commissioner Carr specified that the black helmet was to be worn in the winter, and the pearl gray helmet worn during summer months. The helmet at that time was significant of rank, only patrolmen and sergeants wore it. The Marshal and his Deputy Marshal as well as all Captains and Lieutenants wear the regular cap of the period. Similar to that worn by the Fire Department, known today as a Bell cap/hat)

1908 – 7 Nov, 1908 After 22 years, The Baltimore Police Department stopped using the Police Helmet, (Bobby Cap), and chose a more modern round, or oval top, police hat.

From the Baltimore Sun - The Baltimore Police go from the Bobby Type Helmet to the more modern cap and Officers donned new uniforms, veteran Captains returned to old Districts, caps supplant helmets and Espantoons are in use once again.

1944 – 7 Oct, 1944 The Baltimore police switches from the round, or oval top police caps that were worn for nearly 30 years after the "Bobby Cap" type helmet was introduced, to the current "Octagonal" or "Eight point" hat we wear today.

9 October - 1936

On this day in Baltimore Police History, 1936 we lost our brother, Police **Officer Leo Bacon**. His death came during surgery resulting from a Line of Duty injury that occurred sometime some four years earlier. The details of this injury and the circumstances of intervening four years were not clear from the information we were able to ascertain. However, information drawn from correspondence between Commissioner Charles D. Gaither and the Law Offices of Hargest, LeViness, Duckett and McGlannan on 26 February, 1932 indicates that Officer Bacon was injured while helping move a semaphore (a traffic signaling device) through traffic at the intersection of Eutaw and Saratoga Streets.

Officer Bacon, assigned to the Traffic Division, was on duty directing this movement. During this incident, Officer Bacon somehow received an injury to his kidneys – we have been unable to determine exactly how the injury was sustained or what type of injury it was. However, it is known that the injury continued to aggravate him until he was finally forced to seek the medical advice of a doctor.

After initial treatment for the injury, it continued to disturb him, and Dr. A. J. Gillis made a diagnosis of epididymitis (a medical condition characterized by discomfort and pain in the epididymis, or testicle) on Officer Bacon's right side.

Officer Bacon was also diagnosed with a stone in the left kidney severe enough to warrant emergency surgery. Dr. Gillis believed that this was also related to the accident and injury sustained on in February of 1932.

That surgery caused the officer's passing as a result of pneumonia on 9 October, 1936. The Department awarded Line of Duty Death benefits to Mrs. Leo Bacon in January 1937.

As his brothers and sisters of the Baltimore Police Department we will not let him be forgotten. His service honored the City of Baltimore, and the Baltimore Police Department. May he rest in peace, and may God bless him.

8 October - 1985

On this day in Baltimore Police History 1985 we lost our brother, **Officer Richard J. Lear** to an auto accident based on the following:

Shortly after 11:00 pm alarms sounded at several locations in the 5300 block of York Road. A marked police vehicle responded as did foot Officer Richard Lear. To get to the scene, Officer Lear had to cross several lanes of York Road, and as he crossed one of the lanes he was struck by a northbound vehicle traveling well above the posted speed limit. The driver never stopped.

Doctors at Sinai Hospital pronounced Officer Lear dead just before midnight. Meanwhile, miles away in Baltimore County, police stopped a vehicle which they saw was being driven in an erratic manner. The operator was arrested. A short time later, a civilian who knew of the traffic accident that killed Officer Lear spotted the car that killed him in a parking lot and notified Baltimore County police who, in turn, called Baltimore Police Accident Investigators to the scene.

The automobile was seized and transported to the Baltimore Police Headquarters building for processing, and as a result of the investigation, charges of automobile manslaughter, leaving the scene of an accident, driving while intoxicated, and excessive speed were filed against a 29 year old Baltimore resident.

Officer Richard Lear was a veteran of 31 years on the department.

Local newspaper report; dated 13 October, 1985

For over 30 years, Officer Richard J. Lear wore the badge of a Baltimore Police Officer. He walked his beat in the North Baltimore neighborhoods of Hampden and Remington, and he wasn't flashy or dynamic, but he was dedicated to the oath he had taken, and he loved his job.

My bet would be that after 30 years, and still on the beat, still working a foot post, he had a lot of respect for the job, and as for being "flashy or dynamic," that probably left him 10 or 15 years earlier after having completed 15 or 20 years on the job. In most cases, walking a foot beat for 30 years is flashy and dynamic enough. God bless him, he was one of our own.

As his brothers and sisters of the Baltimore Police Department we will not let him be forgotten. His service honored the City of Baltimore, and the Baltimore Police Department. May he rest in peace, and may God bless him.

9 October - 1957

On this day in Baltimore Police History, 1957 we lost our brother, Police **Officer John F. Andrews** to an auto accident based on the following: At approximately 9:50 am, on 9 October, 1957, Officer John Andrews was pursuing a vehicle that had been operating at a high rate of speed while in the 900 blk. of South Monroe Street. Officer Andrews was on a motorcycle with all of his emergency equipment activated and he was traveling at approximately 70 to 75 mph.

The officer was overtaking the speeder, the driver swerved in front of Officer Andrews, causing his motorcycle to jump the sidewalk and hit a cement wall. He was killed immediately. Officer Andrews served in the U.S. Navy from March 9, 1943 to February 5, 1946. He saw three years of combat in the Pacific.

As his brothers and sisters of the Baltimore Police Department we will not let him be forgotten. His service honored the City of Baltimore, and the Baltimore Police Department. May he rest in peace, and may God bless him.

10 October - 1989

On this day in Baltimore Police History, 1989 we lost our brother, Police **Officer William J. Martin** to gunfire based on the following:

Two Central District officers were shot when they responded to a complaint of narcotics being sold in an apartment building in the 1500 block of Pennsylvania Avenue. Officer William J. Martin, 38, a ten-year veteran, entered the building and walked up a flight of stairs to the second floor landing where he encountered two subjects, a 21 year-old and a 20 year-old suspect who without warning or provocation shot Officer Martin twice in the head, and once in the left shoulder. He died at the Shock Trauma Unit at University Hospital.

Detectives believe that the suspects then ran to the lower level in an attempt to escape through a rear door, where they encountered Officer Herman L. Brooks, Jr., 36. The two-year veteran had former police training and experience with the Philadelphia Police Department, and was covering the back of the building for just such an eventuality. Immediately upon their face-to-face confrontation at the rear door, the suspect began firing at the officer, and Officer Brooks returned fire.

During this furious exchange of gunfire, both the suspect and Officer Brooks were wounded.

As a result of this furious but brief gunfight, Officer Brooks was struck twice, once in the chest and the other in his left ring finger. He was treated for his wounds, and recovered. The suspect was wounded in the abdomen during the exchange. He was treated for his wounds and recovered.

Central District officers had responded to two previous calls at that address earlier that morning; one for a narcotics complaint and the second for a disorderly person.

The 21 year-old suspect was also arrested by officers as he attempted to escape from the building. Officers recovered a .38 caliber Colt automatic from the lower level hallway. Officer Herman Brooks, Jr.'s life was saved, the University Hospital doctors say, by the departmentally issued soft-body armor.

Both Will Martin and Herman Brooks were well liked, good police, and as such, we their brothers and sisters of the Baltimore Police Department will not let them or this incident be forgotten. Their service honored the City of Baltimore, and the Baltimore Police Department. May Officer Brooks rest in peace, and may God bless him.

11 October - 1857

Possibly the first Police Involved Shooting with Baltimore Police "Issued" firearms took place on this day, 11 October, 1857, based on the follow:

The officers involved were, Deputy Marshall Manly and Officers G.H.E. Bailey, Nicholson Saville, Lee George Bailey, Andrew Presto, and Chapman Englar.

Shot was Deputy Marshall Manly, the suspect that shot the Deputy Marshal was Andrew Hesslinger. He along with an African American, named Ramsey were both killed when police returned fire on the pair. The shooting took place in a bar called Seager's Lager Beer Brewery, at 7 o'clock on that Sunday, the establishment situated upon Frederick Road at its intersection with West Pratt Street.

Firearms were approved for issuance on 11 December 1856, but they were not purchased until 15 August, 1857, from there it could have taken from two weeks to a month to catalog and issue the firearms. Showing it to be a good chance that the first Police involved shooting with an "issued" firearm.

14 October - 1857

On this day in Baltimore Police History, 1857, we lost our brother, **Sergeant William Jourdan** to gunfire based on the following circumstances:

The 1800's were a mixing pot for Baltimore, made up of different nationalities that were struggling to find a political direction. A city divided into wards, there was literally fighting in the streets for control of everything from polling places to a political party.

There was the "No Nothing Party" and "The Democratic Party" in 1857 alone tons of arrests were made for people shooting at police officers. While the police were charged with keeping the peace and maintaining order, it didn't stop those they swore to protect from turning their guns on us, and police were shot at on a regular basis.

That day was like any other day in Baltimore – a confused society taking their misguided, misinformed political confusion out on the police. At the time, the police "ran" the city. The four member Board of Police Commissioners at that time was made up of Charles Howard, William H. Gatchell, Charles Hinks, and John W Davis. The Board itself was very political, and often these commissioners either went on to become Mayors, or were Mayors that later became police commissioners which ran the city government. It was frustrating to the people of Baltimore, a port town, made up of so many different nationalities, all vying for their place and for political power; some sort of identity and fair treatment, which they often felt they weren't getting from society.

It was in this environment that Sergeant William Jourdan fell victim to a bullet fired at him while keeping order at a polling place, when he was shot for no other reason than that he wore a badge and uniform of a Baltimore Police Officer. He wasn't out to arrest anyone, it wasn't a wanted person, a robber, or thief who shot him - it was a voter in the 5th ward at Gay and Front Street ready to cast his ballot, but several Democratic candidates withdrew their names from consideration for seats on the city council. This served to quiet some of the trouble that had been brewing, but it didn't stop shots from being fired at approx. 1:30 pm, with streets full of voters and political activists. A man on the roof of an omnibus fired a pistol into the crowd. He discharged several rounds, apparently without hitting anyone. Many of the onlookers chased after him, and the shooter ran through a store owned by Jehu Gorsush, at the corner of Front and Gay Street, then onto the roof of that store, and he finally escaped by descending trough an adjacent house. Once again, those in the street began fighting, and the situation demanded action by the police on the scene in order to prevent more fighting and a worsening riot.

Fortunately, for nearly everyone there, one of the groups involved in the fighting retreated down High Street toward French Street. Wanting the retreat to continue, police did all they could to maintain the push moving them further out of the area. As police encouraged the crowd to continue their move, the shots started up again, this time from a window of the Democratic headquarters, "Jackson Hall." One ball of the rounds struck Sgt. Jourdan, killing him within minutes. Lieutenant Carmichael took over, transporting Sgt. Jourdan's lifeless body to his home near Ann Street and Eastern Avenue. 250 or more police attended his funeral, they came from all four districts. At 3:00 pm on 15, October 1857, a procession led by fellow officers carried his body to the Baltimore Cemetery. When his death was reported in the Baltimore Sun, he was remembered as being "Faithful, full of a Zeal for good order, looking for "Peace" in our city"

There were seven people arrested and charged in this killing. They were, 1) M. J. Grady, 2) Henry Burns, 3) Jas. Fawcett, 4) Thomas Murray, 5) William Quinn, 6) Chas. Reilly and 7) Peter Ward, each indicted in Baltimore city for the murder of Sergeant William Jourdan, each as principal and each as an accessory to the murder. To day we have been unable to find documentation of the results of indictments.

As his brothers and sisters of the Baltimore Police Department we will not let him be forgotten. His service honored the City of Baltimore, and the Baltimore Police Department. May he rest in peace, and may God bless him.

14 October - 1994

On this day in Baltimore Police History, 1994, we lost our brother, **Sergeant Richard P. Harris** to an auto accident on his way home from work. He was attempting to make a U-turn on Pulaski Highway at the time, and was struck by a truck that had been traveling behind him.

The following was based on news reports at the time:

Police sergeant killed in crash on Pulaski Highway - October 15, 1994

Baltimore police yesterday were mourning an off-duty sergeant killed in a car crash being investigated as alcohol-related – one week after a Baltimore County officer died in a similar accident.

Sgt. Richard P. Harris, 35, a 13-year veteran who lived with his wife and three children in Parkville, was pronounced dead at the scene of the accident, which occurred about 5:45 am in the 6200 block of Pulaski Highway in east Baltimore. Sergeant Harris, driving a 1994 Ford Mustang, apparently tried to make a U-turn when he was broadsided by a pickup truck.

His passenger and colleague, Officer Jesse K. Schmidt, 38, who has been on the force for four years, suffered internal abdominal injuries and was listed in critical condition at Johns Hopkins Bayview Hospital.

Three others – two civilian passengers in Sergeant Harris' car and the truck's driver – also were injured. One remained in critical condition late yesterday; two others were resting at home.

The accident occurred exactly one week after Scott Michael Kern, a rookie Baltimore County police officer, died in an alcohol-related accident that left one colleague seriously injured and another charged with drunken driving.

All three officers had been at a Parkville bar called Strapps.

Investigators released few details of yesterday's accident. Sam Ringgold, a city police spokesman, said autopsy results were not available as of last night.

Traffic investigators found two beer bottles inside the sergeant's car, police said. A source close to the investigation said both officers had visited McCallister's bar in Northeast Baltimore after their shift ended at 11 pm until the 2 am closing time. Where they were between then and the accident was unknown, police said.

Maj. Bert Shirey, commander of the Northeastern District, where both officers were assigned, said, "Sergeant Harris was well liked and respected in the station house. He will be missed very much."

Sergeant Harris was assigned to the Northeastern District in 1990 upon his promotion. He supervised six officers assigned to foot and bicycle patrols in communities along Sinclair Lane.

"He was the kind of sergeant I liked because he got the job done," Major Shirey said. "Tell him what you want done and you are assured that you didn't have to follow up with him all the time."

Sergeant Harris is survived by his wife Phyllis, a 15-year-old daughter, and 11 and 7-year-old sons.

Family members said they did not want to talk about the accident. The sergeant's neighbor, John Irlbacher, a retired 25-year veteran of the Baltimore County Police Department, said the sergeant was "friendly with everyone in the neighborhood."

His death, Mr. Irlbacher said, choking back sobs, "hits a little hard."

The sergeant supervised Officer Schmidt, who patrolled on foot in the Hollander Ridge neighborhood. He has a wife and two children.

"He was just a very enthusiastic and dedicated officer," Major Shirey said. "He definitely made a difference in that neighborhood. I remember seeing him walking patrol with mud up to his belt. He said he had just chased a drug suspect through the woods. He was right back on patrol without cleaning himself up."

Police said the car driven by Sergeant Harris and a 1994 Chevrolet pickup driven by George E. Young, 37, of the 3800 block of Dunsmuir Circle in Middle River, were headed east on Pulaski Highway.

A police source said witnesses gave investigators two accounts. In one, Sergeant Harris tried to make a U-turn in front of the truck. In the other, the sergeant failed in his attempt to make a U-turn and was backing up in the street to complete the U-turn when his car was struck.

The police spokesman, Mr. Ringgold, said the pickup truck hit the Mustang near the driver's-side door.

Two other people in the Mustang also were injured. Colleen Sneed, 32, of the 4800 block of Richard Ave., a barmaid at McCallister's, was listed in critical condition at Bayview. Her roommate, Joseph Huff, 22, a cook at the bar, was treated and released from Franklin Square Hospital.

The driver of the truck, Mr. Young, also was treated and released from Franklin Square Hospital.

14 October - 2000

On this day in Baltimore Police History, 2000, we lost our brothers, **Sergeant Platt**, and **Officer Kevin McCarthy**, who were killed when their patrol car was broadsided in a Hamilton intersection by a drunk driver.

The two officers were on routine patrol in a residential area when the driver of a full size pickup truck failed to obey a stop sign and T-boned their radio car in an intersection where the officers had the right of way.

The impact caused the officer's patrol car to flip over and strike a utility pole. Both officers were killed instantly. Neither occupant of the pickup truck was injured. The driver of the vehicle was charged with DUI with other charges pending. The driver was found guilty of two counts of involuntary manslaughter and sentenced to two ten year sentences with all but six years suspended. In 2003, after serving just 3 years and 2 months of his sentence the driver of that vehicle was able to go home to his wife and kids, Sgt. Platt and Officer McCarthy's kids are still waiting to meet their dads – for them it will be a lifetime.

Sergeant Platt had been employed with the Baltimore City Police Department for 17 years, and is survived by his wife, 3-year-old daughter, and 4-year-old son.

Officer McCarthy had been employed with the Baltimore City Police Department for 15 years, and is survived by his 9-year-old daughter.

The Sun paper had a lot to say about the funeral of these two fine officers, as they reported the following:

"The deaths of these two police officers remind us not only of their vulnerability, but our own. And, when Mayor O'Malley offered his tender words of comfort, it took some of us back seven years, to another funeral, another slain policeman, and the randomness of life and death.

"That Officer's name was Herman Jones. He was a 23-year veteran in a job in which every day is a roll of the dice. However, the irony of his death, like Platt's and McCarthy's, was that it could have happened to anyone. Jones had gone into an East Baltimore carryout for an evening snack, where a couple teen-age kids that should have been home studying arithmetic pulled out a gun and shot him.

"Then on a summer morning at the Little Ark Missionary Baptist Church, they laid Herman Jones' body in an open casket for everyone to see, Herman Jones' wife Linda and his children were nearby, as a choir sang so hauntingly that it tore everybody in the place up with tears.

"The Mayor of Baltimore was there that day. They saved a front-row seat for Kurt L. Schmoke directly in front of Herman Jones' casket. The mayor looked at poor Jones and he heard the choir chanting its refrain, and you knew that something special was coming from Schmoke. The mayor was so much like Jones. They were kids who'd grown up in post-war America, each a product of the great civil rights movement, each a graduate of Baltimore City College, each a football player for the legendary coach, George Young. This one would come from Schmoke's heart.

"But nothing came.

"By the time the mayor reached the pulpit, he'd had time to think about all the killing in his city, and he'd had time to absorb the emotional singing, and all of the church's mourners with their grief coming out of their pores, and there was nothing he could summon.

"He muttered a few platitudes about the awfulness of killing, and the need for some national sense of urgency, and in a few moments he was done. Whatever passion he felt, he kept it to himself, and there were people who walked out of the Little Ark Missionary Baptist Church that morning feeling they had been cheated.

"Last week, the new mayor of Baltimore spoke quite beautifully. He called the funerals of police officers the toughest part of his job. However, the job is still new for Martin O'Malley. It has been his for less than a year. By the time of Herman Jones' funeral, Kurt L. Schmoke was five years into the job, and maybe 1,500 killings into it, and some of those killed were police officers of his city."

As their brothers and sisters of the Baltimore Police Department, we will not let them be forgotten. Their service honored the City of Baltimore, and the Baltimore Police Department. May they rest in peace, and may God always bless them.

15 October - 1885

Today in Baltimore Police History, 1885, Jacob Frey was appointed Marshal. He remained Baltimore's Marshal until July 12, 1897.

16 October - 1949

On this day in Baltimore Police History 1949 we lost our brother **Police Officer Thomas J. O'Neill** based on the following:

Officer O'Neill suffered a fatal cerebral hemorrhage after escorting an emergency Polio patient to Sydenham hospital at approximately 10 pm. Officers O'Neill, Kemmerzell, and Newman leapfrogged their motorcycles from intersection to intersection in order to get the patient to the hospital as quickly as possible without interruption. The escorted ambulance carrying the Polio patient to the hospital made it there safely, and in record time without incident. After the ambulance arrived at the hospital, the officers left to return to their posts. Officer O'Neill had trouble starting his bike (in 1949 they didn't have electric starters, he had to kick-start his bike), but he managed to catch up to the others an told them about his bike troubles and then made his way back over to his post near Lake Montebello. There can be a lot of stress in police work, often causing high blood pressure and heart trouble from the fast paced lifestyle we as police have to live. In O'Neill's case his body was found face down in the parking lot by a doctor, who realized he had an emergency medical condition so he rushed him into the Sydenham ER where doctors determined that his medical condition was more serious than they were equipped to handle, so they arranged for him to be escorted from Sydenham to Mercy Hospital.

A combination of factors, including the stress of the escort and the effort made to restart his motorcycle, induced a fatal cerebral hemorrhage. Doctors worked for hours to save the Officer O'Neill's life, but at 6:45 AM on October 16, 1949, Officer O'Neill died. Investigation revealed his death was duty related, and so his wife Helen was awarded his LOD pension.

As his brothers and sisters of the Baltimore Police Department we will not let him be forgotten. His service honored the City of Baltimore, and the Baltimore Police Department. May he rest in peace, and may God bless him.

16 October - 2010

We lost brother police **Detective Brian Stevenson**, off duty, and not line of duty, but nonetheless he was our brother, and he was murdered based on the following:

A 25-year-old Southeast Baltimore man has been charged with fatally injuring an off-duty Baltimore police detective by throwing a piece of concrete at the officer's head during an argument over a Canton parking space, according to police.

Detective Brian Stevenson, an 18-year veteran and married father of three, had gone out to have dinner on the eve of his birthday when he and Sian James got into an altercation in a private parking lot in the 2800 block of Hudson St. about 10 pm Saturday, police said. James was charged Sunday with first-degree murder.

James struck Stevenson in the left temple with a "fist-sized" concrete fragment, according to court records. Stevenson suffered "massive head injuries" and was taken to Johns Hopkins Bayview Medical Center, where he died about an hour before he was to have turned 38.

Colleagues who investigate violent crime in the city — much of it over petty disputes and perceived slights — were struggling to cope with Stevenson's death and were baffled by the circumstances. "All of them are terrible," Detective Thomas Jackson said of the city's killings. "But a parking space?"

Stevenson, who lived in Gwynn Oak, grew up in the city and as an officer investigated shootings and robberies in the Northeast District. He is the first city officer to die at the hands of another since Jan. 9, 2007, when Officer Troy Lamont Chesley Sr. was fatally shot during a robbery while he was off duty in Northwest Baltimore.

Rest in Peace to all of our brothers and sister in the BPD who have lost their lives to the senseless violence of this city. They will not be forgotten, as we their brothers and sisters will keep them in our memories

17 October - 1885

Today in Baltimore Police History, 17 October 1885, the department officially tested and put the call box into use. Box number 63, located at Franklin and Charles Streets, was the first to be installed and used.

Successful test of the new appliance in the middle district

The new police patrol system is now in working order at the central police station, North Street near Lexington

Street. The completion of this branch of police work places the department of Baltimore upon an equal footing with that of many other cities in the union. The system is unique and simple. Call boxes are placed at convenient intervals throughout the district.

They are about six feet high, painted red, and made of iron. They are divided into two sections. The upper section is provided with a telephone, which makes possible any verbal communications with the station. The lower section is provided with what may be termed an indicator dial.

When a policeman on his beat needs the assistance of the station he is able by the indicator dial to tell plainly what he wants. The indicator looks like a compass; the needle is the guide for the patrolman using the box. If he wants the wagon, he places the needle on the word wagon and turns the lever on the indicator. This is registered at the station. If he wants the help of additional officers, he can place the needle to suit this purpose.

The call of an officer on a beat is answered from the station by the use of a lever, which rings a bell in the call box. A piece of tape [ticker type tape] makes known to the station the needs of an officer on a beat.

The wagon is located in a stable opposite the central station house. Communication between the station and the stable is made to the ringing of a bell. The workings of the stable are on the same order as those at the firehouse.

The wagon is a combination of beauty and convenience. In its design and workmanship, it is very attractive. It is 11 feet long, and 4'9" wide. It resembles the salvage corpse wagon. The wheels and running gear were red the body is black. It is furnished with a folding stretcher, so the wagon can be turned into an ambulance. The entrance is at the rear. A silver-plated rod surmounts the seat as a protector. The horses, which will be used to tow the wagon, are coal black. They are possessed with great strength. The wagon bears the words, "Central Police Patrol No. 1" on each side.

Police officers David McClellan, Edward Meehan, Thomas W. Mills and James A. Kelly were first to take charge of the wagon.

There will be a day and night relief. The object of the system is to render the officers working beats assistance. Instead of leaving a beat unprotected for any length of time, as in the case of a stupid drunk, or troublesome prisoner, the wagon comes into use.

There are 58 call boxes in the Central District, located as follows:

Baltimore and Calvert, Baltimore and Charles, Lombard and Hanover, Baltimore and Liberty, Pratt and Howard, Pratt and Light, Gay and 2nd, Pratt and Frederick, Pratt and East Falls Ave., Eastern Avenue and Mill, Norfolk Steamboat Company, Union dock, City dock, Canton Avenue and W. Falls Ave., Central Avenue and Pratt, Central Avenue and Baltimore, Lombard and Albemarle, Baltimore and Exeter, Chestnut and Fayette, Chestnut and Douglas, Asquith and Orleans, Front and Fayette, Baltimore and Harrison, Gay and Saratoga, Gay and Exeter, Western Maryland Depot (Hillen Street,) Chestnut and Jones Falls, Gay and Forrest, Asquith and Madison, Front and Forrest, Eager and Greenmount Avenue, Eager and Jones Falls, Preston and Greenmount Avenue, Federal and Greenmount Avenue, Boundary Avenue and Greenmount Avenue, Lanvale and Calvert, Boundary Avenue and Charles, Boundary Avenue and Jones Falls, Charles and Jones falls, Calvert and Preston, Chase Street and Hargrove Alley, Preston and Cathedral, Chase and Cathedral, Charles and Read, Richman and Park, Calvert and Madison, Charles Street and Peabody Alley, Center and Park, Saratoga and Park, Saratoga and Charles, Franklin and Charles, Franklin and Calvert, North and Bath, Pleasant and Calvert.

The Police Officials made a very satisfactory test of the system on Saturday night [17 Oct 1885]. Box 63, Franklin and Charles Streets, was used first. A call was turned in, and four minutes later, the wagon was at the box.

Those who saw the test were police Commissioner George Colton and Jay. D. Ferguson, ex-Commissioner John W. Davis, Marshal Jacob Frey, Deputy Marshal John Lannan, Captains Delaney, Farnan and Cadwellader, fire Commissioner Samuel Kirk, J. Frank Morrison and a number of detectives. The system was put up by the southern electric company, of which Mr. J. Frank Morrison is agent. Marshal Frey was particularly pleased with the system, and believes it will greatly enhance the efficiency of the department.

17 October - 1895

On this day in Baltimore Police History, we lost our brother, **Police Officer John J. Dailey** to gunfire based on the following:

As the result of arresting three men during a struggle at Charles and Conway Streets, Officer Dailey walked to a local doctor to have first aid applied to what he thought was superficial scrapes. On route, he felt blood trickling down his back, but didn't pay it much attention as he continued along his way. While at the doctors it was discovered that Officer Dailey had been shot in the small of his back, he was advised to go to the hospital.

At this point, he walked back to the station house where a horse and wagon was waiting to take him to University Hospital. There a staff Doctor advised him that his wound was serious, and could prove fatal. Officer Dailey felt it was not that serious, after all he just walked to a doctor, and then to the station where he was then driven to the Hospital, and he insisted on going home.

The shooting of officer Dailey occurred on August 26, 1895, he would eventually die of blood poisoning on this day, 17 October, 1895.

From an 1895 *News Article* entitled "His Dying Statement"

This is a story which the patrolmen's brother and sister told on the witness stand at a Towson court house. The defense tried to have the testimony excluded, but failed.

The Dying Statement of Patrolman John J. Dailey, of Baltimore, to the effect that Roger Dougherty, Patrick Kane, and John Diviney killed him, was admitted as evidence yesterday at a Towson court house where the trial of the three men was continued.

The statement was repeated by the dead man's brother, William Dailey, who is a member of the Baltimore Fire Department, and by his Sister Mrs. Baunah Frank.

Firemen Daily visited the wounded patrolman twice a day while the latter was at the hospital and three times a day when he was at his home. Wednesday, October 16th the day before the patrolman died, his brother was with him in the morning, when the sick man said he was dying and requested the brother to send for a Doctor...

It was the testimony of Firemen Daily that he tried to reassure the suffering man, but the latter replied, "No Bill, the death pain has struck me. I will not live to see Sunday."

"Tell me all about the shooting then," implored William Dailey. "I was on the east side of Charles Street," said the dying man according to his brother's testimony, "When the three men came down the street, making a disturbance on the opposite side. I crossed over and warned them to stop. Dougherty called me an Irish _____ and I grabbed him to arrest him. With that Kane grabbed my club and struck me over the head, knocking me down. I was trying to get up from my hands and knees when Diviney kicked me. Kane then yelled to Dougherty get his pistol and give it to him. Dougherty took the pistol out of my pocket and shot me in the back."

Corroborated by Mrs. Frank

Mrs. Frank was called to the stand and repeated the statement almost word for word as it was given by her brother, before Justice Schenkel arrived to take a sworn statement of the dying man. These two witnesses said that the Patrolman became unconscious. The next morning he died without having regaining consciousness.

Trying to exclude testimony

While the brother and sister were on the stand the crowd in the courtroom was still; the jury leaning forward in their seats to catch every word, and the three prisoners showing more interest in the proceeding than they had before expressed in the matter. The testimony of the two witnesses had not been admitted until nearly an hour had been consumed in an effort by the prisoners and lawyers to have it excluded. William Campbell Duncan read authorities as to the admission in testimony of dying statements, and asserted that the charge of Patrolman Dailey was not made when he was in fear of death. Another argument was that he was not responsible for this statement because it was made when his mind was clouded by opiates that had been administered to deaden of the excruciating pain that he suffered. The brother's interest in securing a conviction was also alluded to.

His Mind Was Clear

The foundation of the statement had been carefully laid by the authorities for the prosecution, State's Attorney John Kansan of Baltimore County, and State's Attorney Duff of Baltimore City. Patrolman Dailey sister and brother were recalled by them to say that his mind was clear, and that on the day the statement was made a dose of opiate mixer had not been given to him until after he had made a declaration as to the guilt of the prisoners and when his pain became so great that he begged for relief.

The Evidence is Admitted

Judge Fowler said in ruling on the objection that the state has shown that Dailey's mind was clear and that he believed he was about to die. We can do nothing else but admit the testimony. It is for the jury to determine as to its value and truth.

The Patrolman's Widow

The patrolman's widow, Mrs. Magee Dailey, stated that her husband announced on the day before his death that he was dying. She was overcome by grief and immediately left the room, just as she heard him say, "Dougherty did it."

Mr. and Mrs. Dailey had been married 30 years and had four children of whom the eldest is a boy of 10 and the others girls, the youngest being 18 months old.

As his brothers and sisters of the Baltimore Police Department we will not let him be forgotten. His service honored the City of Baltimore, and the Baltimore Police Department. May he rest in peace, and may God bless him.

17 October - 1914

On this evening in 1914, **Policewoman Elizabeth Faber** and her partner, **Patrolman George W. Popp** of the Northwest police district were shot on the west end of the Edmondson Avenue bridge by a black male as they attempted to effect his arrest for being a pickpocket. As they approached to arrest him, the suspect suddenly turned and opened fire on the pair. Policewoman Faber was shot in the chest, and Patrolman Popp was wounded in the side and in the thigh.

A newspaper at the time reported, "Little hope was entertained at Franklin Square Hospital for her recovery. At 4 am her recovery chances seemed even less possible. At midnight her deposition was taken by Justice Schirm, and will be used in case of her death, which at the time seemed more than likely."

Officer Pop was also severely wounded and while at the hospital his chances for recovery were listed as good. Policewoman Faber was the first female officer to be shot in the line of duty, and she nearly died as a result of her injuries. A year later she resigned her post as a Baltimore Policewoman. It should be noted that she was a tough cookie, one of the smallest of the female officers (and there weren't many) of her time. She was also one of the most active, often fighting men nearly twice her size.

She later made a full recovery, but retired because of both injuries and stress brought on by the shooting – she was the first female officer to have been shot in the line of duty

History lesson: *The first female officer hired by the Baltimore Police Department was Mary S. Harvey, on June 19, 1912, followed by Margaret B. Eagleston on July 22, 1912. It was in 1937 when Mrs. Whyte became the fifth woman hired by the department that she also became the first ever-black person hired by the Baltimore Police Department. However, not only didn't Mrs. Whyte ever wear a uniform, but she also never carried a gun.*

In fact, none of the first five women hired as policewomen even had any training in the handling or use of firearms. It was not until March 28, 1925, some eleven years after Policewoman Faber was shot that any of the female officers were finally trained and provided with a firearm.

That was the first date that any female members of department were given their first lesson in pistol shooting. The newspaper wrote at the time, "Baltimore policewomen yesterday received their first lesson in the use of firearms. Lieutenant James O. Downes, expert marksman and instructor of the Baltimore Police Department's Pistol Team, explained the use of pistols to policewomen Mrs. Mary J. Bruff and Miss Margaret B. Eagleston. Several minutes after their training began at the Central police station the basement of the building resounded with sharp reports (sounds of gunfire) as efforts were made to pierce the 'Bull's-eye.' The target was 6 feet in distance from the policewomen. Other policewomen will receive their first lessons next week. The distance of the target will be increased as Lieutenant Downes plans to make each of the five into 'Expert Shots.' With the exception of Mrs. Mary Harvey, none of the policewomen are familiar with firearms. The others to be trained next week are Miss Eva Aldridge and Ms. Mildred Campbell."

20 October - 1851 - 1st Issue Badge

The first known metallic badge worn by Baltimore Police Officers was also known as the **1st Issue badge**. It was a large six pointed star with Baltimore's official city seal, the War of 1812 "Battle Monument" over the year 1797 – that being the year Baltimore City was incorporated. This design element was inscribed in an oval center. Also within this oval center, across the top and sides were the words "City Police."

Reissued in 1997 to celebrate our 200th Anniversary, officers at that time purchased this badge and wore it for that year only.

From a Baltimore Sun Article dated - 21 October 1851

The Stars – The badge designed to be worn by the city police was displayed yesterday (Monday 20 Oct 1851) for the first time by Officers Mckinley and Callaway, who were in special attendance at the hall of the Maryland Institute. The new badge, the first known metallic badge for city officers, consists of a heavily gilded, brightly burnished six point star, in the center of which is seen a correct representation of the Battle Monument, surrounded by the words "City Police." Underneath was the date "1797" – the date of our city's charter. The star is worn on the left the lapel of the coat, and is very conspicuous.

20 October – 2010

On this day in Baltimore Police History, 2010 we lost our brother, **Police Officer Thomas Portz Jr.** to an auto accident based on the following:

Police Officer Tommy Portz was killed in an automobile accident when his patrol car struck the back of a parked firetruck on the highway, US Route 83, better know locally as the Jones Fall Expressway. The firetruck had responded to reports of an injured person lying helpless on the side of the highway median strip. The truck stopped in the left lane to investigate. Officer Portz's patrol car was traveling at a high rate of speed in an effort to back-up a fellow officer when he struck the back of the parked fire truck, which caused the fatal injuries. There were no known injuries to any of the firefighters.

Officer Portz had served with the Baltimore Police Department for nearly 10 years. He is survived by his wife and three children.

As his brothers and sisters of the Baltimore Police Department, we will not let him be forgotten. His service honored the City of Baltimore and the Baltimore Police Department. May he rest in peace, and may God bless him.

22 October - 1971

22 October 1971 – The Charles D. Gaither (police boat) is retired from the Police Department and starts a new career as a fire boat.

22 October - 1987

Today in Baltimore Police History, 1987 our Brother **Officer Eugene Cassidy** was shot in the head at point blank range leaving him blinded in the process… based Sun Paper Articles – *A man was charged in shooting of city policeman.*

Oct 24, 1987, *Man is charged in shooting and blinding of city policeman*

An 18-year-old alleged cocaine dealer, accused of shooting a city police officer twice in the head at point-blank range late Thursday night, was charged with attempted murder last night after turning himself into police.

Agent Eugene J. Cassidy, 27, who had approached a group of people on the street while patrolling the Western district, remained in critical condition at the Maryland shock trauma Center, where he underwent six hours of neurosurgery and reconstruction of the bones in his face.

Doctors were able to remove only one of the two bullets in the officer's head.

Anthony Terrel Owens, who just a week ago was arrested on charges of distributing cocaine, turned himself in at the central district shortly after 8 pm shooting.

Police reported that the teenager's mother persuaded him to surrender.

Police began searching for Mr. Allen about 6 pm after a full day of questioning witnesses who were taken into custody after the 11 pm shooting.

Police gave Mr. Owens address as the 3900 block of Penn Hearst Avenue in Northwest Baltimore.

By early yesterday evening, police had pieced together this account of the shooting;

Agent Cassidy had just filed a report at his district and returned to patrol duty when he saw a crowd of 20 to 25 persons at the corner of North Appleton and Mosher streets.

"The officer parked his patrol car on Appleton and walked about 90 feet, around the corner of Moser," said police spokesman Dennis S. Hill.

"He apparently had no idea it was not a crowd idly standing on the corner, it was someone selling cocaine," Mr. Hill said.

He also did not draw his gun, but one man in the crowd "Off the officer and pulled his weapon. The gun was 1, 1½ feet from the officer's head when he pulled the trigger."

The officer "reeled back against the wall. The gunman lowered the gun and walked up to him puts the gun to the left side of his head and pulled the trigger" a second time, "the crowd all scattered," Mr. Hill said.

Agent Cassidy was hit in the left cheek and the left temple.

An unidentified caller notified police at 11:06 pm that the officer was hurt, officer Cassidy apparently had not notified his dispatcher when he left his patrol car and approached the crowd.

Agent Cassidy, who had recently married and moved to Carroll County, had been assigned to the Western district since 1983, when he joined the force.

His title is police agent, rather than officer, because he had a college degree, and that designation gave him equal rank but a slightly higher salary than an officer.

"He was one of the more well-liked officers in the Western," said Sgt. Ernest Judd, "and not everyone at the Western is well-liked,"

Sgt. Bert Ricasa, who supervised Agent Cassidy for some time, described him as "an easy-going guy, happy-go-lucky, most of the officers from his shift stayed over last night and helped with whatever they could do," he said

"He is a fine young man and a good officer – a very good police officer, very thorough, very dedicated," added Lieutenant James W. Madigan acting commander at the Western district.

Through the day, rumors and reports about the officer's condition changed from hopeful to discouraging and back again, but Mr. Hill said it will be "a couple days before they can make a prognosis."

Mr. Hill said he remained hopeful because Agent Cassidy "is a young person in extremely excellent, excellent physical condition."

23 October - 1955

On this day in Baltimore Police History, 1955, we lost our brother **Sergeant James Purcell** to gunfire based on the following;

Sergeant Purnell was shot twice with his own service revolver on a Sunday morning 23 October 1955 during a scuffle with burglar Ronald A. King, in a house at 134 W. Lanvale Street in the Central District. King was killed as he was trying to escape and ran into Officers Leroy Prediger, and Richard Doda. The paroled convict King was still armed with Sgt. Purcell's service revolver and as such, was fired on by Prediger and Doda. The two Northwest officers were initially charged with King's death, but later released to the custody of their Captain, Millard Horton, by Judge Joseph Byrnes following a Habeas Corpus Action.

ASA Preston A. Pairo Jr. reported that an investigation had thus failed to show which of the two had fired the shot that caused King's death... in 1955 they didn't have today's technology (or apparent common sense, as these officers shouldn't have been arrested, they should have been awarded a medal). Sergeant Purcell was acting Lieutenant at the time of his death due to an incident that occurred while working the cellblock. Commissioner Hepbron forgave him of the cellblock incident and obtained the permission of Governor Theodore McKeldin to restore Purcell's Sergeant Powers. During his time as an officer/sergeant Purcell had been awarded several commendations for his hard work and willingness to put the job before himself.

As his brothers and sisters of the Baltimore Police Department, we will not let him be forgotten; his service honored the City of Baltimore, and the Baltimore Police Department. May he rest in peace, and may God bless him.

23 October - 1973

The Evidence Control Unit became the central evidence repository within the department. This unit has the sole responsibility for safeguarding, accounting for, and disposing of non-departmental property that has come into the department's custody. It also acts as the lost and found portion of the department.

24 October - 1978

Baltimore Police promoted the first female Police Major, Lt. Patricia Mullen, elevated two grades as she became Major Patricia Mullen. Promoted from Lieutenant of the Homicide Unit, Major Mullen was put in charge of Youth Section.

24 October - 1987

Baltimore Public Housing Projects were patrolled by "Baltimore Housing Authority Police" a police agency that was State funded and took over private security in the projects of Baltimore city. It initially was patrolled by 15 officers and 6 supervisors. Part of REACT (Responsible Enforcement and Aggressive Community Training) officers, which was designed to eliminate drug trafficking at the 53 public housing projects. These officers trained with City Police, under Maryland Training Commission guidelines.

27 October - 1975

On this day in Baltimore Police History 27 Oct 1975 we lost our brother **Police Officer Timothy Ridenour** to gunfire based on the following: Southwestern District Police Officers Timothy Ridenour and Bernard Harper received a call indicating a man was running nude in the 4400 Blk. of Old Frederick Road. Arriving on the scene they found the suspect, wearing only a shirt, walking around in a grassy area, which is out of view of the thoroughfare.

The man had been placing Christmas decorations on a tree growing in the apartment complex. As the officers approached the man, the suspect bolted past them and sat down on the passenger side of their patrol car. He bounced out again, and ran toward the front steps of his apartment where he apparently began moving a sofa, which had been sitting partly on the grass. As the officers approached he turned and raised his hands in a defensive position, as would a pugilist before a match, he was in a defensive position seemingly ready to ward off the expected blows of his opponent.

Officer Harper explained to the suspect that they were there to help him and not fight or injure him. Officer Harper had already requested back up units. At this point the suspect, who never uttered a word to the officers throughout the entire incident, pointed to Officer Ridenour's service revolver. Officer Ridenour checked the holster strap, assuring that the weapon was secure. The suspect then reached for the weapon. A scuffle ensued as Officer Harper succeeded in pulling the suspect away from the younger officer who dodged through a hedge in order to obtain a better position. The suspect followed, pouncing on Officer Ridenour, tripping him over a hedge. Frantic efforts were made by Officer Harper to pull the suspect away from the downed officer but his efforts failed.

As he recovered from being pushed off the suspect himself he observed the suspect with Officer Ridenour's service revolver, firing point blank into his partners head. Back up Officers arrived as the suspect and Officer Harper traded shots. The officers fired several rounds while Officer Harper retrieved a shotgun from his vehicle and approached the suspect who was attempting to reload Officer Ridenour's weapon with round he was taking from the gun belt of Ridenour's lifeless body. Demands to drop the revolver were shouted at and ignored by the suspect. Then as the suspect leveled the weapon once again at Officer Harper, a single round was fired from the shotgun. When the incident was over, a civilian who had attempted to assist the officers had been shot once. His condition was listed as "serious" but stable.

The medical staff at Saint Agnes Hospital tried vainly to save the life of Officer Ridenour but it was to no avail. Officer Ridenour died in the hospital's emergency room at 1706 hours. The 32-year old assailant, who had a history of mental problems, was pronounced dead at the scene of the incident.

Newspaper Article - Nov 1, 1975

Police honor fallen officer, while across town, Ridenour rites attract big crowd

More than 1,000 law officers from all over Maryland and at least three other states filed silently by a mahogany-stained hardwood coffin in a South Baltimore funeral

establishment yesterday to pay final tribute to Officer Timothy B. Ridenour, who was shot to death on a routine call Monday.

The brief, halting words of the priest conducting the prayer service seemed to reflect the mood of the policemen, the dignitaries and the family of the 26-year-old rookie officer:

"He came to serve, not to be served," the Rev. Joseph F. Martel said. "Through the example of his life and his death, we can ask ourselves to be of service to each other."

Five blocks of East Fort Avenue flanking the McCully funeral establishment were closed off before 8am as sparkling police cruisers from every district began filling the street three abreast.

The slain patrolman's wife, Kathleen Stallings Ridenour, and her oldest son were last out of the funeral chapel after the quiet services. They sat in a limousine with the patrolman's mother, Mrs. Mary Ridenour, while the coffin was wheeled two blocks past an honor guard of officers.

A motorcycle escort led the hundreds of cars through the center of Baltimore, creating traffic jams for an hour and trapping at least one fire truck, on Pratt street bound for a small fire.

The motorcade wound north up Falls road and into the colorful, rich countryside near Timonium, a far cry in distance and atmosphere from the beat In Southwest Baltimore where Patrolman Ridenour died.

He was buried in near silence in the small cemetery under the oak trees behind Mays Chapel Methodist Church, where his family has a burial plot.

As his brothers and sisters of the Baltimore Police Department we will not let him be forgotten. His service honored the City of Baltimore and the Baltimore Police Department. May he rest in peace, and may God bless him.

27 October - 1978

On this day in Baltimore Police History, 1978, we lost our Brother, **K9 Officer Nelson F. Bell** to gunfire based on the following;

On October 22, 1978, shortly after 8:00 pm a Trailways security guard approached two Central District officers and reported that an armed man was menacing citizens at the rear of the downtown Trailways Bus Terminal. The officers quickly passed through the crowded terminal and exited to the bus loading area where they confronted the suspect, who was armed with a rifle.

As the suspect raised the weapon to a firing position, the Central Officers sought cover behind a parked bus. They then ordered the suspect to drop his weapon. He refused and continued to aim at one of the officers. At this point, the officers fired as the suspected retreated into a dark shadow. The officers notified the dispatcher of the situation at hand. Other units immediately began responding, including K-9 Officer Nelson F. Bell.

Officers who began arriving at the scene heard several shots and fellow officers pleading with the suspect to drop his weapon. As they inched their way through three narrow alleyways, which accessed the bus loading area, they observed the officers seeking cover as the suspect threatened them with various weapons. The events were moving quickly; the suspect was not responding to the efforts of the officers who were trying to calm the situation. Two officers began climbing the nearby rooftop in an effort to obtain an advantageous position should additional application of deadly force become necessary. Before they could get to their destination, the suspect, armed with a bow and arrow, lunged at the officers. There was a volley of shots involving several of the many officers who had responded. The suspect went down. Officers went to the suspect's side in order to provide first aid. The suspect was dead. At this time, an officer noticed that Officer Bell had been shot. He sustained a massive head wound and lay bleeding thirty feet from the suspect. He was transported to University of Maryland's Shock Trauma Unit where teams of medical specialists worked to save his life. The injuries were too massive and after five days of treatment on 27 Oct 1978 he died. The question of where the fatal shot came from may never be answered. Officer Bell's position was such that he was not in direct line of fire from any of those Officers who were involved. It may very well have been that he was hit by a shot ricocheting from the tall brick walls, which surrounded the bus loading area. Since the suspect was armed only with a bow and arrow at the time, it was likely a police bullet may have found Officer Bell.

As his brothers and sisters of the Baltimore Police Department we will not let him be forgotten, his service honored the City of Baltimore, and the Baltimore Police Department. May he rest in peace, and may God bless him.

29 October - 1936

On this day in Baltimore Police History, 1936 we lost our brother, **Police Officer Carroll Hanley** in an auto accident based on the following:

Officer Hanley placed a well-dressed man under arrest in the back of a Chevrolet, 10 E. North Avenue, when the suspect hopped in the front seat and sped away. Officer Hanley jumped onto the closest side running board of the vehicle as the car sped through rush hour traffic trying to shake him. Officer Hanley held on for a little more than three blocks but was eventually flung from the car to his death when the driver made a sharp left turn from 20th Street to Hargrove alley.

Newspapers reports:

On 31 October 1936 - The search for Officer Hanley's Killer widened. Authorities of Pennsylvania, Delaware and D. C. asked to help Baltimore Police. Still lacking any definite clue to the slayer in this case, police extend their search to neighboring States; their search for the driver of the automobile from which Patrolman Carroll F. Hanley was thrown to his death, were accepting the offered help of these neighboring agencies.

The casting of a wider net in 1936 pays off, as police in Washington DC nab a suspect based on the following:

On 2 Nov 1936 - *The Baltimore Newspapers reported:*

A 35-year-old advertising agent was arrested in a Washington rooming house yesterday (1 Nov) and held for being the suspected driver of the automobile from which Police Officer Carroll F. Hanley was thrown to his death on 20th Street at Hargrove Alley on Thursday morning. After a brief interview the salesman/suspect admitted to driving the car that caused officer Hanley's death, he went on to tell investigators he was in the rooming house since that Thursday night and that if he could take it all back he would.

On 3 Nov 1936 - The *Baltimore Newspapers reported* the following:

George K. Shea, 35-year-old advertising solicitor, was held without bail in the Central Police Station last night while awaiting the action of the grand jury, which tomorrow will hear allegations that he drove the automobile from which Patrolman Carroll F. Hanley was thrown to his death on Thursday, then drove straight to the DC Rooming house after killing Officer Hanley.

A day later, on the 4th of November, 1936 – The *Baltimore News reported:*

Shea was held for the Officer Hanley Death. The Coroner found the Patrolman was "Deliberately Thrown from Auto" George Shea made several quick turns back and forth, from side to said, in order to shake, and throw him from the vehicle, in order to help facilitate his escape.

Police waited on a Grand Jury Action. On advice of his counsel, George Shea refused to testify on make statements at his inquest.

Coroner Hubert last night reached a verdict that the death of Patrolman Carroll, last Thursday was due to being intentionally thrown from the running board of Shea's moving automobile as it was being driven by Mr. George K. Shea. This was the testimony given to the Grand Jury by Baltimore Coroner Mr. Hubert.

On 1 Dec 1936 – Last night he began serving a five-year term in the Maryland Penitentiary after being found guilty of manslaughter in the death of Patrolman Carroll Hanley.

November 2nd 1936 Funeral Services were held for Officer Hanley in attendance were all of his brothers and sisters of the Baltimore Police Department, along with his wife Katherine and his 5 children, Robert, Angela, Thomas M. Carroll & Albert E. Hanley.

As his brothers and sisters of the Baltimore Police Department we will not let him be forgotten, His service honored the City of Baltimore, and the Baltimore Police Department. May he rest in peace, and may God bless him.

30 October – 1998

On this day in Baltimore Police History, 1998 we lost our brother, **Police Officer Harold Jerome Carey** to an auto accident based on the following;

A Baltimore police officer's call for help led to an accident in which a police van and a cruiser collided at a midtown intersection, killing an officer and injuring two others.

Officer Harold J. Carey, a 28-year old Douglass High School graduate who studied engineering before joining the force six years ago, was killed instantly in the crash that sent the police paddy wagon skidding on its side and into the air, until it came to rest on the wall of a senior citizen's high-rise.

The crushed van landed on top of a parked and running Chevrolet Monte Carlo, injuring its owner, who was sitting in the driver's seat. It took firefighters an hour to extricate Carey and the wagon driver, Officer Keith Owens, who suffered injuries to his head, and spine. The officers were on the way to help a fellow officer who was struggling with a man on North Avenue and Charles Street.

Officer Carey was described by Lieutenant Joesph A. Chianca Jr. as a "good officer" who "really cared for the people in the community he served." Officer Carey was awarded a bronze star in 1993 for shooting a man that was armed with a .357 Magnum.

As his brothers and sisters of the Baltimore Police Department, we will not let him be forgotten. His service honored the City of Baltimore, and the Baltimore Police Department. May he rest in peace, and may God bless him.

31 October - 1935

On this day in Baltimore Police History, 1935, we lost our brother, **Police Officer Arthur H. Malinofski** to gunfire based on the following:

Officer Malinofski was discovered several feet from his patrol car dead from two gunshot wounds. A milkman discovered the body lying on the ground on Main Avenue near Gwynn Oak Avenue at approximately 4 am According to news reports at the time, "it was about 4 o'clock when Patrolman Malinofski, flashlight in hand, parked his car on a lot just off Maine Avenue, and begun a routine inspection of rear doors.

The beam of his light, General Gaither, Commissioner of Police surmised, fell on 'somebody doing something he shouldn't have been doing.' Caught in the flood of light then 'somebody' fired at the patrolman before the latter had a chance to reach for the gun that hung in a holster on his hip. This was possible, the police said, for the holster was untouched, the gun not moved and 'no good officer who arrests a man would continue to hold his flashlight in his hand.' Patrolmen Anthony Staylor and Henry Levinson arrested the suspect, Oscar Norfolk, 30. Mr. Norfolk was questioned by Lieutenant Edward Hitzelberger and then booked as "suspected of assault and shooting." Officer Malinofski had 9 years of service with the police department and was survived by his wife Gladys.

1 November - 1935

A man was arrested as a suspect in the police murder of Patrolman Malinowski. He was said to have a long criminal record; and he was being quizzed at Northwestern held for further questioning today in reference to Patrolman Malinowski's having been shot through heart early yesterday. A man arrested early this morning was docketed as James Snail, from the 1000 block Walbrook Avenue.

Off. Malinofski was checking businesses on the midnight shift near Maine Ave. & Gwynn Oak Avenue. As he was checking businesses he came upon a man trying to pry open a rear door to one of them. The man spun around and fired two shots striking the officer. A milkman making deliveries nearby was drawn to the gunfire and discovered P/O Malinofski laying near the curb. He died from his wounds shortly thereafter.

As his brothers and sisters of the Baltimore Police Department we will not let him be forgotten. His service honored the City of Baltimore, and the Baltimore Police Department may he rest in peace, and may God bless him.

1 November - 1925

On this day in Baltimore Police History, 1925, we lost our brother, **Motorcycle Patrolman Leroy Mitchell** to an auto accident based on the following:

Man is released on bail after auto accident - Newspaper Article; Oct 30, 1925

George Cooley was charged with striking Patrolman Mitchell on Wednesday. Charged with assaulting with an automobile Motorcycle Patrolman Leroy Mitchell on Reisterstown Road Wednesday, was George Cooley, of Bucks Ave., West

Arlington. Yesterday Cooley was released on $1,000 bail from the Northwestern Police Station pending the outcome of Mitchell's injuries.

Cooley is alleged to have abandoned the injured patrolman after the accident. He was arrested after license tags on the automobile which is said to have struck the patrolman were traced.

The accident occurred when Mitchell was chasing a speeding car on Reisterstown Road, the police said. Mitchell, who is at the Maryland General Hospital suffering with possible fracture of the skull, is said to be in critical condition.

<u>Patrolman Struck by Automobile Dies</u> - Newspaper Article; Nov 2, 1925

Patrolman Leroy Mitchell succumbs. Leroy Mitchell, 1002 West Cross Street, Motorcycle patrolman of the Baltimore traffic division died yesterday at the Maryland General Hospital of injuries received in a Wednesday hit and run when he was struck by an automobile.

George Cooley, Bucks Ave., West Arlington, driver the car, was re-arrested yesterday and held at Northwestern police station on charges of having caused the patrolman's death.

As his brothers and sisters of the Baltimore Police Department we will not let him be forgotten. His service honored the City of Baltimore, and the Baltimore Police Department. May he rest in peace, and may God bless him.

1 November - 1938

On this day in Baltimore Police History, 1938, we lost our brother **Chief Engineer Joseph Edward Keene** to a work related illness based on the following:

On 24 October, 1938 at approximately 8:10 am Chief Engineer Joseph Keene was having engine trouble on a departmental boat, this trouble forced Chief Keene to work the engine while out in the Baltimore Harbor (the harbor was nothing like it is today) while working in the cabin on the boats engine unbeknownst to Chief Keene the engine had two small holes in the muffler of the engine with carbon monoxide escaping into the cab.

He was at the foot of Wells Street on Philpot, while working on a boat engine, he became sick, and dizzy. They managed to get the boat ashore and the Chief was taken to a hospital for treatment and to his home where he died on this date 1 Nov

1938. It was determined that Mr. Keene died as a result of Carbon Monoxide poisoning. Mrs. Anna Keene was awarded a full police pension by Commissioner Robert F. Stanton.

As his brothers and sisters of the Baltimore Police Department we will not let him be forgotten, his service honored the City of Baltimore, and the Baltimore Police Department. May he rest in peace, and may God bless him.

2 November - 1934

On this day in Baltimore Police History 1934, we lost our brother **Police Officer John A. Stapf** to a trolley accident based on the following;

Having completed his tour of duty, and waiting at the North Avenue call box over the Western Maryland Railway Bridge with his side partners Officer John Schmidt, and Edward Burns, as they awaited their relief officers. Once their relief arrived, the trio parted ways.

Their eastbound trolley had pulled up and was standing as Schmidt and Burns boarded. Patrolman Stapf, rounded their trolley in an attempt to ready himself for the boarding of his westbound trolley, (Officer Staph lived at 5102 Elmer Avenue.) In his haste to get home to his family he quickly rounded their trolley and crossed over and onto the westbound trolley's tracks where he was struck by said trolley. Witnesses said the officer ran in front of a standing eastbound car, and into the path of a car going in the opposite direction.

Radio cars were dispatched to the scene and took him to the West Baltimore General Hospital, where he was pronounced dead of a compound skull fracture. He was hit so hard that he was thrown into the air, and back into the eastbound trolley where he landed close to his partners Schmidt and Burns. They later reported to the Department that Stapf's injuries were so bad, his chances for survival were grim; still he was transported to West Baltimore General Hospital where he died due to a severe skull fracture.

Officer John A Staff, was 63 years old at the time of his death; he had served the citizens of Baltimore for nearly 34 years, receiving numerous awards, commendations and citations. He was survived by his wife Katherine and sons George, William, John and Garland along with his daughters Lillian, Margaret, and Florence.

As his brothers and sisters of the Baltimore Police Department we will not let him be forgotten, his service honored the City of Baltimore, and the Baltimore Police Department. May he rest in peace, and may God bless him.

4 November - 1968

<u>A National First</u>: The Baltimore Police Department inaugurates its *In-service training*. The education and training program expanded beyond the traditional entrance level training for recruits to a forty-hour annual In-Service Training course attended by all personnel from the rank of Patrolman through Captain. It was an annual weeklong, forty-hour course, designed to instruct our police officers in the latest developments in the law and techniques in professional law enforcement. The concept of In-Service Training demonstrates the department's goal in development of an officer's capabilities to function amid the complexities of an ever-changing society. This coupled with daily Roll Call training keeps our Officers up to date on the most current police procedures and newest law changes.

4 November - 1998

On this day in Baltimore Police History, 1998 we lost our brother, **Flight Officer Barry Winston Wood** to a flight accident and crash.

All too often police officers face life and death situations alone. During a typical tour of duty, they run after dangerous criminals, confront armed people in the dark, deserted alleys, and pray for fellow officers to arrive during those difficult moments. Police officers claimed the Archangel Michael as their patron saint, and in Baltimore the sound of the beating blades of a helicopter they call Foxtrot represents the closest manifestation to a guardian angel, an unequalled source of comfort as it tracks criminals and helps protect officers from the sky.

When an officer needed a reliable protector, Flight Officer Barry Wood always did his utmost to provide that assistance. The beam of his powerful searchlight brought daylight into darkness. His soothing voice, a hallmark of the foxtrot crew, allayed the fears of officers on foot. As flight officer Wood patroled the skies over this city, he never took lightly the duty of watching over the neighborhood below from his aircraft, but he also knew that he and his crew had a still higher mission: to safeguard the city's protectors.

On 4 November 1998, as Baltimore mourned the loss of Officer Harold Carey and hundreds of highly polished police cars formed a long procession that would lay him to rest, Barry Wood took to the skies over Pratt Street to answer another call for help. Minutes later, trainees directing traffic listened in disbelief as their radios crackled:

"Signal 13, a Signal 13, 1050 RED, Foxtrot has Gone Down." The wail of sirens pierced the crisp morning air, and officers raced to help. What had begun as a routine for call for assistance over Pratt Street ended with engine failure and a catastrophe. In an attempt to land his doomed aircraft with a maneuver called "autorotation," Barry tried to touch down in the B&O Railroad Museum Parking Lot. Foxtrot's tail rotor apparently struck either a power line, or a tree that changed the attitude of the helicopter and drove it into the ground, killing one of Baltimore's finest. Though severely injured, Barry's partner and aerial observer, Mark Keller would survive the crash, most credit Barry with Mark's survival, I am sure Mark leads the group of those that praise Barry in saving his life.

When the time came to lay Barry to rest, helicopters from many different agencies flew overhead in tribute as officers below saluted his flag draped coffin. In the background, a speaker broadcast the dispatcher's last call for him, "KGA to Foxtrot - KGA to Foxtrot - Foxtrot 10-5 not acknowledging." The loss of flight officer Wood profoundly affected every officer in the Baltimore Police Department because the Foxtrot fleet remained grounded during the extensive follow-up investigation, leaving Baltimore City's Police Officers to face danger zone until a new fleet of aircraft arrived and resumed the role of guardian angels.

From news reports:

Barry W. Wood didn't join the Baltimore Police Department to cruise city streets. He joined to fly over them.

Coming straight from the battlefields of Vietnam, the then 23-year-old came to Baltimore less than a month after he was honorably discharged from the Army in 1971 - part of a bold experiment for building a police helicopter unit.

Unlike other cities that took street officers and trained them to fly, Baltimore sought battle-hardened pilots and trained them to be police officers. "When we started, we said, 'Why not get the best pilots available?'" said Frederick Police Chief Regis

Raffensberger, who started the city chopper unit known as "Foxtrot" and made Wood one of his first hires.

Wood, a 27-year veteran, died Wednesday when his two-seat Schweizer crashed at the B&O Railroad Museum. "His manner epitomized professional law enforcement and aviation," said Raffensberger, who left the city department in 1992. Wood, 50, was the second city officer to be killed in five days and the 99th to die in the line of duty since the department was formed in 1870. The deaths -- the other from a car accident -- have rocked the department's 3,200 officers. The department's aviation unit is a small group of officers who work at Martin State Airport in Middle River, where they are well-known to other aviators, including flight officers from Baltimore County.

Pilots gathered Wednesday evening at the wreckage that had been moved to the airport and remembered their fallen colleague. "We were in tears," said Roy Taylor, a former flight officer for Baltimore County who flies the news helicopter for WJZ-TV (Channel 13). "Barry did what he loved to do," Taylor said. "He loved to fly." Wood had lived with his wife, Martha, in Abingdon, a small community south of Aberdeen in Harford County. Friends said the couple was devoted to each other and recently went on a romantic getaway to celebrate their wedding anniversary.

Yesterday, neighbors drove by the couple's neatly kept house, leaves scattered in the front yard. "If he was home right now, he'd be cleaning up those leaves and working on one of his projects," said next-door neighbor Rick Stelmack. "He was just such a fantastic guy and his whole life was work, his wife and taking care of his home."

Wood was born in Taunton, Mass., and graduated from a high school in Manassas, Va., in 1966. He attended Northern Virginia Community College for a year before going to Army Helicopter School at Fort Rucker, Ala.

He served in Vietnam for three years, and he once safely landed a Huey packed with soldiers after another helicopter flew too close and clipped off his landing gear. He was honorably discharged from the Army on April 1, 1971, and joined the city police force 26 days later. Wood spent more than 42,000 hours flying over Baltimore in his quarter-century of chasing stolen cars and helping officers find elusive suspects. He once piloted one of the choppers from Los Angeles, where the aircraft were made, to Baltimore, a seven-day trip. "It's a very sad day here at the airport," said Jake West, manager of Martin State Airport.

West said it appeared as if Wood maneuvered his crippled aircraft away from homes and tried to crash-land in the parking lot of the museum. "He tried to make a clearance and he couldn't make it," he said. Stelmack said he last saw his neighbor the morning of the crash, leaving for work with his partner, Officer Mark A. Keller, 43, who was seriously injured in the accident. "He's the kind of guy who would have tried to land that chopper in such a way that would have saved his partner even if it meant he got hurt," Stelmack said. "He's that kind of man."

Many praised Wood, 50, for piloting his crippled Schweizer 300C away from rowhouses and tilting the aircraft so it hit the pavement on its left side, where he was sitting. "Barry took the brunt of that crash," said Sal Milizano, who served with Wood in Vietnam.

That thought was not lost on Officer Mark A. Keller, who was sitting beside Wood on Nov. 4. Quoting from the Gospel of St. John, Keller said, "There is no greater love than this: to lay down one's life for one's friends. Barry did that for me," Keller told the small room packed with 100 friends, family, aviators and Army veterans. "Because of that, I will always love him, and my family will always love him, all the days of our lives."

From the website BaltimorePoliceHistory.com:

November 4, 1998 a Baltimore Police helicopter piloted by Flight Officer Barry W. Wood experienced mechanical problems while chasing down a car thief, and crashed into the parking lot at the B&O Railroad Museum on West Pratt St. According to witnesses, a loud bang came from the helicopter and plumes of smoke were seen pouring out the back. Remaining calm and courageous until the end, Officer Wood dispatched a distress signal over his radio, declaring "10-50 RED, 10-50 RED" which indicates that a crash is imminent. Then, the former Vietnam War pilot did all he could to maneuver his aircraft away from people on the ground. There were more than 60 people inside the museum at the time of the crash. A ten-year-old boy playing near the accident site said, "It was coming down with smoke. When I saw it hit the gate, I ran because I was so scared." Fortunately, no one on the ground was hurt.

On the way down, the helicopter struck a light pole and then crashed through an iron fence in the museum parking lot before coming to a rest on its left side. The cockpit was destroyed. The two Officers were immediately removed from the helicopter and rushed to Shock Trauma Center. Flight Officer Wood, 50, made it into surgery, but was pronounced dead at 5 pm, less than three hours after the *accident. Officer Mark Keller, 43, suffered a number of serious injuries, including a broken elbow and a spinal fracture, but survived the accident.*

At the funeral, Barry was compared to "David, the Warrior," a Biblical figure who was renowned for the love, compassion and strength of character he exemplified. Officer Wood's wife of 28 years, Martha, spoke eloquently and powerfully at the funeral. She praised her husband as a great planner and excellent provider, and talked about the special relationship they had. "No one on earth has ever experienced the love that Barry and I shared. He was a loving, caring man who touched everyone that he came in contact with" Officer Keller expressed great admiration for his partner of more than a year and a half when he said, "Barry laid down his life for a friend. Our family will always love him and so will I." Officer Barry Wood's service, dedication to duty, and compassion honored the City of Baltimore and the Police Department.

As his brothers and sisters of the Baltimore Police Department, we will not let him be forgotten; his service honored the City of Baltimore, and the Baltimore Police Department. May he rest in peace, and may God bless him.

5 November - 1858

On this day in Baltimore Police History, 1858 we lost our brother, **Police Officer Robert M. Rigdon** in an Assassination by Gunfire.

From the newspapers of the 1800's

The Examination before the Mayor – Investigation and Verdict of the Coroner's Jury – The Excitement and Incidents of the Tragedy. – and the killing of our brother Robert M. Rigdon, an officer of the Western District, who was assassinated in the bosom of his family, at 468 West Baltimore street, the night previous, out of revenge for his testimony delivered in the case of Gambrill, concluded in Criminal Court on the very same afternoon for the murder of officer Benjamin Benton, a brother officer of the deceased...

The assassination appears to have been one of deliberate premeditation. Officer Rigdon, after answering roll call at the station house on Green Street, retired into the privacy of his home, which was in the back part of a store operated by his wife. During the evening, and while Mr. Rigdon was in the back-room of his dwelling, a

man (since recognized as Peter Corrie) entered the store, which is in the front part of the house, and looked at some undershirts and other articles displayed for sale.

In the store, he conducted himself like a drunken man, but that was evidently feigned. His actions becoming repulsive to Mrs. Rigdon and a female attendant, she called on her husband to eject him from the premises. Fearful that the thing was a ruse to draw him within the reach of his enemies, Rigdon hesitated, and said to his wife, who stood in the doorway leading to the storeroom, "I don't attend the store – tell him to go out," or words to that effect. At that moment, while resting with his elbow against the mantel of the fireplace, where he had laid his pistol belt, the weapon of the crouching assailant in his rear was fired through the little window, which opens into the yard from the sitting room. Rigdon, who, from the position of the mantel, must have been but three or four feet distant from the weapon, received five slugs in his back, near the left side. His only exclamation was, "My God! I'm shot!" and attempted to reach for the sofa, but sank on the floor and died after heaving an audible groan.

Persons passing upon the street and the residents alarmed by the shot, hastened into the store, where they stood horrified and trembling at the deed of blood before them, for a moment transfixed and unable to act. His wife is said to have acted heroically, and neither shrieked nor fainted, but recited all with coolness and self-possession which was remarkable. Officer J. Cook being in the vicinity hastened in the direction of the shot, and fell upon Peter Corrie as he was running away from the alley behind Rigdon's house.

The officer gave chase, when another man (since recognized as Mal Cropps,) followed, and ran along on the other side of the street. Cook singled out Corrie, and came up with him on the run, calling on him to stop. Corrie did not heed but ran down Baltimore to Pine and to Penn streets, the pursued and pursuer exchanging shots occasionally. At Penn Street, Cook was joined by officers Jamison and Huggins, one of whom sprang his rattle in advance of Corrie, which so alarmed him, that he slackened his pace and was easily captured. When he found himself in the hands of the officers, he begged for life, and said as "God lived" he was innocent of the murder. He then in his fear, confessed, and said "Mal Cropps did it." He was locked up in a cell at the Western District.

<u>The Excitement and Incidents of the Tragedy</u>

The Sun Newspaper of Saturday contained the startling announcement of the killing of Robert M. Rigdon, an officer of the Western district, who was assassinated in the

bosom of his family, No. 468 West Baltimore Street, the night previous. This cowardly act was apparently committed out of revenge for Rigdon's testimony delivered in the case of Gambrill, concluded in Criminal Court on the same afternoon for the murder of Officer Benjamin Benton, a brother officer of the deceased. The assassination appears to have been one of deliberate premeditation. Officer Rigdon, after answering roll call at the station house on Green Street, retired into the privacy of his home. During the evening, and while Mr. Rigdon was in the back room of his dwelling, a man (since recognized as Peter Corrie) entered the store, which is in the front part of the house, and looked at some undershirts and other articles displayed. In the store he conducted himself like a drunken man, but that was evidently feigned. His actions becoming repulsive to Mrs. Rigdon and a female clerk, she called on her husband to eject him from the premises.

Fearful that the thing was a ruse to draw him within the reach of his enemies, Rigdon hesitated, and said to his wife, who stood in the doorway leading to the store, "I don't attend the store – tell him to go out," or words to that effect. At that moment, while resting with his elbow against the mantel of the fireplace, where he had laid his pistol belt, the weapon of the crouching assailant in his rear was fired. Rigdon, who, from the position of the mantel, must have been but three or four feet distant from the weapon, received five slugs in his back, near the left side. His only exclamation was, "My God! I'm shot!" and attempted to reach for the sofa, but sank on the floor and died after heaving an audible groan. Persons passing upon the street and the residents, alarmed by the shot, hastened into the house, where they stood horrified and trembling at the pool of blood before them, for a moment transfixed and unable to act. His wife is said to have acted heroically, and neither shrieked nor fainted, but recited all with coolness and self-possession which was remarkable.

Officer J. Cook being in the vicinity hastened in the direction of the shot, and fell upon Peter Corrie as he was running away through the alley of Rigdon's house.

The officer gave chase, when another man (since recognized as Mal Cropps,) followed, and ran along on the other side of the street. Cook singled out Corrie, and came up with him on the run, calling on him to stop. Corrie did not heed but ran down Baltimore to Pine and to Penn streets, the pursued and pursuer exchanging shots occasionally. At Penn street, Cook was joined by officers Jamison and Huggins, one of whom sprang his rattle in advance of Corrie, which so alarmed him, that he slackened his pace and was easily captured. When he found himself in *the hands of the officers, he begged for his life, and said as "God lived" he was innocent of the murder. He then in his fear, confessed, and said "Mal Cropps did it." He was locked up in a cell at the western district.*

<u>Baltimore Sun Article</u> Dated January 27, 1859

At about 10 o'clock it was announced that the jury, who had been out all night in the case of Corrie, had agreed upon a verdict, and they soon after entered the court. Their names having been called, and the prisoner directed to hold up his right hand, the court said the verdict must be received in silence, and without demonstration whatever on the part of the spectators. The clerk then, amid breathless silence, asked – "What say you, is the prisoner at the bar guilty or not guilty?" The foreman replied, "Guilty of murder in the first degree."

<u>Baltimore Sun Article</u> Dated April 9, 1859

Yesterday was the day fixed upon by the Governor of the State of Maryland for the execution of the four condemned murders, Henry C. Gambrill (Note; this is the person who murdered Officer Benton), Marion Cropps, Peter Corrie and John Stephens. Many persons had arrived in the city during Thursday to witness the scene – all parts of the State, the District of Columbia, Virginia and Pennsylvania, and even New York City and Buffalo being represented on this occasion. Early in the morning throngs of persons began to pour in from Baltimore, Howard, Anne Arundel, Harford and adjacent counties, and the houses of the city appeared themselves empty of their inhabitants – all wending their way to the streets and hills to the west and north of the jail, which commanded full view of the gallows erected within the jail yard. The housetops, windows, trees and all other places from whence a more enlarged view could be obtained were crowded with human beings. A sea of faces met the eye far and near – men, women and children – old age and infancy – white and black – swelled up the vast multitude, drawn to witness the horrible spectacle...

The execution throughout was conducted with the greatest precision and humanity, the orders and arrangements of Sheriff Creamer being carried out with the most scrupulous fidelity. To the sheriff and those deputies who assisted him every credit is due for the faithful discharge of their duties – No execution that ever occurred in Baltimore was performed with more strict regard to mercy and humanity, and not a single circumstance occurred which could cause regret, the performance of the stern demands of the law.

As his brothers and sisters of the Baltimore Police Department, we will not let him be forgotten, his service honored the City of Baltimore and the Baltimore Police Department - may he rest in peace, and may God bless him.

7 November - 1908 – Round Hat

Today in Baltimore Police History, the Department stopped using the Police Helmets that in 1886 had become part of the Baltimore Police Department uniform. The helmets had been worn for decades, but on this day (1908) they were replaced with the more modern round, or oval top, police hat

Note that the Helmets themselves had replaced the original derby caps, (Bell Cap) that had been used for decades before that in Baltimore. Also, note that the Helmets replaced on this day are still used in many parts of the world, most notably London.

7 November - 1943

On this day in Baltimore City Police History, 1943 we lost our brother Police **Officer William S. Knight**, who along with his partner, Officer John J. Bianca, was sent to the 1100 block of Rutland Avenue to investigate the trouble at a private political club.

Upon arrival, the officers were informed that the people involved in the argument that had precipitated the call, had left the club. As they received this information, gunshots rang out from a nearby alley. A black male was seen running from the alley and across the street. The officers gave chase and the suspect was caught by Officer Knight.

The captured suspect told the officers, he saw a man in a tan jacket firing a pistol, and that he was only running to get out of the area. That suspect was placed in the rear of their radio car (keep in mind this was 1943 and the idea of a cage car wouldn't come along for some time). The area was then further searched for the suspect in the tan jacket that was mentioned by the first suspect. As they were in the radio car discussing how to handle the situation, they observed a man wearing a tan jacket run into an alley where the patrol car could not go. Officer Bianca chased the man on foot, while Officer Knight stayed with the first suspect and the radio car.

The suspect dressed in tan reportedly doubled back to the radio car where he was confronted by Officer Knight. Shots were fired by both the suspect and the officer, each striking the other in the chest. Officer Knight staggered back to his radio car to call for help; he made that call and then passed out on the front seat. He was later taken to St. Joseph's Hospital where he was pronounced dead. The first man who was originally placed in the car, left the scene when Officer Knight died, he was never identified. The suspect shot by Officer Knight, Thomas Toler, a 20-year-old male died the next day.

Officer Knight had served the City for 7 years before this incident and as his brothers and sisters of the Baltimore Police Department, we will not let him be forgotten. His service honored the City of Baltimore, and the Baltimore Police Department. May he rest in peace, and may God bless him.

9 November - 1880

Today in Baltimore Police History, the Motto of the department was established based on the following:

On the wall of the gymnasium in the Central District was displayed a plaque with the following word, "Ever on the Watch" written in English, under the Latin words "Semper Paratus" and "Semper Fideles." The Latin word "Semper" can mean either, "Always" or "Ever" - so our motto could either be read as "Ever Ready / Ever Faithful / Ever on the Watch" or "Always Ready / Always Faithful / Ever on the Watch".

Throughout history, "Semper Paratus" and "Semper Fideles" have consistently been read as "Always." However in Baltimore, we used *"Ever on the Watch"* over *"Always on the Watch"* leading us to believe that in our case "Semper" stood for "Ever," giving us *"Semper Paratus - Semper Fideles - Semper Alapa Buris Pervigil"* or in English, *"Ever Ready - Ever Faithful - Ever on the Watch."*

The meaning of Semper for Baltimore Police being "Ever," instead of "Always" was a theory based on logic, and logic that paid off. We have found another source that confirms our thoughts. Meaning the Motto of the Baltimore Police department since 1880, has been ""Semper Paratus – Semper Fideles – Ever on the Watch"

13 November - 1856

On this day in Baltimore Police History, 1856, we lost our Brother, Patrolman **John O'Mayer** to gunfire based on the following:

When a call came in to stop the violence at the Belair Market at 500 N. Gay Street, city police found themselves fighting both sides of an argument leading to what would become a gunfight rather than just a disagreement.

An astounding ten of our brothers were shot in action during the conflict; most of them suffering only minor injuries. Patrolman O'Mayer's wound was accidental – in the excitement he shot himself in the hand. For the next several days the men of the Eastern District slowly recovered from their "ugly but not-too dangerous wounds." All but Officer John O'Myer, whose condition steadily worsened, becoming seriously infected. Over the next week, the infection spread, and spread quickly… until it had become apparent that the infection threatened the patrolman's life.

The treating physician, Dr. Yates had no choice but amputate O'Mayer's hand. At the time, that seemed to be the only answer, and even then it was only an attempt to stop the spread of the nasty infection… It would be a few days before Doc Yates would know if his efforts were successful.

On 13 November 1856, with his family, a wife, and child by his side, Patrolman O'Mayer would draw his last breath. Doc Yate's surgery was a valiant effort, but an effort that was but too late, as the infection grew into a severe case of lockjaw, and nothing could be done at that point to save him.

His funeral was held on the 15th of that November, and he was given the honors bestowed upon a soldier, when "the military fired three volleys over the grave, and cortege retired." The leaders of the city mourned the death of the watchman by flying the flags at half-staff.

As his brothers and sisters of the Baltimore Police Department, we will not let him be forgotten. His service honored the City of Baltimore, and the Baltimore Police Department. May he rest in peace, and may God bless him.

16 November - 1960

On this day in Baltimore Police History, 1960, we lost our Brother, Police **Officer Warren Eckert**.

On November 16, 1960 at approximately 12:35 pm, Officer Warren Eckert was responding to a call for service using his lights and sirens. At the intersection of Pratt and Carey Streets, Officer Eckert was struck by another motorist, throwing him from his motorcycle. He struck his head against the street, causing fatal injuries. Officer Eckert served with the Baltimore Police department for 5 years. Before being appointed to the Baltimore Police Department in 1955, Officer Eckert was a member of our United States Navy where he served from April 19, 1951 until March 22, 1955.

Motorist Faces Jury Action in Fatal Accident - 21 Dec 1960

A motorist who was involved in an accident in which a traffic policeman was killed last month was held for grand jury action yesterday after a hearing in Central District Police Court - Police said the defendant Thomas A Goins, Jr., 42, suspect, was the driver of a pick-up truck that collided with the motorcycle being operated by Patrolman Warren V. Eckert

The Officer was dead on arrival at Franklin Square Hospital after the accident.

Police testified Patrolman Eckert was westbound on Pratt Street with his siren operating and red light flashing when his vehicle was hit the truck which was traveling northbound on Carey Street, and had run the red light entering the intersection into the path of Patrolman Warren V. Eckert

Goins, a resident of 600 Block of Baker Street was charged with manslaughter. He was held on $1,000 Bail

$70,000 Granted Kin of Policeman - Dec 12, 1962

Damages totaling $70,000 were awarded in superior court yesterday to the widow and three minor children of Officer Warren V. Eckert, a motorcycle patrolman who was killed in a traffic accident while escorting an emergency ambulance to a hospital in November 1960.

The jury under Judge Anselm Sodaro returned a consent judgment of $27,750 for Mrs. Katheryn A. L. Eckert: $19,000 for Maureen S Eckert, 6, $11,500 for Beverly C Eckert, 10, and $2,250 for Mrs. Eckert as administratrix.

Testimony produced by James R. White, A. Davis Gomborov and Matthew Swerdloff, Council for the plaintiff, disclosed that Patrolman Eckert was leading an Ambulance with his siren on, and lights flashing when he was hit by a truck at Carey and Pratt Streets.

Thomas A. Goins Jr. was the driver of the truck, owned by the Baltimore Beverage Distribution Company of Maryland, Inc. of the 2600 Blk. Pennsylvania Avenue. Mr. Goins violated the red light, entering the intersection and causing the collision.

As his brothers and sisters of the Baltimore Police Department, we will not let him be forgotten. His service honored the City of Baltimore, and the Baltimore Police Department. May he rest in peace, and may God bless him.

16 November - 1994

The department ended authorized use of the Slap Jack

18 November - 1985

On this day in Baltimore Police History, 1985; we lost our brother, Police **Officer Vincent J. Adolfo** to gunfire based on the following:

At approximately 5:30 pm on Monday, 18 November, 1985, Eastern District Officer Vincent J. Adolfo was operating his marked police vehicle when he saw an automobile headed eastbound on Biddle Street. Running a routine check of its license plate, via police communications, revealed the vehicle to be stolen. Seeing there were four occupants in the vehicle, he notified other Eastern units of its location and direction of travel. Two additional marked units responded and began heading westbound on Biddle Street. All of the police vehicles displayed their flashing blue emergency lights (from 1970 until 1993 the Baltimore Police Department used only blue lights on our emergency vehicles' light bars). The suspect vehicle slowed but never came to a complete stop before the driver bailed-out, leaving the moving vehicle to collide head-on into approaching traffic including both civilian and police vehicles. While Officers secured the three passengers of the vehicle, Officer Adolfo gave chase to the driver, north from Biddle Street into a cluttered thoroughfare called, "Iron Alley." Vince caught the suspect in the 1200 block of Iron Alley and attempted to place him against the wall.

As Officer Adolfo attempted to place the suspect's right hand behind him, the suspect grabbed a nearby traffic sign pole, used it for advantage to pull away from the Officer, twisting in such a way as to resist the arrest.

At this time, according to witnesses, the suspect turned and lunged at the officer, pushing him backwards, causing him to trip over the debris on the ground in Iron Alley, lose his balance and fall to the ground.

As Officer Adolfo struggled to regain his feet, the suspect pulled a gun from his waistband, turned and fired, striking Officer Vincent Adolfo once in the chest. Officer Adolfo then staggered several feet north, and the suspect fired a second round, striking Adolfo in the back.

Other Eastern District Officers heard the reports of the gunshots, and ran into the alley to find their 25-year-old side partner crumpled to the ground, mortally wounded with two gunshots, one to the chest, and one to his back.

Fellow officers immediately initiated CPR, and were relieved after a few minutes by firefighters and paramedics from the Baltimore City Fire Department. As they attempted to stabilize the wounded officer, doctors at Johns Hopkins Hospital, just a few blocks away, were alerted as to the nature, and seriousness of the injuries coming in, and knowing it was a police officer, they were prepared to help him in any way they could.

Officer Vincent Adolfo arrived at Johns Hopkins Hospital to the waiting hands of a trauma team where every effort of that medical team was used in an attempt to save the life of our brother. As quickly as their efforts began, they ended. The injury to his heart was massive, and irreversible. Sadly, the surgeon pronounced Vince dead at 6:00 pm.

Investigating officers and detectives quickly ascertained the identity of the suspect and efforts to apprehend him began. As word of what had happened spread, reports of sightings of the suspect came into the CID - Criminal Investigation Division. During the days that followed, news accounts on television and in the newspapers repeated praise for young officer Adolfo. He was dedicated, caring, and he loved his job. Reports of specific instances in which Officer Adolfo went out of his way to help people were legend.

He was born not too many blocks from where he gave his life. He knew the city, its people and its problems. That's why he became police officer. At the time of his death he was living in the county, and he could have easily become a county officer, but Vince wanted to give back to the community he grew up in, and he became a police officer in the city, the city he loved. Instead of pursuing other careers that were open to bright young men, young men with his intelligence, and his character, Vince held a strong belief that it was his mission to serve as an officer in Baltimore.

Friday, 22 November, 1985, was rainy, it was cold and it was gray… members of the Baltimore Police Department, his brothers, and sisters, along with numerous local, state, and Federal law enforcement agencies arrived for his funeral services at Our Lady of Fatima; a Roman Catholic Church on East Pratt Street.

Inside the church, the Priest talked about the sacrifices that were made by Officer Adolfo and what it meant. Although only 25 years of age, his example can be followed by every man and every woman in law enforcement. His time of service to the citizens of his community was brief, but exemplary. We have all heard the saying, "It is not how one dies that makes them a hero; but how they lived!" In that sense, too, Vince was a hero. He was proud to a Baltimore Police Officer, and it made him feel complete.

The truth of the matter was that the department was more complete to have an Officer like Vince wear its badge. Police work is not a competition, but ask anyone and you will learn, good police flock together, and they become better just by being around one another. Vince had some of the best around him, they drew to him, and he to them… making some of the best Police in Baltimore better. It is how Vince was… to be near him, made you feel you had to be better, just to be worthy of his company. The sad ride to the cemetery was observed by concerned citizens who lined nearly shoulder to shoulder for the entire length of the funeral procession. Services at the graveside were brief, and then our brother Officer Vincent J. Adolfo was buried.

As his brothers and sisters of the Baltimore Police Department, we will not let him be forgotten. His service honored the City of Baltimore, and the Baltimore Police Department. May he rest in peace, and may God bless him.

18 November - 1946

On this day in Baltimore Police History, 1946, we lost our brother Police **Officer Elmer A. Noon**, to a heart attack. Officer Noon was 41 years old, and died of a heart attack shortly after returning home from work. His daughter, Elizabeth-Ann used to wait for her dad to get home to tell her how his day went. This was normally achieved by his telling her a police war story, though he would always tone it down for her four-year-old ears.

On this day however, as he came into the house he was visibly ill. Not wanting their daughter to see him this way, patrolman Noon's wife, Elizabeth bypassed the evening ritual with Elizabeth-Ann and took her husband straight in to bed, then went and called immediately for medical attention. By the time the Doctor arrived, Officer Noon had died. The Doctor determined that the cause of death was a massive heart attack.

His commanders and wife were confused by the cause of death because he had always appeared to be in such good shape, and had not exhibited any of the warning signs, or physical symptoms related to heart attack. The Doctor explained the possibility that, "great physical exertion" by even a healthy man, could sometimes result in a heart attack.

Investigators focused their attention on his last several calls for service for the day. They quickly honed in on a call he handled at 10 minutes to four, when Officer Noon and his partner, Patrolman Otto Leyhe, had responded to the intersection of Gay and Forrest Streets, outside of the Belair Market, to assist a Special Police Officer, Fred Thomas, who was attempting to subdue a disorderly drunk. The drunk man, Albert Thomas Rogers, in addition to being intoxicated, was large and he was strong. Citizens stood by watching as the much larger, Rogers, tossed the Special Police Officer around like a rag doll. As Officer Noon and Leyhe pulled up on scene Officer Noon could see the security officer in need of assistance, so before their patrol car could come to a complete stop, Officer Noon had leapt from the passenger seat to the street, and joined in the fight. Patrolman Leyhe had not made it to the tussling officer's before he saw Rogers toss Officer Noon aside. It was like two warriors fighting a giant, and the giant was winning, but the warriors were not giving up.

Officer Noon was thrown with such force that he didn't touch the ground until his body was slammed onto the side of their police vehicle. Stunned, Officer Noon got up and shook it off. Showing no fear, he went right back in after Rogers, but this time he removed a device from his belt called an "Iron Claw" (for those that don't know, "The Iron Claw" was mix between the old "Come Along" [a choke chain device used to latch onto a suspects wrist] and the more modern day, police handcuff." When Officer Noon latched this device onto Roger's wrist, the fight was not completely over, but it was more controlled by the police than by Rogers.

Not long after this (Officer Leyhe estimated it to be about 5 to 10 minutes), another officer, patrolman William Ervine, arrived to help subdue Rogers. It took four officers to control the violent drunk, and get him into the patrol wagon. The wagon, driven by patrolman Hue Law took Rogers to the Northeastern Station House for booking. However, due to his combative behavior, an officer would have to ride in the wagon with him. Being the second officer in a two-man car, Officer Noon was elected for the ride to keep Rogers from escaping or assaulting anyone else.

The entire trip from the scene to the station house, to the cellblock and to the holding cell was one continuous battle. Still, Officer Noon declined to charge Roger's with anything other than his initial act of drunk and disorderly. We'll never know if this was out of compassion for a drunk that didn't know fully what he was doing, or his being anxious to get home to Elizabeth-Ann and tell her about this, one of his more action-packed war stories.

Members of Patrolman Noon's family waited anxiously for the outcome of the investigation into his death. Because without the determination that it had occurred in the line of duty, and the modest financial benefit that decision would permit, Elizabeth faced the difficult time of raising their daughter on her own. On January 7, 1947, Raymond Noon penned a letter to Police Commissioner Hamilton R. Atkinson, praising the department's decision to consider his brother's death to be line of duty. In it he wrote, "The decision rendered is a credit to the department, and proves that the men in charge have their interests of those under them at heart."

Officer Noon, 41 years old, died two hours after the altercation; he was married and had a four year daughter.

As his brothers and sisters of the Baltimore Police Department, we will not let him be forgotten. His service honored the City of Baltimore, and the Baltimore Police Department. May he rest in peace, and may God bless him.

19 November - 1928

On this day in Baltimore Police History, 1928, we lost our brother, **Detective Sergeant Frederick W. Carroll** to gunfire based on the following:

Captain John Carey, night commander of police, received word that a man answering the description of a man wanted in New York for armed robberies and the shooting of a New York City Police officer was in a Baltimore Street hotel. Three detectives were detailed to go to the location and bring the suspect to police headquarters for questioning. The detectives found the person that was being reported, but felt he was not the suspect wanted by NYPD. Captain Carey said he told the three officers sent earlier of the dangers of this suspect, and let them know he was a dangerous and desperate character. While the Detectives didn't think the guy they received the tip about was the actual person involved with the NYPD Officer's death, they still brought him in for questioning. The subject was cleared and released shortly after.

Later the same morning Detective Sergeant Frederick W. Carroll received a phone tip of a wanted suspect at a downtown hotel. Sergeant Carroll didn't have any additional information on the suspect, didn't know what he was wanted for, and most importantly did know that three Detectives had already gone out on this tip. He did know, from the tipster, that police had been there earlier looking for a suspect but that the suspect was there now.

Det. Sgt. Frederick Carroll then left for the hotel. We don't have any idea who phoned in the tip; it may have been the person police brought in earlier and then released, or a hotel employee. We'll never know. Likewise, we'll never know why Sergeant F. Carroll didn't look into it any further, or didn't take back-up. He just took the name the caller gave him, grabbed a set of keys, and went alone… While at the hotel, he located the wanted suspect and arrested him without incident. As Sergeant F. Carroll and the suspect proceeded from the hotel, they got to Fayette Street and Fallsway (right next to the Headquarters building), when the suspect pulled a pistol, and demanded that Detective Sergeant F. Carroll put his hands up. Detective Sergeant Elmer O'Grady and Detective Joseph Carroll (no relation), who were looking out a window of the police building at the time, ran out to assist Det. Sgt. F. Carroll, only to be met by the gunman's fire. Detectives O'Grady and Joseph Carroll were both hit by gunfire, but were reported as doing well at the hospital. However, Det. Sgt. Frederick Carroll died a few minutes after being taken to the hospital.

The suspect in this case also was shot and died of his injuries, but not before admitting to police that he was in fact the suspect wanted in New York for robberies and shooting two police officers in the NYPD.

As his brothers and sisters of the Baltimore Police Department, we will not let him be forgotten. His service honored the City of Baltimore, and the Baltimore Police Department. May he rest in peace, and may God bless him.

[Author's Note: Several things that should be known about the Baltimore Police 1928. First, Baltimore Police didn't cuff people in public; Second, we didn't search people in public, nor did we stand by and watch as others searched people in public. To explain that, Commissioner Charles Gaither read the following from the rulebook to the media:

"Members of the force shall not search, or act as witness to the searching of any person in any place other than the station house, or headquarters, unless such search be made for dangerous or deadly weapons suspected to be upon the person of the prisoner."

In this case, Det. Sgt. F. Carroll had no information that the suspect was wanted for shooting other police officers or that he might be armed, and so was within the rules of the Baltimore Police Department. It is because of cases like this that we have the rules we have today; cases like this that let us handcuff people that are only suspected of a crime. And, of course, cases like this that let us search incident to an arrest.]

20 November - 1930 - Weitzel

On this date, **Patrolman Edward T. Weitzel** of the Central District was stabbed and shot twice by a theft suspect early yesterday morning (20 November 1931). He was reported in good condition last night at Mercy Hospital.

Patrolman Weitzel was attacked by a man in Hargrove alley after he had taken him into custody for stealing garments from a clothesline. The man stabbed him in the hip with an ice pick, took his pistol and fired at him six times, hitting him in the left hand with one bullet and in the back with another before running away.

Despite his wounds, the patrolman commandeered a taxicab and gave chase, but the suspect disappeared on Greenmount Avenue and the wounded officer was taken to the hospital by the taxicab driver.

Nine months later on the 27th of August 1932, the newspapers reported:

Stabbing Suspect Was Arrested After Nine Months

A search of more than nine months was ended yesterday with the arrest of Hubert Austin, 20, Negro, in a house in the 900 block of Brevard Street.

Austin was booked at Central Police Station on charges of stabbing and shooting Patrolman Edward Weitzel in a backyard in the 1700 block of Charles Street, on November 20th 1931.

Weitzel Goes to House

Weitzel and two plainclothes patrolmen went to the house yesterday afternoon after information had been received that the suspect was there after having been out the city for some time.

On the day of the November attack, Weitzel was patrolling his post when he noticed a subject in the vicinity of Hargrove Alley and Lanvale Street with a large bundle clothes under his arm. When confronted, Austin admitted the clothes had been stolen and offered to take the officer to the place from which he obtained them.

When they reached the yard, Austin suddenly threw the clothes in the officer's face and attacked him with an ice pick, stabbing him in the side. In the struggle that followed, Austin got possession of Officer Weitzel's pistol and fired a shot through the officer's hand. He then backed out of the gate, firing several more shots, one of which hit the patrolman in the back.

Sergeant Weitzel joined the Baltimore Police Department on 8 October 1923. He was assigned to the Central District. He was promoted to Sergeant on 19 October 1939 and was transferred to the Southern District. In 1941, he received a commendation while he held the rank of Sergeant in the Southern District.

He was born in late 1893 and in 1920 he married Barbara Weitzel, and together they had 8 children: Frank, Helen, Marie, Catherine, Margaret, Edward Jr, Robert, and Wayne. They lived at 604 Boldin Street with his father William Weitzel. He was the oldest of three boys, with his brothers being Amon and William Weitzel. He passed away on 5 March, 1952. He was a Baltimore hero and will always be remembered...

Credit: Courtesy of Robert D. Weitzel

His son, Robert D. Weitzel, later joined the Baltimore Police and had a similar incident in career

Sgt. Edward Weitzel had eight children, and we could spend hours writing about each of them, but for now, let's concentrate on just one, Robert Weitzel. Why Robert? Well, because Robert was also a Baltimore Police officer, and here is part of his story…

Robert's Father, Sgt. Edward Weitzel passed away in 1952 just one year before his wife, Barbara died. Robert was 16 at the time, his younger brother Wayne was just 13. Robert lived with one of his sisters in Edmondson Village until he turned 18.

At age 18, Robert enlisted in the United States Air Force and was off to the Korean War. After 13 weeks of basic training in Upstate, N.Y., he was sent to communication school (26 weeks), and then he was to be sent overseas to Korea. However, he was diverted to Japan because of the agreement being signed at the 38th parallel between N. Korea, and S. Korea ending the Korean War. From there Robert was shipped to Goose Bay Labrador. At the time the United States and Canada had agreed to build radar stations all along the northern part of Canada, called the defense early warning (DEW) line. This was during the cold war with Russia. Robert traveled all over the artic for 15 months setting up communications and radar sites. In 1957, he was sent back to Upstate, N.Y. and assigned to the ready reserves until 1961.

While working as a patrolman for the Baltimore Police Department there was an incident in which the young Weitzel, Robert, was trampled by a herd of stampeding cows that had escaped from the Ruppersberger Slaughterhouse located in the 2600 block of Pennsylvania Ave. The Slaughterhouse was founded in 1868 and notably, at the time of this writing (2015) still exists and is open for business.

Officer Weitzel worked the Northwest District, and was near Pennsylvania and North Avenues when the cows stampeded and trampled him. In a different incident just below Pennsylvania Avenue, during an altercation inside a sub-shop at North and Linden Avenues a suspect bit officer Weitzel on the hand during a violent struggle to resist being arrested. These were the days of callboxes and few radios, so like his father's case from years earlier, Weitzel was unable to call for assistance, and the suspect was able escape.

In a similarity to his father's case years earlier, the detainee didn't really get away; he merely postponed his arrest. Young Officer Robert Weitzel, like his dad, never gave up, and he identified the suspect and arrested him at a later date. Like father like son… the original Blue Bloods – police work was really in their blood. You can run, but you can't hide, and both Weitzel's never quit until they got their man.

22 November - 1872

On this day in Baltimore Police History, 1872, we lost our brother, **Patrolman Franklin Fullum** of the Southern District to a Line of Duty Illness.

Death of a Policeman - Newspapers reported at the time:

Patrolman Francis Fullum, of the South District, died on Friday night. Officer Fullum died at his residence, 42 South Oregon St., of smallpox. Officer Fullum was regarded as a very efficient Officer. During his term of service, he was instrumental in the rescue of a large number of persons from drowning at the docks skirting Federal Hill.

Some two or three months earlier, duty brought him in contact with a man delirious from the smallpox, and notwithstanding the fact that the man was covered with evidence of this dreadful malady, Fullum did his job, grappling with the suspect, and succeeding in getting him in a place of safety, and out of the public's eye. This was done to protect others from possible infection. Officer Fullum did not take the disease at that time, but continued in the service until Tuesday last (19 November, 1872) when he was confined with the smallpox, which resulted in his death. His remains were interred on Saturday.

As his brothers and sisters of the Baltimore Police Department, we will not let him be forgotten. His service honored the City of Baltimore, and the Baltimore Police Department. May he rest in peace, and may God bless him.

23 November - 2002

On this day in Baltimore Police History, 2002 we lost our brother, **Detective Thomas G. Newman**, to gunfire based on the following;

Some six months before he was killed, on 21 April, 2001 to be exact, one of my best friends, Detective Tommy Newman, drove his Chevy S-10 pickup onto an Amoco gas station lot in South Baltimore. While there, he encountered four men who began taunting him. Tommy identified himself as a police officer, in hopes that would diffuse the situation. And for a short time it did, and the men walked away, but not before one of them boldly made eye contact with Tommy, then reached back and touched his back to indicate he had a weapon.

Tommy was a super calm and easy going, level headed officer. Tommy used his cell phone to call 911 from his vehicle, as he followed the men and their vehicle, a dark red Mazda MPV. Believing at least one of the men was armed, Tommy kept his distance and did not approach them, nor however, did he want to lose sight of their vehicle. Able to alert authorities, Tommy gave the 911 operator his location, and attempted to summon sufficient police units to his location. Before police could get to Newman's location, the men pulled over and exited their vehicle. Each of the men would run off in a different direction. Tommy waiting in his truck for police to arrive so he could pass on the information, had no idea that one of the men in the Mazda had doubled back around the buildings and was approaching the rear of his truck.

Tommy was on his cell phone with the 911 dispatcher when the man opened fire on him, sending five shots into his truck. Wounded in the attack, Tommy nevertheless remained committed to the department and, once healed, came back to the job he loved. Moreover, he helped convict the man who shot him.

Because of that incident and Tommy's testimony in court sending his attacker to jail, there was a contract out on Tommy's life. At approximately 1:50 am on 23 November 2002, Tommy was off duty and leaving Joe's Tavern on Dundalk Avenue, at which time he was ambushed by three men waiting outside of the Tavern with a plan to take his life in retaliation for his testimony in the shooting that left him wounded six months earlier.

Tommy was killed that night, in a most cowardly attack. One of the suspects responsible for Tommy's murder was the half-brother of the suspect who was convicted and imprisoned for the attempted murder of our Brother Detective Thomas "Tommy" Newman in April of 2001.

Detective Newman was a twelve-year veteran of the Baltimore Police Department, and is survived by his son, daughter, mother, sisters, brother, nieces and nephews. Detective Newman was a key part of his family unit; his strength and love are a painful loss. His death also saddened his squad members in the Check and Fraud Unit. In mourning his loss, Tommy's desk was as he left it. His jacket hung on the back of his chair. Photographs of his children hung on the surrounding walls, and slips of phone messages were neatly stacked one on top of the other. Anyone that knew Tommy, knew how devoted he was to his family, his friends, and to the Baltimore Police Department.

Tommy was a good guy, good police and a good friend, he will never be forgotten by us, his brothers and sisters of the Baltimore Police Department. RIP Tommy, you know how much you meant to those of us that were lucky enough to have gotten to work with you, and become your friend.

As his brothers and sisters of the Baltimore Police Department, we will not let him be forgotten. His service honored the City of Baltimore, and the Baltimore Police Department. May he rest in peace, and may God bless him.

25 November - 1912

On this date in Baltimore Police History, 1912 we lost our brother, Police Officer **John McGrain** to an auto accident based on the following newspaper account. No further details have been uncovered.

Newspaper Article; Nov 25, 1912; pg. 4

On 25 November, 1912 Officer John McGrain, an injured patrolman died. John McGrain was badly injured in peculiar accident last February while riding in the Northwestern District Auto Patrol. Patrolman McGrain, was forced to retire at 56 years old due to these injuries, and as a result died at his home at 1519 Myrtle Avenue some months later. While the attending physicians said that heart disease was the cause of his death, McGrain's family insist he never fully recovered from injuries received in that auto accident and that is what ultimately led to his death.

McGrain was widely known in the city while in the Central District, where he met and knew personally many in the financial district.

One day last February he was instructed to hold a loose windshield in the police patrol while it was being taken to Northern police station for repairs. When the turn was made at North and Pennsylvania Avenue, McGrain was thrown forward, striking his forehead against the windshield he held. His head was badly cut and he was taken to St. Luke's Hospital.

Born in Baltimore Officer McGrain was appointed a member of the Police Department in 1891. He is survived by his widow, Miss Ann McGrain, his three sons, John W., Joseph W., and William F. McGrain and two brothers, Thomas L. and James McGrain.

As his brothers and sisters of the Baltimore Police Department, we will not let him be forgotten. His service honored the City of Baltimore, and the Baltimore Police Department. May he rest in peace, and may God bless him.

26 November - 1904 - Fingerprints

Today in Baltimore Police History, 1904, Sergeant John A. Casey became the first Police Officer in this country to fingerprint a suspect. He fingerprinted a man by the name of John Randles, who was being held on the charge of larceny, and of course, Randles himself became the first US citizen to be fingerprinted under this brand new system of identification.

The fingerprint system was initiated and championed in the United States by Marshal Farnan, who while attending a Chiefs of Police seminar in St Louis, first learned of the system. Afterwards, he came back to Baltimore, whereupon he directed Sergeant John Casey of Baltimore's Bureau of Identification Section, to investigate the idea of collecting, filing and storing (but not efficiently searching for) fingerprints – an efficient system of finding and matching fingerprints would come later with the creation of the Henry System of classification used in Europe. After due investigation of the idea during his own trip to St. Louis, Sergeant Casey, though initially a skeptic, became a convert.

Sergeant Casey then set up and perfected an efficient method of running a fingerprint system, which he came to believe would complement, or even supplant, the Bertillion (named after the Frenchman who initially created it) system of identification theretofore in use. In fact, the system Sgt. Casey developed became the leading fingerprint system in this country, run so efficiently that Sgt. Casey's model was often used by other agencies throughout the United States.

The unit would go on to continue setting things up, collecting prints and establishing a workflow until Wednesday, 7 December, 1904, when the system was accepted as a permanent part of Baltimore Police Department's Bureau of Identification.

28 November - 1955

A First-in-Maryland Polygraph Unit Established

Commissioner Hepbron purchased the first in the state "Lie Detector" machine to help build a polygraph unit within the Rackets Division of the department. In 1966, this unit was transferred to the Crime Lab Section, but for now we'll focus on the 28th of November 1955, when Baltimore began its use of the State's first polygraph machine. It was approved by Commissioner Hepbron, and first used by Lieutenant Frank W. Grunder

Baltimore Newspaper reports of 29 Nov 1955 – *Lie Detector Machine is Unveiled*

On 28 November 1955, Commissioner James Hepbron unveiled the state's first Lie Detector (Polygraph) Machine. His idea was to use it as part of the department's increased program of scientific crime detection.

Installation of the instrument went into effect under the direct supervision of Lieutenant Frank W. Grunder. Lt. Grunder recently returned to the department with the machine after a six-week training course in Chicago.

A special examination room is under preparation by the Rackets Division to house the "lie box" in the enforcement section's sixth floor offices of the police headquarters building.

To Train Assistants

Lieutenant Grunder, a former instructor at the police academy, is now assigned to the Rackets Division, and will train five or six assistants to operate the polygraph.

Results of the lie-detector examination, voluntarily given, cannot be admitted in court, but police claim they are a useful adjunct in the interrogation process.

Commissioner Hepbron, who approved purchase of the machine and the training of Lieutenant Grunder is familiar with the development of the lie detector technique and strongly supported its use by the department.

"Aids the Innocent"

In the past, out-of-state experts have been called in by Maryland police authorities to conduct polygraph tests in such major criminal investigations as the Carolyn Wasilewski and John Adams murder cases.

"The only thing we want to establish with the machine is the truth," Lieutenant Grunder said, "and this machine aids the innocent as well as weeding out the guilty."

"A polygraph operates on the theory that when you tell a lie you think the truth," the lieutenant explained. "The subconscious knowledge of this fact causes physiological changes in the body which can be measured and interpreted by the operator," he continued.

Three measuring devices are attached to the subject to record reactions. One about the chest for breathing; another around the upper arm for blood pressure, and a third around the palm of the hand to note changes in Galvanic Skin Response (perspiration).

[Author's Note – When I started using *Statement Analysis* in the early 90's, it was used to clear people as well as for revealing them as deceptive. In fact, I had a few Sergeants and Lieutenants quite excited that we could use it to clear, or eliminate, suspects.]

"Subdued Colors" Needed

In conducting the examination, Lt. Grunder said, the examiner must gain the subject's confidence and impart an "impartial" attitude in his role. The person to be examined is also explained the operation of the machine.

Questions requiring only yes or no answers are posed by the interrogator. A complete examination includes an unspecified number of tests each containing eight or twelve questions.

A series of questions, in which the true answers are known, such as name, age, address, sex, etc. are asked to establish a truth pattern. Pertinent questions relative to the investigation at hand are interjected to ascertain any change in the recorded patterns.

The examining room should be free of distracting influence, the lieutenant recommended. He said, "The colors of the room should be subdued. The furnishing plain and everyday noises evident only to a slight degree."

The subject and the examiner sit alone together in the room. However, most police agencies construct a one-way mirror and connect a microphone to allow other interested parties to view and hear the proceedings.

"Key to effectiveness of the test is interpretation of the results." The lieutenant declared.

"There can be only three results," he said, "Indications of Deception, of the truth, or that it is inconclusive."

During the demonstration yesterday (28 Nov 1955) in the commissioner's office for high ranking police officials, Police Commissioner Hepbron remarked that many subjects confess to crimes before an actual test is begun.

Only one in the State

"This reflects on the fine reputation accorded the machine by the public." He commented. He said one police agency reported that ten percent of the total volunteers for examination confessed before the test could be completed.

Lieutenant Grunder, who is also a lawyer and a graduate of the National Police Academy, is enthusiastic about the possibilities of the polygraph. "It's practically foolproof," he exclaimed. "Even if someone attempts to alter the results by moving, yawning, coughing, whatever – we can detect it," he said.

The Lie Detector, the only one in the state, will be made available to other police departments, Lieutenant Grunder said. It is portable and weighs only about 46 pounds.

Lieutenant Grunder was the first police official to operate a Polygraph in the state of Maryland.

For those readers who think the name Frank Grunder sounds familiar, it is probably because his son, Sergeant Frank W. Grunder, Jr. was killed in the line of duty on 1 August 1974 while in the process of apprehending a bank robbery suspect.

28 November - 1995

On this date in 1995, CBIF (the Central Booking Intake Facility) opened, closing down police cellblocks and courtrooms all over the city. Moving court from the districts to the Eastside court at North Avenue and Harford Road was the first step in taking prisoners and court proceedings out of the police districts.

1 December - 1973

On this day in Baltimore Police History 1 Dec 1973, we lost our brother Detective **Wiley M. Owens, Jr.** in the line of duty to poisoning based on the following Newspaper articles:

Newspaper Article - Feb 27, 1974; pg. C24 - *Crime Prober Poisoned*

A city police officer assigned to investigate organized crime who died December first of last year was poisoned, an assistant state medical examiner confirmed yesterday.

Dr. William S. Medart said that Officer Wiley M. Owens, Jr., 31, died after consuming ethylene glycol, the active ingredient in antifreeze.

The Police Department is conducting an investigation of the death to determine if the poisoning was accidental, a suicide or a homicide. Dennis S. Hill, a police spokesman, said homicide detectives have not "ruled out any of the three possibilities."

Odorless and colorless

Officer Owens, who had been assigned to the super-secret Inspectional Services Division for the past year, but whose specific assignment has not been revealed, was admitted to Union Memorial Hospital on November 25th of last year. The officer went into a coma the next day. He died the following Saturday without gaining consciousness after extensive tests failed to reveal the nature of his illness, according to another assistant medical examiner.

The poison, which is odorless and colorless, could be given to a victim in a glass of water or mixed drink without his knowledge, Dr. Medart said. He added that the poison enters the bloodstream and causes kidney failure. About twelve hours after ingestion, the victim will go into a coma. After the original autopsy made medical examiners "99 per cent sure that he had been poisoned," samples of the officer's kidneys were sent to the Armed Forces Pathological Laboratory in Washington. The findings returned this week confirmed those results, he said.

Our Investigation is continuing

Mr. Hill said that, "We've talked to all types of people. We're conducting a thorough investigation. There have been some rumors that his death may have had

something to do with his work," Mr. Hill added, but police have been unable to substantiate that.

He predicted that the Investigation would take at least "several more weeks." In 1972, Officer Owens was the main witness against Jackson Pennington, a lawyer who was convicted of offering the policeman a $100 bribe to give false testimony in a drunken driving case.

Before joining the department, Officer Owens spent several years with the Special Forces.' He was the father of three children.

<u>Newspaper Article</u> - Nov 13, 1976 - <u>Suit by Police Widow Remanded to City Court</u>

Annapolis - The Court of Special Appeals yesterday sent back the Baltimore Superior Court a suit by the widow of a Baltimore city police officer who has been trying to get records on her husband's death from the department.

Wiley M. Owens, Jr., a detective with the department's secret inspectional Services Division, died in December, 1973, after consuming ethylene glycol, an active ingredient in antifreeze.

Although medical examiners at first said the death was most probably a homicide, an investigation by the Police Department ruled that the death was not murder and was not in the line of duty.

But Thelma J. Owens, his widow, demanded records from the department on the investigation, claiming that her husband had feared there was a "contract" on his life.

Mrs. Owens has been trying to claim special death benefits from the board of trustees of the Fire and Police Employee Retirement System, and the board at her lawyer's request also went after the police records.

But the department has steadfastly refused to release the information claiming there was no "imperative duty" to disclose the records and that such action was not in the public interest.

Millard S. Rubenstein, the assistant attorney general representing the police commissioner, said that the city State's Attorney had been involved in the investigation and had found nothing that would lead to an indictment.

Mrs. Owens took her efforts to the city Superior Court, but Judge Shirley, B. Jones technically upheld the Police Department's position with a ruling on preliminary motion.

In remanding the case, the appeals court held that a decision on the matter should be based on Maryland's 1970 Public Information Act, which calls for general disclosure of public records with exceptions only when disclosure would be against the public interest.

The initial petition by Mrs. Owens did not seek the information under that law, though the matter was raised on appeal.

In most cases arguments on appeal can only be those made on the lower court level, but a Maryland rule permits a remand on other issues when the "purposes of justice will be advanced by permitting further proceedings."

The court's ruling allows Mrs. Owens to amend her petition to allege an action under the public information law.

3 December - 1937

Today in Baltimore Police Department History, 1937, the Department hired **Policewoman Violet Hill Whyte**… the first African American Officer of any gender on the Department. In an editorial, the Baltimore Sun said, "She worked in an all-white, mostly male dominated institution, and won the respect of all those she worked with. She did it through hard work, and human understanding." The Sun report went on to say she explained her success by saying, "I'm not afraid of hard work." During her 30 years on the police force, she proved "hard work" time and time again, she worked 16 to 20 hour days. Often she would begin her shift at 6 am and not leave until midnight or 1 am only to go home and be back in the station by 6 am She worked cases, as well as collecting clothing for inmates, and the poor. She made holiday baskets for the needy and counselled delinquent kids and their families. She once said, "Being first at anything is hard because you represent so many others; if you do poorly, everyone will think all those you represent will also do poorly."

[Author's note: *I understand what she means, and how that can be hard. If I were voting for someone to become a County Councilman, and I heard one of the guys running was an Irish and a retired Baltimore Police Officer, some might think he would automatically have my vote. However, I would first want to make sure I knew he would represent me well, and that is what Lieutenant Whyte was saying; if she had done poorly, it would have reflected on all of her sex and all of her race, and would have had people saying that "they" must all be like that. So if we are all going to be judged on the acts or conduct of one, then let us send the best we have. Let's not just send the first that asked to go. Mrs. Whyte went in alone, she was notably the first African American Police Officer, and she represented all police well. Thirty years, not one day missed; thirty years, she did more than she was asked, she worked doubles and more. She was an example not just for Women and African American police, but for all police. It is sad that she is only remembered for being the first African American Officer on the Baltimore Police Department, because she was so much more. Lieutenant Whyte was by all accounts a good police officer, she was a hard working police officer, a caring police officer... and she should be known for that... more than the color of her skin.*

Sadly, Lieutenant Violet Hill Whyte passed away on 17 July 1980 while in the Keswick nursing home where she had been since November 1979. - God bless her, and thank her for her service. There is no use in being first, if you can't also be the best, and she was said to have been the best by any standard.

The following is based on several newspaper articles from 1920:

On 3 July 1920, the headline of the Baltimore paper read: *"No African-American Policemen, and General Gaither's Dictum"* – It was subtitled; *"Announces none will be appointed, even if they pass examination – Declares time is not ripe"*

Another headline read: *"Representatives of the colored race informed of decision; can maintain order without them, Commissioner Rules"*

Police Commissioner Charles D. Gaither has decided that African-Americans, although they take and pass the examination, will not be appointed to the police force. General Gaither declared yesterday (2 July 1920) that "The psychological time had not yet come in Baltimore for the appointment of African-Americans to the force." The African-American population was informed of General Gaither's stand through the Afro American newspaper.

Carl Murphy, colored editor of the paper, called on General Gaither Tuesday and asked for the General's "position on the subject of appointing colored men to the force providing they are successful in passing the examination and their names were entered on the eligible list." The General told Murphy the time has not come for such action and that he positively would not appoint a colored man as a member of the Department. Murphy pointed out that New York City with the force of nearly 11,000 policemen had only 8 black policeman. General Gaither replied that if the same percentage were applied to the local Department, Baltimore would have no African-American policemen. There is no doubt, said General Gaither, "That colored policeman could be of value to the Department under certain conditions, but Baltimore does not need African-American policeman at this time. Our officers and patrolmen have for many years maintained law and order in the African-American neighborhoods and we propose to continue do so in the future. As far as I am concerned the question of appointment of African-Americans to the police force is settled." Colored men interested in having African-Americans appointed to the force made an appeal to the former police board headed by General Lawrason Riggs. At that time information was submitted showing that the following cities had African-American policemen, Pittsburgh 65, Trenton 2, Philadelphia 300, Cincinnati 9, Chicago 95, New York 8, Los Angeles 18, Cleveland 15, Detroit 14, Indianapolis 13, Boston 25. Figures were also submitted showing the cities which did not employ colored policemen. The large southern cities not having African-American policemen were New Orleans, and Atlanta. General Riggs told the African-American delegation then that he did not think the time had come for the appointment of African-Americans to the force.

Police Commissioner Charles Gaither was our First Commissioner, not to fall under a Board of Commissioners; he sat in that seat from 1920, until 1937 when Commissioner William Lawson took office.

Commissioner Lawson, sat one year 1937-1938, during his time in office, on the 3rd of December, 1937, he appointed Policewoman Violet Whyte, as can be seen in the following article dated, 4 Dec, 1937, titled:

Police Work Begun by Colored Woman - Mrs. Whyte, First Negro Member of Force, Assigned to Northwestern - Newspaper 4 Dec, 1937,

Mrs. Violet Whyte, Baltimore's first colored member of the Police Department, last night took over her duties as policewoman, assigned for the moment to the Northwestern District. William P. Lawson, Commissioner of Police, in a statement outlining her qualifications for the post, said last night that after her work in Northwestern is finished, she would be available for duty elsewhere in the city.

Appointee Lauded

Policewoman Whyte is "one of the best-prepared women among the colored people of Baltimore for the work she is to do," Commissioner Lawson said. He mentioned that she is the daughter of the late Rev. Daniel G. Hill, for many years pastor of Bethel AME (African Methodist Episcopal) Church. Lanvale Street, and Druid Hill Avenue, and that among her brothers, and sisters are a Vice-President of Howard University, and an instructor at Lincoln University, an instructor at Princess Anne Academy, and another instructor in Southern College. Policewoman, Whyte, is 40, married and the mother of four children, her husband George Whyte, has been a principal in the public schools of Baltimore for the last ten years, she lives at 623 North Carrollton Avenue.

Various Posts Named

Among the posts she has held, or now holds, which fit her for her job, Commissioner Lawson named the following: Teacher in the School of Christian Education, Member, advisory board, Civic League. President, Intercity Child Study Association, Teacher, Department of Parent Education, Executive secretary, Parent-Teacher Federation, Policewoman Whyte is an active member of the Negro State Republican League.

It would be 30 years before Lieutenant Violet Whyte would retire, 30 years of long days, 30 years of never missing a single day, and 30 years of promotions, promotions that took her from policewoman, to Sergeant, and from Sergeant to Lieutenant.

Her career can be seen in the following article:

"Lady Law" Leaves the Force after 30 Years - But Only Formally: as Volunteer, She Still Helps All

3 December 1967 – "Lady Law" as Lieutenant Violet Hill Whyte is known to hundreds of persons in West Baltimore, has formally retired from the Baltimore Police Department. But Lieutenant Whyte, the soft-spoken slender woman who made headlines as the first Negro police woman to join the force 30 years ago, (7 Dec 1967) still comes to her office at 6:00 am every morning. She organized the distribution of Thanksgiving baskets to needy families throughout the city, and is now planning a Christmas party for 4,000 children at the Royal Theatre on Pennsylvania Avenue.

Holiday Project Goes

She councils as many as 125 persons a month who come from the city and county to see her and in addition, works a regular 8 hours a day as a member of the Western District force.

Although she officially retired December 3, Lieutenant Whyte will continue those, and other activities on a volunteer bases until the end of her "Holiday" projects.

So she continues to collect Christmas toys in laundry baskets in the police station, and to gather clothes for prisoners and their families. She is still awakened at all hours of the night by those who want her help, or sometimes they call about the "Good News" she said, referring to a woman who phoned at 1:30 am because she was, "so glad" about the birth of her first grandson.

She would described by retired Judge Charles E. Moylan Sr. of the supreme bench of Baltimore as a "one-woman-police-force, and a one-woman-social-worker combined" she has worked narcotics cases, homicides, assaults, sexual abuse, and robberies during her 30 year career.

She is known for Bravery

Once she played the part of a "drunkard, cigarette smoking, dope addict" to help bring about the capture of a narcotics gang. For that she received a Federal citation, and was invited to appear before the Keauver committee investigating criminal rackets.

Lieutenant Whyte, rarely carried a gun, in one incident she declined an escort as she went to help a 12 year-old-girl being held by an armed man.

She said she enjoys testifying in court, and disliked child abuse cases more than any other assignments

I Get Emotionally Involved

"It's with the children that I find I get emotionally involved," she said. "Emergencies always seem to happen before 6:00 AM" she said, adding she never needed a sleeping pill to go back to sleep when she was awakened, and never missed a day at work on account of illness, or otherwise.

Lieutenant Whyte, the only Female Lieutenant of the 46 women on the police force, was born in Washington, and came to Baltimore as a young girl. Her father the Rev. Daniel G. Hill was a Methodist Minister (Bethal AME), and her mother a teacher.

Has Five Children

She graduated from Douglass High School, and Coppin State College. She was married to a public school teacher, who went on to become a principal himself, and who is now dead. She has five grown children.

"Retirement from one's job doesn't mean actual retirement" she said. She has spoken in every State in the country, and expects to continue her speaking career. She is also thinking of taking a job in the community service field. But after 30 years of work on countless crimes, and a lifetime of participating in church, and civic activities, she has one more wish – Time to grow flowers at her house on Elsinore Avenue.

A testimonial fete will be held at 7:30 pm today in her honor at the Blue Crest North

After retiring in 1967, she would enjoy 13 years of retired life, where she still gave to the community, working to help whoever needed her help, before passing away on 17 July 1980 as can be seen in the following article

Whyte, Black Police Pioneer, Dies - 22 July 1980

Lieutenant Violet Whyte who in 1937 became the first black officer to be appointed to the city's police force always said "I'm not afraid of work" The lieutenant passed away on [Thursday] 17 July, 1980 at the age of 82 proved during her 30 years on the police force, she meant what she said. Lieutenant Whyte often worked as many as 16 hours a day collecting clothing to the inmates and Thanksgiving baskets for the needy, and counseling to like what youngsters and their families in addition to handling cases that ranged from homicide, to child abuse. The late juvenile court Judge Charles E Moylan Sr. once called her a, "One-Woman-Police-Force and One-Woman-Social-Worker Combined!" Known as, "Lady Law" to her co-workers, the former police Lieutenant, and social activist never carried a gun. Born in Washington, she was the daughter of a Methodist minister, "My father taught me young, not to fear death, nothing has helped me as much in police work!" she said once, after helping the capture a narcotic gang, and impersonating a drunken, cigar smoking, dope addict on one of the most of the chilling of winter nights! For this action she was invited to appear before *The Kefauver committee*, which was investigating organized crime in 1952. She moved to Baltimore as a child and was a graduate of Douglass senior high school and Coppin State Teachers College. For about six years, she taught grammar school in Frederick County, then marrying the late George Sumner Whyte, a city school principal. She stopped teaching, and raised four children. Two of them were adopted. In 1937 she became the first black police officer in the city of Baltimore and was assigned to the Northwestern District. In 1955, she was promoted to the rank of sergeant, and was in charge of the policewomen, and transferred to the newly opened Western District Because of the uniqueness of her occupation at the time she was asked to appear on The TV game show *"To Tell the Truth"* in 1962 and channel thirteen's *"The Brent Gunts show."* In October 1967, just too months before retirement she was promoted to the rank of Lieutenant. She once told a reporter that of all the cases she ever worked to dislike child abuse the most "It's with the children that I find I get emotionally involved," she said After retiring from the police force in December of 1967, she became a field work supervisor for Planned Parenthood of Maryland and "continued visiting inmates and nursing homes with her sunshine bag of gifts and toiletries," her daughter, Esther C Bailey, said yesterday "I belonged to everything in Baltimore!" Lieutenant Whyte once said, when questioned about her numerous affiliations. She was appointed by both governors McKeldin, and Tawes to the board of managers of Boise a village in Cheltenham. She was also on the Board of Directors of Provident Hospital, a board member for the former Maryland safety council, a member of the speakers' bureau of the women's Christian temperance union, a member of the Lambda Kappa Mu sorority, and the Charmettes, a social group. The Phi Beta Sigma Wives, the F.E.W. Harper Elks Lodge No. 429 and the Matinee Ensemble, a civic association. She in addition to her daughter in Baltimore is survived by two other daughters Grace and Danielle of war Simpson and Grace Virginia of Waynesboro, Pennsylvania, a sundial rustle of Eden Maryland three sisters Esther hill Isaiah and grace hill Jake up and Lea hill Fletcher all of Petersburg, a Brother Joseph N. Hill of New York City and five grandchildren. Services for the lieutenant will be held at noon today at Bethel AME church 1300 to 110. The family suggests that expressions of sympathy be in the form of a memorial contributions to the acute stroke care unit of Dr. Elijah Sanders, Provident Hospital, 2600 Liberty Heights Avenue.

3 December - 1984

On this day in Baltimore Police History, 1984 we lost our brother Police **Detective Marcellus Ward** to gunfire based on the following:

Detective Marcellus Ward was shot and killed while working on an undercover assignment. He was shot and killed as he and other Baltimore officers along with a DEA agent attempted to arrest a heroin dealer on the third floor of a Baltimore row house. The suspect was taken into custody following the shootout, and was later convicted of Detective Ward's murder, and sentenced to life in prison.

Newspaper Articles released the following transcripts from court testimony:

Detective Ward had been with the agency for 13 years, and was assigned to the Drug Enforcement Administration's Baltimore District Office Task Force. He was survived by his wife and son. While undercover working narcotics, Detective Marcellus Ward was shot and killed as he was making a narcotics related buy prior to a raid on 3 December 1984.

Detective Marcellus Ward, 36, and other members of a specialized DEA task force were in the closing stages of an investigation with a final "heroin buy" from the suspects. It was shortly after 5:00 pm when one of the targets left 1829 Frederick Avenue to go to Pennsylvania Station to get the money with which the narcotics were to be purchased. Det. Ward was supposed to go with him, but for some reason at the last minute, plans were changed. Det. Ward waited with Lascell Simmons from whom he was to buy the high grade heroin, when suddenly, "Where they at, what the fuck happened?" was heard on the surveillance tape. "Oh Shit!" was heard from Det. Ward as he was hit by gunfire.

Ward's partner was Sgt. Gary Childs, who was outside, one of the members of the raid team. Hearing the shots, Sgt. Childs yelled up the steps, "Marty, where you at?" There were two more shots, and Det. Ward could be heard on the surveillance equipment moaning. Simmons then traded shots with officers coming up the steps. Sgt. Childs told Agt. Richard Boronyak, of the DEA to get down, and then yells for Marty, three times, "Marty! Marty! Marty!" But Marty couldn't answer as he lay choking, three floors up from his partners. Sgt. Childs began a desperate attempt to get Simmons to throw down his gun, yelling up to him to, "Throw the gun down and come out." Simmons, apparently in fear for his own life, thinking they might not be police at all but rival drug dealers, yelled back that he "ain't throwing his gun down until the police show up." He continues telling the police, "don't come up here, because I don't know who ya'll is, man!"

Sgt. Childs politely tells him, "I am the fucking police man, here's my badge, now throw down your gun, and walk out..." Getting no response, Sgt. Childs yelled, "If that man dies, I will kill you – I will fucking kill you!" Simmons says, "Man, I don't know if you are the police!" Sgt. Child responded, "Here's my mother fucking badge!" Simmons asks, "You sure yall's the police?" In response, Sgt. Childs threw his badge and wallet up the steps to the third floor, within the sight of Simmons. When Simmons saw the badge, he realized Sgt. Childs was who he said he was, and then Simmons threw his gun down, and surrendered.

Federal prosecutors contend that Simmons killed the 36-year-old detective assigned to the Baltimore task force because he suspected he was a police officer. They contend the killing was deliberate and premeditated, a virtual "execution." There was no struggle, which they say is clearly shown by the tape recording. Simmons's lawyer on the other hand said the Detective was shot as Simmons struggled with him, with both of their guns drawn. The defense contended the shooting was either accidental or in self-defense. He claimed Simmons would not have known Ward was "a police."

Earlier that day, Detective Ward went to the Kandy Kitchen to buy heroin from Simmons and Mark Byron Walker, his alleged partner in the West Baltimore heroin operation from whom Det. Ward had twice previously bought heroin, Sgt. Childs testified. When he was shot, Det. Ward was waiting with Simmons for Walker's return; Walker had gone to the train station to meet a man that was supposed to provide the money for the drug buy. Det. Ward had been supposed to go with Walker, to meet the guy and get the money, but from the tape, it was suggested by Simmons that Ward stay with him. Through an intermediary, Sgt. Childs relayed a message to his partner over the phone telling him to, "Leave the building, and failing that to be ready to take Simmons off." As police stormed the house, Det. Ward indicated he could not leave, the Sergeant testified during the trial.

Detective Ward had already informed Sgt. Childs that Simmons had a nickel-plated .357 close at hand. The tape was crucial to the government's case against Simmons and prosecutors played the 90 minute tape for the jury. Jurors heard only the first half-hour or so, but by the end of the day are expected to hear the remainder of the tape the following day, and to hear the portion where the detective is shot. Copies of the full transcript of the tape were made available to the press by Judge James Miller Jr. In releasing the transcript the Judge made clear that the transcript was only to be used as a guide. In the first part of the tape, Simons, Ward, and Walker are talking about a man that threatened to kill Ward. Walker and Simmons talk about killing the man.

Det. Ward was a Baltimore hero, well known, and well liked. Detective Ward was shot as he sat on Simmons' couch. Valiant efforts to preserve his life failed. Detective Marcellus Ward was a member of the Department for 13 years. He was married and the loving father of two children. Detective Ward was laid to rest on December 7, 1984.

As his brothers and sisters of the Baltimore Police Department we will not let him be forgotten. His service honored the City of Baltimore, and the Baltimore Police Department. May he rest in peace, and may God bless him.

3 December - 1970

Police Commissioner Donald D. Pomerleau introduced the Department's first Police Flag. It has remained our flag ever since with no changes. At the time the flag cost the department $180, today having that flag, in the same quality would cost more than $700, perhaps as much as $850.

7 December - 1904

While researching Marshal Thomas "Tom" Farnan of the Baltimore Police Department for this book, we came across the following 1907 newspaper report that indicates Baltimore's Police Department was the first agency in our country to officially use fingerprinting to catalog and identify criminals. – The 1907 article would provide us with information that would lead us back to the original 1904 report, and to the following information:

Finger Prints of Crooks are Now Aids of Police – Baltimore News of the Time, April 21, 1907

The article went on to say: *Finger Prints of Crooks are Now Aids of Police - Baltimore, the first American city to Adopt the New Identification Method*

THE THUMB-PRINT CARD USED BY THE BALTIMORE POLICE DEPARTMENT

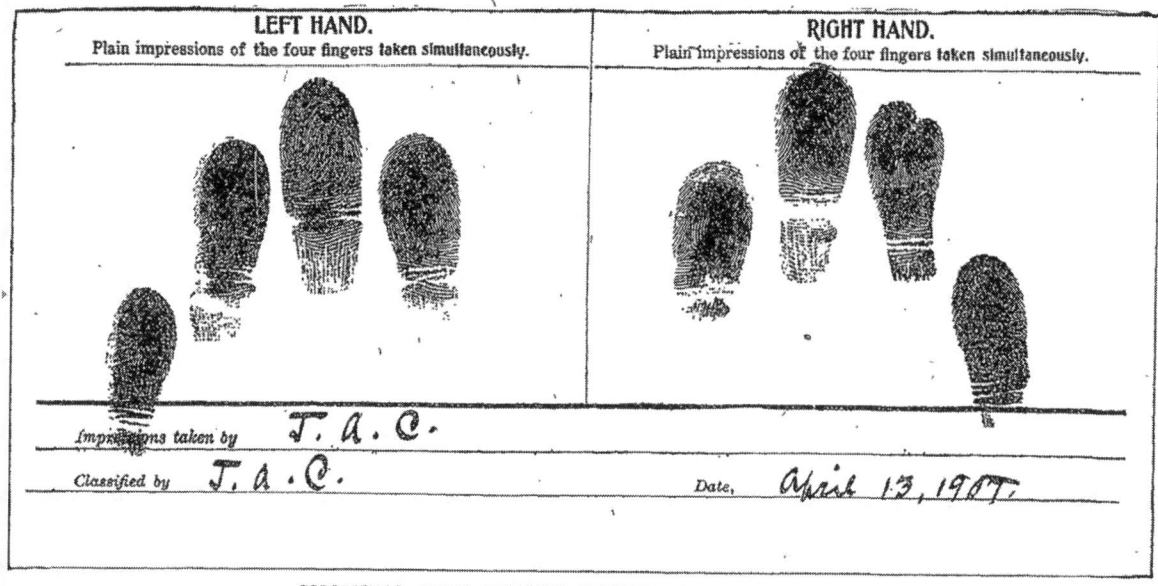

SHOWING THE FINGER-PRINTS OF BOTH HANDS

Thief catching is becoming more and more a matter of applying modern systems. As with every other profession, police investigatory work shares the tendency to utilize methodically new methods of technology from the new century.

In the old days, it used to be a free chase in the open with no odds given, and a scrimmage at the end between the defenders of the law and its violators. However, all that has passed. Criminals are now catalogued. When they are wanted, the apprehension is conducted in a matter-of-fact, systematic manner. There is nothing left to chance.

In line with this tendency in the ancient trade is the fingerprint classification method of identification, invented by E. R. Henry, of Scotland Yard, London, and lately tried in Baltimore for the first time in the United States. By its means, a criminal is tagged and recorded without the possibility of error. His identity, once his fingerprints have been taken, can never be disputed, and his life story, with a summary of his habits and personal characteristics, is always where it can be reached at a minutes notice.

<u>Keeping Track of Crooks</u>

For the last half century, the constant effort in police circles has been to find some means by which a criminal's identity could be permanently and accurately fixed.

The great utility of the rogue's gallery and the system of keeping a record of all persons convicted in the upper courts has made this an evidently desirable outcome. However, a rogue's gallery or cabinet of biographies is of little use, it can be seen, if the identity of the lawbreakers is a matter of uncertainty. An alias or disguise is easily assumed, so if there is no other way of fixing the identity of the person by name or photograph the rogue's gallery and criminal record might as well go to the trash pile.

To accomplish the desirable end of absolute identification various schemes have been proposed and tried. All have been based upon the principles that there are certain parts of the human body whose form cannot be changed without detection.

First came photography. This was in the days when the art was new and was thought to have marvelous value. At one time, for instance, it was believed that a photograph was a sure means of telling whether or not a person was going to develop an eruptive sickness, for it was said that the irruption would show on the photograph even if it had not yet made its appearance on the subject's face. Despite its many real virtues, however, photography did not fully cover the ground desired.

Failure of Photography

It had been supposed that a series of photographs showing a criminal in various poses – full face, half face, profile and so on – would be a complete means of identification should that criminal be apprehended at any time after the photographs had been made. This idea was proved a misconception, mainly through the shrewdness of the criminals, who found that a simple flexing of the facial and neck muscles distorted these features significantly and altered the value of their photographic representation.

As a result, the system was proven entirely inadequate for the task it was supposed to perform. Consequently, many criminals began looking similar, and in some notable cases their mugshots were hardly distinguishable.

The idea of these photographs demonstrated such additional value as a means of apprehension of criminals, that the gallery, and camera were made a permanent part of most police identification bureaus. Still something other than pictures would be needed for an absolute means of identification.

The Bertillon method was the next thing of consequence to make its appearance. Much had been written about the Bertillon method, and by many criminals and criminal-takers (Police, Bounty Hunters, Pinkerton, etc.) it was regarded with a

sort of superstitious admiration, its essentials seeming a sacred rite. At one time it had been proven very effective, but since has been shown as not so altogether infallible, as was shown in a case that occurred in London about 10 years ago which serves to show a troublesome flaw.

At that time two criminals were measured and it was found that their Bertillon records were exactly the same. This is rather a marvelous coincidence and is the only one recorded in the entire history of the system. Nevertheless, it shows that it is not absolutely dependable. Other points to be urged against the Bertillon method are that it is complicated, time-consuming, and can only be applied to adult prisoners.

The Fingerprint System

Then comes promise of what might be the final answer to a genuine method of positive identification. The latest claim, "The Finger-print System," a system that has none of the known faults of the Bertillon method, and that it has all of its virtues. This is rather a broad assertion, but to prove it they point out that the finger-print method is simple, quick, absolutely accurate, and applicable to an individual of any age. They are intensely enthusiastic, but the process is rather new and with any new system we are always apt to go to the extremes.

If the E. R. Henry finger-print system of identification really does pan out in its practical working – and its test in Baltimore seems to show that it will – Palmists will be jubilant and materially-minded of the world reproved, for the principle upon which it rests is one that fortunetellers have long banked upon.

It is the theory that the lines of the fingers of every person in the universe form patterns, which have no exact duplicate, and moreover that these lines remain unchanged in an individual's hand from his birth to his death.

It is a rather awesome reflection. Look at your finger-ends and consider that there is nothing else like them in the entire universe and that there never will be. It reminds us of the story of the little boy who after having been told of the wonders of nature looked up at his teacher with a puzzled air and asked if the Lord didn't ever run out of ideas. It seemed too big to be true. Still that is the principle upon which the E. R. Henry's finger-print system was based.

Taking the Prints

If the skin on our hand somehow becomes damaged and can grow back in a natural manner, its lines, after it has completed the healing process, will be identical to those of the skin that was destroyed. It really seems as if fate has stamped a permanent trademark upon the hand of each individual. At all events, the only thing that will permanently destroy these revealing lines would be an everlasting scar. Nevertheless, that scar, now becomes a part of the permanent identification.

If you have ever gone to a palmist and had him (or her, as the case is more apt to be) smear your hand with black ink and press it on a piece of white paper, you will understand that once just how the fingerprint system is worked. If the palmist as afterward examined this impression with a magnifying glass and discovered interesting things in it you will know also how the print is classified and filed in the Henry system of criminal identification.

The taking of fingerprints consists of a clever use of glass and printers ink and a bit of care. The ink is usually black, or if not that, of some intense color, and is the same as that used for printing fine cuts or engravings. The glass is a strip about 5 x 6". Upon the glass the ink is spread in a thin coating with a printer's roller.

Then a paper form with spaces reserved for the impression of the different fingers is laid upon the table beside the ink and the glass and all is in readiness to take the prints of the fingers of the person whose record is desired.

Prisoners are Frightened

These preparations are all very simple. They certainly don't seem to have anything in them to frighten a person. But prisoners in the Baltimore Bureau who are to be finger-printed seem always to regard them in a respectfully timid way. They think that there is some sort of a "hoodoo" about them. With the colored gentry, this is especially true. The idea of making a finger-print evidently seems possessed of menace of some kind to some.

Twelve prints were initially made from each individual to be recorded. First each of the 10 fingers were printed separately; then the forefingers of each hand together. (Eventually this number would increase to include both palms.) A simple roll of the ink out on a piece of glass, and a pressure upon the paper constituted the entire mechanical portion of the operation.

The next step in the taking of a fingerprint record was the classification, and filing.

The first term may not be understood, but the second seems simple enough. Filing; the word instantly brings to mind a picture of cabinets with their content arranged alphabetically.

Filing a fingerprint to us seems to be very easy in comprehension. In reality, it is the most difficult part of the process. Fingerprints cannot be filed according to the alphabet or numerically. They must be put away according to fixed characteristics of their own, and this is why they must be classified before they can be filed. Enter E. R. Henry.

Suppose a man is in custody. It is thought that he has a fingerprint card on record, and that this individual is desired by police officials. Would it be possible to look for it under the name the man gives? Yes and No, you could check the name given to see if you have a match, but that would only show that he has been arrested under that name in the past. So, we would need to take it a step further, his alias should provide us with the filing code for his finger-print type, and from there we should more easily be able to identify him under all names he has used in the past, providing us with a more positive identification. In which case if there were outstanding wants or warrants we would be able to hold him for the proper authorities.

That is the whole point. If names were affixed and could not be changed, they would serve as a means of identification. Otherwise, identity must be ascertained by means of an individual's personal characteristics. In this case, a fingerprint record must be found by means of a finger-print and not by a name. We can use a name to perhaps lead us to the fingerprint for verification purposes, but it will always be the fingerprints, that verify the name, and not a name to verify the fingerprint.

<u>Sorting the Prints</u>

The task of devising a means by which fingerprints could be filed was one of the greatest difficulties. By successfully carrying it through Mr. Henry gave his name to the process now standing as a monument to him. The peculiar virtues of fingerprints as a means of identification were known before his time, but there was no way to classify them. So often when we tell people this was first designed in 1903, we are told, old Asian findings, and India use of prints, a thousand or more years ago, to which we cannot deny, but what has to be pointed out is, the use of prints before 1903, and Mr. Henry's categorizing prints for the purposes of identification, we had no way of truly using the fingerprint to identify someone, all we could do then was use the name to match the print, but we could not use the print, to identify the name. In other words, where today we can find a name from the print i.e. someone commits a crime and leaves a print, we can now use that print to find a name. Before, all we could do was take a name, and verify that it matches a print we might have on file. Consequently, Mr. Henry's system was quite important, and changed the way crimes were solved, and people were positively identified.

Through the study of several thousand fingerprints which he had collected while he served in India, where the government has long had fingerprints used for signatures among the lower class natives, Mr. Henry came to the conclusion that there were two great classes into which all fingerprints could be divided. In other words, he found that there were certain general designs upon which the patterns of which all fingerprints could be based.

These designs he named "Arches, Loops, Whirls and Composites." Arches or loops occur wherever no single line of the finger-tip makes a complete circle. Whirls are formed wherever a line does complete a circle. Composites are a kind of hybrid pattern partaking more of the nature of the whirl than of a loop. The proportions of these three classes he found to be as follows:

Arches, 5%.

Loops, 60%.

Whirls and composites, 35%

Since the number of arches was found to be inconsiderable, Mr. Henry placed them in a single class with the loops. Whirls and composites were very easily associable. Thus, Mr. Henry had two great natural classes, within which all finger-prints could be divided.

The 1,024 Classes

In every fingerprint record there are 10 separate prints to be considered. Either one of these prints can be one of two classes, or there are a number of combinations that might be formed among fingers of different classes. For instance, there might be five loops, and five whirls, or there might be four loops and six whirls, and so on. The point was to find out how many classes there might be. This Mr. Henry set himself to do. If he discovered exactly the number of classes in a primary classification of his fingerprints he would be able to commence a system of filing. One of the simplest propositions and higher mathematics is the find out the number of possible combinations among a given number of objects. A very simple formula *has been worked out for this purpose. By this formula Mr. Henry ascertained that with sets of two and 10 objects there was a possibility of 1,024 combinations.*

Accordingly, if a cabinet should be constructed to hold 1,024 drawers, the bases of a reliable system of filing fingerprints was… well… right at their finger-tips. Now 1024 is a square of 32, so the cabinet might very conveniently be made with 32 drawers each way.

It is useless to follow the process of finger-record filing further. It simply becomes more complicated as one goes on. It is sufficient to say that the 1024 primary classes can be subdivided by minor peculiarities of fingerprints, which Mr. Henry enumerates in his book dealing with the subject, and so the process is elastic and will accommodate any number of records. In an up-to-date print Bureau a record can be found, or filed in less than two minutes time.

Originated in India

The fingerprint system originated in India, and came from that country by way of British conquest, and the St. Louis exposition to Baltimore and America. In all the Eastern countries, the value of fingerprints has been known from time immemorial. In China, indeed, there is a pleasing little story about an ancient Empress whose official seal for all the coinage of her realm was her finger, and Prussian. At any rate, for many centuries before the British took possession of India, fingerprints had been used as signatures among the lower castes.

After the Empire had been established governmental difficulties with natives who impersonate each other for the sake of fraudulently receiving pensions became so great that some method had to be found by which one Indian could be told from another. The fingerprint method, which had been observed among the natives themselves, was adopted as a happy solution and proved itself all that could be desired.

At first finger-prints were used only in the government departments in India in lieu of signatures. Then they were taken up by the police department also. Notably this was the case in the Bengal Bureau. Mr. E. R. Henry was then a young subaltern in the branch.

Years afterward, when Mr. Henry was appointed chief of Scotland Yard, in London, he took his Indian method with him. When he saw the immense need of a systemized use of fingerprints he perfected his method of classification and filing alluded to above, and gave his invention to the world.

Scotland Yard the First

Scotland Yard was, of course, the first police Bureau among civilized nations to receive the benefit of the Henry method. His introduction there took place in 1897, and it was made an adjunct to the Bertillon method. Its complete adequacy for attending to the duties of identification by itself, however, soon convinced the English officials of the superfluity of the older method, so the time tried Bertillon system was dropped.

When the St. Louis exposition was opened in 1904 the British government sent a delegation from Scotland Yard to demonstrate the effectiveness of its new system. The National Association of Chiefs of Police was in session in St. Louis at that time, and the English representative took advantage of the opportunity to address them upon the new method of identification. This is the combination of circumstances that brought the system to the United States.

Marshall Farnan of the Baltimore Police Department was one of those who heard the lecture upon the fingerprints method. He was much impressed and sought an opportunity to speak personally with the lecturer. When he returned to Baltimore at the conclusion of the convention he sought out Sgt. John Casey, of the Department's Bureau of Identification, confided to him his knowledge, and delegated him to visit St. Louis and receives special lessons in this new system.

Sgt. Casey departed an incredulous scoffer, and returned an enthusiastic convert. His zeal in the work has made the Baltimore Bureau one of the most favorably known in the country.

The Fingerprint Identification section of the Department's Bureau of Identification first put the technique into practice on 26 November 1904, when Sgt. Casey printed a prisoner that was being held on a theft charge. With all their training, and practice, the official date used to establish the Fingerprint Identification section was 7 December 1904, and this date was followed shortly by others in other big cities of the United States.

Exit, M. Bertillon

At the time, it was been often asked of late in police circles if the fingerprint method will ever wholly supersede the Bertillon method in the United States. In case the example of Europe be followed, it most certainly will. At the time of these writings; some 112 year later; it has without any question outlasted the Bertillon method. But, the question asked was, "Wholly Supersede?" and in that case, the answer is,

"No!" as one to the most important aspects of the Bertillon method was the photograph, and when we take finger-prints, we also take, "Mug shots," a forward, and a profile. Therefore, while the fingerprint method has without a doubt, changed the way we categorize, identify, and track criminals, without a photo, it would be much harder. There is now no great nation in the old country, with a single exception of France, where the Bertillon method was born, that does not use the fingerprint system somewhat exclusively.

The advantages of the fingerprint method are that it is cheaper, simpler, and more reliable. The personal element of the operators of efficiency or non-efficiency does not materially alter the results. Finally, the instruments of its use are neither many nor costly. In this last point especially the Bertillon method lags far behind. Special and delicate instruments of much cost have been installed before it can be successfully practiced.

An application of fingerprints that has caused much interest is in the detection of criminals. Suppose a burglar enters the house and leaves his finger-mark upon the windowpane. No other clue was wanted by the enterprising police of today. The pane is carefully taken out and sent to the Bureau of identification. There the prints are classified.

Then someone looks into the file, turned over a few leaves and, presto! If the burglar is an old offender, his name, photograph, criminal record and habits of living are staring one in the face. It sounds like a fairytale, but the experiment really has been tried with complete success in England.

Where Science Failed

In Baltimore, not long since it was thought that this same idea could be given an application in connection with the Cunningham murder case. The search was for the murderer. In the victim's room were found the number of checks with black finger marks upon them. The police generally were jubilant, and Sgt. Casey exalted. Here at last, it was thought, was a chance to throw the limelight on the fingerprint Bureau. Finally, it transpired that the marks were not those of the murder, but of an enthusiastic member of the detective corps who, in raking around among the ashes of the hearth for clues, had gotten his fingers dirty and had then picked up the bunch of checks. Science had a downfall.

Whenever scientific knowledge develops unique features it is immediately applied in a popular form for the pastime of the people. In this case, finger-prints have

received an ingenious embodiment by a novelty house, which is sold a little book containing a pad of ink, and a number of blank pages. "Flugeraphs" are to take the place of autographs. Soon, instead of the fiend who want your name and favored bit of poetry, one will be pursued by the hobbyists in fingerprints. Smutty fingers and black nails will be all the rage. Since some say, at all events. It remains to be seen.

10 December - 1974

On this day in Baltimore Police History, 1974, we lost our brother Police **Officer Martin J. Greiner** to gunfire. According to a Sun Paper article dated 10 December, 1974; On 30 November Officer Greiner responded to the corner of Huntington Avenue and 27th Street for multiple calls of armed person, shots fired, fire crackers, and numerous other duplicate and similar calls. Upon arrival he was approached by four adults; two female, and two male, all seemingly terrified by an armed person and the shots being fired. As Officer Greiner exited his car to investigate, several shots rang out, the group gathered in closer; Greiner, put his arms around the group the way a quarterback might in a game time huddle. His attempt was to push them down, and to take cover behind his car to prevent them from being injured. Before he knew it, the shooting had stopped. Officer Greiner began to ask for information from his witnesses, but as quickly as they approached him for help, they were gone. Then all of a sudden he felt a burning in his abdomen, and left side. He realized that he had been shot, and at a very close range. He fell to the ground while getting back into his car, while lying on the ground his attention was drawn over to a nearby alley where again he saw a suspect holding a gun; laughing at the Officer as he lay helpless in the street, the suspect pointed his handgun at the Officer Greiner and fired several more shots; Officer Greiner was shot one or two more times before the suspect vanished from his sight into the alley. Officer Greiner managed to get back into his car where he was able to call for help. He let KGA know he had been shot, giving a full and complete description of the suspect. Before long Officer Greiner was with medics, and other officer's. He was stabilized and taken to University Hospital. Meanwhile, the shooter, William E. Teves 3rd, of the 2600 block of North Charles Street was arrested by Officer's Stephen McGowan, and David Crites, just outside of his home in the 2600 block of North Charles Street (it was as if they were waiting for him). Officer's McGowan and Crites then took the suspect to University

Hospital for treatment to an injury on his hand, with hopes that he might be identified by Officer Greiner.

Upon seeing Officer Greiner in the hospital bed two things happened; First, Officer Greiner did positively identify Teves as the person that had shot him while he lay injured in the street. Realizing he was caught, Teves lunged at and began to attack Officer Greiner. There are few things that affect police more than seeing a brother officer injured; one of those is to see someone trying to injure someone that an officer feels a personal obligation to protect, i.e. an officer as he lay helpless in his hospital bed. With this Teves was either thumped with an Espantoon, or Buffaloed by a nearby officer with the butt end of a Smith and Wesson .38 Cal. pistol. We may never know which, because to Buffalo someone in Baltimore was rare, and not part of our training, as well to carry a nightstick into a hospital detail was 50/50 - some officers did, others left it in their car. In either case, Teves himself quickly became in need of medical attention, and was taken from University Hospital, to Mercy Hospital where he was admitted for a serious head injury, and of course that original boo boo to his hand.

While in the hospital Teves was guarded by two officers; Officer John Provenza, and Officer John Burns, Officer Provenza stepped in the hall for a minute, some reports say to take a smoke, (In those days smoking in buildings, including hospitals was more liberal) others say he was just guarding from a chair in the hallway. While alone with that single officer, the suspect seized the opportunity, and lunged from his bed, attacking Officer Burns. A struggle ensued, and Teves managed to get Officer Burns' gun; Officer John Provenza heard the commotion and quickly came back into the room; just as Provenza entered the room, Teves managed to fire off several rounds, two of which struck Officer Burns. As Officer Provenza re-entered the room he drew his service revolver and squeezed off a round or two at Teves thereby ending the threat and saving Burns' life.

Officer Burns would go on to survive his injuries. Officer Greiner would not be as lucky, as it would be 11 days after being shot, on 10 December, 1974, that Officer Greiner would die due to complications that had set in from one of the rounds perforating his colon, and ending up lodged against his spine.

The suspect in this case, William E. Teves III, was an orphan, and was no stranger to police; even less, a stranger to police-involved shootings, as a little more than a year earlier he was arrested for shooting Central District Officer James H. Harris, on Tuesday, 18 April 1972 – just outside the White Coffee Pot Jr. when the two attempted to rob a vagrant in the restaurant rest-room; the vagrant had no money, so he was pistol whipped. As Officer Harris entered the restaurant Teves and Jenkins [the suspects] were exiting the restaurant and walked past the young officer, a few seconds later an un-known customer shouted that there had been a man beaten up in the men's room. Patrolman Harris rushed to the street to grab the two men he had just seen leaving the restroom as he entered the establishment. Witnesses said just that fast they heard a volley of shots, and saw Patrolman Harris stagger back, and fall to the pavement on his back. Harris was forced to undergo a four hour surgery; as the shooting had caused damage to his left lung, his liver, and doctors had to remove his spleen. They said Patrolman Harris, was unmarried but had recently become engaged, he was a probationary officer. The victim of the beating at the restaurant was identified as John Grimes, 47, he was staying at the Armistead Hotel, (Fayette and Holliday Streets.) Grimes was treated for cuts, and bruises at Mercy Hospital, and later released. Grimes told police the suspects had accosted him in the men's restroom, and had began beating him on the head with their pistol. He said they attempted to take money from him, but he had none. When it came down to it, the young officer never got a good look at Teves, nor did Grimes, so charges against Teves were dropped.

But that didn't mean the judge forgot about them. Likewise, while in the hospital when Teves attacked Officer Burns taking his gun, and then shooting him, making Burns the 3rd officer Teves was known to have shot, though Teves wouldn't be charged with the first two shootings, or the beating of Grimes in the men's room of the white coffee pot Jr. Judge Basil A. Thomas didn't just forget about those incidents. It may not have been entered in as evidence, and wasn't marked as a conviction so to speak… Judge Basil A. Thomas still remembered it; his memory was obvious when he imposed a sentence on Teves, having just been convicted of 1st degree murder in the shooting death of 25 year old, Northern District Officer Martin J Greiner . Teves so lackadaisical that he would yawn when the jury foreman announced the verdicts convicting Teves of murder, use of handgun commission of a violent crime, and unlawful possession of a concealed weapon. Teves was quick to demand his right to file a motion for a new trial, telling the judge and courts, "This was a mock trial, and anything I would say would not make a difference." Judge Thomas after a brief recess granted the defendants request for an immediate sentencing. "This was an unexplained, unprovoked and coldblooded shooting of Officer Greiner, which ultimately resulted in his demise." The judge said, "It is a crime that has shocked, and is shocking to the entire community, and it deserves the harshest penalty that this court can impose." The Judge was told Teves was the product of a broken home, and that he had begun living in and out of orphanages since the age of 10, he never felt loved, and turned to alcohol for comfort. The Defense went on to ask that Teves be sent to Patuxent Institution for Psychiatric Treatment. Judge Thomas refused that request – giving Teves, "Life plus 18 years", saying, "I couldn't take the shooting of Officer in Harris a little over a year ago April of 72 into consideration; nor could I take the more recent shooting of Officer Burns, into consideration!" he went on to say, "Just as I couldn't take those into consideration, nor can I take being an orphan as a mitigating factor, or any drinking problems to be blamed for a shooting rampage!" The judge basically sent Teves to a place where they don't serve alcohol!"

Commissioner Donald Pomerleau saw 1973 as a particularly bad year for Baltimore Police. Greiner was the fourth officer killed in the line of duty that year, and the Commissioner had finally had enough, he determined based on Greiner's death it was time to issue bullet proof vests for all of patrol. A step in the right direction, it wouldn't be until 1985 with the loss of Vincent J. Adolfo that we would get better vests, and over the years the vest would get better and better. During Teves' trial, his defense tried every trick in the book, from saying he was crazy, to saying he was an orphan, to saying he was a drunk…. None of it worked… while it wasn't admissible, it was unforgettable what Teves did in 1972 to Officer Harris, and then after shooting, and attacking Officer Greiner, to attack and shoot Officer Burns… unforgettable, Teves needed to be sent to jail and he was.

As his brothers and sisters of the Baltimore Police Department, we will not let him be forgotten, his service Honored the City of Baltimore, and the Baltimore Police Department. May he rest in peace, and may God bless him.

11 December - 1856

On this date in 1856 City Council voted on, and passed a bill to "Arm" Baltimore Police Officers - 1857 was a date given by History Channel's "Tales of the Gun" - the "Police Guns" Episode, with an original air date, of 2 April, 2000, in which they reported, "Baltimore as having become the first Department in the nation to issue, and provide each police officer with a firearm." The documentary went on to state The Colt, 1849, Pocket Model, was the weapon of choice, and was 1st issued, and used by the BPD, and it's Officers.

Sometimes information contradicts other information and as such, we located two Sun Paper articles; one dated, 11 December, 1856, entitled "Proceeding of City Council", in which arming the individual City Police Officer was voted into law, then on 25 December, 1856 an article titled "The New Police Bill" the bill was released. While all of the actual revolvers may not have been provided in 1856, they were approved into law on that 11 December, 1856.

[Author's Note: We're only providing the aforementioned contradictory information about, "Baltimore being first to arm their police" out of respect for the Discovery Channel and their source(s), but I suggest, at least for now, that we take that information with a grain of salt. Still, I will leave this until we find further info, or others that read this line from a Sun Paper article, Dated, 11 December, 1856, in which a member of City Council at the time while they were trying to pass his bill to "Arm Baltimore Police" said, "In New York, and Philadelphia where there is a penalty for carrying concealed weapons, the police are armed by the city authorities." This is being taken by us to mean, we may have been 3rd in the issuance of firearms, but by these reports, we were not first.]

13 December - 1988

Today in Baltimore Police history, 1988, our brother **Officer Gene Cassidy** was awarded the **Medal Of Honor** and **Citation of Valor** for a shooting that occurred on 22 October, 1987; a shooting that took his eye sight, injuring him to a point in which he could have easily just, up and quit, retired and done nothing for the rest of his life, instead he stayed on the job, worked the Academy as an instructor, teaching recruits how to become better police.

Newspaper Article - Dec 13, 1988; pg. 1F – *Citations for a Hero*

Agent Eugene Cassidy. 28, a Baltimore police officer blinded by a bullet fired by a drug suspect on 22 October. 1987, was awarded the Police Department's Medal of Honor and Citation of Merit [Valor] during a ceremony yesterday (12 December, 1988) at the Western District Police Station. He was accompanied by his guide dog. Izzy; his wife. Patty; their 6-month-old daughter, Lauren; and his mother, Mary Cassidy.

18 December - 1948 - K9

On this Day in Baltimore Police History, 1948 - we lost our four legged brother, **K9 dog Socolow McGee** who died in the line of duty to a traffic accident;

Based on Sun Paper report dated, 19 December, 1948. Dog Policeman Killed in Duty - Four Footed Volunteer Struck by Car While on His Beat.

[Author's Note: *Some may be confused about the report that K9 Dog Police Officer Killed in the line of Duty in 1948, because elsewhere in this book it is firmly stated that Baltimore didn't have a K9 unit for another 8 years to the day, as they started training on 18 December, 1956. Kind of interesting, as I have spoken to several old timers, Retired Officer Jim Mitchell is one of my favorites, as we had become close friends pretty fast, and he once said, "I know they say the K9 unit started in 1956, and I remember it being a big deal, I even remember one of the first times I heard a dog chasing a guy down," he paused to think about it, and then continued, "It was up on Pennsylvania Ave, and that dog chased the suspect down and held him on a wall until his handler caught up to him. The sound of his paws, or nails running on the street, is a sound I won't forget," again he needed to stop and think, Jim was like that, he wanted to make sure he had his facts straight, and when he was sure of what he was talking about he would continue on, as he did on this day, "but I seem to remember police dogs before that too, I just don't know too much more about them." Well, through some research the earliest I could find our department associated with trained K9 dogs, was 1914, when we had use of two dogs, the report named one dog, as "Luxe," and the second dog as "Morpheus." The two dogs were privately trained and handled. Note: We'll have more on them elsewhere in these writings*].

18 December - 1956

Today in Baltimore Police History, 1956, it was the start of what would become Baltimore's K9 unit, and what would become the best K9 training program in the world. On December 18, 1956, two dogs that had previously been in training were offered to the Baltimore Police Department. Two officers also with previous dog experience joined in, and the program was put into effect on an experimental basis. By the middle of January 1957, fourteen dogs had been acquired as potential candidates, and fourteen men were selected and assigned to the K9 Corps. These men were chosen because of a questionnaire that was sent to all members of the department asking for volunteers. The men and dogs were trained daily until March 1, 1957. At that time, they were put on the streets to work Friday and Saturday nights, in areas where crime was most prevalent. Shortly after this, actually on April 17, 1957. Commissioner Hepbron, considering the experiment a success, went before the Mayor and City Council where appropriations were made through the Board of Estimates, resulting in the K-9 Corps becoming a permanent part of our Police Department

Therefore, Turk, and Major Grunts could be the most well know K9 Dogs in the department, unless we go back to 1914, where instead of today's German Sheppard, we may have found two Airedale Terriers - check out the following Article:

"A little known fact, while not an official unit, Baltimore had two Police Dogs at their call when two Airedale Terriers from London came to enroll as members of the Baltimore Police Force. Their owners learned two dogs were already here, privately owned, one belonging to Mr. Jere Wheelright, and the other to Dr. Henry Barton Jacobs. "Luxe," Mr. Wheelright's dog was a superb example of a highly trained equine aristocrat, big, powerful and intelligent to a degree that was truly remarkable. Morpheus, Dr. Henry Barton Jacobs' dog also a superb example of a highly trained K9. It would be 42 years before we would have an official K9 Unit, but off and on from 1914, until 1956 we had, had Police Dogs used in both a private and official capacity. Nevertheless, not until 1956 did we establish an official unit, with an official methodology that would go on to become world known as the best K9 unit in the country, and then in the world.

By December, Marshals Carter and House decided they should have their own K9 unit with-in the Baltimore Police department, as is found in the following news article dated 18 Sep 1914:

Newspaper Articles – 18 September, 1914; pg. 12: *Trying Police Dogs*

To Try Police Dogs - Departments Here Will Use Belgian Hounds in Suburbs - Their Job to Chase Crooks - Success in Other Cities Prompts Experiment Here For Detection and Protection

Four Belgian hounds, trained to attack a burglar or murderer or to assist anyone who needs protection, will soon be doing police duty for the Baltimore Police Department in the suburban districts. At a meeting of the Police Board Wednesday it was decided to give the police dog a tryout in Baltimore and Marshal Carter and

Deputy Marshal House were instructed to create a dog squad as an aid to policemen who work extensive posts.

As soon as the dogs were bought, they were to be placed in the custody of four night policemen, who will care for them, being amply repaid for the care by the department.

While the board's action is one of an experiment, it is believed that the dog squad will meet with favor and be an important adjunct of the police force.

The policemen who will have the dogs as aids will take them from their homes directly to their posts. Journeying with the policemen the dogs will work until 5 o'clock in the morning. The dogs will be taught to make detours around houses to detect possible marauders.

The record of police dogs in New York, Brooklyn and cities of the West is said to be a surprising one, many notable captures having been made by the animals. According to Marshal Carter and Deputy Marshal House the Belgian hounds can be trained in criminal detection as well as in protective work. As a constant colleague of the patrolman and as a detective he is considered by police as invaluable.

"When the dogs are in regular police service," declared Deputy Marshal House, "They can be put on guard at the door of a house and no one will be permitted to pass in or out. If one is rash enough to try it, the dog will knock him down and sit on him. He does this by getting between the legs of the would-be fugitive and causing him to lose his balance and fall."

Marshal Carter said last night that he would arrange immediately to get at least four dogs in the department within the next two weeks. It is expected that a Belgian hound will cost about $100. Marshal Carter was in Milwaukee several years ago and in looking over the police situation here, he learned of the work that the Belgian police dogs do there.

This is only one of the many new ideas that the Police Board has to better the police system. It is probable that within the next six months the department will increase the dog squad.

1914-1916 - "Luxe" and "Morpheus" Baltimore's first K9 dogs - A little known fact:, while not an official unit, Baltimore had two Police Dogs at their call when two Airedale Terriers from London came to enroll as members of the Police Force.

Their owners learned two dogs were already here, privately owned, one belonging to Mr. Jere Wheelright, and the other to Dr. Henry Barton Jacobs. "Luxe", Mr Wheelright's dog was a superb example of a highly trained equine aristocrat, big, powerful and intelligent to a degree that was truly remarkable. It would be 42 years before we would have an "Official" K9 Unit, but, off and on, since 1914, we had, had Police Dogs used in both a private, and official capacity. Still it wasn't until 1956 that we establish an official unit, with an official methodology that would go on to become world known as the best K9 unit in the country using a system known as the, "Baltimore System".

Add to this information a dog we used in 1948 - Socolow McGee - 18 Dec 1948, "McGee," as this dog was better known, was killed in the line of duty, while patrolling the Central District, he was struck by a car. The driver of that car rushed him to an emergency Veterinarian Hospital where he was pronounced dead.

This based on a Newspaper Paper Article dated 19 Dec 1948 - But this my friends is not to say anything less of our current K9 unit, as with most units, in the department there were some start up attempts, The Marine unit started in 1861 using row boats out of the three districts that were on the waterfronts, Southern, Central and Eastern. The Bicycle Unit had first started in 1917, and the again 1972, and finally 1992. Each of these had multiple start-up attempts, one, two, maybe three tries before they got it right, the odd thing, with the K9 Unit, in the 1917 article, they mentioned the dogs going home with their handlers. Something Baltimore became known for, rather than crating the dogs between shifts... a big part of the Baltimore system was in taking the dogs home to make them, "people friendly."

20 December - 1934

On this day in Baltimore Police history we lost our Brother **Patrolman Henry W. Sudmeier** to accidental friendly gunfire. A little more than 8 years prior to his death Patrolman Henry Sudmeier was walking his beat in the Northern District. He was aware of a suspect robbing the poor boxes of local churches and of the Sacred Heart, so he stayed close to the Sacred Heart, a Catholic Church located in Mount Washington.

It was during the night shift on a cool October night 1926, when he heard gunshots coming from inside the church, knowing of the recent poor box thefts, he grabbed his flashlight (the papers back then called it an electric torch) and ran in. Like all police he didn't know what would be waiting for him inside, he didn't know a suspect by the name Henry "Hank" Connelley, recently released from the Maryland State Penitentiary had entered the church earlier to steal money from the poor box.

He didn't know Captain Frank Gatch had sent two plain clothes officers inside the church on a detail to catch "Hank" Connelley; he also didn't know that when those detail officers, Patrolman Melvin Jackson and Patrolman Joseph Young, spotted Connelley and commanded him to "HALT"; Connelley would refuse and broke for the church entrance. This is what caused Officers Jackson and Young to begin firing on Connelley, and as a chain of events went, it would be those gunshots that would cause Connelley to duck down near the pews where Officer Sudmeier was about to enter.

As Sudmeier entered the church he didn't know lighting his flashlight would cause the young officers on this detail to mistake him for Connelley, and begin firing on him. Once shot, Patrolman Sudmeier fell to the floor. Hank Connelley got up and started to run, but was quickly captured by Officers Jackson and Young.

It was only as they were leaving the church that they would discover Officer Sudmeier was shot; he was lying there on the floor bleeding from a wound in the right side of his abdomen, (an extremely painful injury), but he didn't say a word, not a single moan. So while one policeman handcuffed Hank Connelley, the other summoned an ambulance to hurry Patrolman Sudmeier to the hospital. Once there it was found that he had suffered a severe wound, and an operation was performed immediately. Surgeons were not confident regarding his chance for recovery.

Nonetheless, Patrolman Sudmeier was as tough as they get, he had faith, and was optimistic. He also had one thing every good man has, and needs... a good woman to stay by his side. From his bed at Mercy Hospital, he was recovering in leaps and bounds, above what any of the doctors had expected. He would eventually be moved from Mercy Hospital to Mercy Villa, on Bellona Avenue.

His condition improved beyond anyone's expectations; he was able to get in and out of bed, to and from his wheelchair, (with assistance). He was paralyzed, so he knew he would never walk again. There is a certain amount of psychological grief, depression and other things to deal with when you love your job, and after an injury you learn of things like this; but at the time of his injury he had only about a year on the force, and a newlywed of just two months. His wife, Mrs. Lentha Sudmeier, gave him hope; she made him push forward, and without a single word made him work harder (<u>Author Note</u>: *I know the feeling, and the benefits of a good wife. In this type condition, in front of the woman of your dreams, you don't want to fail, you don't want her to see your pain, and as you always try to impress her, you give it everything you have.*) Mrs. Lentha, came to the hospital to be with her husband every day, her love for him became his strength… and it seemed to be working – On one of his biggest nights of his life in the police force, came in June 1930 (It had been 4 years since being shot) and he was the guest of honor in the hospital auditorium where a party, or Policemen's Ball was being held. It was attended by 1,800 patrolman of the day, the Police Commissioner "Charles D. Gaither" (he was the first PC in the modern police department, a department with just one commissioner instead of the board of commissioners that previously held his position) alongside the Commissioner was, Chief Inspector, George D. Heary, Inspector Stephen G. Nelson and every captain on the force. Patrolman Henry W. Sudmeier was about as proud as anyone could be that night. All that for him, all of it in front of his wife, and family; it had to make them proud of him as well. It was a great day/night.

After that he was in and out of bed; he was able to be rolled out to the garden/park for some sun and fresh air. However, his injuries unfortunately were too many, and caused more weakness, with weakness came a decreased immune system, and before long infections were more than he could handle. He was taking several small steps forward, and then huge leaps back. This went on for four more years, looking good, and then looking bad, until an infection would set in that was so strong Officer Sudmeier would be forced to go back to Mercy Hospital for treatment, and like his first trip to Mercy eight year earlier; immediately upon his arrival, he was rushed into surgery. Surgeons would try everything in their power, but still he grew worse steadily, if not rapidly and before long, there was nothing the doctors could do.

Then on this day, 19 Dec 1934 at 7:30 o'clock death would come to him. Physicians said it was due to congestion in his lungs, brought on by his decreased vitality that was indirectly attributable to the gunshot wound from eight years earlier. Patrolman Sudmeier was just 36 years old at the time of his death.

As his brothers and sisters of the Baltimore Police Department, we will not let him be forgotten. We will remind all of his service, a service that honored the City of Baltimore, and the Baltimore Police Department. May he rest in peace, and may God bless him always.

20 December - 1977

Colonel Bishop Robinson was promoted to Deputy Commissioner of the Services Bureau. He was now third in line to the Police Commissioner. He was already the highest-ranking black officer in the history of the Baltimore Police Department. This rank reports directly to the Police Commissioner, and makes him one of only three Deputy Commissioners. The next step for this man is Police Commissioner, and that would happen in 1984, making him not only the first Black Deputy Commissioner, but also the first Black Commissioner of the Baltimore Police Department.

25 December - 1964

On this day in Baltimore Police History, 1964, we lost our brother, **Sgt. Jack L. Cooper**.

Sgt. Jack L. Cooper was shot to death early on December 25, 1964 as he was searching for a robbery suspect who had wounded a police Lieutenant in a Christmas Eve liquor store hold up. Sgt. Jack L. Cooper, 43, was shot twice through the heart shortly before 5 am Christmas Day as he was working by himself (which was the norm in Baltimore at the time, and still is) in the 2600 block of Kennedy Avenue. Lt. Joseph T. Maskell, 40, was shot twice but was not fatally wounded as he struggled with the suspect shortly before 10 pm Christmas Eve outside a liquor store in the 2000 Block of Greenmount Avenue. He was in fair condition at St. Joseph's Hospital.

Police said Sergeant Cooper apparently had stopped the 25-year old suspect identified by witnesses as one of four men who robbed the liquor store proprietor and several of his customers of $2,399.80. Police found a black leather card case containing the name of the 25-year-old man lying near Sergeant Cooper's body. They also found a driver's license issued to the same man lying on the floor of his radio car near the clutch pedal. Sergeant Cooper's pistol was still in its holster when he was found sprawled on the sidewalk about 10 feet from the open door of his radio car.

At about 4:45 am, Sergeant Cooper, Patrolman Charles Kopfelder and Officer Daniel Sobolewski met in the 1600 block of Carswell Street, about eight blocks northeast from the holdup scene. The two patrolmen left in their police vehicle to cruise along Gorsuch Avenue. They last saw the Sergeant sitting alone in his car. Just before 4:50 am, as they continued looking for the suspect who had shot the Lieutenant. they heard shots and hurried back toward the 1600 block of Carswell Street. They found Sergeant Cooper lying on the sidewalk in the 2600 block of Kennedy Avenue. He was bleeding from three bullet wounds. The dome light of his radio car was turned on.

It was apparent that he had stopped a man fitting the description of the shooting suspect, and had taken the man's ID back to his radio car to call in to communications, either to run a wanted check or to call for additional units. Clearly, the suspect had followed the Sergeant back to the car and shot him.

Both Sergeant Cooper and Lieutenant Makell worked out of the Northeastern District.

Sgt. Cooper served in the U.S. Coast Guard from June 3, 1941 to November 1945, he served in the North Atlantic convoy routes, and was discharged as Radio Man, First Class.

As his brothers and sisters of the Baltimore Police Department, we will not let him be forgotten. His service honored the City of Baltimore and the Baltimore Police Department. May he rest in peace, and may God bless him.

The Rest of the Story of the Veney Brothers:

Joseph T. Maskell, the officer shot in the notorious 1964 Veney brothers Case

17 April, 1998; *Newspaper Story by Fred Rasmussen*:

Joseph T. Maskell, a retired Baltimore Police Lieutenant who was shot in a 1964 robbery that began the notorious case of the Baltimore Police Department versus the Veney Brothers, died of lung cancer April 10, 1998 at his Mount Washington home. He was 73.

Lieutenant Maskell joined the Police Department in 1946 and, after recovering from his wounds in 1964, retired in 1966. After retiring, he became an adjuster for an insurance company, and was appointed Vice President of Marketing at Freestate Adjusting Co. in 1979. He retired again in 1986, and then was a rental car sales representative until 1990, when he retired for the third time – this time for good.

At about 10 pm on Christmas Eve in 1964, Lieutenant Maskell, assigned to the Northeastern District, responded to a robbery in progress call at the Luxies Liquor

store in the 2000 block of Greenmount Ave. "He saw something going on and walked right into a robbery. He was shot twice, and then he staggered to Worsley Street, about 25 feet from Greenmount Avenue, where he was later found," said Bill Rochford, a police lieutenant at the time. "It was a miracle he survived." said Mr. Rochford, a boyhood friend who grew up with Lieutenant Maskell in Northeast Baltimore.

Samuel J. Veney and Earl Veney became the targets of what was at the time the city's largest manhunt. The Veney brothers made the FBI's 10-most-wanted list, the first time two brothers had been on the list. "The search was intense and went on through the night and into Christmas morning, when Sgt. Jack Lee Cooper was killed by Samuel Veney," said Bill Talbott, a retired Evening Sun reporter who covered the case. During the 19-day manhunt, police searched 200 homes in black communities without obtaining search warrants.

The patently illegal searches prompted the National Association for the Advancement of Colored People to file a federal lawsuit that resulted in a 1966 injunction against the city police. The Veney brothers, who had fled the state, were captured in March 1965 while working in a zipper factory on Long Island, N.Y.

They were tried and convicted in Frederick, Maryland, where the case was moved because of pretrial publicity. Earl Veney was sentenced to 30 years in prison and in 1976 was found hanged in the House of Correction in Jessup, where Samuel Veney continues to serve a life sentence. Lieutenant Maskell was awarded two official commendations and received 10 letters of commendation. "He was a very decent guy who never really held any animosity about what happened," Mr. Rochford said. "I think the only regret he had was the fact that it ended his career. In later years, he really never talked about it."

Retired Sun reporter Robert A. Erlandson said, "He was the prototypical Irish cop with a big smile and very caring and most of all was well-liked." A 1942 graduate of City College, Lieutenant Maskell served in the Army Coast Artillery from 1942 to 1945 and was discharged as a staff sergeant. He earned a law enforcement certificate from the University of Maryland in 1963. Graveside services were held Monday. He is survived by his wife of 46 years, the former Gloria Bauer; three daughters, Cynthia DiLiello of Jarrettsville, Mindy Sturgis of Joppatowne and JoAnne Bell of Fallston; and nine grandchildren.

Newspaper Reports - Sam Veney Gets Death Sentence

Frederick, MD: Samuel Jefferson Veney, 27, convicted of the Christmas, 1964 murder of Police Sgt. Jack Lee Cooper, must die in the gas chamber. So ruled a two-judge Frederick County Circuit Court panel here late Monday. Sam, the second half of the first brother team ever to make the FBI's "Ten Most Wanted" list, stood impassively as Judge J. Dudley Diggs pronounced the Supreme penalty. Execution of sentence will be delayed pending outcome of an appeal to the Md. Court of Appeals.

Charges of armed robbery and shooting with intent to murder Police Lt. Joseph T. Maskell were stetted by Baltimore State's Attorney Charles E. Moylan, who headed the weeklong prosecution before a two-woman and ten-man jury which returned the guilty verdict of first degree murder. While imposing sentence Judge Diggs said he and associate Judge Robert E. Clapp Jr. decreed the death penalty after "consciously and unconsciously" searching their minds and concluding there was no justification for not imposing capital punishment. Chief defense counsel John R. Hargrove, arguing against the extreme penalty said Sam should not be made a "scapegoat" while others involved in the crime are out walking the streets. Mr. Moylan, on the other hand declared that he could not think of any case where the death penalty would be imposed if it were not imposed in a case of the convicted police killer. Mr. Hargrove posted an immediate intention to appeal.

12 August 1993 - *Putting a Price Tag on that which is Priceless – Life Itself*

Convicted cop killer Samuel Veney, who was returned to a Maryland prison Monday, walked away the same weekend two Los Angeles police officers were found guilty of violating Rodney King's civil rights. That was a coincidence, but both Sam Veney and Rodney King were involved in cases where police misconduct became at least as notorious as the misdeeds of either man. Before his brutal beating, King had led police and highway patrolmen on a high-speed car chase. He was quite drunk at the time. My guess is that he had broken at least four laws by the time of his arrest, crimes that were all but forgotten in the furor that resulted from the video of those 82 seconds it took police to subdue him.

The case of Sam Veney and his brother Earl is different because their crime was more heinous. They gunned down two Baltimore Police Supervisors – killing one and wounding another – after robbing a liquor store on Greenmount Avenue. The Veney brothers were probably the most notorious and feared criminals in Baltimore history, but police misconduct figured prominently in their crime, too.

After the shootings, the Baltimore Police Department declared war on the city's black population. Police broke into scores of homes without warrants or the slightest pretext of probable cause. The search teams were called "flying squads," as delicate a euphemism for police state terror as it should ever be our disgust to encounter. Juanita Jackson Mitchell had to take city police to federal court and remind them that Baltimore was in America, not Nazi Germany or the Stalinist Soviet Union.

As a young boy living in the Murphy Homes housing project at the time, I vividly remember wondering whether I had more to fear from the Veney brothers or Baltimore Police. Years later I remember thinking that whatever the iniquities of the Veney brothers, it was their act that had exposed the Baltimore Police Department for its brutal, racist treatment of Baltimore's black citizens in 1964 and before. Should we forget how bad it was, we need only remind ourselves that Commissioner Donald Pomerleau – hardly a flaming liberal – was brought in to nudge the department into the 20th century. Now Sam Veney comes back to haunt us again.

It seems that every time a Veney screws up, a larger issue is brought into focus. The issue this time is the parole policy of the state of Maryland. Many were wondering – Evening Sun columnist Dan Rodricks among them – why a lifer like Veney who was not being considered for parole was given weekend home visiting privileges. I'm sure Sam Veney looked at the situation differently, as did his family. He figured that with a good behavior record and a 10-year history of returning from weekend visits, why shouldn't he be considered for parole? So old Sam simply initiated self-parole. And to give the devil his due, Sam Veney has a point.

Yes, he killed a cop. Yes, he was given a life term. But everyone in the state knows that some murderers are given life terms and then are paroled. Others, like Sam Veney, are given life sentences and won't ever be considered for parole. The criteria for determining which murderers get paroled and which do not sound good – prior criminal record, the impact on the victim's family, the convict's progress while in prison – but ultimately lead to charges that the race, class and occupation of the victim come into the equation.

How it is that Sam Veney can see the absurdity of such a policy and we civilized, law-abiding citizens can't? All murder victims are equally dead. There are none deader than others. If some lifers have a shot at parole, all should have a shot. Or none should have a shot. Equally absurd is the case of Terrence Johnson, sentenced

to 25 years for killing two Prince George's County police officers. Johnson has been a model prisoner for years, even taking the time to further his education while in prison.

But don't look for him to be paroled. Gov. William Donald Schaefer found the heart to pardon women convicted of killing husbands and boyfriends on the grounds that the women had suffered brutality at the hands of the men. Even though the prosecution in Johnson's case conceded the cops were brutalizing him at the time of the killings, the governor apparently can't see any justification for granting Johnson not a pardon, but a parole.

We ought to be concerned that Maryland law allows for the parole of murderers given life sentences. As former city police commissioner, state public safety commissioner and current Mercy Hospital brain surgery patient Bishop L. Robinson has pointed out, if we don't want murderers paroled after they've been handed life sentences, we need only express our wishes to our state legislators and get them to work changing the law. Let's put a no-parole-for-lifers law on the books. Paroling some murderers and denying parole to others puts a price tag on that which should be priceless – human life.

9 June, 2001 – Column by Gregory Kane – *Retired Officer Remembers Veney Brother Raids Held in 1964*

What, some curious readers have asked, were the Veney Brother raids?

I'm older than I'd like to think. At one time, most Baltimoreans knew what the Veney raids were. As those of us in the baby boomer generation get older, we assume those younger know what we know. We assume that events from December 1964 are common knowledge. But they aren't. Sam and Earl Veney robbed a liquor store in December 1964. The two black men also shot two police officers, killing one. They were caught and convicted.

But the police manhunt in Baltimore for the Veney brothers became almost as infamous as their crimes. Without warrants, police broke into scores of homes in black neighborhoods. (Some put the number as high as 300.) Some critics protested that the raids were a widespread violation of civil liberties. Federal courts and the National Association for the Advancement of Colored People had to get involved.

In a recent column, I referred to the Veney raids as "notorious." One man who remembers the raids well – much better than 13-year-old Gregory Kane could have – took umbrage with the use of the word. He's Paul Lioi, now retired and living in

Florida. In December 1964, he was 25-year-old Officer Paul Lioi of the Baltimore Police Department. He sent this letter to The Sun: "That [notorious] remark hit a sensitive chord with me," Lioi wrote. "Let's go back to 1964. It was Christmas Eve, and the children of two police officers wrapped their fathers' gifts, went to bed, and could hardly wait until morning when their daddies would return home from work to open their gifts and celebrate Christmas together."

This was not to be, because one daddy, a police lieutenant, was shot and wounded during a hold-up at a liquor store on Greenmount Avenue. "And later that same day, the second daddy, a police sergeant, was killed. Neither family celebrated Christmas that day, and for one family, Christmas and every day thereafter, the dad would no longer be with them. The investigation at the robbery scene revealed that the suspects responsible for the robbery and shooting of a police lieutenant were the Veney brothers. As the police went looking for the brothers, one of [them] shot and killed a police sergeant. Two police officers shot, one seriously wounded and one killed. They happened to be my lieutenant and sergeant.

"The police department went on a manhunt to try and locate and apprehend these police assassins known as the Veney brothers. They felt compelled to follow up on any lead they received. The tips they received came from the black community. I was part of the raiding party and felt that the tips received were authentic." Its 37 years later, and Lioi - who won four Bronze Stars, a Distinguished Service Medal and the Medal of Honor in his police career – knows that many of the tips were nowhere near authentic. "Most turned out to be bogus," Lioi said yesterday from his Orlando home. The reason baffles him. This was a search for cop-shooters. "Why," Lioi wondered, "were they giving us these bogus tips?" Lioi also feels empathy with those who lived in the raided homes. "Come to think of it," he said, "it was a bad thing. We had our guns pointed at the houses. We weren't going to walk up to a suspect and say, `Sir, are you Mr. Veney?'"

Lioi says he arrested one of the Veney brothers - he doesn't remember which one - several months before that fateful Christmas Eve. He and his partner - whose regular beat included the liquor store that was robbed - were off the night the store was robbed. He often wonders what would have happened if they had been working instead of Lt. Joseph Maskell, who was wounded in the liquor store robbery, and Sgt. Jack Lee Cooper, whom Sam Veney fatally shot after Cooper confronted him in East Baltimore. "He was a decent guy, a real gentleman," Lioi said of Cooper.

"His death just about ruined my Christmas. I went up to my room and closed my door because I didn't want my children to see a grown man cry. And I did."

Other memories of his East Baltimore beat are happier. He remembers when he was "fighting some mental case" and, unable to call for assistance, finally received it when concerned residents called for him. Moreover, he became a fan of legendary black comedian Jackie 'Moms' Mabley while walking his beat on the graveyard shift. "It was about two in the morning," Lioi recalled. "I was walking by this house and the door was open. I heard a comedian doing a routine." He listened a bit and was delighted to hear one of the funniest comedians he'd ever come across in his life. A woman who lived in the house told him who it was and where to buy the album.

The next day, Lioi was in a store on Greenmount Avenue, buying it. When his beat-walking days were over, he was promoted to sergeant and later became a detective with the arson squad. He retired in 1984 after 23 years on the force. Lioi offers no apologies for his role in the Veney raids. It was mischievous tipsters, he insists, who were responsible. But that may be why the 4th U.S. Circuit Court of Appeals was critical of the raids. Federal judges realize that any crackpot can give a tip and lead even good cops to do bad things.

The suspects in this case have gained a sort of finger pointing at the police, as if we did something wrong in getting them off the streets. So I think it may be appropriate to show these suspects were not mellow, or meek looking individuals, that were being picked on singled out by the Police. They were two brothers that regularly robbed individuals in the area as well as many A&R's at the neighborhood liquor store. When police went to arrest them, they shot a lieutenant first, then later in the same night shot and killed a police sergeant.

As a result of their actions and the discontent of these brothers by the neighborhood, hundreds of tips came in to police hot lines giving information on the two, sometimes the tips were false, sometimes they were real... But it was out of fear of the Veney Brothers, not the police that brought the tips in.

28 December - 1936

On this day in Baltimore Police History, 1936 we lost our brother, **Officer John T. King, Jr.** as he was killed when he was stuck by a Vehicle on 27 December 1936

at 11:20 pm. Officer King was struck by a motorist while crossing the intersection of Hoffman and Caroline Streets. He was treated for serious fractures of both legs, internal injuries, abrasions and shock. The next morning (this day 28 Dec 1936) Officer King succumbed to his injuries. He had joined the BPD on 10 April, 1923 and served 13 years and 8 months.

Newspaper Article; Dec 28, 1936; pg. 14 – *Man Is Killed When Struck By Automobile*

Patrolman John T. King, 43, of the 500 block of Morello Avenue, Northeastern district, was seriously injured early this morning 28 December 1936 when he was struck by an automobile at Caroline and Hoffman streets. He was taken to St. Joseph's Hospital, where his injuries were diagnosed as possible internal injuries and compound fractures of both legs.

William F. Higgins, the driver of the car, was charged with failing to give right away to a policeman and failing to have a registration card in his possession.

Newspaper Article; Jan 21, 1937; pg. 24 – *Held For Grand Jury*

William Higgins, 20, was held for the action of the grand jury yesterday by Dr. Gurley on the charge of causing the death of patrolman John T. King, 42, of the Northeastern District. The accident occurred at Hoffman and Caroline streets December 27, 1936, and the patrolman died the next day in St. Joseph's Hospital

Newspaper Article; Feb 11, 1937; pg. 11 – *Youth Is Exonerated In Policeman's Death*

William S. Higgins cleared in traffic accident fatal to Officer, John T. King. William F. Higgins, 20, yesterday was acquitted by Judge Roland K. Adams of the charge of manslaughter growing out of the killing by an automobile of patrolman John T. King at Hoffman and Caroline streets on December 27.

In clearing Higgins, Judge Adam said he was not convinced beyond a reasonable doubt that the policeman was in the pedestrian lane when hit.

Testimony was that Higgins had drank a small quantity of beer before the accident, and Judge Adams commented on this feature of the case, saying that the trail, as in other cases, led to a Tavern.

As his brothers and sisters of the Baltimore Police Department, we will not let him be forgotten. His service honored the City of Baltimore, and the Baltimore Police Department. May he rest in peace, and may God bless him.

30 December - 1948

On this day in Baltimore Police History, 1948, we lost our brother, **Patrolman John W. Arnold** to gunfire based on the following:

On December 12, 1948 while investigating a call for shots fired with his partner fellow Officer Norman Mike, the officers approached 41-year-old Edward L. Grear, who at the time was involved in some sort of altercation with his girlfriend, Miss Mary Alston, and had her in a choke hold. This all took place in the vicinity of Little Pine and Biddle streets. When the Officers called out to Grear he said nothing to them, ignoring their commands to release the woman; Grear waited for the officers to advance on him and then without a word, Grear turned and opened fire; shooting Officer Mike in the knee, and Officer Arnold numerous times hitting him in his thigh, and abdomen. The two officers were rushed to Maryland General Hospital for treatment while for a brief time Grear escaped. The more seriously wounded of the patrolmen had been given several blood transfusions by his fellow officers in an effort to save his life.

Meantime, Grear was arrested later that day in front of Camden station by Sgt. Edward Manning and patrolman George Jackson, while the arrest was made without firing a single shot, it was not made without incident, as Grear was being approached he did pull his pistol a .45 cal semi-automatic handgun and point it in the direction of Sgt. Manning. It is unclear as to whether he didn't fire, or the gun misfired, but Grear was unable to get a shot off and was taken into custody not long before he would be taken before magistrate, Thomas L. Fitzpatrick in Northwestern Police Court. Grear, a packing house worker, was ordered held without bail pending a preliminary hearing.

Eighteen days later on this day, 30 December, 1948 Officer John W. Arnold succumbed to his injuries. Edward R. Grear was charged with fatally shooting patrolman John W. Arnold and several more counts of assault, and assault with attempted murder for shooting and injuring Officer Norman Mike along with Officer Arnold's killing. With those charges came five other counts, including assaults on the two policemen, firearms violations, discharging, etc. With this Grear was returned to the city jail.

On 21 March, 1949, Edward Grear was convicted in criminal court of first degree murder in the 12 December 1948 shooting of Patrolman Arnold - Judges Herman

M. Mosher and E. Paul Mason deferred sentence pending the filing of a motion for a new trial. Speaking for the two Judge Court, Judge Mason said all the elements necessary to prove murder in the 1st degree were present in the case. The shooting was held deliberate; the court pointed out that the identification of the defendant as the person who fired the fatal shots was unquestioned and that Grear knew he was firing at policeman who were attempting to arrest him. One of the identifiers was a woman companion of the defendant, (she was being choked while the officers approached) the second witness was Officer Norman Mike, fellow radio-car partner of the victim. Judge Mason stated further, the court found that the shooting was deliberate and with intent to kill the officers.

In connection with the defense of intoxication, Judge Mason said the court found "no circumstances of intoxication which tends to reduce the degree of the crime which he committed." Testimony at the two-day trial disclosed that patrolmen Arnold and Mike were investigating a report that someone had been firing a gun earlier in the morning of December 12 (1948) in the vicinity of Argyle Avenue.

William J. O'Donnell and James F. Price, the prosecutors concluded the state's case after they were successful in getting a signed confession from the defendant into evidence.

In the confession, Grear admitted firing shots at police, but said his memory was hazy as to the details.

"I know there wasn't no fight and I didn't have words with an officer. But I remember firing some shots in the air and one at police." He said in the confession, "I remember seeing them there, but I don't remember any fights with them, but I remember firing shots at them."

T. Barton Harrington, court-appointed defense counsel, disclosed that Grear is a native of Oklahoma City, Oklahoma, who came to Baltimore in 1929 after holding jobs as a resource exercise boy, and a circus employee. The judges were told that at the time of his arrest, Grear was employed at a local meatpacking house.

Mr. Harrington said that Grear was 11 years old when he was shot through the brain by a playmate and the pellet is still lodged in the head of the accused. The defense attorney pointed out that Dr. Manfred S Guttmacher, Court psychiatrist, had reported that persons with a brain injury are "particularly liable to abnormal behavior when intoxicated"

On 16 December, 1949 Grear would tell the Maryland court of special appeals his confession was forced and that he was beaten by as many as 32 officers at a time, and as little as 4 at a time, they would line up and beat him until they were tired, even saying at one point one of the officer took a swing at him missed and struck another officer in the mouth. These beatings went on for 15 hours knocking Grear unconscious twice.

The state simply put one person on the stand to refute Grear's charges; a nurse that had seen Grear just two days after his confession testified that Grear didn't have a single mark on him.

Convicted of the murder of patrolman John W. Arnold last December, Edward L Grear yesterday, 22 June 1949, was sentenced to hang until dead. Judges E. Paul Mason and Herman M. Mosher imposed the penalty on the 43-year-old in criminal court. The same judges tried the man last February for the slaying. Pointing out that Grear had a record of gun toting, and shooting at police. Judge Mason, speaking for the court said; "The maximum sentence was fully justified in the case" and that, "If any murder is to be punished by capital punishment," this was it, because the full sentence was compulsory. William J. O'Donnell the assistant state's attorney who prosecuted case dropped the assault with intent to murder charge in connection with the shooting of Patrolman Norman Mike pointing out sometimes too many charges can confuse the issues.

A court-appointed defense attorney, T. Barton Harrington, declined to say whether he would appeal. The sentencing followed a denial last Monday by the supreme bench on the new trial motion.

Court-ordered medical reports showed Grear to be sane, but stated an old brain injury caused a tendency toward excitement while drinking and under stress. Judge Mason said the court sided on the basis of all the witnesses and victims and was therefore convinced that Grear purposely shot the policemen.

The woman who had been with Grear at the time of the shooting testified she knew it was policemen who had approached them in the small street that is practically an alley.

On 26 December, 1950 Gov. Lane announced he had signed a death warrant for Edward Grear, the Baltimore police slayer.

Grear, 44-year-old at the time was to be hanged until dead the following January (26th, 1951) for the murder of patrolman John W. Arnold, "After an exhaustive study of the case" the governor said, "I can find no justifiable reason to interfere with the death sentence that has been imposed upon him."

As his brothers and sisters of the Baltimore Police Department, we will not let him be forgotten. His service honored the City of Baltimore, and the Baltimore Police Department. May he rest in peace, and may God bless him.

31 December - 1937

On this date in Baltimore Police History, 1937 we lost our brother Patrolman **Thomas J. Barlow** to an automobile accident at approximately 2:00 am, while investigating a call of for a woman screaming for help, as she was having trouble with her drunken boyfriend based on the following:

Officer Barlow and his partner Officer James M. Leverton were handling the accident call when they were both struck by a car driven by John E. Kelly, of the 3300 block of Hamilton Avenue (Kelly was the son of a retired Central District officer). Officer Barlow was killed instantly, and Officer Leverton was seriously injured at the intersection of Belair Rd. and Pelham Ave. It was nearly one mile from the scene of the accident before Kelly was stopped by another radio car operated by Patrolmen John M. Dippel and John W. Campbell. Once stopped, Kelley was arrested, and charged with Driving While Intoxicated, Driving under the Influence, Hit and Run personal injury, Hit and Run Property Damage and numerous other vehicular and Criminal Offenses.

Kelly was held in city jail without bail from the time of his arrest until the 6th of January 1938, because Dr. F. L. C. Helm, "Acting Automobile Coroner", declined to set bail after his arrest. It would be a week later before Kelly would receive a hearing via a Habeas Corpus Hearing when we would hear a defense attorney make a statement that tells us that things back then were just as bad and seemingly unjust as they are today, and that Defense Attorneys in general were just as heartless then as now. Kelly was represented at the time by attorneys John E. Magers and Bernard H. Herzfeld.

Attorney Magers uttered one of the most disgusting and disturbing things I may have ever heard come from the mouth of someone who is supposed to represent integrity and equality in our court system. He said, "If he were not a policeman involved in this case, the defendant would have been admitted to bail." Then he went on to say, "Defendants in cases more serious than this one have been released on bail." A valid, if irrelevant, observation. But this Attorney said it as though the life of a Police Officer, the life of our Brother, the life of Officer Thomas J. Barlow was no big deal. Like he was disposable, a police officer to a city, a husband to Mrs. Irene M. Barlow and Daddy to his four children.

Disposable to a drunk driver, to a defense attorney, and sadly to a court system that would set bail on a man's freedom, that valued another man's life at just $3,000, or roughly $51,000.00 in today's money. I'm not sure what crawled up Stanton's court dress that day, for he was normally a pretty good judge, and even pro-police, especially in cases where police were injured or killed, and in this case we have both. Yet he did what he did, and Kelly was bailed out by his wife, Mrs. Leopoldina "Leo" Kelly, who lived with her husband in the 3300 block of Hamilton Avenue.

On 10 Febuary, 1938 Kelly had his day in court and was convicted of manslaughter charges by Judge J. Abner Saylor in criminal court in the death of our brother Thomas J. Barlow, based on the testimony of the arresting officers, the injured officer and a cab driver who saw the entire incident. The sentencing was suspended on the request of Kelly's attorney, pending a motion for a new trial.

But this was not the end… while I couldn't find anything more on this case, I did find the following: In a Sun Paper Article dated 8 April 1939 concerning a suit involving vehicular manslaughter that added up to more than $125,000.00 (in today's money that would be $2,125,000.00). One of those actions involved Mrs. Irene M. Barlow, the widowed mother of four who had been married to Patrolman Thomas J. Barlow. I excerpted just the part of the article that pertained to this story.

"Mrs. Barlow seeks $50,000 ($850,000.00) – Mrs. Irene M. Barlow, widow of patrolman Thomas J. Barlow who was killed in a hit-and-run accident last December, filed an action in Superior Court seeking $50,000 from John E. Kelly, who was serving a one year in the House of Corrections for manslaughter in connection with the death of patrolman T. J. Barlow. The suit was entered jointly by Mrs. Barlow and her three juvenile children." (Apparently, one of their children had reached the age of 18 - or we have a newspaper error.)

OK… so from this brief article we learn - John E. Kelly received a one year sentence in the House of corrections for killing a police officer, manslaughter taking the life of our brother Patrolman Thomas J Barlow. Not as much time as one should get for a simple DWI, let alone a hit and run that killed a police officer… but it's better than a suspended sentence. And while we don't know if Mrs. Barlow and her three children won their civil suit, we can only hope they did, as $50,000.00 in 1939/1940 would be worth $850,000.00 in today's currency. And it would show Tommy Barlow's life was more important than taking away a year of Kelly's life.

Thomas J. Barlow, was a member of the Baltimore Police Department since 1919. He was husband to Mrs. Irene M. Barlow and was the father of four children.

As his brothers and sisters of the Baltimore Police Department, we will not let him be forgotten. His service honored the City of Baltimore and the Baltimore Police Department. May he rest in peace, and may God bless him.

Fallen Hero's Wall Locations

Baltimore's Fallen Hero's on the National Law Enforcement Memorial in Washington, D.C.

Finding Names on the Wall

The following list is of our fallen brothers and sister of Baltimore's Police Department whose names appear on the National Law Enforcement Memorial in Washington DC. The associated names, panels, and line numbers listed below can assist you in finding the names of the officers you are looking for on those hallowed walls

Panels on the West (W) and East (E) walls are numbered from 1 to 64 (The panel number is engraved at the bottom of each panel). Line 1 is at the top of the panel. Count down from the top of the panel to locate the Officer you are seeking.

For example: Det. Tommy Newman, "27-W, 23" we would go to west wall, then to Panel 27, where we would count from the top down to Line 23 of the memorial. Using the following list, either printed out or carried on your iPhone, will assist you in locating our Baltimore Officers during your next visit to the National Law Enforcement Memorial Wall.

If you don't mind, while you're there, make as many rubs from as many officers as you can, then either scan them, and email them to us so we can add them to our site. Or mail a copy to us.

Our email address for this is **Memorial@BaltimoreCityPoliceHistory.com** and our mailing address is: Baltimore City Police History – Attn: Ret. Det. Kenny Driscoll – 8138 Dundalk Ave. Baltimore, Md. 21222

~ Alphabetical Listing of Our Fallen Officers ~

VINCENT J ADOLFO
12-W: 13
End of Watch: November 18, 1985

WILLIAM D ALBERS
41-E: 8
End of Watch: August 19, 1979

ROBERT ALEXANDER
1-W: 12
End of Watch: September 20, 1986

JOHN F ANDREWS
21-E: 9
End of Watch: October 9, 1957

LEO BACON
40-E: 1
End of Watch: October 9, 1936

TEDDY L BAFFORD
25-E: 5
End of Watch: October 15, 1964

THOMAS J BARLOW
52-E: 13
End of Watch: December 31, 1937

ROBERT JOHN BARLOW
54-W: 22
End of Watch: April 23, 1978

WILLIAM C BAUMER
18-E: 15
End of Watch: January 25, 1967

JOHN B BEALEFELD
29-E: 15
End of Watch: September 10, 1945

WILLIAM A BELL
41-E: 14
End of Watch: January 2, 1932

NELSON F BELL JR
17-W: 16
End of Watch: October 27, 1978

JOSEPH DANIEL BENEDICT
11-W: 11
End of Watch: February 13, 1948

BENJAMIN BENTON
35-E: 21
End of Watch: September 22, 1858

ALONZO B BISHOP
32-E: 15
End of Watch: August 29, 1899

JOHN BLANK
11-W: 16
End of Watch: February 12, 1934

JOHN R J BLOCK
28-E: 13
End of Watch: April 21, 1933

ALFRED P BOBELIS
23-E: 17
End of Watch: February 14, 1954

RICHARD F BOSAK
9-W: 8
End of Watch: April 18, 1968

NORMAN FREDERICK BUCHMAN
11-W: 12
End of Watch: April 6, 1973

JOHN P BURNS
41-E: 9
End of Watch: January 7, 1931

THOMAS J BURNS
56-W: 9
End of Watch: October 1, 1948

ANTHONY A BYRD
45-E: 25
End of Watch: May 19, 2006

HAROLD J CAREY
5-E: 21
End of Watch: October 30, 1998

JOSEPH F CARROLL
30-E: 7
End of Watch: November 19, 1928

TROY LAMONT CHESLEY SR
8-W: 26
End of Watch: January 9, 2007

JOHN CHRISTOPHER
21-W: 10
End of Watch: August 18, 1872

JOSEPH CLARK
47-E: 14
End of Watch: May 22, 1871

JACK LEE COOPER
17-W: 3
End of Watch: December 25, 1964

MICHAEL JOSEPH COWDERY JR
21-E: 22
End of Watch: March 12, 2001

JOHN J DAILEY
17-E: 3
End of Watch: October 17, 1895

WALTER D DAVIS
27-E: 13
End of Watch: July 1, 1954

WILLIAM F DOEHLER
49-E: 8
End of Watch: August 5, 1927

CHARLES J DONOHUE
56-W: 14
End of Watch: May 20, 1902

JAMES T DUNN
25-E: 17
End of Watch: June 20, 1894

RICHARD H DUVALL
8-E: 17
End of Watch: January 11, 1959

WARREN V ECKERT
63-E: 17
End of Watch: November 16, 1960

JAMES E FOWLER III
16-E: 27
End of Watch: September 27, 2010

CHARLES S FRANK
24-E: 14
End of Watch: June 20, 1924

KEVON MALIK GAVIN SR
14-W: 22
End of Watch: April 21, 2000

LORENZO ARNEST GRAY
13-W: 11
End of Watch: July 26, 1972

MARTIN JOSEPH GREINER
20-W: 2
End of Watch: December 10, 1974

FRANK WILLIAM GRUNDER JR
23-E: 4
End of Watch: August 1, 1974

JIMMY DALE HALCOMB
34-E: 8
End of Watch: April 16, 1976

CARROLL HANLEY
29-E: 4
End of Watch: October 29, 1936

GEORGE D HART
19-E: 1
End of Watch: January 2, 1925

GEORGE F HEIM
64-E: 12
End of Watch: January 16, 1970

CHARLES M HILBERT
39-E: 12
End of Watch: August 4, 1950

MAX HIRSH
37-E: 17
End of Watch: February 14, 1935

ROBERT MAYNARD HURLEY
46-W: 29
End of Watch: March 28, 1973

HERMAN A JONES SR
57-W: 19
End of Watch: May 26, 1993

WILLIAM JORDAN
23-E: 21
End of Watch: October 14, 1857

JAMES L JOYCE
25-E: 8
End of Watch: April 4, 1949

JOHN T KING JR
11-W: 6
End of Watch: December 28, 1936

WILLIAM S. KNIGHT
20-E: 4
End of Watch: November 7, 1943

FREDERICK K. KONTNER
59-E: 17
End of Watch: February 10, 1967

EDWARD J. KOWALEWSKI
15-W: 15
End of Watch: July 2, 1962

ROBERT HENRY KUHN
28-E: 11
End of Watch: July 22, 1965

JOHN LANAHAN
25-E: 1
End of Watch: July 3, 1919

FRANK L LATHAM
6-E: 3
End of Watch: March 2, 1924

RICHARD J LEAR
20-E: 15
End of Watch: October 8, 1985

JOHN T LLOYD
16-E: 5
End of Watch: July 4, 1889

AUBREY L LOWMAN
9-W: 12
End of Watch: April 19, 1954

ARTHUR H MALINOFSKI
62-E: 7
End of Watch: October 31, 1935

WILLIAM J MARTIN
37-E: 1
End of Watch: October 10, 1989

WALTER PATRICK MATTHYS
53-E: 5
End of Watch: September 11, 1964

GEORGE M J MAY
1-E: 10
End of Watch: February 12, 1928

KEVIN JOSEPH MCCARTHY
45-W: 22
End of Watch: October 14, 2000

HENRY M MICKEY
64-W: 6
End of Watch: March 24, 1970

RICHARD THOMAS MILLER
17-E: 17
End of Watch: July 21, 1986

ROY L MITCHELL
5-W: 1
End of Watch: November 1, 1925

ROLAND WALLACE MORGAN
19-W: 3
End of Watch: January 6, 1951

JAMES MURPHY
37-E: 4
End of Watch: July 5, 1870

MICHAEL NEARY
31-E: 8
End of Watch: June 20, 1894

ROBERT K NELSON
5-W: 2
End of Watch: September 19, 1958

THOMAS G NEWMAN
27-W: 23
End of Watch: November 23, 2002

ELMER A NOON
59-E: 9
End of Watch: November 20, 1946

THOMAS JOSEPH O'NEILL
14-W: 26
End of Watch: October 16, 1949

CARL PETERSON JR
14-W: 5
End of Watch: June 12, 1971

JOHN R PHELAN
12-W: 15
End of Watch: September 29, 1956

JOHN DAVID PLATT
60-W: 22
End of Watch: October 14, 2000

THOMAS RUSSELL PORTZ JR
51-E: 27
End of Watch: October 20, 2010

CLAUDE J PROFILI
1-W: 17
End of Watch: February 6, 1964

JAMES J PURCELL
6-W: 12
End of Watch: October 24, 1955

JOHN RICHARDS
45-W: 24
End of Watch: September 14, 1871

TIMOTHY B RIDENOUR
32-E: 5
End of Watch: October 27, 1975

ROBERT M RIGDON
24-E: 21
End of Watch: November 8, 1858

CALVIN M RODWELL
1-W: 2
End of Watch: September 22, 1973

JAMIE ALLEN ROUSSEY
7-W: 22
End of Watch: March 8, 2000

EDGAR J RUMPF
1-E: 11
End of Watch: February 16, 1978

WILLIAM L RYAN
12-W: 10
End of Watch: June 13, 1940

DONALD W SAGER
21-W: 3
End of Watch: April 24, 1970

GEORGE C SAUER
38-E: 1
End of Watch: April 18, 1915

JAMES L SCHOLL
62-E: 13
End of Watch: August 1, 1953

WEBSTER E SCHUMANN
59-E: 9
End of Watch: June 29, 1926

RICHARD D SEEBO
8-E: 5
End of Watch: May 26, 1962

CRYSTAL DENEEN SHEFFIELD
14-E: 23
End of Watch: August 22, 2002

EDWARD S SHERMAN
62-E: 14
End of Watch: September 13, 1975

HENRY SMITH JR
64-W: 7
End of Watch: April 7, 1962

MILTON I SPELL
17-E: 2
End of Watch: August 15, 1974

JOHN A STAPF
62-E: 5
End of Watch: November 2, 1934

THOMAS F STEINACKER
16-W: 14
End of Watch: September 29, 1932

FRANCIS R STRANSKY
28-E: 15
End of Watch: January 10, 1964

HENRY W SUDMEIER
37-E: 4
End of Watch: December 20, 1934

OWEN EUGENE SWEENEY JR
34-E: 20
End of Watch: May 7, 1997

FORREST EDWARD TAYLOR
25-E: 28
End of Watch: August 29, 2012

WILLIAM HENRY TORBIT JR
42-W: 28
End of Watch: January 9, 2011

RONALD L TRACEY
19-E: 1
End of Watch: July 20, 1981

FRED R UNGER
34-E: 11
End of Watch: January 13, 1947

MARCELLUS WARD
6-W: 13
End of Watch: December 3, 1984

MARTIN WEBB
39-E: 17
End of Watch: August 9, 1971

IRA NEIL WEINER
44-E: 18
End of Watch: September 21, 1992

FRANK WARREN WHITBY JR
49-E: 8
End of Watch: May 5, 1974

JOHN C WILLIAMS
35-E: 16
End of Watch: August 21, 1967

BRIAN DONTE WINDER
63-W: 24
End of Watch: July 3, 2004

BARRY WINSTON WOOD
3-E: 21
End of Watch: November 4, 1998

WILLIAM J WOODCOCK
18-E: 9
End of Watch: June 13, 1943

GEORGE WORKNER
33-W: 24
End of Watch: March 15, 1808

JACOB ZAPP
18-W: 8
End of Watch: July 15, 1891

Line of Duty & On-Duty Deaths

Chronological List

The following is a complete and up to date list of officers of the Baltimore Police Department who have died in the line of duty, or while working on-duty, as far as we currently know.

This list will have names that do not appear on any other lists, recognizing Officers that have not been recognized elsewhere. Their complete stories can be found on the BaltimoreCityPoliceHistory.com website or in the Day-to-Day Timeline in this book.

We are not sure why some have not been previously recognized. With some it can be somewhat understood, for instance in the case of the officer shot in the line of duty and seriously injured, blinded in one eye, and with a bullet lodged in his chest next to his heart, who did not die for 35 years before he passed away from his wounds, but it was clear his death was caused from the round, an indication to us that his death was from a line of duty shooting. Other cases, involved illnesses caused by on-the-job contamination, can be understood by not forgotten. Three of these died from Smallpox, another from Pneumonia, several from Heart Attacks, or accidental discharges with their weapons, and other such causes.

What we are doing is including a list of officers that died on the job, or due to job related injury/illness. The list is unofficial, but we feel the stories need to told, the families deserve closure, etc. If you know of someone who is not on this list but you think should be, feel free to contact us through the site, and provide us with the information so we can look into it, and hopefully we will add them to the list in forthcoming editions.

The all-inclusive listing is presented in reverse chronological order using the End of Watch (EOW) date, from the most recent to the oldest.

Police Officer Craig Chandler EOW: Wednesday, January 9, 2015 Cause: Automobile accident

Police Officer Forrest "Dino" Taylor EOW: Wednesday, August 29, 2012 Cause: Automobile accident

Police Officer William Henry Torbit, Jr. EOW: Sunday, January 9, 2011 Cause: Gunfire (Accidental)

Police Officer Thomas Russell "Tommy" Portz, Jr. EOW: Wednesday, October 20, 2010 Cause: Automobile accident

Police Officer James Earl Fowler, III EOW: Monday, September 27, 2010 Cause: Automobile accident

Detective Troy Lamont Chesley, Sr. EOW: Tuesday, January 9, 2007 Cause: Gunfire

Police Officer Anthony A. Byrd EOW: Friday, May 19, 2006 Cause: Automobile accident

Police Officer Brian Donte Winder EOW: Saturday, July 3, 2004 Cause: Gunfire

Lieutenant Walter A. Taylor Jr. EOW: Tuesday, April 17, 2003 Cause: Heart Attack

Detective Thomas G. Newman EOW: Saturday, November 23, 2002 Cause: Gunfire

Police Officer Crystal Deneen Sheffield EOW: Thursday, August 22, 2002 Cause: Automobile accident

Agent Michael Joseph Cowdery, Jr. EOW: Tuesday, March 13, 2001 Cause: Gunfire

Police Officer Kevin Joseph McCarthy EOW: Saturday, October 14, 2000 Cause: Vehicular assault

Sergeant John David Platt EOW: Saturday, October 14, 2000 Cause: Vehicular assault

Police Officer Kevon Malik Gavin EOW: Friday, April 21, 2000 Cause: Vehicular assault

Police Officer Jamie Allen Roussey EOW: Wednesday, March 8, 2000 Cause: Automobile accident

Flight Officer Barry Winston Wood EOW: Wednesday, November 4, 1998 Cause: Aircraft accident

Police Officer Harold Jerome Carey EOW: Friday, October 30, 1998 Cause: Automobile accident

Lieutenant Owen Eugene Sweeney, Jr. EOW: Wednesday, May 7, 1997 Cause: Gunfire

Police Officer Herman A. Jones, Sr. EOW: Wednesday, May 26, 1993 Cause: Gunfire

Police Officer Ira Neil Weiner EOW: Monday, September 21, 1992 Cause: Gunfire

Police Officer William J. Martin EOW: Tuesday, October 10, 1989 Cause: Gunfire

Police Officer Robert Alexander EOW: Tuesday, September 20, 1986 Cause: Struck by vehicle

Police Officer Richard Thomas Miller EOW: Monday, July 21, 1986 Cause: Vehicular assault

Police Officer Vincent J. Adolfo EOW: Monday, November 18, 1985 Cause: Gunfire

Police Officer Richard J. Lear EOW: Tuesday, October 8, 1985 Cause: Struck by vehicle

Detective Marcellus Ward EOW: Monday, December 3, 1984 Cause: Gunfire

Police Officer Ronald L. Tracey EOW: Monday, July 20, 1981 Cause: Gunfire

Police Officer William D. Albers EOW: Sunday, August 19, 1979 Cause: Gunfire

Police Officer Nelson F. Bell, Jr. EOW: Friday, October 27, 1978 Cause: Gunfire

Sergeant Robert John Barlow EOW: Sunday, April 23, 1978 Cause: Heart attack

Police Officer Edgar J. Rumpf EOW: Wednesday, February 15, 1978 Cause: Fire

Police Officer Jimmy Dale Halcomb EOW: Friday, April 16, 1976 Cause: Gunfire

Police Officer Timothy B. Ridenour EOW: Monday, October 27, 1975 Cause: Gunfire

Police Officer Edward S. Sherman EOW: Saturday, September 13, 1975 Cause: Duty related illness

Police Officer Martin Joseph Greiner EOW: Tuesday, December 10, 1974 Cause: Gunfire

Police Officer Milton I. Spell EOW: Thursday, August 15, 1974 Cause: Gunfire

Detective Sergeant Frank William Grunder, Jr. EOW: Thursday, August 1, 1974 Cause: Gunfire

Police Officer Frank Warren Whitby, Jr. EOW: Sunday, May 5, 1974 Cause: Gunfire

Police Officer Calvin M. Rodwell EOW: Saturday, September 22, 1973 Cause: Gunfire

Detective Wiley M. Owens EOW: December 1, 1973 Cause: Questionable poisoning

Police Officer Robert M. Hurley EOW: Friday, 29 March, 1973 Cause: Gunfire

Police Officer Norman Frederick Buchman EOW: Friday, April 6, 1973 Cause: Gunfire

Police Officer Lorenzo Arnest Gray EOW: Wednesday, July 26, 1972 Cause: Gunfire

Lieutenant Martin Webb EOW: Tuesday, August 3, 1971 Cause: Drowned

Police Officer Carl Peterson, Jr. EOW: Saturday, June 12, 1971 Cause: Gunfire

Police Officer Donald W. Sager EOW: Friday, April 24, 1970 Cause: Gunfire

Police Officer Henry M. Mickey EOW: Tuesday, March 24, 1970 Cause: Gunfire

Police Officer George F. Heim EOW: Friday, January 16, 1970 Cause: Struck by vehicle

Detective Richard F. Bosak EOW: Thursday, April 18, 1968 Cause: Gunfire

Police Officer Frank Ankrom Cause: Illness brought on by being struck by a stolen automobile

Police Officer John C. Williams EOW: Monday, August 21, 1967 Cause: Fire

Police Officer Frederick K. Kontner EOW: Friday, February 10, 1967 Cause: Gunfire

Police Officer William J. Baumer EOW: Wednesday, January 25, 1967 Cause: Heart attack

Police Officer Robert Henry Kuhn   EOW: Thursday, July 22, 1965 Cause: Gunfire

Police Officer Charles R. Ernest   EOW: Wednesday, January 20, 1965 Cause: Struck by vehicle

Sergeant Jack Lee Cooper   EOW: Friday, December 25, 1964 Cause: Gunfire

Police Officer Teddy L. Bafford   EOW: Thursday, October 15, 1964 Cause: Gunfire

Police Officer Walter Patrick Matthys   EOW: Friday, September 11, 1964 Cause: Gunfire

Police Officer Claude J. Profili   EOW: Thursday, February 6, 1964 Cause: Gunfire

Police Officer Francis R. Stransky   EOW: Friday, January 10, 1964 Cause: Heart attack

Police Officer Edward J. Kowalewski   EOW: Monday, July 2, 1962 Cause: Gunfire

Police Officer Richard D. Seebo   EOW: Saturday, May 26, 1962 Cause: Gunfire

Police Officer Henry Smith, Jr.   EOW: Saturday, April 7, 1962 Cause: Gunfire

Police Officer Warren V. Eckert   EOW: Wednesday, November 16, 1960 Cause: Motorcycle accident

Police Officer Richard H. Duvall, Jr.   EOW: Sunday, January 11, 1959 Cause: Gunfire (Accidental)

Police Officer Robert K. Nelson   EOW: Friday, September 19, 1958 Cause: Motorcycle accident

Police Officer John F. Andrews   EOW: Wednesday, October 9, 1957 Cause: Vehicle pursuit

Police Officer John R. Phelan   EOW: Saturday, September 29, 1956 Cause: Gunfire

Sergeant James J. Purcell   EOW: Monday, October 24, 1955 Cause: Gunfire

Police Officer Walter D. Davis   EOW: Thursday, July 1, 1954 Cause: Automobile accident

Police Officer Aubrey L. Lowman   EOW: Monday, April 19, 1954 Cause: Gunfire

Police Officer Alfred P. Bobelis   EOW: Sunday, February 14, 1954 Cause: Vehicular assault

Police Officer James L. Scholl   EOW: Saturday, August 1, 1953 Cause: Gunfire

Police Officer Roland W. Morgan   EOW: Saturday, January 6, 1951 Cause: Vehicular assault

Police Officer Charles M. Hilbert   EOW: Friday, August 4, 1950 Cause: Vehicular assault

Police Officer Thomas J. O'Neill   EOW: Sunday, October 16, 1949 Cause: Duty related illness

Police Officer James L. Joyce   EOW: Monday, April 4, 1949 Cause: Automobile accident

Police Officer John W. Arnold   EOW: Thursday, December 30, 1948 Cause: Gunfire

Police Officer Thomas J. Burns   EOW: Friday, October 1, 1948 Cause: Motorcycle accident

Police Officer Joseph Daniel Benedict   EOW: Friday, February 13, 1948 Cause: Gunfire

Patrolman Charles Heart   EOW: Thursday 13 October 1947 Cause: Illness

Police Officer Fred R. Unger   EOW: Monday, January 13, 1947 Cause: Gunfire

Police Officer Elmer A. Noon   EOW: Wednesday, November 20, 1946 Cause: Heart attack

Patrolman James M Shamer   EOW: Thursday 27 June 1946 Cause: Illness

Police Officer John B. Bealefeld   EOW: Monday, September 10, 1945 Cause: Duty related illness

Police Officer Patrolman Joseph Waldsachs   EOW: Monday, January 29, 1944 Cause: Struck by vehicle

Police Officer William S. Knight   EOW: Sunday, November 7, 1943 Cause: Gunfire

Police Officer William J. Woodcock   EOW: Sunday, June 13, 1943 Cause: Assault

Police Officer William L. Ryan   EOW: Thursday, June 13, 1940 Cause: Stabbed

Chief Engineer Joseph Edward Keene   EOW: Tuesday, November 1, 1938 Cause: Fall

Police Officer Thomas J. Barlow   EOW: Friday, December 31, 1937 Cause: Vehicular assault

Police Capt. Charles A Kahler   EOW: Monday, November 17, 1937 Cause: Heart Attack during interrogation

Police Officer John T. King, Jr.   EOW: Monday, December 28, 1936 Cause: Struck by vehicle

Police Officer Carroll Hanley   EOW: Thursday, October 29, 1936 Cause: Vehicular assault

Police Officer Leo Bacon   EOW: Friday, October 9, 1936 Cause: Accidental

Police Officer Arthur H. Malinofski   EOW: Thursday, October 31, 1935 Cause: Gunfire

Police Officer Max Hirsh   EOW: Thursday, February 14, 1935 Cause: Accidental

Police Officer Henry W. Sudmeier   EOW: Thursday, December 20, 1934 Cause: Gunfire (Accidental)

Police Officer John A. Stapf   EOW: Friday, November 2, 1934 Cause: Struck by streetcar

Police Officer John Blank   EOW: Monday, February 12, 1934 Cause: Gunfire

Police Officer John R. J. Block   EOW: Friday, April 21, 1933 Cause: Gunfire

Police Officer Thomas F. Steinacker   EOW: Tuesday, October 4, 1932 Cause: Accidental

Police Officer William A. Bell   EOW: Saturday, January 2, 1932 Cause: Gunfire

Police Officer John P. Burns   EOW: Wednesday, January 7, 1931 Cause: Gunfire

Patrolman James M. Moore   EOW: Friday, July 26, 1929 Cause: Gunfire

Sergeant Joseph F. Carroll   EOW: Monday, November 19, 1928 Cause: Gunfire

Sergeant George M. J. May   EOW: Sunday, February 12, 1928 Cause: Automobile accident

Police Officer William F. Doehler   EOW: Friday, August 5, 1927 Cause: Gunfire

Police Clerk Thomas J. Dillon   EOW: Monday, July 12, 1926 Cause: Gunfire

Police Officer Milton Heckwolf   EOW: Monday, February 9, 1926 Cause: Illness

Police Officer Webster E. Schumann   EOW: Tuesday, June 29, 1926 Cause: Gunfire

Police Officer Roy L. Mitchell   EOW: Sunday, November 1, 1925 Cause: Struck by vehicle

Police Officer John E Harris   EOW: Sunday, July 3, 1925 Cause: Struck by a student driver in public park

Police Officer Patrick J Coniffee   EOW: Sunday, May 17, 1925 Cause: Struck by a streetcar / fractured skull

Police Officer George D. Hart   EOW: Friday, January 2, 1925 Cause: Motorcycle accident

Patrolman John Edward Swift   EOW: Sunday, 1925 Cause: illness brought on by an assault

Police Officer Charles S. Frank   EOW: Friday, June 20, 1924 Cause: Gunfire

Police Officer Frank L. Latham   EOW: Sunday, March 2, 1924 Cause: Gunfire

Police Officer John J. Lanahan   EOW: Thursday, July 3, 1919 Cause: Gunfire

Patrolman Michael J Egan   EOW: Sunday, 2 October 1920 Cause: Heart Attack

Police Matron Teresa Foll   EOW: Tuesday, 19 March 1918 Cause: Illness

Patrolman Michael Burns   EOW: Tuesday, 22 January 1917 Cause: Electrocuted

Policeman Herbert Bitzel   EOW: Tuesday, 21 September 1915 Cause: Hit by Trolley Car

Police Officer George C. Sauer   EOW: Sunday, April 18, 1915 Cause: Gunfire

Police Officer John McGrain   EOW: Monday, 25 November 1912 Cause: Injury

Police Officer Thomas H. Worthington   EOW: Thursday, March 4, 1909 Cause: Electrocuted

Police Officer Charles Spitznagle   EOW: Wednesday, 25 December 1905 Cause: Paralyzed

Police Officer John G. McNamara   EOW: Wednesday, 22 March 1905 Cause: Gunfire

Police Officer Mathew Boone   EOW: Thursday, 26 January 1905 Cause: Illness

Police Officer John a McIntyre   EOW: Wednesday, 30 July 1902 Cause: Illness

Police Officer Charles J. Donohue   EOW: Tuesday, May 20, 1902 Cause: Gunfire

Police Officer Alonzo B. Bishop   EOW: Tuesday, August 29, 1899 Cause: Automobile accident

Police Officer John J. Dailey   EOW: Thursday, October 17, 1895 Cause: Gunfire

Police Officer Michael Neary   EOW: Wednesday, June 20, 1894 Cause: Struck by train

Police Officer James T. Dunn   EOW: Wednesday, June 20, 1894 Cause: Struck by train

Police Officer Jacob Zapp   EOW: Wednesday, July 15, 1891 Cause: Struck by train

Police Officer John T. Lloyd   EOW: Thursday, July 4, 1889 Cause: Gunfire

Police Officer Charles W. Fisher   EOW: Sunday, January 6, 1884 Cause: Drowned

Policeman James T. Harvey   EOW: Sunday, January 12, 1873 Cause: Line of Duty Illness (Small Pox)

Policeman John H. Dames EOW: Sunday, January 12, 1873 Cause: Line of Duty Illness (Small Pox)

Patrolman Franklin Fullum EOW: Friday, November 22, 1872 Cause: Line of Duty Illness (Small Pox)

Police Officer John Christopher EOW: Sunday, August 18, 1872 Cause: Gunfire

Detective John H. Richards EOW: Thursday, September 14, 1871 Cause: Gunfire

Police Officer Joseph Clark EOW: Monday, May 22, 1871 Cause: Gunfire

Police Officer Charles J. Walsh EOW: Thursday, 12 January 1871 Cause: Gunfire (Accidental)

Police Officer James Murphy EOW: Tuesday, July 5, 1870 Cause: Assault

Police Officer Robert M. Rigdon EOW: Monday, November 8, 1858 Cause: Gunfire

Police Officer Benjamin Benton EOW: Wednesday, September 22, 1858 Cause: Gunfire

Sergeant William Jourdan EOW: Wednesday, October 14, 1857 Cause: Gunfire

Night Watchman John O'Mayer EOW: Saturday, November 13, 1856 Cause: Gunfire (Accidental)

Night Watchman George Workner EOW: Tuesday, March 15, 1808 Cause: Stabbed,

Excerpts - 1856 Proceeding of City Council

(During this December 11th session in 1856)

Mr. Boyd moved to strike out all of the section providing for arming the police with revolvers and other suitable weapons and placing muskets at the station-houses. Mr. Boyd said the cost of arming the police with revolvers would alone amount to $5,161.00; that there were men in the police not fitted to trust with arms, and if the amendment was not adopted he feared he should be compelled to vote it was necessary to arm the police, as long as rowdies were armed with revolvers and other weapons. In New York and Philadelphia where there is a penalty for carrying concealed weapons, the police are armed by the city authorities. The muskets at the stations houses were to be KEPT there under the charge of the Mayor, to be used only in case of riot, where such arms were necessary to compete with armed mobs.

Mr. Boyd replied that only a few weeks since one of the police had drawn his revolver at Carroll Hall on one of the night police - he reiterated that there were men not fit to be trusted with such arms. The time was when twenty-six men kept this city quiet and in good order without being armed. As to giving the police muskets, we might as well have a standing army. If muskets are necessary at any time, the military are always ready to obey any call of the Mayor. Mr. Pinkney again urged that it was necessary to arm the police - you must arm them to have any effect at all. If the military were called out at the present state of feeling in the public mind, instead of preventing or suppressing riot, it would lead to one of the bloodiest riots on record.

Mr. Howard opposed the amendment - he believed that it was necessary to arm the police in order to protect the citizens - to put down the riots that had so often of late violated the law and shot down peaceable persons. We may have seen outrages heretofore, but we have not seen orderly citizens shot down at their own doors - men driven from the polls when only seeking their right of exercising the elective franchise – polls obstructed and men leading armed mobs with apparent impunity - Mr. Boyd was willing to judge the present by the past - If we are to have no better men on the police than for time past, he was not willing to place arms in their hands. If the police are armed, no man is safe in this community. The question being taken on Mr. Boyd's proposed amendment, it was rejected by yeas 3, (Messrs. Boyd, Tidy, and Carroll,) and nays 16.

Mr. Nalls moved to strike out that portion of the ordinance placing muskets at the station houses rejected by yeas 6, (Messr Daiger, Boyd, Green, Tidy, Carroll and Nalls,) and nays 13. Section 8 was reconsidered, on motion of Mr. Handy, who moved to amend it by making the police officers to be confirmed by the city council, as other city officers are; which was adopted with but one dissenting voice.

During the times the city was nearly taken over by several gangs involved in politics, they would travel the various wards making it nearly impossible for honest voters to vote. As such elections were not fair, the same people won every time. I wouldn't be surprised to hear Mr. Boyd was benefiting more by having the Know Nothings, Plug Ugglies, Bloody Tubs, etc. ruling the city with an unarmed, or under-armed police force, at the time police carried their own weapons, usually single shot pistols, or some other small pocket pistol, ill-equipped to fight these gangs. We lost several officers at the times. Still arming police, wasn't as much to help, or protect the police, so much as it was to allow politicians to receive fair votes.

It may also be worth reminding readers of the **Know-Nothing Riot of 1856**, in which some of the worst rioting of the Know-Nothing era in the United States occurred in Baltimore. It was the fall of 1856, street tensions had escalated sharply over the preceding six-dozen years as neighborhood gangs, most of them operating out of local firehouses, became increasingly involved in party politics. Know-Nothing candidate Thomas Swann was elected Mayor of Baltimore in 1856 amidst violence and a heavily disputed ballot. Police Commissioner Kane was also involved in this, and in fact testified in open court for the defence in a trial against a Know Nothing that was charged with killing one of Kane's Officers. Kane was more dedicated to his party than he was his own men. Based on what these gangs were doing, it is obvious what some politicians wouldn't want to fight it. The point being, City Council wasn't interested in Officer Safety, or even Public Safety at the time, as much as they were in getting voters to the polls.

Baltimore's Police Commissioners

In the earliest days of the Baltimore Police Department, the Mayor and City Council appointed the Board of Police Commissioners to oversee the police department. This board in turn appointed a Marshal, who was in charge of the day-to-day operations of the department.

In June of 1861 the United States Military took control of the Baltimore Police Department, it would be nearly a year before March of 1862 would come and the power to appoint the members of the BOC, and eventual single Police Commissioners would be turned over to the Governor of the State of Maryland. That arrangement would last until 1978, when control of the department went back to Baltimore's Mayor and City Council.

What follows is a complete list of Baltimore Police Commissioners, in Chronological Order:

Charles D. Gaither
1920-1937

William Lawson
1937-1938

Robert F. Stanton
1938–1943

Hamilton R. Atkinson
1943-1949

Beverly Ober
1949-1955

James M. Hepbron
1955 - 1961

Interim Bernard Schmidt
1961-1966

Maj, Gen, George M. Gelston
22 January 1966 - 22 September 1966

Donald D. Pomerleau
1966-1981

Frank J. Battaglia
1981-1984

Bishop L. Robinson
1984-1987

Edward J. Tilghman
1987-1989

Edward W. Woods
1989-1993

Thomas C. Frazier
1994-1999

Edward T. Norris
2000-2002

Kevin P. Clark
2003-2004

Leonard D. Hamm
2004-2007

Frederick H. Bealefeld III
2007-2012

Anthony W. Batts
2012 - 8 July 2015

Interim Commissioner
Kevin Davis
8 July 2015 - 19 Oct 2015
Commissioner
Kevin Davis
19 Oct 2015 – Present

Baltimore's Board of Police Commissioners

As noted in the previous section of this book, until 1920 rather than a single Police Commissioner the Baltimore Police Department was overseen by a Board of Commissioners (BOC). The following is a list of BOC members

1840-1850
The Honorable John Quincy Adams Robson

1850-1861 (Mayor member Ex-officio)
Charles Howard
William H Gatchell
Charles d Hinks
John W Davis

June 22 1861 until March 29 1862 (Under control if the United States Military authorities)
Police Commissioners Appointed by the Military authorities
Columbus O'Donnell
Archibald Sterling Jr. Thomas Kelso
John R Kelso
John W Randolph
Peter Sauerwein
John B Seidenstricker
Joseph Roberts
Michael Warner

March 29 1862 to Nov 15 1866 (Mayor member Ex-officio)
Samuel Hindes
Nicholas L Wood

Nov 15 1866 to March 1867 (Mayor member Ex-officio)
William T Valiant
James Young

March 1867
Lefevre Jarrett
James E Carr
William H B Fusselbaugh

March 14 1870
John W Davis
James E Carr
William H B Fusselbaugh

March 15 1871
William H B Fusselbaugh
James E Carr
Thomas W Morse

March 15 1875
William H B Fusselbaugh
Harry Gilmor
John Milroy

March 15 1877
William H B Fusselbaugh
Harry Gilmor
James R Herbert

April 12 1878
William H B Fusselbaugh
James R Herbert
John Milroy

March 15 1881
George Colton
James R Herbert
John Milroy

March 15 1883
George Colton
James R Herbert
John Milroy

Aug 5 1884
George Colton
John Milroy
J D Ferguson

Feb 25 1886
George Colton
John Q A Robson
John Milroy

Jun 25 1886
George Colton
John Q A Robson
Alfred J Carr

March 15 1887
Edson M Schryver
Alfred J Carr
John Q A Robson

Jan 23 1888 Edson
M Schryver John
Gill Jr
John Q A Robson

Dec 1 1894
Edson M Schryver
John Gill Jr
John C Legg

March 27 1896
Daniel C
Heddinger John
Gill Jr
Edson M Schryver

March 15 1897
Daniel C
Heddinger William
W Johnson Edson
M Schryver

May 7 1900
George M Upsher
Edward H Fowler
John T Morris

March 23 1904
George M Upsher
John T Morris
Thomas J Shryock

May 2 1904
George R Willis
James H Preston
Thomas J Shryock

May 4 1908
Sherlock Swann
John B A Wheltle
Peter E Tome

May 2 1910
John B A Wheltle
Peter E Tome
C Baker Clotworthy

April 4 1912
John B A Wheltle
Peter E Tome
Morris A Soper

May 6 1912 Morris A Soper Daniel C Ammidon Alfred S Niles

Dec 31 1913 James McEvoy Daniel C Ammidon Alfred S Niles

Dec 28 1914
Daniel C Ammidon
Clarendon I T Gould
Alfred S Niles

March 22 1916
Lawrason Riggs
Daniel C Ammidon
Alfred S Niles

May 1 1916
Lawrason Riggs
Edward F Burke
Daniel C Ammidon

Baltimore Police Weapons

Courtesy Robert Lee Keene

The primary service weapon today is the **Glock 22** .40 caliber pistol. Officers are also issued a Monadnock expandable straight baton, Taser X26 and pepper spray. Remington 870 shotguns are available, as well as a less-than-lethal model of the 870. In certain situations, SWAT officers may employ the use of the G36, which fires the 5.56 NATO round, the H&K UMP40, and M4 variants.

The Espantoon is a type of wooden police baton, or more commonly known as a nightstick or billy club, that is distinct to the city of Baltimore and has been in use for generations. It is an ornate straight baton equipped with a swivelled leather strap with which it can be twirled. Between 1994 and 2000, the Espantoon was abandoned in favor of the Koga stick due to police commissioner Thomas Frazier's perception that its twirling intimidated the citizenry. In 2000, Edward T. Norris assumed the office of police commissioner and lifted the ban on the Espantoon, although he did not mandate its use. The move was made as part of a general effort to boost morale and instil a more aggressive approach to policing in Baltimore. Norris stated, "When I found out what they meant to the rank and file, I said, 'Bring them back.' ... It is a tremendous part of the history of this Police Department." While the move did not make the Espantoon an issued item by the department as it once was, it remains to this day an optional piece of carry equipment.

Baltimore Police Department
242 W. 29th St., Baltimore, MD.
Emergencies: 9-1-1   -   Non-emergencies: 410-396-2037
BALTIMORE POLICE Web Site: **http://www.baltimorepolice.org**

Contact Ret. Det. Kenny Driscoll if you have pictures of you, your family, or other members of the Baltimore Police Department and wish to see them remembered on our tribute website. We are anxious to honor the fine men and women who have served this fine police department. Also if you have comments about the book, positive or negative we want to hear them. Don't forget to visit our history site. And if you have memorabilia that you want to donate or sell let us know.

Ret. Det. Kenny Driscoll can be reached at: **Kenny@BaltimoreCityPoliceHistory.com.** Also "Like" us on Facebook (Baltimore City Police History), follow us on Twitter (BaltoPoliceHistory) or contact us for a mailing address.

Highly Recommended

PERFECTION COLLECTION
BALTIMORE CITY POLICE
★ ESPANTOONS ★
DEPARTMENTAL ISSUE ★ CARL HAGEN
★ EDWARD BREMMER ★
JOE HLAFKA

"This is where I have my Espantoons made!"
Retired Detective Kerry Driscoll

K & I Creative Plastics And Wood, LLC
582 Nixon Street
Jacksonville, FL. 32204
Plastics Dept: (904) 387-0438
Wood Dept: (904) 981-8011

https://www.kicreativeplastics.net/espantoon_results.php

A Blue & White Life

Policing Baltimore in the 1970's & 1980's
by Wesley Wise (Author), Mark Keller (Author), Chris Streett (Author), Ken Driscoll (Author, Illustrator), Richard Price (Author), Victor Gearhart (Author), William Gordon (Author), Kurt Lurz (Author), Jeff Rosen (Author)

This book is a compilation which describes in great detail some true stories the author and his fellow contributors experienced during their time first as rookies and then as veteran Baltimore Police officers as they advanced through their careers in the Southeast section of Baltimore in the 1970's & 1980's. These are true stories told by the officers who lived them. Some are humorous, some are sad, some are surprising, but all are stark and real. It contains several stories from other Baltimore Police Officer contributors, in addition to the forty-five stories lived through and told by the Author, a thirty-six year veteran of the department who retired as a Major in 2006, after 18 years in the ghettos of Baltimore's Southeastern District. These stories come primarily from the Author's time as a street officer and Sergeant from 1970 until 1989. They've seen it, they've lived it, and now they've told it. These stories are told in gritty detail with a good dose of dry humor and thought-provoking insight into big city policing during a particularly troubled time in our history. Full of harsh realities and aberrant adventures of a group of veteran street officers - you couldn't make this stuff up if you tried.

$14.95

http://www.amazon.com/Blue-White-Life-Policing-Baltimore/dp/1503266532/ref=tmm_pap_swatch_0?_encoding=UTF8&qid=1458960797&sr=8-1

Made in the USA
Lexington, KY
10 July 2016